T0324997

# Virtual Team Leadership and Collaborative Engineering Advancements: Contemporary Issues and Implications

Ned Kock
*Texas A&M International University, USA*

**INFORMATION SCIENCE REFERENCE**

Hershey · New York

| | |
|---|---|
| Director of Editorial Content: | Kristin Klinger |
| Director of Production: | Jennifer Neidig |
| Managing Editor: | Jamie Snavely |
| Assistant Managing Editor: | Carole Coulson |
| Typesetter: | Jeff Ash |
| Cover Design: | Lisa Tosheff |
| Printed at: | Yurchak Printing Inc. |

Published in the United States of America by
Information Science Reference (an imprint of IGI Global)
701 E. Chocolate Avenue, Suite 200
Hershey PA 17033
Tel: 717-533-8845
Fax: 717-533-8661
E-mail: cust@igi-global.com
Web site: http://www.igi-global.com

and in the United Kingdom by
Information Science Reference (an imprint of IGI Global)
3 Henrietta Street
Covent Garden
London WC2E 8LU
Tel: 44 20 7240 0856
Fax: 44 20 7379 0609
Web site: http://www.eurospanbookstore.com

Library of Congress Cataloging-in-Publication Data

Virtual team leadership and collaborative engineering advancements : contemporary issues and implications / Ned Kock, editor.
     p. cm.
Summary: "This book addresses a range of e-collaboration topics, with emphasis on two particularly challenging ones: virtual team leadership, and collaborative engineering"--Provided by publisher.

Includes bibliographical references and index.

ISBN 978-1-60566-110-0 (hardcover) -- ISBN 978-1-60566-111-7 (ebook)

1. Virtual work teams--Management. 2. Virtual reality in management. 3. Leadership. 4. Academic-industrial collaboration. 5. Research--International cooperation. 6. Intellectual cooperation. I. Kock, Ned F., 1964-

HD66.V557 2008
658.4'092--dc22
                    2008014460


British Cataloguing in Publication Data
A Cataloguing in Publication record for this book is available from the British Library.

All work contributed to this book set is original material. The views expressed in this book are those of the authors, but not necessarily of the publisher.

*Virtual Team Leadership and Collaborative Engineering Advancements: Contemporary Issues and Implications* is part of the IGI Global series named *Advances in E-Collaboration Book (AECOB)* Series, ISBN: 1935-2883

# Advances in E-Collaboration Book Series (AECOB)

ISBN: 1935-2883

## Editor-in-Chief: Ned Kock, Texas A&M International University, USA

### Virtual Team Leadership and Collaborative Engineering Advancements: Contemporary Issues and Implications

*Ned Kock, Texas A&M International University, USA*
Information Science Reference • copyright 2009 • 263pp • H/C (ISBN: 978-1-60566-110-0) • $195.00 (our price)

Virtual team leadership and collaborative engineering bring teams, product engineering, and processes into the 21st century through the use of e-collaboration technologies. These powerful tools accomplish work efficiently and effectively, whether communication takes place only through e-collaboration technologies or in combination with face-to-face interaction. Virtual Team Leadership and Collaborative Engineering Advancements: Contemporary Issues and Implications addresses a range of e-collaboration topics, with emphasis on two particularly challenging ones: virtual team leadership and collaborative engineering. With contributing authors among the most accomplished e-collaboration, virtual team leadership, and collaborative engineering researchers in the world today, this book presents a blend of conceptual, theoretical, and applied chapters creating a publication that will serve both academics and practitioners.

### E-Collaboration in Modern Organizations: Initiating and Managing Distributed Projects

*Ned Kock, Texas A&M International University, USA*
Information Science Reference • copyright 2008 • 320pp • H/C (ISBN: 978-1-59904-825-3) • $180.00 (our price)

E-Collaboration in Modern Organizations: Initiating and Managing Distributed Projects combines comprehensive research related to e-collaboration in modern organizations, emphasizing topics relevant to those involved in initiating and managing distributed projects. Providing authoritative content to scholars, researchers, and practitioners, this book specifically describes conceptual and theoretical issues that have implications for distributed project management, implications surrounding the use of e-collaborative environments for distributed projects, and emerging issues and debate related directly and indirectly to e-collaboration support for distributed project management.

*The Advances in E-Collaboration (AECOB) Book Series publishes books that address the design and implementation of e-collaboration technologies, assess the behavioral impacts of e-collaboration technologies on individuals and groups, and present theoretical considerations on links between the use of e-collaboration technologies and behavioral patterns. Examples of such technologies are web-based chat tools, web-based asynchronous conferencing tools, e-mail, listservs, collaborative writing tools, group decision support systems, teleconferencing suites, workflow automation systems, and document management technologies. Considering the aforementioned areas of focus, the Advances in E-Collaboration (AECOB) Book Series seeks to fulfill the need for a platform to address the emerging principles of e-collaboration technologies. This book series aspires to supply researchers, practitioners and academicians, a high-quality and prestigious channel of publication for these areas of immediate social implication. The ongoing efforts of the series to bridge the gaps of existing literature within e-collaboration and its surrounding disciplines will foster further growth and influence the knowledge society in whole.*

Hershey • New York

Order online at www.igi-global.com or call 717-533-8845 x 100 –
Mon-Fri 8:30 am - 5:00 pm (est) or fax 24 hours a day 717-533-7115

# Table of Contents

**Section I**
**Emerging Issues and Debate**

*David Gefen, Drexel University, USA*
*Nitza Geri, The Open University of Israel, Israel*
*Narasimha Paravastu, Metropolitan State University, USA*

*Lior Fink, Ben-Gurion University of the Negev, Israel*

*Patricia McManus, University of Western Sydney, Australia*
*Susan Standing, Edith Cowan University, Australia*
*Craig Standing, Edith Cowan University, Australia*
*Heikki Karjaluoto, University of Jyväskylä, Finland*

*Ned Kock, Texas A&M International University, USA*
*Pedro Antunes, University of Lisboa, Portugal*

## Section II
## Virtual Team Leadership

## Section III
## Collaborative Production and Engineering

## Section IV
## Advanced Conceptual and Theoretical Issues

# Detailed Table of Contents

**Section I**
**Emerging Issues and Debate**

**Chapter I**

*David Gefen, Drexel University, USA*
*Nitza Geri, The Open University of Israel, Israel*
*Narasimha Paravastu, Metropolitan State University, USA*

The differences among peoples and how their respective culture and history may affect their adoption of information and communication technologies (ICT), as well as their preferred usage patterns, are often discussed in the literature. But do we really need to look that far to find such cross-cultural differences? Considering language is one of the major defining attributes of culture, this chapter takes a sociolinguistic approach to argue that there is a cross-cultural aspect to ICT adoption also within the same culture. Sociolinguists have claimed for years that to a large extent, communication between men and women, even within the supposedly same culture, has such characteristics due to their different underlying social objectives which affect their communication patterns. This chapter examines this sociolinguistic perspective in the context of online courses, where students are often requested to collaborate with their classmates in online threaded discussions. Although the stage is set in online courses to smother cultural and gender differences if participants wish to do so, a key finding is that gender based cultural patterns still emerge. These differences were strong enough to allow significant identification of the student gender, despite the gender neutral context of the course discussions. Implications for ICT in general in view of this Vive la Différence are discussed.

**Chapter II**

*Lior Fink, Ben-Gurion University of the Negev, Israel*

This chapter develops an organizational view of the roles and impacts of e-collaboration. Drawing on the dynamic capabilities perspective, e-collaboration is conceptualized as a change-oriented capability that enables a firm to identify, integrate, and apply its knowledge assets to meet competitive demands. Therefore, e-collaboration potentially has three organizational roles – coordination, learning, and innovation – that are associated with either efficiency impacts or competitive impacts. Drawing on contingency theory, the main argument developed in this chapter is that firms in less dynamic business environments need e-collaboration for operational purposes, emphasizing the coordination role, whereas firms in high-velocity business environments need e-collaboration for strategic purposes, emphasizing the learning and innovation roles. An analysis of the way in which business environment characteristics interact with media characteristics serves to demonstrate the importance of strategic characteristics – in addition to media and task characteristics – in determining the organizational effectiveness of e-collaboration.

Mobile services (m-services) have become an important part of the e-commerce landscape. Although research has been conducted on which services people use and the benefits they attach to those services, the values associated with the adoption and use of m-services at the individual level is still unclear. This paper addresses the question of why and how individuals adopt and appropriate m-services with a particular focus on m-communication? In the information systems field various technology adoption models have been proposed and validated in relation to technology adoption within an organisational setting but personal adoption and use of technology is less researched. We propose the use of means-end chains and laddering techniques to determine the basic primitive values that are fulfilled for the individual by using various m-services. The examples presented show that mobile services often fulfil such basic needs as self-esteem, achievement, individuality, belonging and well-being. Exploring the realization of values as a theoretical framework offers researchers a way forward in environments characterised by individual technology decisions.

Much of the funding for research and development initiatives in the area of e-collaboration comes from government agencies in various countries. Government funding of e-collaboration research in the European Union (EU) and the United States (U.S.), in particular, seems to be experiencing steady growth in recent years. In the EU, a key initiative to promote governmental investment in e-collaboration research is the Collaboration@Work initiative. This initiative is one of the EU's Information Society Technologies

Directorate General's main priorities. In the U.S., government investment in e-collaboration research is channeled through several government branches and organizations, notably the National Science Foundation. There are key differences in the approaches used for government funding of e-collaboration research in the EU and U.S. Among other differences, the EU model appears to foster research that is aligned with the action research tradition, whereas the U.S. model places emphasis on research that is better aligned with the experimental research tradition.

## Section II
## Virtual Team Leadership

**Chapter V**

*Kathryn R. Wickham, LiveOps, Inc., USA*
*Joseph B. Walther, Michigan State University, USA*

While considerable research has explored perceptions of groups and members in computer-mediated communication (CMC), and leadership behaviors in face-to-face groups, little research has examined how leadership is identified in CMC groups. Contemporary CMC theories alternatively stress the impact of salient, stereotyped roles on CMC groups' perceptions, or the accretion of exaggerated impressions based on behavioral cues. These perspectives, in turn, coincide with predictions about the predominance of alternative forms of leadership: Assigned versus emergent. This study draws on traditional leadership theories from face-to-face group research and applies them to CMC to examine dynamics related to assigned and emergent leaders in online groups. The results of the study demonstrate that CMC groups may identify more than one leader. When identifying emergent leaders, regardless of whether a leader was assigned or not, group members consider perceived amounts of communication, intelligence, and encouraging and authoritarian behaviors.

**Chapter VI**

*Halbana Tarmizi, University of Nebraska at Omaha, USA*
*Gert-Jan de Vreede, University of Nebraska at Omaha, USA*
*Ilze Zigurs, University of Nebraska at Omaha, USA*

Organizations have the potential to achieve advantage through communities of practice (COPs) initiatives. However, establishing and sustaining COPs is a challenging task. Facilitation is needed to help COPs overcome difficulties throughout their life stages. Facilitators take on leadership roles within these virtual communities, yet little is known about the challenges related to their roles. This paper contributes in helping to improve leadership in COP by highlighting challenges in facilitating COP and by providing potential solutions addressing those challenges. A recent survey of facilitators reveals challenges faced by facilitators in performing their tasks within COPs. The issue of participation was identified as the main concern in COP facilitation. Several design and technology initiatives are discussed for their potential to help facilitators in coping with the participation issue and providing essential leadership roles within communities of practice.

The purpose of this study was to improve the understanding of virtual team leadership occurring within existing virtual teams in a range of organizations. Qualitative data were collected through comprehensive interviews with nine virtual team leaders and members from six different organizations. A semi-structured interview format was used to elicit extensive information about effective and ineffective virtual team leadership behaviours. Content analysis was used to code the interview transcripts and detailed notes obtained from these interviews. Two independent raters categorized results into themes and sub-themes. These results provide real-world examples and recommendations above and beyond what can be learned from simulated laboratory experiments. The four most important overarching findings are described using the following headings: 1) Leadership critical in virtual teams, 2) Virtual team meeting effectiveness, 3) Personalizing virtual teamwork, and 4) Learning to effectively use different media. These findings represent the most significant and pertinent results from this qualitative data and provide direction for future research, as well as practical recommendations for leaders and members of virtual teams.

# Chapter VIII

Teams whose interactions might be mediated entirely via Internet-based communication, virtual teams, are emerging as commonplace in business settings. Researchers have identified trust as a key ingredient for virtual teams to work effectively (Aubrey & Kelsey, 2003; Beranek, 2000; David & McDaniel, 2004; Iacono & Weisband, 1997; Jarvenpaa, Knoll, & Leidner, 1998; Jarvenpaa, Shadow, & Staples; 2004). However, researchers have not identified scalable methods that consistently promote trust within virtual teams. Improved interface design for communication support systems used by virtual teams may contribute to solving this problem. Interface cannot solve the problem of members trusting each other, but it can support the type of activities that do. This paper describes the development and some initial experiences with a Web-based, template-driven, asynchronous communication support tool and how this system can be used to support trust development in virtual teams and performance goals of virtual teams. This article presents the capabilities and features of the communication support system. More detailed findings from an experimental study of this system's use can be found in another publication (Remidez, 2003).

In this study we examined the perceived importance of line managers and middle managers in virtual teams of what work roles and leadership functions are necessary to promote virtual team success and performance. Using Quinn's (1988) competing values framework it was found that control-related roles of directors and producers were perceived to be most important. With years in a leading position, the repertoire of leadership roles needed to successfully lead virtual teams declined. Additionally, middle managers compared to line managers perceived people oriented leadership functions (i.e., mentor and facilitator roles) and flexibility-related work roles (i.e., innovator and mentor roles) as more important whereas line managers compared to middle managers perceived stability leadership functions (i.e., monitor and coordinator roles) as more important. Limitations, implications for virtual team leadership, and suggestions for future research are discussed.

*Johannes Glückler, Catholic University of Eichstätt, Germany*
*Gregor Schrott, University of Frankfurt, Germany*

This article explores the structural foundations of leadership and performance in virtual project teams. In an experimental business case, the article demonstrates the effect of structural brokerage in team communication on leadership and team performance. This research suggests that social roles as well as the acknowledgement of leadership and performance are conditional to the way individuals and teams relate to their environment. It supports structural hole theory in that leaders and a winner team achieved the highest values of flow betweenness and network efficiency. Strategically, managers of virtual knowledge networks should focus their attention not only on the qualifications of individuals, but also on communication structures within their work groups.

## Section III
## Collaborative Production and Engineering

*Walter Rodriguez, Florida Gulf Coast University, USA*
*Janusz Zalewski, Florida Gulf Coast University, USA*
*Elias Kirche, Florida Gulf Coast University, USA*

This paper presents a new concept for supporting electronic collaboration, operations, and relationships among trading partners in the value chain without hindering human autonomy. Although autonomous intelligent-agents, or electronic robots (e-bots), can be used to inform this endeavor, the paper advocates the development of e-sensors, i.e., software based units with capabilities beyond intelligent-agent's functionality. E-sensors are hardware-software capable of perceiving, reacting and learning from its interactive experience thorough the supply chain, rather than just searching for data and information through the network and reacting to it. E-sensors can help avoid the 'bullwhip' effect. The paper briefly reviews the related intelligent-agent and supply-chain literature and the technological gap between fields.

It articulates a demand-driven, sense-and-response system for sustaining e-collaboration and e-business operations as well as monitoring products and processes. As a proof of concept, this research aimed a test solution at a single supply-chain partner within one stage of the process.

**Chapter XII**

*Fredrik Elgh, Jönköping University, Sweden*
*Staffan Sunnersjö, Jönköping University, Sweden*

Many companies base their business strategy on customized products with a high level of variety and continuous functional improvements. For companies to be able to provide affordable products in a short time and be at the competitive edge, every new design must be adapted to existing production facilities. In order to ensure this, collaboration between engineering design and production engineering has to be supported. With the dispersed organisations of today combined with the increasing amount of information that has to be shared and managed, this collaboration is a critical issue for many companies. In this article, an approach for sharing and managing product and production information is introduced. The results are based on the experiences from a case study at a car manufacturer. By ontology-based integration, work within domains engineering design, production engineering and requirement management at the company was integrated. The main objectives with the integration were: support the formation of requirement specifications for products and processes, improve and simplify the information retrieval for designers and process planners, ensure traceability from changes in product systems to manufacturing systems and vice versa, and finally, eliminate redundant or multiple versions of requirement specifications.

**Chapter XIII**

*Vladimir Tarasov, Jönköping University, Sweden*
*Kurt Sandkuhl, Jönköping University, Sweden*
*Magnus Lundqvist, Jönköping University, Sweden*

Collaborative design in dispersed groups of engineers creates various kinds of challenges to technology, organization and social environment. This paper presents an approach to description and representation of the competences needed for a planned collaborative design project. The most important competence areas are identified starting from the nature of design work, problem solving in design teams, and working in distributed groups. The competence model is built structuring these areas according to three perspectives: general, cultural, and occupational competences. An ontological representation is proposed to implement the described model for collaborative design competence. Using an ontology language for representation of collaborative design competence models makes it possible to identify those individuals who are best suited for the collaboration by ontology matching. Furthermore, a software design team consisting of two persons was interviewed and competence profiles were created using the developed ontological representation. Modeling of the team members has confirmed that the proposed approach can be applied to modeling competences needed for collaborative design in engineering fields.

# Chapter XIV

Developing service-laden products in a virtual extended enterprise implies a wider distribution of resources and product development (PD) team members than what is the case today. In this setting, the challenge is getting a cross-disciplinary distributed team to collaborate effectively over distance using not only the tools available today, but also new tools and approaches. One such activity-based approach, based on an actual Volvo Aero service-provision process, is presented in this article. Supplying a physical product as part of a service contract within an extended enterprise demands increased speed and quality of the predictions the supplier wants to make in order to keep track of the product functionality, its cost effectiveness and lifecycle cost. One approach that has been proven in engineering is modeling and simulation, here implemented as activity-based simulation of an actual industrial work process that provides a maintenance service. The activity-based simulation approach is realized in the industry standard simulation environment MATLAB. It is created as a demonstrator of one of several future tools that may help a virtual extended enterprise to face the challenge of supplying function or services to the customer more effectively. Conclusions regarding Collaborative Working Environments include new requirements on quality of tools for supporting functional product development regarding knowledge availability, usability, security and interoperability. Conclusions also support the suggested approach concerning development of distributed, modular activity-based process simulation models as a suitable approach for supporting functional product development.

# Chapter XV

Traditionally management schools of thought that emphasize certain types of work structures usually appear earlier than information technologies (IT) geared at supporting those work structures. This situation has undoubtedly changed recently, arguably around the mid-1990s, with the explosion in the commercial use of the Internet and particularly the Web. This calls for the development of a generic framework that ties together relevant management ideas that help organizations strategically and operationally align themselves with new Web-based IT. Our goal with this chapter is to provide some basic elements that can be used by managers and researchers as a starting point to develop this generic framework. As such, we focus on a particular set of activities associated with team coordination and communication in production and service delivery business processes through the Internet and the Web.

# Chapter XVI

New challenges result from the virtualization and distribution of product development activities. This article analyzes problems of cooperative engineering as well as methods and tools for the virtual engineering of extended products. Based on these analyses, a broad road map is proposed that articulates public- and civil-sector roles in coping with future engineering challenges. With a strategic horizon, the public-sector role targets the creation of a knowledge-intensive global business ecosystem conducive to balanced civil-sector innovation and sustainable growth. The civil-sector roles evolve tactics that implement proven cooperative and virtual engineering practices with a focus on value creation.

**Section IV**
**Advanced Conceptual and Theoretical Issues**

**Chapter XVII**

*Ned Kock, Texas A&M International University, USA*
*Vanessa Garza, Texas A&M International University, USA*

This chapter reviews theoretical research on e-communication behavior, identifying two main types of theories: technological and social. Based on this review, it provides the rationale for the development of a new theory that is neither technological nor social. The new theory is based on evolution theory, whose foundations were laid out by Darwin. Three theoretical principles are developed from evolution theory: media naturalness, innate schema similarity, and learned schema variety. The chapter concludes by illustrating how the theoretical principles can be used as a basis for the development of a simple predictive model in the context of an online broker.

**Chapter XVIII**

*Julie E. Kendall, Rutgers University, USA*

What constitutes regional commerce? What creates and enhances a regional identity? In the United States, regions can be quite large and may even cover geographical territory from several surrounding counties or states. They are larger than any one individual company, shopping street, or district. Regional cooperation of commercial businesses is often manifested through special events, cooperative advertising with coordinated signage, extended opening hours, and special discounts that contribute to building a sense of community, and which eventually develop a sense of region. The political and environmental exigencies for the creation and expansion of regions have meant an increase in the popularity and importance of regions and a subsequent movement to enhance and differentiate their identities. We now see the rise of regional governments, water authorities, and educational institutions among many others. One little-explored idea has been the use of e-collaboration to forge, reinforce, and sustain a regional identity via the virtual world. Although geographical separation of many miles might dictate that bricks-and-mortar theatres cannot easily collaborate physically (i.e., they cannot share costumes, props, ushers, and so on), the possibility of e-collaboration opens potential opportunities for attracting wider audiences, reaching and ultimately casting fresh talent, and building reciprocal audiences who possess a passion for the arts and who have the means and desire to travel to attend performances throughout the geographical region. In this study, a methodology built on the conceptual foundation of metaphor research was used to comprehend and then interpret the Web presence of 15 nonprofit theatres that comprise the total regional theatre of southern New Jersey that exists on the Web. In order to add additional insight, our earlier research findings from working with off-Broadway and regional theatre festivals were extended to analyze the Web presence of the theatres in southern New Jersey. We contribute to the literature by systematic and deep investigation of the strategic importance of the Web for nonprofit theatre groups in the southern New Jersey region. In addition, our use of the metaphor methodology in order to create a telling portrait of what transpires on the Web in relation to nonprofit organizations is also an original contribution. Our work is meant to heighten the awareness of administrators to the rapidly accelerating need for the strategic use of e-collaboration. We propose that with the use of the Web, administrators can move toward creating a regional theatre Web presence for South Jersey, one which would make use of an evolutionary metaphor. To this end, we suggest the use of an organism metaphor. Through the creation of reciprocal hyperlinks, theatres can be supported in improving their practice of colocation on the Web, wherein they will be taking strides to cooperate as a regional theatre community.

## Chapter XIX

*Jeffrey Wong, University of Nevada, USA*
*Kevin Dow, Kent State University, USA*
*Ofir Turel, California State University, USA*
*Alexander Serenko, Lakehead University, Canada*

E-mail is a critical component of most e-collaborative environments. This chapter describes an application of the American Customer Satisfaction Index (ACSI) framework to model the antecedents and consequences of customer satisfaction with e-mail systems. The ACSI framework is an established methodology in the marketing literature and appeared to be useful to assess the antecedents and consequences of individual satisfaction in many more circumstances than external customer purchases. We surveyed e-mail users to gather data to utilize in an ACSI model modified for e-mail systems. Our findings indicate that the ACSI model can yield useful insights into factors that contribute to and result from user satisfaction.

## Chapter XX

*Anita Blanchard, University of North Carolina at Charlotte, USA*

This study examines how a Listserv affects its members' sense of community (SOC) with the sponsoring organization. It was expected that the Listserv would increase members' knowledge about and participation in the sponsoring organization department, which, in turn, would increase their SOC. The study examined Listserv members and nonmembers before and after implementation of the Listserv. As expected, Listserv membership increased knowledge and face-to-face activity, and knowledge and face-to-face activity increased sense of community. However, there was ironically no effect of Listserv membership on sense of community. These findings challenge previous theories about the development of sense of community while nonetheless demonstrating the positive effects of Listserv membership.

Agile methods are lightweight, iterative software development frameworks used predominantly on small and mid-sized software development projects. This chapter introduces a project structure and management practices creating agile conditions for large software projects outsourced either offshore or onshore. Agility is achieved by slicing a large project into a number of small projects working in agile settings. Development is divided into research and development activities that are located on-site, and production activities located off-site. The proposed approach makes agile methods applicable to the stressed conditions of outsourcing without compromising the quality or pace of the software development effort. Creating an agile environment in an outsourcing project relies on maintaining a balance between the functions and sizes of on-site and off-site teams, on redefining the developers' roles, and on reorganizing the information flow between the different development activities to compensate for the lack of customers on-site, team colocation, and tacit project knowledge.

# Chapter XXII

The management of virtual projects is fundamentally different from that of traditional projects. Furthermore, the research in this area comes from different reference disciplines and perspectives, and a unified view or theory of best practices does not yet exist. We use the theoretical frame of patterns to propose a unified view. We focus on three concepts as the underlying theoretical elements for identifying patterns of effectiveness in virtual project management: (a) coordination, (b) communication, and (c) control. As a first step in the identification of specific patterns, we conducted a series of virtual focus groups with participants from industry who had real experience with virtual projects. The brainstorming data from the focus groups were analyzed to develop an initial set of patterns. Based on this first step, we also present a structured process for the discovery and continuing validation of patterns of effectiveness in virtual projects, and discuss the issues involved in applying the process.

# Preface

This book addresses a range of e-collaboration topics, with emphasis on two particularly challenging ones: virtual team leadership, and collaborative engineering. Virtual team leadership refers to the task of leading teams using e-collaboration technologies to accomplish work efficiently and effectively; whether communication takes place only through e-collaboration technologies or in combination with face-to-face interaction. Collaborative engineering is a broad and emerging concept, and generally refers to the task of engineering new processes and products using e-collaboration technologies; again, with or without resorting to face-to-face interaction. The book also addresses issues related to e-collaborative production and delivery of goods and services in the context of operational business processes.

The book is organized in four main sections – Section I: Emerging Issues and Debate; Section II: Virtual Team Leadership; Section III: Collaborative Production and Engineering; and Section IV: Advanced Conceptual and Theoretical Issues. Each section contains several chapters written by experts. In Section I a range of emerging e-collaboration topics are discussed, setting the stage for the next two sections, which are the core sections of the book. Those two core sections then explore in more detail the topics of virtual team leadership, and collaborative production and engineering. The fourth and final section discusses advanced conceptual and theoretical issues related to the topics covered in the previous sections. Most of the chapters in this book are revised versions of selected articles published in the *International Journal of e-Collaboration*. I have had the pleasure and honor of serving as Founding Editor-in-Chief of that Journal since its first issue was published in 2005.

The contributing authors are among the most accomplished researchers in the world today in the areas of e-collaboration, virtual team leadership, and collaborative engineering. I am most grateful for their hard work in connection with the development of this book, which has been a great pleasure to edit together with my colleagues at IGI Global. The blend of conceptual, theoretical and applied chapters found here makes me confident that this book will serve both academics and practitioners very well. I hope that the book will stimulate further research on virtual team leadership, collaborative engineering, and related e-collaboration issues. It is also my hope that this book will serve as a valuable source of ideas for managers involved in projects that rely heavily on e-collaboration technologies.

*Ned Kock*

# Acknowledgment

No book project can be completed successfully without the support of a dedicated editorial team. I would like to thank the team at IGI Global for that. Special thanks go to Kristin Klinger, Carla Hackman, and Deborah Yahnke. Many thanks are also due to Heather Probst, Elizabeth Duke, and their journal editorial team for their support in the development of several issues of the *International Journal of e-Collaboration*. Since most of the chapters in this book are revised versions of articles previously published in that journal, many of the chapters published here would not exist without Heather's and Elizabeth's excellent support.

I thank Texas A&M International University for their institution support. Special recognition in that respect is due to Ray Keck, the University's President; Dan Jones, Provost; and Jacky So, Dean of the College of Business and Economics. Thanks are also due to the great group of colleagues with whom I have been sharing the third floor of Pellegrino Hall on the University's beautiful campus. They make up the Division of International Business and Technology Studies, which I have had the pleasure to serve since 2006 in the capacity of Founding Chair. My special thanks go to Cindy Martinez, Jacques Verville (now at the University of British Columbia), Jackie Mayfield, Milton Mayfield, Ananda Mukherji, Pedro Hurtado, Balaji Janamanchi, Leonel Prieto, and Hugo Garcia for the leadership roles that they have played in the Division.

Last, but most important of all, I would like to thank my family for their love and support. This book is dedicated to them.

*Ned Kock*

# Section I
# Emerging Issues and Debate

# Chapter I
# Vive la Différence:
## Communicating Across Cultural Boundaries in Cross-Gender Online Collaborative Discussions

**David Gefen**
*Drexel University, USA*

**Nitza Geri**
*The Open University of Israel, Israel*

**Narasimha Paravastu**
*Metropolitan State University, USA*

## ABSTRACT

*The differences among peoples and how their respective culture and history may affect their adoption of information and communication technologies (ICT), as well as their preferred usage patterns, are often discussed in the literature. But do we really need to look that far to find such cross-cultural differences? Considering language is one of the major defining attributes of culture, this chapter takes a sociolinguistic approach to argue that there is a cross-cultural aspect to ICT adoption also within the same culture. Sociolinguists have claimed for years that to a large extent, communication between men and women, even within the supposedly same culture, has such characteristics due to their different underlying social objectives which affect their communication patterns. This chapter examines this sociolinguistic perspective in the context of online courses, where students are often requested to collaborate with their classmates in online threaded discussions. Although the stage is set in online courses to smother cultural and gender differences if participants wish to do so, a key finding is that gender based cultural patterns still emerge. These differences were strong enough to allow significant identification of the student gender, despite the gender neutral context of the course discussions. Implications for ICT in general in view of this Vive la Différence are discussed.*

## INTRODUCTION

One of the major manifestations of culture is language and the way it affects communications: who we prefer to talk to and the some of the underlying objectives of the communication. Communication is not a mere exchange of words or information. It is a social process and, as such, it is imbued with a social meaning of inclusion, exclusion, and social hierarchy. These cultural aspects are a prime aspect of cross-cultural research, including in the context of Information and Communication Technology (ICT) adoption and usage patterns (Kayworth & Leidner, 2000). But one need not look that far to find cross-cultural differences. They are here among us all the time – that at least is the basic premise of sociolinguistics.

Sociolinguistics deals, among other things, in the way culture affects and determines communication. Most import in the context of this study is that culture is not only a manifestation of language and national heritage. Culture is also a matter of gender. Men and women communicate differently, and do so with different underlying social objectives. This is part of our evolutionary past (Brizendine, 2006), which also affects online collaboration (Kock & Hantula, 2005). Gender is so much a part of communication in communication that in many languages there are distinct rules in the language about how men and women should conjure the sentences they speak and their expected speech patterns. But it is much more than superimposed linguistic gender segregation. It is, at least in the view of sociolinguists, a matter of a cultural difference between men and women.

In general terms, men, according to sociolinguistics, communicate more with the objective of creating and preserving their social status, while women do so more with the objective of creating rapport and social inclusion. Not surprisingly, the result of this is that communication across genders is often an exercise in cultural miscommunication (Brizendine, 2006; Tannen, 1994, 1995). Indeed, when men communicate with each other it is often on a basis of exchanging information, or as Tannen calls it "report talk", while women do so to exchange emotions, or as Tannen calls it "rapport talk" (Tannen, 1994). The consequence of this is often communication that are gender segregated (Hannah & Murachver, 1999; Yates, 2001).

Looking at this distinction in the context of virtual communities and supporting it, Gefen and Ridings (2005) commented that when men joined virtual communities composed of mostly male members, they did so with the declared objective of sharing information, while when they joined mixed gender virtual communities it was more for emotional support. In contrast, women who joined mixed virtual communities did so for information exchange but when they looked for emotional support they too joined mostly female ones. Indeed, even in what should be a gender and emotion neutral settings, women perceive more social presence in email (Gefen & Straub, 1997) and ecommerce websites (Gefen, 2003).

The objective of this study is to examine whether the expected gender-related cultural differences in oral communication, predicted by sociolinguists regarding oral communications, hold true also in the explicitly created gender-neutral ICT environment of online courses where the nature of the controlled course conversations make social dominance and rapport rather irrelevant. If these gender communication patterns hold true also in this scenario, then how much more so that such cross-cultural differences should hold true in other ICT induced environments. This is a crucial question, because if true, then cross-cultural research in ICT should look not only across the border, but also within.

The data support the basic *Vive la Différence* proposition of the study even in the stoic context of online course discussions. Male students did prefer to respond to other male students and female ones to females, and men did show a more domineering attitude in their postings. Therefore, cross-cultural studies in ICT should consider gender as another dimension of culture.

## THEORY

The tendency of society toward being masculine or feminine is a central aspect of the cultural dimensions of peoples (Hofstede, 1980; Hofstede, Neuijen, Ohayv, & Sanders, 1990). But is gender also an aspect within a culture? According to sociolinguistics, it is (Yates, 2001). Actually, the popular press sometimes even takes it a step further claiming, perhaps jokingly, that this gender difference might even take on celestial proportions (Gray, 1992). If this is so then gender-related social behavior should come through even in the stoically enforced context of online courses. Thus, demonstrating the need to include gender as an aspect of culture even within a given national and linguistic culture, as also biology implies (Brizendine, 2006). Moreover, previous research reports on gender differences in online shopping (Venkatesh & Agarwal, 2006; Zhang, Prybutok, & Strutton, 2007), computer training (Venkatesh & Morris, 2000), organizational innovation initiatives related to ICT (Ahuja & Thatcher, 2005), and adoption of advanced mobile applications (Hong & Tam, 2006).

One of the major manifestations of culture is in language and communication. Communication carries with it not only information but often also a very strong social message, a social message which is interpreted, and sometimes also misinterpreted, within the cultural context of the speaker and listeners. Even the very way words are pronounced carries a cultural burden with it, making people identify or not with the speaker based on the national or local culture implied in the accent (Deaux, 1984; Deschamps, 1982). Speaking in the accepted dialect can in fact make all the difference between whether people agree or disagree with a speaker based almost purely on the manifestation of the presumed culture of the speaker (Abrams & Hogg, 1987). This additionally crucial social level of communication is a function not only of national and local culture but, according to sociolinguists (Tannen, 1994; Yates,

2001) and hormones (Brizendine, 2006), also of gender. Men and women may communicate in what on a superficial level may seem as the same language, but the social message behind the words and this message is interpreted is quite different between the average man and the average woman. This is because men and women, on average, imbue and insert different social nuances into the message and do so even in languages, such as English, where there are no linguistically gender enforced styles. These gender related nuances can be so manifest as to result in the equivalent of cross-culture miscommunication (Tannen, 1994). Picking up on this idea Gefen and Straub (1997) showed that women, across cultures, sense more social presence in work-related emails and that increased sense of social presence affect their perceptions of the usefulness and ease of use of the ICT and ultimately its usage. Expanding on this theme, Venkatesh and Morris (2000) showed that women are more affected by social norms in their adoption of ICT.

A salient example of this underlying social message in communication brought by Tannen (1994) is asking for directions. On the face of it, asking for direction is no more than just asking a stranger a question in what may seem as a neutral environment. It could be regarded as information exchange and no more. But this is not the case. Asking for directions also carries a social meaning. That is why men will often drive around for hours rather than ask for directions, while women will think nothing of it and do so without hesitation when they think they are lost. The reason for this, sociolinguists say, is that in asking for directions men are subconsciously implying at least to themselves, certainty women are often surprised to hear this, that the other guy knows more than they do. The person being asked for directions certainly may know more, after all that is why they are being asked for directions, but it is admitting this that bothers men and makes them drive around for hours. Admitting someone else knows more than I do, to men, carries with it a social inferiority message of the other guy is better than I am in something. Men, unless aware of the stupidity of this underlying message, are loath to admit this supposedly social inferior standing. The same communication with women, however, carries no such subconscious implication. If anything, to women this creates a chance to engage with others, rapport, which they more willingly do than men are (Tannen, 1994).

This example, adapted from Tannen (1994), highlights the cultural social difference in communication between men and women. Beyond the meaning conveyed in the words themselves, men tend to communicate with the objective of exchanging information and in doing so establish their social pecking order. This is why men tend to try to control the conversation by talking more than others and employing various methods to silence or demote those who disagree with them. Generally, men, unless aware of the need to do otherwise, also tend to center the conversation more on themselves (Anderson & Leaper, 1998; Coates, 1986). Again, this is a manifestation of using conversation as a way of establishing the social pecking order. Tannen (1994) classes this communicational behavior *report* talk. In contrast, women tend more than men do to be inclusive in their conversational styles. This is because women are more centered on creating rapport, rather than self promotion (Holmes, 1992; Johnson, 1993; Kilbourne & Weeks, 1997; Lakoff, 1975; Mulac, Erlandson, Farrar, & Hallett, 1998; Tannen, 1994, 1995). Tannen (1994) classes this communicational behavior *rapport* talk.

Supporting this report versus rapport distinction, previous research has claimed a greater tendency by men, at least in oral conversations, to try to dominant (Herring, 1993; Holmes, 1992) and control the discussion (Edelsky, 1993), to be more competitive (Kilbourne & Weeks, 1997) and more assertive by interrupting others (Anderson & Leaper, 1998; West & Zimmerman, 1983; Zimmerman & West, 1975), and generally be more forceful (Guiller & Durndell, 2007; Weatherall, 1998) and

less complementary (Coates, 1986; Yates, 2001). These gender-based differences in the cultural message imbued into the conversation are evident across cultures (Costa, Terracciano, & McCrae, 2001; Hofstede, 1980) and seem to carry over also to listserves (Herring, 1996b; Stewart, Shields, & Sen, 2001) and to email in general (Boneva, Kraut, & Frohlich, 2001; Parks & Floyd, 1995). A direct consequence of these gender-based differences and preferences is that men and women tend to congregate into same-gender conversations (Tannen, 1994). Men talk more to other men than to women; women talk more to other women than to men. Interestingly, this happens also online in virtual communities where people have a much broader choice of communities to join and where they can hide their gender and identities or even masquerade as anything they wish to be known as (Gefen & Ridings, 2005).

The ICT in charge of discussions in online courses provides a unique opportunity to examine these cross-gender differences because it is possible to create what are arguably gender-neutral settings. If also in these induced gender-neutral ICT settings, cross-gender differences exist then these differences are probably not a matter of setting alone, but are a matter of the ingrained nature or nurture considerations extensively discussed in the cross-culture literature (Hofstede, 1980; Hofstede et al., 1990) and should thus be controlled for in the context of cross-cultural ICT research.

Whether cross-gender differences, such as gender congregation, apply also in online courses is actually an open question because parallels cannot be drawn with the closest equivalent, virtual communities, where these do apply (Gefen & Ridings, 2005). Virtual communities are not regulated by a moderator and people are free to come and go as they wish, without being graded on it. Moreover, in typical online courses, students do not interact with other students except in controlled threaded discussion settings where the teacher posts a question and the class then discusses it. This discussion is usually graded. The discussion is asynchronous so it is impossible to dominate air time or control the discussion and who talks when as in oral discussions. Inserting socially loaded comments and body language cues is also impossible. It is as close as possible to a gender neutral setting. Moreover, in contrast to virtual communities where people join for many reasons, including the stereotypical feminine rapport and the stereotypical masculine information exchange, the reason people join online class discussions is usually a matter of being forced to by the grading policy, a matter antitypical of both masculine and feminine stereotypical and sociolinguistic behavior. While gender-based communication patterns do occur in the regular classroom (Tannen, 1991), and some evidence does exist that men use the online environment more to access information and women more to converse (Herring, 1996a; Yates, 2001), how these apply to a supposedly gender-neutral setting, such as an online class, remains an open question. Should these gender-related communication behaviors carry over to these neutral settings then it could be argued that they are another aspects of culture induced behaviors.

## HYPOTHESES

Accordingly, applying the underlying proposition that gender differences are not induced by the settings alone but rather are a matter of culture, then even in the relatively gender neutral ICT setting of online course discussions some typical gender communication patterns should be evident. While the basic cross-gender difference of rapport versus report might be somewhat mute in these settings, other aspects, such as gender congregation, should still be evident. The rapport versus report distinction should be rather mute because online class discussions are deliberately not conductive for the feminine rapport type communication and are explicitly managed to

discourage the male dominating status building communication styles. Moreover, the technical settings in these ICT, such as the asynchronous nature of online course discussions, do not permit the students to control who speaks, when, what they say, and for how long – again making aspects of stereotypical male alleged domination conversation styles immaterial (Tannen, 1995; West & Zimmerman, 1983).

And yet, other aspects of typical gender behavior should come through if the proposition holds. Primary among these is gender congregation during discussions. Men's preference to respond to other men more than to women and vice versa could still come through even in these settings because there is nothing in the technical aspects of the ICT or in the way these conversations can typically be managed to exclude this possibility. There are no technical ICT aspects or plausible conduct rules that can make a student address comments, or not be able to address comments, by any other specific given student. Practically speaking, this should translate to a gender preference with men preferring to refer to other men and women to other women.

**H1:** *The number of references to postings by students of the same gender is higher than the number of references to posting of students from the opposite gender.*

Although we do not expect students to resort strongly to their alleged stereotypical report versus rapport conversational styles in these ICT in general, some weaker aspects of these styles should still come through in conversational aspects which are not forced by ICT or typical course conduct regulations. One aspect in which these aspects should come through is in the extent of support given to positions presented by other students. Conventional political correctness in online courses may not be overly encouraging of blunt disrespect and challenging others, but there is a nuance students can play in whether they choose to be explicitly supportive of the postings of others or not. Extrapolating from the literature about typical gender conversational styles, and hence assuming these styles are culture induced and should therefore carry over also to gender neutral ICT settings, men should be less supportive of the positions of other students. Generally, men are supposed to be more assertive, competitive, and dominating (Anderson & Leaper, 1998; Edelsky, 1993; Guiller & Durndell, 2007; Herring, 1993; Holmes, 1992; Kilbourne & Weeks, 1997; Weatherall, 1998; West & Zimmerman, 1983; Zimmerman & West, 1975), and less complementary (Coates, 1986; Yates, 2001) than women. All these mount up to ways of shoring up one's own social standing, a motive strong among men but rather absent among women (Tannen, 1994). This behavior should especially come through strongly when male students refer to other male students because, extrapolating from sociolinguistics, they should be competing with each other. When male students refer to postings by female students the competition should be one way, only by the male student.

**H2:** *Men referring to postings by other men will be less supportive than women are.*

With female students, on the other hand, inclusion should be a more dominant feature of the conversation, as it is in other settings (Guiller & Durndell, 2007; Tannen, 1994). A central strategy in creating inclusion is showing support and encouragement toward the other person. If this carries over to gender neutral ICT then it could be expected that women will be more supportive of other women because of their tendency to be inclusive among other women.

**H3:** *Women referring to postings by other women will be more supportive than men are.*

## METHOD AND DATA

The data for this study were extracted from online course discussions in 14 online courses. There was an average of eight online course discussions in each online course. Every one of these online discussions was analyzed. For each student in each online course discussion we recorded how many postings there were, how many related to a previous posting by other students in this discussion, how many of these references to previous posting were to postings by male students, how many of these were supportive, how many were to postings by female students and how many of these were supportive. A posting was counted as supportive if the student posting it explicitly stated agreement or support with a previous posting in this discussion. We then removed those records that related to students who did not refer to postings by other students in this specific online discussion. These records were removed from the analyses because evidently these students were not taking an active part in the specific conversation but only posting to fulfill the course requirements. This left us with 599 records, dealing with 83 students who each participated on average in 7.2 online course discussions. Among these 599 records, 381 were of men who took an active part in the online course conversation and referred to postings by other students in the specific conversation and 218 were by women. The data were classified by two raters. On the overlapping sample of 100 posting which was classified by both raters there was absolute agreement.

Supporting the stereotype of men trying to control the conversation (Edelsky, 1993), men did significantly (T=2.751,p=.006) post more (mean = 3.00, standard deviation= 2.096) than women (mean = 2.55, standard deviation= 1.542) and did significantly (T=3.959,p<.001) post longer messages (mean number of words = 346.30, standard deviation= 205.903) than women (mean = 286.99, standard deviation= 154.767).

## DATA ANALYSIS

To examine hypotheses H1 through H3 we compared the means of men and women with a set of T tests. Men in a given online course discussion did not significantly (T=1.067, p=.286) refer more to others (mean=.69, standard deviation=1.255) than women did (mean=.58, standard deviation=1.032). But, men did significantly (T=2.525, p=.012) refer more to other men (mean=.45, standard deviation=.913) than women did (mean=.28, standard deviation=.605), although women did not significantly (T=.692, p=.489) refer more to other women (mean=.28, standard deviation=.620) than men did (mean=.24, standard deviation=.602). These results give partial support to H1. Gender congregation does occur, but primarily among men.

Surprisingly however, men in a given online course discussion were significantly (T=2.082, p=.038) more supportive of other men (mean=.14, standard deviation=.445) than women were (mean=.07, standard deviation=.254). This contradicts the expected direction in H2. Also, men did not significantly (T=1.544, p=.123) refer in a supportive manner to other students in general (mean=.20, standard deviation=.540) more than women did (mean=.13, standard deviation=.414). In fact, women were not significantly (T=.148, p=.882) more supportive of even only other women (mean=.06, standard deviation=.264) than men were (mean=.06, standard deviation=.289). This does not support H3. Unlike Guiller & Durndell's (2007) findings, that women students, who participated in online discussions, were more likely to support others and their postings were more personal and emotional than those of the male students, the hypothesized differences in the supportive behavior of students in online course discussions were not supported in this study. Apparently, the courses were sufficiently gender neutral to make this otherwise typical behavior mostly insignificant.

We then examined if the gender of the student could be identified in a linear regression by the characteristics of postings the student made in the online course discussion. If this is so, it would lend more support to the claim that gender and communication style, also in these gender neutral settings, are related. In the linear regression the gender of the student making the posting was the dependent variable. The length of the posting in words, whether this posting was supportive, and whether it was addressed to a student of the same or opposite gender were the independent variables. In all, the explained variance was low at .02. The only significant determinant of student gender was the length in words of the postings the student made in this online discussion (β=.149, p<.001). However, when only the more active students were examined, the results became more convincing. When the analysis was limited to only those students who posted at least 3 postings in the conversation, there were 268 such records, the degree of explained variance became .15. The significant determinants were the length in words (β=.175, p=.004), the number of postings referring to previous postings by women (β=-.173, p=.006), and the number of postings referring to previous postings by men (β=.123, p=.048). In other words, among more students who participated actively in the online course conversation, students who referred more to previous postings by men and less to previous postings by women were mostly significantly more likely to be men.

## DISCUSSION

Language is a central pillar of culture and subcultures within the dominant culture. It is a central pillar even within what may otherwise be considered the same national or historical culture. It is enough to read the famous words of George Bernard Shaw in *Pygmalion* "An Englishman has only to open his mouth, in order to have another Englishman despise him." to realize how even dialects create a cross-cultural event. This is a conclusion supported by research (Abrams & Hogg, 1987). Along those lines of brilliant eloquence, this study presents another aspect of cross-cultural communication, the *Vive la Différence*, according to which gender too is a central cultural difference.

As sociolinguistics claim, men and women apply language, and communication in general, to such a differing social objectives that cross-gender communications can be sometimes best seen as nothing less than cross-cultural miscommunications among people with differing cultural backgrounds (Tannen, 1994). Examining a derivative of this sociolinguistic viewpoint, this study hypothesized that even in the gender neutral ICT environment of online course discussions with their asynchronous and topic focused orientation, cross-gender communication would show some aspects of a cross-cultural communication. These hypotheses were partially supported, but, the pattern in the data was strong enough to significantly allow the correct identification of the gender of the student participating in the online course discussion.

That gender should come through significantly in this otherwise deliberately gender and culture independent ICT setting lends support the claim that there is a need to include gender as another significant aspect of culture, even within the same national culture environment. One should pay special heed to this conclusion because to some extent there is a voluntary gender segregation going on in these discussions. This is something quite amazing when one stops to think about because it is going on despite the gender neutral environment which supports neither the typical male report type communication nor the typical female rapport type communication.

Before discussing these implications in detail, a word should be said about the limitations of the study. The data in this study came from a convenience sample. This is adequate because the objective of the study was to demonstrate sup-

port for the need to include gender as an aspect of culture. Generalization of the findings was not an objective per se. Generalization requires replication in other and more varied ICT settings, including, but not limited to, other online courses and ICT supported business interactions. To this, one should add that no two courses are the same. Having said this though, the data of this exploratory study do warrant further investigation. Some gender behavior patterns did come through and did allow a significant identification of student gender.

So what do the data tell us? Gender, as sociolinguists and eminent playwrights tell us, is also about culture. Cross-gender communications have cross-culture aspects to them. While it is as yet unknown if these gender differences are ingrained or are learnt, they did come through even when the settings, such as the one of this study, should have made them mute. When considering how culture affects ICT adoption and usage patterns, and it does (Gefen & Straub, 1997; Leidner & Kayworth, 2006; Rose & Straub, 1998; Straub, 1994), this aspect should be considered too. Although more research is needed, sociolinguistics is one possible theory base to support this inclusion. On a practical level these conclusions imply some interesting tentative implications. If men and women communicate with different objectives and so understand messages differently, then awareness and practical steps to address these misunderstandings should be taken both in online conversations and in other instances of ICT.

Explaining the gender effect by focusing on the culture of language may also explain some previous research results. People are generally more accepting of answers given by a computer generated cartoon when the topic of the answer provided through this cartoon corresponds to its gender stereotypes: male cartoons about sports and female cartoons about fashion (Lee, 2003). If gender preference is so much part of our everyday behavior that people show a tendency to congregating by gender even in gender neutral discussions, then this carryover of oral discussion gender behavior might explain why this happens. The results also provide additional explanations why women sense more social presence in business email than men do (Gefen & Straub, 1997). Again, the carryover of the respective gender aspects of communication to an ICT environment which is supposed to be gender neutral might explain this.

Looking at the results in a broader manner, the results of the study, if generalized, tentatively suggest that just as culture should be a major aspect of ICT research so should gender. ICT research, and especially human computer interaction research, is about many things, but one of its central topics of research is about how people use ICT to communicate with other people, be it through email, ecommerce, or virtual communities. A key aspect in such communication, determining its meaning and success, is the use of language. Since language cannot be understood properly when analyzed devoid of its social underpinnings, these socially overlaid meanings should be part of any research on how ICT is used and how it supports communication among people. Ignoring these central social components, how they contribute to the meaning and value of ICT based communication, and especially how misunderstandings may arise when communicating across genders as they are across cultures, is tantamount to ignoring a central tenet of the ICT interaction process itself.

Including gender into human computer interaction research, however, requires a solid theoretical base. This lack of a strong theory base may explain why gender has not come up often before as a central aspect of this research. It is not enough to say there is a significant T statistic. There must also be a theory base which can explain why there is this significance and so tie it into other research and a broader understanding. There might be undeniable physiological reasons which affect gender differences in ICT behavior, as some research suggests (Cutmore, Hine, Maberly, Langford,

& Hawgood, 2000), but there are also cultural reasons, such as those presented in this study. These cultural psychological reasons are central in determining behavior. Sociolinguistics could be one theory base on which such understanding could be achieved. Looking at things through this theory could make our understanding richer and broader, and, more importantly, avoid a joint misclassification of men and women into one group which ignores the different social meanings men and women attach to communication.

Unfortunately, while culture is recognized as a key issue in ICT adoption and usage patterns (Leidner & Kayworth, 2006), most such research has chosen to ignore this aspect of gender. This may be because of politically correctness constraints, but it is taking the unnecessary risk of being scientifically wrong. Smothering this cultural aspect not only hides significant relationships and blotches construct validity, but it also skews our understanding of the world. We know men and women have different managerial styles (Beasley, 2005; Boon, 2003) and handle domination and conflicts differently (Chan, Monroe, Ng, & Tan, 2006). And, we all know men and women think and communicate differently, whether saying so is or is not politically correct. It is about time ICT research also paid homage to gender. Ignoring gender may be a mistake, if gender differences come through even in the controlled settings of this study, how much more so that they should be evident in less controlled settings.

## REFERENCES

Abrams, D., & Hogg, M. A. (1987). Language Attitudes, Frames of Reference, and Social Identity: A Scottish Dimension. *Journal of Language and Social Psychology, 6*(3-4), 201-213.

Ahuja, M. K., & Thatcher, J. B. (2005). Moving Beyond Intentions and Toward the Theory of Trying: Effects of Work Environment and Gender on

Postadoption Information Technology Use. *MIS Quarterly, 29*(3), 427–459.

Anderson, K. J., & Leaper, C. (1998). Meta-analyses of Gender Effects on Conversational Interruption: Who, What, When, Where, and How. *Sex Roles, 39*(3/4), 225-252.

Beasley, A. L. (2005). The Style Split. *Journal of Accountancy, 200*(3), 91-92.

Boneva, B., Kraut, R., & Frohlich, D. (2001). Using e-Mail for Personal Relationships: The Difference Gender Makes. *American Behavioral Scientist, 45*(3), 530-549.

Boon, M. v. d. (2003). Women in International Management: An International Perspective on Women's Ways of Leadership. *Women in Management Review, 18*(3/4), 132-146.

Brizendine, L. (2006). *The Female Brain*. USA: Morgan Road Books.

Chan, C. C. A., Monroe, G., Ng, J., & Tan, R. (2006). Conflict Management Styles of Male and Female Junior Accountants. *International Journal of Management, 23*(2), 289-295.

Coates, J. (1986). *Women, Men and Languages: Studies in Language and Linguistics*. London, UK: Longman.

Costa, P. T. J., Terracciano, A., & McCrae, R. R. (2001). Gender Differences in Personality Traits across Cultures: Robust and Surprising Findings. *Journal of Personality and Social Psychology, 81*(2), 322-331.

Cutmore, T. R. H., Hine, T. J., Maberly, K. J., Langford, N. M., & Hawgood, G. (2000). Cognitive and Gender Factors Influencing Navigation in a Virtual Environment. *International Journal of Human-Computer Studies, 53*, 223-249.

Deaux, K. (1984). From Individual Differences to Social Categories. Analysis of a Decade's Research on Gender. *American Psychologist, 39*(2), 105-116.

Deschamps, J. (1982). Social Identity and relations of Power Between Groups. In H. Tajfel (Ed.), *Social Identity and Intergroup Relations* (pp. 85-98.). UK: Cambridge University Press.

Edelsky, C. (1993). Who's Got the Floor? In D. Tannen (Ed.), *Gender and Conversational Interaction* (pp. 189-227). New York, NY: Oxford University Press.

Gefen, D. (2003). Tutorial Assessing Unidimensionality through LISREL: An Explanation and Example. *Communications of the Association for Information Systems, 12*(2), 1-26.

Gefen, D., & Ridings, C. (2005). If You Spoke as She Does, Sir, Instead of the Way You Do: A Sociolinguistics Perspective of Gender Differences in Virtual Communities. *The DATA BASE for Advances in Information Systems, 36*(2), 78-92.

Gefen, D., & Straub, D. W. (1997). Gender Differences in Perception and Adoption of E-mail: An Extension to the Technology Acceptance Model. *MIS Quarterly, 21*(4), 389-400.

Gray, J. (1992). *Men are From Mars, Women Are From Venus*. New York, NY: HarperCollins.

Guiller, J., & Durndell, A. (2007). Students' Linguistic Behaviour in Online Discussion Groups: Does Gender Matter? *Computers in Human Behavior, 23*(5), 2240-2255.

Hannah, A., & Murachver, T. (1999). Gender and Conversational Style as Predictors of Conversational Behavior. *Journal of Language and Social Psychology, 18*(2), 153-174.

Herring, S. C. (1993, January 20). Gender and Democracy in Computer Mediated Communication. *Electronic Journal of Communication 3(2)* Retrieved July 29, 2006, from http://www.cios.org/www/ejc/v3n293.htm

Herring, S. C. (1996a). Posting in a Different Voice: Gender and Ethics in Computer-Mediated Communication. In C. Ess (Ed.), *Philosophical*

*Perspectives on Computer-Mediated Communication* (pp. 115-145). Albany: State University of New York Press.

Herring, S. C. (1996b). Two Variants of an Electronic Message Schema. In S. C. Herring (Ed.), *Computer-Mediated Communication Linguistic, Social and Cross-cultural Perspectives* (pp. 81-106). Philadelphia, PA: John Benjamins Publishing Company.

Hofstede, G. (1980). *Culture's Consequences: International Differences in Work Related Values.* London, UK: Sage.

Hofstede, G., Neuijen, B., Ohayv, D. D., & Sanders, G. (1990). Measuring Organizational Cultures: A Qualitative and Quantitative Study Across Twenty Cases. *Administrative Science Quarterly, 35,* 286-316.

Holmes, J. (1992). Women's Talk in Public Contexts. *Discourse and Society, 3*(2), 131-150.

Hong, S. J., & Tam, K. Y. (2006). Understanding the Adoption of Multipurpose Information Appliances: The Case of Mobile Data Services. *Information Systems Research, 17*(2), 162-179.

Johnson, B. (1993). Community and Contest: Midwestern Men and Women Creating Their Worlds in Conversational Storytelling. In D. Tannen (Ed.), *Gender and Conversational Interaction* (pp. 62-80). New York, NY: Oxford University Press.

Kayworth, T., & Leidner, D. E. (2000). The Global Virtual Manager: A Prescription for Success. *European Management Journal, 18*(2), 183-194.

Kilbourne, W., & Weeks, S. (1997). A Socio-economic Perspective on Gender Bias in Technology. *Journal of Socio-Economics, 26*(1), 243-260.

Kock, N., & Hantula, D. A. (2005). Do We Have e-Collaboration Genes? *International Journal of e-Collaboration, 1*(2), i-ix.

Lakoff, R. T. (1975). *Language and Woman's Place.* New York: Harper & Row.

Lee, E.-J. (2003). Effects of "Gender" of the Computer on Informational Social Influence: The Moderating Role of Task Type. *International Journal of Human-Computer Studies, 58,* 347–362.

Leidner, D. E., & Kayworth, T. (2006). Review: A Review of Culture in Information Systems Research: Toward a Theory of Information Technology Culture Conflict. *MIS Quarterly, 30*(2), 357-399.

Mulac, A., Erlandson, K. T., Farrar, W. J., & Hallett, J. S. (1998). Uh-huh. What's That all About? Differing Interpretations of Conversational Backchannels and Questions as Source of Miscommunication Across Gender Boundaries. *Communication Research, 25*(6), 641-668.

Parks, M. R., & Floyd, K. (1995, January 10, 2003). Making Friends in Cyberspace. *Journal of Computer Mediated Communication 1(4)* Retrieved October 3, 2007, from http://www.ascusc.org/jcmc/vol1/issue4/parks.html

Rose, G., & Straub, D. W. (1998). Predicting General IT Use: Applying TAM to the Arabic World. *Journal of Global Information Management, 6*(3), 39-46.

Stewart, C. M., Shields, S. F., & Sen, N. (2001). Diversity in On-Line Discussions: A study of Cultural and Gender Differences in Listervs. In C. Ess & F. Sudweeks (Eds.), *Culture, Technology, Communication: Towards an Intercultural Global Village* (pp. 161-186). Albany, NJ: State University of New York Press.

Straub, D. W. (1994). The Effect of Culture on IT Diffusion: E-mail and FAX in Japan and the U.S. *Information Systems Research, 5*(1), 23-47.

Tannen, D. (1991). Teachers' Classroom Strategies Should Recognize that Men and Women Use Language Differently. *The Chronicle of Higher Education, June 19*, B1-B3.

Tannen, D. (1994). *You Just Don't Understand Women and Men in Conversation.* New York, NY: Ballantine Books.

Tannen, D. (1995). The Power of Talk: Who Gets Heard and Why. *Harvard Business Review, 73*(5), 138-148.

Venkatesh, V., & Agarwal, R. (2006). A Usability-Centric Perspective on Purchase Behavior in E-Channels. *Management Science, 52*(3), 367-382.

Venkatesh, V., & Morris, M. G. (2000). Why Don't Men Ever Stop to Ask for Directions? Gender, Social Influence, and their Role in Technology Acceptance and Usage Behavior. *MIS Quarterly, 24*(1), 115-139.

Weatherall, A. (1998). Re-visioning Gender and Language Research. *Women and Language, 21*(1), 1-9.

West, C., & Zimmerman, D. (1983). Small Insults: A Study of Interruptions in Cross-sex Conversations between Unacquainted Persons. In B. Thorne, H. Kramarae & N. Henley (Eds.), *Language, Gender and Society* (pp. 103-118). Rowley, MA: Newbury House.

Yates, S. J. (2001). Gender, Language and CMC for Education. *Learning and Instruction, 11*(1), 21-34.

Zhang, X., Prybutok, V. R., & Strutton, D. (2007). Modeling Influences on Impulse Purchasing Behaviors during Online Marketing Transactions. *Journal of Marketing Theory & Practice, 15*(1), 79-89.

Zimmerman, D., & West, C. (1975). Sex-roles, interruptions and silences in conversation. In B. Thorne, H. Kramarae & N. Henley (Eds.), *Language and Sex: Difference and Dominance* (pp. 89-101). Rowley, MA: Newbury House.

# Chapter II
# Toward an Organizational View of E-Collaboration

**Lior Fink**
*Ben-Gurion University of the Negev, Israel*

## ABSTRACT

*This chapter develops an organizational view of the roles and impacts of e-collaboration. Drawing on the dynamic capabilities perspective, e-collaboration is conceptualized as a change-oriented capability that enables a firm to identify, integrate, and apply its knowledge assets to meet competitive demands. Therefore, e-collaboration potentially has three organizational roles – coordination, learning, and innovation – that are associated with either efficiency impacts or competitive impacts. Drawing on contingency theory, the main argument developed in this chapter is that firms in less dynamic business environments need e-collaboration for operational purposes, emphasizing the coordination role, whereas firms in high-velocity business environments need e-collaboration for strategic purposes, emphasizing the learning and innovation roles. An analysis of the way in which business environment characteristics interact with media characteristics serves to demonstrate the importance of strategic characteristics – in addition to media and task characteristics – in determining the organizational effectiveness of e-collaboration.*

## INTRODUCTION

Firms are increasingly adopting electronic communication tools to facilitate collaboration among individuals and groups, both within and beyond organizational boundaries. This trend is driven by the motivation of firms to take advantage of the collaborative potential of such tools as discussion boards, instant messaging, and groupware for facilitating communication and coordination without the limitations of time and place. To promote theory development and to provide practical guidelines, substantial research has been conducted to identify the conditions under which certain collaboration tools and practices are more productive than others (e.g., Daft and Lengel, 1986; Dennis and Valacich, 1999; Dennis et al., 2001; Easley et al., 2003; Majchrzak et al., 2005; McGrath, 1984; Nunamaker et al., 1991; Short et al., 1976; Zigurs and Buckland, 1998). This research tends to focus on the direct consequences of e-collaboration in group contexts. Considerably less research has been conducted on the importance of organizational conditions. Overall, it seems that e-collaboration research has underestimated the significance of the organizational and environmental context.

In this chapter, I conceptually address two research questions:

(1) What are the differences between the roles of e-collaboration in dynamic versus static business environments?

(2) What are the implications of role differences for the implementation of e-collaboration?

To answer these questions, I develop an organizational view of e-collaboration by conceptualizing e-collaboration as a dynamic capability. I draw upon three strategic management frameworks – the resource-based view of the firm, the knowledge-based view of the firm, and the dynamic capabilities perspective – to describe how specialized knowledge assets can be integrated through e-collaborative processes to create and sustain a competitive advantage. I then use this conceptualization as a platform for defining the organizational roles of e-collaboration and the potential impact of each role on organizational performance. The conceptualization thus suggests that different roles of e-collaboration should be emphasized in different business environments. Finally, I discuss the implications of the proposed organizational view by demonstrating the interaction between business environment characteristics and communication characteristics, whose importance has been established in the literature.

## AN ORGANIZATIONAL VIEW OF E-COLLABORATION

### Knowledge as a Strategic Resource

The resource-based view of the firm (Barney, 1991; Dierickx and Cool, 1989; Grant, 1991; Wernerfelt, 1984) argues that heterogeneity and immobility of firm resources can provide the basis for superior competitive performance. Firm resources that are strategically valuable, because they enable the implementation of strategies that exploit opportunities or neutralize threats in the business environment, and that are heterogeneously distributed enable firms to outperform the competition. However, such a competitive advantage cannot be sustained if competitors can acquire strategically equivalent resources to implement the same valuable strategy. Therefore, for a firm to sustain its competitive advantage, its valuable and rare resources should not be open to imitation or substitution.

The knowledge-based view of the firm (Grant, 1996; Kogut and Zander, 1996; Nonaka and Takeuchi, 1995) extends the resource-based view by defining organizational knowledge as a valuable subset of the firm's resources, capable of generating and sustaining a competitive advantage. The knowledge-based view perceives a firm as a knowledge-creating entity; it argues that the capability to create and utilize knowledge is the most valuable source of the firm's sustainable competitive advantage (Nahapiet and Ghoshal, 1998; Nonaka et al., 2000; Spender, 1996). Specialized, firm-specific knowledge resources are those that are valuable, scarce, and difficult to imitate, transfer, or substitute. By utilizing such resources in the attainment of organizational goals, a firm could gain an advantage in its markets that competitors would find difficult to overcome. Tangible resources are more susceptible to imitation and substitution because their origin lies outside the firm. Sustained competitive advantage is more likely to come from intangible firm-specific knowledge that adds value to the incoming means of production in a unique manner (Spender, 1996).

One of Grant's (1996) underlying assumptions is that knowledge is created and held by individuals, not organizations. Individuals' specialized knowledge is integrated within an organization through four coordination mechanisms: rules and directives, sequencing, routines, and group problem solving and decision making. Whereas the former three coordination mechanisms seek the integration of knowledge by minimizing the necessary communication between individuals, the latter represents a communication-intensive form of integration. Directives, sequencing, and routines are organizational practices that aim at integrating knowledge efficiently with minimal costs. Conversely, group coordination modes are more costly in terms of communication overhead but carry a potential of improved performance. While it is beyond the scope of this chapter to analyze the differences between coordination mechanisms that seek to minimize communication and those that seek to capitalize on it, the knowledge-based view highlights the strategic value of organizational knowledge and the role of coordination mechanisms in realizing this value.

## E-Collaboration as a Coordination Mechanism

Applying Grant's (1996) view of coordination mechanisms, e-collaboration is conceptualized here as a group coordination mechanism. Kock, Davison, Wazlawick, and Ocker (2001) define e-collaboration as "collaboration among individuals engaged in a common task using electronic technologies" (p. 1). This definition encompasses different types of systems, ranging from computer-mediated communication (CMC), through group decision support systems (GDSS), to Web-based collaboration tools (Kock and Nosek, 2005). The jury is still out on the effectiveness

of different collaborative technologies compared with traditional face-to-face (FTF) collaboration. The literature typically proposes a contingency approach, which matches the communication medium to the characteristics of the task. On the one hand, theories such as the media richness theory (Daft and Lengel, 1986) argue that the FTF medium is richer (the ability of information to change understanding within a time interval) than CMC. On the other hand, theories such as media synchronicity (Dennis and Valacich, 1999) propose that the importance of media capabilities depends on the characteristics of the situation. Therefore, "the 'richest' medium is that which best provides the set of capabilities needed by the situation: the individuals, task, and social context within which they interact" (Dennis and Valacich, 1999, p. 3). Nevertheless, the common denominator among researchers is that e-collaboration tools are vehicles for information and knowledge sharing that transcends traditional limitations of time and space. The ubiquitous Internet enables these tools to provide significantly larger reach and richness of services (Evans and Wurster, 2000). Therefore, compared with traditional coordination mechanisms, e-collaboration is a group coordination mechanism with wider capabilities because it enables and facilitates the work of *virtual* groups, giving firms extra degrees of freedom in establishing and managing knowledge-sharing mechanisms.

## E-Collaboration as a Dynamic Capability

*"Because many of the most valuable assets inside the firm are knowledge related and hence nontradable, the coordination and integration of such assets create value that cannot be replicated in a market."* (Teece, 2007, p. 1341)

While e-collaboration is commonly described as a coordination mechanism for knowledge sharing, in dynamic business environments, characterized by rapid strategic and technological change, it has potential strategic value. In this section, I draw upon the dynamic capabilities perspective (Eisenhardt and Martin, 2000; Teece et al., 1997) to promote an understanding of the strategic potential of e-collaboration in dynamic business environments.

The dynamic capabilities perspective is an extension of the resource-based view to dynamic markets (Eisenhardt and Martin, 2000). It has evolved to account for the deficiencies of the resource-based view in explaining how firm resources are developed and renewed in response to shifts in the business environment. The resource-based view identifies a subset of resources as a potential source of competitive advantage. However, this is a static view of the relationship between firm resources and competitive advantage. When change occurs in the business environment, firm resources should evolve to enable new and innovative forms of competitive advantage. By adopting a process approach, the dynamic capabilities perspective argues that dynamic capabilities are the process mechanisms responsible for the continuous development of resources in the face of rapidly evolving strategic needs. Dynamic capabilities are defined as "the firm's ability to integrate, build, and reconfigure internal and external competences to address rapidly changing environments" (Teece et al., 1997, p. 516). Hence, such capabilities are critical in high-velocity business environments, where change can quickly erode the strategic value of resources that had previously been a source of competitive advantage. Dynamic capabilities are less significant in more static business environments, where a firm's superior asset position is more durable and able to sustain a competitive advantage for substantial periods of time.

Dynamic capabilities are, therefore, change-oriented competencies that enable firms to reconfigure and redeploy their resource bases to meet competitive demands (Zahra and George, 2002; Zhu and Kraemer, 2002). By viewing specialized, firm-specific knowledge resources as a strategic asset and e-collaboration processes as a dynamic capability, I propose that e-collaboration is a potential source of competitive advantage, generated by its ability to foster organizational innovation. The distinctive strategic value of specialized knowledge assets has already been discussed previously in presenting the knowledge-based view. In rapidly changing business environments, knowledge assets that have enabled superior competitiveness can quickly lose their strategic relevance, calling for the fast identification and utilization of novel, possibly tacit and distributed knowledge bases to maintain a favorable market position. The frequency of such renewal processes should increase with the degree to which the business environment is dynamic. In these situations, e-collaboration can provide a unique mechanism for the persistent identification, organization, integration, and utilization of knowledge assets. By creating webs of collaborations among various business segments, firms are able to generate new and synergistic resource combinations (Eisenhardt and Galunic, 2000). The dynamic capability of e-collaboration enables the frequent introduction of organizational innovations, which, in turn, can provide a source of sustained competitive advantage.

## The Organizational Roles of E-Collaboration

Prior to identifying the role of e-collaboration in different business environments, it is necessary to generally define the organizational roles of e-collaboration processes. Teece et al. (1997) describe organizational processes as having three roles: coordination/integration (a static concept), learning (a dynamic concept), and reconfiguration (a transformational concept). Teece (2007) refers to them as asset 'orchestration' processes. Building upon this framework, the following sections describe coordination, learning, and innovation as the three organizational roles of e-collaboration.

**Coordination.** The primary functional role of e-collaboration is to facilitate coordination among individuals, groups, and organizations. Coordination is strongly related to the effectiveness of management in virtual settings (Khazanchi and Zigurs, 2006). Malone and Crowston (1994), who define coordination as "managing dependencies between activities" (p. 90), describe communication and group decision making as two processes that are important in almost all instances of coordination. Collaborative technologies are typically designed to facilitate communication and decision making and therefore enable firms to manage dependencies between activities more efficiently and effectively, whether those dependencies are intra- or inter-organizational. The ability of collaborative technologies to enhance coordination among organizations is frequently discussed in the context of interorganizational systems (e.g., Chi and Holsapple, 2005; Kumar and van Dissel, 1996). Bafoutsou and Mentzas (2002) demonstrate that all categories of electronic tools for communication and collaboration address some of the coordination problems created by recent organizational trends, such as decentralization and outsourcing.

**Learning.** E-collaboration may serve as a mechanism for facilitating learning, both individual and organizational, by boosting knowledge creation and sharing processes. Kogut and Zander (1996) view firms as organizations that represent social knowledge of coordination and learning. According to Teece et al. (1997), learning processes are intrinsically social and collective and result from joint contributions to the understanding of complex problems. Collaborative technologies may enable individuals to arrive at new insights by providing an extended field for interaction among members of an organization (Alavi and Leidner, 2001). While individual learning skills are important, their value depends on their utilization to enhance collective learning skills through collaborative mechanisms. Huysman, Creemers, and Derksen (1998) argue that all forms of problematic organizational learning (filtered, egocentric, unbalanced, or autonomous learning) are caused by limited access to information. Therefore, Internet technologies and the new collaboration capabilities they enable increase the efficiency and effectiveness of learning processes (Alavi and Leidner, 2001; Huysman et al., 1998).

The use of collaborative technologies improves the three aspects of knowledge management – knowledge creation, knowledge discovery, and knowledge transfer (Paul, 2006). Leidner, Alavi, and Kayworth (2006) describe two fundamental approaches to knowledge management: the process approach and the practice approach. The process approach attempts to codify organizational knowledge through formalized processes. In contrast, the practice approach attempts to build social environments necessary to facilitate the sharing of tacit knowledge. According to Leidner et al. (2006), both approaches involve the use of collaborative technologies – either to enhance the quality and speed of knowledge creation and distribution or to facilitate conversations and transfer of tacit knowledge. Based on Argyris and Schon (1978), Scott (2000) suggests that e-collaboration facilitates both lower and higher levels of learning. While e-collaboration enables fast feedback to promote greater efficiency at the lower level, it catalyzes the learning process by stimulating reassessment of current practices at the higher level, reflecting a more innovative role of e-collaboration.

**Innovation.** Innovation may be perceived as a mechanism underlying the ability of specialized knowledge assets to sustain a competitive advantage. Knowledge can provide a firm with a competitive advantage, because it is through this knowledge that the firm is able to introduce innovation in processes, products, and services (Nonaka et al., 2000). Nonaka (1991) describes the "knowledge-creating company" as a company "whose sole business is continuous innovation" (p. 96). Collaborative technologies play a significant role in creating business innovation (Eden and Ackermann, 2001). Wheeler (2002) proposes the *net-enabled business innovation cycle* (NEBIC) as an applied dynamic capabilities theory for understanding how pervasive digital networks can enable growth through business innovation. The role of collaboration in fostering business innovation is also demonstrated in *absorptive capacity* research. Cohen and Levinthal (1990) show that a firm's absorptive capacity – its ability to recognize, assimilate, and apply new information based on prior related knowledge – is critical to its innovative capabilities. E-collaboration as a platform for interaction and learning creates opportunities for integrating new external knowledge into existing knowledge assets. Virtual collaboration spaces increase the probability that external knowledge will be identified, assimilated, and implemented to facilitate innovation, because such spaces intensify knowledge flows both internally and externally. Hargadon and Sutton (1997) note that "ideas from one group might solve the problems of another, but only if connections between existing solutions and problems can be made across the boundaries between them" (p. 716). The authors describe how a firm can exploit its network position to become a knowledge broker by gaining knowledge of existing solutions in various industries, creating new products that are original combinations of

existing knowledge, and introducing them into existing and new markets.

Figure 1 summarizes graphically the conceptualizations developed so far in this chapter about e-collaboration as a dynamic capability and about its three organizational roles.

## The Business Value of E-Collaboration

The implementation of collaborative technologies can facilitate coordination, learning, and innovation at the organizational level. However, these organizational roles of e-collaboration, in themselves, are not direct sources of business value. Coordination, learning, and innovation are of no consequence if they do not result in organizational performance impacts. Therefore, to demonstrate the potential business value of e-collaboration, it is necessary to associate the three organizational roles of e-collaboration with their expected performance impacts, as is done in this section.

In a comprehensive review of the literature on IT and organizational performance, Melville, Kraemer, and Gurbaxani (2004) develop an integrative model of IT business value. The authors' analysis highlights the existence of two formulations of performance, efficiency and ef-

*Figure 1. E-collaboration as dynamic capability*

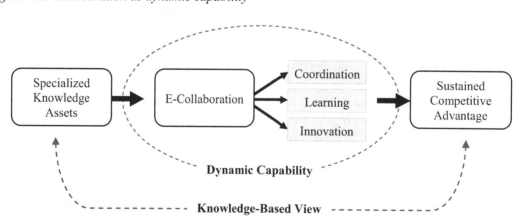

fectiveness. The former, designated *efficiency impacts*, adopts an internal process perspective using such metrics as cost reduction and productivity enhancement. The latter, designated *competitive impacts*, focuses on the attainment of organizational objectives in relation to the external environment, possibly resulting in a competitive advantage. Melville et al. (2004) note that efficiency and competitive impacts are independent of one another, i.e., IT may generate efficiency impacts even if it is quickly imitated by competitors, or it may be a source of competitive advantage based on a superior market position without process efficiency improvements.

I propose that e-collaboration roles are associated with both efficiency and competitive impacts. However, the particular roles differ in their impacts on organizational performance: coordination leads primarily to efficiency impacts, whereas learning and innovation are more strongly associated with competitive impacts. One of the most fundamental performance impacts attributed to IT is the reduction of coordination costs (Shapiro and Varian, 1999). Malone and Crowston (1994) expect three effects from using IT to reduce the cost of coordination: substituting human coordination, increasing the overall amount of coordination used, and encouraging a shift toward the use of more coordination-intensive structures (i.e., previously "expensive" coordination structures become more feasible and advantageous). Efficiency impacts also result from better coordination with the external business environment. Collaborative supply chain management (SCM) systems, which strengthen coordination among partners in a supply chain, offer inventory, process, and product cost reductions, while lowering the total cost of system ownership (McLaren et al., 2002). Coordination-based efficiency impacts are apparent at the organizational and interorganizational levels, but also at lower levels. Huang and Newell (2003) empirically demonstrate that the level of coordination positively affects integration efficiency in the context of cross-functional project teams. In conclusion, implementing collaborative technologies for the purpose of enhancing coordination, at different organizational levels, can deliver a wide range of organizational efficiency impacts.

Conversely, organizational learning has the potential to generate both efficiency and competitive impacts, depending on its objectives and level. Electronic links enhance lower and higher levels of learning (Argyris and Schon, 1978; Scott, 2000). At the lower level, collaborative technologies are used to integrate explicit knowledge for the purpose of reducing process and product costs, shortening cycle times, improving productivity, enhancing quality, and streamlining business processes. By integrating knowledge from diverse organizational perspectives, enabled by e-collaboration, learning processes have the potential to improve the efficiency of business processes. At the higher level, collaborative technologies are used to facilitate systems thinking (Senge, 1990), strengthening the ability of firms to identify opportunities and threats in the business environment, to understand their strengths and weaknesses, to formulate an organizational vision, and to develop creative solutions to organizational problems. By identifying, integrating, and utilizing organizational sources of tacit knowledge, a firm can outperform the competition and gain a competitive advantage. However, at the higher level, the competitive impacts of learning are not direct but rather mediated through innovation. There is a causal relationship between organizational learning capabilities, process and product innovation, and competitive advantage (Adams and Lamont, 2003). A firm that is able to learn effectively, but is unable to use the products of learning in the service of innovation, would not gain performance advantages. Therefore, organizational learning and innovation may be viewed as complementary processes: the former is a mechanism for generating alternatives and solutions, and the latter is an implementation mechanism. While collaborative technologies may be viewed as commodity resources that are susceptible to imitation, a firm's ability to exploit their potential in facilitating its learning and innovation capabilities is critical in gaining IT-based competitiveness. The strategic importance of learning comes from implying path-dependency and specificity in organizational transformations preventing imitability, which is crucial for competitive advantage (Andreu and Ciborra, 1996). In recent years, it seems that continuous business innovation has repeatedly been identified, more than any other organizational capability, as a potential source of competitive advantage in contemporary business environments (e.g., Adams and Lamont, 2003; Goh, 2005; Roberts and Amit, 2003; Santos et al., 2004; Sawhney et al., 2006).

## Modes of E-Collaboration in Different Business Environments: A Contingency Perspective

In this section, I draw on contingency theory to integrate the conceptualizations developed thus far in this chapter into a process view of e-collaboration at the organizational level. Contingency theory, one of the most dominant theories in the study of organizational design and performance, is based on the assumption that there is no one best way to organize, and that any one way of organizing is not equally effective under all conditions (Galbraith, 1973; Ginsberg and Venkatraman, 1985). Central to this theory is the proposition that the structure and process of an organization must fit its context, if it is to be effective (Drazin and Van de Ven, 1985). The contingency approach to information systems research suggests that the better the fit between contingency variables and the design and use of IT, the better the IT performance and the organizational performance (Weill and Olson, 1989).

The organizational view developed here focuses on the business environment, specifically on the extent to which it is dynamic, as the primary contingency variable determining the preferred mode of e-collaboration. The business environment has been conceptualized as one of the key constructs for understanding organizational behavior and performance (Hofer and Schendel, 1978; Prescott, 1986). One of its important characteristics is the rate of change in products, production process, and organizational factors (Eisenhardt and Brown, 1998; Fine, 1998). The rate of change in the business environment has been found to be a moderator of the relationship between IT use and organizational performance (Guimaraes et al., 2002).

I propose that firms can implement collaborative technologies in two different modes, operational and strategic. The former is more valuable when a firm's business environment is static, whereas the latter is more valuable when the business environment is dynamic.

**Operational e-collaboration mode.** Firms can implement collaborative technologies to improve their efficiency of scale and scope by building upon their ability to facilitate organizational coordination. Such an IT investment is more lucrative for firms that operate in less dynamic business environments and aim at gaining efficiency advantages in their markets. When market conditions are relatively stable, market entry barriers are high, new technologies are developed along an evolutionary path, and business models are established and steady, then a firm may pursue market advantages that are based on superior cost and time-to-market positions. To gain IT-based efficiency advantages, the firm can implement collaborative technologies that emphasize the coordination role of e-collaboration. For instance, the use of asynchronous communication tools, such as electronic mailing lists and discussion boards, may enable better exchange of information and explicit knowledge, improved coordination, and, eventually, cost and cycle time reductions. Such use of collaborative technologies aims at enhancing the operational capabilities of the firm.

**Strategic e-collaboration mode.** Firms can also use collaborative technologies to gain competitive advantages by capitalizing on their ability to facilitate organizational learning and innovation. Such an IT investment is more lucrative for firms that operate in high-velocity markets and repeatedly seek to exploit opportunities and neutralize threats in their external environments. When market conditions are dynamic, market entry barriers are low, new technologies are developed along a revolutionary path, and business opportunities are proliferating, then a firm has to continuously find new organizational sources of competitiveness. To gain an IT-based competitive advantage, the firm can implement collaborative technologies that emphasize the role of e-collaboration in enabling learning and innovation processes. For example, by using synchronous collaboration tools (e.g., instant messaging, video conferencing, and groupware) to support the cross-organizational identification and integration of tacit knowledge, knowledge creation and renewal processes can generate new

opportunities for innovation and, consequently, superior competitive performance.

Malhotra (2000) distinguishes between two models of knowledge management, an information-processing model and a sense-making model. Whereas the former is optimization driven and efficiency oriented, the latter is directed at knowledge creation and knowledge renewal. The conceptual framework presented in Figure 2 is based on the same underlying logic: IT can be implemented to enhance efficiency, by emphasizing its operational capabilities, and competitiveness, by emphasizing its strategic capabilities. In the particular case of e-collaboration, efficiency impacts are gained by leveraging its coordination role, whereas competitive impacts are gained by capitalizing on its role as a catalyst of learning and innovation.

*Figure 2. An organizational view of e-collaboration*

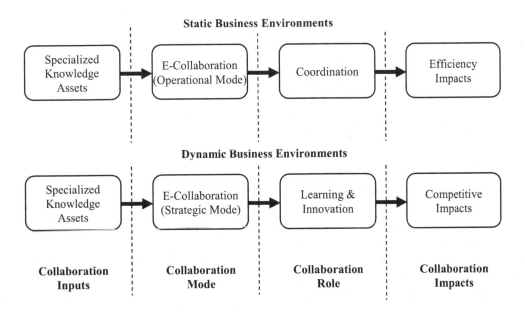

## IMPLICATIONS OF AN ORGANIZATIONAL VIEW OF E-COLLABORATION

The organizational view of e-collaboration, developed in this chapter, describes the role and potential organizational impact of e-collaboration in different business environments. While this view represents a conceptual framework, it can be extended to offer practical guidelines for the selection and implementation of collaborative technologies based on business environment characteristics. Considerable research has been done to identify which collaborative technologies should prove most effective in certain situations (e.g., Daft and Lengel, 1986; Dennis and Valacich, 1999; Dennis et al., 2001; Zigurs and Buckland, 1998). This research has attempted to associate specific media and task characteristics with the most effective collaboration tools, given their different communication and information processing capabilities. An organizational view of e-collaboration may broaden this line of research by arguing that collaborative technologies should be selected and implemented on the basis of strategic characteristics, specifically business environment characteristics, in addition to media and task characteristics. Business environment characteristics should be considered because of their criticalness to the ability to align the use of collaborative technologies with business strategies. Therefore, a collaboration tool that is selected on the basis of media characteristics, but does not provide a good fit to strategic objectives, would probably allow individuals to communicate effectively without significant strategic value. To demonstrate the validity of this argument, as well as to extend the proposed organizational view to offer practical guidelines, I draw on Dennis and Valacich (1999) to describe which media characteristics have greater importance in dynamic versus static business environments. Given that the interaction between media characteristics and the effectiveness of collaborative technologies

has already been described, understanding the interaction between media characteristics and the extent to which the business environment is dynamic makes it possible to identify the collaborative technologies that should be more effective in different business environments.

Dennis and Valacich (1999) describe five media characteristics that can affect communication: (1) immediacy of feedback – the extent to which a medium enables rapid bidirectional communication; (2) symbol variety – the variety of ways in which information can be communicated; (3) parallelism – the number of simultaneous conversations that can exist effectively; (4) rehearsability – the extent to which the medium enables the rehearsal or fine tuning of the message prior to sending it; and (5) reprocessability – the extent to which a message can be reexamined or reprocessed within the context of the communication event. Table 1 describes the level of importance of these five media characteristics in static and dynamic business environments.

The table shows that in less dynamic business environments, where e-collaboration should be implemented in an operational mode to facilitate coordination, rehearsability and reprocessability are the more significant media characteristics. To improve coordination, the immediacy, "depth" (symbol variety), and "width" (parallelism) of the communication channel are less important than the clarity, accuracy, and completeness of the communicated information, given the high cost associated with inaccuracies and misunderstandings when coordination and efficiency are the objectives. Table 1 also shows that in high-velocity business environments, where e-collaboration should be implemented in a strategic mode to enhance learning and innovation, the significant media characteristics are feedback immediacy, symbol variety, and parallelism. In such environments, the interactiveness and richness of the communication channel are crucial to the creative thinking of individuals and their ability to learn and innovate. Rather than increase

*Table 1. Importance of media characteristics in static and dynamic business environments*

| Media Characteristic | Static Business Environment | Dynamic Business Environment |
|---|---|---|
| Immediacy of feedback | Less important | Important |
| Symbol variety | Less important | Important |
| Parallelism | Less important | Important |
| Rehearsability | Important | Less important |
| Reprocessability | Important | Less important |

communication effectiveness, rehearsability and reprocessability may inhibit free expression and associative thinking, which are extremely valuable in such situations.

Based on Table 1, it is possible to identify which collaborative technologies should prove more effective in different business environments. Technologies high in rehearsability and reprocessability, such as electronic mail and discussion boards, should be more effective in less dynamic environments (operational e-collaboration mode). In contrast, technologies that are relatively high in feedback immediacy, symbol variety, and parallelism, such as synchronous groupware, should be more effective in high-velocity environments (strategic e-collaboration mode). It is important to note here, however, that very few collaborative technologies are high in all three media characteristics that are important in enhancing learning and innovation. Future research may further examine interactions between strategic characteristics and media, task, or social characteristics to identify situations in which the successful implementation of collaborative technologies warrants an organizational view.

## CONTRIBUTIONS TO RESEARCH

Beyond practical implications, an organizational view of e-collaboration offers several research contributions. Firstly, as discussed in the previous section, an organizational view extends previous research on media and task characteristics as key determinants of collaborative technology effectiveness. It does so by demonstrating that strategic characteristics, specifically the degree to which the business environment is dynamic, may be crucial for the success of e-collaboration. Because strategic characteristics interact with media and task characteristics, understanding the specific organizational situation is essential for implementing collaborative technologies effectively.

Secondly, considerable research has been conducted to account for the potential of specialized knowledge assets to create and sustain a competitive advantage. Grant (1996) describes four coordination mechanisms that seek the integration of knowledge. Others turn to learning or innovation as the mechanisms underlying the strategic benefits of knowledge assets (e.g., Adams and Lamont, 2003; Andreu and Ciborra, 1996; Cohen and Levinthal, 1990; Goh, 2005; Hargadon and Sutton, 1997; Nonaka, 1991; Wheeler, 2002). By conceptualizing e-collaboration as a dynamic capability, which potentially has three organizational roles, the organizational view developed in this chapter represents an overarching conceptualization of how collaborative technologies mediate the organizational impacts of specialized knowledge assets. Furthermore, it is argued that two routes exist for knowledge to have an organizational impact through e-collaboration. Distinguishing between the operational and strategic modes of e-collaboration offers a broad theoretical explanation of its potential organizational consequences.

Finally, the proposed organizational view promotes the empirical investigation of the organizational roles and impacts of e-collaboration. The conceptualizations developed in this chapter can be used straightforwardly to formulate research hypotheses about relationships among collaboration tools, roles, organizational impacts, and business environment characteristics. For example, empirical research may investigate whether collaborative technologies high in feedback immediacy, symbol variety, and parallelism are associated with collaboration-based learning and innovation, resulting in competitive impacts, and whether those relationships are more significant in dynamic business environments than in static environments.

## CONCLUSION

While there is an increasingly growing body of research that explores the organizational implementation of collaborative technologies, a significant part of that research typically focuses on the context of the individual or the group. As a result, studies that use an organizational lens to explore e-collaboration are lacking. In this chapter, I develop an organizational view of e-collaboration. A view of e-collaboration as having three organizational roles – coordination, learning, and innovation – associated with either efficiency impacts (operational mode) or competitive impacts (strategic mode) offers valuable practical guidelines and, at the same time, advances theory development. The next conceptual step should be to link this organizational view to previous, more established views of e-collaboration, which focus

on processes that individuals or groups undergo. I demonstrate one avenue in which such links between different views can be identified. This is done by exploring the interaction between strategic and media characteristics. The existence of such an interaction validates the criticalness of strategic characteristics to the successful implementation of collaborative technologies. While further conceptual and empirical research is warranted to fully identify the operational and strategic value of e-collaboration, the organizational view developed in this chapter represents a theoretical foundation for future research that aims at understanding e-collaboration through an organizational lens.

## REFERENCES

Adams, G. L., & Lamont, B. T. (2003). Knowledge management systems and developing sustainable competitive advantage. *Journal of Knowledge Management, 7*(2), 142-154.

Alavi, M., & Leidner, D. E. (2001). Knowledge management and knowledge management systems: Conceptual foundations and research issues. *MIS Quarterly, 25*(1), 107-136.

Andreu, R., & Ciborra, C. (1996). Organizational learning and core capabilities development: The role of IT. *Journal of Strategic Information Systems, 5*(2), 111-127.

Argyris, C., & Schon, D. A. (1978). *Organizational learning: A theory of action perspective.* Reading, MA: Addison-Wesley Publishing Company.

Bafoutsou, G., & Mentzas, G. (2002). Review and functional classification of collaborative systems. *International Journal of Information Management, 22*(4), 281–305.

Barney, J. (1991). Firm resources and sustained competitive advantage. *Journal of Management, 17*(1), 99-120.

Chi, L., & Holsapple, C. W. (2005). Understanding computer-mediated interorganizational collaboration: A model and framework. *Journal of Knowledge Management, 9*(1), 53-75.

Cohen, W. M., & Levinthal, D. A. (1990). Absorptive capacity: A new perspective on learning and innovation. *Administrative Science Quarterly, 35*(1), 128-152.

Daft, R. L., & Lengel, R. H. (1986). Organizational information requirements, media richness and structural design. *Management Science, 32*(5), 554-571.

Dennis, A. R., & Valacich, J. S. (1999). Rethinking media richness: Towards a theory of media synchronicity. In R. H. Sprague (Ed.), *Proceedings of the 32nd Hawaii International Conference on System Sciences* (pp. 1-10). Los Alamitos, CA: IEEE Computer Society Press.

Dennis, A. R., Wixom, B. H., & Vandenberg, R. J. (2001). Understanding fit and appropriation effects in group support systems via meta-analysis. *MIS Quarterly, 25*(2), 167-193.

Dierickx, I., & Cool, K. (1989). Asset stock accumulation and sustainability of competitive advantage. *Management Science, 35*(12), 1504-1511.

Drazin, R., & Van de Ven, A. H. (1985). Alternative forms of fit in contingency theory. *Administrative Science Quarterly, 30*(4), 514-539.

Easley, R. F., Devaraj, S., & Crant, J. M. (2003). Relating collaborative technology use to teamwork quality and performance: An empirical analysis. *Journal of Management Information Systems, 19*(4), 247-268.

Eden, C., & Ackermann, F. (2001). Group decision and negotiation in strategy making. *Group Decision and Negotiation, 10*(2), 119–140.

Eisenhardt, K. M., & Brown, S. L. (1998). Time pacing: Competing in markets that won't stand still. *Harvard Business Review, 76*(2), 59-69.

Eisenhardt, K. M., & Galunic, D. C. (2000). Co-evolving: At last, a way to make synergies work. *Harvard Business Review, 78*(1), 91–101.

Eisenhardt, K. M., & Martin, J. A. (2000). Dynamic capabilities: What are they? *Strategic Management Journal, 21*(10), 1105–1121.

Evans, P., & Wurster, T. S. (2000). *Blown to bits: How the new economics of information transforms strategy.* Boston, MA: Harvard Business School Press.

Fine, C. (1998). *Clockspeed: Winning industrial control in the age of temporary advantage.* Reading, MA: Perseus Books.

Galbraith, J. (1973). *Designing complex organizations.* Reading, MA: Addison-Wesley.

Ginsberg, A., & Venkatraman, N. (1985). Contingency perspectives of organizational strategy: A critical review of the empirical research. *Academy of Management Review, 10*(3), 421-434.

Goh, A. L. S. (2005). Harnessing knowledge for innovation: An integrated management framework. *Journal of Knowledge Management, 9*(4), 6-18.

Grant, R. M. (1991). The resource-based theory of competitive advantage: Implications for strategy formulation. *California Management Review, 33*(3), 114-135.

Grant, R. M. (1996). Toward a knowledge-based theory of the firm. *Strategic Management Journal, 17*, 109-122.

Guimaraes, T., Cook, D., & Natarajan, N. (2002). Exploring the importance of business clockspeed as a moderator for determinants of supplier network performance. *Decision Sciences, 33*(4), 629-644.

Hargadon, A., & Sutton, R. I. (1997). Technology brokering and innovation in a product development firm. *Administrative Science Quarterly, 42*(4), 716-749.

Hofer, C. W., & Schendel, D. (1978). *Strategy formulation: Analytical concepts*. St. Paul, MN: West Publishing Company.

Huang, J. C., & Newell, S. (2003). Knowledge integration processes and dynamics within the context of cross-functional projects. *International Journal of Project Management, 21*(3), 167–176.

Huysman, M., Creemers, M., & Derksen, F. (1998). Learning from the environment: Exploring the relation between organizational learning, knowledge management and information/communication technology. In E. D. Hoadley & I. Benbasat (Eds.), *Proceedings of the 4th Americas Conference on Information Systems* (pp. 598-600). Atlanta, GA: Association for Information Systems.

Khazanchi, D., & Zigurs, I. (2006). Patterns for effective management of virtual projects: Theory and evidence. *International Journal of e-Collaboration, 2*(3), 25-49.

Kock, N., Davison, R., Wazlawick, R., & Ocker, R. (2001). E-collaboration: A look at past research and future challenges. *Journal of Systems and Information Technology, 5*(1), 1-9.

Kock, N., & Nosek, J. (2005). Expanding the boundaries of e-collaboration. *IEEE Transactions on Professional Communication, 48*(1), 1-9.

Kogut, B., & Zander, U. (1996). What do firms do? Coordination, identity, and learning. *Organization Science, 7*(5), 502-518.

Kumar, K., & van Dissel, H. G. (1996). Sustainable collaboration: Managing conflict and cooperation in interorganizational systems. *MIS Quarterly, 20*(3), 279-300.

Leidner, D., Alavi, M., & Kayworth, T. (2006). The role of culture in knowledge management: A case study of two global firms. *International Journal of e-Collaboration, 2*(1), 17-40.

Majchrzak, A., Malhotra, A., & John, R. (2005). Perceived individual collaboration know-how development through information technology–enabled contextualization: Evidence from distributed teams. *Information Systems Research, 16*(1), 9–27.

Malhotra, Y. (2000). Knowledge management and new organization forms: A framework for business model innovation. *Information Resources Management Journal, 13*(1), 5-14.

Malone, T. W., & Crowston, K. (1994). The interdisciplinary study of coordination. *ACM Computing Surveys, 26*(1), 87-119.

McGrath, J. E. (1984). *Groups: Interaction and performance*. Englewood Cliffs, NJ: Prentice-Hall.

McLaren, T., Head, M., & Yuan, Y. (2002). Supply chain collaboration alternatives: Understanding the expected costs and benefits. *Internet Research, 12*(4), 348-364.

Melville, N., Kraemer, K., & Gurbaxani, V. (2004). Information technology and organizational performance: An integrative model of IT business value. *MIS Quarterly, 28*(2), 283-322.

Nahapiet, J., & Ghoshal, S. (1998). Social capital, intellectual capital, and the organizational advantage. *Academy of Management Review, 23*(2), 242-266.

Nonaka, I. (1991). The knowledge-creating company. *Harvard Business Review, 69*(6), 96-104.

Nonaka, I., & Takeuchi, H. (1995). *The knowledge-creating company: How Japanese companies create the dynamics of innovation*. New York: Oxford University Press.

Nonaka, I., Toyama, R., & Nagata, A. (2000). A firm as a knowledge-creating entity: A new perspective on the theory of the firm. *Industrial and Corporate Change, 9*(1), 1-20.

Nunamaker, J. F., Dennis, A. R., Valacich, J. S., Vogel, D. R., & George, J. F. (1991). Electronic meeting systems to support group work. *Communications of the ACM, 34*(7), 40-61.

Paul, D. L. (2006). Collaborative activities in virtual settings: A knowledge management perspective of telemedicine. *Journal of Management Information Systems, 22*(4), 143-176.

Prescott, J. E. (1986). Environments as moderators of the relationship between strategy and performance. *Academy of Management Journal, 29*(2), 329-346.

Roberts, P. W., & Amit, R. (2003). The dynamics of innovative activity and competitive advantage: The case of Australian retail banking, 1981 to 1995. *Organization Science, 14*(2), 107-122.

Santos, J., Doz, Y., & Williamson, P. (2004). Is your innovation process global? *MIT Sloan Management Review, 45*(4), 31-37.

Sawhney, M., Wolcott, R. C., & Arroniz, I. (2006). The 12 different ways for companies to innovate. *MIT Sloan Management Review, 47*(3), 75-81.

Scott, J. E. (2000). Facilitating interorganizational learning with information technology. *Journal of Management Information Systems, 17*(2), 81-113.

Senge, P. M. (1990). *The fifth discipline: The art and practice of the learning organization.* New York, NY: Doubleday/Currency.

Shapiro, C., & Varian, H. R. (1999). *Information rules: A strategic guide to the network economy.* Boston, MA: Harvard Business School Press.

Short, J., Williams, E., & Christie, B. (1976). *The social psychology of telecommunications.* London, England: John Wiley and Sons.

Spender, J. C. (1996). Making knowledge the basis of a dynamic theory of the firm. *Strategic Management Journal, 17*, 45-62.

Teece, D. J. (2007). Explicating dynamic capabilities: The nature and microfoundations of (sustainable) enterprise performance. *Strategic Management Journal, 28*(13), 1319–1350.

Teece, D. J., Pisano, G., & Shuen, A. (1997). Dynamic capabilities and strategic management. *Strategic Management Journal, 18*(7), 509–533.

Weill, P., & Olson, M. H. (1989). An assessment of the contingency theory of management information systems. *Journal of Management Information Systems, 6*(1), 59-85.

Wernerfelt, B. (1984). A resource-based view of the firm. *Strategic Management Journal, 5*(2), 171-180.

Wheeler, B. C. (2002). NEBIC: A dynamic capabilities theory for assessing net-enablement. *Information Systems Research, 13*(2), 125-146.

Zahra, S. A., & George, G. (2002). The net-enabled business innovation cycle and the evolution of dynamic capabilities. *Information Systems Research, 13*(2), 147-150.

Zhu, K., & Kraemer, K. L. (2002). E-commerce metrics for net-enhanced organizations: Assessing the value of e-commerce to firm performance in the manufacturing sector. *Information Systems Research, 13*(3), 275-295.

Zigurs, I., & Buckland, B. K. (1998). A theory of task/technology fit and group support systems effectiveness. *MIS Quarterly, 22*(3), 313-334.

# Chapter III
# The Drivers for the Adoption and Use of M–Services:
## A Consumer Perspective

**Patricia McManus**
*University of Western Sydney, Australia*

**Susan Standing**
*Edith Cowan University, Australia*

**Craig Standing**
*Edith Cowan University, Australia*

**Heikki Karjaluoto**
*University of Jyväskylä, Finland*

## ABSTRACT

*Mobile services (m-services) have become an important part of the e-commerce landscape. Although research has been conducted on which services people use and the benefits they attach to those services, the values associated with the adoption and use of m-services at the individual level is still unclear. This paper addresses the question of why and how individuals adopt and appropriate m-services with a particular focus on m-communication? In the information systems field various technology adoption models have been proposed and validated in relation to technology adoption within an organisational setting but personal adoption and use of technology is less researched. We propose the use of means-end chains and laddering techniques to determine the basic primitive values that are fulfilled for the individual by using various m-services. The examples presented show that mobile services often fulfil such basic needs as self-esteem, achievement, individuality, belonging and well-being. Exploring the realization of values as a theoretical framework offers researchers a way forward in environments characterised by individual technology decisions.*

## INTRODUCTION

Various theories are used in information systems to determine the patterns of adoption of technologies at an organisational level. However, the reasons for adoption of technologies and services at the individual level are less understood. The aim of this paper is to determine the reasons for m-services adoption and usage at the individual level. Means-end chains and laddering are explained and examples are used to show the reasons underpinning different consumer value choice perceptions. Finally, the significance of value based theories as an explanatory theory at the individual level is assessed.

Industry analysts have high expectations of the consumers' willingness to adopt mobile services. However, there is still uncertainty in relation to understanding why an individual adopts electronic channels, and the intrinsic influential factors, such as consumers' attitudes and values in relation to electronic channels (Venkatesh & Brown, 2001; Anckar, 2002). Anckar (2002, p3) pointed out that "the main reason for value-adding elements in m-commerce, the consumers' actual reasons – the primary drivers for adopting m-commerce remain unclear". The importance of understanding what motivates adoption becomes even more critical for m-services as adoption rates are expected to rapidly increase (Anckar, 2002). Some of the reasons behind this optimistic forecast are the low cost associated with m-commerce hardware (e.g. mobile telephones) and consumers' familiarity with mobile telephones (Ropers, 2001; Anckar, 2002).

## DEFINITIONS OF MOBILE SERVICES AND MOBILE COMMERCE

Mobile services embrace terms such as mobile communication, mobile collaboration and mobile commerce (Sarker & Wells, 2003). Whilst there is some overlap between these terms it can be argued that mobile communication includes voice, Short Messaging Service (SMS) and Multimedia Messaging Service (MMS) whilst the same services can be used to collaborate on projects and can additionally draw upon information and news from Web sites. Mobile commerce involves information, news, and the purchase of physical goods and services. In this paper the term m-services is used to describe the ability to send and receive communication and purchase goods/services through a wireless public (e.g. Internet) or private network enabled device like a mobile telephone or a personal digital assistant (Balasubramanian, Peterson & Jarvenpaa., 2002; Clark, 2001, Han, Harkke, Landor, & Mio, 2002; Junglas, 2002).

It is argued that the main difference between e-commerce and m-commerce is that m-commerce is associated with wireless technologies (Clark, 2001; Anckar & D'Incau, 2002; Han et al., 2002; Turban, McLean & Wetherbe, 2002*)*. For example, Turban et al. (2002, p28) have defined m-commerce as the "Conduct of e-commerce via wireless devices". The basic definition of wireless is: "The absence of a physical link between the sending and receiving devices" (Balasubramanian et al., 2002). It is important to clarify the terminology since it is easy for the concept of m-commerce to be mistaken for its underlying technologies (applications and devices) (Balasubramanian et al., 2001; Han et al., 2002).

Three key characteristics of m-commerce are portability, ubiquity and addressability.

## Portability

Portability refers to the mobility aspects of communication devices. The portability construct implies that there is no fixed physical location at the device or application level, i.e. an individual can take the device anywhere (Muller, 1999; Balasubramanian et al., 2001; Turban et al., 2002; Junglas, 2002; Microsoft, 2003).

## Ubiquity

The ubiquity construct comprises the two characteristics of reach and accessibility. The combination of these two characteristics mean that an individual can be contacted or make a contact at any time from anywhere, in other words time and space are made irrelevant (Muller, 1999; Balasubramanian et al., 2002; Turban et al. 2002; Junglas, 2002; Lyytinen & Yoo, 2002).

## Addressability

Blattberg and Deighton (1991, p.6) have defined an address as "Anything that locates the customer uniquely in time and space". In most m-commerce definitions authors have used the word localization (see Muller, 1999; Junglas, 2002; Turban et al., 2002) to describe the characteristics of positioning services like Global Positioning System (GPS) that enable consumers and marketers to push (send) or receive information in the context of where the consumer is located at that moment.

These three concepts help us to define the conceptual significance of mobile commerce independent of the hardware.

## THEORETICAL PERSPECTIVES ON M-SERVICES ADOPTION AND USE

This section of the paper examines the factors that drive consumers' adoption and willingness to adopt and use m-services.

There has been a number of m-commerce consumer adoption studies conducted. Barnes and Huff (2003) use Rogers' (1995) innovation and diffusion theory to examine the diffusion of Internet access via mobile telephones (iMode). Rogers developed a number of characteristics that explain innovation diffusion: 1) Relative advantage: the degree to which the technology provides an advantage over other methods, 2) Compatibility: the degree to which the technology

is compatible with how people work or behave, 3) Complexity: whether people perceive the technology as easy to understand and use, 4) Trialability: the degree to which a technology can be trialled before being adopted, 5) Observability: the level of visibility of the product to the other members of the adopter's social group.

Barnes and Huff (2003) conclude that iMode's success in Japan is unlikely to be replicated to the same extent in other countries since the conditions that prevailed in Japan do not exist elsewhere to the same extent. The low level of PC adoption, high market saturation of mobile telephones and fierce competition between trusted brands who are putting together cost-effective mobile Internet packages enable consumers in Japan to readily access mobile services.

Studies related to advertising and marketing are closely associated with consumer attitudes and built around the Theory of Reasoned Action (TRA) (Ajzen & Fishbein, 1980; Fishbein & Ajzen, 1975) and its applications to IT settings. The theory provides a framework to understand why people behave as they do when making decisions. TRA proposes that the use of technology can be predicted by a person's behavioural intention and that this is determined by a person's attitude towards using the technology. A person's attitude is shaped by their positive or negative feelings towards performing a specific behaviour (or using a technology) and whether people who are personally important, typically in the workplace, think that they should or should not perform the behaviour.

Using a form of TRA Tsang, Ho and Liang (2004) examine the link between attitude, intention and behaviour in relation to m-marketing. In their model entertainment, information content, irritation and credibility are seen to shape attitudes with permission having a major impact. The availability of incentives, such as free calls, impacts on the intention to receive m-marketing for certain attitudes. Intention is directly related to behaviour in relation to m-marketing. Their study findings indicate that consumers have a negative attitude towards mobile advertising unless they have consented to it. All four attributes of mobile advertising impact significantly on attitude towards mobile advertising. Attitude was significantly correlated to intention with incentives also positively impacting on intention. There was a strong correlation between intention and behaviour. This study was conducted in Taiwan with a large percentage of respondents regularly using SMS, although it is unclear from the results presented the extent to which respondents had received mobile advertising.

The Technology Acceptance Model (TAM) (Davis, 1989; Davis, Bagozzi & Warshaw, 1989; Davis & Venkatesh, 1996; Mathieson, 1991) is tailored to information systems contexts and is designed to predict IT acceptance and usage in the workplace. It focuses on perceived usefulness of the technology and perceived ease of use. In m-commerce adoption research conducted by Wu and Wang (2004) perceived ease of use was not found to be significant. TAM has been extended to include a third belief called perceived enjoyment (Davis, Bagozzi & Warshaw, 1992) where using the computer is perceived to be enjoyable in its own right (hedonic) and quite separate from performance issues (Van der Heijden, 2004). The consumer behaviour literature shows that utilitarian, in the sense of instrumental value, or hedonic benefits determine the intention to consume. In some m-commerce studies hedonistic factors including entertainment value have been considered as significant (Bauer, Barnes & Reichardt, 2005).

As there are a number of adoption models available to researchers, Venkatesh, Morris, Davis and Davis (2003) synthesized the main models in order to provide a unified view of user acceptance. The unified model identifies determinants and moderators related to intention and it suggests intention is a predictor of use behaviour. Four factors impact on intention and usage: performance expectancy, effort expectancy, social influence

and facilitating conditions. The key moderators are gender, age, experience and voluntary use. Interestingly, attitude was considered to overlap with performance and effort expectancies. The non-significance of attitude in the presence of these two other constructs has been supported in a number of other studies (Taylor & Todd, 1995). In empirical studies the unified model was found to be a substantial improvement on any of the other earlier models. Standing, Benson and Karjaluoto (2005) used a version of the unified theory to determine significant factors in the decision to participate in m-marketing schemes and found that granting permission, financial savings and highly relevant information were significant factors in the decision to participate but that the time and effort involved in processing m-marketing messages were not considered important. Work on technology acceptance is still evolving with, for example, studies that integrate user satisfaction constructs with technology acceptance constructs (Wixom & Todd, 2005).

Consumer adoption related factors can be summarized as including the consumer's general attitude toward the technology, level of involvement, innovation, response to stimuli, trust and perceptions of utility, choice, control and risk. Demographic factors (age, gender, income, education) have also been found to be important control variables to consider when looking at consumer acceptance of m-services (Barnes & Scornavacca, 2004; Tsang, Ho & Liang, 2004).

Although it is widely recognized that younger consumers have embraced mobile technology it is being increasingly recognized that factors beyond age or gender may be important. It can be argued that segmenting people on the basis of their acceptance and use of technology as well as their lifestyle motivations is more representative of their actual behaviour (Sultan & Rohm, 2005). Consumers' adoption of new technologies/services depends on a number of factors, for example, the type of service to be offered, how comfortable people feel using the technology, how user friendly the service interface is, socio-economic factors, motivations (benefits), culture, demographics and psychographics, amount of time that the customer expects to use the service and past experience (Daghfouls, Petrof & Pons, 1999; Sultan & Henrichs, 2000). Sarker and Wells (2003) provide a framework for understanding the adoption and use of mobile devices that includes most of these factors. Their model considers not only the decision made in the initial adoption but also how users appropriate the technology and services through exploration and experimentation. They argue that users assess their experiences on three dimensions: functional (e.g. time savings), psychosocial (e.g. safety, elevated self-worth, sense of freedom) and relational (building relationships).

## THE CONCEPTUALISATION OF VALUE AND VALUES

The concept of values is a theme of research in a range of social science disciplines including: anthropology, economics, education, history, marketing, political science, psychology and sociology (Rokeach, 1973). Generally, the concept of value has two different connotations: Values as an individual core belief, and as a perceived direct or indirect benefit of a product/service (Rokeach, 1973). The meaning of "perceived value" (or value) is drawn from definitions related to the "value-for-money" concept. Valerie Zeithaml's (1988) definition is one of the most widely accepted (see Woodruff, 1997, Sweeney et al., 1999; Anckar & D'Incau, 2002). She depicts value as: "The consumers' overall assessment of the utility of a product based on their perception of what is received and what is given" (Zeithaml, 1988, pp14). The concept of perceived value can be called product value as it refers to what consumers' value in terms of product characteristics/benefits. This concept has been considered an important source of competitive advantage for

manufactures and retailers (Sheth, Newman & Gross, 1991a; Woodruff, 1999; Forester, 1999; Sweeney & Soutar, 2001).

Sheth, Newman and Gross (1991a, 1991b) conceptualized a model to help explain how consumers make decisions in the marketplace. They based their model on the principle that the choices consumers make are based on their perceived values in relation to what the authors called "market choice". Sheth et al., (1991a) classify five categories of perceived value. Functional values are associated with the utility level of the product (or service) compared to its alternatives. Social values could be compared with the subjective norm dimension in the Theory of Planned Behaviour, as it is associated with willingness to please and social acceptance. Emotional values are those choices made based upon feelings and aesthetics. Epistemic values can be used to describe the early adopters in the sense that it relates to novelty or knowledge searching behaviour. Finally, the conditional value refers to a set of circumstances that depend upon the situation (e.g. Christmas, wedding etc.). Socio-economic and physical aspects are included in this value. These five values were conceptualised based on a diversity of disciplines including social psychology, clinical psychology, sociology, economics and experimental psychology (Sheth et al., 1991a).

### Means-End Chains

The concept of values is also addressed through means-end chains. The means-end chain concept concentrates on the systematic relationship between three level of values: product/service attributes, consequences and personal values (Gutman 1982; Reynolds & Gutman 1988). This model represents how the consumption of a product enables the consumer's realization of his/hers desired ends. The central aspect of this theory is that "...consumers choose actions that produce desired consequences and minimize undesirable consequences" (Gutman, 1982 p 61).

In Gutman's (1982) model, product attributes are understood as all tangible and intangible product characteristics such as size, weight, colour etc. Consequences are defined as the physiological or psychological results acquired directly or indirectly by the consumer from his/her behaviour (product or service use). Sheth's et al. (1991a) theory of Consumption Values does not represent end states of existence but expected benefits (consequences) from consuming that particular product or service.

The personal value construct in this model is drawn from the concept used in psychology and sociology and relatefs to Rokeach's construct of human/personal values. Rokeach (1973) identified two types of values: instrumental and terminal. Instrumental values relate to those values that act like tools in achieving end-state behaviours (values like courage, honesty, ethics, etc.). Terminal values, also used by Gutman (1982), refer to "Preferred end-states of existence" (Gutman, 1982 p.63) for example: accomplishment, happiness and satisfaction. Gutman's model (1982) has two basic underlying assumptions: 1) Values are connected to consequences as long as the consequences have positive or negative connotations and 2) Consequences have a direct relationship with product attributes as long as consumers obtain the products which may cause the desired benefits.

The three levels of product attributes, consequences and personal values are hierarchically

*Table 1. Personal values (Gutman 1982; Rokeach, 1973)*

| | |
|---|---|
| Self esteem | Achievement/fulfilment |
| Security | Nurturer |
| Belonging | Well Being |
| Independence | Honesty/responsibility |
| Acceptance | Grounded |
| Individuality | Moral |
| Happiness | |

*Figure 1. Means-end chain*

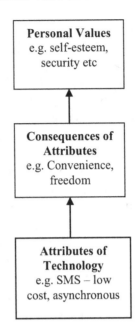

interconnected (Figure 1). The lower level values are an instrument for consumers to reach their desirable end values (higher levels) (Gutman, 1982; Reynolds & Gutman, 1988). The central aspect of this model assumes that consumers will behave in a way to obtain the desired or positive consequences and minimize the undesirable or negative consequences (Leao & Mello, 2001, 2002). The end values as explained above are ideal end-states or goals.

## Laddering Technique

The laddering technique is a method used to reveal the means-end hierarchy (Gutman 1982; Reynolds & Gutman 1988; Leao & Mello 2002). This ladder refers to the relationship between the three levels of values or abstractions (attribute, consequence and value). It represents the connection between the actual product and the user's cognitive process that leads to a direct and useful understanding of his/hers perceptual orientation in relation to the service. The laddering technique is an in-depth individual interview used to understand consumers' decisions. It translates product attributes into associations relevant to the users "self", based on the means-end chain model. This is done through sequentially asking the respondent the reason why that attribute/consequence was important to him or her (Reynolds & Gutman, 1988). The goal of this strategy of enquiry is to allow the researcher to get to users' actual root reasons for using that particular mobile service (Reynolds & Gutman 1988). Because this technique can be perceived by the respondent as obvious and intrusive it is paramount that the researcher pays particular attention to the interview environment. The environment needs to be friendly and conducive to introspection in order to seek the underlying drivers behind a given mobile service (Reynolds & Gutman, 1988). It is fundamental that the interviewee perceives the interviewer as very interested at the same time as neutral; his only job is to record the information provided (Reynolds & Gutman, 1982).

The result of the laddering process is a series of cognitive maps or hierarchical value maps (HMV) that show the aggregate consumer means-end chains that link the product or service characteristics with consumer's values.

We applied the mean-end chain and laddering approach to the investigation of the adoption of m-services. For each person an interview lasting between forty minutes to an hour involving closed and open-ended questions was carried out. The questions asked addressed issues related to the respondents' background, personal and family life (significant life events), and personality traits. Then questions were asked about the mobile services they use, usage intensity and reasons for using those particular services/features. An assessment of motives for using particular services was analysed following a laddering approach. This involved why they used the service and what benefits they obtained and this line of enquiry was pursued to obtain the personal values behind the consequences. The following conceptual maps are the result of analysing 28 interviews with mobile

service users. The interviewees represent a convenience sample of m-service users and covered late teenagers through to retirees.

When the data are synthesised from the 28 interviews and analysed three broad patterns emerge. These patterns can be classified under relational, achievement and individual/well-being. The relational map (Figure 2) centres around the use of communication to keep in contact and stay connected in order to achieve a sense of belonging and/or acceptance by a group (typically work group). Both of these values can have a positive impact on self-esteem.

Mobile services including games, streaming video and ring tones provide fun and entertainment which create a sense of well-being and individuality which also links to self-esteem. The aesthetic appeal of mobile phones (colour, style) can make a positive impression on people and can support the value of individuality (Figure 3). Figure 4 revolves around the use of communication to provide convenience and organisation to improve efficiency. The key value here is sense of achievement that also links to self-esteem.

## CONCLUSION

In this paper we have proposed that adoption of m-services at the individual can be better understood through the use of means-end theory and a laddering methodology. We argue that the emphasis given to values through means-end theory takes research on the adoption of technology and services to another level. Much of the research to date on technology adoption has examined technology adoption in organisational settings. Adoption of mobile services typically requires decisions to be made at the individual level yet few researchers are investigating the primitive value drivers. Our study with a small sample of mobile-service users illustrates how means-end chain theory and a laddering style of enquiry can uncover the real value of m-services.

*Figure 2. Relational map*

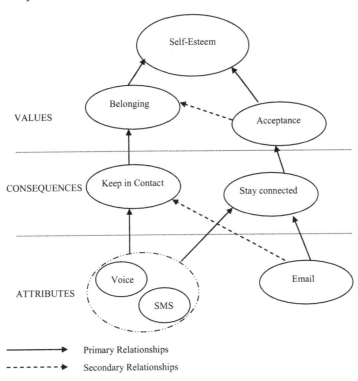

*Figure 3. Individuality/well-being map*

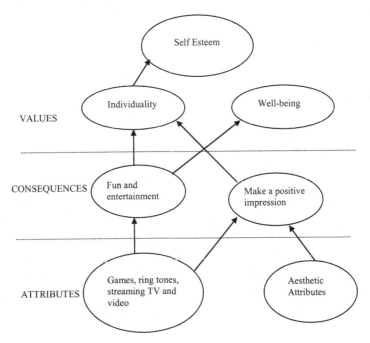

*Figure 4. Achievement map*

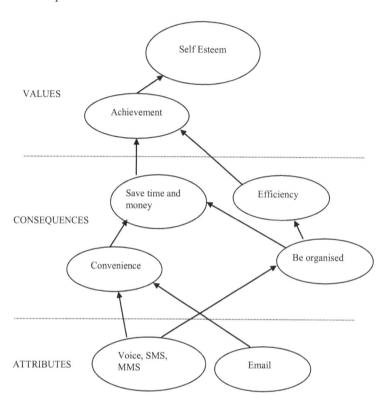

The three cognitive association maps may not be a definitive group for the m-services area. Rather we propose them as a starting point for further research. Nor are the maps mutually exclusive. Mobile services have a functional value as they are convenient but the decision to adopt may often be combined with the desire to feel part of a group or community of use. Indeed, the erosion of boundaries between work, home, leisure, learning and education, partly brought about by mobile technology, means that people may have multiple reasons for adopting or using services. Mobile technology can serve multiple needs including, family, friends, work and curiosity or learning.

Castells (1996) suggested we have moved from an information society to a networked society. This Network Society is characterised by the network flows (capital, information, images, etc.) which become more important than the social interests which they represent. Mobile services have accelerated the evolution of the networked society and the network of flows have become more significant than the sometimes seemingly trivial nature of the service itself. In other words, being connected via these services can develop a sense of achievement, self-esteem, feelings of belonging and acceptance. With these powerful primitive values being fed then it highly likely the rapid developments in mobile service adoption will continue.

The ideas proposed in this paper are currently being tested through a large scale study that involves interviewing over a hundred users of m-services. When this is completed we should be nearer developing a predictive model of m-service adoption. These findings may also be applicable to the adoption of other technologies at the individual level.

# REFERENCES

Anckar, B. (2002). Adoption drivers and intents in the mobile electronic marketplace: Survey findings. *Journal of Systems and Information Technology, 6*(2), 1-17.

Anckar, B., & D'Incau, D. (2002). Value creation in mobile commerce: Findings from a Consumer Survey. *The Journal of Information Technology Theory and Application (JITTA), 4*(1), 43-64.

Ajzen, I., & Fishbein, M. (1980). *Understanding attitudes and predicting social behavior.* Englewood Cliffs: NJ: Prentice-Hall.

Balasubramanian, S., Peterson, R. A., & Jarvenpaa, S. L. (2002). Exploring the Implications of M-Commerce for Markets and Marketing. *Journal of the academy of Marketing Science, 30*(4), 348-36

Barnes, S. & Huff, S. (2003). Rising Sun: iMode and the Wireless Internet. *Communications of the ACM, 46*(11), pp. 79-84.

Barnes, S., & Scornavacca, E. (2004). Mobile marketing: the role of permission and acceptance. *International Journal of Mobile Communications, 2*(2) 128-139.

Bauer, H.H., Barnes, S.J., Reichardt, T., & Neumann M.M. (2005). Driving consumer acceptance of mobile marketing: A theoretical framework and empirical study. *Journal of Electronic Commerce Research, 6*(3) 181-192.

Blattberg, R. C., & Deighton, J. (1991). Interactive marketing: Exploiting the age of Addressability. *Sloan Management Review, Fall,* 5-14.

Carroll, A., Barnes, S.J., & Scornavacca, E. (2005). Consumers perceptions and attitudes towards SMS mobile marketing in New Zealand. *In Proceedings of the Fourth International Conference on Mobile Business (ICMB), Sydney, Au*stralia, July 11-13, pp. 434-440.

Castells, M. (1996). *The Rise of the Network Society, The Information Age: Economy, Society and Culture, Vol. I.* Cambridge, MA; Oxford, UK: Blackwell.

Clark III, I. (2001). Emerging value propositions for m-commerce. *Journal of Business Strategies, 18*(2), 133-148.

Daghfous, N., Petrof, J. V., & Pons, F. (1999). Values and adoption of innovations: A cross cultural study. *Journal of Consumer Marketing, 16*(14), 314-331.

Davies, F. (1989). Perceived Usefulness, Perceived Easy of use and user acceptance of Information Technology. *MIS Quarterly, 13*(3), 319-340.

Davis, F. D., Bagozzi, R. P., & Warshaw, P. R. (1989). User Acceptance of Computer technology: A comparison of two theoretical Models. *Management Science, 35*(8), 982-1003.

Davis, F.D., Bagozzi, R.P., & Warshaw, P.R. (1992). Extrinsic and intrinsic motivation to use computers in the workplace. *Journal of Applied Social Psychology, 22*(14), 1111-1132.

Davis, F.D., and Venkatesh, V. (1996). A critical assessment of potential measurement biases in the technology acceptance model: three experiments. *International Journal of Human-Computer Studies, 45*(1), 19-45.

Dickinger, A., & Haghirian, P. (2004). An investigation and conceptual model of SMS marketing. *In Proceedings of the 37th Hawaii International Conference on System Sciences (HICSS-37),* Hawaii, USA, January 5-8, CD-ROM.

Fishbein, M., & Ajzen, I. (1975). *Belief, Attitude, Intention, and Behavior: An Introduction to Theory and Research.* Reading, MA: Addison-Wesley.

Forester, M. (1999). Deja vu discussion delivers message emphasizing value. *Chain Store Age, 75*(April), 12.

Gutman, J. (1982). A Means-End Chain Model Based on Consumer Categorization Processes. *Journal of Marketing, 46*(Spring), 60-72.

Haghirian, P., & Madlberger, M. (2005). Consumer attitude toward advertising via mobile devices - an empirical investigation among Austrian users. In *Proceedings of the 13th European Conference on Information System*s, Regensburg, Germany, May 26-28: http://is2.lse.ac.uk/asp/aspecis/20050038.pdf (Accessed February 21, 2006).

Han, J., & Han, D. (2001). A framework for analysing customer value of internet business. *Journal of Information Technology Theory and Application (JITTA), 3*(5), 25-38.

Han, S., Harkke, V., Landor, P., & Mio, R. R. d. (2002). A foresight framework for understanding the future of mobile commerce. *Journal of Systems & Information Technology, 6*(2), 19-39.

Junglas, I. A. (2002). *U-Commerce an experimental investigation of ubiquity and uniqueness.* Unpublished Dissertation, University of Georgia, Athens.

Leao, A. L. M. d. S., & Mello, S. C. B. d. (2002). *Conhecendo o valor do cliente virtual: Uma analize utilizando a teoria de cadeias de meios-fim.* Paper presented at the XXVI ENAMPAD, Salvador, Bahia, Brazil.

Lyytinen, K., & Yoo, Y. (2002). Issues and Challenges in Ubiquitous Computing. *Communications of the ACM, 45*(12), 63-65.

Mathieson, K. (1991). Predicting user intentions: comparing the Technology Acceptance Model with the Theory of Planned Behavior. *Information Systems Research, 2(3),* 173-191.

Microsoft (2003). *Internet &networking dictionary.* Redmond: Microsoft Press.

Muller, F. (1999). *Mobile commerce report* [Internet]. Durlacher. Retrieved June 11, 2003, from the World Wide Web: http://www.durlacher.com/bbus/resreports.asp

Rettie, R., & Brum, (2001). M. M-commerce: the role of SMS text messages. In *Proceedings of the Fourth Biennial International Conference on Telecommunications and Information Markets (COTIM 2001)*, Karlsruhe, Germany; http://www.ebusinessforum.gr/content/downloads/047_brum_mcommerce.pdf

Reynolds, T., & Gutman, J. (1988). Laddering Theory, Theory, Method, Analysis, and Interpretation. *Journal of Advertising Research, 28*(1), 11-31.

Rogers, E. M. (2003). *Diffusion of Innovations* (5th ed.). New York: Free Press. A division of Simon & Schuster , Inc. 1230 Avenue of the Americas.

Rokeach, M. (1973). *The nature of human values.* New York, NY: The Free Press a division of Mc-Millan Publishing Co.Inc.http://www.wirelessreview.com/ar/wireless_numbers_sky/

Ropers, S. (2001). New business models for the mobile revolution. *EAI*(February), 53-57.

Sarker, S. & Wells, J. D. (2003). Understanding Mobile handheld Device use and Adoption. Communications of the ACM, 46(12), p.35-40.

Sheth, J. N., Newman, B. I. & Gross, B. L. (1991a). *Consumption values and market choice: Theory and applications* (1991 ed.): South-Western Publishing Co.

Sheth, J. N., Newman, B. I., & Gross, B. L. (1991b). Why we buy what we buy: A theory of consumption values. *Journal of Business Research, 22,* 150-170.

Standing, C., Benson, S., & Karjaluoto, H. (2005). Consumer perspectives on mobile advertising and marketing. In *Proceedings of the Australia and New Zealand Marketing Academy Conference*, Perth, Australia, December 5-7, pp. 135-141 [CD-ROM].

Sultan, F. & Rohm, A. (2005). The Coming of the Era of "Brand in the hand" Marketing. MIT Sloan Management Review, 47(1), p.83-90.

Sultan, F. & R. B. Henrichs (2000). "Consumer preferences for Internet services over time: Initial explorations." Journal of Consumer Marketing 17(no. 5): 386-402.

Sweeney, J. C., Soutar, G. N., & Johnson, L. W. (1999). The Role of Perceived risk in the quality-value relationship: A study in a retail environment. *Journal of Retailing, 77*(1), 75-105.

Sweeney, J. C., & Soutar, G. N. (2001). Consumer Perceived Value: The development pf a multiple item scale. *Journal of Retailing, 77*(2001), 203-220.

Taylor, S., & Todd, P.A. (1995). Assessing IT usage: the role of prior experience. *MIS Quarterly, 19*(2),561-570.

Tsang, M.M., Ho, S., & Liang, (2004). T. Consumer attitudes toward mobile advertising: an empirical study. *International Journal of Electronic Commerce, 8*(3), 65-78.

Turban, E., McLean, E., & Wetherbe, J. (2002). *Information Technology for Management: Transforming Business in the Digital Economy* (Third ed.). Milton, Queensland: John Wiley & Sons.

Van der Heijden, H. (2004). User acceptance of hedonic information systems. *MIS Quarterly, 28*(4), 695-703.

Venkatesh, V., & Brown, S. A. (2001). A longitudinal investigation of personal computers in homes: adoption determinants and emerging challenges. *MIS Quarterly, 25*(1), 71-102.

Venkatesh, V., Morris, M.G., Davis, G.B., & Davis, F.D. (2003). User acceptance of information technology: toward a unified view. *MIS Quarterly, 27*( 3), 425-479.

Wixom, B., & Todd, P.A. (2005). A theoretical integration of user satisfaction and technology acceptance. *Information Systems Research, 16*(1), 85-102.

Wu, J.-H., & Wang, S.-C. (2004). What drives mobile commerce? An empirical evaluation of the revised technology acceptance model. *Information & Management, 42*(5), 719-729.

Woodruff, R. B. (1997). Customer Value: The Next Source of Competitive Advantage. *Journal of the Academy of Marketing Science, 25*(2), 139-153.

Zeithaml, V. A. (1988). Consumer Perception of Price, Quality, and Value: A Means-End Model and Sythesis of Evidence. *Journal of Marketing, 52*(July), 2-22.

# Chapter IV
# A Comparative Analysis of E–Collaboration Research Funding in the European Union and the United States

**Ned Kock**
*Texas A&M International University, USA*

**Pedro Antunes**
*University of Lisboa, Portugal*

## ABSTRACT

*Much of the funding for research and development initiatives in the area of e-collaboration comes from government agencies in various countries. Government funding of e-collaboration research in the European Union (EU) and the United States (U.S.), in particular, seems to be experiencing steady growth in recent years. In the EU, a key initiative to promote governmental investment in e-collaboration research is the Collaboration@Work initiative. This initiative is one of the EU's Information Society Technologies Directorate General's main priorities. In the U.S., government investment in e-collaboration research is channeled through several government branches and organizations, notably the National Science Foundation. There are key differences in the approaches used for government funding of e-collaboration research in the EU and U.S. Among other differences, the EU model appears to foster research that is aligned with the action research tradition, whereas the U.S. model places emphasis on research that is better aligned with the experimental research tradition.*

## INVESTMENT IN ICT RESEARCH IN THE U.S. AND EU

Information and communication technologies (ICT) have been among the main drivers of both the European Union (EU) and United States (U.S.) economies. In the last 30 years, they have been the source of a significant growth in labor productivity in the manufacturing sectors of both the EU and U.S. In the service sector, ICT have not had the same impact in terms of labor productivity improvement. Yet, they have revolutionized delivery models, and allowed for a tremendous growth in revenues generated by service organizations. This is reflected in the size of the service sector of the economy, which now account for most of the jobs and wealth generated in both the U.S. and EU.

Given the above, one would expect investment in research on ICT to be significant, which seems to be the case in both the EU and the U.S. There have been many estimates of investment in ICT research in the EU, in both the public and private sectors (EC, 2005). Some of those estimates point at $28 billion as a recent figure for total annual private sector investment in ICT research. The same estimates put the EU's public sector investment in ICT research at around $10 billion. By comparison, the private sector in the U.S. invests over 3 times more; and the public sector about 2.5 times more.

The above differences become even more significant when we take into account differences in population size. While in the EU the total investment in ICT research per person annually is estimated at about $100, including both the private and public sectors. In the U.S., that investment is likely to be over $400.

Not surprisingly, there is a general perception among research funding agencies in the EU that it is lagging behind the U.S. in terms of its ICT development and use capabilities. This is a major source of concern in the EU, because ICT are perceived as a major driver of labor produc-tivity improvement (EC, 2005b), accounting for as much as 40 percent of the variation in labor productivity in recent years. (In the U.S., ICT are perceived as accounting for an even higher percentage of variation in labor productivity, namely 60 percent).

## E-COLLABORATION VERSUS ICT RESEARCH

E-collaboration can be defined as collaboration among individuals engaged in a common task us-ing electronic technologies. As such, e-collabora-tion can be seen as an "umbrella" term that can be used to refer to a range of fields of research, such as those of computer-mediated communication, computer-supported cooperative work, and group support systems (Kock, 2005; 2008).

Some examples of e-collaboration technolo-gies are e-mail, group decision support systems, instant messaging, web-based bulletin boards, teleconferencing suites, and supply-chain man-agement systems. E-mail, arguably one of the most widely used computer applications today, is an e-collaboration technology aimed at supporting fast and relatively simple forms of communication. Certain e-collaboration technologies are more geared at supporting complex communication and decision making, such as group decision support systems. Other e-collaboration technologies, such as supply-chain management systems, are aimed at supporting the flow of information among vari-ous departments engaged in the production and delivery of goods and services.

There are many areas of ICT that are not seen as directly related to e-collaboration. Some examples are database and telecommunications technologies. There is a great deal of research being conducted aimed at the development of new database technologies. The same is true for telecommunications technologies. Incidentally, both database and telecommunications technolo-gies are necessary for the implementation of e-collaboration technologies.

Nevertheless, research on e-collaboration has been steadily increasing in importance recently. Evidence of this, as recently as 2005, comes from two key publication initiatives. One is the establishment of a new journal dedicated to e-collaboration research, the *International Journal of e-Collaboration* (Kock, 2005). The other initiative is the publication the Special Issue on Expanding the Boundaries of E-Collaboration of the prestigious journal *IEEE Transactions on Professional Communication* (Kock & Nosek, 2005).

Much of the past and recent research on e-collaboration falls into one of two broad categories: (a) applied research, which often attempts to provide solutions to technological problems; and (b) behavioral research, whose main goal is to understand how e-collaboration technologies affect group behavior. The former type, i.e., applied research, is often favored by industry; while the latter type incorporates elements (see e.g., Rosenthal & Rosnow, 1991) that make it more prevalent in academic journals such as the ones mentioned above.

## THE EUROPEAN RESEARCH FRAMEWORK PROGRAM

The European Commission is the executive branch of the EU, which comprises 25 European countries – Austria, Belgium, Cyprus, Czech Republic, Denmark, Estonia, Finland, France, Germany, Greece, Hungary, Ireland, Italy, Latvia, Lithuania, Luxembourg, Malta, Netherlands, Poland, Portugal, Slovakia, Slovenia, Spain, Sweden, and the United Kingdom.

The European Commission finances ICT research mostly through the Information Society Technologies Directorate General, currently concluding the 6th Framework Program, which covered the period from 2002 to 2006. This Directorate General adopts two fundamental objectives: strengthen the scientific and technological bases of the EU industry, and encourage the EU

international competitiveness. However, these objectives are combined with other policies, the fundamental one being the subsidiary principle: projects must have a trans-national nature and be inclusive in terms of members' participation, which includes the EU, candidate and affiliated countries. The international successes of the Global System for Mobile Communications (usually referred to by the acronym GSM) and Airbus technologies have been considered exemplary of the European research approach.

The Information Society Technologies Directorate General integrates several research and development instruments and thematic priorities, assembling a very complex framework. The available instruments include Integrated Projects (large-scale, focusing on technology integration and public-private partnerships), Networks of Excellence (large-scale, basically supporting researchers' mobility) and Specific Targeted Research Projects (smaller and focused). The thematic priorities are further organized in vertical issues, such as e-Health, e-Inclusion, cognitive systems, nano-technologies; and horizontal issues, including specific research for small and medium enterprises (also referred to as SMEs), research helping the formulation of European Commission policies and support to international cooperation activities. The thematic priorities are approved after consultation with advisory groups invited by the European Commission and web-based public consultations. The gap between the production of consultation reports and project submission deadlines is about one year.

The European Commission's interest in financing e-collaboration research emerged as a confluence of various concerns defined at a political level. One notable example is the so-called "Lisbon Agenda", a political statement about how to improve European competitiveness, developed in the year 2000 in Lisbon. The primary concern is the development of pan-European ICT infrastructures and services, including interoperability and multi-lingual support. Another important concern reflects a user-centered view of work, focusing on the "quality of experience" and seamless integration of co-workers through technology.

## THE COLLABORATION@WORK INITIATIVE

The Collaboration@Work initiative is one of the Information Society Technologies Directorate General's main priorities. Its focus is on research proposals that address the development of an "upper-layer" collaboration platform, residing on top of middleware platforms currently offering basic collaboration services such as person-to-person communication, web services, remote object invocation, persistency, reliability, and security (Laso-Ballesteros & Salmelin, 2005). This upper-layer would allow co-workers to orchestrate their work while moving between different work contexts, places and connected/disconnected modes. The underlying services would be used in a flexible way and customized to the users' communities.

The proposed vision is that a large "suite" of collaborative activities will seamlessly utilize the upper-layer collaboration platform. These are expected to include e-business, e-commerce, e-manufacturing, e-government, e-health and e-learning initiatives. The standardization of collaborative activities and services is considered necessary and regarded as strategic for obtaining critical mass and giving leadership to Europe in the e-collaboration field.

The Collaboration@Work initiative specifically indicates several technical challenges regarded as necessary to accomplish the above vision and expected to be present in the proposals. These include the development of reference architectures for collaboration at work; high-level orchestration and composition of collaborative services; support mobility and ubiquity; and ontologies for semantic interoperability.

The research proposals must also combine three additional key attributes. They are expected to be ambitious in terms of their expected technological impact on the society and on SMEs, which are operationally defined as organizations with less than 250 employees and "turnover" (equivalent to "revenues" in the U.S.) of approximately $60 million. In fact, research projects that do not only involve but are led by SMEs are quite welcome. Also, proposals are expected to involve a broad practical implementation component, carried out cooperatively by a variety of organizations from different countries. And, proposals are expected to include a "demonstration" component, where the impact of the research on individuals, organizations, and society is clearly demonstrated.

## FUNDING PRIORITIES AND CRITERIA IN THE EU

Proposing highly innovative ideas, with high potential industry impact, is not, in and of itself, a sufficient condition for obtaining funding from the Information Society Technologies Directorate General. It is mandatory that the identified research objectives be fully aligned with the thematic priorities. An interesting consequence of this supplementary criterion is that most times highly innovative ideas appear "behind" other fairly common research goals, many times shared by several proposals. The situation is even more complex if we consider that "horizontal" goals must also be explicitly addressed by the research, where the expected technological impact on SMEs assumes a critical importance. Our general observation is that under these conditions the projects' research objectives tend to be both broad and somewhat homogeneous.

The publication of project results in journals and conferences is not seen as very important. On the contrary, project proposals should identify a list of technical reports, usually associated to the project's milestones, which tend to be carefully scrutinized both during the evaluation and review. The funding criteria also emphasize the evaluation of project outcomes through what are called "large-scale demonstrators" (i.e., applied sub-projects), instead of controlled or semi-controlled empirical experiments. For instance, the Collaboration@ Work initiative requires that Integrated Projects adopt a new evaluation method designated "living labs." Living labs consist of community-wide environments (such as rural areas) where systemic innovation may be experimented and evaluated in a fairly open and interdisciplinary way. Although this idea is quite interesting, the evaluation context often tends to be highly exploratory.

The proposal submission and evaluation process also has interesting and defining characteristics. First of all, it should be mentioned that the overhead associated with documenting the project proposal is generally very high. There is no page limit specified for the proposals, which quite often go beyond 100 pages; and the list of requested items goes beyond scientific issues, often comprising organizational, management and administrative issues. Secondly, successful research projects must represent a balanced consortium, consisting of industry, SMEs, developers, research organizations and demonstrators. Experience with previous EU projects is also positively evaluated. Furthermore, the consortium should also reflect a good diversity of countries, either members of or affiliated with the EU. Consequently, each consortium tends to be quite large, often with more than 10 organizations.

Concerning the evaluation process, the adopted criteria require that at least three (five, in the case of Integrated Projects) evaluators analyze each project and reach consensus in one or more face-to-face meetings. Each meeting is usually preceded by a careful on-site reading of the proposal. Printed versions of the proposals are distributed to evaluators for review only in the building where the face-to-face consensus meetings take place, and cannot be taken outside that building. Moreover, evaluators are asked not to discuss the proposal they are reading with anyone prior or after the face-to-face consensus meetings. The only time in which proposals are discussed by a larger group of evaluators, which can be more than 40, is when a shortlist of proposals is ranked. This is done in one large face-to-face meeting, which can last several hours.

In the cases where consensus cannot be obtained, additional evaluators are invited to analyze and discuss the proposals. This approach is fair, but is also time consuming and quite expensive, considering that the reviewers must travel from all over Europe, and stay in Brussels for a relatively long period of time (e.g., a week). European Commission officials carefully and systematically instruct the reviewers to stay in line with the thematic initiatives, vertical and horizontal objectives, and technical challenges specified by the Information Society Technologies Directorate General program for which they are serving as evaluators. The aim is to evaluate all projects consistently, but the approach necessarily reduces the reviewers' latitude of decision. It could be argued that wider decision latitude would be important in situations where the project proposals deviate from the norm.

## A COMPARISON WITH THE U.S. MODEL

Table 1 summarizes the discussion above regarding characteristics of the funding model adopted by the EU. It also contrasts key elements of that funding model with that employed by the main equivalent funding agency in the U.S., namely the National Science Foundation. The term "principal investigator" is used to refer to the researcher who is the main coordinator of a research project.

As it can be seen from Table 1, there are key differences in the funding models employed by the EU and the U.S. It is beyond the scope of this chapter to provide a detailed discussion of the merits of each funding model, or a detailed

*Table 1. Priorities and criteria for funding in the EU and the U.S.*

| EU (European Commission) | US (National Science Foundation) |
|---|---|
| Funding is provided to a consortium involving several organizations from different EU countries. Often more than 10 organizations and countries are represented. | Funding is provided to a principal investigator and co-investigator, which usually are based in universities and/or research centers. Often less than 3 organizations from the U.S. are represented. |
| Emphasis is placed on integration with other research projects and broader EU initiatives. | Self-contained projects of high scientific impact are quite welcome. |
| Explicit emphasis is placed on desirable peripheral impacts of the project, such as impact on SMEs, gender diversity, and rural development. | Explicit emphasis is placed on the research component of the project, with some interest in minority inclusion and diversity, and the project's relationship with education activities. |
| Publication of results is not seen as very important. Development of tools-methods and their practical use is. The expectation is that practical use will be part of the project. | Publication of results is seen as fairly important. Less emphasis is placed on practical use of tools-methods as part of the project. The idea here is that the tools-methods will be disseminated through publications, and later used by non-project participants. |
| Less emphasis is placed on a controlled or semi-controlled empirical evaluation of impacts of the research project. Controlled laboratory experiments are not very welcome. | More emphasis is placed on a controlled or semi-controlled empirical evaluation of impacts of the research project. Controlled laboratory experiments are welcome. |
| No strict limit on number of pages in proposal. | Usually limited to 15 pages, with additional material provided in appendices. |
| More guidance is provided to expert reviewers, and stricter interpretation of rules is expected. | Less guidance and more leeway on what to look for as "good" elements are left at the discretion of the expert reviewers. |
| Evaluation is by consensus meetings where all expert reviewers have to unanimously agree on a score in connection with an aspect of a proposal (e.g., quality of consortium, impact etc.). Unanimous consensus is required for a funding decision to be made. | Evaluation is conducted by expert reviewers independently at first, based on an online version of the proposal. A group discussion is conducted at the end. Unanimous consensus is not needed for a funding decision to be made. |
| Evaluation process is very expensive and time consuming. Expert reviewers are brought in from several countries (including countries outside the EU), and work together for several days or more (often several weeks). | Evaluation process is relatively inexpensive and not very time consuming for reviewers. Expert reviewers work together for a day, after they produce their independent reviews. |

analysis of the likely consequences of each model in terms of research impacts on ICT development in the EU and the U.S. While such discussion would undoubtedly add value to the chapter, the complexities associated with such a broad comparison would probably be better addressed through a book-length publication. Also, much more consultation is needed with researchers in the EU and U.S. to produce such a detailed discussion.

Hopefully this chapter will provide the motivation for this and other related initiatives.

Interestingly, one could argue that the EU model fosters research that is better aligned with the "action research" tradition (see, e.g., Kock, 2003; 2006), in which inquiry is seen as aimed at having a positive impact on the participating organizations and society at the same time as the investigation is being conducted. The U.S. model arguably fosters research that is better aligned with the "experimental research" model, whereby inquiry is guided by the goal of testing theory and related hypotheses either in laboratories or the field.

It is important to note that comparing the European Commission with the National Science Foundation presents several challenges, which means that the discussion presented in this chapter should be examined with some caution. One of the problems is that there are other research funding bodies in the EU other than the European Commission. The situation is the same in the U.S., with several other research funding organization other than the National Science Foundation; e.g., DARPA, Office of Naval Research, Army Research Institute, Air Force Research Laboratory. Nevertheless, it seems that the National Science Foundation, due to its breadth of research coverage, is the organization the fits best the notion of a U.S. counterpart of the European Commission in the EU.

It is also important to note that comparing the EU with the U.S. leads to some unavoidable limitations in the conclusions drawn from that comparison. While the EU and the U.S. present some macro-level similarities, such as economic size and overall level of development, they also are different in many aspects. While the EU is a multination body with diverse constituents, the U.S. is one single country. (Although some would argue that there is a lot of diversity among the States that make up the U.S. – e.g., a visit to the southern part of Texas may conceivably look like an overseas trip to a New York State resident). Also, many different languages are spoken in the EU, whereas in the U.S. English is spoken by the vast majority of the population. (Spanish is also spoken, but far behind English, and is often spoken among bilinguals).

## CONCLUSION

Investment in ICT research seems to have been growing both in the U.S. and EU, which is likely a direct consequence of the fact that the ICT sector of the economy has also been one of the main wealth and job creators in both the U.S. and EU. There is a general perception that the EU is trailing behind the U.S. in ICT research investment. This is true both in absolute amounts invested, as well as in per-capita terms. The lag in terms of per-capita ICT research investment is more accentuated, since the EU population is about 50% larger than that of the U.S.

The area of research and industry development known as e-collaboration generally comprises electronic technologies and related methods that enable collaboration among groups of individuals engaged in common tasks. While not all ICT research involves e-collaboration study, investment in both ICT and e-collaboration research seem to go hand-in-hand. In the EU, a key initiative to promote governmental investment in e-collaboration research is the Collaboration@Work initiative. This initiative is one of the EU's Information Society Technologies Directorate General's main priorities. In the U.S., government investment in e-collaboration research is channeled through several government branches and organizations, notably the National Science Foundation.

When we look at e-collaboration funding priorities in the EU and U.S., some marked differences emerge. EU funding seems to be more geared at promoting large applied projects, modeled on the action research tradition, with broad organizational participation. In the U.S., funding seems to be geared at promoting focused projects modeled on the natural sciences approach to inquiry, often involving only one or a few research organizations. The process of selection of research proposals for funding in the EU is significantly more expensive and consensus-oriented than that adopted by the U.S. That process also relies on published guidelines a lot more strongly in the EU than in the U.S.

Which is the "best" e-collaboration research funding approach, the one employed by the EU, or that employed by the U.S.? The answer to this question is a lot more difficult to provide than could be inferred at first glance. If we look at the societal and organizational impact of research projects, while the projects are being conducted, one could argue that the EU approach is better, given its action research orientation. Besides, its focus on multi-organizational collaboration in large research projects is well-aligned with what many see as the ultimate goal of e-collaboration research – to allow for seamless collaboration among individuals who are geographically distributed and yet have to accomplish joint tasks.

However, one could argue that under the EU model research goals are more strongly defined and enforced by European Commission officials than in the U.S., thus decreasing the research funding system's flexibility while increasing latency. Furthermore, the more focused U.S. approach arguably creates and strengthens focused centers of excellence contained in single organizations. Past experience suggests that work in these focused centers ends up leading to the development of breakthrough technologies. One example that could be mentioned here is the largely government-funded National Center for Supercomputing Applications at the University of Illinois in Urbana, whose research led to the development of the first graphical browser for the World Wide Web. That Web browser, dubbed Mosaic, opened up the doors for the Internet technological revolution, whose developments underlie many of the ideas behind government funding of e-collaboration research in both the U.S. and EU.

Two reasonable conclusions that one could reach trying to answer the question as to which government e-collaboration funding approach is better are that: both, the EU and U.S. funding models, are likely to lead to highly desirable results; and each approach has its pros and cons.

Given that, perhaps they could be made a little more like each other. For example, the research proposal selection approach employed by the EU could be made less expensive by employing a combination of online and face-to-face consensus meetings. The approach employed by the U.S. could be made more applied, by the funding agencies placing more emphasis on problem-solving aspects of projects in their selection of proposals to be funded.

We hope that this discussion brings to light the differences in funding approaches in the U.S. and the EU, and promotes more discussion about the merits and consequences of each of the key defining characteristics of each approach. More than anything, we hope to see in the future more funding of e-collaboration research in both the U.S. and EU, without which neither will make progress in the development of e-collaboration technologies and methods or the understanding of the impact of those technologies on individuals, groups and society.

## ACKNOWLEDGMENT

A previous version of this chapter has been published in the *International Journal of e-Collaboration*. The authors thank Isidro Laso-Ballesteros and Bror Salmelin, both officers with the EU's Information Society Technologies Directorate General, for several discussions that formed the basis for this chapter. Those discussions gravitated around ways in which the project proposal selection processes employed in the EU and U.S. differ, and how each can be made more efficient. Thanks are also due to Arden L. Bement, Jr., Director of the National Science Foundation, for his comments on a previous version of this chapter and for information about the National Science Foundation's funding of e-collaboration research. The opinions expressed in this chapter are not meant to be presented as being shared by the EU or the U.S. governments, their branches, or any of their officers. Any errors and omissions are the sole responsibility of the authors.

## REFERENCES

EC (2005). *i2010 – A European Information Society for Growth and Employment.* Brussels, Belgium: Commission of European Communities.

EC (2005b). *i2010 – A European Information Society for Growth and Employment: Extended Impact Assessment.* Brussels, Belgium: Commission of European Communities.

Kock, N. (2003). Action research: Lessons learned from a multi-iteration study of computer-mediated communication in groups. *IEEE Transactions on Professional Communication*, 46(2), 105-128.

Kock, N. (2005). What is E-Collaboration? *International Journal of e-Collaboration*, 1(1), i-vii.

Kock, N. (Ed) (2006). *Information systems action research: An applied view of emerging concepts and methods.* New York, NY: Springer.

Kock, N. (Ed) (2008). *Encyclopedia of e-collaboration.* Hershey, PA: Information Science Reference.

Kock, N., & Nosek, J. (2005). Expanding the Boundaries of E-Collaboration. *IEEE Transactions on Professional Communication*, 48(1), 1-9.

Laso-Ballesteros, I., & Salmelin, B. (2005). AMI-endowed collaboration@work. In G. Riva, F. Vatalaro, F. Davide, & M. Alcaniz (Eds.), *Ambient Intelligence: The evolution of technology, communication and cognition towards the future of human-computer interaction (pp. 237-265).* Amsterdam, The Netherlands: IOS Press.

Rosenthal, R., & Rosnow, R.L. (1991). *Essentials of Behavioral Research: Methods and Data Analysis.* Boston, MA: McGraw Hill.

# Section II
# Virtual Team Leadership

# Chapter V
# Perceived Behaviors of Emergent and Assigned Leaders in Virtual Groups

**Kathryn R. Wickham**
*LiveOps, Inc., USA*

**Joseph B. Walther**
*Michigan State University, USA*

## ABSTRACT

*While considerable research has explored perceptions of groups and members in computer-mediated communication (CMC), and leadership behaviors in face-to-face groups, little research has examined how leadership is identified in CMC groups. Contemporary CMC theories alternatively stress the impact of salient, stereotyped roles on CMC groups' perceptions, or the accretion of exaggerated impressions based on behavioral cues. These perspectives, in turn, coincide with predictions about the predominance of alternative forms of leadership: Assigned versus emergent. This study draws on traditional leadership theories from face-to-face group research and applies them to CMC to examine dynamics related to assigned and emergent leaders in online groups. The results of the study demonstrate that CMC groups may identify more than one leader. When identifying emergent leaders, regardless of whether a leader was assigned or not, group members consider perceived amounts of communication, intelligence, and encouraging and authoritarian behaviors.*

## INTRODUCTION

Early research on computer-mediated communication (CMC) suggested that, due to the lack of nonverbal cues in the new medium, leadership in online decision-making groups was unlikely to take place. According to Kiesler (1986, p. 48),

*without nonverbal tools, a sender cannot easily alter the mood of a message, communicate a sense of individuality, or exercise dominance or charisma. . . . Communicators feel a greater sense of anonymity and detect less individuality in others.*

Such a state might affect the ability of appointed leaders to lead. In terms of emergent leaders, the prospects for such were considered unlikely even to occur (Rice, 1984).

As the field has matured, many types of groups have emerged that use CMC, but a mainstay of CMC research has involved task-oriented, decision-making, and problem-solving groups (see, e. g., Hinds & Kiesler, 2002). Moreover, prognoses about stark social dynamics online have given way to alternative frameworks, in which it is becoming recognized that social effects indeed arise in CMC, albeit through alternative cues and frameworks. On the basis of these frameworks, the capacity for individuals to be recognized in certain roles, and/or to distinguish themselves individually online seems most likely, under many circumstances. Indeed, the hyperpersonal model of CMC suggests that, rather than detecting no individuality in online groups, behavioral hints about individual characteristics early in the course of online exchanges become magnified through online social interaction. These processes lead to behavioral confirmation and exaggeration of such perceptions over time (Walther, 1996). Alternatively, from a social identification/deindividuation (SIDE) perspective, if a particular role or power position is ascribed to an online group member, members self-stereotype around those preconcep-

tions and reify them (Postmes & Spears, 2002). These theoretical perspectives, while potent, have not yet been applied to leadership identification in online groups. Moreover, what specific behaviors individuate a CMC member as a leader, or what intragroup stereotypes lead to reification of leadership online is as yet not well known. It is clear that advanced information technologies can help leaders scan, plan, decide, disseminate, and control information (see Avolio, Kahai, & Dodge, 2001). How communication technology facilitates the recognition or emergence of an ad hoc small group leader may be less clear.

In traditional groups literature, while leadership is easy to recognize, it is not always easy to define and predict. An individual who aspires to group leadership may enact specific behaviors that will achieve this position. Behaviors identified with emergent leadership have previously been studied in face-to-face groups (Hollander, 1964; Kickul & Neuman, 2001). Do leaders in CMC groups behave as those in traditional groups? Do behaviors differ if leaders are assigned or if they simply emerge?

This study reports an experiment intended to address the questions of assigned versus emergent leadership identification in CMC groups. In this study, online groups participated in a decision-making discussion, with a leader appointed or with no leader appointed. Comparisons were drawn between perceived behaviors of an assigned leader and those of emergent leaders in online groups. The individuals nominated post hoc by others as the group leaders were perceived to exhibit several behaviors theoretically connected to leadership tendencies in traditional groups research. Surprisingly, assigned leaders did not reflect traditional expectations for group-related behavior and individual attributes as often, and were less likely to be recognized as the groups' leaders, despite their public appointment as such. It appears that the reification of behavioral stereotypes through hyperpersonal CMC allows emergent leaders to develop greater recognition. The background, methods, and analyses leading to these conclusions are enumerated in the following.

## LEADERSHIP IN GROUPS

In an early definition of the subject, Allport (1924, p. 419) stated that leadership means direct, face-to-face contact between leader and followers it is personal social control. Allport's explanation of leadership provides this study with two immediate problems: a circular definition using "leader" to describe "leadership," and the assumption that leadership requires a face-to-face setting.

Researchers have spent the eighty years following Allport's 1924 definition attempting to craft broad yet operational definitions of leadership. Approaches to defining leadership include, but are not limited to, how to influence group behavior, how to realize goal achievement, ways to modify perceptions within a group, and how to enhance a group's performance level (see for review Shaw, 1981). Leadership studies have identified types of leaders in goal-oriented groups. Two specific types of leaders are of interest to this study: appointed and emergent.

### Appointed Leaders

An appointed, or assigned leader is a member designated by a superior authority to a leadership position (Hollander, 1964). For example, if a group of colleagues is asked to look through resumes of job applicants, a senior manager may ask one member to monitor and direct his or her peers to ensure the completion of the task. Although several group members may naturally possess a variety of leadership capacities, appointed leaders often adopt behaviors stereotypically associated with their given position. Once an individual attains leadership status, that individual often begins meetings by speaking first, organizing activities, and leading discussion. An assigned leader may take it as his or her duty to let other

members know when it is time to shift activities or when the group has deviated from the task at hand. As the assigned leader knows that other group members will be looking to him or her for guidance, the leader may be more conscious of what he or she says and how it may be interpreted by other members. In assigned leadership, the assigned status precedes the associated behaviors (see for review Lawler, 2005).

The principles of the SIDE model of CMC predict that an appointed leader should garner clear leadership consensus in an online group. The SIDE model argues that in CMC there is visual anonymity which obscures the recognition of interpersonal differences among group members. Rather, group members relate to one another as interchangeable group members per se. However, when stereotypical role, status, or social category identifiers are made salient to a group, members perceive one another in line with these identifications, and behave in ways that reinforce and maximize the stereotypical differences among them (Postmes & Spears, 2002; Postmes, Spears, & Lea, 1998; see also Hogg & Tindale, 2005).

These dynamics are suggested to affect individuals' self-categorizations as well as their deference to others. Indeed, Weisband, Schneider, and Connolly (1995) created online groups in which a higher-status member was either correctly identified or mis-identified. When a higher-status member was identified as such, behavior that was consistent with that status (frequent comments and arguments) was valued by others, and influential in the group. However, when an individual who was aware of his or her higher status was experimentally introduced to other members as if s/he was a lower-status member, the individual engaged in the same level of behavior, but was denigrated and uninfluential as a result. The identification of status and leadership may have robust effects on CMC groups' cognitions, behaviors, and evaluations.

From this perspective, in a CMC group with an assigned leader, there should be strong agreement when identifying the assigned group leader, regardless of the presence of specific leadership duties. What would preclude an ambitious follower of an appointed leader from becoming an emergent leader in an assigned-leader group? Bell and Kozlowski's (2002) argument of "member roles" states that virtual teams rely more heavily on the function of a specific group member than teams in a face-to-face environment. Thus, when a team relies on an assigned leader, group members will not want to upset the structure of the team and no emergence will occur.

## Emergent Leaders

When no leader has been assigned to a group, an alternative leader type occurs. The second type of leader considered in this study is the emergent leader, a group member who is perceived by the other members through the process of interaction to be in command, as a director or facilitator, whom they willingly accept (Hollander, 1964). For example, an emergent leader may appear in a group project as the self-appointed note-taker or in a "task-master" position. When no one assigned leader is named, members' own behaviors and characteristics are displayed such that leadership-related behaviors may become apparent. One (or more) group member may naturally fill that role and will be followed and recognized by other group members. Unlike assigned leaders, where the given role precedes the leaders' behaviors, emergent leaders may arise through the enactment of behaviors or characteristics, and perceptions by partners of those enactments, that garner leadership recognition.

While many mechanisms are associated with the emergence of leadership in face-to-face group situations, some of these characteristics are unavailable in CMC, while the role of others warrants examination. Early studies found an association between physical traits and leader emergence, such as gender or height (see for review Shaw, 1981), and spatial location with respect to other

members (Burgoon, Buller, & Woodall, 1996), none of which are apparent online. Will other, communicative behaviors fill this void?

The frequency of messages and chronology of messages have been found to be important characteristics that predict who group members perceive as their leader. One study found that the quantity of verbal interaction is the only factor found to affect the perception of leadership in face-to-face groups significantly (Sorrentino & Boutillier, 1975). Hollander (1964) notes that the more contributions an individual makes towards a group's activities, the higher the status that peers will give to the contributing members. Research has shown that the quantity of verbal interaction is correlated with perceived emergent leadership (see Kickul & Neuman, 2000, for review). Stogdill (1974) found evidence of both frequency and primacy of communication as key factors in determining the identity of leaders, as he discovered that the person who participates earliest and most often is likely to be the identified as the emergent leader.

Many studies have found that emergent leaders are more likely to express their opinions, initiate ideas, and ask other group members questions. Others have noted that the behaviors of emergent leaders include opinion expression and initiation of ideas (Morris & Hackman, 1969). All of these specific behaviors involve great amounts of communication, thus we may assume that frequent communication may be the superordinate consideration.

In addition to these behavioral correlates, a number of trait attributions are associated with face-to-face leadership emergence. When testing for emergent leadership, Kickul and Neuman (2000) found that behaviors displaying cognitive ability, extroversion, and openness also correlate with emergent leadership. Intelligence is another such judgment. Perceived idea initiation, cognitive ability, and task competence are also associated with leadership emergence (Bass, 1990; Hollander, 1964). When attempting to link an individual's qualities with emergent leadership, Taggar, Hacket, and Saha found that cognitive ability was associated most strongly with leadership (1995).

The question remains whether these behaviors and traits are recognizable in the limited-bandwidth environment of CMC. We have previously discussed the potential for *a priori* specification of a leader to have great potency on leader recognition, according to the SIDE perspective. When no such specification is made, will the CMC environment lead to status equalization due to the lack of nonverbal cues and communication through text alone, as suggested in some research (Dubrovsky, Kiesler, & Sethna, 1991)?

The hyperpersonal model of CMC (Walther, 1996) recognizes that there is less information about members initially than in face-to-face groups, but that emergent CMC behaviors lead to identification of members, and on that basis, to exaggerated impressions of one another, and mutual shaping of perceived characteristics and behaviors online, leading to complementary relations. The hyperpersonal model draws on the social information processing theory of CMC (Walther, 1992), which explains how CMC users use verbal behavior to achieve the social and interpersonal impressions typically conveyed nonverbally. From there, the hyperpersonal model suggests that behavior/impression cycles are reciprocated online, leading to exaggerated relational states. Consistent with this framework, Hollingshead and Contractor (1994) argued that the lack of social cues in CMC creates an initial obstacle for recognition of leadership but that there should be eventual consensus as to who has become a group's leader.

In order for this perspective to apply to leader emergence through the exhibition and perception of verbal behavior, CMC groups must be able to substitute verbal for nonverbal cues. Research in dyadic CMC shows that the language of CMC generates as much variance in interpersonal affect as do nonverbal cues face-to-face, and users

adapt fluidly to language in attempting these effects (Walther, Loh, & Granka, 2005). Related to the timing and primacy of messages - a potent leadership emergence cue face-to-face - the timing of messages has significant and complex effects in CMC dyads as well, where variations in the time messages are sent, and replied to, affect the perceived status and dominance/submission of those involved in CMC exchanges (Walther & Tidwell, 1995). Weisband (1992) found that those who spoke their opinions first in CMC groups were most often perceived as the leaders.

Whether these adaptations lead so far as to members ascribing more global traits to one another is another question. Drawing on the hyperpersonal model, Hancock and Dunham (2001) found that trait perceptions of CMC partners were more extreme than were those of face-to-face partners, even though CMC trait perceptions were less detailed. George and Sleeth (2000) have proposed that writing skills displayed via CMC are adequate means through which group members may determine the intelligence level of their group mates.

Thus, the two major theoretical models offer promise for the recognition of CMC leaders. The SIDE perspective favors consensus around assigned leaders. In contrast, the hyperpersonal model stakes no such claim, favoring the potency of enacted online behaviors, whether they emanate from assigned leaders (who, once assigned, may enact them) or from individuals who, through their behavior, emerge as leaders in CMC groups. In which condition - assigned or unassigned - will there be greater leadership recognition and consensus?

Additional research has shown that leaders do emerge from leaderless online groups, but group members may identify more than one person as the leader (Heckman & Misiolek, 2005). Although every member of a virtual team may believe that one of their peers has risen to a position of "leader," the members may not agree on which member has obtained the position. While members are in groups, it is important to note that not every member may define leadership in the same terms. For example, while one member may consider the leader as the person who has dictated tasks, another may believe that the member who has focused on group maintenance was the actual leader (Bales, 1953). If a group has needs for multiple types of leaders, different people may rise to fill each needed role, thus creating multiple emergent leaders. These findings suggest that leadership consensus may indeed be greater in leader-assigned rather than unassigned conditions. Thus, the following hypotheses were generated.

*Hypothesis 1*: Group members of assigned leader groups achieve greater consensus as to the identification of their leader than group members of unassigned leader groups.

*Hypothesis 2*: Assigned leaders are more likely to be identified by members as a group's leader than are other members who are not assigned as leaders.

In addition to the prediction of leader consensus outcomes, above, the relationship of perceived behaviors and capacities associated with leader recognition in traditional groups are examined for their potency in CMC groups as well, both for their association with (a) assigned leaders, and (b) emergent leaders.

*Hypothesis 3a*: The assigned leader is perceived to be the most frequent communicator.

*Hypothesis 3b*: The member perceived as the most frequent communicator is perceived to be an emergent leader in initially leaderless group discussions.

*Hypothesis 4a*: The assigned leader is perceived to be the earliest communicator.

*Hypothesis 4b*: The member perceived as the earliest communicator is perceived to be an emergent leader in initially leaderless group discussions.

*Hypothesis 5a*: Assigned leadership is related to perceived intelligence.

*Hypothesis 5b*: Emergent leadership is related to perceived intelligence.

Whereas the above characteristics are hypothesized to pertain equally well to assigned or emergent leaders, a final characteristic identified in leadership research presents disparate predictions for the two kinds of leaders under consideration. Emergent face-to-face group leaders have been found to be perceived by group members as displaying authoritarian behavior. In face-to-face studies, the emergent leader often focuses on goal achievement and pushes group members to the end task (Bass, 1990). The emergent leader is also perceived to be more highly motivated and self-oriented (Shaw, 1981). If members are self-oriented, they may want their ideas to be the focus of discussion, and will likely be perceived as trying to control the conversation. This contention is also supported by early research by Carter, Haythorn, Shriver, and Lenzetta (1951) who found that emergent leaders are significantly more authoritarian than their appointed counterparts.

The authoritarian behaviors of the emergent leaders in face-to-face groups stand in contrast to the encouraging behaviors of appointed leaders. Manz and Sims (1987) found that assigned external leaders of self-managed groups are perceived as encouraging to group members. Another quality of appointed leaders is their desire to minimize conflict. Appointed leaders try to maintain an atmosphere of cooperation and encourage others to share their opinions (Carter et al., 1951). This is in contrast to the emergent leaders who are perceived as mostly interested in their own contributions. Although both types of leaders work to achieve the same end result, their methods of doing so appear to be in stark contrast.

*Hypothesis 6a*: Emergent leader identification is related to perceived authoritarian behavior.

*Hypothesis 6b*: Assigned leaders are greater than others in perceived encouraging behavior.

## Methods

The study involved 18 groups, composed of three to four members, in CMC small group decision-making discussions. The participants were recruited from a northeastern US university's undergraduate communication courses. As incentive to participate, subjects received extra credit in their courses, and four participants were selected at random to receive a $50 gift certificate to the campus store. Participants' ages ranged from 18 to 22, who signed up for time slots during which to attend a computer-equipped interaction laboratory. Groups at various time slots were randomly assigned to experimental conditions, as follows. The research employed a 2 (no assigned leader vs. assigned leader) x 1 factorial design. Nine groups met within each condition: Six groups of four members and three groups of three members were run with no assigned leader, and eight groups of four members and one group of three members were run with an assigned leader.

The group task involved an information-sharing, decision-making task similar to those used in a variety of group studies both with and without CMC (e. g., McLeod, Baron, Marti, & Yoon, 1997; Stasser, Vaughan, & Stewart, 2000). The discussion involved how the imaginary city of Brooksfield should spend a 10 million dollar Urban Renewal Grant, with the final decision requiring a rank-ordering of three specified alternatives. Each group member was given a packet of information, containing pros and cons related to each decision alternative, but each packet included discrepant information items, which created the need for members to collaborate and work together to share all of the available information in order to make the best decision. Groups were provided 45 minutes, an ample amount of time in which to come to a consensus decision, and no groups

failed to complete their discussion in that time interval.

Among half of the groups, a research assistant instructed group members that it is often helpful to have a leader in discussions such as these, and one of the members had been chosen to be the group's leader for their impending discussion. These announcements did not offer any basis for the selection of a leader, nor were specific responsibilities of leaders enumerated. The name of the leader, which was actually chosen at random, was provided to all group members including the specified individual. Although real-world groups and leadership assignments may reasonably be accompanied by additional rationale, we did not wish to bias the participants' expectations about the intelligence or accomplishments of the assigned leader, since the focus of this research was on whether leader assignment per se affected perceptions and behavior. Groups' CMC discussions involved each member physically isolated in different rooms. The CMC discussions took place using Microsoft Netmeeting, as it allowed the groups to communicate in real time, was similar in appearance to common online messaging programs, and allowed four individuals to communicate within a single discussion space. Netmeeting clients were prepared in advance for each group and participant, so that each individual's name appeared with every comment he or she posted in the discussion. Although most participants (87%) were unfamiliar with NetMeeting before the experiment began, only three participants were new to real-time online chat programs altogether. Brief explanations and demonstrations of the software were provided, which were readily learned; prior experience levels with Netmeeting or chat had no demonstrable effect on the results reported below.

Following the CMC discussion, participants completed an online questionnaire regarding their perceptions of each other member's behaviors, as well as their own. Authoritarian leader behavior and encouraging leader behavior were assessed using subsets of items from Morris and Hackman's (1969) leadership-oriented Behavior Description Questionnaire (BDQ). These seven-interval Likert scales indicted how strongly participants perceived each member to have displayed leaders' behaviors such as "Person 1 generated many ideas in the group, suggesting new ways of handling the group's problem; Person 1 influenced the opinions of others." Authoritarian leadership behavior was assessed with a composite of items measuring perceived criticism, interrupting behaviors, disruptive behaviors, and being concerned only with his or her own viewpoint. Encouraging leader behavior was measured using scales assessing how cooperative a member seemed, how much s/he appeared to listen to other members' ideas, and having worked well with others. In addition to these composites, participants were asked which of their group members they perceived to have communicated the most frequently, both by rating individuals ("In your opinion, Person 1 contributed what percentage of the group conversation?") and of the group as a whole ("Which one of the group member do you believe communicated the most throughout the experiment?"), as well as which of the members they perceived as having the communicated first ("Did Person 1 present the group with its first idea?" and "Which one of the group members do you believe spoke/wrote first on your online chat system?"). Perceived intelligence was measured by the item, "Person 1 is an intelligent person."

Finally, each member was asked which of the group members he or she perceived to be the leader, using a Likert-type item for each member ("Person 1 was a leader of the group") and later in the questionnaire by nominating "Which group member(s) do you consider to be the leader of your online task group?" Group members could select more than one person as the group leader, including themselves, thus a method of determining who the leaders were was developed. Following the procedures of Heckman and Misiolek (2005),

a leadership index was created by dividing the number of times an individual was nominated by the number of opportunities for nomination to occur (e.g., if Member 1 was in a four person group and one person recognized her as the leader, her leadership index score =.25).

## Results

The first hypothesis stated that members of groups with an assigned leader achieve greater consensus about who their leader is than do their counterparts in unassigned leader groups. To compare the agreement regarding assigned leaders to agreement about emergent leaders, we first eliminated from comparison the group members who had a leadership index score of zero. (A score of zero showed perfect group consensus, yet the consensus was regarding the lack of leadership, not the existence of leadership.) The mean of the leadership indices for the assigned leaders was .45 (SD = .26) and the emergent leaders' was .48 (SD = 36). A Student $t$-test for two samples found no significant difference between the two means, $t$ (42) = .24, $p < .81$. The hypothesis was not supported.

In a post hoc examination, the frequency with which there was consensus among members' leader nominations was noticeably greater for emergent leader groups than in assigned-leader groups. The rate of perfect consensus (i.e., individuals who had been noted as leaders by all members of their group, culminating in a leadership index score of 1.0) was higher in emergent groups (five out of nine groups) than in assigned-leader groups (two out of nine groups). Testing the binomial proportions of groups with a consensual leader between the two conditions, a significant difference obtained, $z = 4.02$, $p < .001$, meaning that emergent groups were more likely to identify a consensual leader than assigned-leader groups, even though the assigned leader was introduced to group members as their leader. It appears that appointing a member to a leadership position does not ensure that the assigned member will remain in that position; there is no evidence to support the notion that members will continue to view the appointed member as being in a leadership position throughout a CMC group task.

To analyze the second hypothesis, that group members recognize the randomly appointed leader as the actual leader of the group, we listed all participants with high leadership scores (i.e., index score of .66 or higher), and counted the number of times that the randomly assigned leader was indeed recognized as a leader by the group members. Out of the nine assigned leader groups, only three of these groups gave their appointed leader a leadership index score equal to or greater than .66. Thus, six groups, the majority, did not recognize their assigned leader as an actual leader of the group. Assigning a group member to the position of leader holds little clout with other group members. Even when a leader was assigned, the group seemed to recognize a different individual as the actual leader on an emergent basis.

The next four hypotheses involve relationships between leadership identification and various perceived behaviors and traits. Hypothesis 3 concerned the relationship between group members perceived as the most frequent communicators and the members recognized as leaders. Specifically, the first part of the hypothesis (3a) predicted a relationship between the appointed leader and perception of communication frequency. This was analyzed by comparing the individuals who were nominated as being the most frequent communicator to those who were the appointed leaders. Of 33 nominations for most frequent communicators, only 8 named appointed leaders. The *chi*-square test for the relationship between communication frequency and appointed leadership was significant, $\chi^2 (1, N = 33) = 4.52, p < .05$, but given the array of the frequency data, these results indicate that assigned leaders were significantly *less* likely to be among those perceived to have written the most.

Hypothesis 3b predicted that members perceive the individuals whom they believe to be the emergent leaders as the most frequent communicators within the group. In the groups with no assigned leaders, 34 different leaders were recognized. (Each member was able to identify more than one leader, thus causing more identified emergent leaders than may be expected.) Of those 34 leaders, 27 were perceived as the most frequent communicators in the group. A *chi* square test determined a significant relationship between frequent communication and leadership nomination, $\chi^2 (1, N = 34) = 14.26, p < .001$.

The fourth hypothesis (4a) predicted a relationship between assigned leaders and perceived first communicators. Of the 33 identified leaders within assigned leader groups, 24 were remembered as having sent the first message. A *chi*-square test failed to find significance, $\chi^2 (1, N = 33) = 3.41, p > .05$.

The data also did not support hypothesis 4b, which predicted a relationship between perceived communication primacy and recognition of emergent leadership. Among groups with no assigned leader, 18 of 31 leadership nominations aligned with members perceived to have sent the first messages. A *chi*-square analysis, $\chi^2 (1, N = 31) = .5806, p > .05$, was not significant. There is no significant relationship between speaking first and recognition as the emergent leader.

Hypothesis 5 predicted a relationship between members' perceived intelligence and leadership. Since participants rated each and every partner on perceived intelligence, a hierarchical, or mixed-model analysis (SPSS MIXED) was employed; as observations were nested within groups which are further nested within two types of conditions, analyzing the subjects' data with a simple between-groups approach might lead to inflated error (Anderson & Ager, 1978). Mixed model analysis takes into account the common error variance due to the random factor of belonging to one group versus another, and incorporates that error term, along with the residual (within-subjects) error, in testing the effects of independent variables, leaving the researcher with a more appropriate analysis (Kenny, Manetti, Pierro, Livi, & Kashy, 2002).

Within assigned-leader groups, the appointed leaders ($M = 5.50$, $SE = .30$) were not rated more intelligent than non-leaders ($M = 5.24$, $SE = .18$), $t$ $(77.63) = .82$, $p = .42$, failing to support hypothesis 5a. Indeed, within assigned-leader groups, there was no significant relationship between perceived intelligence and leader consensus at all; a test for a linear association between a leadership index scores and perceived intelligence ratings was not significant, $t$ $(68.47) = 1.20$, $p = .24$. Using a similar test but considering non-leader assigned groups (hypothesis 5b), a significant relationship was obtained between perceived intelligence and leader index scores, offering support for the hypothesis, $t$ $(69.84) = 2.68$, $p = .009$. Apparently recognizing that a randomly-chosen leader is not necessarily more intelligent than other members, there was no recognition that anyone was smarter than anyone else in the group, and no "halo effect" derived from being the appointed leader. However, when no leader was assigned, perceived intelligence seemed to go hand-in-hand with leader recognition.

Hypothesis 6a predicted a relationship between perceived authoritarianism and leadership index for emergent leaders. The authoritarian leader behavior scales achieved a Cronbach's *alpha* reliability score of .77. Using hierarchical mixed-model analysis, a test of the linear relationship between authoritarianism and leader index score found no support for the hypothesis, $t$ $(80.78) = .75$, $p = .46$.

Hypothesis 6b predicted that assigned leaders are perceived as being encouraging by other group members. The measure of perceived encouragement achieved *alpha* reliability of .83. Within the assigned-leader groups, a mixed-model analysis for being an assigned leader ($M = 5.23$, $SE = .28$) or not an assigned leader ($M = 4.89$, $SE = .16$) had no effect on perceived encouragement, $t$ $(79.84) =$

1.13, $p = .26$. However, in contrast to predictions about authoritarian versus encouraging behavior, a post hoc analysis of perceived encouragement and leadership index score in unassigned-leader groups did reveal a significant relationship, $t$ $(76.80) = 3.32$, $p = .001$.

After splitting the groups into assigned leader groups and non-assigned leader groups to examine the sixth hypothesis, we then collapsed the two conditions and tested the relationship between all leaders, regardless of group type, and the aforementioned perceived behaviors. We found a significant relationship between the perception of encouragement and perception of leadership among the combined group of all leaders, $t$ $(150.267) = 2.21$, $p = .029$. There was also support for a linear relationship between perception of authoritarianism and perceived leadership, $t$ $(140.246) = 2.10$, $p = .037$.

## DISCUSSION

While leadership has been a subject of study for many decades, the implications for online leadership, or 'tele-leadership' are just beginning to be discovered (see for review Avolio et al., 2001). This study examined the perceived behaviors of leaders in online groups. After completing a group decision-making discussion using CMC, members rated assigned leaders and other members, or in leaderless group discussions participants rated all members, on several measures of behaviors and traits. Analyses of these data provided varying levels of support for the experiment's predictions. However, even the results that were unanticipated suggest interesting concepts in online leadership.

The first observation of this study is that more than one leader may emerge from a group. There was little consensus about who were the group leaders (showing no support for hypothesis 1), with most groups nominating at least two different emergent leaders. Perhaps this is due to the different roles, such as task director or group maintenance, that leaders may be expected to fill (Bales, 1953). If each role was being filled by a different person, different people may then be nominated as leaders.

When comparing consensual leader recognition between leader-assigned and non-assigned groups, we found that non-assigned groups were more likely to identify a consensual leader than assigned-leader groups, even though the assigned leader was introduced to group members as such. It appears that there is less confusion about who a leader is, or fewer members vying for that role, in groups in which no one individual is named as the leader per se. If the appointed leaders did not display leadership behaviors, members may have been more uncertain about what constitutes leadership that their non-assigned counterparts. The low number of consensual leaders in both types of groups may mean that different members perceive different leadership qualities in their teammates.

Thus, one important result of this study is to question the importance of an assigned leader as far as CMC groups are concerned. Even if there is an assigned leader, a different group member may exhibit behaviors associated with leadership, an occurrence that nullifies the second hypothesis. Despite the potential for intragroup differentiation to occur on the basis of a salient role assignment, it appears that some behaviors carry precedence with other members in identifying who a group leader is. Appointing a member to a leadership position does not ensure that the assigned member will remain in that position; there is no evidence to support that members will continue to view the appointed member as being in a leadership position throughout a CMC group task. Assigning a group member to the position of leader holds little clout with other group members.

These results stand in stark contrast with early prognoses about CMC's incapacity to allow leader emergence, or its tendency to mask inter-individual differences. Rather, given the relatively short time interval that these experimental groups experienced, it appears that hyperpersonal dynamics (Walther, 1996) were more likely to be operating. Subtle behaviors such as communicating most frequently engendered stereotyped impressions of leadership, powerful enough in the case of the assigned-leader groups to overcome the imposition of a leader designation from the experimenters. These results were surprising with respect to hypotheses. They also refute group identification-based approaches to CMC (e.g., SIDE theory; Postmes et al., 1998), that argue that social categorical information - such as leader and follower designations - would drive perceptions. It seems that the stereotypes that affected members' perceptions of who was a leader occurred in a bottom-up, rather than a top-down, fashion, consistent more with hyperpersonal than social identification approach.

Another potential contribution of this study is the confirmation of the significant relationship between frequent communication and leader identification. This relationship is well-known in the face-to-face groups literature, but one of the few to be sustained in online interaction. Frequent communication is emerging as one of the most vital of cues in virtual groups, associated in other research with increased trust and affinity for online colleagues (Walther & Bunz, 2005). Both emergent leaders and assigned leaders were perceived to have been the most frequent communicators within their groups. This suggests that assigned leaders may indeed believe that they must communicate often to help direct the group's activities, and that group members perceive the most frequent communicator to be a group leader. While we cannot be certain whether frequent communication causes leadership to be identified, or if the role of the assigned leader causes frequent communication, we can be certain that the two concepts are related.

Unlike frequency of communication, primacy of communication had no relationship with perceived leadership. Although assigned leaders were more likely to speak first in the online chat room than their non-assigned teammates, no significant relationship was found between leadership recognition and the first message sent. Unlike in face-to-face settings, this experiment found that communication primacy has little bearing on leadership. Previous CMC studies have found links between primacy of *opinion contribution* and leadership (Weisband, 1992); this study did not look at content, simply who sent the first message.

Also of note in this study is the support the hypothesized relationship between leadership identification and perceived intelligence. Emergent leaders were believed to be more intelligent by their group members. This study provides support for the idea that task competency is associated with leadership. Again, we cannot be sure if being a leader causes the perception of intelligence or if intelligence prompts the behaviors that lead to leadership recognition; however, we can state that the two concepts are related.

The final contribution of this study is the finding of relationships between perceived authoritarian behaviors and leadership, and perceived encouraging behaviors and leadership. The hypothesis that leaders would be perceived as encouraging to other group members was supported, and leader nomination was related to perceived encouragement when all types of leaders were considered. This shows that group members who appear to be listening to their teammates and who care about the project are more likely to be accepted as the leader than other teammates.

It may be important to note than when considering *all* leaders in this study, both encouraging and authoritarian behaviors were found to have a linear relationship with leadership. As with the links between leadership and communication frequency and leadership and intelligence, we cannot be certain if the perceived behaviors lead to leadership identification, or if leadership identification creates a bias that makes salient these behaviors. The two significant behavioral qualities appear to conflict; authoritarian behaviors are not something generally considered to be encouraging. Although some theorists suggest that task-oriented and socially-oriented leadership are likely to be engendered by different members of a group (e.g., Bales, 1953), other theorists suggest that an optimal leader, in some groups, provides both task and social direction (e.g., Blake & Mouton, 1994). The latter configuration seems to fit CMC decision-making groups: Leaders must fill several roles for the group, and two of those roles may be authoritarian and encouraging.

This study joins a growing body of literature examining types of leadership in various online forums and discussion systems. Previous studies have compared the impacts of behaviors consistent with leadership styles such as participative versus directive (Kahai, Sosick, & Avolio, 2004) or transformational versus transactional (Kahai & Avolio, 2006; Kahai, Sosick, & Avolio, 2003), which have found differences in other members' discussion patterns and in decision-making as a result of the leader's (or confederate's) behavior. Taken as a whole, these studies all indicate that the structure and nature of a leader's online group behavior does affect a variety of perceptions and actions in electronic groups. The question of whether leadership *behavior* must be vested in a specifically recognized individual, and whether it is less important in online than offline groups, remains to be formally examined. Although many of these studies involved student subjects and real-time discussions, they are intended to apply both to synchronous electronic groups such as those seen using group decision support systems, as well as distributed and potentially asynchronous teams, where messaging may still be sporadic and where little information by and about participants generally leads to large-scale attributions and interpretations (see Walther, 1996).

## Limitations

Each group discussion in this study was completed in one, 45 minute session. It is possible that the divergence among members in their nomination of individual leaders is partly a function of the limited opportunities to identify and differentiate among their partners. This contention is consistent with the SIP theory of CMC (Walther, 1992), which explains that ample time and interactions are required for online partners to develop individuated perceptions of one another. With more time, it is possible that consensual leadership may become more consistent across groups. If more time is spent within the group, perhaps one person may emerge as having all qualities expected of the leader once the alpha role has been established. Due to time constraints, the task assigned to the students was fairly straightforward and was solvable in less than an hour. Groups facing more complex tests might lead to different findings.

## Implications for Future Research

While linking several perceived behaviors with CMC leadership, this study provides many opportunities for future research. Future CMC leadership behavior researchers may find different, significant results by running similar tests over a longer period of time. While these results are applicable to groups working on short-term projects, long-term work groups may associate different behaviors and traits with their identified leaders.

This study shows that multiple leaders may emerge among peers who remain mostly anonymous through the entire process. Different results may be achieved by work associates who have developed face-to-face relationships or have already established a system of hierarchy and leadership through working on previous task-oriented projects. These associates may be more likely to subscribe to behaviors that follow the guidelines of impression formation/management, as online communication may foster and protect their already-made perceptions (see, e.g., Finholt & Sproull, 1990). Populations of people who have already worked together in other online groups or face-to-face conditions deserve further attention.

Other future research relevant to this work is content analysis based on similar studies. While the present research focused on perceived behavior, future research may examine actual behaviors of the identified emergent and assigned leaders. What happens in reality and what is perceived to have happened by group members may be different. However, that opens the field to yet another question: What is more important to group members identifying a leader, perceived leader behaviors, or actual leader behaviors? Additionally, whether the frequent communication and perceived intelligence of online leaders facilitate information exchange and consensus, or whether these perceived behaviors and traits simply dominate discussion, remains for further analyses to resolve.

## REFERENCES

Allport, F.H. (1924). *Social psychology.* Boston: Houghton Mifflin.

Anderson, L.R., & Ager, J.W. (1978). Analysis of variance in small group research. *Personality and Social Psychology Bulletin, 4,* 341-345.

Avolio, B. J., Kahai, S., & Dodge, G. E. (2001). E-leadership: Implications for theory, research, and practice. *Leadership Quarterly, 11,* 615-668.

Bass, B. M. (1990). *Bass and Stogdill's handbook of leadership.* New York: Free Press.

Bell, B.S., & Kozlowski, S.W.J. (2002). A typology of virtual teams: Implications for effective leadership. *Group and Organization Management, 27,* 14-50.

Blake, R. R., & Mouton, J. S. (1994). *The managerial grid* (4th ed.). New York: Gulf Publishing.

Burgoon, J. K., Buller, D. B., & Woodall, W. G. (1996). *Nonverbal communication: The unspoken dialogue* (2nd ed.). New York: McGraw-Hill.

Carter, L., Haythorn, W., Shriver, B., & Lanzetta, J. (1951). The behavior of leaders and other group members. *Journal of Abnormal and Social Psychology, 46,* 589-595.

Dubrovsky, V.J., Kiesler, S., & Sentha, B.N. (1991). The equalization phenomenon: Status effects in computer-mediated and face-to-face decision-making groups. *Human Computer Interaction, 6,* 119-146.

Finholt, T., & Sproull, L. (1990). Electronic groups at work. *Organization Science, 1,* 41-64.

George, G., & Sleeth, R.G. (2000) Leadership in computer-mediated communication: Implications and research directions. *Journal of Business and Psychology, 15,* 287-310.

Hancock, J.T., & Dunham, P.J. (2001). Impression formation in computer-mediated communication revisited: An analysis of the breadth and intensity of impressions. *Communication Research, 28,* 325-347.

Heckman, R., & Misiolek, N. I. (2005, January). *Leaders and followers in student online project teams.* Paper presented at 38th Hawaii International Conference on System Sciences, Waikoloa, HI.

Hinds, P. J., & Kiesler, S. (Eds.) (2002). *Distributed work: New research on working across distance using technology.* Cambridge: MIT Press.

Hogg, M. A., & Tindale, R. S. (2005). Social identity, influence, and communication in small groups. In J. Harwood & H. Giles (Eds.), *Intergroup communication: Multiple perspectives* (pp. 141-164). New York: Peter Lang.

Hollander, E. P., (1964). *Leaders, groups, and influence.* New York: Oxford University Press.

Hollingshead, A. B., & Contractor, N. S. (1994, November). *The dynamics of leader consensus in continuing face-to-face and computer-mediated work groups.* Paper presented at the annual meeting of the Speech Communication Association, Chicago.

Kahai, S. S., & Avolio, B. J. (2006). Leadership style, anonymity, and the discussion of an ethical issue in an electronic context. *International Journal of e-Collaboration, 2,* 1-26.

Kahai, S. S., Sosick, J. J., & Avolio, B. J. (2003). Effects of leadership style, anonymity, and rewards on creativity-relevent processes and outcomes in an electronic meeting system context. *Leadership Quarterly, 14,* 499-524.

Kahai, S. S., Sosick, J. J., & Avolio, B. J. (2004). Effects of participative and directive leadership in electronic groups. *Group & Organization Management, 29,* 67-105.

Kenny, D. A., Manetti, L., Pierro, A., Livi, S., & Kashy, D. A. (2002). The statistical analysis of data from small groups. *Journal of Personality and Social Psychology, 83,* 126-137.

Kickul, J., & Neuman, G. (2000). Emergent leadership behaviors: The function of personality and cognitive ability in determining teamwork performance and KSAS. *Journal of Business and Psychology, 15,* 27-51.

Kiesler, S. (1986, January-February). The hidden messages in computer networks. *Harvard Business Review*, pp. 46-54, 58-60.

Lawler, E. J. (2005). Role of status in group processes. In M. C. Thomas-Hunt (Ed.), *Status and groups* (pp. 315-325). New York: Elsevier.

Manz, C. C., & Sims, H. P. (1987). Leading workers to lead themselves: The external leadership of self-managing work teams. *Administrative Science Quarterly, 32,* 106-128.

McLeod, P. L., Baron, R. S., Marti, M. W., & Yoon, K. (1997). The eyes have it: Minority influence in face-to-face and computer-mediated group discussion. *Journal of Applied Psychology, 82*, 706-718.

Morris, C.G., & Hackman, J.R. (1969). Behavioral correlates of perceived leadership. *Journal of Personality and Social Psychology, 13*, 350-361.

Postmes, T., & Spears, R. (2002). Behavior online: Does anonymous computer-mediated communication reduce gender inequality? *Personality and Social Psychology Bulletin, 28*, 1073-1083.

Postmes, T., Spears, R, & Lea, M. (1998). Breaching or building social boundaries? Side-effects of CMC. *Communication Research, 25*, 689-716.

Rice, R. E. (1984). Mediated group communication. In R. E. Rice & Associates (Eds.), *The new media: Communication, research, and technology* (pp. 129-156). Beverly Hills, CA: Sage.

Shaw, M.E. (1981). *Group dynamics: The psychology of small group behavior.* New York: McGraw-Hill Book Company.

Sorrentino, R.M., & Boutillier, R.G. (1975). The effects of quantity and quality of verbal interaction on ratings of leadership ability. *Journal of Experimental Social Psychology, 11*, 403-411.

Stogdill, R.M. (1950). Leadership, membership, and organization. *Psychological Bulletin, 47*, 1-14.

Stogdill, R.M. (1974). *Handbook of leadership.* New York: The Free Press.

Stasser, G., Vaughan, S. I., & Stewart, D. D. (2000). Pooling unshared information: The benefits of knowing how access to information is distributed among group members. *Organizational Behavior and Human Decision Processes, 82*, 102-116.

Taggar, S. Hackett, R., & Saha, S. (1999). Leadership emergent in autonomous work teams: Antecedents and outcomes. *Personnel Psychology, 52*, 899-926.

Walther, J. B. (1992). Interpersonal effects in computer-mediated interaction: A relational perspective. *Communication Research, 19*, 52-90.

Walther, J. B. (1996). Computer-mediated communication: Impersonal, interpersonal, and hyperpersonal interaction. *Communication Research, 23*, 3-43.

Walther, J. B., & Bunz, U. (2005). The rules of virtual groups: Trust, liking, and performance in computer-mediated communication. *Journal of Communication, 55*, 828-846.

Walther, J. B., Loh, T., & Granka, L. (2005). Let me count the ways: The interchange of verbal and nonverbal cues in computer-mediated and face-to-face affinity. *Journal of Language and Social Psychology, 24*, 36-65.

Walther, J. B., & Tidwell, L. C. (1995). Nonverbal cues in computer-mediated communication, and the effect of chronemics on relational communication. *Journal of Organizational Computing, 5*, 355-378.

Weisband, S. P. (1992). Group discussion and first advocacy effects in computer-mediated and face-to-face decision making groups. *Organizational Behavior and Human Decision Processes, 53*, 352-380.

Weisband, S. P., Scheider, S. K., & Connolly, T. (1995). Computer-mediated communication and social information: Status salience and status differences. *Academy of Management Journal, 38*, 1124-1151.

# Chapter VI
# Supporting Facilitators in Communities of Practice via Design and Technology

**Halbana Tarmizi**
*University of Nebraska at Omaha, USA*

**Gert-Jan de Vreede**
*University of Nebraska at Omaha, USA*

**Ilze Zigurs**
*University of Nebraska at Omaha, USA*

## ABSTRACT

*Organizations have the potential to achieve advantage through communities of practice (COPs) initiatives. However, establishing and sustaining COPs is a challenging task. Facilitation is needed to help COPs overcome difficulties throughout their life stages. Facilitators take on leadership roles within these virtual communities, yet little is known about the challenges related to their roles. This paper contributes in helping to improve leadership in COP by highlighting challenges in facilitating COP and by providing potential solutions addressing those challenges. A recent survey of facilitators reveals challenges faced by facilitators in performing their tasks within COPs. The issue of participation was identified as the main concern in COP facilitation. Several design and technology initiatives are discussed for their potential to help facilitators in coping with the participation issue and providing essential leadership roles within communities of practice.*

## INTRODUCTION

Communities of practice (COPs) have become an important part of an organization and are increasingly recognized as valuable organizational assets (2001). COPs have been identified as playing a critical role in the promotion of learning and innovation in contemporary organizations (Swan, Scarbrough, & Robertson, 2002). However, establishing and sustaining COPs in organizations is a challenging endeavor and COPs are likely to face various challenges and/or difficulties throughout their life-cycle (Tarmizi & de Vreede, 2005).

Design and technology are two factors that are important for a community. Community design affects how people can interact, the information they receive about one another and the community, and how they can participate in community activities (Ren, Kraut, & Kiesler, 2007). Technology, on the other hand, is the one that makes COP possible as it connects people from different locations and different time zones. At the same time, we believe that the introduction of a facilitator could help in promoting a sustainable COP, since a facilitator can play a crucial role in addressing the challenges of establishing and nurturing a COP (Fontaine, 2001; Kimball & Ladd, 2004). In general, facilitation can be defined as "making things easier by using a range of skills and methods to bring the best out in people as they work to achieve results in interactive events" (Townsend & Donovan, 1999, p. 2). The facilitator role entails a wide variety of behaviors, including leadership behaviors (Schuman, 2005; R. Schwarz, Davidson, Carlson, & McKinney, 2005).

Leadership in communities of practice could be involved in various activities including facilitation and coordination (Stuckey & Smith, 2004). The concept of leadership has been viewed in many ways over its history, including in terms of leader characteristics or traits, leader behaviors, typologies, sources of power or influence, and situational contingencies (Bass, 1990). In virtual environments, leadership is an especially inter-

esting phenomenon because of the distributed nature of the context in which leadership must be exercised (Avolio, Kahai, & Dodge, 2001). Traditional forms of exercising leadership are changed in virtual environments, where the usual face-to-face influence is not possible. Thus, it may be that COP members look to a facilitator to exercise leadership to a greater extent than in other kinds of virtual entities because COPs typically do not have an assigned leader.

Although the concept of facilitation has been acknowledged to be applicable to communities of practice (Johnson, 2001, p. 49), the role of the facilitator in COPs is still under-researched, in contrast to research on facilitation in other fields (Tarmizi, de Vreede, & Zigurs, 2006). Facilitation has been extensively studied and documented in the field of Group Support Systems (GSS) (Clawson & Bostrom, 1996; de Vreede, Boonstra, & Niederman, 2002; Dickson, Limayem, J., & DeSanctis, 1996; Griffith, Fuller, & Northcraft, 1998; Niederman, Beise, & Beranek, 1993; Romano, Nunamaker, Briggs, & Mittleman, 1999). COPs could draw benefit from those extensive studies, although there are differences in the nature of COPs and GSSs that should be taken into consideration. Based on the GSS literature, Tarmizi and de Vreede (2005) proposed a facilitation task taxonomy for COPs. This taxonomy took into consideration key differences between facilitation in COP environments and in GSS-supported meetings. Furthermore, the taxonomy included several tasks that reflect leader behaviors within groups, e.g., providing information, encouraging group members, keeping the group focused, and managing conflict.

Yet this taxonomy does not explicitly address the challenges that facilitators experience in executing the various tasks that are part of their COP facilitation duties. While knowing what tasks a COP facilitator has to undertake helps to prepare for this responsibility, having insight into the relative difficulty and importance of the various facilitation tasks would improve the facilitator's preparation. This in turn could help a facilitator to consciously allocate available cognitive resources more efficiently. For example, attention is a scarce resource and a facilitator could be helped to focus more on important yet difficult tasks, while focusing less on difficult yet unimportant tasks. Finally, this knowledge would inform training efforts for novice COP facilitators. Therefore the goal of the study reported in this paper is to answer the following two research questions:

- What are the most challenging facilitation tasks in COPs?
- How can facilitators be supported in addressing the most important challenges?

To address the first question, we conducted a survey of professional COP facilitators to determine their perceptions of the relative difficulty and importance of COP facilitation tasks. The second question was addressed by analyzing previous studies that focused on one or more COP facilitation challenges and extrapolating our own findings in relation to technology developments. Our research contributes in the following ways: (i) organizations can see how to help COP facilitators in more systematic ways; (ii) COP facilitators can learn how to allocate their limited attention in more efficient ways; and (iii) COP researchers can learn from other fields and develop tools for supporting the most challenging tasks.

The remainder of this paper is structured as follows. The next section provides background information on COPs and facilitation tasks in COP environments. Section 3 provides details on the research methodology employed in this study. Section 4 discusses our findings, followed by discussion of a number of ways to help COP facilitators in facing the COP facilitation challenges that were identified. We conclude the paper with a discussion of implications of our findings and directions for future research.

# BACKGROUND

## Communities of Practice

Wenger, McDermott and Snyder (2002) define a COP as a group of people informally bound together by shared expertise and/or passion for a joint enterprise. COPs emerge more or less spontaneously from informal networking among groups of individuals who share similar interests or passions (Lave & Wenger, 1991). In recent years, however, organizations have played an increasingly significant role in initiating COPs (Bourhis, Dubé, & Jacob, 2005; Fontaine, 2001). Within an organization, a COP can serve several purposes, including a forum for sharing ideas, solving problems, disseminating best practices, and organizing knowledge (Wenger et al., 2002). Robey, Ross and Boudreau (2002) also suggest that a COP can serve a role in overcoming knowledge barriers at the time of an IT adoption process in an organization.

Various challenges have been identified for establishing and sustaining COPs within organizations. Those challenges include, but are not limited to, the following:

- making a case for a COP (Muller & Carey, 2002),
- finding common interesting topics for members (Dubé, Bourhis, & Jacob, 2005),
- securing trust of shared information (Van House, Butler, & Schiff, 1998),
- lowering barriers among members to become involved in knowledge-sharing activities (Ardichvili, Page, & Wentling, 2003),
- recruiting the right members, e.g., knowledgeable members who have enough time for social interaction (Pawlowski, Robey, & Raven, 2000), and
- sustaining members' participation, since "… participation is central to the evolution of the community and to the creation of relationships that help develop the sense of

trust and identity that defines the community" (Hildreth, Kimble, & Wright, 2000, pp. 30-31).

Overcoming these challenges could be key for a COP to survive and to serve organizations in a better way. A number of approaches might be used to help overcome these challenges, including technology, management policy, and COP design. No single approach is likely to provide a stand-alone solution, however. Facilitation is a potentially powerful way to address some of these challenges and help the community and its members to navigate through existing obstacles (Fontaine, 2001). The importance of facilitation has been shown in the GSS field, which reinforces the need to study its potential in the COP environment.

## Facilitation in Communities of Practice

Facilitation is often described as the preparation and guidance of a process to help a group achieve its goals, e.g., Hunter, Bailey, & Taylor (1995) and Schuman (2005). In the context of technology-supported groups, facilitators are considered instrumental in helping a group capitalize on the technology's potential (Bostrom, Anson, & Clawson, 1993). However, the facilitator's role goes beyond technology support. A facilitator leads a group towards achieving its objectives through designing and offering effective and efficient process structures, whether this takes place during a focused two-hour workshop or a multi-month period, e.g., Schuman (2005) and Schwartz (2002). The facilitator role has been studied extensively in the GSS field, e.g., Bostrom et al. (1993), Dickson et al. (1996), Griffith et al. (1998), Niederman et al. (1996), while only a few articles in the COP domain have addressed this issue, e.g., Kimball & Ladd (2004), Johnson (2001), Fontaine (2001), Gray (2004), Tarmizi et al.(2006) and Tarmizi, de Vreede, & Zigurs (2007). Therefore, learning

from the GSS field could help us to understand facilitation in COPs.

In order to provide a sufficient background for the context of this study, we describe in some detail the development of the task taxonomy that was the basis for the study. We used the processes that were identified by Gongla and Rizzuto (2001) in their study of COPs at IBM as a starting point for developing an overview of facilitation tasks in COPs. Some COP processes were decomposed into sub-processes to enable a more finely-grained description of the activities within a community. For example, "finding new members" was decomposed into: (i) identifying potential members; (ii) locating potential members; and (iii) discovering what they already know. To identify the tasks a facilitator has to perform for each process, we asked the question: in what way can a facilitator be helpful in this process? To answer this question, we used the following approach. We first mapped each of Clawson and Bostrom's (1996) facilitation tasks to each appropriate COP (sub)process. We adopted Clawson and Bostrom's model since it can be considered to be the most specific and comprehensive model available, covering the facilitation tasks proposed by other researchers, e.g., Dickson et al. (1996), Niederman et al. (1996), de Vreede et al. (2002). However we dropped two of their sixteen items, since those two were more about a facilitator's characteristics than tasks.

After mapping Clawson and Bostrom's (1996) tasks, we identified new tasks to cover several processes specific to COP that were not covered by Clawson and Bostrom. Each (sub)process was critically examined to identify further facilitation tasks. A more detailed elaboration of this exercise can be found in Tarmizi and de Vreede (2005). For some processes, Clawson and Bostrom's (1996) facilitation tasks appeared to comprehensively cover that specific process, e.g., for "defining the roles" (Tarmizi & de Vreede, 2005). One can argue that the process of "defining the roles" for a COP would include (prospective) members gathering offline or online and discussing the roles within the community. Therefore, the facilitator in this process should (i) listen to, clarify, and integrate information from those participants; (ii) develop and ask the right questions that could help participants in this process; and (iii) encourage multiple perspectives during this process in order to achieve the best outcomes.

There were some cases where a combination of Clawson and Bostrom's (1996) facilitation tasks and new tasks were needed. An example of such a process is "introducing new members," where the facilitation task "creates comfort with and promotes understanding of the technology and technology output" is considered one relevant facilitation task. However, additional facilitation tasks were considered necessary to adequately support this process. Those new tasks were: "presenting important information to new members," "encouraging new members to participate," "presenting new members to community members," and "answering new members' concerns."

Some facilitation responsibilities were not covered by Clawson and Bostrom's (1996) tasks at all, especially when the COP processes were related to interaction with the COP's external environment. An example is "positioning the COP in its environment," including its subprocesses "integrating with organizational processes," "linking with other communities," and "mentoring the formation of new communities." These subprocesses required new facilitation tasks such as "guiding the community to match organizational process," "communicating with other communities," and "responding to outside requests." Through this approach we were able to identify 19 new tasks in addition to the 14 original tasks that we adopted from the Clawson and Bostrom (1996) model.

Table 1 shows the COP facilitation task taxonomy that we developed, consisting of 33 COP facilitation tasks. Based on these facilitation tasks, we argue that facilitators can play their role in many capacities in a COP. Therefore, we proposed a categorization of the tasks into several

categories. In labeling the categories, we followed the following approach. First, we divided the tasks into two broad categories: internal and external. "Internal" refers to tasks that are directed toward the internal functioning of the COP, i.e., toward the processes inside the community. "External" refers to tasks that are related to the functioning of the COP as a whole in its broader organizational environment. The "internal" category can be subdivided into three facilitator roles:

- Information source, including all tasks that are related to providing information to the COP's members,
- Inspirator, including all tasks that focus on encouraging members to be active in the community, and
- Guide, including all tasks that concern assisting and advising the COP and its members.

The "external" category can also be subdivided into three facilitator roles:

- Information source, including all tasks that are related to providing information about the COP to the outside world.
- Public relations manager, including all tasks that focus on representing the interests of the COP and its members to the outside world, and
- Investigator, including all tasks that concern searching for and/or collecting useful information for the COP and its members.

The COP facilitation task taxonomy shows that the COP facilitator role appears to be broader and more complex than the GSS facilitator role, although there are many similarities. An important reason for this greater complexity is that the COP facilitator has more of an external representative role than a GSS facilitator.

The taxonomy also shows that many of these tasks reflect leadership roles or behaviors within the COP. The term "distributed leadership system" has been used to describe the phenomenon of members of virtual teams being jointly responsible for the leadership-related tasks or behaviors that need to be carried out for effective virtual functioning (Y. Yoo & Alavi, 2004). The related concept of "total leadership development" (Avolio, 1999) is also relevant to our taxonomy and our view of leadership requirements for facilitators. As the taxonomy shows, facilitators are expected to carry out a wide variety of tasks, many of which are leadership types of tasks. The distributed nature of COPs and the lack of an assigned leader makes it particularly important to ensure that such tasks are carried out.

Although we could consider all of the tasks in Table 1 as important, knowing which of them is the most difficult and/or most important would help would-be COP facilitators in their preparation. It also would help organizations in designing training for their COP facilitators. Knowing the most difficult ones would help organizations and facilitators to work harder on them, while knowing the most important ones would help facilitators in allocating more attention to those important tasks.

## Research Methodology

The data was collected through an online survey among experienced COP facilitators. An online survey offers several advantages including: (i) quick distribution and response cycle (Yun & Trumbo, 2000); (ii) low cost; and (iii) no human

*Table 1. Taxonomy of COP Facilitation Tasks*

| INTERNAL | EXTERNAL |
|---|---|
| INFORMATION SOURCE:<br>• Listening, clarifying and integrating information (2)<br>• Understanding community tools and their capability (14)<br>• Creating comfort with and promoting understanding of the tools and tool outputs (15)<br>• Presenting information to the community (16)<br>• Bringing important information to new members<br>• Answering new members' concerns<br>• Informing members regarding management concerns | INFORMATION SOURCE:<br>• Communicating with other existing communities<br>• Responding to outside requests regarding the community<br>• Sharing experience in serving the community with other potential communities<br>• Reporting to management about the community's progress |
| INSPIRATOR:<br>• Creating and maintaining an open, positive, and participative environment (5)<br>• Developing and asking the right questions (8)<br>• Promoting ownership and encouraging group responsibility (9)<br>• Encouraging multiple perspectives (13)<br>• Encouraging new members to participate in the community's activities<br>• Presenting new members to the community | PUBLIC RELATIONS MANAGER:<br>• Initiating contact with potential community members<br>• Promoting the community to potential members<br>• Implementing a strategy for attracting new members<br>• Advocating community independency to management<br>• Acting as moderator between management and the community |
| GUIDE:<br>• Planning community meetings (1)<br>• Keeping community focus on its purpose (4)<br>• Selecting appropriate tools for the community (6)<br>• Managing the community through guidelines and rules (7)<br>• Building cooperative relationships among members (10)<br>• Mediating conflicts within the community (12)<br>• Scanning community for ongoing / current activities<br>• Coming up with suggestions, if necessary<br>• Guiding the community to match with organizational processes and standards | INVESTIGATOR:<br>• Gathering community relevant information from various sources<br>• Scanning environment outside of the community |

*Note: the numbers behind the items relate to Clawson and Bostrom's facilitation tasks*

intervention in entering responses into a database. A Web site containing the questionnaire was set up, since Web-based surveys have an advantage over email surveys (Andrews, Nonnecke, & Preece, 2003). The questionnaire consisted of (i) background information, such as gender, years of experience with COP, years of experience as a COP facilitator, and number of COPs facilitated; (ii) choosing the ten most difficult facilitation tasks based on the respondent's experiences; and (iii) choosing the ten most important facilitation tasks based on their experiences. Respondents were asked to choose up to ten of the most difficult facilitation tasks as well as the ten most important tasks from a list of 33 facilitation tasks. In order to minimize bias due to position of the tasks on the list, the position of each task in the list was randomly generated. Prior to the survey, the questionnaire, including the list of 33 facilitation tasks, was pre-tested among several doctoral students with relevant experience. As a result, definitions for each of the tasks were added to make sure that respondents would have a deeper understanding of the listed tasks. Respondents were also given space to add additional facilitation tasks.

An invitational email to participate in this survey was sent to three mailing-list groups of facilitators: (i) onlinefacilitation group at Yahoo!; (ii) com-prac group at Yahoo!; and (iii) a facilitators' mailing list. We identified those groups, based on their postings, as venues where facilitators of various organizations exchange information, experiences and advice. Most of their members have experience with COPs and facilitation activities. Andrews et al. (2003) argue that "… when a Web-based survey is preceded by email inviting individuals to the URL to participate, the Web-based survey outperforms email survey participation significantly" (p. 197). The online survey was available for 2 weeks. A reminder email was sent at the beginning of week two, in order to spike participation.

## DATA ANALYSIS

### Demographics

One-hundred-fourteen visitors viewed the survey during the two weeks that it was posted on the Web. From those who visited, 79 people (69.3%) started taking the survey. The number of those who actually finished the survey is 45 (56.96% of those who started). However, one respondent had to be dropped from consideration because of a technical problem that failed to record that person's response on the Web survey system. Therefore, we have complete data from a total of 44 respondents. The respondents come from 18 different countries, with the majority from the US (17 respondents), followed by Canada (7 respondents). Other countries include Columbia, Chile,

*Table 2. Facilitation experience of respondents*

| COP experience | Less than 2 years | 20% |
|---|---|---|
| | At least 2 years, but less than 5 years | 30% |
| | At least 5 years, but less than 10 years | 32% |
| | At least 10 years | 18% |
| | | |
| Facilitation experience | Less than 2 years | 30% |
| | At least 2 years, but less than 5 years | 43% |
| | At least 5 years, but less than 10 years | 16% |
| | 10 years or more | 11% |

UK, Netherlands, France, Denmark, Portugal, Spain, Turkey, Italy, Israel, Hong Kong, Malaysia, India, Bangladesh and Australia. There were 19 female (43%) and 25 male (57%) respondents. Table 2 shows the facilitation experience of the respondents.

## Challenging Tasks in COP Facilitation

When confronted with the question of identifying the ten most difficult tasks in COP facilitation, 70.5% of the respondents in this survey clearly identified *"Encouraging new members to partici-pate in the community's activities"* as one of the most difficult tasks. *"Promoting ownership and encouraging group responsibility"* was identi-fied by 61.4% of the respondents. This task was defined as how the facilitator helps a group take responsibility for the community and ownership of the community's activities and outcomes, stays out of their content, and turns the floor over to the members. The majority of the respondents (56.8%) also found that *"Creating and maintaining an open, positive, and participative environment"* was not an easy task. One of the keys of community building, i.e., *"Building cooperative relationships among members,"* was also seen by 45.5% of the respondents as a difficult task. *"Mediating conflict*

*in the community"* was considered by 45.5% of the respondents as difficult. Table 3 shows the ten most difficult tasks in COP facilitation as identified by the respondents.

In identifying the most important tasks in COP facilitation, most respondents (55.6%) regarded *"Creating and maintaining an open, positive, and participative environment"* as one of the most important tasks. *"Encouraging new members to participate in the community's activities"* and *"listening, clarifying and integrating information"* were each identified by 52.3% of the respondents. Half of the respondents (50%) considered *"keeping community focus on its purpose"* as one of the most important tasks. Table 4 shows the ten most important tasks in COP facilitation as identified by the respondents.

If we classify tasks that were mentioned by 20 respondents or more as high in difficulty or high in importance, while those tasks that were mentioned by less than 20 respondents as low in difficulty or low in importance, then we can compare them. Table 5 maps the facilitation tasks into importance and difficulty (low vs. high). The table shows that most of the tasks are not considered difficult, but also not high in importance. Other tasks are considered high in importance, but also high in difficulty. The remaining tasks are considered high in either one of those dimensions.

*Table 3. Most difficult facilitation tasks*

| No. | Tasks | % of Respondents |
|-----|-------|------------------|
| 1. | Encouraging new members to participate in the community's activities | 70.5% |
| 2. | Promoting ownership and encouraging group responsibility | 61.4% |
| 3. | Creating and maintaining an open, positive, and participative environment | 56.8% |
| 4. | Building cooperative relationships among members | 45.5% |
| 5. | Mediating conflicts within the community | 45.5% |
| 6. | Creating comfort with and promoting understanding of the tools and tool outputs | 40.9% |
| 7. | Keeping community focus on its purpose | 38.6% |
| 8. | Implementing a strategy for attracting new members | 38.6% |
| 9. | Advocating community independency to management | 34.1% |
| 10. | Encouraging multiple perspectives | 31.8% |

*Table 4. Most important facilitation tasks*

| No. | Tasks | % of Respondents |
|-----|-------|------------------|
| 1. | Creating and maintaining an open, positive, and participative environment | 56.8% |
| 2. | Encouraging new members to participate in the community's activities | 52.3% |
| 3. | Listening, clarifying and integrating information | 52.3% |
| 4. | Keeping community focus on its purpose | 50.0% |
| 5. | Encouraging multiple perspectives | 47.7% |
| 6. | Promoting ownership and encouraging group responsibility | 47.7% |
| 7. | Developing and asking the right questions | 47.7% |
| 8. | Mediating conflicts within the community | 43.2% |
| 9. | Building cooperative relationships among members | 40.9% |
| 10. | Selecting appropriate tools for the community | 34.1% |

## DISCUSSION

## Participation as the Most Challenging Task

Most of the tasks were considered by respondents as low in terms of difficulty and importance. This fact could help us in thinking about integrating some of those tasks into COP technology, so that it will (partly) automate those tasks and take some of the burden from the facilitator. Tasks such as "presenting new members to the community," "presenting information to the community," and "answering new members' concerns" are good candidates to be (partly) automated and to be integrated into future COP technology. If facilitators are relieved from some of these tasks, they can focus more on tasks considered high in importance. Some of those highly important tasks are relatively low in terms of difficulty, so that facilitators can accomplish those tasks without much problem. Surprisingly, the highly difficult tasks, "building cooperative relationships among members" and "mediating conflicts within the community," were rated low in terms of importance. These hints could help facilitators in prioritizing their attention, although further study is needed to verify this finding.

"Encouraging new members to participate in the community's activities," "promoting ownership and encouraging group responsibility," and "creating and maintaining an open, positive, and participative environment" were considered high in terms of difficulty as well as importance. All of those tasks are related to participation. In this paper, we define participation as "to take part in or share in some process or activity" (Cluts, 2003, p. 146). Participation itself is central to a community, since it is key for the evolution of the community and the creation of relationships that help develop a sense of trust and identity that define the community (Hildreth et al., 2000). Furthermore, participation could be one of the key measurements for evaluating the quality of a community (W. S. Yoo, Suh, & Lee, 2002), and it could be used as an indicator of whether the approach used in developing a community is the right one or not (Gongla & Rizzuto, 2001). For any community, social interaction is not possible without participation and without interaction, no social organization would emerge (Girgensohn & Lee, 2002).

An open, positive and participative environment should lower the barriers to participation among members, which in turn might encourage them to take more responsibility regarding

*Table 5. Importance vs. difficulty of facilitation tasks*

| | | difficulty | |
|---|---|---|---|
| | | low | high |
| importance | low | • Bringing important information to new members<br>• Answering new members' concerns<br>• Informing members regarding management concerns<br>• Presenting new members to the community<br>• Scanning community for ongoing / current activities<br>• Coming up with suggestions, if necessary<br>• Guiding the community to match with organizational processes and standards<br>• Communicating with other existing communities<br>• Responding to outside requests regarding the community<br>• Sharing experience in serving the community with other potential communities<br>• Reporting to management about the community's progress<br>• Initiating contact with potential community members<br>• Promoting the community to potential members<br>• Implementing a strategy for attracting new members<br>• Advocating community independency to management<br>• Acting as moderator between management and the community<br>• Gathering community relevant information from various sources<br>• Selecting appropriate tools for the community<br>• Scanning environment outside of the community<br>• Creating comfort with and promoting understanding of the tools and tool outputs<br>• Presenting information to the community<br>• Planning community meetings<br>• Understanding community tools and their capability<br>• Managing the community through guidelines and rules | • Building cooperative relationships among members<br>• Mediating conflicts within the community |
| | high | • Listening, clarifying and integrating information<br>• Developing and asking the right questions<br>• Keeping community focus on its purpose<br>• Encouraging multiple perspectives | • Creating and maintaining an open, positive, and participative environment<br>• Encouraging new members to participate in the community's activities<br>• Promoting ownership and encouraging group responsibility |

their community. As Ardichvili et al. argue, "the challenge in enabling virtual communities of practice is not so much that of creating them, but of removing barriers for individuals to participate …" (2003, p. 75). As depicted in Table 6, difficulty in encouraging participation, especially that of new members, is faced not only by new facilitators, but also by those with five or more years of experience in facilitation.

While most facilitators recognize the problem with participation, especially for new members, they also admit that offering an open, positive and participative environment is important for their communities. Assisting a facilitator in overcoming challenges with participation issues becomes crucial to any organization that is looking for benefits of having a COP. In this paper, we address our second research question by focusing specifically on two factors that we consider to have high correlation with participation, namely design and technology. Technology is taken into consideration, since one of its characteristics is to extend human capability (Satchwell & Dugger, 1996), in this case a facilitator's capability, while a good community design can invite, even evoke aliveness (Wenger et al., 2002). The importance of technology in COP is also supported by Pan and Leidner who note that "…information technology…is a key part of establishing a global knowledge-sharing culture" (2003, p. 83).

## Helping Facilitators via Design and Technology

Participation in an online community such as a COP can take several forms. The most obvious one is through posting questions, requests, or responses to other members' postings. Interaction among members can also take place in the form of chatting or emailing. However, interac-

tion with content or resources within an online community, such as through reading postings or accessing stored files, should also be considered as participation. As Bento and Schuster's (2003) taxonomy for online interaction shows, community members could have high interaction with community resources while showing low interpersonal interaction. This type of participation could also help in sustaining online communities, since such members could become what Takahashi, Fujimoto and Yamasaki (2003) describe as active lurkers, i.e., those who never post a message but propagate information or knowledge gained from a community to those outside it. This type of participation could bring more benefit to the community than those with high interpersonal interaction but low content interaction within this COP ( e.g., posting messages, but having low interaction with content or resources). Interaction with a community's content or resources could help in making the community become a center of knowledge for its members. Therefore, those members who never consider a community as a center of knowledge, but rather only as another type of mailing list, are less likely to advance the community. Not posting is sometimes better than a low-quality posting, as Cosley, Frankowski, Kiesler, Terveen and Riedl (2005) argue. In fact, "too many low-quality contributions can actually drive away valuable members who decide that the cost of participating is too high" (Cosley

*Table 6. Most difficult tasks by experience level*

| Experience in Facilitation | Tasks | % of Respondents |
|---|---|---|
| Less than 5 years | Encouraging new members to participate in the community's activities | 71.9% |
| | Promoting ownership and encouraging group responsibility | 62.5% |
| | Creating and maintaining an open, positive, and participative environment | 53.1% |
| | | |
| 5 years or more | Encouraging new members to participate in the community's activities | 66.7% |
| | Creating and maintaining an open, positive, and participative environment | 62.5% |
| | Creating comfort with and promoting understanding of the tools and tool outputs | 62.5% |

et al., 2005, p. 13). This argument is in line with Kahai, Sosik and Avolio's (2004) finding that participation is negatively related to satisfaction. They argue that without any tool to help members focus, too many ideas or contributions could make it difficult to sort out good ideas or quality contributions. This difficulty in turn could reduce member satisfaction.

Increasing participation, including increasing the number of quality postings, should be one of the facilitator's main goals in a COP. However, a facilitator cannot act alone to achieve this goal. Community designers have to make large and small design decisions that can influence the way the community motivates participants (Ren et al., 2007). Design that can evoke aliveness (Wenger et al., 2002) and technology that is able to extend human capability (Satchwell & Dugger, 1996) are two factors that could have a high impact on participation. A poorly designed community, e.g., one without a clear goal or one focusing on topics that are irrelevant to the members (Dubé et al., 2005), is unlikely to survive, even with the help of an experienced facilitator. An experienced facilitator without adequate supporting technology would also face difficulties in fulfilling her tasks and in helping her community to be successful. For this reason, we look next at studies in various fields that are highly relevant in addressing the issue of participation in COPs using technology and design. We include those studies that address online communities design and those that focus on technology for increasing participation.

## Design

The issue of participation needs to be addressed at early stages of community development. A COP that has neither a clear purpose nor focuses on topics that are applicable for potential members in an organization is doomed to fail (Dubé et al., 2005). The facilitator of such a poorly-designed COP would face difficulty in motivating members to participate. As Alem and Kravis (2004) also found in their study of online learning communities, the lack of perceived clarity of purpose can be a major problem. Sheard (2004) suggested that the purpose of a community or forum should be clear at the very beginning. Participation in online communities could also be affected by uniqueness and group dissimilarity (Ludford, Cosley, Frankowski, & Terveen, 2004), which would have a positive effect on participation. For this reason, in designing a community, potential members from different backgrounds, expertise, and character should be taken into consideration. Providing incentives for participation would help as well (Romano et al., 1999; Smith & McKeen, 2003). Incentives could take several forms, including financial rewards in the form of bonus or salary increase as practiced by DaimlerChrysler (APQC, 2000), or non-financial rewards in the form of recognition from peers as practiced by Ford (APQC, 2000). Still, consideration needs to be given in offering rewards in an appropriate manner by taking into account the nature of the reward and the social context (Kahai, Sosik, & Avolio, 2003). Having a clear policy within an organization regarding how information is to be shared via electronic media or within an online community would also have a positive impact on the sharing activity (Staples & Jarvenpaa, 2000). A positive impact on sharing would in turn increase members' participation. A regression analysis by Millen and Patterson (2002) revealed that prior experience with other communication applications by each individual, e.g., email lists and chat services, predicted increased participation in an online community. Socialization of new members has been recognized as the most challenging in the community (Ren et al., 2007). Ren et al. (2007) noted that having mechanism to mentor new members could help them feeling comfortable in the community. This can lead to a willingness to engage more in the community. Another potential problem is off-topic discussion. Off-topic discussion could increase information overload among members that could lead to them leaving the community. At the same time, however, off-topic discussion could increase personal relationship among members, as they start revealing their personal information (Ren et al., 2007). Therefore, a community designer needs to recognize this potential as well as this risk. One way to address this issue is by having facilitator controlling, not prohibiting, off-topic discussion. As members are the core of a community, Tarmizi, de Vreede, & Zigurs (2007) found in their study among COP facilitators that a community with voluntary based membership will be more likely to success. A voluntary based membership appears to be more appropriate in advancing a community than a compulsory one. One of the reasons is probably that by letting individuals to choose which of the existing communities they want to join, they will join those that have high relevance to their activities or interests. Those in turn will trigger commitment from them toward their communities. Table 7 summarizes potential design strategies for COPs based on our discussion.

## Technology

COPs involving geographically dispersed participants cannot exist without technology, and there are many different forms of such technology. Technology should help facilitators in performing their duties in a COP, including improving members' participation. Wenger (2001) has argued that there is no ideal system to support a COP available on the market and that ideal systems will arise as combinations and convergence of existing systems in the market as the market matures. Nonetheless, several studies examined technologies used to increase member participation in online communities. Millen and Patterson (2002) argue that *channeling participants* through a common entry point would help them in becoming aware of interaction within a community, since this entry point would become the most active part of the community in terms of the number of postings or number of visits. Furthermore, these authors believe that *notification alerts* would raise awareness among participants about COP activities. Their study showed that a community will get more traffic from active participants as well as passive participants, i.e., lurkers, in response to a notification alert. They also showed that as days pass without any alert, the traffic in the community declines.

Awareness, i.e., the state of knowing or being informed, is one aspect of social interaction (Girgensohn & Lee, 2002). Providing a listing of what has changed since the last visit and displaying discussion threads and messages in chronological order could raise awareness among visitors (Girgensohn & Lee, 2002), which in turn could increase participation. Promoting visibility of

*Table 7. Design strategies for increasing participation*

| Strategy | Authors |
| --- | --- |
| Making the purpose of the community clear as early as possible | Sheard (2004), Alem and Kravis (2004) |
| Finding relevant topics for potential members | Dubé et al. (2005) |
| Providing incentives or rewards for participations | Smith and McKeen (2003) |
| Considering individuals with different background and expertise | Ludford et al. (2004) |
| Including individuals with experience in mailing lists and chat | Millen and Petterson (2002) |
| Having a clear policy on information sharing within the organization | Staples and Jarvenpaa (2000) |
| Having mentorship mechanism for new members | Ren et al. (2007) |
| Controlling off-topic discussions through facilitation | Ren et al. (2007) |
| Building community based on voluntary membership | Tarmizi et al. (2007) |

people and their activities is also key in a community (Girgensohn & Lee, 2002), since identity is an important condition for cooperation and people like to interact with people they know, people they like, and people who are similar to them (Constant, Sproull, & Keisler, 1997). Providing a profile of each member and having the ability to track each member's contribution should help in promoting members' visibility and their activities.

Recognition and identification encourage participation (Constant et al., 1997). Kapoor, Konstan and Terveen (Kapoor, Konstan, & Terveen, 2005) found that providing photo galleries of members could lead to greater participation in an online community, which suggests that providing members' profiles would encourage participation. Vassileva and Sun (2007) designed a motivational visualization design to encourage participation. This visualization uses a night-sky metaphor with four dimensions, i.e., size (reflecting numbers of contributions), color (reflecting membership status), level of brightness (reflecting quality of contributions) and shade (indicating current online or offline status). They showed that this visualization stimulates social comparison, which in turn becomes a source of motivation to members to contribute and to participate actively in the community. Since participation could also include interaction with resources or content in a community (Bento & Schuster, 2003), having technology that tracks lurkers' activities would be useful to a community's facilitator. Nonnecke and Preece (1999) point out that lurkers have received very little attention, despite the high number of lurkers compared to active posters. Carroll and Rosson (1996) estimate that the ratio of lurkers to posters is as high as 100 to 1. This estimation gives us a sense of urgency for developing technology to track those lurkers and convert them to active posters. However, we have to acknowledge that tracking lurkers could lead to privacy concern among users, since the majority of Internet users voice concern about accepting Internet cookies (Teltzrow & Kobsa, 2004). For this reason, in the

future a more user-oriented approach of tracking should be proposed to address this privacy concern. To address low-quality contributions that could drive away valuable members (Cosley et al., 2005), COP can allow members to rate a post. Members rate posts in a forum for relevance and quality and they can then decide to view messages rated above some threshold (Ren et al., 2007). A reputation system for members based on their contribution (Kelly, Sung, & Farnham, 2002) could have a positive impact on participation, since it would allow other members to judge each contribution by looking at its author's reputation. Table 8 summarizes technology features that may increase participation among COP members.

## CONCLUSION

This study provides several major contributions to our understanding of the challenges faced by facilitators as part of their leadership role in communities of practice. First, we identified the highly important and difficult tasks that need special attention from facilitators in order to manage their communities of practice. Second, participation was identified as the major challenge for facilitators. Third, we developed recommendations for solutions to overcome this major challenge, based on existing research on design and technology.

The findings of this empirical study indicate that most of the facilitation tasks were considered low in difficulty and importance. These types of tasks are good candidates to be (partly) automated or to be built in as part of future COP technology. Some of the highly difficult tasks were also highly important for the community, while others were less important. This finding could help a facilitator to prioritize her limited attention in order to provide optimal support for the community.

Furthermore, while increased participation has the potential to help a community of practice to thrive and serve its purposes in an organization, encouraging members' participation has been

*Table 8. Technology for addressing participation in COPs*

| Technology | Authors |
|---|---|
| Channeling participants through a common entry point | Millen and Patterson (2002) |
| Notification alert | Millen and Patterson (2002) |
| Listing of what has changed | Girgensohn and Lee (2002) |
| Member profiles and activity tracking | Girgensohn and Lee (2002) |
| Providing photo galleries of members | Kapoor et al. (2005) |
| Visualization of quantity and quality of contributions, membership status, and current online/offline status | Vassileva and Sun (2007) |
| Lurker tracking | Nonnecke and Preece (1999) |
| Reputation system based on contribution | Kelly et al. (2002) |
| Rating for messages and filtering capability | Cosley et al. (2005), Ren et al. (2007) |

identified as a major challenge for facilitators. For this reason, facilitators need support in overcoming this major challenge, and design and technology are two such approaches. Deciding how to encourage participation needs to be addressed as early as possible, when a community of practice is in its building phase. In a well-designed COP, a good facilitator will be more likely to be successful in encouraging participation than a facilitator in a poorly-designed community. Technology could also help a facilitator, and several available technologies have potential as partial solutions to overcome this challenge.

Given its exploratory nature, the study has some limitations. Those limitations include the use of descriptive instead of inferential statistics due to the limited data set. Furthermore, since the majority of our respondents were from North America, our findings might be biased toward that region. Our data also represents only the perspective of the facilitator, since the data was collected among facilitators and not community of practice members. A COP member could have different perceptions about facilitation. The limitations of this exploratory effort provide fertile ground for future research.

Next steps include measuring how various technologies might help in fostering participation for a well-designed community of practice. We

also envision proposing COP technology that we believe would help in lifting some of the burdens from the facilitator. When the burden is reduced, facilitators should be able to focus more and to use their expertise in addressing more demanding challenges.

This study lays the ground work for future development of communities of practice technology. It also informs COP practitioners regarding facilitation challenges and how to overcome them. There is still much work to be done to gain a thorough understanding of the complex picture of COP facilitation. This study brings us one step closer to that goal.

## REFERENCES

Alem, L., & Kravis, S. (2004). Design and evaluation of an online learning community: a case study at CSIRO. *SIGGROUP Bulletin, 25*(1), 20-24.

Andrews, D., Nonnecke, B., & Preece, J. (2003). Electronic Survey Methodology: A Case Study in Reaching Hard-to-Involve Internet Users. *International Journal of Human-Computer Interaction, 16*(2), 185.

APQC. (2000). *Building and Sustaining Communities of Practice-Final Report.* Houston, TX: American Productivity and Quality Center.

Ardichvili, A., Page, V., & Wentling, T. (2003). Motivation and barriers to participation in virtual knowledge-sharing communities of practice. *Journal of Knowledge Management, 7*(1), 64-77.

Avolio, B. (1999). *Full Leadership Development: Building the Vital Forces in Organizations.* Thousand Oaks, CA: Sage Publications, Inc.

Avolio, B., Kahai, S., & Dodge, G. E. (2001). E-Leadership: Implications for theory, research, and practice. *Leadership Quarterly, 11*(4), 615-668.

Bass, B. M. (1990). *Bass & Stogdill's Handbook of Leadership: Theory, Research, and Managerial Applications.* New York, NY: Free Press.

Bento, R., & Schuster, C. (2003). Participation: the online challenge. In A. K. Aggarwal (Ed.), *Web-based education: learning from experience table of contents* (pp. 156-164). Hershey, PA, USA IGI Publishing.

Bostrom, R. P., Anson, R., & Clawson, V. K. (1993). Group facilitation and group support systems. In L. M. Jessup & J. S. Valacich (Eds.), *Group Support Systems: New Perspectives* (pp. 146-168.). New York, NY: McMillan Publishing Company.

Bourhis, A., Dubé, L., & Jacob, R. (2005). The Success of Virtual Communities of Practice: The Leadership Factor. *Electronic Journal of Knowledge Management Volume, 3*(1), 23-34.

Carroll, J. M., & Rosson, M. B. (1996). Developing the Blacksburg electronic village. *Communications of the ACM, 39*(12), 69-74.

Clawson, V. K., & Bostrom, R. P. (1996). Research-driven facilitation training for computer-supported environments. *Group Decision and Negotiation, 5*(1), 7-29.

Cluts, M. M. (2003). *The evolution of artifacts in cooperative work: constructing meaning through activity.* Paper presented at the International ACM SIGGROUP Conference on Supporting Group Work 2003.

Constant, D., Sproull, L., & Keisler, S. (1997). The Kindness of Strangers: On the Usefulness of Electronic Weak Ties for Technical Advice. In S. Kiesler (Ed.), *Culture of the Internet* (pp. 303-322). Mahwah, NJ: Lawrence Erlbaum Associates.

Cosley, D., Frankowski, D., Kiesler, S., Terveen, L., & Riedl, J. (2005, April 2–7, 2005, ). *How oversight improves member-maintained communities.* Paper presented at the SIGCHI 2005 Conference on Human factors in Computing Systems, Portland, Oregon, USA.

de Vreede, G. J., Boonstra, J., & Niederman, F. (2002). What is effective GSS facilitation? A qualitative inquiry into participants' perceptions. *System Sciences, 2002. HICSS. Proceedings of the 35th Annual Hawaii International Conference on,* 616-627.

Dickson, G., Limayem, M., J., L.-P., & DeSanctis, G. (1996). Facilitating computer supported meetings: A cumulative analysis in a multiple criteria task environment. *Group Decision and Negotiation, 5*(1), 51-72.

Dubé, L., Bourhis, A., & Jacob, R. (2005). The impact of structuring characteristics on the launching of virtual communities of practice. *Journal of Organizational Change Management, 18*(2), 145-166.

Fontaine, M. (2001). Keeping communities of practice afloat: understanding and fostering roles in communities. *Knowledge Management Review, 4*(4), 16-21.

Girgensohn, A., & Lee, A. (2002). *Making Web Sites be places for social interaction.* Paper presented at the ACM 2002 Conference on Computer Supported Cooperative Work.

Gongla, P., & Rizzuto, C. R. (2001). Evolving communities of practice: IBM Global Services experience. *IBM Systems Journal, 40*(4), 842-862.

Gray, B. (2004). Informal Learning in an Online Community of Practice. *Journal of Distance Education, 19*(1), 20-35.

Griffith, T., Fuller, M., & Northcraft, G. (1998). Facilitator influence in Group Support Systems. *Information Systems Research, 9*(1), 20-36.

Hildreth, P., Kimble, C., & Wright, P. (2000). Communities of practice in the distributed international environment. *Journal of Knowledge Management, 4*(1), 27-38.

Hunter, D., Bailey, A., & Taylor, B. (1995). *The Art of Facilitation*. Cambridge, MA: Perseus Book Group.

Johnson, C. M. (2001). A survey of current research on online communities of practice. *Internet and Higher Education, 4*(1), 45-60.

Kahai, S. S., Sosik, J. J., & Avolio, B. J. (2003). Effects of leadership style, anonymity, and rewards on creativity-relevant processes and outcomes in an electronic meeting system context. *The Leadership Quarterly, 14*(4-5), 499-524.

Kahai, S. S., Sosik, J. J., & Avolio, B. J. (2004). Effects of participative and directive leadership in electronic groups. *Group & Organization Management, 29*(1), 67-105.

Kapoor, N., Konstan, J. A., & Terveen, L. G. (2005). *How peer photos influence member participation in online communities*. Paper presented at the 2005 Conference on Human Factors in Computing Systems.

Kelly, S. U., Sung, C., & Farnham, S. (2002). *Designing for Improved Social Responsibility, User Participation and Content in On-line Communities*. Paper presented at the SIGCHI conference on Human factors in computing systems.

Kimball, L., & Ladd, A. (2004). Facilitator toolkit for building and sustaining virtual communities

of practice. In P. M. Hildreth & C. Kimble (Eds.), *Knowledge Networks: Innovation through Communities of Practice* (pp. 202-215). Hershey, PA: Idea Group Pub.

Lave, J., & Wenger, E. (1991). *Situated Learning: legitimate peripheral participation*. Cambridge, UK: Cambridge University Press.

Lesser, E. L., & Storck, J. (2001). Communities of practice and organizational performance. *IBM Systems Journal, 40*(4), 831-841.

Ludford, P. J., Cosley, D., Frankowski, D., & Terveen, L. (2004). *Think different: increasing online community participation using uniqueness and group dissimilarity*. Paper presented at the 2004 conference on Human factors in computing systems.

Millen, D. R., & Patterson, J. F. (2002). *Stimulating social engagement in a community network*. Paper presented at the ACM 2002 Conference on Computer Supported Cooperative Work.

Muller, M. J., & Carey, K. (2002). *Design as a minority discipline in a software company: Toward requirements for a community of practice*. Paper presented at the SIGCHI conference on Human factors in computing systems.

Niederman, F., Beise, C. M., & Beranek, P. M. (1993). Facilitation issues in distributed group support systems. *Proceedings of the 1993 conference on Computer personnel research*, 299-312.

Niederman, F., Beise, C. M., & Beranek, P. M. (1996). Issues and concerns about computer-supported meetings: The facilitator's perspective. *MIS Quarterly, 20*(1), 1-22.

Nonnecke, B., & Preece, J. (1999). *Shedding light on lurkers in online communities*. Paper presented at the Ethnographic Studies in Real and Virtual Environments: Inhabited Information Spaces and Connected Communities, Edinburgh, Edinburgh, Scotland.

Pan, S. L., & Leidner, D. E. (2003). Bridging communities of practice with information technology in pursuit of global knowledge sharing. *Journal of Strategic Information Systems, 12*(1), 71-88.

Pawlowski, S. D., Robey, D., & Raven, A. (2000). *Supporting shared information systems: boundary objects, communities, and brokering.* Paper presented at the 21st International Conference on Information Systems.

Ren, Y., Kraut, R., & Kiesler, S. (2007). Applying Common Identity and Bond Theory to Design of Online Communities. *Organization Studies, 28*(3), 77-408.

Robey, D., Ross, J. W., & Boudreau, M.-C. (2002). Learning to implement enterprise systems: An exploratory study of the dialectics of change. *Journal of Management Information Systems, 19*(1), 17-46.

Romano, N. C. J., Nunamaker, J. F. J., Briggs, R. O., & Mittleman, D. D. (1999). Distributed GSS facilitation and participation: field action-research. [Conference paper]. *System Sciences, 1999. HICSS-32. Proceedings of the 32nd Annual Hawaii International Conference on,* 1-12.

Satchwell, R., & Dugger, W. (1996). A united vision: Technology for all Americans. *Journal of Technology Education, 7*(2), 5-12.

Schuman, S. (2005). *The IAF Handbook of Group Facilitation: Best Practices from the Leading Organization in Facilitation.* San Francisco, CA: Jossey-Bass.

Schwarz, R. (2002). *The Skilled Facilitator.* San Francisco, CA: Jossey-Bass.

Schwarz, R., Davidson, A., Carlson, P., & McKinney, S. (2005). *The Skilled Facilitator Fieldbook: Tips, Tools, and Tested Methods for Consultants, Facilitators, Managers, Trainers, and Coaches.* San Francisco, CA: Jossey-Bass.

Sheard, J. (2004). *Electronic learning communities: strategies for establishment and management* Paper presented at the 9th annual SIGCSE conference on Innovation and technology in computer science education.

Smith, H. A., & McKeen, J. D. (2003). The Evolution of the KM Function. *Journal.* Retrieved from http://business.queensu.ca/knowledge/working-papers/working/working_03-07.pdf

Staples, D. S., & Jarvenpaa, S. L. (2000). *Using Electronic Media for Information Sharing Activities: A Replication and Extension.* Paper presented at the 21st International Conference on Information Systems.

Stuckey, B., & Smith, J. D. (2004). Sustaining communities of practice. *Proceeding of WBC2004 - The IADIS International Conference on Web-based Communities,* 24–26.

Swan, J. A., Scarbrough, H., & Robertson, M. (2002). The Construction of'Communities of Practice'in the Management of Innovation. *Management Learning, 33*(4), 477-496.

Takahashi, M., Fujimoto, M., & Yamasaki, N. (2003, November 9–12, 2003). *The active lurker: influence of an in-house online community on its outside environment.* Paper presented at the 2003 international ACM SIGGROUP conference on Supporting group work, Sanibel Island, Florida, USA.

Tarmizi, H., de Vreede, G.-J., & Zigurs, I. (2007). A Facilitators' Perspective on Successful Virtual Communities of Practice. *Proceedings of the 13th Americas Conference on Information Systems.*

Tarmizi, H., & de Vreede, G. J. (2005). A Facilitation Task Taxonomy for Communities of Practice. *Proceedings of the Eleventh Americas Conference on Information Systems,* 1-11.

Tarmizi, H., de Vreede, G. J., & Zigurs, I. (2006). Identifying Challenges for Facilitation in Communities of Practice. *System Sciences, 2006. HICSS'06. Proceedings of the 39th Annual Hawaii International Conference on, 1*, 1-10.

Teltzrow, M., & Kobsa, A. (2004). Impacts of User Privacy Preferences on Personalized Systems: a Comparative Study. In J. Karat, J. Vanderdonekt, C.-M. Karat & J. O. Blom (Eds.), *Designing personalized user experiences in eCommerce* (pp. 315 - 332). Norwell, MA: Kluwer Academic Publishers.

Townsend, J., & Donovan, P. ( 1999). *The Facilitator's Pocketbook*. Hants, UK: Management Pocketbooks.

Van House, N. A., Butler, M. H., & Schiff, L. R. (1998). *Cooperative knowledge work and practices of trust: Sharing environmental planning data sets*. Paper presented at the ACM Conference on Computer Supported Cooperative Work.

Vassileva, J., & Sun, L. (2007). An Improved Design and a Case Study of a Social Visualization Encouraging Participation in Online Communities. In J. M. Haake, S. F. Ochoa & A. Cechich (Eds.), *Groupware: Design, Implementation, and Use* (Vol. 4715, pp. 72-86).

Wenger, E. C. (2001). Supporting Communities of Practice: A Survey of community-oriented Technologies, Available from http://www.ewenger.com/tech

Wenger, E. C., McDermott, R., & Snyder, W. M. (2002). *Cultivating Communities of Practice: A Guide to Managing Knowledge*. Boston, MA: Harvard Business School Press.

Yoo, W. S., Suh, K. S., & Lee, M. B. (2002). Exploring the Factors Enhancing Member Participation in Virtual Communities. *Journal of Global Information Management, 10*(3), 55-71.

Yoo, Y., & Alavi, M. (2004). Emergent leadership in virtual teams: what do emergent leaders do? *Information and Organization, 14*(1), 27-58.

Yun, G. W., & Trumbo, C. W. (2000). Comparative response to a survey executed by post, e-mail & web form. *Journal of Computer Mediated Communication, 6*(1).

# Chapter VII
# Virtual Team Leadership:
## Perspectives from the Field

**Laura A. Hambley**
*University of Calgary, Canada*

**Thomas A. O'Neill**
*University of Western Ontario, Canada*

**Theresa J.B. Kline**
*University of Calgary, Canada*

## ABSTRACT

*The purpose of this study was to improve the understanding of virtual team leadership occurring within existing virtual teams in a range of organizations. Qualitative data were collected through comprehensive interviews with nine virtual team leaders and members from six different organizations. A semi-structured interview format was used to elicit extensive information about effective and ineffective virtual team leadership behaviours. Content analysis was used to code the interview transcripts and detailed notes obtained from these interviews. Two independent raters categorized results into themes and sub-themes. These results provide real-world examples and recommendations above and beyond what can be learned from simulated laboratory experiments. The four most important overarching findings are described using the following headings: 1) Leadership critical in virtual teams, 2) Virtual team meeting effectiveness, 3) Personalizing virtual teamwork, and 4) Learning to effectively use different media. These findings represent the most significant and pertinent results from this qualitative data and provide direction for future research, as well as practical recommendations for leaders and members of virtual teams.*

## INTRODUCTION

Rapid technological advancements have led to a new paradigm of work — it can now be conducted anytime, anywhere, in real space or through technology (Cascio & Shurygailo, 2003). The virtual workplace is a reality, and all indications are that technology-mediated communications will become increasingly prevalent in the future (Martins, Gilson, & Maynard, 2004). Leaders are finding themselves directing portions of, or even entire projects, solely through communication technologies (Avolio & Kahai, 2003). Virtual teams require new ways of working across boundaries through systems, processes, technology, and people (Duarte & Snyder, 1999), which require effective leadership. Despite the widespread increase in virtual teamwork, there has been relatively little focus on the role of leaders within these teams (Bell & Kozlowski, 2002).

Descriptive field studies examining virtual team leadership have been recommended as valuable by Bell and Kozlowski (2002), as there is currently a paucity of such data. Most of the existing research on virtual team leadership consists of anecdotal case studies of virtual teams in single organizations (e.g., Kirkman, Rosen, Gibson, Tesluk, & McPherson, 2002) or laboratory studies using *ad hoc* student teams (e.g., Balthazard, Waldman, Howell, & Atwater, 2002; Kahai, Sosik, & Avolio, 2003). The purpose of this field study was to improve the current understanding of leadership within virtual teams in a range of organizations by interviewing virtual team leaders and members. The findings outline specific leadership behaviours involved in successful virtual teamwork, thereby providing tangible recommendations for organizations implementing virtual teamwork and providing the basis for future theory development.

## LEADERSHIP RESEARCH

Previous leadership theories have used trait, behavioural, and contingency-based approaches to describing leadership effects at the individual, team, and organizational level (Yukl, 2006). Recently, these theories have received less attention, as an alternative paradigm has come to the forefront of leadership research. This paradigm has inspiration as a key tenet and the theories using the paradigm have been coined "the New Leadership theories" (Bryman, 1993). One similarity among the new theories is that they provide a rationale to explain how leaders can increase organizational effectiveness, and inspire followers to achieve outstanding levels of motivation, admiration, respect, trust, and commitment. These outcomes are the result of an emphasis on symbolism and emotionally-based leader behaviours (e.g., visioning, role modeling, risk-taking), in addition to cognitively oriented leader behaviours (e.g., adaptation, versatility, intellectual stimulation) (House & Aditya, 1997).

Of particular interest to the present study is the theory posited by Bass (1985) and later revised and updated by Bass and Avolio (1994, 1997). This theory, called the Full Range Leadership Theory (FRLT; Sivasubramaniam, Murray, Avolio, & Jung, 2002), was developed to integrate transformational, transactional, and laissez-faire leadership styles, and has been supported empirically (Judge & Piccolo, 2004; Lowe & Kroeck, 1996). It is widely accepted in the management and leadership literatures (Antonakis & House, 2002) and has served as the conceptual basis for many studies of virtual team leadership (e.g., Kahai & Avolio, 2006; Kahai, Sosik, & Avolio, 1997; 2003).

How leadership works within the contexts of different communication media, however, has received relatively little attention in the literature. Furthermore, the extant research that has considered possible interactions between leadership and communication media is comprised of mostly laboratory-based studies. The nature and results of these studies as well as the few relevant field studies on virtual team leadership are discussed next.

## Virtual Team Leadership Research

Although some research on virtual team leadership styles exists, there is relatively little research on how leadership affects virtual team interaction and performance. Some idea about how leadership may affect virtual team interaction and performance is provided by laboratory studies of transactional, transformational, participative, and directive leadership in computer-mediated teams (e.g., Kahai & Avolio, 2006; Kahai, Sosik, & Avolio, 1997, 2003, and 2004; Sosik, Avolio, & Kahai, 1997; Sosik, Avolio, Kahai, & Jung, 1998). For example, Sosik et al. (1997) found that transformational leadership was associated with higher levels of group potency (the group's belief that it can be effective) than transactional leadership in a Group Decision Support System setting, and that group potency was related to group effectiveness. More recent research found that teams of participants working with a confederate transformational leader made more arguments challenging the copying of "copyrighted" software compared to teams that were working with a transactional confederate (Kahai & Avolio, 2006). In contrast, the participants in the transactional condition were more likely to make arguments in support of copying the copyrighted materials.

There also exist a small number of field studies on virtual team leadership. For example, a field study involving 68 managers of global virtual teams from many countries compared the relationships between laissez-faire, transactional, and transformational leadership on team effectiveness and commitment (Davis et al., 2003). They found that team leaders displaying transformational leadership characteristics had more effective and committed teams.

Kirkman et al. (2002) interviewed members and leaders of 65 virtual teams in a single organization, resulting in five broad challenges of virtual teams as opposed to specific effective and ineffective virtual team leadership behaviours. Similarly, Furst, Reeves, Rosen, and Blackburn (2004) followed six virtual project teams within a single large organization to see how they developed and determine what factors contributed to performance. They make suggestions for managers at various stages in a virtual team's development, but the major focus of their study was on virtual team development as opposed to leadership. Other papers present some challenges and recommendations for leading virtual teams, but are not based on empirical data (e.g., Zaccaro & Bader, 2002; Zigurs, 2002).

In sum, studies on leadership in virtual and computer-mediated teams, most of which are limited to temporary, *ad hoc* student groups in laboratory settings, suggest that leadership style does significantly impact various aspects of team performance. Some researchers argue that the complexity of virtual teams cannot be adequately captured in the laboratory, yet most virtual team leadership research is laboratory-based (Martins et al., 2004). Those studies that are field-based tend to focus mainly on virtual teamwork as opposed to leadership, and do not examine virtual team leadership at a detailed, behavioral level. Clearly, more field research on specific leadership styles and behaviours within virtual teams is needed to fill this gap in the literature, which this study sought to address.

## METHOD

The method employed for this study entailed semi-structured interviews. An inductively-based qualitative approach was used to gain a more detailed understanding of virtual team leadership. This was not a grounded study as our purpose was not to build theory but instead to uncover content about specific virtual team leadership behaviours to guide future research and theory building.

## Participants

A sample of nine leaders and members of virtual teams from six organizations in Western Canada were interviewed for this study. These organizations represented the following industries: professional/consulting, oil and gas, financial services, government/public, IT, and legal. Participants consisted of seven males and two females. In order to be included in this study, participants had to be: 1) involved in at least one virtual team that communicated at least 75% of the time virtually (i.e., through non-face-to-face (FTF) media), and 2) a virtual team member for at least three months. All participants met these criteria, with one having recently left her position but who could still respond as a subject matter expert to all of the questions.

## Procedure

Participants were recruited through convenience and snowball sampling, which involves beginning with one or more contacts within a given population and asking participants to nominate others (Goldenberg, 1992). No more than two individuals were interviewed from any single organization, and an attempt was made to have representation from a range of industries.

Those participants who met the criteria for inclusion were individually interviewed at their workplace. Seven of the nine interviews were taped and transcribed. Detailed notes were taken for the other two interviews, one of which was conducted via long distance telephone. All participants worked in two large, Canadian cities.

The interview consisted of a series of semi-structured questions, including a combination of closed and open-ended questions, as well as probes to elicit further information (see Appendix). Each participant was asked this same set of

items aimed at gaining a better understanding of current virtual team leadership practices. The interviews lasted about an hour.

## Data Analyses

Content analysis (Berg, 1989) was used to code the interview transcripts and detailed notes obtained from the interviews. Two of the authors discussed an explicit rule set, or criteria of selection for how to handle the data, which is recommended in qualitative research before the data is analyzed. The unit of analysis for this data was at the "statement" or "phrase" level, meaning specific statements or phrases were analyzed as opposed to words. These will be referred to as "sub-themes." When applicable, sub-themes were grouped into themes. The broadest level of analysis was by category under which the themes were organized. A category could be based on a single interview question or on two questions that elicited similar information.

Upon agreeing on a rule set, each researcher independently organized the sub-themes in each category into themes. Some categories with only a few statements represented a single theme, while others were organized into several themes. The researchers also kept a quantitative record by tracking the number of participants who mentioned each sub-theme. According to content analysis (Berg, 1989), the process used to establish these themes and sub-themes was "inductive," meaning they were identified by immersing oneself in the data rather than pre-established according to existing theory.

The researchers met to compare their coding schemes, discussing how to categorize and name each category, theme, and sub-theme. Where they disagreed they discussed the issue until they came to an agreement as to how the category, theme or sub-theme should be handled. Edits to sub-themes were made for the purposes of making them more succinct, but the content itself was not changed and every effort was made to preserve the original terminology. Due to the extensive number of decisions (hundreds of decisions ranging from minor wording changes to major reorganization), the rate of agreement between coders could not be accurately recorded. Full agreement was achieved, however, through discussion and collaboration throughout the coding process.

## RESULTS

Results are organized by categories stemming from one or more interview questions. Due to the volume of these qualitative results, generally only the statements made by two or more participants will be described for each theme. (Note that the frequencies often add up to more than nine because each participant could give more than one response per question.) We used two as cut-off so that we could present and comment on as many unique themes as possible within the constraints of a single study. As we were not developing theory in this study *per se*, this approach satisfied the need for both parsimony and inclusiveness.

### Nature of Participants' Involvement in Virtual Teams

This first category captured participants' responses to interview question 1: Describe the virtual team(s) in which you are involved (number of members, activities the team engages in, roles of the members, where they are located, etc.) (see Table 1).

Participants were almost equally as likely to be involved in ongoing virtual teams versus short-term project teams. Teams were most commonly composed of members from various countries, and the most frequently reported size of a virtual team was 7-10 members, which is typical given that the mean of such teams has been found to be 7.7 members (Kinney & Panko, 1996).

*Table 1. Nature of participants' involvement in virtual teams*

| Theme | Frequency |
|---|---|
| **Type of Virtual Team** | |
| Ongoing virtual teams | 6 |
| Short-term project teams | 5 |
| **Location of Virtual Team Members** | |
| Various Countries | 7 |
| Different Canadian cities/ provinces | 2 |
| **Virtual Team Size** | |
| 7-10 members | 4 |
| 10-15 members | 2 |
| 4-7 members | 2 |
| 2-5 members | 1 |

## Participants' Roles in Virtual Teams

Question 2 asked: Describe your role in the virtual team(s). Are you in a leadership position? Participants' roles were evenly split between leading short-term ($n = 4$) and ongoing ($n = 4$) virtual teams. Three of the eight participants who had leadership roles were also virtual team members in other virtual teams. One participant was solely in a member role on a virtual team, although this person had previously taken on leadership roles in virtual teams. Thus, all participants could speak to their experiences leading virtual teams.

## Percent of FTF Communication in Participants' Virtual Teams

Question 3 asked participants the following: Approximately what percent of your virtual team's communication is FTF? The most common amount of FTF communication mentioned was 5% ($n = 4$). This translates to meeting FTF very rarely, such as once or twice per year for a team meeting. Three participants indicated that their virtual teams had no FTF contact, while two participants estimated having about 8% FTF contact (monthly meetings).

## Importance of FTF Meetings in Virtual Teams

Question 4 asked: Did your virtual team members meet FTF prior to working together virtually? If so, do you think this had any impact on how the team worked? If not, do you think that the members should have? If you were to work on other virtual teams would you want to meet the members FTF prior to working together virtually? (see Table 2)

Three themes emerged from this question. The first was that meeting FTF is important at the conception of a virtual team. In particular, most participants indicated that a FTF kick-off is important. A second theme was that FTF meetings have important impacts, such as facilitating the development of trust, comfort level, and rapport between team members more quickly than solely communicating virtually would allow. A third theme was the significance of meeting FTF, further supporting its importance for virtual teams. For example, three participants noted that virtual teams *should* meet FTF periodically if economically feasible.

## Behaviours of Effective Virtual Team Leaders

Question 5 asked: To be effective in a virtual setting, what does a team leader need to do? Similar information was also obtained through and question 6, which asked: Describe examples of effective leadership in a virtual team. Table 3 combines the data obtained from both questions 5 and 6.

The statements resulting from these two questions were organized into five major themes. The first theme of effective virtual team leadership was the ability to *build* a virtual team. In particular,

*Table 2. Importance of FTF meetings in virtual teams*

| Theme | Frequency |
|---|---|
| **FTF Meeting at Virtual Team Conception** | |
| FTF kick-off is very important | 6 |
| FTF meetings needed if members have not met | 2 |
| New team member always meets rest of team FTF | 2 |
| **Impact of FTF meetings** | |
| Trust develops faster if first meet FTF | 2 |
| Increased comfort level and rapport if first meet FTF | 2 |
| **Significance of Meeting FTF** | |
| Meet FTF if economically feasible | 3 |
| Nothing replaces FTF (a must) | 2 |
| Important for leader to meet team members FTF | 1 |

many participants mentioned the importance of the leader providing role and expectation clarity for virtual team members. Also, participants emphasized that effective virtual leaders need to encourage regular communication and establish various channels to support team communication, captured by the following interview quote:

*Let your project team members know how important it is to communicate on a regular basis and encourage it and be a leading example of that.*

Setting goals for the team was also brought up as an important responsibility of the leader.

The second major theme was that the virtual leader needs to possess a set of specific virtual team leadership skills. Many of these are similar to skills important in leading FTF teams, with a few being specific to virtual teams. The importance of the virtual leader obtaining training to lead a virtual team was also noted. Additionally,

*Table 3. Behaviors of effective virtual team leaders*

| Theme | Frequency |
|---|---|
| **Building a Virtual Team** | |
| Provide role and expectation clarity | 6 |
| Encourage regular communication and establish various communication channels to support it | 5 |
| Set goals for the team | 3 |
| Establish a vision/mission for the team | 2 |
| Facilitate team members getting to know each other | 2 |
| Create team operating principles (e.g., appropriate behaviours, ground rules) | 2 |
| Help engage people to communicate effectively though different media | 2 |
| Pre-qualify people for their tolerance for isolation | 1 |
| Build trust in the team | 1 |
| **Virtual Team Leadership Skills** | |
| Obtain training to lead a virtual team | 2 |
| Lead by example (work alongside team when needed) | 2 |
| Manage to results (hold people accountable) | 1 |
| Strong facilitation skills | 1 |
| Try to simulate as if team was co-located (e.g., invest in technologies to do so) | 1 |
| Keep team members feeling connected to rest of team | 1 |
| Promote an information sharing environment | 1 |
| Theme | Frequency |

| | |
|---|---|
| Celebrate and reward successes | 1 |
| Make projects fun | 1 |
| Allow for and create opportunites for virtual workers to balance isolation with social (e.g., allow them time to network in community | 1 |
| Obtain coaching to work in a new medium | 1 |
| Leader-follower relationships | |
| Establish regular one-on-ones with followers | 6 |
| Invest time getting to know followers | 2 |
| Periodically visit followers FTF in their own environment | 2 |
| Respect people's lives (e.g., personal responsibilities, holidays) | *Data needed* |
| **Virtual Team Meetings** | |
| Establish regular virtual team meetings (typically teleconference | 4 |
| Ensure meetings are well organized | 3 |
| "Share the pain" (rotate virtual meeting times to be convenient for different time zones) | 2 |
| Control side-bar conversations in virtual meetings | 1 |
| Make sure introverts get a chance to contribute | 1 |
| "Be here now" (leader needs to be 100% Focused during virtual team meetings) | 1 |

*continued on following page*

*Table 3. continued*

| Theme | Frequency |
|---|---|
| Follow-up after virtual meetings to ensure understanding of participants | 1 |
| Be able to ad lib when technology fails (always have a Plane B | 1 |
| **Virtual Team Management** | |
| Have a strong, dedicated project manager | 4 |
| Tailor amount and type of communication to suit individual needs | 1 |
| Establish tools to track progress (e.g., project management software) | 1 |
| Regularly review issues and obstacles | 1 |
| Make effective virtual teamwork part of performance appraisals | 1 |

leading by example through working alongside the team when needed was emphasized as being important.

The third major theme captured the importance of the virtual leader in establishing and maintaining effective relationships with his/her followers. Participants emphasized that this requires the virtual leader to conduct regular one-on-one meetings; invest time getting to know his/her followers; and periodically visit followers in their own environments.

The fourth theme was the virtual leader's responsibility for ensuring that virtual team meetings are effective. This requires holding regular virtual team meetings, typically done via teleconference, and ensuring these are well organized. Furthermore, effective virtual leaders "share the pain" amongst team members by rotating virtual meeting times to be convenient for different time zones. The following interview

quote focuses on the importance of preparation for a virtual team meeting:

*I've been in other conference calls over video-conferencing when no one was actually taking control of the logistics of the meeting, and there are interruptions, there are silences, there is frustration. I think for virtual meetings there has to be much more preparation upfront.*

The final theme of effective virtual team leadership addressed the establishment of strong virtual team management. This involves setting up processes and tools to ensure that the team is well managed. For example, the virtual leader should ensure that the team has a skilled, dedicated project manager. The leader may fill this role, or alternatively delegate or hire a project manager. Regardless, strong project management appears to be key to virtual team effectiveness.

## How an Effective Virtual Leader Impacts Team Interactions

Participants were asked about how an effective virtual leader impacts a team's interactions. These results were elicited from question 8 (see

*Table 4. How an effective virtual leader impacts team interactions*

| Theme | Frequency |
|---|---|
| Builds a cohesive team | 3 |
| Creates a team culture | 1 |
| Helps team members develop relationships and business contacts to share knowledge across geographical lines | 1 |
| Builds social connections between virtual team members | 1 |
| Prevents silos in different locations from forming | 1 |
| Will cause followers to mimic or pick up his/her behaviors | 1 |

Table 4): In your experience, how has a virtual leader been able to impact his/her/your team's interactions?

The most commonly cited way that an effective virtual leader can impact a team's interactions was by building a cohesive team. Participants described a cohesive virtual team as a "jelled" team that works very well together. Leaders can build cohesive virtual teams by demonstrating many of the behaviours of effective virtual leaders listed in Table 3.

## Behaviours of Ineffective Virtual Leaders

Participants were asked about the behaviours of ineffective virtual leaders in two different questions. The second part of question 5 asked about ineffective virtual team leadership: To be effective in a virtual setting...are there things he/she should NOT do? Also, question 7 asked: Describe examples of poor leadership in a virtual team (see Table 5).

The behaviours of ineffective virtual leaders identified by participants were organized into two themes. The first captured examples of ineffective virtual team leadership behaviours. The most frequently mentioned sub-theme was that ineffective virtual leaders, like their FTF counterparts, lack vision, strategy, and direction. Participants also noted that the same leadership issues that co-located teams experience are amplified in a virtual setting. In other words, poor leadership behaviours are even more detrimental when communication is virtual.

The second theme in the category of ineffective virtual team leadership behaviours was virtual team meetings. This theme again emphasized that the leader plays an important role in the success of virtual team meetings, and ineffective behaviours by the leader, such as cutting off conversation or dominating the meeting, can decrease success.

*Table 5. Behaviours of ineffective virtual leaders*

| Theme | Frequency |
|---|---|
| **Ineffective virtual team leadership** | |
| Lack of vision, strategy and direction | 3 |
| Same leadership issues experienced in co-located teams are amplified virtually | 2 |
| Many are the same ineffective leadership traits that happen in co-located teams | 1 |
| Keep people isolated (e.g., create barriers to keep them from collaborating with others; not acknowledging isolation is an issue | 1 |
| One-way communication (top-down) | 1 |
| Not responding to e-mails/ voice mails in a timely manner | 1 |
| **Virtual team meetings** | |
| Cutting off conversation (e.g., during delays in a VC) | 1 |
| Dominate the meeting | 1 |
| Assume that silence from team members means everything is fine | 1 |

## Challenges of Leading Virtually

Although not included as a specific question, the challenges of leading virtually emerged as important when respondents were questioned about ineffective virtual team leadership. In particular, challenges were mentioned in response to question 7 (see Table 6): Describe examples of poor leadership in a virtual team.

The most commonly mentioned challenge faced by a virtual leader was working with followers in different time zones. This requires

*Table 6. Challenges of leading virtually*

| Theme | Frequency |
|---|---|
| Working with different time zones | 3 |
| Cross-cultural differences | 1 |
| Establishing and maintaining self as a leader virtually | 1 |
| Lack of training for employees to be effective in a virtual environment | 1 |
| Making time to visit virtual team members at their locations | 1 |
| Greater potential for misunderstandings virtually than FTF | 1 |
| More time to accomplish tasks when communicating through technology than FTF | 1 |

having to coordinate meetings to work for all team members, and to face the challenge of different energy levels across team members, and the logistics of different working hours, lunch breaks, etc.

## Comparing Effective Leadership in Virtual vs. FTF Settings

Next, participants were queried about the differences between effective leadership in virtual versus FTF settings. Question 9 asked: Do you think team leadership differs in FTF, versus other forms of communication? (see Table 7)

The responses to this question were organized into two themes. The first captured the different process issues experienced when leading virtually versus FTF. Participants emphasized that project management needs to be stronger in virtual than

*Table 7. Comparing effective leadership in virtual vs. FTF settings*

| Theme | Frequency |
|---|---|
| **Process Issues** | |
| Project management needs to be stronger in virtual than FTF teams | 2 |
| Need to learn to read cues and behaviours specific to non-FTF communication | 2 |
| Effective virtual team leadership is more difficult than FTF leadership | 1 |
| Create rules and norms up front concerning how/when to use certain media | 1 |
| Leaders must exhibit a lot of patience when listening and waiting for feedback in virtual communications | 1 |
| FTF allows for impromptu and spontaneous discussions | 1 |
| Always try to model FTF though other media | 1 |

| Theme | Frequency |
|---|---|
| **Social Issues** | |
| Difficult to establish personal connections virtually, thus creating the potential for losing the "human element" because of increased task focus | 2 |
| Virtual team leadership requires conscious effort to encourage sharing of non-work information | 2 |
| Virtual leaders must watch for unhappy members and address problems promptly | 1 |
| Maintaining rapport is more important in virtual than FTF | 1 |

FTF teams. Further, a virtual leader needs to learn to read cues and behaviours specific to non-FTF communication.

A second theme was the different social issues inherent when leading virtually versus FTF. Participants mentioned the difficulty leaders face in establishing personal connections virtually, thus creating the potential for losing the "human element" because of increased task focus. Another sub-theme related to maintaining the human element was that virtual leaders needed to make a conscious effort to encourage the sharing of non-work related information. This tends to occur more naturally for leaders in a FTF setting, but must be more deliberately implemented in virtual teams.

## Effective Telephone Use in Virtual Teams

Participants were asked how leadership differs when communicating FTF versus through various specific media. The first of these communication media is the telephone. Specifically, question 10a

asked: How does leadership differ between FTF and telephone interactions? (see Table 8)

Participants mentioned how leaders must learn to "hear" body language through the telephone. For example, if a team member is silent, the virtual leader should follow-up with that individual to determine if he/she has any feedback. In addition, the virtual leader needs to read pauses through the telephone, such as recognizing whether the pause means a certain reaction and to be aware of the cues followers give (or do not give) through the telephone. The telephone was also mentioned as an important media for the leader to use when regularly meeting individually with his/her followers.

*Table 8. Effective telephone use in virtual teams*

| Theme | Frequency |
|---|---|
| Leaders must learn to "hear" body language (e.g., follow-up with silent members, read pauses, be aware of cues) | 2 |
| Useful for discussions that require substantial time (e.g., 20 minutes or more) | 1 |
| Effective in times of crisis | 1 |
| Helpful when conveying detailed information that is too complex for written media | 1 |
| Leader should regularly make use of the telephone to connect with each team member individually (to discuss issues that the team member may not have wanted to share with the team) | 1 |

*Table 9. Effective teleconference use in virtual teams*

| Theme | Frequency |
|---|---|
| Seek each member's input rather than allowing the loudest voices to dominate (e.g., use checklists, ask specific people for input to ensure they are engaged) | 4 |
| Encourage the sharing of non-work related information so teleconference is not too task focused | 2 |
| Establish protocols and rules for teleconference sessions, and periodically revisit them | 1 |
| Be alert that team members may be tempted to disengage from the call  (e.g., by checking e-mail) | 1 |
| Don't put shy or introverted people on the spot ("are you ok with this" rather than "what do you think?") | 1 |
| If some team members are co-located, it is important to make sure virtual members are equally included | 1 |

## Effective Teleconference Use in Virtual Teams

Another medium about which participants were queried is the teleconference. Specifically, question 10b asked: How does leadership differ between FTF and teleconference interactions? (see Table 9)

The most commonly mentioned sub-theme was that the leader of the teleconference should seek each member's input rather than allowing the loudest voices to dominate. What might be helpful in monitoring team members' inclusion is using checklists and asking specific people for input to ensure that they are engaged. Another sub-theme was that the leader should encourage the sharing of non-work related information so the teleconference is not entirely task focused. In other words, remaining solely task focused results in a teleconference that is depersonalized.

## Effective E-mail Use in Virtual Teams

Another commonly used medium about which participants were queried is e-mail. Question 10c asked: How does leadership differ between FTF and e-mail interactions? Table 10 summarizes responses to this question.

Responses were organized into two themes, the first of these being the social aspects of e-mail use. As with teleconference, personalization was brought up in regards to e-mail. Participants recommended that the leader should take a moment to personalize e-mails, at least some of the time. For example, leaders should ask how the individual is doing or what they are doing for the weekend rather than solely addressing work.

A second theme in regards to e-mail was protocol. The leader needs to establish acceptable ground rules for the use of e-mail. Examples of ground rules brought up by participants were keeping e-mails concise (e.g., maximum one thought or idea per e-mail) and only sending the e-mail to whom it directly relates (not "over-copying").

*Table 10. Effective e-mail use in virtual teams*

| Theme | Frequency |
|---|---|
| **Social Aspects** | |
| Take a moment to personalize the email (e.g., ask how they are doing) | 2 |
| Learn to read body language over e-mail | 1 |
| Never discuss emotional or sensitive issues through e-mail | 1 |
| E-mail can more easily seem rude and be misunderstood | 1 |
| **E-mail Protocol** | |
| Leader must establish acceptable ground rules for use of e-mail | 1 |
| e-mail is a poor media choice to show leadership | 1 |
| Leader an show recognition and praise though e-mail | 1 |
| Keep e-mails concise (e.g., maximum one thought or idea per e-mail | 1 |
| Only send the e-mail to whom it directly related to (don't over-copy) | 1 |
| Useful for transferring documents and other information | 1 |

## Effective Videoconference (VC) Use in Virtual Teams

Participants were also queried about the use of videoconference (VC). Question 10d asked: How does leadership differ between FTF and videoconference interactions? (see Table 11)

Responses were organized into three themes. The first theme was boardroom videoconference, consisting of a VC system set-up in a meeting room with one camera that typically focuses on all participants. In some cases the camera is operated so that it zooms in on whoever is speaking.

*Table 11. Effective Videoconference (VC) use in virtual teams*

| Theme | Frequency |
|---|---|
| **Boardroom Videoconference** | |
| Boardroom VC is used less now because the lack of quality creates some problems (e.g., can't capture entire room, delays, sideline conversations) | 4 |
| Boardroom VC must be carefully managed and facilitated | 1 |
| In boardroom VC, it is important for each person to say their name before speaking (allowing sufficient time for the camera to zoon in on them) | 1 |
| Zooming in is helpful to see expressions, but may make some people uncomfortable | 1 |
| **Desktop Videoconference (DVC)** | |
| DVC would be fantastic for picking up on non-verbals and body language, but not yet affordable for many organizations | 3 |
| DVC may be more productive and flexible than boardroom VC(it is the future of VC) | 2 |
| VC would be more effective one-to-one | 1 |
| Most employees don't have DVC | 1 |
| Theme | Frequency |

| Utility of Videoconference | |
|---|---|
| VC is appropriate when it is critical to see body language (e.g., strategic project meetings, not necessary for weekly meetings) | 2 |
| VC is better than telephone, but mostly just matches a face to a name and isn't the best for reading nonverbal cues | 2 |
| Training is needed for team members to use VC/DVC effectively | 1 |

Several participants mentioned that boardroom VC is used less now because its lack of quality created some challenges. For example, it often does not capture the entire room, there are delays, and sideline conversations are common (e.g., individuals engaged in separate conversations, to the exclusion of participants in the other location).

The second theme was the use of Desktop Videoconference (DVC). This involves the VC being conducted from an individual's PC, and is usually one-on-one, although multiple points can be connected to allow for team meetings with the appropriate technology and bandwidth.

Several participants commented that DVC would be fantastic for picking up on non-verbal cues and body language, but may not yet be affordable for many organizations. Participants also mentioned that DVC may be more productive and flexible than boardroom VC, and therefore represents the future of videoconferencing.

A third theme regarding the effective use of VC was its utility. This theme is applicable to both boardroom VC and DVC. Participants mentioned that VC is appropriate when it is critical to see body language (e.g., strategic project meetings), but that it is not necessary for weekly virtual team meetings. Another sub-theme was that VC is better than telephone, but mostly just matches a face to a name and is not the best medium for reading nonverbal cues.

## Effective Use of Chat in Virtual Teams

Another communication medium about which participants were queried is chat. Specifically, question 10e asked: How does leadership differ between FTF and chat interactions? Table 12 summarizes responses to this question.

Having a facilitator to help keep a chat session on track was mentioned as important. Also

*Table 12. Effective use of chat in virtual teams*

| Theme | Frequency |
|-------|-----------|
| Everything is recorded permitting easy consolidation of information | 1 |
| Chat is more efficient than e-mail because it allows work to be carried out in real time | 1 |
| Having a facilitator can help keep a chat session on track | 1 |
| Leader should monitor and encourage team member participation (because it may be tempting to stay silent when not seen) | 1 |
| Training should be provided for those unfamiliar with chat | 1 |

*Table 13. Effective use of instant messaging in virtual teams*

| Theme | Frequency |
|-------|-----------|
| Effective for quick messages/ requests, not for sharing lots of information | 3 |
| Very useful during negotiation or sales conference calls because it allows team members to "whisper" comments to each other during the call | 2 |
| Much more interactive than e-mail | 2 |
| Allow for personalized messages that help build virtual team rapport (e.g., "how are you doing?") | 1 |
| Don't use instant messaging because not secure and impossible to document | 1 |

recommended was to have the leader monitor and encourage team member participation, as it may be tempting for some members to stay silent when they are not seen.

## Effective Use of Instant Messaging in Virtual Teams

The final communication medium about which participants were asked was instant messaging (instant messaging differs from chat in that a history of communications is not typically maintained). Specifically, question 10f asked: How does leadership differ between FTF and instant messaging interactions? Table 13 summarizes responses to this question.

One commonly mentioned sub-theme was that instant messaging is most effective for quick messages and requests (e.g., 30 second messages), but *not* for sharing more detailed information. Participants also mentioned its utility during negotiation or sales conference calls because it allows team members to "whisper" comments to each other during the call. Another sub-theme regarding instant messaging is that it is much more interactive than e-mail, and therefore comes closer to approximating FTF communication than does asynchronous communication.

## Other Communication Media and Issues

Participants were also asked about other communication media relevant to their work, in question 10g: How does leadership differ between FTF and other media interactions? (see Table 14)

A few participants mentioned the utility of team collaboration tools to allow virtual teams to post documents, have online discussions, track project advancement, and record the history of the project (e.g., E-Rooms, share point, lotus notes, project forums, collaborative space). Participants also mentioned that web-conferencing is a useful tool (i.e., to demo software or applications). The importance of various communication media in virtual teamwork is captured by the following interview quote:

*Table 14. Other communication media and issues*

| Theme | Frequency |
|---|---|
| Team collaboration tolls allow virtual teams to post documents, have online discussions, track project advancement, and record the history of the project (e.g., e-rooms, share point, lotus notes, project forums, collaborative space) | 3 |
| Web-conferencing useful (i.e., demo software or application) | 2 |
| Photos of team members are a good compromise if video is not available | 1 |
| Tools help to create a sense of togetherness | 1 |
| Tools do not guarantee virtual team success | 1 |

*The end goal is to try to simulate the real environment as much as you can and you are always looking for tools that are coming closer and closer to simulating everyone being in the same office.*

## DISCUSSION

The field interviews yielded an extensive amount of data, meeting the goal of increasing the understanding of leadership within existing virtual teams. Due to the descriptive nature of the findings, each of the categories presented in the Results will not be described. Rather, the most important findings transcending more than one category are discussed. Four overarching findings represent the most significant and pertinent learnings from this qualitative data and provide direction for future research and theory-building, as well as practical recommendations for virtual team leaders.

## Leadership Critical in Virtual Teams

The necessity for strong leadership of virtual teams was highlighted throughout the interview data. This corroborates a field study in which employees rated leadership as critical to the success of their virtual teams (Webster & Wong, 2003). Participants provided numerous examples of effective and ineffective virtual team leadership and were able to describe the behaviours that they believed exemplify strong leadership in virtual contexts. They emphasized the necessity of a leader to build the virtual team and the fact that he/she needs a certain set of virtual team leadership skills, some of which are qualitatively different from those used in FTF settings. Interviewees mentioned the leader's role in providing vision and direction as very important to virtual team success, supporting the findings of a recent field study by Staples, Wong, and Cameron (2004). Interestingly, participants noted how ineffective leadership is amplified or compounded in virtual settings. This points to the importance of virtual leaders understanding the challenges associated with different communication media, and learning the behaviours and skills necessary to effectively lead virtual teams. Thus, leaders cannot simply lead the virtual team exactly the same as if it were FTF.

Many of the leadership behaviours identified in this study can be linked to the transformational and transactional styles of the FRLT. For example, "set goals for the team" reflects the *inspirational motivation* factor of transformational leadership (Bass & Avolio, 1993). Also, "establish regular one-on-ones with followers" and "periodically visit followers FTF in their own environment" reflect the *individualized consideration* factor of transformational leadership. Similarly, "provide role and expectation clarity" could fit with the contingent reward factor of transactional leadership. Through linking the themes identified in this study with the FRLT factors, these findings can be framed within an existing theory.

There are, however, some themes identified in this study that cannot be framed within the FRLT. For example, the finding that "leaders must learn to hear body language" and the many suggestions for leading through various communication media are qualitatively different from the skills needed to lead FTF. Perhaps these behaviours could be framed within a new "virtual team leadership" factor added to this existing theory. Alternatively, they could possibly be thought of as types of facilitation falling under the instrumental behaviours identified by Antonakis and House (2002) in their extension of FRLT.

## Virtual Team Meeting Effectiveness

Another recurring theme throughout the interviews was the importance of running effective virtual team meetings. Given the frequent lack of FTF contact in virtual teams, meetings take on increased importance as a chance to collaborate, build relationships, and make sure everyone is on the "same page." Participants emphasized the importance of the leader in establishing regular virtual team meetings and ensuring that these meetings are well organized. Many specific recommendations were provided on exactly how virtual team meetings can be successfully conducted, many of which require skills above and beyond those needed to facilitate FTF meetings. For example, the leader needs to use specific techniques in dealing with aggressive and passive (e.g., introverted) team members in virtual meetings.

These data indicate that one should not simply apply FTF meeting facilitation skills when conducting a virtual meeting. Indeed, the importance of carefully orchestrating conference calls was found to be important for virtual team success in a recent case study by Majchrzak, Malhotra, Stamps, and Lipnack (2004). Researchers have recommended various aspects of facilitation that improve effectiveness of virtual team meetings (Rangarajan & Rohrbaugh, 2003). The leader

would be wise to receive coaching or training on the techniques of facilitating virtual team meetings to maximize productivity.

## Personalizing Virtual Teamwork

Another recurring theme was that the virtual leader needs to ensure the team goes beyond solely focusing on the work itself to personalizing virtual work relationships. Participants noted that it is easy to become too task-focused, resulting in virtual work becoming depersonalized and lacking a "human element." Personalizing the relationships between the leader and his/her virtual followers, as well as between the team members, was deemed important. This finding corroborates past research by Kimball and Eunice (1999) who found that virtual teams can more easily lose focus on relationship building. Moreover, Jarvenpaa and Tarniverdi (2002) noted that electronic communication methods coupled with compressed project deadlines may impair team member relationships. Leaders that personalize relationships, however, can increase virtual team trust. Interestingly, research on global virtual teams by Jarvenpaa and Leidner (1999) found that teams with higher levels of trust tended to engage in more personalized, social communications.

Recommendations for the leader to build strong relationships with followers included conducting regular one-on-one meetings with followers, investing time getting to know followers, and periodically visiting followers in their own environments if possible. These suggestions can help alleviate the challenge other researchers have noted: that the spatial distance between team members and using non-FTF communication can impede the ability of the virtual leader to mentor and develop followers (e.g., Bell & Kozlowski, 2002). Building relationships with team members reflects individualized consideration, a factor of transformational leadership, and enables the leader to better understand and accommodate individuals' needs, abilities, and goals (Bass & Avolio, 1993).

Participants recommended that the leader should also facilitate the building of social connections between virtual team members so that their relationships become personalized as well. Effective relationships between team members was mentioned by participants as a component of successful virtual teamwork that leads to team satisfaction, and the desire to continue working together (i.e., team cohesion). These observations are in agreement with previous findings that leaders need to allocate more time for communication and be proactive in pursuing relationships (Hart & McLeod, 2002). Taken together, virtual team leaders that explicitly cultivate team member relationships will foster team member satisfaction, development, and trust.

## Learning to Effectively Use Different Media

The final recurring theme and major learning from the data was that virtual leaders and team members need to learn how to use different media effectively. Different communication media and technologies require certain rules and norms for use, and cues and behaviours occur differently through these media. One cannot assume that the skills to lead or work within a virtual team are the same as in a FTF team. Virtual leaders and workers must learn how to "read" and "hear" body language through non-FTF media. Interview data indicated that different skills were required to effectively work FTF as compared to interacting via telephone, teleconference, e-mail, VC, chat, instant messaging, and other non-FTF media. Participants suggested that virtual leaders and team members should be trained on how to utilize these communication media effectively. In their field study of six virtual teams, Staples et al. (2004) also found that virtual team members need to find the best communication and IT tools for their needs, and receive the training necessary to effectively use these systems. Additionally, Hart and McLeod's (2002) findings from a study of 126

virtual team member relationships suggested that the use of appropriate communication methods was key to developing effective work interactions. As described by Wakertin, Sayeed, and Hightower (1997), it is important for virtual teams to foster familiarity and proficiency with these new tools and techniques of social interaction.

In addition to learning to effectively use various media, the leader needs to establish norms and ground rules for their use. Virtual leaders and team members need to learn that computer-mediated communication may be more beneficial for some tasks than for others (Wiggins & Horn, 2005). Disagreements should be discussed over the telephone or in a conference call rather than handled through text-based media (Majchrzak et al., 2004). The specific recommendations for each media are included in the Results tables, and provide useful suggestions for how virtual leaders and teams can make better use of each medium.

## Contributions

This study contributed to future development of theory on virtual team leadership through identifying behaviours, observations, and insights from virtual leaders and members. These findings serve to highlight salient issues and learnings from the field, which provide directions for future theory-building and empirical research.

This study contributes beyond existing field studies of virtual team leadership by presenting more specific leadership behaviours that contribute to effective and ineffective virtual teamwork. These behaviours are organized into themes and categories, an approach not done in past virtual team leadership research. For example, the present study goes into more detailed behaviours than did the study of 65 virtual teams by Kirkman et al. (2002). Although some of the lessons learned in that former study are corroborated by the present study, the four overarching themes in the present study were not directly discussed, and that study was not specific to virtual team leadership.

The present study also contributes beyond that of Furst et al. (2004), who studied six virtual project teams in a single organization to explore team development and what factors contribute to high performance. A few of their suggestions for managers are corroborated by the present study, but our study offers many more behaviours specific to leadership, and explores virtual team leadership at a much more detailed level. Furthermore, the present study includes participants from six organizations and a variety of industries as opposed to single organizations used in these earlier field studies.

Findings from the field interviews also provided many recommendations that can be practically helpful for virtual leaders and teams. The findings represent areas that virtual leaders should be aware of and focus upon, especially in the early stages of a virtual team's development. Furthermore, the detailed information in the Results tables provides many specific recommendations that would be useful to virtual team leaders in developing and maintaining successful virtual teams.

## Limitations and Future Research

One limitation of this study was that the sample was relatively small ($n = 9$), therefore only representing the viewpoints of a limited number of virtual team leaders and members. Thus, additional research is needed to validate these findings with larger and more diverse samples. Although these participants represented a range of industries, they by no means captured the large number of industries currently using virtual teamwork. Future research should explore similarities and differences in virtual team leadership across different industries.

A second limitation of this study was that participants were all from two western Canadian cities. Despite working from only two cities, however, seven of the participants worked on global virtual teams (with members from various countries), and two participants worked on virtual teams with members from different Ca-nadian cities/provinces. Thus, the perspectives of these participants were certainly not limited to one geographic region. Future research should continue exploring virtual teams from different cities and countries, and examining virtual team leadership across various cultures. For example, exploring whether virtual team leadership differs across individualistic versus collectivist cultures might provide some interesting findings.

Another limitation of this study was that a comparison between responses from virtual leaders and their followers was not gathered, because typically only one person from an organization was interviewed. It will be important in future research to determine whether the issues and recommendations of followers corroborate those of their leaders and vice versa. This type of research would provide a better understanding of the similarities and differences in their perceptions.

A recommendation for future research is for quantitative studies to validate the themes found in this study. Such research could compare these themes across successful and unsuccessful virtual teams to determine which are most critical. Also, future research could focus on creating a modified measure of virtual team leadership, as current popular measures such as the Multifactor Leadership Questionnaire (MLQ; Bass & Avolio, 1990) do not capture many of the behaviours specific to virtual team leadership as evidenced by this field data. The qualitative data presented in this study would provide useful material for generating potential items for a virtual team leadership measure.

This study has demonstrated that virtual team leadership is indeed an important component of virtual teamwork that definitely warrants future research. Developing effective training programs for virtual leaders and team members, and testing their effects on team cohesion and performance is an important area to pursue. Clearly, there are still many more questions than answers about virtual team leadership, and given the continued growth of virtual teams across industries, this exciting area of research is ripe with future potential.

## ACKNOWLEDGMENT

This research was funded by SSHRC (Social Sciences and Humanities Research Council of Canada).

We would also like to thank the virtual team leaders who participated in this study for their time and input.

## REFERENCES

Antonakis, J., & House, R. J. (2002). The full-range leadership theory: The way forward. In B. J. Avolio & F. J. Yammarino (Eds.). *Transformational and charismatic leadership: The road ahead* (Vol. 2, p. 3-33). Oxford, UK: Elsevier.

Avolio, B. J., & Kahai, S. S. (2003). Adding the "e" to e-leadership: How it may impact your leadership. *Organizational Dynamics, 31*(4), 325-338.

Balthazard, P., Waldman, D. A., Howell, J., & Atwater, L. E. (August, 2002). *Modeling performance in teams: The effects of media type, shared leadership, interaction style, and cohesion.* Paper presented at the meeting of the Academy of Management, Denver, Colorado.

Bass, B. M., & Avolio, B. A. (1990). *The multi-factor leadership questionnaire.* Palo Alto, CA: Consulting Psychologists Press.

Bass, B. M., & Avolio, B. J. (1993). Transformational leadership: A response to critiques. In *Leadership Theory and Research: Perspectives and Directions* (pp. 49-80). New York: Academic Press.

Bell, B. S., & Kozlowski, S. W. J. (2002). A typology of virtual teams: Implications for effective leadership. *Group and Organization Management, 27*(1), 14-49.

Berg, B. L., (1989). *Qualitative Research Methods for the Social Sciences.* Needham Heights, MA: Allyn and Bacon.

Bryman, A., (1993). Charismatic leadership in business organizations: Some neglected issues. *Leadership Quarterly, 4,* 289-304.

Cascio, W. F., & Shurygailo, S. (2003). E-leadership and virtual teams. *Organizational Dynamics, 31*(4), 362-376.

Davis, D. D., Mihalescz, M., Bryant, J. L., Tedrow, L., Liu, Y., & Say, R. (2003, April). *Leadership in global virtual teams.* Paper presented at the meeting of the Society for Industrial and Organizational Psychology, Orlando, Florida.

Den Hartog, D. N., & Koopman, P. L. (2001). Leadership in organizations. In N. Anderson, D. S. Ones, H. K. Sinangil, & C. Viswesvaran (Eds.). *Handbook of Industrial, Work and Organizational Psychology* (Vol. 2, p. 166-187). London, England: Sage.

Duarte, D. L., & Snyder, N. T. (1999). *Mastering virtual teams.* San Francisco: Jossey-Bass Inc.

Furst, S. A., Reeves, M., Rosen, B., & Blackburn, R. S. (2004). *Managing the life cycle of virtual teams. Academy of Management Executive, 18*(2), 6-20.

Goldenberg, S., (1992). Thinking Methodologically. New York, NY: HarperCollins Publishers Inc.

Hart, R. K., & McLeod, P. L. (2002). Rethinking team building in geographically dispersed teams: One message at a time. *Organizational Dynamics, 31,* 352-361.

House, R.J., & Aditya, R.T. (1997). The social scientific study of leadership: Quo Vadis? *Journal of Management, 23,* 409-473.

Jarvenpaa, S. L., & Leidner, D. E. (1999). Communication and trust in global virtual teams. *Organizational Science, 10*(6), 791-815.

Jarvenpaa, S. L., & Tanriverdi, H. (2002). Leading virtual knowledge networks. *Organizational Dynamics, 31,* 403-412.

Judge, T. A., & Piccolo, R. F. (2004). Transformational and transactional leadership: A meta-analytic test of their relative validity. *Journal of Applied Psychology, 89,* 755-768.

Kahai, S., & Avolio, B. (2006). Leadership Style, Anonymity, and the Discussion of an Ethical Issue in an Electronic Context. *International Journal of e-Collaboration, 2*(2), 1-26.

Kahai, S, Sosik, J., & Avolio, B. (1997). Effects of leadership style and problem structure on work group process and outcomes in an electronic meeting system environment. *Personnel Psychology, 50,* 121-146.

Kahai, S. S., Sosik, J. J., & Avolio, B. J. (2003). Effects of leadership style, anonymity, and rewards on creativity-relevant processes and outcomes in an electronic meeting system context. *Leadership Quarterly, 14*(4-5), 499-524.

Kahai, S, Sosik, J, & Avolio, B. (2004). Effects of Participative and Directive Leadership in Electronic Groups. *Groups & Organization Management, 29*(1), 67-105.

Kimball, L., & Eunice, A. (1999). The virtual team: Strategies to optimize performance. *Health Forum Journal, 42*(3), 58-62.

Kinney, S. T., & Panko, R. R. (1996). Project teams: Profiles and member perceptions - Implications for group support system research and products. *Proceedings of the 29ᵗʰ Annual Hawaii International Conference on System Sciences,* 128-137.

Kirkman, B. L., Rosen, B., Gibson, C. B., Tesluk, P. E., & McPherson, S. O. (2002). Five challenges to virtual team success: Lessons from Sabre, Inc. *Academy of Management Executive, 16*(3), 67-79.

Lowe, K. B., & Kroeck, K. (1996). Effectiveness correlates of transformational and transactional leadership: A meta-analytic review of the MLQ literature. *Leadership Quarterly, 7*(3), 385-426.

Majchrzak, A., Malhotra, A., Stamps, J., & Lipnack, J. (2004). Can absence make a team grow stronger? *Harvard Business Review, 82*(5), 131-137.

Martins, L. L., Gilson, L. L., & Maynard, M. T. (2004). Virtual teams: What do we know and where do we go from here? *Journal of Management, 30*(6), 805-835.

Rangarajan, N., & Rohrbaugh, J. (2003). Multiple roles of online facilitation: An example in any-time, any-place meetings. *Group Facilitation: A Research and Applications Journal, 5,* 26-36.

Sivasubramaniam, N., Murray, W. D., Avolio, B. J., & Jung, D. L. (2002). A longitudinal model of the effects of team leadership and group potency on group performance. *Group and Organization Management, 27,* 66-96.

Sosik, J. J., Avolio, B. J., & Kahai, S. S. (1997). Effects of leadership style and anonymity on group potency and effectiveness in a group decision support system environment. *Journal of Applied Psychology, 82*(1), 89-103.

Sosik, J. J., Avolio, B. J., Kahai, S. S., & Jung, D. I. (1998). Computer-supported work group potency and effectiveness: The role of transformational leadership, anonymity, and task interdependence. *Computers in Human Behavior, 14*(3), 491-511.

Staples, D.S., Wong, I. K., & Cameron, A. F. (2004). Best Practices for Virtual Team Effectiveness. In D. Pauleen (Ed.). *Virtual teams: Projects, protocols and processes* (pp. 160-185). Hershey, PA: Idea Group Publishing

Wakertin, M. E., Sayeed, L., & Hightower, R. (1997). Virtual teams versus face-to-face teams: An exploratory study of a web-based conference system. *Decision Sciences, 28*(4), 975-996.

Webster, J., & Wong, W. K. P. (2003, April). *Comparing traditional and virtual group forms: Identity, communication and trust in naturally occurring project teams.* Paper presented at the meeting of the Society for Industrial/Organizational Psychology, Orlando, Florida.

Wiggins, B., & Horn, Z. N. J. (2005, April). *Explaining effects of task complexity in computer-mediated communication: A meta-analysis.* Paper presented at the meeting of the Society for Industrial and Organizational Psychology, Los Angeles, CA.

Yukl, G. A., (2006). *Leadership in organizations* (6th ed.). Upper Saddle River, NJ: Pearson Prentice Hall.

Zaccaro, S. J., & Bader, P. (2002). E-leadership and the challenges of leading E-teams: Minimizing the bad and maximizing the good. *Organizational Dynamics, 31*(4), 377-387.

Zigurs, I., (2002). Leadership in virtual teams: Oxymoron or opportunity. *Organizational Dynamics, 31*(4), 339-351.

## APPENDIX A. FIELD INTERVIEW QUESTIONS

The following questions are meant to be used in a 1-1.5 hour individual interview with a leader or member of a virtual team. Participants interviewed should be involved in at least one virtual team that communicates at least 75% of the time virtually, for a minimum of three months.

### Description of Team and Role

1. Describe the virtual team(s) in which you are involved (number of members, activities the team engages in, roles of the members, where they are located, etc.).
2. Describe your role in the virtual team(s). Are you in a leadership position?
3. Approximately what percent of your virtual team's communication is FTF?
4. Did your virtual team members meet FTF prior to working together virtually? If so, do you think this had any impact on how the team worked? If not, do you think that the members should have? If you were to work on other virtual teams would you want to meet the members FTF prior to working together virtually?

### Virtual Team Leadership

5. To be effective in a virtual setting, what does a team leader need to do? Are there things he/she should NOT do?
6. Describe examples of effective leadership in a virtual team (e.g., when your virtual team performed successfully, what behaviours did the leader demonstrate?)
7. Describe examples of poor leadership in a virtual team (e.g., if/when your virtual team performed poorly, what behaviours did the leader demonstrate?)
8. In your experience, how has a virtual leader been able to impact his/her/your team's interactions?
9. Do you think team leadership differs in FTF, versus other forms of communication? Please explain.
10. How does leadership differ between FTF and:
    a. Telephone
    b. Teleconference
    c. E-mail
    d. Videoconference
    e. Chat
    f. Instant messaging
    g. Other

Thank you for participating

Chapter VIII
# Web-Based Template-Driven Communication Support Systems:
## Using Shadow netWorkspace to Support Trust Development in Virtual Teams

**Herbert Remidez, Jr.**
*University of Arkansas at Little Rock, USA*

**Antonie Stam**
*University of Missouri, USA*

**James M. Laffey**
*University of Missouri, USA*

## ABSTRACT

*Teams whose interactions might be mediated entirely via Internet-based communication, virtual teams, are emerging as commonplace in business settings. Researchers have identified trust as a key ingredient for virtual teams to work effectively (Aubrey & Kelsey, 2003; Beranek, 2000; David & McDaniel, 2004; Iacono & Weisband, 1997; Jarvenpaa, Knoll, & Leidner, 1998; Jarvenpaa, Shadow, & Staples; 2004). However, researchers have not identified scalable methods that consistently promote trust within virtual teams. Improved interface design for communication support systems used by virtual teams may contribute to solving this problem. Interface cannot solve the problem of members trusting each other, but it can support the type of activities that do. This paper describes the development and some initial experiences with a Web-based, template-driven, asynchronous communication support tool and how this system can be used to support trust development in virtual teams and performance goals of virtual teams. This article presents the capabilities and features of the communication support system. More detailed findings from an experimental study of this system's use can be found in another publication (Remidez, 2003).*

## INTRODUCTION

Communication support tools mediate an increasing amount of communication in work settings. In particular, communication support systems are critical to the functioning of virtual teams, as the systems often times mediate all interactions (Powell, Piccoli, & Ives, 2004). Although the importance of the systems in the communication process continues to grow, they do not provide support for constructing messages. They do not support creating a good introduction message or other key communication actions researchers have found to be characteristic of high functioning teams. This lack of support presents a problem for workers but at the same time an opportunity for system designers and researchers.

The use of templates is a framework for designing systems that engage forms of communication that support trust development. An example of a successful use of templates to support communication can be found in Microsoft Word. A Microsoft Word user who has no experience creating a professional letter can choose to create a new document based on the "Professional Letter" template available in the system. By using this template, a novice user can take advantage of the knowledge and experience of the publisher and is more likely to succeed in creating a professional letter. Similar templates are available for supporting the creation of brochures, resumes and memos. These templates no doubt have helped many workers communicate more effectively; similarly, we suggest message templates in online communication systems can facilitate successful collaborative work.

Trust has been identified as a key, yet challenging, ingredient for the effectiveness of virtual teams (Aubrey & Kelsey, 2003; Beranek 2000; Coppola et al., 2004; David & McDaniel, 2004; Iacono & Weisband, 1997; Jarvenpaa et al., 1998; Jarvenpaa et al., 2004). Researchers have not developed scalable methods that consistently promote trust within virtual teams. Given that virtual teams often interact entirely via communication support systems, part of the solution to promoting trust might lie in the design of the communication support systems these teams utilize. For a discussion of the multifaceted nature of virtual teams see Dubé and Paré (2004). Semi-structured message templates have been found to be helpful in designing a variety of computer-based communication and coordination systems (Malone, Grant, Lai, Rao, & Rosenblitt, 1987) and might be a basis for designing communication systems that support trust. Specifically, Malone et al., (1987) conclude that semi-structured messages can serve as aids for composing messages to be sent; selecting, sorting, and prioritizing messages that are received; responding automatically to some messages and suggesting likely responses to other messages. Researchers have found that one key characteristic of high-trusting teams is the inclusion of affective statements early in teams' lifecycles, suggesting that message templates of appropriate affective statements might be a useful means by which computers could support the inclusion of such statements and indirectly promote the development of trust. Te'eni (2001) proposed the use of message templates to promote the inclusion of affective statements in his discussion of a new model of organizational communication, Cognitive-Affective Model of Organizational Communication (CAMOC), which he used as the basis for suggesting design principles for future communication support systems. CAMOC takes into consideration the impact of the communication strategy, task inputs, message form, and medium selection on cognitive and affective goals of the sender.

This paper focuses on the design of the communication support tool itself. We present the flexibility of the tool, in terms of the user interface and interaction, the design and nature of the message templates and how they are organized. Our motivation for presenting details of the communication tool is that journal articles reporting on experimental studies often lack the space to detail the specifics of the tools used. In our case, this is unfortunate, because – in contrast to the vast majority of systems used in other research studies – the system we used is custom-designed with a number of special features; moreover, as we will detail below, the system is available free of charge to anyone in the research community.

Throughout this article we strive to keep the focus on the tool, because we believe that understanding how tools can be developed to match with organizational goals has value for the IS community. The purpose of this paper is not to present a tool that can be used to investigate trust development per se. Instead, by keeping the focus on the tool, and using the investigation of trust development as an illustration of the tool's capabilities, we hope to promote the development and use of tools for use in the investigation of multiple phenomena (team cohesion, decision quality, shared mental model development, the use of message labels to promote information processing, etc.).

We next review the importance of trust in virtual teams, followed by the development and implementation of a Web-based template-driven asynchronous communication support tool that we have used in several ongoing experimental research projects in which we investigate how systems like ours can be used to support trust development in virtual teams. Findings from our customized system implementation in three such experiments are summarized, and we explain how our particular choice of template structure is rooted in the existing theory on trust in virtual teams and empirical results generated by Jarvenpaa and her colleagues (Jarvenpaa et al., 1998; Jarvenpaa & Leidner, 1999).

## TRUST IN VIRTUAL TEAMS

We have long known that forcing people to cooperate requires expensive and constant surveillance; in addition, it engenders distrust, and can have various negative effects (Kelman, 1958). This is especially true in today's organizations, where traditional controls based on authority have been replaced with self-directed teams and empowered workers (Golembiewski & McConkie, 1975; Jarvenpaa et al., 1998; Larson & LaFasto, 1989). The phenomenon that the control mechanisms work against the development of trust appears to hold true even in virtual team settings. A recent study by Piccoli and Ives (2003) encouraged participants to employ behavioral controls within virtual teams. For example, team members were to prompt a tardy member to participate. Unfortunately, in this study teams using the behavioral control mechanisms reported lower levels of trust than the teams that did not use the control mechanisms.

A large and expanding body of literature demonstrates the importance of trust in facilitating cooperation (Krackhardt & Stern, 1988; Mayer, Davis, & Schoorman, 1995), a more productive free flow of information (Hart & Saunders, 1997; Nelson & Cooprider, 1996), communication (Dore, 1983; Griffin, 1967; Williamson, 1975), collaborative relationship performance (David & McDaniel, 2004), leadership (Atwater, 1988), self-managed work teams (Lawler, 1992; Claus, 2004), the improvement of organizations' abilities to adapt to complexity and change (Korsgaard, Schweiger, & Sapienza, 1995; McAllister, 1995), collective learning, knowledge sharing, and creative problem solving (Argyris, 1999; Reina & Reina, 1999; Senge, 1990), and the design, implementation and evaluation of trust-supporting components in virtual communities (Ebner & Krcmar, 2005).

Given what we know about forcing people to work together and the benefits of trust, promoting trust appears to be the more productive option. However, organizations might find it difficult to promote trust between people who hardly ever meet (Handy, 1995). As a result of little physical interaction, communication support systems will play a greater role in promoting "not only task-oriented goals, but also relationship-oriented goals" (Te'eni, 2001). Communication support systems can influence not only how a message is delivered but also the effect of the message on both task-oriented and relationship-oriented goals. Designers of communication support systems now face the task of developing systems that stimulate more effective communication by changing the medium and attributes of the message depending on the goal or goals of the user.

## TRUST TEMPLATES

Although Te'eni (2001) suggested that message templates might be used to encourage the inclusion of affective statements, he did not suggest the format or content of such templates. A comprehensive study by Jarvenpaa et al. (1998) found several characteristics of high-trusting teams: getting started early, early positive interactions, high levels of activity, communication about communication strategies, expressions of time orientation, robust feedback, and confrontation of slackers or other areas of conflict. This section explains how Jarvenpaa et al.'s (1998) and Jarvenpaa and Leidner's (1999) work provided the empirical basis for the contents of a set of message templates.

In Jarvenpaa et al. (1998), the interactions of 75 teams with four to six members per team were analyzed in order to extract communication characteristics that resulted in trust formation or degradation. Team members lived in different countries and worked together for eight weeks. Participants were asked to conduct two voluntary exercises and were required to complete a third exercise. Based on their findings, Jarvenpaa et al. (1998) suggested strategies like encouraging "proactive behavior, empathetic task communication, positive tone, rotating team leadership, task goal clarity, role division, time management, and frequent interaction with acknowledged and detailed responses to prior messages" (p. 60),

that virtual teams might employ to reinforce trust and improve team process outcomes. They also found that the initial interactions between team members are critical to trust development and the team's overall functioning. This finding is consistent with other studies (Beranek, 2000; Chidambaram, 1996; Clear & Daniels, 2001; Huff, Cooper, & Jones, 2002; Iacono & Weisband, 1997; Meyerson, Weick, & Kramer, 1996).

In another paper, Jarvenpaa and Leidner (1999) reported that communication that rallies around the project and tasks, social communication that complements rather than substitutes for task communication, meaningful and timely responses, and members explicitly verbalizing their commitment, excitement, and optimism are behaviors that strengthen trust. As an example of how we implemented Jarvenpaa et al.'s (1998) concepts in our studies, we outline in Table 1 how we aligned the templates used in our research studies with the activities identified by Jarvenpaa et al. (1998) and Jarvenpaa and Leidner (1999).

We next give descriptions of each of the seven templates. Included in the template descriptions are "Strategy" sections with statements explaining the purpose of the template. The example statements were taken from the statements Jarvenpaa and her colleagues (Jarvenpaa et al., 1998; Jarvenpaa & Leidner, 1999) selected as representative of communications that promoted trust. For example, "Looking forward very much to working with you all" was identified as an expression of excitement about the forthcoming collaboration. Other examples include "Great job" and "I shall keep in touch soon to congratulate us all on winning." The motivation for each template is summarized in Table 1.

*Introduction Template*

>*Introduce yourself. Members of a strong team will get to know each other a little before beginning work. A good introduction includes: 1) information about yourself and your background, 2) your past job experi-*

*Table 1. Characteristics of High Trusting Teams and Template Titles*

| Characteristics of High Trusting Teams (Jarvenpaa et al. 1998; Jarvenpaa & Leidner, 1999) | Templates |
|---|---|
| Positive initial interactions | Introduction |
| Early starters | Getting Started |
| Discussed communication plans | Communication Issues |
| Time and goal oriented | Time management/ Milestones |
| Provided robust feedback | Feedback |
| Addressed and managed conflict | Issue/Conflict |
| Task oriented | Task completion/ Questions |

*ences, 3) your current focus of study, 4) why you chose to study this subject, and 5) what are your aspirations. In addition, you should address any skills you have that might help your team solve this problem. Also, you should raise any concerns you have about the successful completion of the project.*

*Strategy:* Expressing positive emotions throughout the project will help your team succeed. For example, "I am looking forward to working with you all." would be a good comment to include.

The "Introduction" message template includes several *individual prompts*: "Provide a little information about yourself and your background," "How often you plan to check the system for new messages (early and often is better)," "Times you will not be available to communicate during the course of this project," and "Address any skills you have that might help your team solve this problem. Also, you should raise any concerns you have about the successful completion of the

project." Each of these prompts is followed by fields for users to enter their answer.

*Getting Started Template*

Begin the problem-solving process by sharing your understanding of the goals. Adopt a role that will help your team reach its goal and begin acting the part of that role.

*Strategy:* It is a good practice to state positive feelings about the project or the work of team members. For example, "Well, done" or "I like this group" are good types of comments to include. In addition, it is best to do what you can to get the project started early and to keep it moving through regular communication with your teammates.

*Communication Issues Template*

Discuss how often you would like to communicate with your teammates and any other communication practices you would like to see everyone use.

*Strategy:* Expressions of enthusiasm are always a good thing to include in your messages. For example, "I think we are going to win," or related statements help your teammates feel good about their work.

*Time Management/Milestones Template*

— Suggest deadlines and milestones for completing the task (e.g., "I think we can get this done by Tuesday.").

*Feedback Template*

You can use this option to reply to any message that your teammates have posted. Good feedback goes beyond simple statements such as "ok" and "looks good." It includes thoughtful compliments, critiques, edits and additions.

*Strategy:* Expressions of social greeting and positive statements are good items to include in your feedback statements (e.g., "Hi everyone, I think we can win this.").

*Issue/Conflict Template*

Use this option to address any concerns about the process being followed or the participation of others. If a team member is not participating and you feel it is hurting the team, it is important to address it in front of the entire team.

*Strategy:* It is better to address concerns in the open, even if they lead to conflict. For example, if you do not hear from someone, it is good to address it in front to the entire team (e.g., "Where is Joe?").

*Task Completion/Questions Template*

If you have completed a task or have questions about something, select this option. For example, if you wish to post individual or final team rankings of the items in the problem, this is the option you should choose. You also can take advantage of the ability to compile your results in MS Word or Excel and attach these files to messages.

*Strategy:* Social greetings included in messages are a good way to keep team members feeling close to each other and to keep your team functioning well (e.g., "I like working in this team"). In addition, expressions of enthusiasm are always a good thing to include in your messages, and they help keep your team working well.

## SHADOW NETWORKSPACE (SNS)

The template-driven discussion board application that we will introduce and discuss in the next sections was implemented within Shadow net-Workspace (SNS) (http://sns.internetschools.org) (Laffey, Musser, Remidez, & Gottdenker, 2003). SNS is a Web-based work environment originally designed for and extensively tested in education settings. Although SNS was designed with the education environment in mind, the template-driven discussion application we describe was designed

to be flexible enough to support discussions in multiple settings. Much like a personal computer's desktop, SNS provides a personal workspace for organizing, storing, and accessing files, and an environment for running applications. SNS also provides the ability to create groups, and for each group to have a "group desktop" for file sharing, communication and collaboration. As such, SNS is capable of supporting a wide variety of virtual collaboration and online communication needs. Our use of SNS to design a virtual team environment that fosters trust is just one of many potential applications. SNS is freely available for downloading from the SNS website to all users under the GNU free software license.

## CREATION OF THE TEMPLATE-DRIVEN SYSTEM ENVIRONMENT

This section describes the creation of a template-driven discussion board intended to support trust development. Illustrating the flexibility of the template structure will facilitate the subsequent example of how we have used these types of templates in our experimental studies of trust development in virtual teams. Throughout, we focus on creating template-based discussion boards; however, the application we use to create the template-driven discussion boards can also be used to create a typical non-template driven discussion board. A non-template-driven discussion board shares all the features of the template version except for the ability to choose a message type and view customized message input screens. In addition, a non-template-driven board does not display message type labels and all messages are displayed in a single non-interrupted field, whereas messages created with a customized input screen (e.g. Introduction messages) are displayed in sections corresponding to the input template's sections.

*Figure 1. Creating a template-driven discussion board*

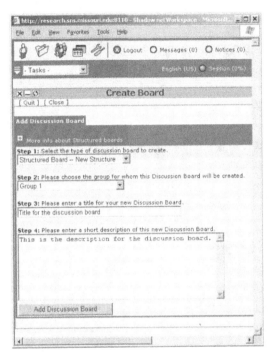

## Creating a Board

In order to create a template-driven (i.e., structured) forum, the board creator must enter a title and description for the discussion forum (see Figure 1), define the specific templates (e.g., Introduction, Time Management, Issue/Conflict, etc.), and specify a name and description for each template (see Figure 2).

After specifying all of the message templates to be available to users of a given discussion board, the next step is optional for the board creator, but allows the creation of an input format for each message template (see Figure 3). For example, in building a specific template-driven discussion board which was intended to promote trust within virtual teams, we specified that all "Introduction" messages should be composed of several different text blocks: (1) a text block (i.e. text area in HTML) with the prompt "Provide a little information about yourself and your background", (2) another single text line for responding

to the question "How often do you plan to check the system for new messages (early and often is better)?", (3) a text block with the prompt: "Times you will not be able to communicate during the course of the project," and (4) a text block with the prompt: "Address any skills you have that might help your team address this problem. Also, you should raise any concerns you have about the successful completion of this project."

There is no limit to the number of text blocks or text lines that a single message template can contain. In addition, there is no limit to the number of message templates that accompany a single discussion board or the number of template-driven discussion boards a user can have access to at any one time. If the board creator chooses not to specify the input format for a message template, the input screen for that message template will include the familiar subject line and a text block, that are the input means for standard discussion boards.

*Figure 2. Creating message templates*

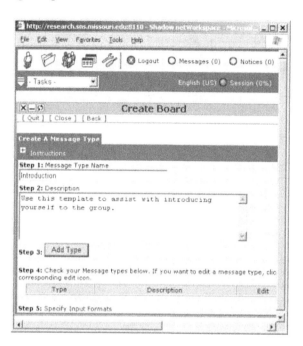

*Figure 3. Creating the input format for message templates*

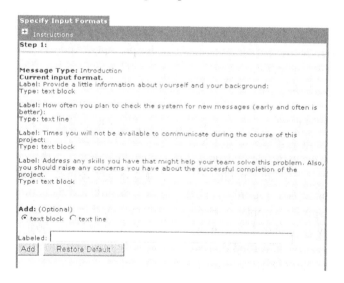

*Figure 4. Defining relationships between message templates*

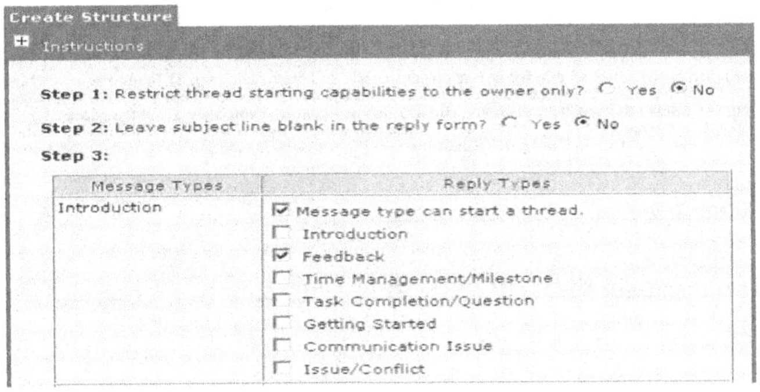

*Figure 5. Users select the type message template to author*

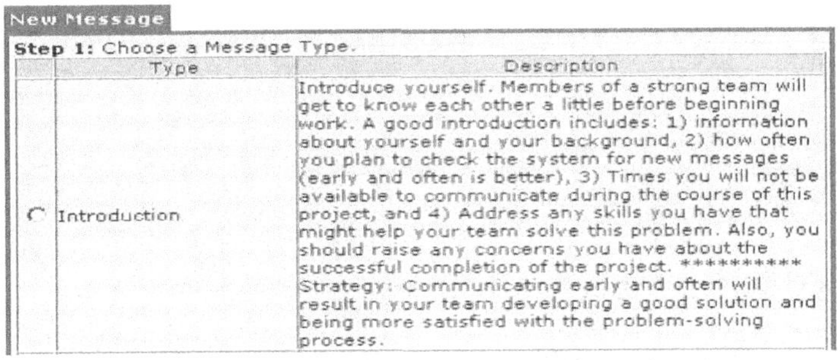

The next step for the board creator is to specify the relationships between message templates (see Figure 4), by checking which message templates are allowed to respond to other message templates. The resulting hierarchical structure constrains and streamlines users' comments and message response structures. After specifying the relationship the message types can take, the next step is to complete the creation of the board. In addition to supporting the creation of template structures, the system supports the ability to save, load, and share template structures.

Once a template-driven discussion board has been created, users can choose to create a new message in much the same way they would with a traditional discussion board. However, once a user has chosen to create a new message or reply to an existing message they are presented with a list of the available message templates along with their associated description. Figure 5 shows a partial screen capture of the message selection screen. This screen would contain a list of all the available message templates.

After making a selection from the available message templates, the user is then presented with that template's associated input screen (see Figure 6), the format of which was previously specified by the author of the template-driven discussion board (see Figure 3). The message description is restated at the top of the input screen in hopes of providing additional support for the user.

Template-driven communication support systems have been developed to support domain-specific conversations and problem solving (e.g. KIE [Bell & Linn, 2000], CaMILE [Guzdial et al., 1996], the Collaboratory Notebook [O'Neill & Gomez, 1994] and CSILE [Scardamalia & Bereiter, 1994]). Many of these systems are used

113

*Figure 6. Message Input Screen for the Introduction Message Template*

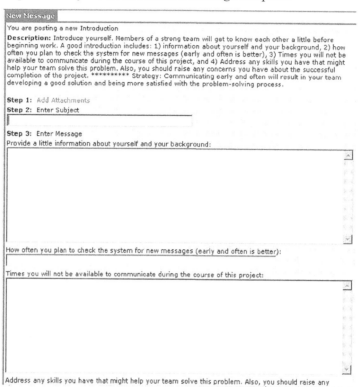

in an education setting and have graphical interfaces that "utilize node-link graphs representing argumentation or evidential relationships between assertions" (Suthers, 1998, p. 8) and provide users with a visual representation of the conversation. Similar systems have been proposed to support argumentative decision processes in organizations (Ramesh & Whinston, 1994; Bui, Bodart, & Ma, 1998). To the best of our knowledge, the system that we created is the first template-driven communication support system implemented to support relationship development as opposed to cognitive development or information processing.

## THREE EXPERIMENTAL STUDIES

We tested our template-driven communication support system with the trust templates described in the previous section in several experimental studies. In this section, we highlight the results of three experimental studies that we have conducted using the system. These experiments are part of our ongoing research on template-supported virtual teamwork, and represent a progression of efforts to assess the effectiveness of our approach. Preceding these three studies, several pilot studies were conducted as well, but those merely served to try out and refine different features and screens in the system. With some very minor variations of negligible consequence, the template-based system as described in this paper corresponds to that used in each of the experiments. Although there were slight differences between the experiments, these were very minor. Therefore, the experiments were very similar in nature.

As we used the template-based system described above, our experiments are based on the rational definition of trust by Mayer et al. (1995), build on the trust model used by Jarvenpaa et al.

(1998) and extend the CAMOC-DIT framework of Te'eni (2001), which proposes that templates might be an effective strategy for promoting the inclusion of affective statements in messages. Moreover, the system was designed to stimulate the flow of information between team members, and is grounded in the work by Hart and Saunders (1997) and Nelson and Cooprider (1996). These authors found that mutual trust facilitates a freer flow of information.

The research questions studied in the experiments are based on the studies mentioned in the previous paragraph, and revolve around the following issues: (1) do users of a template-driven system show evidence of higher levels of perceived ability, perceived integrity and or perceived benevolence (these are antecedents of trustworthiness) and/or overall trustworthiness, as compared with users of a regular discussion board without templates; (2) to what extent do message templates influence the free flow of information; and (3) how does the situational context affect the use of the template-based system? MANOVA analyses were used in each experiment to address these research questions.

The first experiment, Experiment I, involved 40 students in a graduate level MIS course. As discussed below, this experiment yielded quite interesting results (see also Remidez, 2003). However, as the sample size in Experiment I was limited, we conducted a follow-up experiment in a large undergraduate Management course involving a total of 432 students. In the analysis we omitted those teams that had at least one member cheating or dropping out, reducing the number of students analyzed substantially. We discovered that in Experiment II a number of students dropped out just after the experiment had started, effectively reducing the sample size suitable for inclusion in the analysis. We determined that this was due to us assigning students to teams at an early point of time, prior to distributing the preliminary survey and other initial administrative activities. We corrected this anomaly in Experiment III,

by postponing the actual assignment of students to teams as long as possible, thus reducing the number of incomplete teams we had to exclude from the analysis. The number of participants in Experiment III was 415. The write-ups of the extended results of Experiments II and III are still in process.

Each experiment involved teams of five randomly assigned students solving a mountain survival scenario problem. The task was to rank order the importance of available items for use by survivors of a plane crash in a remote, mountainous location. The relevance and the correct solution to this problem were validated by several experts. The total duration of the task was approximately five weeks. In order to stimulate the team discussions and complicate the decision task, each team member received partial (but no conflicting) information. Each scenario was missing 10 percent of the descriptive information and 10 percent of the survival items. In Experiment I the only treatment was the use (or non-use) of the templates; Experiments II and II included a second treatment, consisting of e-mail messages that were sent to students anytime when a teammate posted a note on the discussion board. In addition to the information and descriptive statistics provided directly through the discussion boards, the students filled out pre- and post-test surveys to assess any changes in trust development. These participant surveys closely followed those used by Jarvenpaa et al. (1998). In Experiment II, the Sarker, Valacich, and Sarker (2003) trust questionnaire was used as well. In addition, Experiment I included selective post-test interviews to check for undetected problems that might be unique to the context of the experiments.

In Experiment I, we found that both the flow of information (as measured by the number of messages authored and the number of messages viewed) and perceived ability were significantly higher ($p<.05$) for users of the template-driven system, but the other two antecedents of trust, perceived integrity and perceived benevolence were not significantly higher. The increase in information flow may indicate higher levels of mutual trust or be antecedents to trust development. The most interesting finding in Experiment II was that, among those teams that used the template-based system, the teams that also received e-mail notifications exhibited significantly higher levels ($p<.05$) of perceived ability and benevolence than teams that did not receive e-mail notifications. Among teams that used the regular discussion board, no such effect was detected. Experiment III showed strong evidence that template-based systems can enhance overall trustworthiness ($p<.05$), but this result was found only for those teams that also received e-mail notifications. In addition, the number of messages authored, and therefore the flow of information, was significantly enhanced ($p<.05$) for those template-driven teams that received e-mail prompts, again suggesting the possibility that mutual trust did develop.

The variable that improved most consistently through the use of templates and/or e-mail notification in Experiments I – III was the flow of information. Although Experiments I – III did not yield consistently increased levels for all three antecedents of trust and/or for trustworthiness, each study showed clear effects with respect to some of the variables involved, confirming that template-based systems at least hold significant promise as a means to enhance trust development in the virtual team environment.

Summarizing, we have established that there are significant differences in the interaction patterns and trust development between users of the template-driven system and those using a traditional discussion board. On the negative side, interviews with students suggest that, while most find the message templates helpful, some find them to be distracting. This is not unexpected given previous work in the area of the perceived restrictiveness of decision support systems (Silver, 1988). We are working on making the templates optional much the way that templates in Microsoft Office are optional. We are also learning from others us-

ing the system to successfully support classroom discussion (Jonassen & Remidez, 2002).

## FUTURE DIRECTIONS

Message templates can be viewed as behavior/process controls because they work to promote team members' conformity to predefined communication strategies (Kirsch, 1997). Behavior controls have been used in colocated and virtual teams with different levels of success. Henderson and Lee (1992) fond that high-performing colocated IS teams exihibited high process control by managers and high outcome control by team members. In a virtual team setting, Piccoli and Ives (2003) found that teams using process controls experienced greater levels of vigilance, increased saliencey of reneging and incongruence, and decreased levels of trust.

Any action to make intentions and obligations more explicit increases the probability that deviations will be detected and viewed negatively by the team. It is possible that by prompting team members to be more explicit about their intentions that messages templates might promote the salience of reneging and incongruence, which was associted with lower levels of trust in the Piccoli and Ives study (2003). One advantage of using message templates to facilitate process control procedures is that, like this set of templates, message templates can be created to help team members address deviations when they are first detected, before they impact team preformance and permanently damange team trust. The ability to embed process support for dealing with infractions is one of the advantages that message templates have over training alone.

Trust, although important, is just one of the many types of affect that might be supported by a template-driven discussion board. In addition, through our experiments we have come to realize that the templates we created emphasize ability and integrity aspects of the conversation. While these are two important antecedents of trust (Jarvenpaa et al., 1998), benevolence is another important antecedent that our templates seem to underemphasize. One future direction might be to develop a template structure specifically designed to promote benevolence.

Moreover, as our studies support the finding by Hart and Saunders (1997) and Nelson and Cooprider (1996) that trust and a freer flow of information are associated, and indeed this flow may be enhanced particularly in the presence of both a template-based system and e-mail notification, one may seek ways to fine-tune the system design in order to optimize the communication patterns. Presumably, these patterns may lead to increased perceptions of ability, integrity and benevolence.

Other types of affect that might benefit from this type of communication support include feelings of satisfaction, cohesion and decision confidence. Each of these types of affect might require different kinds of communication support for them to fully develop in a virtual team setting. The SNS system is very versatile, and with appropriate choice and design of message templates might accommodate some of these needs. The flexibility of this system allows us to easily create and re-use entire sets of message templates and allows us to control the label, description, input format, and relationship of the messages. In effect, we can map a discourse structure onto the conversation, which opens up a new set of possibilities for understanding human computer interactions.

From a research perspective, we face issues of how to control for the effects of the system vs. the effects of the content in the system. For example, would teams benefit just the same if we simply gave them the information in the templates? Also, what is the right number of templates? Too few might have no effect, while too many might cause the user to become frustrated or not accurately use the system. Would making the templates optional, like Microsoft Word templates, be a good idea or

not? These are all interesting questions that invite others to investigate along with us.

The experiments that we have conducted to date have been limited to populations of college students. It is certainly worthwhile to study the effectiveness of template-based systems such as ours in a "real world" virtual work environment. One would expect that different types of template-based systems might be more effective in a real-world environment, and that strategies effective in terms of promoting trust in teams of college students might not be useful in real-world work settings, and vice versa.

While the possible combinations of message labels, relationships, descriptions, etc. are limitless. It is important to keep in mind that message templates are inherently restrictive. Their use immediately raises questions about how much support to provide. Support can be limited to requiring students to label incoming and outgoing messages (Hilmer & Dennis, 2001) or as elaborate as forcing users to select message types (Request, Offer, Answer, etc.) and then providing custom templates for each type of message Winograd (1987-1988). A finding by Silver (1988) that different users viewed the same set of supports differently complicates template structure decisions.

Another large area that has yet to be explored is the cultural interpretation of various template sets and their impact on the team development process. For example, some of the included statements would be less natural in a non-US setting (e.g. "Hi everyone, I think we can win this"). For a discussion on cultural effects on virtual teams, see Sarker and Sahay (2004).

One strategy for overcoming the lack of explicit theoretical guidance is to draw from communication models such as Te'eni's (2001) model for guiding the design of IT. His model offers insights into how the use of message templates might impact participants' cognitive and affective load, understanding and relationships. The lack of explicit empirical guidance for designing templates might also be mediated by using software development techniques for ill-structured problems (e.g. rapid prototyping). Only after multiple sets of templates have been developed and employed can the IS community hope to develop a theoretical basis for determining the appropriate amount of support to provide for a given task and setting.

In closing, we emphasize that, in contrast with most other studies of communication support systems, SNS allows for a custom-designed structure and interface, offering ample opportunity for future research involving virtual team work, especially since the software can be downloaded free of charge from the SNS website at http://sns.internetschools.com. It is our hope that researchers will make use of this unique research opportunity.

## REFERENCES

Argyris, C., (1999). *On Organizational Learning* (2nd Ed.). Mallden, MA: Blackwell.

Atwater, L. E., (1988). The relative importance of situational and individual variables in predicting leader behavior: The surprising impact of subordinate trust. *Group and Organization Studies, 12*(3), 290-310.

Aubrey, B., & Kelsey, B. (2003). Further understanding of trust and performance in virtual teams. *Small Group Research, 34*(5), 575-619.

Bell, P., & Linn, M. C. (2000). Scientific arguments as learning artifacts: Designing for learning from the Web with KIE. *International Journal of Science Education, 22*(8), 797-817.

Beranek, P., (2000). The impacts of relational and trust development training on virtual teams: An exploratory investigation. Paper presented at the *33rd Hawaii International Conference on System Sciences.* Honolulu, HI.

Bui, T., Bodart, F., & Ma, P. C. (1998). ARBAS: A formal language to support argumentation in network-base organizations. *Journal of Management Information Systems, 14*(3), 223-237.

Chidambaram, L., (1996). Relational development in computer-supported groups. *MIS Quarterly, 20*(2), 143-163.

Claus, L., (2004). Too much of a good thing? Negative effects of high trust and individual autonomy in self-managing teams. *Academy of Management Journal, 47*(3), 385-400.

Clear, T. & Daniels, M., (2001). *"A Cyber-Icebreaker for an Effective Virtual Group?,"* 6th Annual Conference On Innovation and Technology In Computer Science Education (ITiCSE), June 25-27, Canterbury.

Coppola, N., Hiltz, S., & Rotter, N., (2004). Building trust in virtual teams. *IEEE Transactions on Professional Communication, 47*(2), 65-105.

David, P., & McDaniel, R., (2004). A field study on the effect of interpersonal trust on virtual collaborative relationship performance. *MIS Quarterly, 28*(2), 183-227.

Dore, R., (1983). Goodwill and the spirit of market capitalism. *British Journal of Sociology, 34*(4), 459-482.

Dubé, L., & Paré, G., (2004). The Multi-Faceted Nature of Virtual Teams. In D.J. Pauleen (Ed.), *Virtual teams: projects, protocols, and processes* (pp. 1-39). Hershey, PA: Idea Group Publishing.

Ebner, W., & Krcmar, H., (2005). Design, implementation, and evaluation of trust-supporting components in virtual communities for patients. *Journal of Management Information Systems, 21*(4), 101-135.

Golembiewski, R. T., & McConkie, M., (1975). The centrality of interpersonal trust in group processes. C.L. Cooper (Ed.). *Theories of Group*

*Processes.* New York: John Wiley & Sons, 131-185.

Griffin, K., (1967). The contribution of studies of source credibility to a theory of interpersonal trust in the communication process. *Psychological Bulletin, 68*(2), 104-120.

Guzdial, M., Kolodner, J. L., Hmelo, C., Narayanan, H. Carlson, D. Rappin, N., Hubscher, R., Turns, J., & Newsletter, W. (1996). Computer support for learning through complex problem-solving. *Communications of the ACM, 39*(4), 43-45.

Handy, C., (1995). Trust and the virtual organization. *Harvard Business Review, 73*(3), 40-50.

Hart, P., & Saunders, C., (1997). Power and trust: Critical factors in the adoption and use of electronic data interchange. *Organization Science, 8*(1), 23-42.

Henderson, J. C., & Lee, S., (1992). Managing I/S design teams: A control theories perspective. *Management Science, 38*(6), 757-777.

Hilmer, K., & Dennis, A. (2001). Stimulating thinking: Cultivating better decisions with groupware through categorization. *Journal of Management Information Systems, 17*(3), 93-114.

Huff, L. C., Cooper, J., & Jones, W., (2002). The development and consequences of trust in student project groups. *Journal of Marketing Education, 24*(1), 24-34.

Iacono, C. S., & Weisband, S., (1997). Developing trust in virtual teams. Paper presented at the *30th Annual Hawaii International Conference on System Sciences.* Honolulu, HI.

Jarvenpaa, S., Knoll, K., & Leidner, D., (1998). Is anybody out there? Antecedents of trust in global virtual teams. *Journal of Management Information Systems, 14*(4), 29-64.

Jarvenpaa, S., & Leidner, D., (1999). Communication and trust in global virtual teams. *Organization Science, 10*(6), 791-815.

Jarvenpaa, S., Shadow, T., & Staples, S., (2004). Toward contextualized theories of trust: The role of trust in global virtual teams. *Information Systems Research, 15*(3), 250-267.

Jonassen, D., & Remidez, H., (2002). Mapping alternative discourse structures onto computer conferences. Gerry Stahl, (Ed.). *Computer Support for Collaborative Learning: Foundations for a CSCL Community.* Hillsdale, NJ: Erlbaum, 237-244.

Kelman, H. C., (1958). Compliance, identification and internalization: Three processes of attitude change. *Journal of Conflict Resolution, 2*(1), 51-60.

Kirsch, L. J., (1997). Portfolios of control modes and IS project management. *Information Systems Research, 8*(3), 215-239.

Korsgaard, M. A., Schweiger, D. M., & Sapienza, H. J., (1995). Building commitment, attachment, and trust in strategic decision-making teams: The role of procedural justice. *Academy of Management Journal, 38*(1), 60-84.

Krackhardt, D., & Stern, R. N., (1988). Informal networks and organizational crises: An experimental simulation. *Social Psychology Quarterly, 51*(2), 123-140.

Laffey, J., Musser, D., Remidez, H., & Gottdenker, J., (2003). Networked systems for schools that learn. *Communications of the ACM, 46*(9), 192-200.

Larson, C. E., & LaFasto, F. M. J., (1989). *Teamwork: What must go right/what can go wrong.* Newbury Park, NJ: Sage.

Lawler, E., (1992). *The ultimate advantage: Creating the high-involvement organization.* San Francisco: Jossey-Bass.

Malone, T. W., Grant, K. R., Lai, K.-Y., Rao, R., & Rosenblitt, D., (1987). Semi-structured messages are surprisingly useful for computer-supported coordination. *ACM Transactions on Information Systems, 5*(2), 115-131.

Mayer, R. C., Davis, J. H., & Schoorman, F. D., (1995). An integration model of organizational trust. *Academy of Management Review, 20*(3), 709-734.

McAllister, D. J., (1995). Affect and cognition-based trust as foundation for interpersonal cooperation in organizations. *Academy of Management Journal, 38*(1), 24-59.

Meyerson, D., Weick, K. E., & Kramer, R. M., (1996). Swift trust and temporary groups, in R. M. Kramer and T. R. Tyler (Eds.). *Trust in Organizations: Frontiers of Theory and Research.* Thousand Oaks, CA: Sage Publications.

Nelson, K. M., & Cooprider, J. G., (1996). The contribution of shared knowledge to IS group performance. *MIS Quarterly, 20*(4), 409-432.

O'Neill, D. K., & Gomez, L. M., 1994. The collaboratory notebook: A distributed knowledge building environment for project learning. *Proceedings of ED MEDIA* 94. Vancouver B.C., Canada.

Piccoli, G., & Ives, B., (2003). Trust and the unintended effects of behavior control in virtual teams. *MIS Quarterly, 27*(3), 157-180.

Powell, A., Piccoli, G., & Ives, B., (2004). Virtual teams: A review of current literature and directions for future research. *The Data Base for Advances in Information Systems, 35*(1), 6-36.

Ramesh, R., & Whinston, A., (1994). Claims, arguments, and decisions: Formalisms for Representation, Gaming, and Coordination. *Information Systems Research*, 5(3), 294-325.

Reina, D., & Reina, M., (1999). *Trust and betrayal in the workplace.* San Francisco, CA: Berrett-Koehler.

Remidez, H., (2003). System structure design and social consequence: The impact of message templates on affectivity in virtual teams. Unpublished doctoral dissertation. University of Missouri, Columbia.

Sarker, S., & Sahay, S., (2004). Implications of space and time for distributed work: an interpretive study of US-Norwegian systems development teams. *European Journal of Information Systems, 13*(1), 3-20.

Sarker, S., Valacich, J., & Sarker, S., (2003). Virtual team trust: Instrument development and validation in an IS educational environment. *Information Resource Management Journal, 16*(2), 35-55.

Scardamalia, M., & Bereiter, C., (1994). Computer support for knowledge-building communities. *The Journal of Learning Sciences*, 3(3), 265-283.

Senge, P., (1990). *The fifth discipline: The art and practice of the learning organization.* New York: Doubleday.

Silver, M., (1988). User perceptions of decision support system restrictiveness: An experiment. *Journal of Management Information Systems, 5*(1), 51-65.

Suthers, D., 1998. Representations for scaffolding collaborative inquiry on ill-structured problems. Paper presented at the *1998 AERA Annual Meeting.* San Diego, CA.

Te'eni, D., (2001). Review: A cognitive-affective model of organizational communication for designing IT. *MIS Quarterly*, 25(2), 251-312.

Williamson, O.E., (1975). *Markets and hierarchies.* New York: The Free Press.

Winograd, T., (1987-1988). A language/action perspective on the design of cooperative work. *Human-Computer Interaction, 3*(1), 3-30.

*This work was previously published in International Journal of e-Collaboration, Vol. 3, Issue 1, edited by N. Kock, pp. 65-73, copyright 2007 by IGI Publishing (an imprint of IGI Global).*

# Chapter IX
# Exploring the Virtual Team Leaders' Perspective:
## Efficient Work Roles and Leadership Functions

**Udo Konradt**
*University of Kiel, Germany*

**Julia E. Hoch**
*University of Technology Dresden, Germany*

## ABSTRACT

*In this study we examined the perceived importance of line managers and middle managers in virtual teams, and what work roles and leadership functions are necessary to promote virtual team success and performance. Using Quinn's (1988) competing values framework it was found that control-related roles of directors and producers were perceived to be most important. With years in a leading position, the repertoire of leadership roles needed to successfully lead virtual teams declined. Additionally, middle managers compared to line managers perceived people oriented leadership functions (i.e., mentor and facilitator roles) and flexibility-related work roles (i.e., innovator and mentor roles) as more important whereas line managers compared to middle managers perceived stability leadership functions (i.e., monitor and coordinator roles) as more important. Limitations, implications for virtual team leadership, and suggestions for future research are discussed.*

## INTRODUCTION

In virtual teams, team members are geographically distributed and coordinate their work predominantly via electronic information and communication technology (Duarte & Snyder, 1999; Gibson & Cohen, 2003). The lack of face-to-face interaction in virtual teams and the impact of electronic communication media exert a strong influence on social processes and effective collaboration (Hertel, Geister, & Konradt, 2005; Hinds & Kiesler, 2002; Hollingshead & Contractor, 2002; Wegge, 2006). With regard to the leader he/she has less information to assess the team's situation and instances to recognize necessary modifications. As a consequence, managing the dynamics of social behavior in virtual teams and the development of adequate practices and critical team processes is impaired, i.e. to uncover conflicts, to motivate team members who are working at disparate sites, and to develop trust and team cohesion (Avolio, Kahai, & Dodge, 2001). Moreover, it has been argued that due to the physical distance between the vertical leader and the team members, the amount and quality of dyadic leader-member exchange (Gerstner & Day, 1997) is reduced and the leadership process is shared by team members, which spread across units and organizations (Pearce & Conger, 2003). Consequently, the changing role of leadership in virtual teams has been discussed (Duarte & Snyder, 1999; Gibson & Cohen, 2003; Hinds & Kiesler, 2002) and management concepts have been proposed that shift parts of managerial functions either to situational substitutes, e.g., task interdependence or incentives (Kahai, Sosik, & Avolio, 2003), or that is directed to empower the team members to make decisions by themselves in self-managing teams (Conger & Kanungo, 1988; Manz & Sims, 1993). Within empowered teams leadership functions, which were formerly in the responsibility of the team leader are delegated to the team members.

Referring to leadership in dispersed organizational structures, several scenarios have been suggested (e.g., Avolio et al., 2001; Murphy & Jackson, 1999; Shamir, 1999). A prominent scenario assumes leadership tasks to be broadly distributed among and shared by a set of team members in ad-hoc arrangements. Shared leadership (Pearce & Conger, 2003) occurs when there is no formal authority, all leadership responsibilities are distributed and collectively enacted among the members and decisions are made collectively. Scholars on virtual teams, however, have argued that leadership in virtual teams generally needs more structure and procedural assistance than leadership in conventional teams (Bell & Kozlowski, 2002; Gibson & Cohen, 2003; Hinds & Kiesler, 2002). Support for this argument is provided by field studies with computer-supported teams. For example, team members who were allowed to communicate in written form were shown to be less satisfied than those with face to face contact and teams with a formal team leader were more efficient and more satisfied than those without (Fjermestadt & Hiltz, 2000; Hollingshead & Contractor, 2002). In addition, meta-analytic findings demonstrate that physical distance was negatively related to subordinate's performance (Podsakoff et al., 1996).

While past research on leadership in virtual teams emphasized the impact of communication on team performance and member satisfaction (Hofner-Saphiere, 1996; Maznevski & Chudoba, 2000), work roles and leadership functions have received comparatively little attention in the empirical literature (e.g., Zigurs & Kozar, 1994). In the present study, we thus examined roles and functions of virtual teams leaders related to effectiveness in virtual teams. Additionally, we investigated whether virtual leadership experience and organizational position moderate the way in which leaders interpret their leadership behavior in virtual teams.

## THEORETICAL BACKGROUND AND HYPOTHESIS DEVELOPMENT

### A Framework of Work Roles

Work roles are defined as positions within an occupational social framework (Katz & Kahn, 1978; Oeser & Harary, 1964). In contrast to duties that comprise established tasks and formalized expectations, work roles comprise a set of emerging tasks and informal expectations within a particular group context (Ilgen & Hollenbeck, 1991). The function of work roles is to define permissions and obligations of organizational behavior and to provide guidelines for appropriate behavior. In research of managerial behavior, numerous conceptions for the description and classification of managerial roles and role behavior were proposed (McGrath, 1984; Mintzberg, 1973; Quinn, 1988). A widely accepted model of managerial roles is the Competing Values Framework Model (CVF) by Quinn (1988).

As illustrated in Figure 1, eight work roles are distinguished within the CVF along the di-

mension of type of focus (internal vs. external focus) and, amount of flexibility exerted by the leader (flexibility vs. control). Given these two dimensions, four quadrants and eight work roles are described which will be briefly outlined (for more details, see Quinn, Faerman, Thompson, & McGrath, 1996).

The first quadrant is characterized by the *adaptability leadership function*. The adaptive leadership quadrant is characterized by a flexible orientation and a focus on the external environment of the unit, and emphasizes developing innovations and obtaining resources for the unit. This quadrant contains the innovator and broker roles. An innovator is expected to pay attention to changes in the environment and to identify and facilitate adaptations to changes. A broker is expected to meet with people from outside the unit, represent the unit, to negotiate and acquire resources for the unit. The second quadrant, the *people leadership function* quadrant, is characterized by a flexible orientation and a focus on the internal functioning of the unit. It emphasizes mentoring subordinates and facilitating group

*Figure 1. The competing values framework*

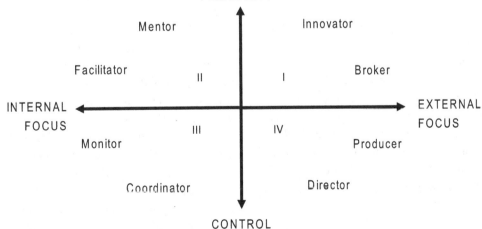

*Note: I: Adaptive leadership function, II: People leadership function, III: Stability leadership function, IV: Task leadership function.*

processes in the unit. This quadrant contains the facilitator and mentor roles. A facilitator is expected to foster collective effort, build cohesion and teamwork, and manage interpersonal conflicts. A mentor is expected to support people in a caring and empathetic way. In this role, the manager is helpful, considerate and sensitive to the members' feelings and perceptions. The third quadrant emphasizes stability, characterized by control and a focus on the internal functioning of the unit. Core tasks of *stability leadership function* are monitoring and coordinating the work. This quadrant contains the coordinator and monitor roles. A coordinator is expected to maintain the structure and flow of the system, coordinate the scheduling of staff efforts, handle crises, and attend to technical and logistical issues. A monitor is expected to know about current issues of the unit, to see if people comply with rules and regulations, and to see whether the unit is meeting its quotas. Finally, the fourth quadrant of *task leadership function* is characterized by a control orientation and a focus on the external environment. This quadrant contains the producer and director roles. A producer is expected to motivate members to increase production and accomplish their goals. As a director, a manger is expected to clarify expectations, outline problems, establish objectives, generate rules and policies, and give instructions.

There is consistent research that has shown the effectiveness of the Competing Values Framework as a means to describe leadership and organizational behavior in different domains, including commercial, public services and non-profit fields. Moreover, the CVF was shown to have satisfying discriminant, convergent, and nomological validity (Denison, Hooijberg & Quinn, 1995; Buenger, Daft, Conlon, & Austin, 1996; Hooijberg, 1996; Hooijberg, Hunt, & Dodge, 1997; Panayotopoulou, Bourantas, & Papalexandris, 2003).

## Control-Related Roles in Virtual Teams

In organizational research on leadership of telecommuters and virtual teams, it has been argued that dispersed teams do not need strong leadership (for reviews, see Axtell, Fleck, & Turner, 2004; Hertel et al., 2005; Konradt, Schmook, & Maelecke, 2000). However, there has as yet been very little empirical exploration of this contention. Instead, related research in the area of virtual teams provides a different view that leadership functions are directed toward control-related activities. As Antonakis and Atwater (2002) argue, the physical distance of leader and members will reduce social interaction and will have the effect that the leader cannot directly observe follower behavior and performance. Distance will also make it more difficult for the leader to coach individual team members and moderate team processes because this would assume that a leader directly interacts with his/her team members. Hertel, Konradt and Orlikowski (2004) provided empirical evidence for this contention. In their study on virtual teams, a positive relation between the quality of goal setting as perceived by the team members and effectiveness was observed. In a study with telecommuters, control-related leadership tasks (i.e., delivering and clarifying goals) were positively related to job satisfaction and negatively related to perceived stress (Konradt, Hertel, & Schmook, 2003). Hoch (2007) found a positive relationship between reward and communication systems and virtual team success, thereby suggesting the significance of non-directional leadership functions.

A further argument is provided by DeSanctis and Monge (1998) who suggest that communication processes in virtual teams are more formal than in traditional settings. They argue that a lower hierarchical level leads to an increasing volume of communication and two-way exchanges among team members, and thus communication needs to be more formal or programmed to achieve efficiency in work (Hollingshead & Contractor, 2002; Straus, 1997). Research on computer-mediated communication has consistently shown that in computer-mediated communication more formal contexts are transmitted than informal or social contents (Marshall & Novick, 1995).

Finally, role-based theories hold that the content of roles has to be clearly known and that the set of behavior is available to the role incumbent. One problem of such a view is the possible difficulty for leaders to realize the environmental expectancies due to organizational factors, e.g., leader distance or amount of communication. Managers in virtual teams are in a peripheral position with fewer opportunities for receiving social cues and feedback (Daft & Lengel, 1986). Qualitative data on role perception in computer supported groups suggest that participants had difficulties in identifying correctly the roles they would take in their group (Zigurs & Kozar, 1994). As a consequence, the leader may follow well established control-related roles that have been successfully employed in face-to-face teams (Kluger & DeNisi, 1996; Rodgers & Hunter, 1991). Therefore, we hypothesize the following:

**Hypothesis 1:** *Managers of virtual teams perceive control-related work roles as more appropriate (i.e., the roles of a director and a coordinator) than non-control related roles.*

## Role Repertoire

Different from other role concepts (e.g., Mintzberg, 1973; Yukl, 1989), the CVF proposes that not a single role is related to performance, but rather a multidimensional behavioral model of roles is better suited to achieve performance. Hooijberg (1996) argued that the broader a managers' repertoire is, the more appropriately they can respond to the task requirements. A broad behavioral repertoire becomes more important with an increasing complexity of tasks and changing requirements

which is given in new work arrangements (Murphy & Jackson, 1999). We argue that the repertoire of adequate work roles of managers in virtual teams will be more limited than the repertoire of non-virtual team leaders because they have little or no chance to fulfill people work roles which would require face-to-face interaction. As a result, we hypothesize the following:

**Hypothesis 2:** *The repertoire of managerial work roles which is related to virtual team success and performance will be narrowed over years in a leading position.*

## Work Roles in Organizational Positions

Previous research on managerial activities has shown the moderating effect of organizational positions on managerial activities (e.g., Hemphill, 1959; for a review, see Bass, 1990) and has examined the relationship between one's organizational position and the work roles (Salam, Cox, & Sims, 1997; Tsui, 1984). Middle managers, for example, show more activities of planning, controlling, monitoring and networking than line managers (Van der Velde, Jansen, & Vinkenburg, 1999). Also, differences between internal and external networking activities were found, showing that middle managers and upper-level managers who hold a higher position in the organizational hierarchy, involve more in internal and external networking than lower-level managers (Michael & Yukl, 1993).

Virtual teamwork might be managed more effectively by delegating the managerial functions to the team members (Hofner-Saphiere, 1996; Duarte & Snyder, 1999; Harrington & Ruppel, 1999) and by empowerment of the employees (Conger & Kanungo, 1988). In empowered working structures, principles of self-regulating behavior are fostered which allow team members to be personally responsible for carrying out tasks (Hofner-Saphiere, 1996; Jarvenpaa & Leidner,

1999). Accordingly, Kayworth and Leidner (2001) argue that the roles of line managers in virtual teams will change from controlling to people oriented roles of coaching and mentoring.

Virtual team members typically work across a range of projects with responsibilities toward individuals outside of their own department who have no direct authority over them. It has been argued that for managers in global virtual team boundary spanning activities are crucial for team success (Duarte & Snyder, 1999; Wiesenfeld, Raghuram, & Garud, 1999), they are expected to focus more on external management than managers in conventional teams. However, there is little empirical evidence for this suggestion.

We argue that due to the lean team structures in virtual teams, the typical differences between line managers and middle managers should be reduced. Those work roles that are perceived as effective for middle managers are comparable to effective roles as seen by line managers. Referring to Hypothesis 1, line managers, however, will be more directed toward control-related roles of coordinator and director while middle managers will emphasize flexibility-related roles, i.e. mentor and innovators. While both views emphasize that middle managers follow a behavioral concept of flexibility, the first view has an internal focus, whereas the second view has an external focus. These reflections suggest the following:

**Hypothesis 3:** *With regard to virtual team success and performance, middle mangers perceive people leadership functions (i.e., mentor and facilitator roles), and flexibility related roles (i.e., innovator and mentor roles) as more important than line managers (H3a). Line managers compared to middle managers perceive stability leadership functions (i.e., monitor and coordinator roles) as more necessary to promote virtual team success and performance (H3b).*

## METHOD

### Sample

Participants were 97 managers, predominantly male (with the exception of two women), and on average 45.1 years old ($SD = 7.1$), ranging between 26 and 60 years. Their experience in leadership ranged between one and 360 months, with an average of 94 months ($SD = 82.9$ months), thereof experience as a line manager ranged from zero to 324 months ($M = 21.4$, $SD = 21.1$), and in middle management from zero to 28 months ($M = 7.53$; $SD = 1.63$). The tenure in leading virtual teams ranged between one and 144 months ($M = 31.9$; $SD = 30.5$).

### Measures

Quinn's (1988) Competing Values Framework questionnaire was used to measure leadership behavior, working roles and leadership functions. To reach a high response rate, we minimized the number of role items to a total of sixteen which have the highest discriminative power (cf. Hooijberg & Choi, 2000). Each role was therefore measured by two items adapted from Hooijberg and Choi (2000) which characterize work roles by typical managerial activities. All items stated in the questionnaire are reported in the Appendix. Since the frequency of managerial activities does not always show significant relationships with effectiveness (e.g., Shipper, 1991), participants were asked to assess the *importance* of managerial activities to promote virtual team success and performance. A seven point difference scale based on the observer's judgments was used to indicate the extent to which each leadership activity substantially impedes (score of -3) to substantially promotes (score of +3) virtual team effectiveness.

Analyses of the 16-item scale revealed that the two corresponding items on each leadership role were significantly and positively related ($r = .27$ and $.81$, all $p < .001$). Given the small sample size-to-item ratio in this study, an Exploratory Factor Analysis (EFA) instead of a confirmatory analysis was selected. The Procrustes rotation which rotates the extracted factors to the target matrix of loadings was used to maximize congruence to the CVF and to demonstrate adequate fit to the 8-factor structure. Parameters were estimated by a Maximum Likelihood method because this method allows goodness-of-fit tests (cf. Fabrigar, Wegener, MacCallum, & Strahan, 1999). The results revealed the 8-factor model as an adequate fit ($\chi^2(20) = 20.13$, n.s.), explaining a total variance of 80.06%. Thus, following the CVF, the sixteen behavioral activities were aggregated to eight role composites, and to four leadership functions, respectively.

The *behavioral repertoire* was calculated by aggregating the means of each role to a composite score. This measure represents the breadth with which work roles are perceived to be related to virtual team success.

The *management level* was measured by asking the participant how long they were working as a line manager (in months) and as middle manager (in months). To compare management levels, line managers (coded as -1) and middle managers (coded as +1) were contrasted (cf. Cohen & Cohen, 1983). Finally, age (in years), gender, total leadership experience (in months), and experience in leading virtual teams (in months) were assessed.

## Procedure

Data were collected from managers of a global company. The purpose of the study was verbally described to the managers and they were assured that data would be kept anonymous and only used for scientific purposes. In case of compliance, a written questionnaire was administered including leadership behaviors, work roles, leadership functions, and demographic questions.

## RESULTS

Means, standard deviations, and bivariate correlations are presented in Table 1. Hooijberg and Choi (2000) found high intercorrelations among the work roles. As shown in Table 1, most roles have significant positive relations. The producer role held the highest correlation with the director role ($r = .55$, $p < .001$). A highly significant positive correlation was also found between the coordinator role and the facilitator role ($r = .54$, $p < .001$). In contrast, the innovator role correlates significantly only with the mentor role ($r = .23$, $p < .05$). As expected, virtual team experience is positively related to age ($r = .36$, $p < .01$), and leadership experience ($r = .47$, $p < .001$), respectively. Thus, the descriptive statistics show good internal validity of the data.

Table 1 shows the descriptive statistics of what work roles and leadership functions are perceived to be most important by virtual team managers to virtual team success and performance. The mean scores of the roles of directors, producers and facilitators are highest (all $M > 1.86$), compared to the lowest mean scores of monitor roles, innovator roles, and broker roles (all $M < 0.93$). Referring to leadership functions, task leadership functions are perceived as mostly important by leaders ($M = 1.98$, $SD = 0.79$), followed by people leadership functions ($M = 1.53$, $SD = 1.04$), adaptive leadership functions ($M = 0.93$, $SD = 0.98$), and stability leadership functions ($M = 0.89$, $SD = 1.02$). A series of one-sample t-tests was performed, separately for each work role and each leadership function. In addition, the Bonferroni method was used to adjust p values for multiple tests. However, all $p$ values remained significant after this adjustment. Results of the role analysis show that task leadership function is rated as significantly more important to virtual team effectiveness than people leadership function ($t(93) = 5.55$, $p < .001$), and people leadership as more important than adaptive leadership function ($t(94)$

*Table 1. Means, standard deviations, and correlations among leadership roles, leadership functions, and controls*

| Variable | M | SD | 1 | 2 | 3 | 4 | 5 | 6 | 7 | 8 | 9 | 10 | 11 | 12 | 13 | 14 | 15 | 16 | 17 | 18 |
|---|---|---|---|---|---|---|---|---|---|---|---|---|---|---|---|---|---|---|---|---|
| *Roles* | | | | | | | | | | | | | | | | | | | | |
| 1 Broker | 0.87 | 1.50 | -- | | | | | | | | | | | | | | | | | |
| 2 Innovator | 0.93 | 1.23 | .08 | -- | | | | | | | | | | | | | | | | |
| 3 Mentor | 1.19 | 1.41 | .14 | .23* | -- | | | | | | | | | | | | | | | |
| 4 Facilitator | 1.86 | 0.97 | .23* | -.03 | .51** | -- | | | | | | | | | | | | | | |
| 5 Monitor | 0.33 | 1.25 | .19† | .01 | -.09 | .17† | -- | | | | | | | | | | | | | |
| 6 Coordinator | 1.46 | 1.22 | .30** | -.05 | .44** | .54** | .37** | -- | | | | | | | | | | | | |
| 7 Director | 2.03 | 0.91 | .11 | -.07 | .44** | .44** | .04 | .31** | -- | | | | | | | | | | | |
| 8 Producer | 1.91 | 0.91 | .17 | .12 | .31** | .33** | .10 | .30** | .55** | -- | | | | | | | | | | |
| 9 Role repertoire | 11.21 | 4.53 | .49** | .30** | .58** | .63** | .43** | .64** | .55** | .62** | -- | | | | | | | | | |
| *Functions* | | | | | | | | | | | | | | | | | | | | |
| 10 Adaptive Leadership | 0.93 | 0.98 | .78** | .68** | .24* | .12 | .13 | .14 | .01 | .20† | .55** | -- | | | | | | | | |
| 11 People Leadership | 1.53 | 1.04 | .19† | .15 | .92** | .81** | .00 | .54** | .52** | .36** | .72** | .22* | -- | | | | | | | |
| 12 Stability Leadership | 0.89 | 1.02 | .29** | -.03 | .20* | .43** | .83** | .83** | .20* | .24* | .65** | .160 | .33** | -- | | | | | | |
| 13 Task Leadership | 1.98 | 0.79 | .15 | .01 | .41** | .43** | .06 | .34** | .88** | .88** | .66** | .10 | .49** | .24* | -- | | | | | |
| 14 Control-related | 1.77 | 0.84 | .25* | -.10 | .50** | .58** | .26* | .86** | .75** | .50** | .74** | .07 | .61** | .67** | .71** | -- | | | | |
| 15 Flexibility-related | 1.09 | 1.01 | .13 | .76 | .81 | .26* | -.01 | .25* | .19† | .27* | .58** | .57** | .70** | .15 | .23* | .23* | -- | | | |
| *Controls* | | | | | | | | | | | | | | | | | | | | |
| 16 Age | 41.1 | 7.1 | .18† | .18† | .12 | .05 | -.02 | .06 | .03 | .13 | .23* | .26* | .11 | .02 | .07 | .08 | .22* | -- | | |
| 17 Managerial level[a] | - | - | .04 | .20 | .18 | .20 | -.10 | -.09 | .14 | .20 | .25† | .17 | .23† | -.11 | .19 | .04 | .22† | .43** | -- | |
| 18 Leadership experience[b] | 94.2 | 82.9 | .16 | .08 | -.03 | -.07 | -.13 | .10 | .05 | .08 | -.29* | .17 | -.05 | -.02 | .07 | -.10 | -.13 | .76** | .50** | -- |
| 19 Virt. team experience[b] | 31.9 | 30.5 | -.09 | .08 | -.23† | -.34* | -.24† | -.15 | -.06 | -.08 | -.12 | .01 | -.31* | -.24† | -.10 | .00 | -.06 | .36** | .31† | .47** |

*Notes.* † $p < .10$. * $p < .05$. ** $p < .01$ (two-tailed).
a: 1 = line manager, 2 = middle manager.
b: in month.

= 5.66, $p < .001$) and stability leadership functions ($t(94) = 5.94$, $p < .001$), respectively.

In Hypothesis 1, we expected that managers in virtual teams view control-related roles as more appropriate for virtual team success and performance than non-control-related roles. To contrast control-related roles with non-control-related roles, we aggregated the scores of the director and coordinator role to high-control roles ($M = 1.77$, $SD = 0.84$), and the role of the mentor and innovator scores to low-control roles ($M = 1.09$, $SD = 1.01$), respectively. The significant mean difference ($t(94) = 7.88$, $p < .001$, $d = 0.73$) provides strong support for Hypothesis 1. The effect strength of .73 indicates a medium-sized to large effect (cf. Cohen, 1988).

Hypothesis 2 predicted that with years in virtual team leadership the role repertoire which is perceived to be related to virtual team success and performance will be narrowed. In a first step, the results of a simple regression analysis show that with increasing experience in leading virtual teams a lower repertoire is perceived to be related to virtual team success and performance ($\beta = -0.29$, $t(47) = -2.11$, $p < .05$), explaining 9% variance in the dependent variable (Adjusted $R^2 = .08$). Because this effect could be traced back to the overall effect of age and professional experience of leaders than specifically to the experience in virtual team leadership, we carried out a hierarchical regression analysis in a second step. In this regression analysis, the influence of leadership experience and age was partialled out in a first step before entering virtual leadership experience as a predictor. In support of Hypothesis 2, the overall leadership experience ($\beta = -.09$, $t(42) = -0.33$, n.s.) and age ($\beta = .14$, $t(42) = 0.53$, n.s.) does not significantly contribute to the leadership repertoire while virtual team leadership was still negatively related to the leadership repertoire ($\beta = -.40$, $t(42) = 2.38$, $p < .01$; $R^2 = .12$, Adj. $R^2 = .06$), supporting Hypothesis 2.

Hypothesis 3a stated that middle managers compared to line managers perceive people

leadership functions and flexibility-related roles as more necessary to promote virtual team success and performance. Regression analysis with the measure of the people leadership function as the dependent variable revealed that middle managers ascribe more importance to people leadership functions ($\beta = 0.30$, $t(60) = 2.40$, $p < .01$); $R^2 = .08$ (Adj. $R^2 = .07$). Moreover, middle managers compared to line managers perceive flexibility-related roles as more necessary to promote virtual team success and performance ($\beta = 0.22$, $t(61) = 1.79$, $p < .05$); ($R^2 = .05$, Adj. $R^2 = .034$), and thus provide support for Hypothesis 3a. Finally, Hypothesis 3b was rejected because line managers compared to middle managers did not perceive stability leadership functions as more necessary to promote virtual team success and performance ($\beta = -0.11$, $t(62) = -0.86$, $p > .10$). The 95% confidence interval (CI) for the sample fails to exclude zero (LCI = -.381, HCI = .152), thereby supporting the rejection of Hypothesis 3b.

## DISCUSSION

The aim of this study was to explore what managerial work roles and leadership functions are perceived by line and middle managers to promote virtual team success and performance. According to the role concept, roles are shaped by the perceived expectations of employees regarding what they should or should not do as part of their role (Katz & Kahn, 1978). Drawing upon the Competitive Value Framework, findings clearly indicate that control-related work roles were predominantly perceived to be related to virtual team success. Control-related work roles include motivating the team to meet expected goals, make the team members' roles clear, and clarify priorities, directions, and efficient ways to increase the behavioral certainty (Murphy & Jackson, 1999). This result is in line with previous studies which found that control-related leadership strategies were positively related to telecommuters' job satisfaction and virtual team success (Hertel et al., 2004, Konradt et al., 2003). It is plausible within virtual work contexts that the co-presence of leader and team members is lowered than in face-to-face contexts, and the exchange of expectations between target person and employees is reduced. Due to the peripheral position in the virtual team network and the restricted communication opportunities for receiving social cues and feedback (Daft & Lengel, 1986), lesser possibilities of employees to influence and shape the manager's perception regarding his/her role is given (Zigurs & Kozar, 1994). Thus, it is possible that executives are more ambiguous and uncertain about the attitudes, beliefs and expectations which form their roles. As a result, leaders might tend to avoid risks and choose a set of typical or consensual roles, such as task leadership functions. Further, the impact of leadership substitutes (Kerr & Jermier, 1978) and team shared leadership (Pearce & Conger, 2003) become more important as it may compensate for team leader interactional leadership (Hoch, 2007).

Besides, it seems plausible that roles of mentors or facilitators need a greater awareness of in-group processes and team mental models which are typically restricted in virtual teams (Hinds & Weisband, 2003). Finally, due to the lack of overt interaction in virtual teams and the characteristics of computer-mediated communication (e.g., Hollingshead & Contractor, 2002) the leader member exchange is restricted, and, thus, leaders might narrow their role to those that are central or want to achieve at all costs.

The second hypothesis, which proposed that with years in position the repertoire of leadership roles which are perceived as adequate will be narrowed, was confirmed. Contrary to the CVF which assumes that a broad repertoire of leadership activities will permit the leaders to successfully engage and sustain members' motivation and performance, a lower repertoire is related to virtual team performance and success. This

result indicates that in order to be effective in virtual teams it is not important to have a broad role set at one's disposal, but to rely on a limited set of role or functions (Hooijberg, 1996; Murphy & Jackson, 1999). An explanation for this result is that leaders in virtual teams have little or no chance to fulfill highly interactive work roles. As a consequence, the repertoire of leadership roles will be narrowed. An alternative explanation is that members of virtual teams compared to members of face-to-face teams have usually attained a high stage of professional maturation (Hinds & Kiesler, 2002) and developed improved shared leadership competencies and self leadership skills, resulting in a lower need for the manager to engage in control-oriented leadership behaviors.

Finally, we examined the relation between one's organizational position and the perceived importance of work roles for team effectiveness. The findings were that middle managers compared to line managers perceive people leadership functions and flexibility-related roles as more necessary to promote virtual team success and performance. Results confirmed previous research which shows that middle managers display more activities of planning, controlling, monitoring, and networking than line managers (Van der Velde et al., 1999) and exercise more internal and external networking than lower-level managers (Michael & Yukl, 1993). Contrarily to our hypothesis, line managers compared to middle managers did not perceive stability leadership functions as more necessary to promote virtual team success and performance. First, the effect can be explained by the flat hierarchies and low formalism in virtual teams. Differences in status, role and activities among virtual team members are typically smaller than in face-to-face teams, because all members are authorized to undertake project management tasks. Another reason for the absence of differences could be that the leader is 'Primus inter pares' and may play the role of a model. Support for this assumption comes from studies on the changing role of middle management (Jaeger

& Pekruhl, 1998). Due to their function as an interface and multiplier, middle mangers play the role of a change agent, they are in charge of communicating and altering cultural values at the operative level.

The findings from the present study provide an initial empirical insight into managerial activities and roles in virtual teams. Consequently, several theoretical and methodological limitations of this study should be noted. First of all, we adopted the CVF which pays particular attention to the employee perspective. Thus this study focuses on reflections of leaders on what leadership managerial behavior should be like, reflecting rather normative aspects how it is supposed be, than how it really is that would reflect descriptive aspects of their behavior and experiences. Indeed, past research indicated that self-perceptions of behavior often differ to judgments of subordinates and peers (e.g., Atwater & Yammarino, 1993; Tsui, 1984). Moreover, self-perceptions are susceptible to socially desirable responding (for a review, see Paulhus, 1991), indicating that self-perceptions may be relatively unreliable measures to judge behaviors (Podsakoff & Organ, 1986). On the other hand, it seems plausible that the conceptions held by managers reveal how they interpret their work roles and direct their behavior. Thus, direct responses from superiors and subordinates (e.g., Hooijberg, 1996) should be examined in future studies in addition to managers' role self-perception to validate our results.

A further limitation of this research is that managers' ratings do not refer to a single team, but to several teams which are differing in several characteristics, e.g. their tenure and their grade of formalization. For example, past research has found that role priority changes with the stages of team development (e.g., Yang & Shao, 1996). Moreover, in virtual teams which are less formalized, priority may be given to aspects of flexibility, whereas control has been less emphasized. It could thus be expected that the roles of coordinator and monitor will receive more emphasis when the

teams are young and less formalized. Furthermore, it is possible that different types of virtual teams (Bell & Kozlowski, 2002) require different leadership behavior to be effective. Additional research is needed to further explore whether role preferences and managerial activities are bound to particular organizational settings and organizational culture (Brodbeck, Frese, Akerblom et al., 2000; Valkeavaara, 1998) and whether our results can be generalized to other companies and female virtual leaders. Eagly and Johnson (1990), for example, found that women used a more participative or democratic style and a less directive style than men did. Another related direction for future research involves pinpointing the extent to which the level of a team's virtuality promotes role rigidity and role ambiguity and may discourage managers from showing preferred roles.

Finally, another open question is whether the managerial activities which were studied address the full scope of the managerial roles in virtual teams. The managerial activities and roles were adopted from the Competing Values Framework which was developed for face-to-face teams. In other role concepts it is proposed that extra-role aspects are critical to team effectiveness, i.e. assist and enable the members to build supporting group norms (Morrison & Phelps, 1999). Moreover, under e-leadership (Avolio et al., 2001) more agents are actively involved in interactions both within and across units and organizations and the role of the leader turns from previously stable into flux. Further, it is possible that in virtual teams roles might be perceived less differentiated than in conventional teams. Observation studies of managers in their workplace will shed light on the appropriateness of the taxonomy for virtual working structures.

In general, it is assumed that leaders in virtual teams have to follow a substantive role change processes to adopt roles of an entrepreneur and boundary spanner (e.g., Duarte & Snyder, 1999). To date, little research has successfully established the validity of this claim. In conclusion, this study adopted a role approach and demonstrated the validity of using the CVF to differentiate between roles in virtual teams. Results further indicate that managers of virtual teams perceive control-related roles to be most important for virtual team success and performance, the repertoire of leadership decline with years of experience, and middle managers compared to line managers perceived people leadership functions and flexibility-related roles as more significant. Work roles provide important behavioral guidelines, reduce uncertainty, and may foster a shared meaning of expectancies in virtual teams. Relating work roles with measures of the followers and situational characteristics, as well as stress reactions in conflicting or uncertain job expectations would be a next step to explore theoretical and empirical relationships between team processes and different outcomes in virtual teams. This would not only broaden our understanding of leadership in dispersed work structures and would have fruitful implications for role theory but would also be useful for management practice in new working arrangements to identify ways to improve their skills and, in turn, enhance their organization's effectiveness.

## REFERENCES

Antonakis, J., & Atwater, L. (2002). Leader distance: A review and a proposed theory. *Leadership Quarterly,* 13(6), 673-704.

Atwater, L.E., & Yammarino, F.J. (1993). Personal attributes as predictors of superiors and subordinates perceptions of military academy leadership. *Human Relations*, 46(5), 645-668.

Avolio, B.J., Kahai, S., & Dodge, G.E. (2001). E-Leadership: Implications for theory, research, and practice. *The Leadership Quarterly*, 11(4), 615-670.

Axtell, C.M., Fleck, S.J., & Turner, N. (2004). Virtual teams: Collaborating across distance. In C.L. Cooper & I.T. Robertson (Eds.), *International review of industrial and organizational psychology* (Vol. 19) (pp. 205-248). Chichester: Wiley.

Bass, B.M. (1990). *Bass & Stogdill's handbook of leadership.* New York: The Free Press.

Bell, B.S., & Kozlowski, S.W.J. (2002). A typology of virtual teams: implications for effective leadership. *Group and Organization Management*, 27(1), 14-49.

Bentler, P.M. (1989). *EQS structural equations program manual.* Los Angeles: BMDP Statistical Software.

Brodbeck, F.C., Frese, M., Akerblom, S. et al. (2000). Cultural variation of leadership prototypes across 22 European countries. *Journal of Occupational and Organizational Psychology*, 73(1), 1-29.

Buenger, V., Daft, R.L., Conlon, E.J., & Austin, J. (1996). Competing values in organizations: Contextual influences and structural consequences. *Organization Science*, 7(5), 557-576.

Cohen, J., & Cohen, P. (1983). *Applied multiple regression/correlation analysis for the behavioral sciences* (2nd ed.). Hillsdale, NJ: Erlbaum.

Cohen, J. (1988). *Statistical power analysis for the behavioral sciences* (2nd edition). Hillsdale, NJ: Erlbaum.

Conger, J.A., & Kanungo, R.N. (1988). The empowerment process: integrating theory and practice. *Academy of Management Review*, 13(3), 471-82.

Daft, R.L., & Lengel, R.H. (1986). Organizational information requirements, media richness and structural design. *Management Science*, 32(5), 554-571.

Davidow, W.H., & Malone, M.S. (1992). *The virtual corporation.* New York: Harper Collins.

Denison, D.R., Hooijberg, R., & Quinn, R.E. (1995). Paradox and performance: Toward a theory of behavioral complexity in managerial leadership. *Organization Science*, 6(5), 524-540.

Duarte, D.L., & Snyder, N.T. (1999). *Mastering virtual teams*. San Francisco: Jossey-Bass.

Eagly, A., & Johnson, B. (1990). Gender and the emergence of leaders: A meta-analysis. *Psychological Bulletin,* 108(2), 233-256.

Fjermestad, J., & Hiltz, S.R. (2000). Group support systems: A descriptive evaluation of case and field studies. *Journal of Management Information Systems,* 17(3), 115-160.

Gerstner, C.R., & Day, D.V. (1997). Meta-analytic review of leader-member exchange theory: Correlates and construct issues. *Journal of Applied Psychology*, 82(6), 827-844.

Gibson, C.B., & Cohen, S.G.(Eds.) (2003). *Virtual teams that work. Creating conditions for virtual team effectiveness*. San Francisco: Jossey-Bass.

Harrington, S.J., & Ruppel, C.P. (1999). Telecommuting: A test of trust, competing values, and relative advantage. *IEEE Transactions on Professional Communication*, 42(4), 223-239.

Hemphill, J.K. (1959). Job descriptions of executives. *Harvard Business Review,* 37(5), 55-67.

Hertel, G., Geister, S., & Konradt, U. (2005). Managing virtual teams: A review of current empirical research. *Human Resource Management Review*, 15(1), 69-95.

Hertel, G., Konradt, U., & Orlikowski, B. (2004). Managing distance by interdependence: Goal setting, task interdependence and team-based rewards in virtual teams. *European Journal of Work and Organizational Psychology,* 13(1), 1-28.

Hinds, P., & Kiesler, S. (2002). *Distributed work*. Cambridge, MA: MIT Press.

Hinds, P., & Weisband, S. (2003). Knowledge sharing and shared understanding in virtual teams. In C.B. Gibson & S.G. Cohen (Eds.), *Virtual teams that work: Creating conditions for virtual teams effectiveness* (pp. 21-36). San Francisco: Jossey-Bass.

Hoch. J.E. (2007). *Verteilte Fuehrung in virtuellen Teams*. Dissertationsschrift an der Universität Kiel [*Distributed leadership in virtual teams*, PhD thesis]. URL: http://e-diss.uni-kiel.de/index.html

Hofner Saphiere, D.M. (1996). Productive behaviors of global business teams. *International Journal of Intercultural Relations*, 20(2), 227-259.

Hollingshead, A.B., & Contractor, N.S. (2002). New media and organizing at the group level. In S. Livingstone & L. Lievrouw (Eds.), *Handbook of new media* (pp. 221-235). London: Sage.

Hooijberg, R. (1996). A multidirectional approach toward leadership: An extension of the concept of behavioral complexity. *Human Relations*, 49(7), 917-946.

Hooijberg, R., Hunt, J.G., & Dodge, G.E. (1997). Leadership complexity and development of the leaderplex model. *Journal of Management*, 23(3), 375-408.

Hooijberg, R., & Choi, J. (2000). Which leadership roles matter to whom?: An examination of rater effects on perceptions of effectiveness. *Leadership Quarterly*, 11(3), 341-364.

Hooijberg, R., & Choi, J. (2001). The impact of organisational characteristics on leadership effectiveness models: an examination of leadership in a private and public sector organisation. *Administration and Society*, 33(4), 403-431.

Ilgen, D.R., & Hollenbeck, J.R. (1991). The structure of work: Job design and roles. In M.D. Dunnette & L.M. Hough (Eds*.), Handbook of industrial and organizational psychology* (pp. 165-207). Palo Alto, CA: Consulting Psychologists Press, Inc.

Jaeger, D., & Pekruhl, U. (1998). Participative company management in Europe: The new role of middle management. *New Technology, Work and Employment*, 13(2), 94-103.

Jarvenpaa, S.L., & Leidner, D.E. (1999). Communication and trust in global virtual teams. *Organization Science,* 10(6), 791-815.

Kahai, S.S., Sosik, J.J., & Avolio, B.J. (2003). Effects of leadership style, anonymity, and rewards on creativity-relevant processes and outcomes in an electronic meeting system context. *The Leadership Quarterly* , 14(4/5), 499-524.

Katz, D., & Kahn, R.L. (1978). *The social psychology of organisations.* New York: John Wiley.

Kayworth, T.R., & Leidner, D.E. (2001). Leadership effectiveness in global virtual teams. *Journal of Management Information Systems,* 18(3), 7-40.

Kerr, S., & Jermier, J.M. (1978). Substitutes for leadership: Their meaning and measurement. *Organizational Behavior & Human Performance*, 22(3), 375-403.

Kluger, A.N., & DeNisi, A. (1996). The effects of feedback interventions on performance: A historical review, a meta-analysis, and a preliminary feedback intervention theory. *Psychological Bulletin,* 119(2), 254-284.

Konradt, U., Hertel, G., & Schmook, R. (2003). Quality of management by objectives, task-related stressors and non-task-related stressors as predictors of stress and job satisfaction among teleworkers. *European Journal of Work and Organizational Psychology,* 12(1), 61-79.

Konradt, U., Schmook, R., & Maelecke, M. (2000). Impacts of telework on individuals, organizations and families - A critical review. In: Cooper, C.L. & Robertson, I.T. (Eds.), *International review of industrial and organizational psychology (*Vol. 15, pp. 63-99). Chichester: Wiley.

Manz, C.C., & Sims, H.P. (1993). *Business without bosses: How self-managing teams are building high performance companies.* New York: Wiley.

Marshall, C., & Novick, D. (1995). Conversational effectiveness and multi-media communications. *Information Technology & People*, 8(1), 54-79.

Maznevski, M.L., & Chudoba, K.M. (2000). Bridging space over time: global virtual team dynamics and effectiveness. *Organization Science,* 11(5), 473-492.

McGrath, J. E. (1984). *Groups: Interaction and performance.* Englewood Cliffs, NJ: Prentice Hall.

Michael, J., & Yukl, G. (1993) Managerial level and subunit function as determinants of networking behavior in organisations. *Group & Organisation Management*, 18(3), 328-351.

Mintzberg, H. (1973). *The nature of managerial work.* New York: Harper and Row.

Morrison, E.W., & Phelps, C. (1999). Taking charge: Extra-role efforts to initiate workplace change. *Academy of Management Journal*, 42(4), 403-419.

Murphy, P.R., & Jackson, S.E. (1999). Managing work role performance: Challenges for twenty-first-century organizations and their employees. In D.R. Ilgen & E.D. Pulakos (Eds.), *The changing nature of performance: Implications for staffing, motivation, and development* (pp. 325-365). San Francisco: Jossey-Bass.

Oeser, O.A., & Harary, F. (1964). A mathematical model for structural role theory, II. *Human Relations,* 17(1), 3-17.

Panayotopoulou, L., Bourantas, D., & Papalexandris, N. (2003). Strategic human resource management and its effects on firm performance: an implementation of the competing values framework. *International Journal of Human Resource Management*, 14(4), 680-699.

Paulhus, D.L. (1991). Measurement and control of response bias. In J.P. Robinson, P.R. Shaver, & L.S. Wrightsman (Eds.), *Measures of personality and social psychological attitudes* (pp. 17-59). New York: Academic Press.

Pearce, C.L., & Conger, J.A. (2003). *Shared leadership: Reframing the hows and whys of leadership.* Thousand Oaks, CA: Sage.

Podsakoff, P.M., & Organ, D.W. (1986). Self reports in organizational research: problems and prospects. *Journal of Management,* 12(4), 531-544.

Quinn, R.E. (1988). *Beyond rational management: Mastering the paradoxes and competing demands of high performance.* San Francisco: Jossey-Bass.

Quinn, R.E., Faerman, S.R., Thompson, M.P., & McGrath, M.R. (1996*). Becoming a master manager: A competency framework.* New York: John Wiley.

Rodgers, R., & Hunter, J.E. (1991). Impact of management by objectives on organizational productivity. *Journal of Applied Psychology,* 76(2), 322-336.

Salam, S., Cox, J.F., & Sims, H.P. (1997). In the eye of the beholder: How leadership relates to 360-degree performance ratings. *Group & Organizational Management,* 22(2), 185-209.

Shamir, B. (1999). Leadership in boundaryless organizations: Disposable or indispensable? *European Journal of Work and Organizational Psychology,* 8(1), 49-71.

Shipper, F. (1991). Mastery and frequency of managerial behaviors relative to sub-unit effectiveness. *Human Relations,* 44(4), 371-388.

Straus, S.G. (1997). Technology, group process, and group outcomes: Testing the connections in computer-mediated and face-to-face groups. *Human Computer Interaction,* 12(3), 227-266.

Tsui, A.S. (1984). A role set analysis of managerial reputation. *Organizational Behavior and Human Performance,* 34(11), 64-96.

Valkeavaara, T. (1998). Human resource development roles and competencies in five European countries. *International Journal of Training and Development,* 2(3), 171-189.

Van der Velde, M.E.G., Jansen, G.W.E., & Vinkenburg, C.J. (1999). Managerial activities among top and middle managers: self versus others perceptions. *Journal of Applied Management Studies,* 8(2), 161-174.

Wegge, J. (2006). Communication via videoconference: Emotional and cognitive consequences of seeing one's own picture, affective personality dispositions and disturbing events. *Human Computer Interaction,* 21(3), 273-318.

Wiesenfeld, B.M., Raghuram, S., & Garud, R. (1999). Managers in a virtual context: The experience of self-treat and its effects on virtual work organizations. In C.L. Cooper & D.M. Rousseau (Eds.), *The virtual organization* (pp. 31-44). Chichester: Wiley.

Yang, O., & Shao, Y. (1996). Shared leadership in self-managed teams: a competing values approach. *Total Quality Management,* 7(5), 521-534.

Yukl, G. (1989). Managerial leadership: A review of theory and research. *Journal of Management,* 15(2), 251-289.

Zigurs, I., & Kozar, K. (1994). An exploratory study of roles in computer-supported groups. *MIS Quarterly,* 18(3), 277-297.

# APPENDIX

*Leadership Roles and Managerial Activities Items (Adopted from Hooijberg & Choi, 2000)*

---

Innovator

      (1) Comes up with inventive ideas

      (2) Experiments with new concepts and procedures

Broker

      (3) Exerts upward influence in the organization

      (4) Influences decisions made at higher levels

Facilitator

      (5) Surfaces key differences among group members, then works participatively to resolve them

      (6) Develops consensual resolution to openly expressed differences

Mentor

      (7) Shows empathy and concern in dealing with subordinates

      (8) Treats each individual in a sensitive, caring way

Coordinator

      (9) Anticipates workflow problems, avoids crisis

      (10) Brings a sense of order and coordination into the unit

Monitor

      (11) Maintains tight logistical control

      (12) Compares records, reports, and so on to detect discrepancies

Producer

      (13) Maintains a results orientation in the unit

      (14) Gets the unit to meet expected goals

Director

      (15) Makes the unit's role very clear

      (16) Clarifies the unit's priorities and direction

---

# Chapter X
# Leadership and Performance in Virtual Teams:
## Exploring Brokerage in Electronic Communication

**Johannes Glückler**
*Catholic University of Eichstätt, Germany*

**Gregor Schrott**
*University of Frankfurt, Germany*

## ABSTRACT

*This article explores the structural foundations of leadership and performance in virtual project teams. In an experimental business case, the article demonstrates the effect of structural brokerage in team communication on leadership and team performance. This research suggests that social roles as well as the acknowledgement of leadership and performance are conditional to the way individuals and teams relate to their environment. It supports structural hole theory in that leaders and a winner team achieved the highest values of flow betweenness and network efficiency. Strategically, managers of virtual knowledge networks should focus their attention not only on the qualifications of individuals, but also on communication structures within their work groups.*

## INTRODUCTION

The project is an important type of organization, as it encourages flexible production and the assembly of a diverse expertise. In contrast to permanent organizational forms, projects often create unique output and are essentially non-routine forms of collaboration in which search procedures are highly complex. Projects are organized in temporary, often multidisciplinary teams. Virtual teams have especially been experiencing considerable expansion in the organization of production and knowledge generation (Cascio & Shurygailo, 2003; Pinsonneault & Caya, 2005). This is largely a consequence of several developments in the current economy: an increase of inter-firm project cooperation, a shift from manufacturing to service and knowledge work, and the ongoing internationalization of factor and commodity markets. Compared to permanent work organizational structures and localized projects, virtual teams offer a number of strategic advantages. Firms can form work groups with optimum membership while retaining the advantages of flat hierarchies (Townsend et al., 1998). Moreover, organizations gain access to formerly unavailable expertise and maximize the potential use of this expertise across geographically disperse locations within the firm. Finally, though reliable statistics are not yet available, firms report that virtual teams cut down the costs of production when compared to alternative forms of collaborative production.

The trend toward physically dispersed work groups with only limited space for intimate communication has necessitated a fresh inquiry into the role and nature of team organization, leadership, and performance in virtual settings (Kayworth & Leidner, 2002). Warkentin and Beranek (1999) found social ties among team members to be a significant contributor to the effectiveness of information exchange in the use of computer-mediated communication systems. Since many managers still tend to base their decisions on intuition rather than structural analysis of virtual communication processes (Cross, Parker, Prusak, & Borgatti, 2001; Cross & Prusak, 2002), more research is needed to explore mechanisms of coordination and communication in virtual teams (Montoya-Weiss, Massey, & Song, 2001).

This article aims at identifying some of the dynamics and drivers of leadership and performance in virtual teams. The objective of the analysis is to understand the basis of leadership and team performance from a network perspective focusing on communication relationships between project participants. The second section develops hypotheses for the effect of network structure on individual and team performance in virtual projects. The third section presents the design of an experiment with students for empirical exploration and introduces the network methods used for analysis. The fourth section presents the results from the social network analysis of the communication patterns. The results are discussed, with respect to leadership and performance, and then the fifth section closes with a conclusion.

## Theory and Hypotheses

Research on leadership and work performance often sticks to the notion that effective leadership or performance increase with the appropriate abilities, characteristics, or qualifications of individuals (e.g., Kayworth & Leidner, 2002; Yoo & Alavi, 2004). Though the analysis of constant conjunctions between a certain type of behavior and particular attributes of actors represents the default mode of establishing cause-effect relationships in many social sciences, it systematically leads us to ignore context and to reduce causality to individual attributes (Granovetter, 1992; Sayer, 2000). Thirty years ago, experiments in social psychology revealed this "attributional bias" in scientific thought, for instance, in leadership research. Staw (1975) randomly assigned failure and success to work groups. When group members were afterwards invited to rate the cohesiveness and leadership within the groups, there was a clear pattern that successful groups perceived high cohesiveness and effective leadership while less successful groups perceived less cohesiveness and leadership. This finding challenges many of the arguments about the association of a style of leadership with organizational performance (McElroy & Shrader, 1986). In consequence of this line of research, Pfeffer and Salancik (1978, p. 8) concluded that

*the concept of the omnipotent actor has led to the search for the unique set of ingredients that produces success in organizations. Originally, the quest was for those traits that distinguish good from poor leaders. [...] Unfortunately, the characteristics could never be found.*

This article adopts a relational or network view of social action, which claims that social structure has a more pronounced effect on human behavior than cultural norms or individual dispositions (Mizruchi, 1994, p. 329). Social structures are typically described and studied as social networks. A social network is

*a specific set of linkages among a defined set of persons, with the additional property that the characteristics of these linkages as a whole may be used to interpret the social behavior of the persons involved.* (Mitchell, 1969, p. 2)

The specific implication intended by this definition is that relations are the unit of analysis and that the particular set of relations can be employed to account for the behavior of particular individuals within the set of relations and for the network as a whole (Knoke & Kuklinski, 1991). This article argues that the analysis of communication flows will lead to a better understanding of the dynamics of virtual teams and potentially enhance future management practice. Particularly, structural aspects of network communication might help to improve the understanding of the processes of emergent leadership within and between teams and team performance.

## Emergent Leadership

Teamwork may imply a division of labor, where some members focus on certain pieces of work and others on the coordination of that work within the team and between teams. Leaders may emerge from ongoing team work and be acknowledged leadership by their peers. The diverse literature on leadership may be grouped into three broad sets of approaches (Kayworth & Leidner, 2002): trait theory, behavioral theory, and contingency theory. While trait theory essentially expects leaders to

benefit from superior or particularly advantageous skills or capabilities—just as criticized before—behavioral theories focus on the actually displayed behavior and actions taken by leaders. Due to the empirical limitation of their predictions, many authors have supported contingency theory in arguing that there is no one-best style of action yielding leadership effectiveness. Instead, they argue that different situations and contexts require different behavioral styles.

This article adopts a fourth approach to leadership inspired by social network theory. McElroy and Shrader (1986) discuss some of the weaknesses of assessing leadership through individual characteristics and propose to compensate for these by applying social network analysis to leadership research. A leader is generally understood to be an individual who takes crucial roles in work processes such as the innovator, motivator, mediator, broker, director, among many other conceivable roles (Kayworth & Leidner, 2002; Zigurs, 2003; Yoo & Alavi, 2004). Network theory focuses explicitly on social roles as a specific pattern of interrelation with other actors. Following this perspective, one would expect individuals to become leaders because they create a specific structure of communication with their peers. One such structure is the brokerage role, which creates a favorable position for the transmission of information, conflict resolution, and coordination. Instead of asking respondents to rate a leader's role—as is common in conventional leadership research—network theory measures this brokerage position formally and thus permits to systematically test the brokerage effect on leadership.

More concretely, two effects of communication networks on leadership are expected: (1) *Size.* People exert leadership if they communicate with more people and therefore, extend beyond the realm of their peers. As a result, one would expect leaders to have bigger ego-networks. (2) *Structure.* Structural hole theory (Burt, 1992; 1997) suggests that actors enjoy advantages of information and control, if they create structural holes around them, that is, engage in non-redundant relations. Relations are redundant whenever an actor can be omitted or substituted by another actor in the network without changing or limiting the flow of communication. In turn, actors engaging in non-redundant relations cannot be substituted. Instead, they control the information flow between their alters and thus become brokers. Brokerage increases with the necessity that other actors in the network need to communicate with a broker in order to reach the other actors. These aspects of network structure inform the following hypotheses:

- **Hypothesis 1:** Team members are more likely to be acknowledged leaders if they communicate with more people.
- **Hypothesis 2:** Team members are more likely to be acknowledged leaders if they take a brokerage position in the flow of communication.

## Group Performance

Following the line of reasoning from above, the brokerage argument may be extended to the expectation about group performance. Empirical research suggests that personality characteristics are unrelated to manager performance such that a network perspective proves largely indispensable for understanding differences in performance (Burt, Janotta, & Mahoney, 1998). Nonetheless, there has been very little research that links structural properties of social networks to the performance of individuals and groups (Reagans & Zuckerman, 2001; Sparrowe, Liden, Wayne, & Kraimer, 2001). Baker and Faulkner (2004) investigated the effect of social networks on investment returns and found that investors who used social ties were less likely to lose capital in the course of their investment. Sparrowe et al. (2001) found that network position is associated with both individual and group performance. The more

central individuals were in an advice network, the higher their performance, and the more central they were in hindrance networks, the lower their performance. Clearly, communication structures need not have universal effects independent of the nature of the work (Tushman, 1979). Hansen (1999) provided empirical support for the notion that weak ties between work groups enhance the search of useful knowledge, but obstruct the transfer of complex knowledge. So, while weak ties speed up routine projects, they, at the same time, slow down non-routine projects. Following this line of research, one would expect network structure to affect overall group performance. In a context of inter-team collaboration, this paper hypothesizes that team performance increases with its degree of brokerage in the inter-team communication:

- **Hypothesis 3:** A team is more likely to outperform other teams if it plays a brokerage role in the interaction between the whole set of teams.

## Communication Media

The communication constraints within projects depend, among other factors, on geography. Whenever teams are co-located, the members in a work group may communicate face-to-face and find themselves in repeated physical interaction. In contrast, in virtual teams team members are geographically dispersed. In this case, work groups communicate predominantly via computer-mediated communication systems, interact without a common past or future, and collaborate with geographically disperse and culturally diverse individuals (Jarvenpaa & Leidner, 1999). Since projects often yield high-risk outcomes, virtual teams require an enormous amount of communication, coordination, and institutional safeguards, such as trust and conventions that minimize the likelihood of failure (Grabher, 2002; Cummings & Cross, 2003; Grabher, 2004).

In most situations of uncertainty and high-risk ventures, face-to-face communication rules out any dislocated form of electronic communication (Guzzo & Dickson, 1996; Zigurs, 2003; Sorenson, Rivkin, & Fleming, 2005). Therefore, one would expect collaborators to opt for face-to-face communication whenever communication is complex, that is, involves conflict, negotiation, or complex knowledge transfer.

Under conditions of geographical dispersion and virtual team organization, individuals are reliant often exclusively on electronic forms of communication. With respect to leadership in virtual teams, empirical research demonstrates that leaders send more and longer messages than their team members (Yoo & Alavi, 2004). As a result, leadership should also become visible in the structure of electronic communication. Empirical research suggests that different communication media affect the structure of communication between people (Sproull & Kiesler, 1986). It is assumed, for instance, that electronic forms of communication (i.e., e-mail messages) are less prone to hierarchical communication in organizations and that they support the emergence of communication relations that cut across formal authority relations (Dubrovsky, Kiesler, & Sethna, 1991). When different media are available to co-workers, the question arises whether the media are only complementary to each other within existing patterns of communication relations or whether their use reflects different structures of communication relations. This article specifically focuses on the different uses of face-to-face meetings and electronic mail communication. Moreover, it distinguishes stationary electronic messages from and electronic message exchanges over mobile devices. This distinction is made to account for differences in comfort of use, functionality, and available memory between desktops and mobile devices.

- **Hypothesis 4:** Complex coordination will more likely be realized in face-to-face rather than in electronic communication

- **Hypothesis 5:** The use of different communication media will produce different structures of communication

## METHODOLOGY

### Research Setting

Sixteen graduate students in information systems joined an experimental business case project over a period of five weeks. The students were asked to imagine that they were employed with a telecommunications company. The major objective was to conceive, plan, and organize a new product launch event under serious time and budgetary restrictions. Each of four departments (i.e., development, marketing, international business, sales) received instructions regarding their specific tasks and the requirements for coordination with the other departments. All tasks were highly interrelated and a great deal of coordination was required from the students to assent on budget allocation, milestones of work delivery and on work results (see Appendix for task descriptions). During the course of the project, two critical interventions were made to compel inter-team communication. First, the budget was reduced shortly after the groups had already planned their course of action, causing them to renegotiate their requirements with other departments. Second, three days later, the deadline was advanced to again stimulate inter-team coordination, accelerate the delivery of a solution, as well as to meet the intended project objective.

### Data

In order to be able to test the impact of electronic and mobile communication on team dynamics, three communication channels were specified:

- **Face-to-face meetings.** Students reported face-to-face meetings individually on data forms which contained a list of the participants of each meeting.

- **Stationary e-mail messages.** All students were given access to a Web-based communication portal which was customized as the company's intranet site.
- **Mobile e-mail messages.** Students were also equipped with mobile devices, which they could use free of any cost for project communication.

All e-mail messages were recorded electronically by log file-analysis and filtered according to some general criteria. Students were instructed to respect a series of conventions on how to use these media. First, all project communication had to be realized exclusively across the project e-mail address (and no other e-mail-accounts). Second, all electronic messages had to be titled in a defined way in order to distinguish administrative questions from content messages, as well as to identify e-mails sent through the mobile channel more easily during the data-analysis. Besides, students were asked to avoid "broadcasting," that is, spreading their messages to everybody in the group, although they were not directly affected by the message. Finally, all communication towards and from the CEO as well as "delivery-failure-notices" and administrative questions were removed from the raw data. In sum, stationary and mobile electronic communication clearly outweighed face-to-face meetings between the students. After the five-week period, students had 46 meetings compared to 2,745 stationary e-mails and 990 mobile e-mails within the project period.

## Measures

*Independent variables.* Network size was measured as the degree, that is, the number of people that a student communicated with during the project; and as effective size (Burt, 1992), that is, the number of non-redundant contacts that a student communicated with. Brokerage position

of individuals and teams was also measured with two parameters: efficiency measures the extent to which communication relations are committed to non-redundant contacts while controlling for network size (see Borgatti, 1997 for further details); and flow betweenness measures the frequency to which a person is on the shortest path connecting any other pair of actors in the network (see Freeman, Borgatti, & White, 1991 for further details).

*Dependent variables.* Two dependent variables were defined in this experiment. (1) *Leadership.* Accurate measures of leadership are difficult to assess (McElroy & Shrader, 1986). Leadership can be assessed internally or externally to the work group. Internal attribution refers to the assessment by team peers or subordinates, whereas external attribution refers to observers who are not dependent on the leader (McElroy, 1982). Instead of defining—largely artificial—measures of leadership external to the work groups, this article, similar to other research such as Kayworth and Leidner (2002), measures leadership as the rate of acknowledgement of a leader role from within the peer group. Instead of arguing that particular objective measures qualified a person as a leader or a team as a winner, we were interested in accounting for a leader and a winner team by vote of their project peers. This operational technique draws on attribution theory, which assigns roles on the basis of other participants' attributions. If it is possible to demonstrate network structure to account for empirically acknowledged leadership and success, we find our analysis more accurate because ultimately, leadership and project performance are socially constructed phenomena embedded into a collective of individuals. We avoid the problem of self-reinforcing attribution since there are no a priori leader roles or status differences pre-determined. Hence, team peers are not biased towards identifying a leader at the beginning. Only after the project had finished were they asked to determine whether there was a leader at all and who that person was. With respect to the measure, therefore, two outcomes are important here: first, whether the peers in a team acknowledged a leader or not, and if yes, who this individual was. (2) *Team performance.* In line with the measure of leadership, team performance was also measured through peer evaluation. After the project had finished, all participants were invited to rank the performance of all teams against a defined set of five criteria: cooperation, quality of work, reliability, communication, and flexibility. With each indicator, students had to rank the teams from first to fourth place. The overall rating was calculated as the sum of scores along these main dimensions. The maximum score possible was 320 points (first rank from all 16 students across all five dimensions). Their scores were used to assess a winner team. In order to ensure commitment and willingness to perform, the entire group was briefed about the following incentive: the best performing team would win an attractive prize right. However, in order to exclude particular team strategies, they would not be informed about the criteria and technique for performance evaluation.

## Methods

Two sets of methods were applied to the data. First, the network measures of size, centrality and brokerage, which are used as independent variables, are computed with a specific software package for social network analysis (Borgatti, Everett, & Freeman, 2002). Where necessary, matrix information was reduced through symmetrization and dichotomization in order to complement with alternative measures such as flow betweenness. The limited number of participants in the case example does not allow for inferential statistical analyses. Therefore, tests for significance of variations between individuals or groups with respect to the network parameters would be inappropriate. Instead, the parameters are tabulated for comparison between groups. For the purpose of the empirical exercise, this

is sufficient because the major contribution of this paper is to open a research perspective that actively seeks to apply network hypotheses on dynamics in virtual teams.

Second, the quadratic assignment procedure (QAP) was used to test for structural coincidence between the communication relations (Krackhardt, 1987; Kilduff & Krackhardt, 1994). The QAP was used to investigate whether the pattern of physical communication through meetings varied significantly from the patterns of stationary and mobile electronic communication. The QAP proceeds as follows: First, for two observed matrices, for instance, meetings and stationary e-mails, the Pearson correlation coefficient is calculated. Then, the rows and columns of the comparative matrix are permuted to provide a new matrix. Now, both matrices are crrelated again and the r-value is compared to the original one. This permutation-correlation process is repeated an arbitrarily large number of times (here 2,500). The individual r-values from the permutations generate an empirical reference distribution against which the observed original r-value is then compared. If fewer than five percent of the r-values from the random correlations are larger than the observed r-value of the original correlation, the correlation is qualified significant at the 0.05 level.

## Results

### Leadership

Two questions were important here. First, did the team members acknowledge leaders; and, second, if yes, who became leader and why? After the project was finished, a questionnaire was used to ask every student to indicate if they acknowledged a leader in their group and who that person was. Although the number of votes that people received varied considerably across the teams, it is striking that there was not a single contradictory vote. In every team, only one person was acknowledged as a leader. As a result, every team had a univocal leader though the degree of leadership acknowledgement varied strongly across the teams (Table 1). At the aggregate level, one might conclude that the two teams of development and international business did not identify leadership in their groups, yet there was unambiguous agreement on the individuals that were acknowledged leadership. The interest of this article is on the individuals who received positive leadership votes and hence includes all four students assigned leadership status.

Structural analysis supports hypotheses one and two. First, the four people acknowledged as leaders communicated with more people. In terms of network size, leaders met with (though slightly) more people, and exchanged e-mails with up to 11 other students as compared to only eight peers in the case of the other team members. Their ego networks were bigger and extended beyond their teams. Leaders had also more effective networks

in that they had, on average, a clearly higher degree of non-redundant contacts than their peers. These findings strongly support hypothesis one. Second, leaders did not only communicate with more people, but also occupied brokerage positions in the overall communication network. Brokerage was measured in terms of efficiency. According to Burt's (1992) conceptualization, networks are efficient to the extent that egos' alters are not connected among each other. Table 2 demonstrates that leaders had more efficient communication structures than their peers in electronic messages, whereas in meetings they were about the same. Another indicator of brokerage is the role of betweenness. Table 2 shows that leaders had higher values in all three communication channels and thus controlled far more information flow than their alters. Thus, both measures support hypothesis two.

These findings confirm the hypothesis that

*Table 1. Did you find someone to be the leader of your team?*

| team | N | no | yes | number of leaders |
|---|---|---|---|---|
| sales | 4 | 0 | 4 | 1 |
| marketing | 4 | 1 | 3 | 1 |
| international business | 4 | 2 | 2 | 1 |
| development | 4 | 3 | 1 | 1 |

*Table 2. Measures for network size and brokerage roles*

|  | face-to-face meetings | | | stationary e-mail | | | mobile e-mail | | |
|---|---|---|---|---|---|---|---|---|---|
|  | peers | leaders | total | peers | leaders | total | peers | leaders | total |
| N | 12 | 4 | 16 | 12 | 4 | 16 | 12 | 4 | 16 |
| size | 3.58 | 3.75 | 3.63 | 6.83 | 10.00 | 7.63 | 7.83 | 11.00 | 8.63 |
| effective size | 2.27 | 2.29 | 2.28 | 2.48 | 4.42 | 2.97 | 2.40 | 4.65 | 2.96 |
| efficiency | 0.59 | 0.61 | 0.59 | 0.33 | 0.41 | 0.35 | 0.27 | 0.36 | 0.30 |
| flow betweenness* | 12.38 | 12.67 | 12.45 | 6.31 | 8.78 | 6.93 | 4.75 | 13.50 | 6.94 |

*normalized values, flow betweenness was measured for each actor across the entire network on the basis of symmetrical valued data.*

people were acknowledged leaders because of corresponding with more people and by taking a brokerage role in their communication with their peers. In the exploratory project studied here it becomes obvious that the four people who were acknowledged leaders—though to a different degree—showed commitment to more people and communicated with more remote and mutually unconnected people. They extended their commitment across team boundaries and thus managed to gain more control of the information flows than their peers. In order to avoid determinism, it has to be stressed that we do not draw these conclusions on the basis of the content and quality of communication, but simply from the very structure of communication.

## Team Performance

Team performance was measured by peer-to-team vote, that is, each of the sixteen team members was asked to rate the performance of all four teams. Interestingly, the number of votes that each team obtained parallels the number of votes that the leaders received from their peers in each team (Table 3). While the sales team won the overall performance evaluation, all four team members agreed on one person being in lead of the team. In contrast, the development team scored lowest in the winner election, and only one student acknowledged leadership. One implication from this finding is the proposition that leadership is closely associated with group performance. Given the small sample size of only four teams, however, such a finding should only be accepted as a preliminary hypothesis, rather than proven evidence. But why did the sales team win?

In order to test the brokerage hypothesis on team performance, the 16-by-16 actor matrices were aggregated into 4-by-4 group-membership (team) matrices. These reduced affiliation matrices formed the basis for analysis. First, the frequency and direction of message exchanges within and between groups were analyzed. To do this, the flow of communication that is directed to the team itself (so called loops) was compared with the flow directed towards other teams. This outward communication ratio may then be

*Table 3. Peer-to-team ratings of team performance*

| team | overall score (no. of votes) |
| --- | --- |
| sales | 250 |
| marketing | 192 |
| international business | 189 |
| development | 172 |

*Table 4. Outward communication ratio (external/internal communication)*

| | meeting | desktop e-mail | | mobile e-mail | |
| --- | --- | --- | --- | --- | --- |
| | | sent | received | sent | received |
| sales | 1.00 | 1.20 | 1.24 | 1.02 | 0.26 |
| marketing | 0.15 | 0.52 | 0.96 | 0.76 | 0.45 |
| international business | 1.60 | 0.54 | 0.41 | 0.16 | 1.45 |
| development | 0.20 | 0.50 | 0.41 | 0.48 | 3.04 |

interpreted as the relative investment that each team assigns to the other teams as opposed to itself. The ratio is one when a team exchanges the same amount of information (frequency) with other teams as within itself. Values below one indicate relatively higher investment to the team itself than to its environment. Table 4 shows that the sales-team invested the majority of their communication to other teams rather than to itself (messages sent). With both desktop and mobile electronic messages, it is the only team to have a ratio higher than one. With regard to desktop e-mails, it is interesting to see that the team also receives more messages from outside than from its own team members. This result suggests that whereas the other teams invested less communication to the other teams than to themselves, the winner team was the only to communicate more with the teams outside than with itself.

The flow betweenness measure is more sensitive to structural characteristics in the network and was also used to identify the degree of betweenness of the teams in inter-team communication. The measure analyzes how the overall pattern of connectedness influences the actual flow (frequency) of communication and calculates

values for each team indicating the control of this flow. A comparison of the flow betweenness centralities confirms our line of argument (Table 5). The sales-team achieves the highest rates of this measure across all three communication channels. Therefore, it controls the largest proportion of message exchanges throughout the entire project group. In sum, the team with the highest commitment to outward communication and with the greatest betweenness centrality in the overall network took a leader role and was acknowledged as clearly the best performing team. This finding strongly supports the brokerage hypothesis three at the aggregate level of groups and not only of individuals.

## Communication Media

Finally, the project was designed to test for differences in the use of distinct communication channels. In the concluding questionnaire, students were asked to rate the effectiveness of each communication channel and to state the reasons for using a particular channel for which kind of transaction. On a four-point rating scale, meetings where qualified most effective: they scored 3.81,

*Table 5. Flow betweenness measures for the project teams*

|  | Face-to-face | Desktop e-mails | Mobile e-mails |
|---|---|---|---|
| sales | 3.00 | 2.12 | 3.74 |
| marketing | 0.25 | 1.50 | 1.84 |
| international business | 3.00 | 1.97 | 0.82 |
| development | 0.25 | 2.08 | 0.76 |

*Table 6. QAP analysis of correlation between communication media*

| Pearson Correlation | Value | Sign. | Avg. | SD | P(large) | P(small) | N perm |
|---|---|---|---|---|---|---|---|
| desktop e-mails * meetings | 0.542 | 0.000 | -0.003 | 0.089 | 0.000 | 1.000 | 2500 |
| mobile e-mails * meetings | 0.523 | 0.000 | -0.000 | 0.087 | 0.000 | 1.000 | 2500 |
| mobile * desktop e-mails | 0.418 | 0.000 | 0.001 | 0.100 | 0.000 | 1.000 | 2500 |

whereas stationary e-mails only scored 3.44 and mobile e-mails 2.38 points on average. Meetings were generally preferred for bargaining the terms of trade, such as budget splits and work delivery. Furthermore, they were better suited to discuss complex matter among various people. Students consistently found electronic one-way messaging inadequate for communication related to creativity, bargaining, and decision taking. In contrast to meetings, mobile e-mails were mainly sent for quick and spontaneous coordination, especially during travel. In all other cases, stationary e-mails outweighed mobile communication. E-mails sent over the desktop were bigger than those sent via mobile devices. The average size of a stationary e-mail was 119.5 kb, while an average mobile e-mail had only 4.1 kb, which is about thirty times less the volume than that of desktop messages. Attachments, such as product specifications, could be handled far easier with a regular desktop than with the mobile devices. Thus, students economized on the comfort, quickness, and the possibility to attach documents and electronic work material to e-mails. In sum, while on the one hand, meetings were clearly found to be superior instruments to handle complex communication (e.g., generating ideas, bargaining, decision taking), electronic messaging was used far more frequently and widely across the group. This finding supports hypothesis four that complex coordination will more likely be realized in meetings if there actually is a possibility to meet.

Despite these differences in frequency, volume, and purpose, there were also a number of commonalities between the use of these media. In a temporal perspective, though there were far more stationary than mobile e-mails, the distribution of the messages was similar over time: mobile and stationary e-mails followed the same temporal pattern and were correlated with $r = 0.68$ ($p <$ 0.01, $N = 33$; see also Schrott & Glückler, 2004). Moreover, we used the quadratic assignment procedure (QAP) in order to check for co-variance between the three communication relations and

to see whether different communication relations supported different patterns of interaction (Krackhardt, 1987). The QAP analysis reported in Table 6 shows that the three communication media meetings, mobile e-mails, and desktop e-mails are highly correlated. In all cases the 2,500 random permutations of the matrices did not produce a single random correlation that exceeded the observed values. Therefore, with significance at level 0.01, the three matrices are statistically associated with each other, that is, they reflect the same communication pattern. The students that committed themselves to other students with meetings were most likely to also commit their mobile and desktop e-mails to these students. Although communication spread across different media, this does not imply that the different media served different communication relations. In conclusion, stationary and mobile electronic communications complement and support existing exchange relations. They are, however, not a means of creating different communication networks or facilitating exchange against established patterns. This finding disproves hypothesis five and is an important proposition for further research: it calls for modest expectations about the flattening of hierarchies or existing communication networks through electronic media (Weisband, Schenider, & Connolly, 1995). Moreover, this finding supports theoretical propositions about the evolving naturalness of electronic communication media by means of schema alignment and cognitive adaptation, as theorized in a psychobiological model of computer-mediated communication (Kock, 2004).

## DISCUSSION AND CONCLUSION

This article has focused on how people structure work relations in a project that requires a certain division of labor within and between the participating teams. In particular, three questions were at the core of analysis:

- Does communication brokerage yield the acknowledgment of leadership?
- Does team brokerage increase group performance?
- Do different communication media affect the flow of communication in different ways?

This research found that leaders, as well as the winning team, had stronger brokerage positions in the network of communication flow. Moreover, personal face-to-face communication was preferred to communicate complex matter such as budget negotiation, creative debate for solutions, and conflict resolution. Despite the fact that students reported meetings to be more adequate to manage complex and creative aspects of their work, they invested most of their communication in electronic messages. However, there was no support for the hypothesis that electronic communication leads to different patterns of communication, as for instance, less hierarchical or more team-boundary spanning communication. A comparison based on the quadratic assignment procedure (QAP) showed that the communication patterns of meetings, e-mails sent over desktops, and e-mails sent from mobile devices reflected nearly identical communication structures.

There are a number of limitations to this research. The student experiment served as an incident of exploration for a new approach to these questions by adopting a network theoretical perspective. Although the findings confirm the network theoretical concepts of the structural hole approach (Burt, 1992), they are somewhat limited to generalization. First, sample size was limited to sixteen team workers in one project. This small size precludes any application of inferential statistics and thus limits statistical generalization. The primary purpose of this examination, however, was not to test given criteria for general validity, but to explore the propositions of a network approach to virtual team dynamics. Given the remarkable coherence of results in the experiment, this should stimulate empirical analyses

with larger samples. Second, a social experiment is quite an artificial context, which cannot fully represent or even substitute fieldwork in real work settings. However, this experiment has set up a realistic project task and has taken care of equal interdependence between the subgroups. Moreover, communication and coordination was repeatedly re-stimulated through external interventions to invoke coordination challenges similar to real project work. The fact that the students shared the same cultural background and worked at the same university restricts inferences from this simulation to the real world of international virtual teams. Nonetheless, most communication was realized electronically and it was also the electronic communication that made role differences between leaders and peers more visible than in face-to-face meetings. Finally, this article has not employed a dynamic perspective on communication and thus misses to grasp variations and transformations of communication patterns over time. Future research should focus on the evolution of network structures in order to understand more deeply the processes of differentiation within networks of project collaborators (Kilduff & Tsai, 2003). In conclusion, the findings reported here should be interpreted as propositions for future research rather than trans-contextual generalizations.

The search for measurable operations of theoretical concepts bears the risk of measuring artifacts without meaning. Communication activity in terms of frequency and structure is not a research goal for its on sake. Instead, researchers address communication relations as expressions of and predictors for the quality of cooperation and performance. However, we have to be careful about the implicit inference from the level of communication on the quality of cooperation. Since communication and performance are often treated as synonyms, management practice might run the risk of wrongly promoting the level of communication in order to enhance cooperation (Sarker & Sahay, 2003). Communication may only be a necessary condition for team collaboration and performance rather than a sufficient condition. In the experimental context, we succeeded in identifying a clear link between communication structure and the concepts of leadership and performance. Generally, it is important to distinguish the means from the ends.

Our findings confirm the brokerage-hypothesis in network theory. Individual leaders as well as the winning team displayed the highest degrees of network efficiency and flow betweenness. They served as brokers for their teams and managed the coordination with the other teams. Burt, Hogarth, and Michaud (2000) provided evidence that structural hole theory seems viable also in contexts other than the American context. French managers displayed the same network structures and were equally associated with performance as in American surveys. This experiment contributes to leadership research with respect to another aspect. Despite relative homogeneity between students and groups, a division of labor emerged between peer members in a group. This division of labor clearly evolved on the basis of emergent patterns of communication because there were no predetermined status or role differences assigned to the students. Moreover, leadership can thus be inferred to some degree as voluntary and consensus-based. It evolves as a result of collective action and not as a result of individual ambition because other team members could have bridged structural holes themselves and thus limited the broker position of the actual leader, if they had bothered about emerging leadership. Instead, they acknowledged the leadership role to one co-worker in order to render their collaboration more effective.

With respect to social theory, it has to be pointed out that our findings are very much in support of a non-deterministic, contextual understanding of social action. Our analysis suggests that it is not necessarily personal traits that determine social behavior. Instead, the way individuals relate to their environment accounted for the role they occupied. Leadership, then, was not determined by personality, but open to any willing individual if he or she developed the corresponding communication pattern within his or her work environment. Ahuja, Galleta, and Carley (2003) support our argument through the research they have carried out on e-mail communication structures in virtual R&D groups. They found that group centrality was a better predictor of performance than any of the individual characteristics considered. In support of this eventual evidence, this article has tried to break ground for network theory as an alternative approach to research on leadership and performance in virtual teams. The findings also suggest pledging further effort to study communication networks through in-depth structural analysis in corporate environments (Krackhardt & Hanson, 1993; Cross et al., 2001). Knowledge officers should focus their attention on the analysis of network structure in order to gain more insights into the dynamics of virtual corporate networks and to take appropriate measures for the support of such networks.

## ACKNOWLEDGMENT

The authors are grateful for the technical and financial support from T-Mobile.

## REFERENCES

Ahuja, M. K., Galleta, D. F., & Carley, K. M. (2003). Individual centrality and performance in virtual R&D groups: An empirical study. *Management Science, 49*, 21-38.

Baker, W. E., & Faulkner, R. R. (2004). Social networks and loss of capital. *Social Networks, 26*, 91-111.

Borgatti, S. P. (1997). Structural holes: Unpacking Burt's redundancy measures. *Connections, 20*, 35-38.

Borgatti, S. P., Everett, M. G., & Freeman, L. (2002). *Ucinet 6 for Windows*. Harvard: Analytic Technologies.

Burt, R. (1992). *Structural holes: The social structure of competition*. London: Harvard University Press.

Burt, R. (1997). The contingent value of social capital. *Administrative Science Quarterly, 42*, 339-65.

Burt, R., Hogarth, R. M., & Michaud, C. (2000). The social capital of French and American managers. *Organization Science, 11*, 123-47.

Burt, R., Janotta, J. E., & Mahoney, J. (1998). Personality correlates of structural holes. *Social Networks, 20*, 63-87.

Cascio, W. F., & Shurygailo, S. (2003). E-leadership and virtual teams. *Organizational Dynamics, 31*, 362-76.

Cross, R., Parker, A., Prusak, L., & Borgatti, S. P. (2001). Knowing what we know, supporting knowledge creation and sharing in social networks. *Organizational Dynamics, 30*, 100-20.

Cross, R., & Prusak, L. (2002). The people who make organizations go - or stop. *Harvard Business Review, June*, 5-12.

Cummings, J. N., & Cross, R. (2003). Structural properties of work groups and their consequences for performance. *Social Networks, 25*, 197-210.

Dubrovsky, V. J., Kiesler, S., & Sethna, B. N. (1991). The equalization phenomenon: Status effects in computer-mediated and face-to-face decision making groups. *Human-Computer Interaction, 6*, 119-46.

Freeman, L. C., Borgatti, S. P., & White, D. R. (1991). Centrality in valued graphs: A measure of betweenness based on network flow. *Social Networks, 13*, 141-54.

Grabher, G. (2002). The project ecology of advertising: Talents, tasks, and teams. *Regional Studies, 36*, 245-62.

Grabher, G. (2004). Learning in projects, remembering in networks? Communality, sociality, and connectivity in project ecologies. *European Urban and Regional Studies, 11*, 103-23.

Granovetter, M. (1992). Problems of explanation in economic sociology. In N. Nohria & R. G. Eccles (Eds), *Networks and organisations: Structure, form, and action* (pp. 25-56). Cambridge, MA: Harvard Business School.

Guzzo, R. A., & Dickson, M. W. (1996). Teams in organizations: Recent research on performance and effectiveness. *Annual Review of Psychology, 47*, 307-38.

Hansen, M. T. (1999). The search-transfer problem: The role of weak ties in sharing knowledge across organizations subunits. *Administrative Science Quarterly, 44*, 82-111.

Jarvenpaa, S. L., & Leidner, D. E. (1999). Communication and trust in global virtual teams. *Organization Science, 10*, 791-815.

Kayworth, T. R., & Leidner, D. E. (2002). Leadership effectiveness in global virtual teams. *Journal of Management Information Systems, 18*, 7-40.

Kilduff, M., & Krackhardt, D. (1994). Bringing the individual back in: A structural analysis of the internal market for reputation in organizations. *Academy of Management Journal, 37*, 87-108.

Kilduff, M., & Tsai, W. (2003). *Social networks and organizations*. London: Sage.

Knoke, D., & Kuklinski, J. H. (1991). Network analysis: Basic concepts. In G. Thompson, J. Frances, R. Levacic, & J. Mitchell (Eds), *Markets, hierarchies and networks* (pp. 173-82). London: Sage.

Kock, N. (2004). The psychobiological model: Towards a new theory of computer-mediated communication based on Darwinian evolution. *Organization Science, 15*, 327-48.

Krackhardt, D. (1987). QAP partialling as a test of spuriousness. *Social Networks, 9*, 171-86.

Krackhardt, D., & Hanson, J. (1993). Informal networks: The company behind the chart. *Harvard Business Review, 71*, 104-11.

McElroy, J. C. (1982). A typology of attribution leadership research. *Academy of Management Review, 7*, 413-17.

McElroy, J. C., & Shrader, C. B. (1986). Attribution theories of leadership and network analysis. *Journal of Management, 12*, 351-62.

Mitchell, J. C. (1969). The concept and use of social networks. In J. C. Mitchell (Ed.), *Social networks in urban situations. Analyses of personal relationships in central African towns* (pp. 1-50). Manchester: Manchester University Press.

Mizruchi, M. S. (1994). Social network analysis: Recent achievements and current controversies. *Acta Sociologica, 37*, 329- 43.

Montoya-Weiss, M., Massey, A. P., & Song, M. (2001). Getting it together: Temporal coordination and conflict management in global virtual teams. *Academy of Management Journal, 44*, 1251-63.

Pfeffer, J., & Salancik, G. R. (1978). *The external control of organizations.* New York: Harper and Row.

Pinsonneault, A., & Caya, O. (2005). Virtual teams: What we know, what we don't know. *International Journal of e-Collaboration, 1*, 1-16.

Reagans, R., & Zuckerman, E. W. (2001). Networks, diversity, and productivity: The social capital of corporate R&D teams. *Organization Science, 12*, 502-17.

Sarker, S., & Sahay, S. (2003). Understanding virtual team development: an interpretive study. *Journal of the Association for Information Systems, 4*, 1-38.

Sayer, A. (2000). *Realism and social science.* London: Sage.

Schrott, G., & Glückler, J. (2004). What makes mobile computer supported cooperative work mobile? Towards a better understanding of cooperative mobile interactions. *International Journal of Human-Computer Studies, 60*, 737-52.

Sorenson, O., Rivkin, J. W., & Fleming, L. (2005) *Informational complexity and the flow of knowledge across social boundaries.* Paper in Evolutionary Economic Geography. Utrecht: University of Utrecht.

Sparrowe, R. T., Liden, R. C., Wayne, S. J., & Kraimer, M. L. (2001). Social networks and the performance of individuals and groups. *Academy of Management Journal, 44*, 316-25.

Sproull, L., & Kiesler, S. (1986). Reduceing social context cues: Electronic mail in organizational communication. *Management Science, 32*, 1492-512.

Staw, B. M. (1975). Attribution of the causes of performance: A new alternative interpretation of cross-sectional research on organizations. *Organizational Behavior and Human Performance, 13*, 414-32.

Townsend, A. M., DeMarie, S. M., & Hendrickson, A. R. (1998). Virtual teams: Technology and the workplace of the future. *Academy of Management Executive, 12*, 17-28.

Tushman, M. L. (1979). Work characteristics and subunit communication structure: A contingency analysis. *Administrative Science Quarterly, 24*, 82-98.

Warkentin, M., & Beranek, P. M. (1999). Training to improve virtual team communication. *Information Systems Journal, 9*, 271-89.

Weisband, S., Schenider, S., & Connolly, T. (1995). Computer-mediated communication and social information: Status salience and status differences. *Academy of Management Journal, 38*, 1124-51.

Yoo, Y., & Alavi, M. (2004). Emergent leadership in virtual teams: What do emergent leaders do? *Information and Organization, 14*, 27-58.

Zigurs, I. (2003). Leadership in virtual teams: Oxymoron or opportunity? *Organizational Dynamics, 31*, 339-51.

# Section III
# Collaborative Production and Engineering

# Chapter XI
# Intelligent Agents for Supporting Supply Chain Collaborative Technologies[1]

**Walter Rodriguez**
*Florida Gulf Coast University, USA*

**Janusz Zalewski**
*Florida Gulf Coast University, USA*

**Elias Kirche**
*Florida Gulf Coast University, USA*

## ABSTRACT

*This paper presents a new concept for supporting electronic collaboration, operations, and relationships among trading partners in the value chain without hindering human autonomy. Although autonomous intelligent-agents, or electronic robots (e-bots), can be used to inform this endeavor, the paper advocates the development of e-sensors, i.e., software based units with capabilities beyond intelligent-agent's functionality. E-sensors are hardware-software capable of perceiving, reacting and learning from its interactive experience thorough the supply chain, rather than just searching for data and information through the network and reacting to it. E-sensors can help avoid the 'bullwhip' effect. The paper briefly reviews the related intelligent-agent and supply-chain literature and the technological gap between fields. It articulates a demand-driven, sense-and-response system for sustaining e-collaboration and e-business operations as well as monitoring products and processes. As a proof of concept, this research aimed a test solution at a single supply-chain partner within one stage of the process.*

# INTRODUCTION: FROM E-BOTS TO E-SENSORS

Today's supply-chain information technologies (IT) allow managers to track and gather intelligence about their customers purchasing habits. In addition to the widely implemented point-of-sale Universal Product Code (UPC) barcode devices, current IT infrastructure may include retail radio frequency identification (RFID) devices and electronic tagging to track product flow. These technologies aid mainly in the marketing and replenishment efforts. However, tracking partners' behavior and decisions in real-time requires an integrated IT infrastructure to support a continuous intelligent sense and response system for collaborative processes in supply chain.

As e-business and e-commerce grows, so has the need to focus attention on the: (1) electronic communications between e-partners; (2) operational transactions (e.g., sales, purchasing, communications, inventory, customer service, ordering, submitting, checking-status, and sourcing, among others); and (3) monitoring improvements in the supply (supply, demand, value) chain of products, systems, and services (Gaither and Fraizer, 2002). Integrating continuous communication protocols and operational considerations early on in the enterprise design process would greatly improve the performance of e-collaboration technologies. It is particularly important to examine the resources and systems that support the electronic communications, and collaborative efforts among partners in the supply-chain. For example, artificial intelligent agents (e-bots) can be deployed throughout the supply chain to seek data and information about competitive pricing; or e-bots can search for the cheapest supplier for a given product and even compare characteristics and functionality. For this reason, the concept of an *agent* is important in both the Artificial Intelligence (AI) and the e-Operations fields.

The term "intelligent agent" or "e-bot" denotes a software system that enjoys at least one of the following properties: (1) Autonomy; (2) "Social" ability; and (3) Reactivity (Wooldridge and Jennings, 1995). Normally, agents are thought to be autonomous because they are capable to operate without direct intervention of people and have some level of control over their own actions (Castelfranchi, 1995). In addition, agents may have the functionality to interact with other agents and automated systems via an agent-communication language (Genesereth and Ketchpel, 1994). This agent attribute is termed here *e-sociability* for its ability to interact with either people, or systems (software).

The next evolution of the intelligent agent concept is the development of integrated hardware-software systems that may be specifically designed to sense (perceive) and respond (act) within certain pre-defined operational constrains and factors, and respond in a real-timely fashion to changes (not a just-in-time fashion) occurring throughout the supply chain. These integrated hardware-software systems are termed *e-sensors*, in this paper. Indeed there is a real opportunity for process innovation and most likely organizations will need to create new business applications to put e-sensors at the centre of a process if they want to be competitive in this new supply chain environment. Aside from asset tracking, each industry will have specialized applications of e-sensors that cannot be generalized. Before getting into the e-sensors details, let's review some key supply chain management (SCM) issues relevant to this discussion.

# SUPPLY CHAIN MANAGEMENT IN THE E-COLLABORATION CONTEXT

*"SCM is the art and science of creating and accentuating synergistic relationships among the trading partners in supply and distribution channels with the common shared objective of delivering products and services to the 'right customer' at the 'right time.'"* (Vakharia, 2002)

In the e-collaboration/e-business context, Supply Chain Management (SCM) is the operations management discipline concerned with these synergistic communications, relationships, processes and operations in the competitive Internet enterprise. SCM involves studying the movement of physical materials and electronic information and communications----including transportation, logistics and information-flow management to improve operational efficiencies, effectiveness and profitability. SCM consists in the strategies and technologies for developing and integrating the operations, communications and relationships among the e-trading partners (producers, manufacturers, services providers, suppliers, sellers, wholesalers, distributors, purchasing agents, logisticians, consultants, shipping agents, deliverers, retailers, traders and customers) as well as improving their operations throughout the products' or services' chain.

Integrated e-business SCM can enhance decision-making by collecting real-time information as well as assessing and analyzing data and information that facilitate collaboration among trading partners in the supply chain. "To achieve joint optimization of key SCM decisions, it is preferable that there be a free flow of all relevant information across the entire chain leading to a comprehensive analysis" (Vakharia, 2002). As shown in Figure 1, IT systems, such as, Enterprise Resource Planning (ERP), Point of Sale (POS), and Vendor Managed Inventory (VMI) systems permit and, to some extend, automate information sharing.

The advent of reliable communication technologies has forced business partners to rethink their strategies as well as change the nature of the relationships with suppliers and customers. Companies that have made the shift have benefited from "reduced operating expenses, increased revenue growth, and improved customers levels," according to IBM ERP/Supply Management Division (Cross, 2000). According to the same source, the companies that have implemented supply chain improvement projects have been able to increase forecast accuracy and achieve significant inventory reduction. Some of the more recent initiatives being implemented include: supply-and-demand auctions, integrated collaborative product design (CAD/CAM), cross-enterprise

*Figure 1. Information flow using electronic information technologies in the supply chain (after Burke and Vakharia, 2002; Vakharia, 2002)*

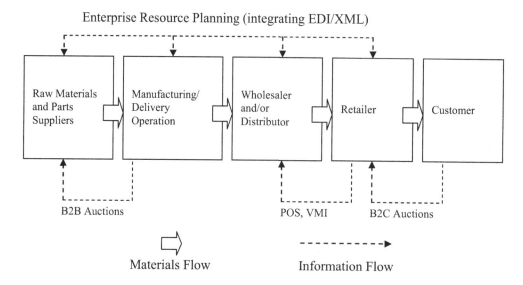

workflow processes, and demand management collaboration. In addition, some companies are even deploying SCM as an offensive tactic to gain a competitive edge (Cross, 2000). We refer the reader to an important literature review recently compiled by Meixell and Gargeya (2005) on decision support models used for the design of global supply chains.

## PARADIGM SHIFT: FROM 'PUSH' (SCM) TO 'PULL' (SRS)

*"We are not smart enough to predict the future, so we have to get better at reacting to it more quickly."* (GE saying quoted by Haeckel, 1999)

E-business forces have shifted both the enterprise landscape and the competitive power from the providers of goods and information (makers, suppliers, distributors and retailers) to the purchasers of goods and information (customers). For this reason, e-businesses must collaborate electronically and sense-and-respond very quickly to the individual customer's needs and wants. So, rather than considering SCM analysis from the "supply" perspective, some researchers and practitioners advocate analyzing the market operations from the "demand" perspective: sensing-and-responding to the consumer changing needs and wants by quickly collaborating and communicating in real-time throughout the chain. Researchers argue that e-businesses should measure and track customers' demand for products and services, rather than relying solely on demand forecasting models.

M. Fisher (1997) studied the root cause of poor performance in supply chain management and the need to understand the demand for products in designing a supply chain. Functional products with stable, predictable demand and long life cycle require a supply chain with focus almost exclusively on minimizing physical costs - a crucial goal given the price sensitivity of most functional products. In this environment, firms employ enterprise resource planning systems (ERP) to coordinate production, scheduling and delivery of products to enable the entire supply chain to minimize costs and maximize production efficiency. The crucial flow of information is internal, within the supply chain. However, the uncertain market reaction to innovation increases the risk of shortages or excess supplies for innovative products. Furthermore, the high profit margins and the importance of early sales in establishing market share for new products, the short product life cycles increasing the risk of obsolescence and the cost of excess supplies, require that innovative product have a responsive supply chain that focuses on flexibility and speed of response of the supplier. The critical decision to be made about inventory and capacity is not about minimizing costs, but where in the chain to position inventory and available production capacity in order to hedge against uncertain demand. The crucial flow of information occurs not only within the chain but also from the market place to the chain.

While Selen and Soliman (2002) advocate a demand-driven model, Vakharia (2002) argues that push (supply) and pull (demand) concepts apply in different settings. That is, since businesses offering mature products have developed accurate demand forecasts for products with predictable life-cycles, they may rely more heavily on forecasting models. While businesses offering new products, with unpredictable short cycles, are better off operating their chains as a pull (demand) system, because it's harder to develop accurate demand forecasts for these new (or fluctuating demand) products.

The difficulty in synchronizing a supply chain to deliver the right product at the right time is caused by the distortion of information traveling upstream the supply chain. One of the most discussed phenomena in e-Operations field is the called the Forrester (1958) or 'bullwhip' effect which portrays the supply chain's tendency to amplify or delay product demand information throughout the chain (Sahin and Robinson, 2002). For instance, a particular supplier may receive a large order for their product and then decides to replenish the products sold. This action provides the quantity to restock the depleted products, plus some additional inventory to compensate for potential variability in demand. The overstated order and adjustments are passed throughout the supply chain causing demand amplification. At some point, the supply-chain partners loose track of the actual customer demand.

Lee et al. (1997) proved that demand variability can be amplified in the supply chain as orders are passed from retailers to distributors and producers. Because most retailers do not know their demand with certainty, they have to make their decisions based on demand forecast. When it is not very accurate, the errors in the retailers forecast are passed to the supplier in the form of distorted order. They found that sharing information alone would provide cost savings and inventory reduction. Other factors that contribute to the distortion of information is over reliance on price promotion, use of outdated inventory models, lack of sharing information with partners and inadequate forecasting methods.

An important question in supply chain research is whether the bullwhip effect can be preventable. Chen et al (2000) quantified the bullwhip effect for a multi-stage system and found that the bullwhip effect could be reduced but not completely eliminated, by sharing demand among all parties in the supply chain. Zhao et al (2002) also studied the impact of the bullwhip effect and concluded that sharing information increases the economical efficiency of the supply chain. In a later study, Chen (2005) found that through forecast sharing the bullwhip effect can be further reduced by eliminating the need for the supplier to guess the retailer's underlying ordering policy.

The causes of uncertainty and variability of information leading to inefficiency and waste in the supply chain can be traced to demand forecasting methods, lead-time, batch ordering processes, price fluctuation and inflated orders. One of the most common ways to increase synchronization among partners is to provide at each stage of the supply chain with complete information on the actual customer demand. Although this sharing of information will reduce the bullwhip effect, it will not completely eliminate it (Simchi-Levy et al 2003). Lee et al (1997-a, 2004) suggests a framework for supply chain coordination initiatives which included using electronic data interchange (EDI), internet, computer assisted ordering (CAO), and sharing capacity and inventory data among other initiatives. Another important way to achieve this objective is to automate collection of Point-of-Sale data (POS) in a central database and share with all partners in real-time e-business environment. Therefore, efficient information acquisition and sharing is the key to creating value and reducing waste in many operations. A specially designed adaptive or sense-and-response system may help provide the correct information throughout the supply chain. The proposed system would have two important system functions – maintaining timely information sharing across the supply chain and facilitating the synchronization of the entire chain.

Haeckel (1999) indicates that "unpredictable, discontinuous change is an unavoidable consequence of doing business in the Information Age." And, since this "intense turbulence demands fast---even instantaneous---response," businesses must manage their operations as adaptive systems. Thus, adaptive (sense-and-response) models may help companies systematically deal with the unexpected circumstances; particularly, e-businesses need to be able to anticipate and preempt sensed problems.

## SENSE-AND-RESPONSE SYSTEM (SRS) MODEL AND FRAMEWORK

Figure 2 shows the proposed SRS model and framework for integrating real-time electronic communications, information-sharing, and materials-flow updating as well as monitoring the e-supply/demand/value chain---towards a new e-collaboration paradigm. The "e-sensors" in the diagram are computer programs (software code) and its associated data and information collection devices (hardware) and communication interfaces. These sensors are designed for e-collaboration, data-capturing (sensing), and information-sharing, monitoring and evaluating data (input) throughout the value chain. Ultimately, this approach would result in semi-automated analysis and action (response) when a set of inputs are determined (sensed) without hindering human autonomy. That is, the sensors will gather the data and monitor and evaluate the exchange in information between designated servers in the e-partners (suppliers and distribution channel) networks. Sensors will adjust plans and re-allocate resources and distribution routes when changes within established parameters are indicated. In addition, sensors will signal human monitors (operations or supply-chain managers) when changes are outside the established parameters. The main advantage of this approach is that sensors will be capable of assessing huge amounts of data and information quickly to respond to changes in the chain environment (supply and demand) without hindering human autonomy. Particularly, e-sensors can provide the real-time information needed to prevent the bullwhip effect.

Companies like Cisco, Dell, IBM and Wal-Mart have led the development of responsive global supply chains. These companies and a few others have discovered the advantages of monitoring changes in near real-time. By doing so, they have been able to maintain low inventories, implement lean production and manufacturing operations, and even defer building and assembly resulting in lower costs and increase responsiveness to variable customer demands. This practice can be extended to incorporate e-sensors and human collaborators throughout the value chain and perceive and react to the demands.

## SYSTEM ARCHITECTURE AND IMPLEMENTATION

To develop the implementation of the entire framework outlined in Figure 2 one faces involvement of multiple supply-chain partners and months, if not years, of work just to develop a reliable communication infrastructure. In order to provide an immediate viable solution to test the concepts, in this research, the authors aimed at a single supply-chain partner/company at only one stage illustrated in Figure 2, to provide interfaces to the immediate preceding and the immediate succeeding stage (Kirche et al., 2005). Choosing a wholesaler/distributor (the middle box in Figure 2) as the company to automate its information flows and material flows with e-sensors and e-controls interfacing to the manufacturers and retailers, as well as to internal storage and distribution centers, we developed the overall design architecture as illustrated in Figure 3. The selected communication architecture is based on CORBA (Common Object Request Broker Architecture), a standard solution available from multiple vendors (Bolton, 2002). CORBA is an open system middleware with high scalability and potentially can serve an unlimited number of players and virtually any number of business processes and partners in the supply chain environment. As a communication infrastructure, it enables an integrated view of the production and distribution processes for an efficient demand management. Other benefits include continuous availability, business integration, resources availability on demand, and worldwide accessibility.

The architecture presented in Figure 3 gives the wholesaler/distributor direct access to the

*Figure 2. SRS framework for integrating communication, information and materials flow and monitoring the e-business supply/demand chain*

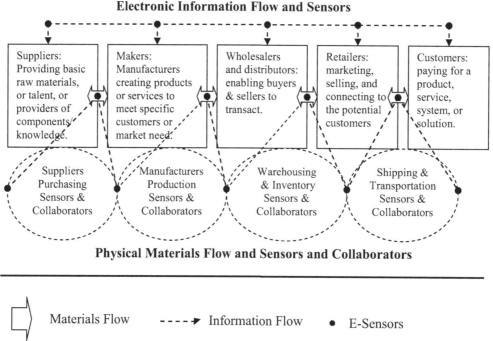

assembly lines of the manufacturers and their shipping/transportation data via the Operational Data Server. Full communication with the retailers is available. The wholesaler/distributor company does have itself full control over their Financial Data Server and Optimization Server. The detailed functions of this architecture are described in (Kirche et al., 2005).

The goal of the real-time system based on this architecture is to dynamically integrate end-to-end processes across the organization (key partners, manufacturers and retailers) to respond with speed to customer changes and market requirements. The real-time CORBA framework enables employees to view current process capability and load on the system and provide immediate information to customers, by enabling tuning of resources and balancing workloads to maximize production efficiency and adapt to dynamically changing environment.

A sample implementation of the system architecture from Figure 3 is presented in the form of a context diagram in Figure 4. To achieve the project's objective, that is, remote data access to enterprise networks with e-sensors/e-controls, we provide the capability of accessing enterprise-wide systems from a remote location or a vehicle, for both customers and employees. The overall view of the system is as follows:

- when access to manufacturers from Figure 2 is considered, the focus can be on *plant access* for immediate availability of data and functions of the system; in that case, a remote *e-sensor/e-control* application using LabVIEW data acquisition software (Sokoloff, 2004) comes into play, with graphical user interface capable of interacting with remote users connected via the Internet
- when access to warehousing from Figure 2 is considered, the focus can be on *business*

*Figure 3. Architecture of distributed services for the wholesaler or distributor (after Kirche et al.)*

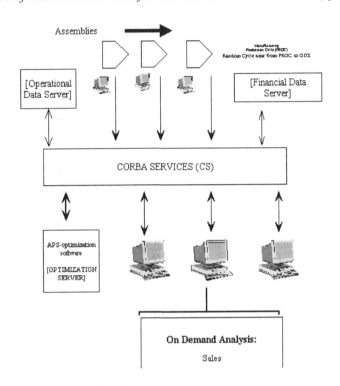

*Figure 4. Context diagram of the system being implemented (DAQ stands for data acquisition and control, 802.11 stands for an IEEE Std 802.11 for wireless networks, SQL stands for standard query language)*

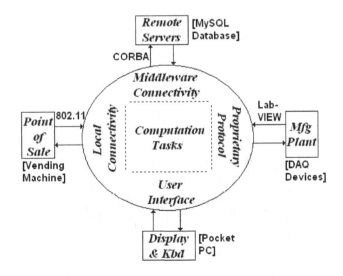

*integration* via a multi-purpose enterprise-wide network; in that case, a CORBA based framework is employed for a remote access to data objects identified as *e-sensors*, that can be stored on typical SQL database servers (Kirche et al., 2005).

From the network operation and connectivity perspective, e-sensors and e-controls provide business services, so they play the role of servers. Access to servers in this system is implemented via two general kinds of clients:

- when focus is on the *customer access* to obtain services, a cell phone location-aware application for business transactions has been developed, using order services as an example
- when focus is on the *employee access* to obtain services, such as conducting business on the road, a wireless PDA application for remote vending machine access, has been developed, using the IEEE Std 802.11 wireless network protocol.

Several tests have been conducted to check behavior and performance of all four applications listed above and presented in Figure 4. For concision, it shows only a sample behavior of a PDA client via connectivity/performance test, in Figure 5. The graph shows how long it takes for the server to receive the connection request from the client application after the application was started. It is marked "Connection time". Another bar on the same chart shows how long the program itself took to load completely after being started (marked "Load time"). The connection graph was created to give an indication of how long, on average, one can expect for requests to be acknowledged and accepted by the server. Since all requests are handled the same way as the initial connection, this average connection time reflects sending and receiving of data to and from the client application. The load time is just a measure of performance for the application on the PDA itself. The data collected that way show the feasibility of all applications built within the SRS framework, as presented in Figure 2, for the architecture outlined in Figure 3.

*Figure 5. PDA client connectivity/performance test*

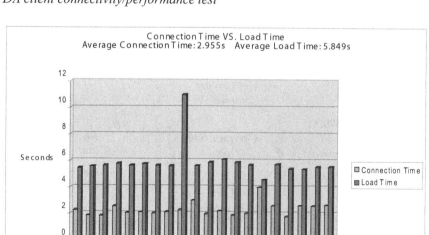

## CONCLUSION

This paper briefly reviewed the current intelligent-agent and supply-chain paradigm and presented a conceptual framework for integrating e-collaboration tools in the operation and monitoring of products and services across value chain networks without hindering human autonomy. The demand-driven, sense-and-response framework model incorporates e-sensors and e-collaborators (humans using communication tools, computer software programs and its associated data-capturing hardware devices) throughout the supply chain. In practice, these e-sensors would be designed for data-capturing (sensing), monitoring and evaluating data (input) throughout the value chain, while humans collaborate and communicate in real-time, as tested in the above solution.

The implications of this new framework are that it enhances current SCM/DCM systems such as Manugistics' Demand Planning System that analyses manufacturing, distribution and sales data against forecasted data, and supports advanced planning systems (APS) for scheduling and Capable-to-Promise (Bixby, Downs and Self, 2006) applications such as Aspen Technology's e-supply chain suite. The addition of SRS sensors would signal human monitors (operations or supply-chain managers) when changes are outside the established parameters. The main advantage of this approach is that sensors would be capable of assessing huge amounts of data and information quickly to respond to changes in the chain environment (supply and demand) without hindering human autonomy.

Ultimately, this approach would result in the semi-automated analysis and action (response) when a set of inputs are determined (sensed) without hindering human autonomy. That is, the e-sensors would gather the data and monitor and evaluate the exchange in information between designated servers in the e-partners (suppliers and distribution channel) networks. E-sensors would adjust plans and re-allocate resources and distri-bution routes when changes within established parameters are indicated. Particularly, the new approach will aid managers in the prevention of the bullwhip effect.

Having real time data is critical in managing supply chain efficiently. Typically companies need to synchronize orders considering type, quantity, location and timing of the delivery in order to reduce waste in the production and delivery process. The data collection and availability provided by the e-sensing infrastructure/architecture will allow for a collaborative environment, improve forecast accuracy and increase cross-enterprise integration among partners in the supply chain. E-sensors will also offer a more proactive solution to current ERP systems by giving them the ability to process in real time relevant constraints and simultaneously order the necessary material type and quantities from multiple sources.

This e-sensor concept opens additional research opportunities within the boundaries of the operations management and information technology fields, particularly in the development of new software-hardware interfaces, real-time data capturing devices and other associated technologies. Finally, it leads to future 'automated decision-making' where IT/operations managers can "embed decision-making capabilities in the normal flow of work" (Davenport and Harris, 2005).

## REFERENCES, SUGGESTED READINGS AND WEB SITES

Bixby, A., Downs, B., and Self, M. (2006). A scheduling and capable-to-promise application for Swift & Company. *Interfaces*, 36(1), 69 – 86.

Burke, G. J., and Vakharia, A.J. (2002). Supply chain management. In H. Bidgoli (Ed.), *Internet Encyclopedia*, New York: John Wiley.

Bresnahan, J. (1998). Supply chain anatomy: The incredible journey. *CIO Enterprise Magazine*,

August 15. [Retrieved from http://www.cio.com site on March 12, 2006.]

Castelfranchi, C. (1995). Guarantees for autonomy in cognitive agent architecture. In Wooldrige, M. and Jennings, N. R. (Eds.), *Intelligent Agents: Theories, Architectures, and Languages*, 890, 56-70. Heidelberg, Germany: Springer-Verlag.

Cheng, F., Ryan, J.K., and Simchi-Levy, D. (2000). Quantifying the 'bullwhip effect' in a supply chain: the impact of forecasting, lead times, and information. *Management Science*, 46(3), 436 – 444.

Chen, L. (2005). *Optimal information acquisition, inventory control, and forecast sharing in operations management*. Dissertation thesis. Stanford, CA: Stanford University.

Cross, Gary J. (2000). How e-business is transforming supply chain management. *Journal of Business Strategy*, 21(2), 36-39.

Davenport, T.H., and Harris, J.G., (2005). Automated decision making comes of age. *MIT Sloan Management Review*, 46(4), 83-89.

Fisher, M. (1997). What is the right supply chain for you? *Harvard Business Review,* March-April, 105-117.

Forrester, J. W. (1958). Industrial dynamics. *Harvard Business Review*, July-August, 37-66.

Frohlich, M.T. (2002). e-Integration in the Supply Chain: Barriers and Performance, *Decision Sciences*, 33(4), 537-556.

Gaither, N. and Frazier, G. (2002). *Operations Management*, 6th Edition, Cincinnati: Southwest.

Genesereth, M. R. and Ketchpel, S.P. (1994). Software agents. *Communications of the ACM*, 37(7), 48-53.

Haeckel, S.H. (1999). *Adaptive Enterprise: Creating and Leading Sense-and-Response Organizations*. Boston, MA: Harvard Business School Press.

Kirche, E., Zalewski, J., Tharp, T. (2005). Real-time sales and operations planning with CORBA: Linking demand management and production Planning. In C.S. Chen, J. Filipe, I. Seruca, J. Cordeiro (Eds.), *Proceedings of the 7th International Conference on Enterprise Information Systems* (pp. 122-129). Washington, DC: IEEE Computer Society Press (in conjunction with ICEIS).

Lee, H., Padmanabhan, V., and Whang, S. (1997). The bullwhip effect. *Sloan Management Review*, 38(3), 93-103.

Lee, H., Padmanabhan, V., and Whang, S. (1997 - a). Information distortion in a supply chain: the bullwhip effect. *Management Science*, 43, 546 – 548.

Lee, H., Padmanabhan, V., and Whang, S. (2004). Information Distortion in a Supply Chain: The Bullwhip Effect/Comments on "Information Distortion in a Supply Chain: The Bullwhip Effect". *Management Science*, 50(12), 1875 – 1894.

Meixell, M.J. and Gargeya, V.B. (2005). Global supply chain design: A literature review and critique. Transportation Research, 41(6), 531-550 [Retrieved on February 15, 2006 from the Science Direct web site resource at http://top25.sciencedirect.com/index.php?subject_area_id=4 .]

Meixell, M.J. (2006). Collaborative Manufacturing for Mass Customization. [Retrieved on February 15 from the George Manson University at http://www.som.gmu.edu/faculty/profiles/mmeixell/collaborative%20Planning%20&%20Mass%20Customization.pdf ]

Sahin, F. and Powell Robinson, E.P. (2002). Flow coordination and information sharing in supply chains: review, implications, and directions for future research. *Decision Sciences*, 33(4), 505-536.

Selen, W., and Soliman, F. (2002). Operations in today's demand chain management framework. *Journal of Operations Management*, 20(6), 667-673.

Schneider, G.P., and Perry, J.T. (2000). *Electronic Commerce*. Cambridge, MA: Course Technology.

Simch-Levy, D., Kaminsky, P., Simchi-Levy, E. (2003). D*esigning and managing the supply chain – concepts, strategies and case studies, Second Edition*. New York: McGraw-Hill.

Vakharia, A.J. (2002). E-business and supply chain management. *Decision Sciences*, 33(4), 495-504.

Wooldridge., M. and Jennings, N.R. (1995). "Intelligent agents: theory and practice." [Retrieved on February 15, 2006 from GRACO web site at http://www.graco.unb.br/alvares/DOUTORADO/disciplinas/feature/agente_definicao.pdf.]

## ENDNOTE

[1]     Based on Rodriguez, W., Zalewski, J., & Kirche, E. (2007). Beyond intelligent agents: E-sensors for supporting supply chain collaboration. *International Journal of E-Collaboration*, 3(2), 1-15.

Chapter XII

# Collaborative Engineering for Enhanced Producibility by Ontology–Based Integration of Design and Production

**Fredrik Elgh**
*Jönköping University, Sweden*

**Staffan Sunnersjö**
*Jönköping University, Sweden*

## ABSTRACT

*Many companies base their business strategy on customized products with a high level of variety and continuous functional improvements. For companies to be able to provide affordable products in a short time and be at the competitive edge, every new design must be adapted to existing production facilities. In order to ensure this, collaboration between engineering design and production engineering has to be supported. With the dispersed organisations of today combined with the increasing amount of information that has to be shared and managed, this collaboration is a critical issue for many companies. In this article, an approach for sharing and managing product and production information is introduced. The results are based on the experiences from a case study at a car manufacturer. By ontology-based integration, work within domains engineering design, production engineering and requirement management at the company was integrated. The main objectives with the integration were: support the formation of requirement specifications for products and processes, improve and simplify the information retrieval for designers and process planners, ensure traceability from changes in product systems to manufacturing systems and vice versa, and finally, eliminate redundant or multiple versions of requirement specifications.*

## INTRODUCTION

Ten years ago, product life cycles in the motor-car industry were such that the development of a new car model usually meant setting up a new assembly line, or even a new manufacturing plant, for the model. This production facility could then be adapted to the requirements of the new model. With today's high product variety and shorter life cycles, this is no longer possible. Instead, new car designs must be adapted to existing production facilities so that they can be used for several car models, often run simultaneously and in an arbitrary, order driven sequence on the same line operated by the same personnel. This change of manufacturing paradigm is illustrated in Figure 1.

This entirely new production paradigm relies on production constraints being well defined, understood and applied by the car designers. Project planning and working practices with frequent interchange of information between production and design departments are a necessity. But manufacturing data and its interrelationships are complex, and there is no universally accepted meaning for terms used in manufacturing (Schlenoff, Ivester, Libes, Denno, & Szykman, 1999). As a result, communication of manufacturing data in a company is afflicted with ambiguous interpretations.

There is also a strong need for a more formalised definition of the manufacturing constraints. A natural way is to represent these constraints as manufacturing requirements analogous to the functional requirements defined by the department for product planning. The designer thus receives a design task together with a requirements list covering both customer specifications and the specifications that certify producibility in existing plants and lines.

### Purpose and Objectives

The purpose of this work was to explore ontology based solutions to handling growing production related information sources, so that relevant information can always be retrieved in a flexible manner for the variety of needs that exist

*Figure 1. Change of manufacturing paradigm results in a need for new methods and tools in the product – production interface. Traditional strategy – A new manufacturing system for every new product. Emerging strategy – Adapt the new products to the manufacturing system that evolves in small steps. Adapted figure from Hannam (1997).*

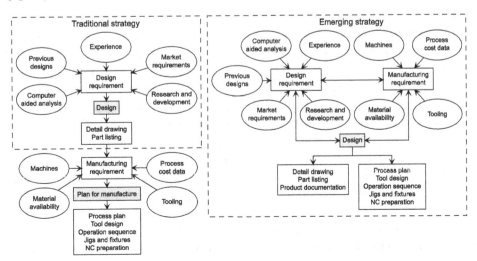

among designers and production engineers. It is important to choose dynamic solutions, which allow the guidelines to change frequently. Such change will occur naturally as product, processes and experiences evolve over time.

The objective is to enable a systematic approach to handling manufacturing requirements. Sharing information is at the core of collaborative engineering. With an ontology approach, work within domains requirement management, production engineering and engineering design can be integrated and their collaboration supported. The main objectives of the proposed approach are to:

- Support the formation of requirement specifications for products and processes by defining an information model including requirement objects, hierarchical tree-structures and links between these.
- Improve and simplify information retrieval for designers and process planners by adding inference functions to the links between requirement objects.
- Allow forward traceability from changes in product systems to manufacturing systems. ("What are the consequences for the manufacturing system if we make these changes in the product systems?")
- Allow backward traceability from changes in manufacturing system to product systems. ("What are the consequences for the product if we make these changes in the manufacturing system?")
- Prevent redundant or multiple versions of requirement specifications, thereby simplifying updating and maintenance of the rule system.

The concepts and tools developed to manage ontologies are proposed in order to realise the modelling of information related to product and process requirements. The feasibility and usefulness of this approach can hardly be evaluated by theoretical reasoning alone. Rather, experimental testing is required. An industrial demonstrator, described in Section *A pilot system*, has thus been built and tested for functionality. In the process of building this demonstrator, a proposal for an information model for rules relating to the manufacture and assembly of motorcars was developed.

## CONCEPTS USED AND RELATED WORK

The suggested systematic approach for management of manufacturing requirements is based on a few well-established concepts. These concepts will be briefly surveyed below, providing an overview of the practice and theory this research is based upon. First, an introduction to collaborative engineering in manufacturing companies is presented. This is followed by introductions to function-means trees, requirement management, information modelling, ontology in knowledge-based systems, and classification of manufacturing processes.

## Collaborative Engineering for Enhanced Producibility

Engineering design is often concerned with striking a good balance between product properties, e.g. performance, and the resources required to manufacture and assemble the product, where the latter aspect is strongly related to cost and lead time. The acronym DFP, Design For Producibility, is used for the process in which a systematic method is used to reach the required functional properties of the product at the same time as good producibility is assured (Elgh, 2007a). The DFP process usually needs to involve several departments simultaneously for the purpose of information and knowledge sharing. In particular, specialists in engineering design need to collaborate with specialists in production engineering to clarify manufacturing constraints and recommendations. Commonly, the engineers of these two branches are not co-located within the company. Further, the organisation for product development can be spread out at different design teams, production units, and first and second tier suppliers. In the most challenging case, this implies collaboration between people working in different domains at different companies over large geographical distances at different times using different methods, tools and concepts in their work. These different types of dispersed organisations, tools, information and knowledge call for new concepts, technologies and solutions for effective and efficient information and knowledge sharing, in order to ensure and enhance the product's producibility.

According to Jacucci, Pawlak, and Sandkuhl (2005), the aim of the research in collaborative engineering is to provide concepts, technologies and solutions for product development in dispersed engineering teams. Collaborative engineering is considered to be the application of the work in the field of Computer Supported Collaborative Work (Lundqvist & Sandkuhl, 2004). The research in the area is based on unsolved problems defined by industrial need, and it addresses technical, social, organisational, and economic aspects of collaborative engineering (Jacucci et al., 2005). The focus of this work is on the technical aspects of an approach for information and knowledge sharing between requirement management, design engineers and production engineers.

## Functions-Means Trees

The aim of functional modelling is to provide an exhaustive and clarifying representation of a product's functions as well as the principles for the realisation of those functions. For this purpose, a graphical representation in the form of a functions-means tree is often created. The logic behind the method is to start by clarifying the details of all product functions and then to proceed to the creation of design solutions. It is an important characteristic that the functions are represented in a solution neutral way so that solutions can be searched with an open mind. A function is defined by means of the commonly used syntax for functional descriptions, i.e. verb + noun. For every function a solution (means) is constructed that by turns can cause sub-functions to be identified. An alternative to functions-means trees is the use of technical system representation. Such use is better suited for products having an input/output character. Functional modelling in various forms has been extensively discussed in literature. Examples include Pahl and Beitz (1996); Hubka, Andreasen, and Eder (1998); and Szykman, Racz, and Sriram (1999).

## Requirement Management

Requirement management is the process of identifying, formulating, allocating, verifying, and managing changes of requirements. Commonly, a distinction is drawn between:

- *Primary requirements*, binding and specified by customers, legislation or other external sources, and
- *Derived requirements,* following from or interpretations of the primary requirements.

In addition, requirements may be *quantitative* or *qualitative,* i.e. defined by measurable quantities or by subjective judgments, respectively. Further, requirements can be classified as *"musts"*, *"wants"* or *"recommendations"*, suggesting three different levels of adherence necessity.

One strong reason for using IT-support to manage requirements is the need for traceability. This implies that changes should propagate to the product definition guided by traceability links. According to Kirkman (1998), a requirement is traceable if one can detect:

- the source that suggested the requirement,
- the reason why the requirement exists,
- what other requirements are related to it,
- how the requirement is related to other information such as function structures, parts, analyses, test results and user documents,
- the decision-making process that led to derivation of the requirement, and
- the status of the requirement.

To map manufacturing requirements for the physical product, Sohlenius (1992) proposes the introduction of a process function domain, with process requirements, in the four domains of the design world (Suh, 1990). However, the focus with this approach is to manage process requirements set by the product. This is in accordance with the traditional strategy and not the emerging strategy at the company in question. Nilsson and Andersson (2004) adopt the new strategy, arguing that manufacturing requirements can be structured according to the product and manufacturing domain. They suggest that the manufacturing structures (processes, functions, functional solutions, and resources) could be used for the structuring manufacturing requirements. However, they do not describe how to support the conceptual phases where different manufacturing alternatives are to be evaluated, or how to model requirements arising from the combination of resources.

## Information Modelling

It is important to distinguish between data, information and knowledge (Figure 2) when discussing information modelling. Data are often described as unprocessed facts, i.e. they are not placed in a context and therefore lack in purpose and relevance. Based on this view, information is regarded as processed data. Information is an aggregation of data that have meaning, implying that the facts have been placed in a context, i.e. the facts have been organised for a purpose. Finally, knowledge is based on information that is contextual, relevant and actionable (Turban & Aronson, 2001).

The development of a manufacturing requirement management system requires the coordination of different concepts of product descriptions, plant resources, manufacturing processes, manufacturing requirements and organisation. Information models can be used to define and communicate these concepts. It also facilitates the coordination and clarification of the relationships between the different concepts, i.e. semantic modelling. Further, the information models are important for the system developers and software programmers. Enhanced Entity Relationships (EER), Express-G and Unified Modelling Language (UML) all have graphical notations and are suitable for the conceptual modelling of information models incorporating semantics.

## Ontology

From a knowledge based systems view, an ontology is a shared understanding with a formal description that is machine executable. When defining an ontology the focus is on "things", not on how to describe data in an efficient way

*Figure 2. The relations between data, information, and knowledge (Turban & Aronson, 2001)*

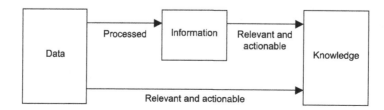

for computer implementations (Noy & McGuinness, 2001). Further, ontologies are broader in scope than semantic data models (Figure 3). An ontology is based on an information model with semantic relationships that has been extended by incorporating different forms of knowledge. The knowledge is represented as concepts, instances, relations, axioms (symmetry, inverse and transitive), and user defined rules (i.e. rules that are fired by an inference mechanism). The axioms and user-defined rules are pieces of knowledge implicitly defined in the knowledge base.

Maier et al. (2003) conclude that ontologies sum up most of the qualities of other knowledge representation models:

- Like Taxonomies, ontologies are able to picture hierarchies.
- Like Thesauri, Semantic Nets and Topic Maps, ontologies contain relations.

- Like the Entity Relationship-Model (ER), ontologies have a data model distinguishing schema information from facts.
- As an object based model, ontologies support inheritance and multiple inheritance of attributes.

## Classification of Manufacturing Processes

A class diagram for manufacturing processes is described by Feng and Song (2000) that includes the classes *Shaping, Surface treatment, Assembly* and *Inspection*. Groover (2001) described another method of classification, with a distinction being made between shaping, property enhancing and surface processing operations. Elgh (2004) proposed a third categorisation (with seven types) involving:

*Figure 3. A tentative semantic model describing parts of the implementation domain of ontology modelling. An ontology is developed if this model is complemented with knowledge.*

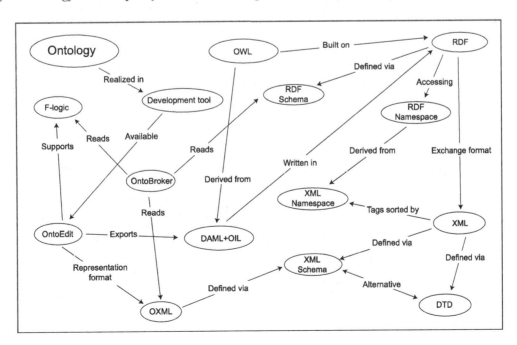

- Pre-treatment
- Shaping
- Property-enhancing
- Surface treatment
- Post-treatment
- Assembly
- Inspection

Pre-treatment involves operations that transform the work piece into a state that facilitates shaping, property-enhancing, surface treatment, assembly or inspection. Post-treatment are subsequent operations that remove properties resulting from shaping, property-enhancing, surface treatment, assembly and inspection.

## CASE STUDY

The case study consists of a study of the initial state of practice, comprising: a study of the present system for management of manufacturing requirements at the company; a description of the collaboration process for enhanced producibility; interviews with company employees; and the elucidation and modelling of present concepts, structures, instances and attributes used in the

context of manufacturing requirements at the studied company.

The car company studied in this work has over the years compiled design rules related to the manufacturing process in order to guide its design work towards solutions with good producibility in existing facilities. The rule base is being gradually expanded and comprises more than 1500 rules. The intention is to extend the guidelines to include rules for first and second tier suppliers as well. It is to be expected that the knowledge base will become substantially larger over time, which may cause problems with maintenance and easy access for designers and production engineers. A need is perceived for a more sophisticated information retrieval system for the future.

## Present System

The system used at the time for this study was a spreadsheet solution, called Function and Requirement Description Process (FRD Process). A version of the FRD Process had been made available as integrated in a Requirement and Traceability Management tool (RTM). The guidelines are documented as text of varying character and stored as chunks of text sorted in a structure of

*Figure 4. Present system. The guidelines are documented and stored as chunks of text sorted in a structure of predefined paragraphs. A problem that has occurred in the present system is redundant guidelines. The system is also afflicted by a number of similar guidelines.*

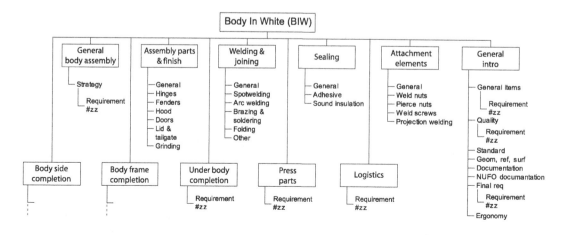

predefined paragraphs (Figure 4). The paragraphs relate to organisational units in product development and manufacturing. Production engineers and designers can access the guidelines on the intranet. Key words relating to organisational units in product development and manufacturing are used for information retrieval.

A problem that has occurred in the present system is redundant guidelines. When examining the content of the system, a number of similar guidelines were found. The redundancy makes it difficult to maintain the system. In addition, the user cannot be sure if he/she has the latest version of the guideline, or if it is still applicable. The system lacks in stringency as a result of guidelines written by different people responsible for different areas using different terminology and guideline classifications. The system also lacks in integrity, i.e. old guidelines are not weeded out.

## Collaboration Process for Enhanced Producibility

Sharing information and knowledge is a core issue at the company for enhancing producibility (Section *Collaborative Engineering for Enhanced Producibility*). The system was originally developed as a tool for production engineers where requirements, constraints, wishes, and lessons learned relating to manufacturing were defined. The production engineers preferably kept a printed hard copy of the guidelines on their shelf. The company wishes to ensure high producibility through formalised collaboration between production engineering and engineering design. Regular meetings mainly achieve this collaboration. In the meetings, the production engineers' experiences and knowledge are applied to different design proposals. The design proposals are evaluated and improvements are discussed from a manufacturing perspective. Between these regular meetings, the designers contact production engineers in manufacturing related issues using e-mail or telephone. Commonly, the production engineers

use the printed hard copy of the guidelines as support when discussing manufacturing issues with the designers.

This working practice is not sufficient, due to: the change of manufacturing paradigm (Section *Introduction*), the ever increasing focus on cost reduction (by enhanced producibility), the growing number of design rules related to the manufacturing process (Section *Case study*), and the outsourcing and globalisation that results in dispersed organisations, tools, information and knowledge (Section *Collaborative Engineering for Enhanced Producibility*).

## Interviews

Interviews were performed (Arrback & Bjelkemyr, 2003) with eight respondents representing engineering design and production preparation. The questions were subdivided into seven main areas and included sub-questions. They were formulated as open questions. The seven main questions addressing manufacturing adaptation and the main results from the interview are summarized in Table 1.

## Concepts, Structures, Instances and Attributes

The elucidation and modelling of present concepts, structures, instances and attributes was done with the purpose of acquiring an understanding of the context in which the guidelines occur. This will support the development of the pilot system. The system requires the coordination of the views different groups of employees at the company have in the area of manufacturing requirements. The modelling and visualization of these views is important. The resulting information model can be used to communicate the different concepts and facilitate the coordination of the different concepts within the company. The purpose is to reach congruence between different stakeholders' concepts and define a terminology to be used

*Table 1. Main questions and summarized answers from the interviews with company employees*

| Main question | Summarized answers |
|---|---|
| 1. Which are the main information channels? | The main information channels are the production preparation meetings held once a week. |
| 2. How is the present system used? | The utilization of the present system is low. |
| 3. Which are the present system's strengths and weaknesses? | The system is perceived as a good tool and a complement to the production preparation meetings. The guidelines are however incoherent, a mixture of "musts", "wants" and "lessons learned". |
| 4. What is the staff's view on the manufacturing adaptation at the company? | The staff considers that the manufacturing adaptation at the company is good comparing to the competitors'. |
| 5. How is the present system maintained and by who? | The staff at the department of production preparation maintains the system. The general opinion is that the maintenance is insufficient. The system is afflicted with old requirements, duplicates and the system lacks in history and traceability. |
| 6. What is the experience of the integration of FRD Process in RTM? | The utilization of FRD Process in RTM version is low. |
| 7. What is the staff's view on future enhancements? | The staff's view on future enhancements include: enhanced user-friendliness, personal views and reports, incorporate history and traceability, improve the means to attach pictures, create relations to other structures, define keywords, and enhance the search mechanism. |

in the area of designers' guidelines concerning manufacturing. The elucidation and modelling of present concepts, structures, instances and attributes is also important for the system developers and programmers because it specifies important items to be incorporated in a system.

The result from the elucidation and modelling is briefly depicted in Figure 5.

## Conclusions from the Study

The purpose of the initial study was to get an overall view of the state of practice at the company: the system used; working routines; the employees' experiences and opinions regarding manufacturing requirements; the context of the domain; and the concepts, structures, instances and attributes used at the company. The conclusions from the study were the following:

- Old requirements, duplicates, and a lack of history and traceability afflict the present system.

- Future enhancements are needed to incorporate traceability, define keywords for formation of requirements and enhance the search mechanism.
- The result from the analysis of the concepts, structures, instances and attributes is that there are missing relationships (connections) between the different structures.

## ONTOLOGY DEVELOPMENT

In order to build, use and maintain a system based on an ontology approach, it is essential to find an information model that agrees well with concepts and working practices used at work daily by the users. Several technical domains are involved, and the objects in these domains are linked in a complex way constituting a semantic data model. Knowledge is to be represented in different ways, allowing for queries that involve inferences regarding the stored data. In the following sections, the chosen semantic data model will be described

*Figure 5. The main concepts and structures in the context of manufacturing requirements. The instances and attributes of the different concepts were also tentatively defined.*

and the background for its structure clarified. The ontology is comprised of the semantic data model extended with different types of knowledge.

## Scenarios and Properties

A number of scenarios and system properties were defined based on the study of the initial state of practise in order to support the development of a new tool. These scenarios and properties together compose the system specification, and they will be used for testing and evaluating the ontology approach. The intended use of the system (i.e. scenarios) and system properties are stated in Table 2, divided into three technical domains: engineering design, production engineering and requirement management.

## Ontology Construction

Several information tree structures relating to the product, the manufacturing system, the organisation and the rule base existed, but they were not formally linked together. In our work, we make use of the existing structures and link those using appropriately named links. The initial information model completed with semantic relations is depicted in Figure 6. The only link between the product and the manufacturing system is through the organisation. As a result, the manufactur-

*Table 2. System scenarios and properties by technical domain*

| Technical domain | Intended use and properties |
|---|---|
| Engineering Design | Early phases (embodiment design) – evaluate different manufacturing alternatives. <br> Detail design phase – adapt the product to the selected manufacturing processes. <br> Find responsible person for a specific manufacturing requirement. |
| Production Planning | Define requirements (how to formulate and where to store). <br> Find people affected by changes in a manufacturing requirement. <br> Map requirements to manufacturing targets. |
| Requirement Management | Prevent redundancy. <br> Enhance integrity. <br> Enhance traceability. |

*Figure 6. Initial model. Manufacturing requirements for a specific part can only be search by the organisation that will give a coarse result.*

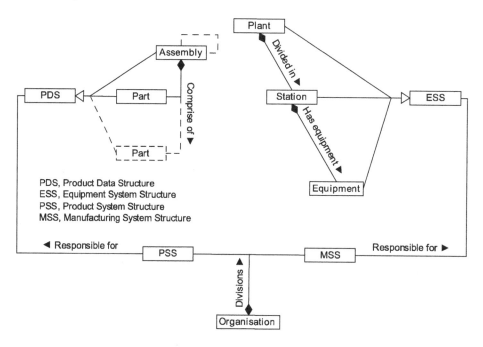

ing requirements for a specific part can only be searched through the organisation structure that leads to a coarse search result. This is because the model incorporates a number of so-called many-to-many relationships

## Manufacturing System Functions (MSF)

To enhance system functionality and support the designer and production engineers in their search for specific information, we propose the introduction of a new structure. This structure describes the generic functions of the manufacturing system. We call this structure MSF, Manufacturing System Functions. It is an analogy to the well-known method of functional modelling of products (See Section *Functions-Means Trees*). This tree structure is a suitable tool to link product related objects to their associated production equipment at varying levels of detailing. In an earlier work at the studied company, the

different manufacturing stations were classified using terms describing their value processing. To some extent, this classification resembles the idea of manufacturing functions.

The adaptation of design proposals to the manufacturing system requires access to information and knowledge early in the product development process. By introducing MSF, the designer is provided with the opportunity to gather information and knowledge about different manufacturing alternatives. Different courses of action can be evaluated, and their implication on the product design can be tested early in the process.

The idea of MSF is considered to be applicable in a broader sense at different companies. However, the introduction of a new concept has to be done with caution. MSF is crucial for system functionality and the users' adoption of the functions it allows for. We believe that to successfully adopt this approach, the MSF has to be defined by the employees at every company. At this point, the main elements of the MSF are the seven categories

*Figure 7. The seven main elements of the MSF, with examples of subdivisions of Surface treatment and Assembly into sub-categories using a functional description of the manufacturing process.*

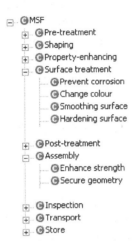

stated by Elgh (2004) in Section *Classification of Manufacturing Processes*. They have been broken down further by means of the commonly used syntax for functional descriptions, i.e. verb + noun (Figure 7).

## Requirement Object (RO)

The next issue to address is how the manufacturing requirements should be modelled to support the defined scenarios and to include the stated system properties. From an engineering design point of view, the origin of manufacturing requirements is the coupled relationship between the product design, the material and the manufacturing process. The main objectives of manufacturing requirements are to ensure the product's conformability with the manufacturing system, i.e. prevent problems in manufacturing from occurring, and to enhance producibility. In this case, the focus is on requirements related to the materials, the stations and the equipments. From a modelling perspective, the manufacturing requirements are considered to arise in the interfaces as depicted in Figure 8.

A number of properties need to be defined (Figure 9) in order to ensure that the ontology fulfils the needs of the different interested parties. This can be achieved by looking at how the requirements relate to the other concepts in the domain. The requirements can have different ranges, be applicable at different company levels, be of different type, be expressed and illustrated in different format, and have a number of links to other concepts and instances.

The manufacturing requirements are modelled using a concept for the definition of the requirement content called Manufacturing Requirement (MR). To enable the MR to cover different ranges

*Figure 8. Manufacturing requirements are in this work limited to those related to the materials, the stations and the equipment. From a modelling perspective, the manufacturing requirements are considered to arise in the interfaces.*

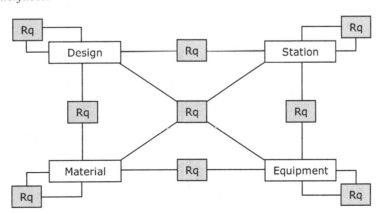

*Figure 9. Manufacturing requirements properties*

| Manufacturing requirement properties | |
| --- | --- |
| □ Range<br>  - Whole domain<br>  - Groups<br>  - Single object | □ Type<br>  - Must<br>  - Wants<br>  - Lessons learned |
| □ Level<br>  - Company<br>  - Fabrication plant<br>  - Department<br>  - Station<br>  - Equipment | □ Format<br>  - Description<br>  - Picture<br>  - Movie<br>  - ...<br>□ Links<br>  - ... |

and levels and enhance the maintenance of the system integrity, the concept of Requirement Object is introduced. RO is used to collect the instances for which a specific MR is valid.

## Information Model

The final information model incorporates the Manufacturing System Function (MSF), the Manufacturing Requirement (MR), and the Requirement Object (RO). Relationships link the different structures, building up a semantic data model. Figure 10 illustrates an overview of the information model upon which the ontology is based.

## Knowledge Representation

A single manufacturing requirement includes information in different formats (e.g. text, pictures and/or movies). When this information is put in a context dynamically related to the other concepts (e.g. organisation, production facilities),

*Figure 10. Final information model with MSF, RO, MR and relationships*

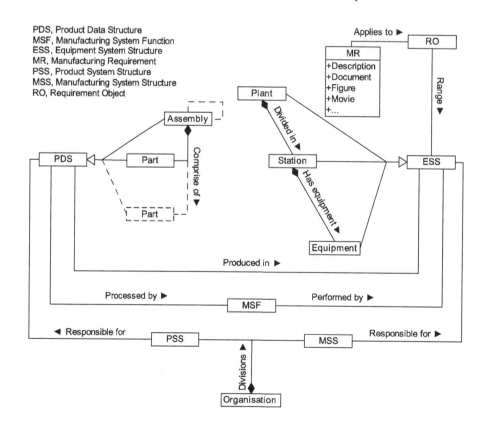

a knowledge base is obtained. From an ontology perspective, the knowledge is composed of concepts, instances, relationships, axioms (symmetry, inverse and transitive), and user defined rules (i.e. rules that are fired by an inference mechanism). The rules are used to reduce the number of explicitly defined relationships. The ontology is to be modelled using a system composed of a database and an inference mechanism. The database can be used for different queries. Some of the queries invoke the inference mechanism when the axioms and the user-defined rules are fired.

## A PILOT SYSTEM

The ontology approach described in a generic way in the previous section is exemplified by a small example relating to the hood system for a car. The pilot system is implemented in an ontology editor for creating, editing and verifying ontologies. The editor is composed of an object oriented database and an inference mechanism. The main concepts, with a number of instances, are depicted in Figure 11, together with examples of relationships and axioms.

## System Testing and Evaluation

The scenarios and properties specified in Section *Scenarios and Properties*, based on the study of the initial state of practise, are used for the testing and evaluation of the functionality and applicability of the ontology approach. The system was tested with a total of 18 different queries. The main queries, related to scenarios in the domain of engineering

*Figure 11. A pilot system based on the ontology approach for the management of designer guidelines for motorcar manufacture. The main concepts, with a number of instances, are illustrated, together with examples of relations, axioms, and the semantics content of the database.*

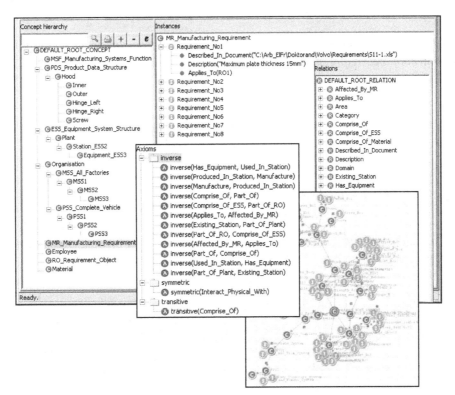

design, are presented below. Further, the system support for the requirement formation in the domain of production engineering is clarified. Finally, a description is given of how the system properties in the area of requirement management are incorporated into the system.

## Queries

The main utilisation of the system in a day-to-day practice is to supply designers and production engineers with valid information. The specific information is searched for and retrieved by querying the vast amount of information. The queries can be standardised using a predefined syntax. In the next level, the user interacts with the system by providing some input to the queries. The user can define individual queries when a more sophisticated and personal search is needed. A selection of queries is presented here. Two are based on the scenarios in the system specification (Section *Scenarios and Properties*), and one illustrates the

use of a rule where the inference mechanism is invoked when the system is searched.

### Scenario 1

The system applicability in the early phases of engineering design (embodiment design) is tested. The designer wants to evaluate different manufacturing alternatives and investigate their implication on the design. The principle search path is illustrated in Figure 12, together with the syntax for the query and some results.

### Scenario 2

In the detail design phase, the designer has to adapt the product to the selected manufacturing processes. A more precise result is obtained by searching the manufacturing resources related to the specific process (Figure 13).

*Figure 12. Which are the stations that can be used for securing geometry by geometrical joining, and what is the content of their requirements?*

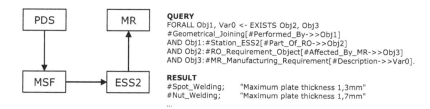

**QUERY**
FORALL Obj1, Var0 <- EXISTS Obj2, Obj3
#Geometrical_Joining[#Performed_By->>Obj1]
AND Obj1:#Station_ESS2[#Part_Of_RO->>Obj2]
AND Obj2:#RO_Requirement_Object[#Affected_By_MR->>Obj3]
AND Obj3:#MR_Manufacturing_Requirement[#Description->>Var0].

**RESULT**
#Spot_Welding;      "Maximum plate thickness 1,3mm"
#Nut_Welding;       "Maximum plate thickness 1,7mm"
...

*Figure 13. What is the content of the requirements related to the manufacturing stations used to manufacture a specific component (Outer_No1)?*

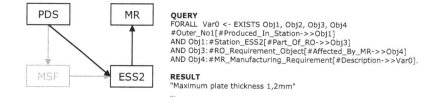

**QUERY**
FORALL Var0 <- EXISTS Obj1, Obj2, Obj3, Obj4
#Outer_No1[#Produced_In_Station->>Obj1]
AND Obj1:#Station_ESS2[#Part_Of_RO->>Obj3]
AND Obj3:#RO_Requirement_Object[#Affected_By_MR->>Obj4]
AND Obj4:#MR_Manufacturing_Requirement[#Description->>Var0].

**RESULT**
"Maximum plate thickness 1,2mm"
...

## An example of a rule

The usefulness of the possibility to define rules and the system's inference mechanism, which is invoked when querying the database, are exemplified here. The relationship between a part and the equipment used for its manufacture is implicitly defined using a rule (Figure 14).

A number of axioms (symmetry, inverse and transitive) have been defined in the system. They also invoke the inference mechanism in the system.

## Other queries

The queries above are just a few examples of different ways to search for information. The system has been tested and evaluated with a total of 18 queries (See Figure 15). The queries have been defined based on scenarios for different groups of people working with manufacturing requirements in various processes and stages of these processes. The system is not limited to answering only these queries. The object-oriented database, with the semantic data model, is perceived as a flexible solution, as it can be further extended with user-defined queries.

## Requirement Formation and Requirement Management

In the process of requirement formation, the system supports the production engineers in two important aspects, as pointed out in the interviews (Section *Interviews*):

*Figure 14. An example of a rule in which the relationship between a part and the equipment used for its manufacture is implicitly defined. The query for the manufacturing equipment used for a specific component invokes the systems' inference mechanism*

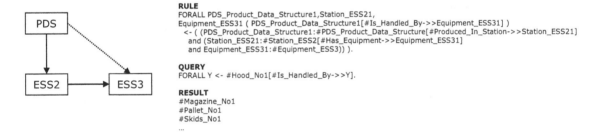

```
RULE
FORALL PDS_Product_Data_Structure1,Station_ESS21,
Equipment_ESS31 ( PDS_Product_Data_Structure1[#Is_Handled_By->>Equipment_ESS31] )
   <- ( (PDS_Product_Data_Structure1:#PDS_Product_Data_Structure[#Produced_In_Station->>Station_ESS21]
   and (Station_ESS21:#Station_ESS2[#Has_Equipment->>Equipment_ESS31]
   and Equipment_ESS31:#Equipment_ESS3)) ).

QUERY
FORALL Y <- #Hood_No1[#Is_Handled_By->>Y].

RESULT
#Magazine_No1
#Pallet_No1
#Skids_No1
...
```

*Figure 15. Examples of the 18 queries used for testing and evaluating the pilot system. The system is not limited to answering only these queries.*

What stations perform joining?
Which requirements govern joining of hood and hinge?
Which requirements govern aligning of hood and hinge?
What MSS is responsible for requirements that govern joining of hood and hinge?
Which are the requirements related the equipments used in the stations performing welding?
Who has the responsibility for the requirements govern joining of hood and hinge?
Which PSS should be notified when the equipment in station XX is changed?
...

1. The ontology defines a terminology for the communication and definition of requirements (how to formulate and where to store).
2. It is possible to map the requirements to the manufacturing targets.

Finally, by recalling the system properties from a requirement management perspective (Section *Scenarios and Properties*), it can be concluded that these have been incorporated in the system (Table 3).

The support for integrity is introduced by the ROs and MRs. The manufacturing requirements are considered to arise in the interfaces between design, material, station and equipment as described in Section *Requirements object (RO)*. The RO is used to collect the instances for which a specific MR is valid. The integrity can then be ensured by checking relations between the ROs and MRs. For example, if a piece of equipment is discarded, all related ROs are to be deleted (See Figure 16).

## Other System Advantages

Compared to the present situation, there are a number of other system advantages that can be of vital importance for the system's usability and maintenance. These include:

*Figure 16. The support for integrity is introduced by checking the ROs and MRs. For example, if a piece of equipment is discarded, all related ROs are to be deleted. The rule for integrity check of the MRs is: an MR should be deleted if all of its ROs have been deleted.*

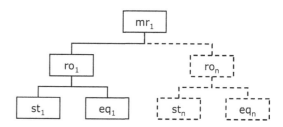

- A consistent information model with sufficient granularity to allow selective search exists.
- The relationships between defined concepts enhance search precision.
- New rules can be tested for consistency with existing rule base.
- Very flexible search attributes exist.
- Redundancy of information can be eliminated.
- Rule search could be made dependent on user and rules activated or deactivated in user profiles.

*Table 3. System incorporated properties related to requirement management*

| System property | Realisation |
| --- | --- |
| Prevent redundancy | Reusing existing requirements can prevent redundancy (e.g. check affected stations and equipments, search for matching text strings). |
| Enhance integrity | Checking the ROs and MRs supports enhanced integrity (e.g. if a piece of equipment is discarded, all related ROs are deleted, and an MR should be deleted if all of its ROs have been deleted. |
| Enhance traceability | The traceability is enhanced by the relationships between the structures. |

The system is based on an ontology model. This model has been developed to fulfil the system specification regarding system supported scenarios and system incorporated properties. In addition, when these fundamental scenarios and properties now have been integrated, the system can be further developed to incorporate functions such as:

- Individual search profiles.
- Regular notification when requirements are added or changed.
- More flexible solutions to add pictures, movies and voice messages to the requirements.
- Automatic compiling of reports for different purposes.
- Enhanced collaboration between first and second tiers by incorporating their manufacturing resources and requirements together with an extended structure for manufacturing system functions.

## Supporting Collaboration

Information sharing is one of the main key features of collaborative engineering. This implies that different individuals and/or domains can express their information and that this information is accessible for others (i.e. understandable and relevant in the individual case). As pointed out in Section *Collaborative Engineering for Enhanced Producibility*, the state of practice at the company is not sufficient due to a number of aspects. The verbal sharing of information and knowledge at the regular meetings has to be more efficient, and other methods for collaboration have to be adopted.

The approach and tool presented in this work are perceived to contribute to a more effective and efficient information and knowledge sharing in the area of manufacturing requirements at the company. As a result, they provide a support in the collaboration process for ensuring and enhancing the products producibility. This is mainly achieved

*Table 4. Supporting collaboration for ensured and enhanced producibility*

| Information sharing feature | Description/example |
| --- | --- |
| Communicable | A defined terminology for communication. |
| Understandable | The semantic model supports the individual's comprehension of the different domains and how they are related. |
| Shared | All individuals have access to the same information and knowledge. |
| Accessible | The access to information and knowledge can be made organisation, language, time, and geographic independent. |
| Relevant | Enhanced support in the search for specific information. |
| Linked | By the introduction of MSF, a link is created between engineering design and production engineering governing collaboration early in the product development process. |
| Managed | It is possible to search for the responsible person to contact for issues regarding a specific object. |

by a number of features of information sharing as illustrated in Table 4.

## SUMMARY OF RESULTS

The purpose of this study was to promote improved collaboration between departments for design and production by exploring an ontology based approach to handling the production related information source, i.e. manufacturing requirements. The objective was to enable a systematic approach to handling a growing number of manufacturing requirements. The main objectives fulfilled by the proposed approach are:

- Support in the formation of requirement specifications for products and processes.
- Improved and simplified information retrieval for designers and process planners.
- Forward traceability from changes in product systems to manufacturing systems.
- Backward traceability from changes in manufacturing system to product systems.
- Redundant or multiple versions of requirement specifications can be prevented, simplifying updating and maintenance of the information.

Recalling the scenarios and properties, a system based on this approach presents support in the area of engineering design, production planning and requirement management described in Table 5.

In the collaboration process for ensuring and enhancing the products producibility, an ontology approach to the management of manufacturing requirements provides an extended support and the possibility of new ways of working. It allows for a flexible and selective accessibility to accurate information and knowledge. The unambiguous interpretations of manufacturing requirements can be limited. The system can be used as a complement to, and to some extent replace, the regular meetings. Further, the meetings' participants can be more prepared, resulting in more effective and efficient meetings.

### Further Achievements

The proposed approach has been further extended and applied for the support of management and maintenance of manufacturing knowledge in design automation systems. A case study was conducted at manufacturing company acting as a sub-supplier providing seat heating elements to different car manufacturer (Elgh, 2007b). The work resulted in a model originating from the results and experiences from a system for automated variant design (Elgh & Cederfeldt, 2007) and the work presented in this article. This new model promotes the integration of properties and func-

*Table 5. System supported scenarios and incorporated properties by technical domain*

| Technical domain | System supported scenarios and system incorporated properties |
|---|---|
| Engineering Design | Early phases (embodiment design) – evaluate different manufacturing alternatives. Detail design phase – adapt the product to the selected manufacturing processes. Find responsible person for a specific manufacturing requirement. |
| Production Planning | Define requirements (how to formulate and where to store). Find people affected by changes in a manufacturing requirement. Map requirements to manufacturing targets. |
| Requirement Management | Prevent redundancy. Enhance integrity. Enhance traceability. |

tions for knowledge execution and information management into one system, i.e. integration of design know-how with life-cycle related know-why. The model offers an expanded support for requirements modelling and mapping addressing different stakeholders' needs of requirement traceability and system maintenance. The model was adopted during the planning and setting up of a first solution for a design automation system. The system ensures the products' producibility in existing facilities and provides the company with opportunity to work with producibility issues in a systematic way.

## CONCLUSION

In order to build, use and maintain a system based on an ontology approach, it is essential to develop an ontology that agrees well with concepts and working practices used in daily work by the users. However, this is not enough when enhanced functionality is required. New solution ideas have to be constructed through innovation in new semantics, structures and concepts. Knowledge has to be represented in different ways, allowing for queries that involve making inferences based on the stored information.

The proposed ontology approach deploys two new ideas: the concept of Manufacturing System Function and the modelling of requirements as two concepts – Requirements Objects and Manufacturing Requirements. A new structure describing the generic functions of the manufacturing system is introduced, MSF. This tree structure is a suitable tool to link product related objects to their associated production equipment at varying levels of detail. The concept Manufacturing Requirement (MR) includes, at instantiation, the requirements' descriptions. To enable the MR to cover different ranges and levels, and enhance the maintenance of the system integrity, the concept

of Requirement Object (RO) is introduced. The RO is used to collect the instances for which a specific MR is valid. In our work we make use of the existing company structures and link those using appropriately named relations. Further, a rule inference facility is used to reduce the number of explicitly defined relations.

The collaboration process practiced at the company for ensuring and enhancing each product's producibility is not sufficient with the dispersed organisations of today. The amount of product and production information and knowledge is increasing. It has to be stored and communicated in a more flexible manner than it has up until now. An ontology approach to the management of manufacturing requirements provides an extended support and the possibility of adopting new ways of working. It is not believed that the presented approach can replace the meetings at the company but, it can be used as a complement. It allows for effective and efficient meetings by enabling the participants to be more updated with the issues to be discussed. The system can also be used as a tool at the meetings to show and evaluate different scenarios (e.g. the implications of a change in one domain and how other domains are affected).

For many manufacturing companies, the collaboration between engineering design and production engineering is a critical issue. The work within domains requirement management, engineering design and production engineering can be integrated by using an ontology management of manufacturing requirements. An ontology approach supports the sharing of information and knowledge between these domains. This allows for the development of products with enhanced producibility in existing plants and lines. The results are product designs with high level of conformability with the production system, decreased manufacturing cost, and shortened manufacturing lead-time.

## ACKNOWLEDGMENT

This work was conducted within the Vinnova program for *Information Technology in the Manufacturing Industry* and financial support is gratefully acknowledged.

## REFERENCES

Arrback, A., & Bjelkemyr, M. (2003). *System to Manage Guidelines for Design for Manufacture.* Technical report. Jönköping, Sweden: Department of Mechanical Engineering, School of Engineering, Jönköping University,

Elgh, F. (2007a). *Computer-Supported Design for Producibility – Principles and Models for System realisation and Utilisation.* Ph.D. thesis. Gothenburg, Sweden: Department of Product and Production Development, Chalmers University of Technology.

Elgh, F. (2007b). Modelling and Management of Manufacturing Requirements in Systems for Automated Variant Design. In Loureiro, G., & Curran, R. (Eds.), *Complex Systems Concurrent Engineering* (pp. 321-328). London: Springer.

Elgh, F., & Cederfeldt, M. (2007). Concurrent Cost Estimation as a Tool for Enhanced Producibility – System Development and Applicability for Producibility Studies. *Journal of Production Economics,* 109(1-2), 12-26.

Elgh, F. (2004). A Generic Framework for Automated Cost Evaluation of Product Variants and Fabrication Plants. *Proceedings of Design Engineering Technical Conferences and Computers and Information in Engineering Conference,* (vol. 3). New York, NY: American Society of Mechanical Engineers.

Feng, S.C., & Song E.Y. (2000). Information Modeling of Conceptual Process Planning Integrated with Conceptual Design. *Proceedings of Design Engineering Technical Conferences and Computers and Information in Engineering Conference.* New York, NY: American Society of Mechanical Engineers.

Groover, M.P. (2001). *Automation, Production Systems, and Computer-Integrated Manufacturing.* Upper Saddle River, NJ: Prentice-Hall.

Hannam, R.G. (1997). *Computer Integrated Manufacturing – From Concepts to Realization.* Harlow, Great Britain: Addison Wesley Longman Ltd.

Hubka, V., Andreasen, M.M., & Eder, W.E. (1998). *Practical Studies in Systematic Design.* London, Great Britain: Butterworth.

Jacucci, G., Pawlak, A., & Sandkuhl, K. (2005). Preface. In Jacucci, G., Pawlak, A., & Sandkuhl, K. (Eds.), *Proceedings of Challenges in Collaborative Engineering Workshop.* Jönköping, Sweden: Department of Computer & Electrical Engineering, School of Engineering, Jönköping University.

Kirkman, D.P. (1998). Requirement Decomposition and Traceability. *Requirements Engineering,* 3(2), pp. 107-111.

Lundqvist, M., & Sandkuhl, K. (2004). Modeling Information Demand for Collaborative Engineering. In Sandkuhl, K., & Kazmierski, T. (Eds.), *Proceedings of Challenges in Collaborative Engineering Workshop* (pp. 111-120). Jönköping, Sweden: Department of Computer & Electrical Engineering, School of Engineering, Jönköping University.

Maier, A., Aguado, J., Bernaras, A., Laresgoiti, I., Pedinaci, C., Pena, N., & Smithers, T. (2003). *Integration with Ontologies.* Paper presented at Professionelles Wissensmanagement - Erfahrungen und Visionen. Luzern, Germany. Retrieved November 3, 2003, from www.ontoprise.de/documents/integration_with_ontologies.pdf.

Nilsson, P., & Andersson, F. (2004). Process-driven Product Development – Managing Manufacturing Requirements, In Horváth, I., & Xirouchakis, P. (Eds.), *Proceedings Fifth International Symposium on Tools and Methods of Competitive Engineering* (pp. 395-404). Rotterdam: Millpress.

Noy, N.F., & McGuinness, D.L. (2001*). Ontology Development 101: A Guide to Creating Your First Ontology*, Stanford Knowledge Systems Laboratory Technical Report KSL-01-05 and Stanford Medical Informatics Technical Report SMI-2001-0880. Stanford University: Stanford Knowledge Systems Laboratory.

Pahl, G., & Beitz, W., (1996). *Engineering Design – A Systematic Approach.* London, Great Britain: Springer-Verlag Ltd.

Schlenoff, C., Ivester, R., Libes, D., Denno, P., & Szykman, S. (1999). An Analysis of Existing Ontological Systems for Applications in Manufacturing. *Proceedings of Design Engineering Technical Conferences and Computers and Information in Engineering Conference.* New York, NY: American Society of Mechanical Engineers.

Sohlenius, G. (1992). Concurrent Engineering. *CIRP annals*, 41(2), pp. 645-655. Retrieved Mars 11, 2005, from http://www.cirp.net/publications.

Suh, N.P. (1990). *The Principles of Design.* New York, NY: Oxford University Press.

Szykman, S., Racz, J., & Sriram, R. (1999). The Representation of Function in Computer-Based Design. *Proceedings of Design Engineering Technical Conferences and Computers and Information in Engineering Conference.* New York, NY: American Society of Mechanical Engineers.

Turban, E. & Aronson, J., (2001), *Decision Support Systems and Intelligent Systems.* Upper Saddle River, NJ: Prentice-Hall Inc.

# Chapter XIII
# An Ontology-Based Competence Model for Collaborative Design

**Vladimir Tarasov**
*Jönköping University, Sweden*

**Kurt Sandkuhl**
*Jönköping University, Sweden*

**Magnus Lundqvist**
*Jönköping University, Sweden*

## ABSTRACT

*Collaborative design in dispersed groups of engineers creates various kinds of challenges to technology, organization and social environment. This paper presents an approach to description and representation of the competences needed for a planned collaborative design project. The most important competence areas are identified starting from the nature of design work, problem solving in design teams, and working in distributed groups. The competence model is built structuring these areas according to three perspectives: general, cultural, and occupational competences. An ontological representation is proposed to implement the described model for collaborative design competence. Using an ontology language for representation of collaborative design competence models makes it possible to identify those individuals who are best suited for the collaboration by ontology matching. Furthermore, a software design team consisting of two persons was interviewed and competence profiles were created using the developed ontological representation. Modeling of the team members has confirmed that the proposed approach can be applied to modeling competences needed for collaborative design in engineering fields.*

# INTRODUCTION

Collaborative design in dispersed groups of engineers creates various kinds of challenges to technology, organization and social environment. Selected examples are knowledge sharing, coordination support, process adaptation or tool integration (Pawlak, Sandkuhl, Cholewa, & Indrusiak, 2007). Work presented in this paper is located in the area of formation of teams for collaborative design. The challenge addressed is how to describe and represent the competences needed for a planned collaborative design project in a way that those individuals best suited for the collaboration can be identified. The proposed approach is to apply ontology engineering to modeling competences of individuals including different competence areas like cultural, professional or occupational competences.

This paper is an extended and improved version of the paper presented in the International Journal of e-Collaboration (Tarasov & Lundqvist, 2006). The presented approach is based on earlier work in the field of competence modeling, both of enterprise competences (Henoch & Sandkuhl, 2002) and of individual competences (Tarassov, Sandkuhl, & Henoch, 2006). Furthermore, earlier work has addressed formation of networks for collaborative engineering (Blomqvist, Levashova, Öhgren, Sandkuhl, & Smirnov, 2005) or flexible supply chains (Sandkuhl, Smirnov, & Shilov), but with a focus on identifying suitable enterprises for a given task description.

The next section will present selected results from an empirical investigation in the field of information use, which confirms the importance of competence when selecting partners for collaboration activities. Section 3 will introduce the structure of competence models with focus on specific elements for collaborative design. The representation of competence models with ontologies is described in section 4. The results of modeling of a software design team are described in section 5. The conclusion presents a summary and an outlook on future work.

# IMPORTANCE OF COMPETENCE: FINDINGS FROM AN EMPIRICAL INVESTIGATION

During March–June 2005, an empirical investigation was carried out in Sweden aimed at studying how information is used in Swedish authorities and small- and medium sized enterprises. The main objective of this investigation was to identify the connection between information use and different work related aspects rather than to focus on collaborative design or formation of teams in collaborative design. The aspects considered in the investigation were work processes, resources, and organizational structures, with the purpose of better understanding the information demands that motivate demand-driven information supply. Nevertheless, the investigation resulted in some interesting findings regarding the importance of competence in the creation of informal information exchange channels.

The investigation comprised 27 interviews with individuals from three different organizations, The Swedish Board of Agriculture, Kongsberg Automotive, and Proton Engineering, the last two being suppliers within the automotive industry. It was performed as a series of semi-structured interviews. Because the results were intended to be used in other research projects, these 27 individuals where chosen in such a way that they constitute a sample of all levels of the investigated organizations, i.e. from top-level management via middle management down to production- and administrative personnel.

To understand and analyze information demands, it is important to examine not only activities, roles and available resources but also in what situations and for what reasons individuals chose to retrieve the needed information from other individuals rather than from existing information systems (Lundqvist, 2005). Without taking into account that all work situations also have a social aspect that is not addressed by means of technology alone, information demand and the fulfillment thereof can never be fully understood. The investigation was expected to result in a number of interesting findings considering this aspect and it really confirmed this idea to a high degree.

The 24 interviewees answered the question: *to what extent do you rely on colleagues for information*? As shown in figure 1, 15 of them replied that they do so to a very high degree, meaning doing so daily and sometimes several times every day. Eight individuals stated that they do this to some extent and only one claimed never doing so at all. These replies suggest that informal information exchange channels are indeed an important issue to consider. It was therefore relevant to find out why this is the case as well as what is the basis for the choice of colleagues. The informants had a large number of motivations for choosing to talk to other individuals rather than retrieving information from readily available systems. This revealed several crucial issues, which concern developing information supply. Some of the reasons mentioned by several of the informants were:

- The social interaction is considered not only nice but also necessary.
- It is perceived to be the fastest, easiest, and in some cases only way to find needed information because existing information systems are considered too hard to use from both user interaction and information retrieval perspective.

- It is common that there is a difference between the information stored in systems and the reality, i.e. information is not updated or correct.

It is however worth noticing that several of the interviewed individuals also claimed that they would prefer not to have to do this. They would like information systems to be designed in a way that render the personal communication unnecessary when it comes to information retrieval.

Even more interesting answers were those received to the question: *what is the basis for your choice of colleague to talk to when you need information?* While in some cases career strategies come into play when choosing, the aspect identified by most informants as the main factor was competence. We believe that when having some information demand, individuals unconsciously do a competence assessment and choose a colleague that is perceived knowledgeable and informed in the relevant subject or area. In some cases the choice is also based on such aspects as geographical location. It is simply convenient to ask people in the immediate vicinity, especially when it comes to information demands of a more general nature[1]. However, it can be claimed that this also relates to competence since in most organizations individuals with similar work tasks are usually grouped together for this very reason. Therefore, it is logical that the best-suited colleagues for fulfilling some information demand,

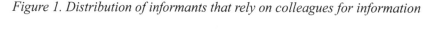

*Figure 1. Distribution of informants that rely on colleagues for information*

11 %

4 %

30 %

55 %

- To a large extent
- To some extent
- Not at all
- No answer

those with the right competence, are the ones placed close by the individual having the information demand.

# COMPETENCE MODEL FOR COLLABORATIVE DESIGN

An individual usually acquires a wide range of different capabilities during his/her life experience. Most of them can be considered as competences possessed by the individual, which can be applied in work situations. More specifically, Bjurklo and Kardemark (1998) define a competence as a set of all knowledge forms and personal abilities that are required for performing tasks. A competence model is a well-defined formal structure allowing for representation of these knowledge forms and abilities for an individual.

In order to develop a competence model for collaborative design, which represents all essential and desirable competences needed, we have to understand the nature of collaborative design. Collaborative design can be defined as design task performed in a dispersed group of workers with a joint collaboration objective. This leads to at least three areas, which should be taken into account:

- The nature of engineering design work itself,
- The work of design teams as compared to individually performed design work,
- The effects of distributing design work as compared to co-located design.

Although all three areas have been thoroughly researched, a systematic analysis of competences required is not available. Our approach is to derive a competence model based on the analysis of literature from the above areas. The next subsection will present this analysis; the proposed competence model is introduced in the subsection after next.

# Required Competences for Collaborative Design

The brief analysis of competences required for collaborative design will focus on engineering design, i.e. the design task within engineering disciplines like mechanical, electrical or computer engineering.

Many researchers consider engineering design a problem solving process involving step-by-step analysis of the problem or task at hand and step-by-step synthesis of solutions or sub-solutions for this problem. Following Pahl and Beitz (Pahl & Beitz, 1996), a general process for problem solving in an engineering context consists of confrontation with the problem, information about constraints, definition of the essential tasks to solve, creation of potential solutions, evaluation of solutions and different variants, and finally decision for the best variant. Pahl and Beitz (1996) propose to use plans and procedures for supporting the problem solving process, i.e. they consider planning and designing as closely interlinked elements of engineering design. These plans and procedures have to be adapted to the problem and to the specific engineering sector, i.e. design processes in mechanical engineering look differently from design in software engineering.

Comparing the way of solving design problems, Ullman (1997) explains that individuals and teams work quite similar. The main difference is that a team integrates different problem-solving styles of the individuals involved and needs an agreement on team roles supporting the problem solving process and to some extend even supporting the social activity in the team. Typical roles would include the coordinator being responsible for clarifying goals and promoting decision making, the creator being imaginative and able to solve different problems, the evaluator focusing on whether a design proposal fits into the overall picture or the implementer who is turning ideas into practical actions. Furthermore, the team will have to include different technical specialist from the same engineering sector, like a user interface designer, a database designer and an architecture designer for solving a design problem in software engineering.

Distributing design work and design team on different locations creates a number of additional challenges, like for example to provide adequate support for communication between the distributed groups, coordination of their work activities or support of collaboration in dispersed groups. These aspects, which are well researched within computer-supported collaborative work (Grudin, 1994), may on the one hand add additional roles to the design team, like local coordinators for the different groups or the facilitator being responsible for the CSCW tools and for operating these tools during team work in a collaboration session. On the other hand, distribution might affect the problem solving style by forcing the groups to divide the design problem in different sub-problems workable at single locations. Work in the field of knowledge co-production shows different organization styles, like teams, communities and networks, which have implications for roles distribution, tool support and organizational environment (Fuchs-Kittowski, 2007).

Furthermore, new issues related to the social activity in the team have to be tackled. In design teams spread over several countries, an obvious issue is to agree on a joint working language mastered by every team member. Another issue is to build trust within these distributed groups (Jones & Marsh, 1997). The latter is of particular importance in a setting with groups that never physically met or have different cultural backgrounds.

Summarizing the aspects discussed above, we see the following competences as important for collaborative design:

- Problem solving competence, including analysis and synthesis
- Planning and designing competences in general

- Competences in the field of engineering in question
- Different technical specialist competences in this engineering area
- Competence for team work, including different roles
- Language competences and competences in integrating different social backgrounds

## Competence Model

The main intention of a competence model is to provide a formally defined way to represent competences of individuals. A competence model for collaborative design should include the different competences listed in the previous section. For this purpose, we propose to distinguish between different competence perspectives and to use selected existing approaches from research on human resource management, healthcare or industrial standardization for these perspectives.

Table 1 gives an overview to the perspectives and the corresponding competences identified in the previous subsection. Each will be briefly described in the following.

The first perspective we considered important is general competences as proposed by Bjurklo and Kardemark. They conducted two studies (Bjurklo & Kardemark, 1998) with the aim to develop a model to control changes in competence. During the studies, they found 21 factors related to competence. The factors were divided into personality, knowledge and proficiency groups. These factors concern abilities general in nature and applicable in different situations, e.g. ability to plan, ability to form teams, creativity, ability to provide support and guidance, etc. The general competences perspective also encompasses design skills identified in (Pahl & Beitz, 1996) and teamwork abilities pointed out in (Grudin, 1994; Ullman, 1997).

The second perspective considers cultural competences. Hammer et al. (2003) describe the concept of intercultural sensitivity, which is use-

*Table 1. Overview to competence perspectives*

| Competence from the previous subsection | Represented by perspective | Based on work from |
|---|---|---|
| Problem solving competence | General Competences | Bjurklo and Kardemark (1998), Pahl and Beitz (1996) |
| Planning and designing competences | General Competences | Bjurklo and Kardemark (1998), Pahl and Beitz (1996) |
| Competences in the field of engineering in question | Occupational Competences | FOET-99 (Andersson & Olsson, 1999) and ISCO-88 (International Labour Organization, 2004) |
| Different technical competences in this engineering area | Occupational Competences | FOET-99 (Andersson & Olsson, 1999) and ISCO-88 (International Labour Organization, 2004) |
| Competence for team work and different roles | General Competences | Bjurklo and Kardemark (1998), Ullman (1997), Grudin (1994) |
| Language competences, competences in integrating different social backgrounds | Cultural Competences | Hammer et al. (2003) |

ful in geographically distributed design groups. Intercultural sensitivity shows how people can perceive cultural differences and act in multicultural environments. Hammer et al. (2003) found that it could be measured against the following scale: denial, defense (reversal), minimization, acceptance, adaptation, integration. The first three items comprise ethnocentric orientations, the last three – ethnorelative ones. Intercultural sensitivity is important for describing intercultural competence that may be expressed as the ability to behave oneself appropriately with respect to intercultural relations.

The third perspective is to show what knowledge and skills the person has acquired during his/her work and education. There is a number of statistical classifications abiding by this perspective. One of them is the International Standard Classification of Occupations, 1988 (ISCO-88) (International Labour Organization, 2004). ISCO-88 divides all possible occupations into ten major groups, 28 sub-major groups, 116 minor groups, and 390 unit groups. All the major groups except for the first and last ones have the corresponding skill levels, from the first to the fourth, required to perform tasks within the occupations of the

groups. There is also a corresponding educational classification – the International Standard Classification of Education (ISCED 1997) (UNESCO Institute for Statistics, 2003). ISCED 1997 defines seven educational levels, from pre-primary to the second stage of tertiary education, and divide 25 fields of educational into nine broad groups. Every educational field must be connected to an appropriate educational level. Another classification of this kind is the classification of fields of education and training developed in Europe in 1999 (FOET 1999) (Andersson & Olsson, 1999). FOET 1999 is based on ISCED 1997 but adds one more level, which is called detailed fields of education and contains 93 items. The first and second levels in FOET 1999 are called broad fields and narrow fields respectively.

## USING ONTOLOGIES TO REPRESENT COMPETENCE MODELS

After having discussed different competence perspectives and particular competences important for collaborative design in the previous section, this one will focus on the implementation of competence models. The main question addressed is which formal representation to use for competence models in order to make competence models available for computer supported retrieval or matching.

We propose to utilize ontologies to represent competence models. An ontology is defined as "an explicit specification of a conceptualization" (Gruber, 1993) and allows for description of a problem domain using concepts, their properties, relations between concepts, and axioms expressing constraints. The same method was part of our approach to represent individual competences of persons who may act as mediators in establishment of business relationships between enterprises in different countries (Tarassov, Sandkuhl, & Henoch, 2006). In our opinion, this method is well suited for formalization of competence models because it allows for capture of the rich semantics of competence and accommodation of the results obtained in the areas of human resource management and statistics. Each competence item can be represented with a concept, description with a property, and competence measurement or competence sub-items with relations to other concepts. Statistical taxonomies can be not only well represented with an *is-a* hierarchy of an ontology but also enriched with adding relations between classification items. When creating ontologies with an ontology editor like Protégé or OntoStudio, an ontology can be stored in a digital form using an ontology language. This provides for further computerized processing of competence models represented in an ontology language, e.g. for searching or matching.

According to the three perspectives described in the previous section, the ontology implementing the collaborative design competence model is built to include three major parts: general competence, cultural competence, and occupational competence. The first part represents general abilities, which are needed for performing general tasks during collaborative design. For this part,

we have chosen 11 competence factors relevant for collaborative design from the ones described in (Bjurklo & Kardemark, 1998), added two new factors, ability to analyze and ability to synthesize based on (Pahl & Beitz, 1996), and organized them in a hierarchy shown in Figure 2. The factors are subdivided into problem solving abilities, planning and designing abilities, and team work abilities. The team role competences identified in (Grudin, 1994; Ullman, 1997) are also included in the model and placed under the Team Work Ability concept. Each factor is to be graded against the scale Very Weak/Weak/Average/Strong/Very Strong when creating competence profiles. The scale is implemented as a set of concepts and each competence factor can be related to any of these concepts (points on the scale) to specify grading. Team roles abilities are also graded ac-

*Figure 2. Personal abilities forming general competences*

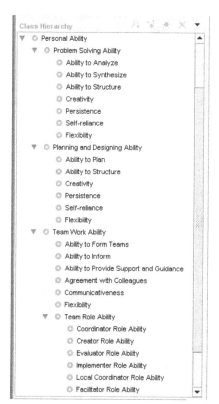

*Figure 3. General competence part of the collaborative design competence model*

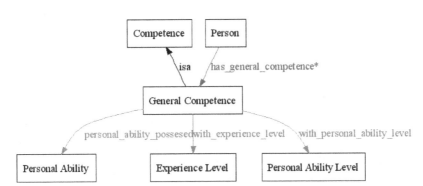

cording to the experience level of a person acting in this role. The experience level scale is Not at All/Little/Medium/Much/Very Much. This scale is only used for grading team roles abilities. Figure 3 depicts relations between concepts representing the grading scales, concepts representing personal abilities and the General Competence concept. A person will normally have a number of general competences, each one being represented by an instance of the General Competence concept related to a particular personal ability concept and a grading concept (or two grading concepts in the case of the team roles abilities) reflecting the ability level. An example of general competence grading is given in the next section.

The cultural competences are important for representation of expertise of individuals of different origin acting as a bridge between groups in the design team from different cultural backgrounds. Hence, the cultural competence part is composed of language competence and intercultural sensitivity to take into consideration abilities to act in a multicultural environment. The language competence includes languages, spoken by a person, which can be related to a language level ranging from a beginner to a native speaker. The Intercultural Sensitivity concept can be related to the intercultural sensitivity orientation described in (Hammer, Bennett, & Wiseman, 2003): ethnocentric orientations – denial, defense (reversal), minimization, and ethnorelative ones – accep-

tance, adaptation, integration. The orientations hierarchy is shown in Figure 4. A person's cultural competence is represented by several instances of the Language Competence concept related to a particular language concept and a grading concept, and an instance of the Intercultural Sensitivity concept related to a particular orientation concept as depicted in Figure 5.

Occupational competences are the major part of a person's abilities and may turn out to be the most important ones in a collaborative design situation. These abilities reflect competences in the field of engineering in question and different technical competences in this engineering area. They are obtained through education and work experience of the person. As soon as we need to model geographically dispersed design teams, we

*Figure 4. Intercultural sensitivity orientations characterizing the intercultural sensitivity*

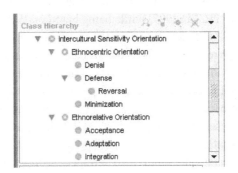

*Figure 5. Cultural competence part of the collaborative design competence model*

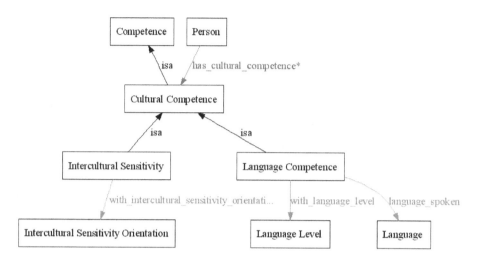

may have to represent very diverse working and educational backgrounds of team members. The Classification of fields of education and training, 1999 (FOET 1999), (Andersson & Olsson, 1999) and International Standard Classification of Occupations, 1988 (ISCO-88) (International Labour Organization, 2004) (which we described in the previous section) are a solid basis for the occupational competence part of our model, which is shown in Figure 6. Overall, the occupational competence of a person is represented by a set of instances reflecting educational programs/subjects studied by the person and his/her past and present jobs.

We have decided to use the European classification FOET 1999 because it provides for a more precise classification of education compared to the International Standard Classification of Education (ISCED 1997) while being based on ISCED 1997. The detailed educational fields of FOET 1999 represent educational areas studied by an individual and relevant for engineering design. The Educational Field concept has sub-concepts representing broad fields that have sub-concepts representing narrow fields and detailed fields of education described in FOET 1999. Each detailed field is further subdivided into specific programs/

subjects (specialization). Each Educational Competence instance representing a program/subject taken must be related to an appropriate educational field, educational level, and country where the education took place.

The occupational groups represent the person's present and past jobs that are of significance for engineering design. The occupational groups are subdivided into major groups, then sub-major, minor and unit groups consecutively as described in ISCO-88. Each unit group is further subdivided into occupational titles corresponding to this group. Each major occupational group is related to a fixed skill level, which in turn is related to a corresponding fixed educational level. Instances of the Work Experience Competence concept are to be related to occupational groups (or titles if possible), countries where a person works/worked, and experience level gained in each job. The latter is graded according to the scale "Not at All/Little/Medium/Much/Very Much". A Work Experience Competence instance can also be related to educational fields to reflect knowledge utilized during the work. An example of interrelationships between concepts in the occupational competence part is shown in the next section.

*Figure 6. Occupational competence part of the collaborative design competence model*

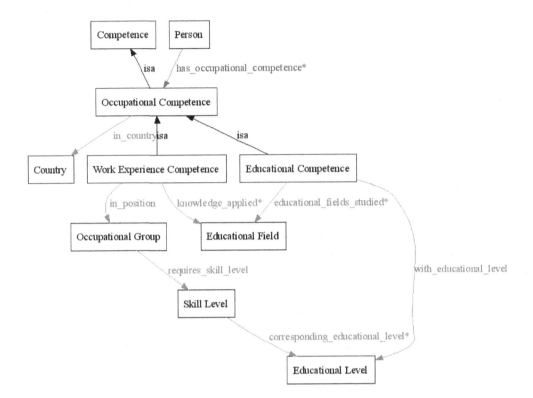

We have created an ontology representing our collaborative design competence model in Protégé 3.3. The ontology includes 494 concepts (classes), 18 relationships/properties (slots), and 59 instances (including instances created as part of two competence profiles – see next section).

## MODELING OF A SOFTWARE DESIGN TEAM

To apply our approach to modeling collaborative design competence with ontologies in practice, we have modeled two persons who have worked as a collaborative software design team in a short-term software development project. The first step was to conduct interviews of the persons. To do that, we created a semi-structured interview guide containing 15 questions about general competences,

eight questions about cultural competences, and 10 questions about occupational competences. The focus of the interviews was on abilities and education/occupations relevant for engineering design. After that the interview answers were analyzed and we built two particular instances of the collaborative design competence model. These instances are called competence profiles and they describe competences of the software design team members.

During creation of the general competence part of the competence profile, each personal ability was graded against the scale described in the previous section. Experience level of team role abilities was also graded. The experience grading was based on the amount of time when the person acted in the corresponding role. Figure 7 shows how one team role and one competence factor (the rest is not shown for brevity) with related grades can be represented by creating two instances of the General Competence concept and setting up appropriate relationships to the personal abilities concepts and their levels. This is part of the competence profile for person B.

The language competence parts were created according to the languages spoken by the team members. The intercultural sensitivity of both competence profiles was represented by relating the Intercultural Sensitivity instance to one concept among denial, defense (reversal), minimization, acceptance, adaptation, and integration. Figure 8 depicts several concepts and instances in the cultural competence part of person's C profile. Only the intercultural sensitivity orientation and two languages are shown for the purpose of brevity.

In the occupational competence parts of the competence profiles of the team members only those occupational groups and educational fields, that represented knowledge and experience relevant for the software design area, were referred to by the instances of Work Experience Competence and Educational Competence. Additionally, each Educational Competence instance was related to educational programs/subjects, corresponding educational levels and countries. In turn, each Work Experience Competence instance was connected to occupational groups, countries, experience level and knowledge applied during the work. The experience level was again graded based on the amount of time spent in the occupation by the person. The knowledge applied shows those disciplines related to software design that were utilized during the work. Figure 9 illustrates part of the occupational competence of person C. It partly shows subjects studied within the Master's Program and experience gained while working as a software engineer (not all subjects are shown for brevity). It is interesting to note that two subjects, Computer System Design and Computer Programming, are referred to by the instances of both the Educational Competence and Work Experience Competence concepts.

*Figure 7. Relations between some concepts and instances of the general competence part of person B's profile*

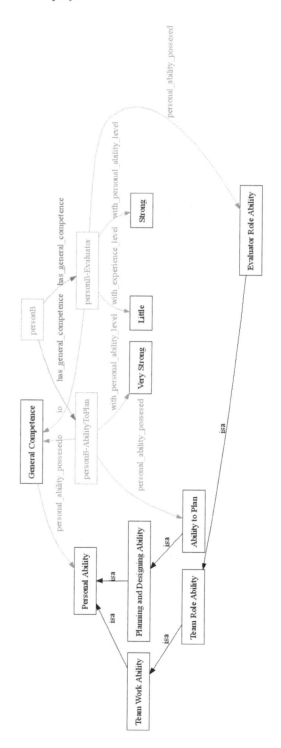

*Figure 8. Cultural competence part of person C's collaborative design competence profile*

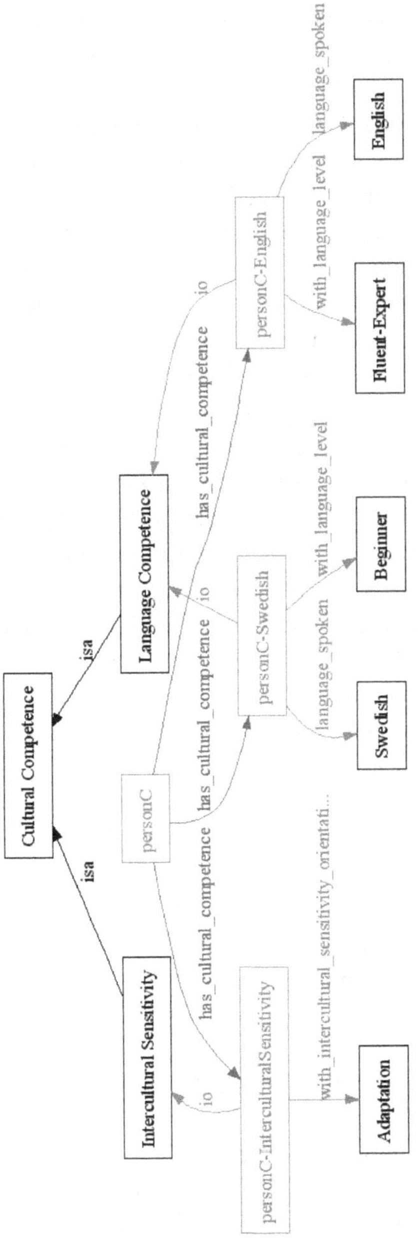

*Figure 9. Relations between some concepts and instances of the occupational competence part of person C's profile*

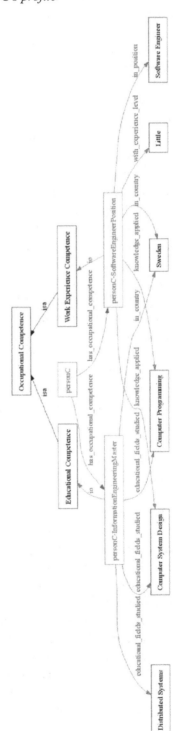

The collaborative design competence profiles were also created with Protégé 3.3. They are integrated in the ontology representing the collaborative design competence model.

## CONCLUSION

Based on the findings from an empirical investigation and literature from CSCW, we consider competence as essential factor when selecting members for a collaborative design team. The most important competence areas were identified starting from the nature of design work, problem solving in design teams and working in distributed groups. These competence areas were matched on competence perspectives, which reflect existing work for structuring capabilities or education profiles of individuals. An ontological representation was proposed to implement the described model for collaborative design competence. Finally, a software design team consisting of two persons was interviewed and two collaborative design competence profiles were created using the developed ontological representation of the model.

Ontologies as representation technique for competence models and the different competence perspectives have already been successfully applied in a research project for the Swedish International Development Agency aiming at capturing competences of migrants in Sweden (Tarassov, Sandkuhl, & Henoch, 2006). The modeling of the software design team members done in this study has proved that the proposed approach can also be applied to modeling competences needed for collaborative design in engineering fields. The developed competence model together with its ontological representation should be refined in a wider study. This especially concerns the general competence part. The accomplished interviews in this study and in the project described in (Tarassov, Sandkuhl, & Henoch, 2006) showed that capturing general abilities of an individual is a laborious task, which might introduce inaccuracy in competence profiles.

Using an ontology language for representation of collaborative design competence models makes it possible to identify those individuals who are best suited for the collaboration by ontology matching. Once competence profiles for potential team members are created, one can compare the profiles to the collaborative design task. The latter may be represented as a task ontology and thus ontology matching can be used to find appropriate team members covering each part of the task. Investigation of different ontology matching techniques enabling computer-based search and selection of individuals possessing needed collaborative design competences is one of the next logical steps in our future work, which so far concentrated on principal matching strategies and how to combine them (Lin & Sandkuhl, 2007).

Another interesting issue is to investigate how well required competences will be represented in a newly formed design team. This will require cooperation with researchers in the psychological field, in particular to provide for a well-balanced team with respect to both technical and social skills. Ongoing work includes an application of the competence modeling experiences in the defense sector. Focus here is on integrating knowledge about relations between individuals into competence models and on combining ontologies and enterprise models.

## ACKNOWLEDGMENT

Part of this research has been done in the project "ICT for the formation of business relationships with developing countries" funded by Swedish International Development Agency within the SPIDER program, 2004 - 2006. Another part of the work was financed by the Swedish Knowledge Foundation (KK-Stiftelsen), grant 2005/0252, project "Information Logistics for SME (infoFLOW)".

# REFERENCES

Andersson, R., & Olsson, A.-K. (1999). Fields of Education and Training. Manual. from http://europa.eu.int/comm/eurostat/ramon/nomenclatures/index.cfm?TargetUrl=LST_NOM

Bjurklo, M., & Kardemark, G. (1998). Social tests in a model for controlling the enhancement of competence. *Journal of Human Resource Costing and Accounting, 3*(2), 51-64.

Blomqvist, E., Levashova, T., Öhgren, A., Sandkuhl, K., & Smirnov, A. (2005). *Formation of Enterprise Networks for Collaborative Engineering.* Paper presented at the Post-conference proceedings of 3. Intl. Workshop on Collaborative Engineering, Sopron, Hungary.

Fuchs-Kittowski, F. (2007). *Integrierte IT-Unterstutzung der Wissensarbeit.* Cologne: EUL Verlag.

Gruber, T. R. (1993). A translation approach to portable ontology specifications. *Knowledge Acquisition, 5*(2), 199-220.

Grudin, J. (1994). Computer-Supported Cooperative Work: History and Focus. *IEEE Computer, May.*

Hammer, M. R., Bennett, M. J., & Wiseman, R. (2003). Measuring intercultural sensitivity: The intercultural development inventory. *International Journal of Intercultural Relations, 27*(4), 421-443.

Henoch, B., & Sandkuhl, K. (2002). Competence modelling as a basis for formation of SME-networks - the SME-chains approach. In *Proceedings of the WWDU 2002 Conference.*

International Labour Organization. (2004, September 18). International Standard Classification of Occupations, 1988 (ISCO-88). Retrieved September 19, 2005, from http://www.ilo.org/public/english/bureau/stat/isco/isco88/index.htm

Jones, S., & Marsh, S. (1997). Human-Computer-Human Interaction: Trust in CSCW. *SIGCHI Bulletin, 29*(3).

Lin, F., & Sandkuhl, K. (2007). Polygon-Based Similarity Aggregation for Ontology Matching. In *ISPA Workshops* (pp. 255-264): Springer.

Lundqvist, M. (2005). *Context as a Key Concept in Information Demand Analysis.* Paper presented at the Proceedings of the Doctoral Consortium associated with the 5th Intl. and Interdisciplinary Conference on Modeling and Using Context (CONTEXT-05), Paris, France.

Pahl, G., & Beitz, W. (1996). *Engineering Design: A Systematic Approach.* London: Springer.

Pawlak, A., Sandkuhl, K., Cholewa, W., & Indrusiak, L. (Eds.). (2007). *Coordination of Collaborative Engineering. 5. Intl. Workshop on Collaborative Engineering.* Krakow, Poland.

Sandkuhl, K., Smirnov, A., & Shilov, N. Configuration of automotive collaborative engineering and flexible supply networks. In P. Cunningham & M. Cunningham (Eds.), *Expanding the Knowledge Economy – Issues, Applications, Case Studies.* Amsterdam: IOS Press.

Tarasov, V., & Lundqvist, M. (2006). Modeling collaborative design competence with ontologies. *International Journal of e-Collaboration: Special Issue on the State of the Art and Future Challenges on Collaborative Design, 3*(4), 46-62.

Tarassov, V., Sandkuhl, K., & Henoch, B. (2006). *Using ontologies for representation of individual and enterprise competence models.* Paper presented at the Proceedings of the Fourth IEEE International Conference on Computer Sciences Research, Innovation and Vision for the Future, RIVF 2006, Ho-Chi-Minh City, Vietnam.

Ullman, D. G. (1997). *The Mechanical Design Process.* Singapore: McGraw-Hill Book Co.

UNESCO Institute for Statistics. (2003, November 25). International Standard Classification of Education (ISCED 1997). Retrieved September 20, 2005, from http://www.uis.unesco.org/ev.php?ID=3813_201&ID2=DO_TOPIC

## ENDNOTE

[1]   It can be possible that different age groups may prefer different types of information sources but our empirical investigation did not address this issue.

# Chapter XIV
# Functional Product Development Challenges Collaborative Work Practices

**Magnus Löfstrand**
*Luleå University of Technology, Sweden*

## ABSTRACT

*Developing service-laden products in a virtual extended enterprise implies a wider distribution of resources and product development (PD) team members than what is the case today. In this setting, the challenge is getting a cross-disciplinary distributed team to collaborate effectively over distance using not only the tools available today, but also new tools and approaches. One such activity-based approach, based on an actual Volvo Aero service-provision process, is presented in this article. Supplying a physical product as part of a service contract within an extended enterprise demands increased speed and quality of the predictions the supplier wants to make in order to keep track of the product functionality, its cost effectiveness and lifecycle cost. One approach that has been proven in engineering is modeling and simulation, here implemented as activity-based simulation of an actual industrial work process that provides a maintenance service. The activity-based simulation approach is realized in the industry standard simulation environment MATLAB. It is created as a demonstrator of one of several future tools that may help a virtual extended enterprise to face the challenge of supplying function or services to the customer more effectively. Conclusions regarding Collaborative Working Environments include new requirements on quality of tools for supporting functional product development regarding knowledge availability, usability, security and interoperability. Conclusions also support the suggested approach concerning development of distributed, modular activity-based process simulation models as a suitable approach for supporting functional product development.*

# FUNCTIONAL PRODUCT DEVELOPMENT CHALLENGES TODAY'S COLLABORATIVE WORK PRACTICE

This paper discusses demands on Collaborative Work and Collaborative Working Environments (EC, 2005) (CWE) originating in companies' transformation from hardware providers to function providers. An activity-based modeling and simulation approach to Functional Product Development (FPD) is suggested as part of a simulation-driven CWE approach to meet the new demands that are placed on tools and methods used in industrial product development due to this transformation.

A shift in view, captured in the concept of functional products, is found within the manufacturing industry. Traditionally, the manufacturing industry has focused on providing excellent goods, i.e., hardware. Services occur on an aftermarket, as add-ons to the developed hardware, and much of the profit is made on activities such as maintenance and spare parts. Nergård (2006) indicates that competition has increased in the manufacturing industries' aftermarket activities; one trigger for the concept of functional products according to information from the case discussed below is seen in the interest to control aftermarket activities associated with the developed hardware. By supplying functions, with hardware components as the core product, instead of merely selling the hardware, companies can control the aftermarket. The responsibility and availability of the functions provided by hardware remains with the service provider, as does the responsibility for maintenance and spare parts. This approach is a response to a necessity for business-to-business collaborators to gain economy-of-scale partnerships in the extended enterprise and ultimately to be able to develop competitive offers, as discussed by Löfstrand, Larsson & Karlsson (2005) and Alonso-Rasgado, Thompson & Elfström (2004) Hence, the shift in view is a move towards provid-

ing services while taking a lifecycle commitment for the hardware as well as optimizing the availability of its function in the customer's system. The redirection from hardware development to a process where the development of functions, comprised of hardware, software and services, or total offers is in focus is hereafter referred to as Functional Product Development (FPD), an area in which technology processes (hardware) and business processes (service add-ons) merge. The function provider needs some partners to act as sub-function suppliers in an extended enterprise fashion. Based on information from the workshops discussed below, this calls for closer collaboration than what is normally the case in a project aimed at hardware development only. Different team members with different functions (e.g., engineering design, production, management, finance and marketing) must be able to share relevant function-specific information while doing distributed collaborative work. O'Donnell (2005) suggests using an approach based on systems thinking for handling business models. This might be carried out by team members in management or economy-related roles.

Product development literature provides a broad view of how to understand customer needs, develop and sell products and includes discussions concerning best practices, (Ulrich & Eppinger, 1995; Wheelwright & Clark, 1992; Cross, 2000) For example, Smith & Reinertsen (1997) offer a general view and aim to describe methods for generating a product (hardware or service) to meet customer needs. Within the hardware product development domain numerous tools have been developed to support the creation of excellent goods; Computer Aided Engineering for geometric representation (LaCourse, 1996) and Finite Element Method for stress calculation. Typically, this work has been about making knowledge explicit and expressible and support tools have over time been developed to aid the creation of the hardware.

On the business side, tools and methods exist for managing the kind of knowledge that is typical for this domain (Porter, 1998; Shostack, 1987; http://www.valuebasedmanagement.net/). Related tools sometimes include functions for project planning and project coordination. Some consist mainly of document templates (http://www.envision-sbs.com/business/index.html). Business-related methods include Total Quality Management, Business Process Reengineering and Process Management. These methods, according to Nilsson (1999) correspond to the second level of development work – organizational development.

It becomes necessary to develop tools and methods for effective and efficient optimization and simulation of future hardware-based services, one way of minimizing the functional product's total lifecycle cost (Boart, 2005).

This paper discusses an activity-based modeling and simulation approach to the FPD process where hardware development activities are combined with service activities in an FPD simulation system. The simulation system is realized in the industry standard simulation environment MATLAB (http://www.mathworks.com/products/matlab/). The approach both challenges and provides new opportunities for distributed collaborative work. A wider distribution of resources and people constitutes the main challenge. This requires an increased need for communication and collaboration between participants. No discipline has a single best tool, which complicates distance collaboration where many tools must be distributed, some of which are not known to all participants. The opportunities include being able to better predict the function and cost of one's development process, which is a prerequisite for daring to enter into business deals where supplying function is a main ingredient. Many approaches may be used to meet the challenge of functional products. They include business process re-engineering (BPR), customer relationship management, marketing,

etc. Tinnilä (1995) has reviewed some of the literature concerned with business process re-engineering. He notes that Davidson (1993) sees that the objective of BPR is usually the optimization of a single process rather than transformation of the enterprise itself. Modeling a single process is the approach has been used for this article. Danesh & Kock (2005) discuss the benefits of using models, as described by Sharp and MacDermott (2001). Modeling is used here, since models are relatively quickly created, safe to manipulate and may allow clarification of non-physical activities of the actual process. Modeling and simulation have long been used in product development research to *verify* a hardware design and are here suggested for the company internal purpose of clarification and optimization of process activities. Since the MATLAB models introduced here are executable and create simulation results, they also allow for work process *predictions* and process *optimization* which may be used externally, for example in business-to-business negotiation. Additionally, models are suitable for remote collaboration, more so because of the modular structure approach used during development. Hence, while modeling in general is not a new approach, to apply it in order to optimize a work process is novel in the field of engineering design and an attempt to allow distributed collaboration through models with a simulation driven approach.

The purposes of the research presented in this article are:

- To identify challenges for distributed collaborative work practices when working with FPD.
- To demonstrate the potential of event-driven simulations of work processes, for supporting distributed collaborative work in functional product development. The demonstrator is based on a case from the aerospace industry.

Based on the need to increase the predictability of design process outcomes, the research question was formulated thus:

*"How is distributed collaborative work affected by functional product development?"*

## THE RATIONALE FOR A SIMULATION APPROACH

Many variables affect the effectiveness and efficiency of the design process (Löfstrand, Larsson & Karlsson, 2005) Identifying how these variables interrelate is crucial for developing adequate models. By applying a simulation rationale in a lifecycle manner and with the idea of simulating not only the hardware but also the service components, the FPD simulation system is achieved, based on the notion that almost anything that can be described can be modeled, simulated and optimized with respect to a desired state. Since the right choices, depending on cost, profit, etc, are desired before any investments in manufacturing and production are actually made, a primary concern is to predict any lifecycle commitment as early as in the concept phase of the development process.

Functional product development may be seen as a response to needs arising in an increasingly globalized market. Here, business-to-business collaboration to gain economy-of-scale partnerships in the extended enterprise is necessary. This has led to an identification of the need to increase the predictability of design in relation to business scenarios.

Given the right variables, activity-based process models may be used to:

- Identify process bottlenecks in collaborative work processes.
- Create material for go/no-go business decisions and causal development decisions.
- Support decision-making by improving the capacity to predict if and by how much a suggested business offer is lucrative.
- Create structures and interfaces which may serve as tools upon which to base discussions in an increasingly cross-functional design team.

These tasks are especially important in the extended enterprise during FPD and must be possible to perform effectively and efficiently over distance in a distributed collaborative environment. This approach is an attempt to identify the design space for the functional product development team member and to alleviate the need for communication, thereby freeing time for more design iterations, producing more concepts and creating better results.

## DATA GATHERING AND ANALYSIS

The research within which this article has been developed includes ongoing investigations with about 10 interviewees at Volvo Aero Corporation concerning their product development practices and goals. Much of the work was carried out during three week-long visits to Volvo Aero, where the researcher observed the daily work and was welcomed to develop a suggestion for improvement concerning how Volvo Aero responds to customers' requests for service provision. The project also included opened-ended interviews (Yin, 1994), document analysis of formal work-process descriptions, archival records, and subsets of what Volvo Aero Corporation calls their Global Development Process or GDP. This first led to the identification of the corresponding process in the Volvo Aero GDP, a hardware-based process for service provision. The information was collected through field notes on a laptop computer when the researcher more or less participated in daily work or interrupted daily work to ask questions. In some cases, formal interviews were recorded. Between visits to Volvo Aero the data was interpreted and modeling was carried out. The information given by interviewees and the researcher's interpretations thereof were then discussed with other Volvo Aero personnel (aside from the interviewees themselves) regularly during the week-long visits, during quarterly project meetings at the university and at Volvo Aero.

In parallel, during the course of 18 months, the researcher's division and Volvo Aero were heavily involved, with other industrial and academic partners, in the planning and formulation of the strategy of the Faste Laboratory – Centre for Functional Product Innovation. During the course of the work, several meetings were held; during these meetings, future challenges concerning Functional Product Development, Simulation Driven Design and Distributed Collaborative Work were discussed; since they are the cornerstones of the Faste Laboratory.

Results from Interviews and Workshops

The information given by interviewees and researcher interpretations thereof were verified through taped interviews with the five most important informants, including the main industrial advisor.

Results indicate that collaborative work will continue to be increasingly distributed. As a consequence, doing research here will require identification of new user needs, evaluation of existing tools and development of new approaches and tools rather than developing technologies for supporting current practices only. The main results from the interviews and workshops follow.

- New distributed tools for CWE are needed to merge the business simulations and hardware-based functional simulations to create a simulation-driven holistic approach to FPD.
- These new tools must be used in an increasingly distributed fashion.
- Tools for distributed work must be simple enough that anybody with little computer skill can use them for communication and collaboration.

- Feedback from the tools needs to be appropriate for the user needs in the specific scenario and may therefore be varied. Different settings would be preferable: fast and relatively inexact (a minute), yet useful; or slower (20 minutes) but more exact simulation results in terms of data maturity or degree of probability.

- One cannot assume that current CWE practices will suffice to support distributed cross-functional teams developing functional products.
- Effects of distribution of the simulation model and results include need for:
  ○ Managing intellectual property rights
  ○ Development of access control technologies to enable black-box simulations and preventing reverse engineering.
- Drivers for industrial FPD interests include: decreasing the competition on the aftermarket, sharing risks and therefore also profits within the extended enterprise.
- Functional Product Development requires closer collaboration, between more disciplines, than what is mostly the case today.

Danesh and Kock (2005) make a case for the importance of placing focus on communication flows rather than on activity-based flows only. In the work leading up to this article it was always necessary to monitor dialogues and to do retrospective studies of communication paths in order to find out what activities people carried out. This is schematically described in Figure 2, below. A main result is the development of a scenario for service provision, which the activity-based simulation models are supporting. The final main result is the developed process for service provision based on an actual hardware-based industrial process. This process is schematically described in Figure 1 and Figure 2 and is included as a component of the scenario.

## THE SCENARIO

In order to show the benefits of the simulation-driven CWE approach a business scenario is created, anchored in the company needs. The scenario is based on a need for predictions concerning company performance that are much faster and more accurate than today's. The changing business demands require that a simulation which today takes two weeks will in the relatively near future have to be done in less than a day. Being able to supply a hardware-based service to a variety of customers is a driving force behind this development. These services include welding, milling, drilling, heat treatments and various types of written instructions, among others.

The work process that is discussed in this article is schematically laid out in Figure 1, below. The process consists of a selection of blocks that correspond to sets of related activities. Through modeling and optimization of the process, based on the available manpower and the cost of this manpower, the corresponding model delivers an indication of which business alternative is best for the company to suggest to the customer; to carry out line one, line two or line three. The approach suggested herein also allows for optimization of the selected line.

Activity-based discrete event simulations as well as dynamic, deterministic simulations are built on sets of rules. The rules used for developing the event-based model discussed here are mainly based on the necessary activities for performing the service. Creating a first version, the demonstrator model requires knowledge of internal aspects such as which capacity, when, for how long and to which cost. Finally, one must have some idea of external aspects such as what customer value is achieved and the risks involved. This becomes important when negotiating issues concerning, for example, profit margin.

A procedural view of the studied process is described in Figure 2.

Here, the process has been described for the purpose of portraying the interaction and communication that must take place internally, before delivery of the intended service. Figure 2 relates to line 1 of Figure 1 as follows: Starting in the lower left corner with a new order from a customer, the order goes though a set of either external activities or internal activities (with no direct feedback to the customer). The order is processed by the customer support department when it is received, an increased cost (through usage of more spare parts) is identified, the service description of work is updated, a price is set and finally the customer receives an offer. The offer may be to repair a component, for example. The outcomes of line 2 and line 3 of Figure 1 represent other services that may be offered to the customer. While the studied

*Figure 1. A schematic layout of the studied process*

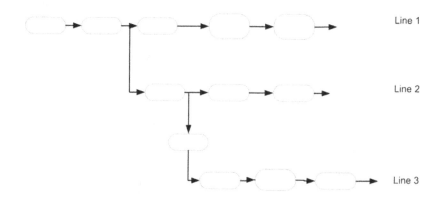

*Figure 2. The work process that provides a service to an internal or external customer*

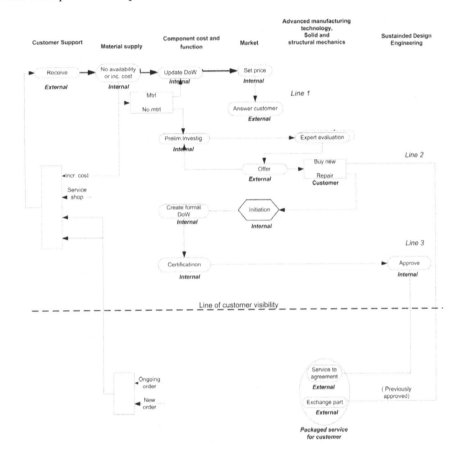

process is an internal one, specific to Volvo Aero, it stands to reason that if this service is part of a larger (functional) product within an extended enterprise, two effects are expected:

- The number of interactions will increase dramatically between companies and competencies, which in turn requires additional resources in terms of distributed collaborative work.
- It will be increasingly important to be able to control the own company-specific process and to predict the performance of one's own products and functional product components, especially for reasons of risk minimization.

## ACTIVITY-BASED SIMULATIONS FOR FUNCTIONAL PRODUCT DEVELOPMENT

Here, the particulars of the MATLAB model structure are discussed. Activity-based simulations are suggested as a suitable approach to making implicit information explicit and thereby enabling the use of late-stage design tools earlier in the development process, thus ultimately improving the quality of the outcome of the development process.

### The MATLAB Model Structure

For decomposition and refinement purposes, the structure and general approach to modeling are

*Figure 3. The structure of the MATLAB FPD models*

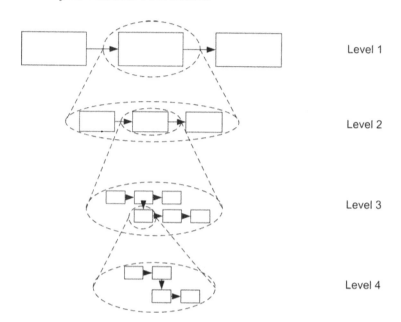

introduced in Figure 3, based on the idea that modeling blocks contain references to other building blocks, creating a modular structure.

At the highest level of model abstraction (see Figure 3 – Level 1) one is interested in which activity blocks a design process consists of as well as the number of people involved and the time and costs associated with the activities. Level one corresponds to the business negotiation level.

A company generally has different levels of knowledge of different clients, and the clients generally have varying degrees of problems and varying knowledge of their own development processes. Say a company has cooperated for decades with some suppliers. Based on that history and your existing knowledge, you would be more likely to create a more accurate model of your collaborative development process than if your company were required to come up with a model for collaborative development in response to a request from a new customer. This aspect is certainly something that may be included in this type of model.

At a second level of simulation the fluctuation of a currency exchange rate might be included, including its likely future fluctuation based on statistics and probability. This aspect would be of interest to many companies, particularly those that buy and sell their products and services at an agreed fixed exchange rate that varies from one business agreement to the next.

At level three the model-associated risks may be included. One can envisage the activity-based model including company-specific gates, each of which imposes new rules on e.g., user feedback concerning the model accuracy or technology readiness level.

At level four the model resembles the approach found in Knowledge Enabled Engineering (Bylund, 2004). The key concepts of Knowledge Enabled Engineering (KEE) are that the logics of the design object and the actual design process are described in a way that allows the automatic generation of design solutions, something which is possible using the activity-based modeling approach described herein. The advantages of KEE are appealing; lead-time for standard work activities can be dramatically reduced in combination with an improved and controllable quality. Standard solutions can be generated, evaluated and reported repeatedly at a low cost for each iteration. Engineers can concentrate on the more intellectual parts of engineering work rather than spending time doing routine work. The design team can thus investigate more design alternatives on a more detailed level than what is possible using today's procedures.

The idea behind this model is somewhat similar to the one developed by Larsson et al. (2001), a tool that supports distribution of multibody dynamic analysis models in a modular way. In that case as in the current activity-based model, the modeling of sub-models is about getting a resemblance between the actual system and the modeled system. That is, between the actual design process and the activity-based model.

The activity-based model allows parallel development of the product development process and the hardware core product by suggesting which line to choose before the hardware has been developed. It facilitates the use of black-box simulation by allowing a partner access to input and output interfaces and not to the model itself. It can be used throughout the different stages of the development process, regardless of geographic location. If changes are made in the existing development process, use of this tool facilitates a simulation-driven design process. Finally, the simulation model allows for storage and retrieval of a number of outputs from execution of the model which, when viewed in retrospect, enhances understanding of the design rationale (Burge, 1998).

## Supporting Collaborative Work Practices: Creating an Interface Between Companies in the Extended Enterprise

Here, a number of potential gains from using a simulation-driven CWE approach are presented.

Then, some plausible positive effects on the actual teamwork are discussed.

Creating and using the activity-based model is an attempt to ensure that the company is working on the most relevant problem, or at least a problem within the most relevant set of problems. (For example, having the model suggest which line to choose, see Figure 1.) Another conceivable benefit is that it is also possible to outsource a part of the activities of the service provision process to an FPD partner, a supplier or a sub-contractor. If running the model, optimizing a selected line, indicates that performing a group of activities within a specific block costs significantly more than if another company performs them, these activities may be outsourced to the lowest qualified bidder. This frees time and resources for the first company to concentrate on activities that create more customer value. Having the two partners developing and tuning their own development processes via the fixed input and output interfaces between the blocks beforehand allows both parties to bring offers to the table that at least formally fulfill the requirements of the partner having the primary customer role.

The process model enables optimization in two ways. First, with known resources, it is possible to optimize how the process should most effectively be carried out, given a known set of goals and a design space for each variable. Second, it is possible to determine how much time and money may be spent, before associated costs equal created value.

This type of model would make it possible for a company to ensure that the same things are requested from a group of competing sub-contractors and act as a measuring device when choosing sub-contractors.

Finally, another benefit of this type of process model is the possibility of comparing the improvement potential of different concepts by simulating cost/gain ratios of the individual concepts and comparing them.

As evidenced by interviews and workshops, one challenge in doing distributed work in the context of the extended enterprise is that the distributed design team is likely to be more culturally, socially and functionally non-uniform than a locally assembled cross-functional team. As a response to this challenge the model may be run remotely by e.g., a sub-contractor with only levels 1 and 2 of the model visible together with audio and video collaboration. The model was discussed with industrialists as a business negotiation tool between two different companies creating a common ground – they are discussing something both have good knowledge of, i.e., their own product development processes. Additionally, both parties are free to use more information then they display – the sub-contractor may also do so if he has accepted responsibility for an outsourced block from the other party. The accuracy of the predicted outcome is thereby greater than it would be if the parties merely exchanged files.

A challenge in allowing a culturally and functionally non-uniform distributed team to collaborate effectively over distance lies partly in describing the design processes and in identifying which activities are truly important for the various aspects of creating a product the team judges to meet its requirements. Effects of a design change, captured as an activity in a simulation tool, could be displayed in different ways to people with different functions in a distributed design team or its management. According to Nemiro (2004), virtual teams run the risk of both information overload (due to the speed of electronic communications) and not getting enough information (due to the inherent limited richness in communication exchanges). The approach presented here would help the team to consider the development process from a few more angles, thus increasing media richness.

The value created by the suggested modeling approach is threefold: technical (identifies the optimal process composition), social (increased safety and security for the project manager) and economic (suggests demands on future business venture intakes through the simulation of time and cost of process activities).

## CHALLENGES FOR DISTRIBUTED WORK PRACTICES POSED BY THE INTRODUCTION OF FUNCTIONAL PRODUCT DEVELOPMENT

Product-development-driven companies work in an increasingly globalized world, implying a need for involved parties to share resources, technologies, risks and profit to a greater extent, especially within FPD. This type of collaboration radically intensifies the demand on various-sized cross-functional teams working over organizational, geographical, functional and cultural borders. Currently, the concept of integrated product development (IPD) (Prasad, 1997) is well understood in the engineering design research community. Differences (in focus and degree) between IPD and FPD are introduced in Table 1.

Clearly, these issues challenge distributed collaborative work. Imagine selling collaboration ability to a global design team engaged in FPD. The demands on CWE methods and tools are increasing in terms of functionality, availability, usability, security, interoperability, personalization and knowledge availability.

To summarize, four different and interrelated issues for CWE have been found as a consequence of development of functional products in the extended enterprise.

- Because of the variety of challenges in functional product development a scenario approach that gives the team members a similar starting point is suggested, based on new user needs.
- Exploration of additional new simulation-driven methods and tools that facilitate other user needs than audio and video and may be used in early concept stages is beneficial. Such user needs include tools for design space exploration, i.e., to define the limitations that exist for the design team (Cost and time have been used as examples of important limiting criteria).

*Table 1. Differences between CWE in a IPD and CWE in a FPD context*

|  | IPD through CWE | FPD through CWE |
|---|---|---|
| **Need:** | personal interaction | hard to identify and express |
| **Problem:** | easily defined | hard to define, wicked |
| **Product:** | hardware | combo of hardware, software, services |
|  | tangible | hardware core probable, not necessary |
| **Ownership:** | transferred | wholly or partly non-transferred |
| **Design space:** | experienced, defined, taught | experienced, not defined, not taught |
| **External limits:** | few | many, increasing policy, law, environment |
| **Setting:** | B2C, (B2B) | B2B, (B2C) |
| **Competitive Differentiation:** | being the best, low price | being the best partner, optimized cost/gain |
| **Value prod. in:** | factory | interactions, consumption, factory |
| **Value prod. by:** | hardware, ownership | FP availability, knowledge, security |
| **Value measured:** | hardware performance | FP functionality, decreased risk |
| **Team bounds:** | interdisciplinary, uniform | interdisciplinary, non-uniform |
| **Crossing:** | time zones, languages | time zones, languages, companies, cultures |
| **Responsibility:** | company individual | Shared in extended enterprise, Life-cycle |
| **Simulations:** | verificational | predictive, optimizing |
|  | local, results shared | simultaneous, real-time |

- Tolerances for problems related to the tool rather than to actual work decrease (Holtzblatt & Jones, 1993).
- Developing the ability to distribute other new tools with extensive demands on usability, interoperability and interface personalization.

Addressing the latter issue would be another step towards enabling relevant views of the same information, displayed differently according to the function of the person seeing it, thereby moving towards a shift from application to activity-oriented systems design. Engineers might need 3D-geometry views, while economists might want to see how the product cost is affected by a design change made by the engineer. One person might prefer dependencies described in terms of a design structure matrix while others prefer a functional breakdown of the product being sold, etc.

The described simulation tool is an attempt to display engineering-design-related information differently, based on what in a generic way may be seen as business information (i.e., cost and time) in a way that makes the information more accessible for business management. Concurrently,

the model layout corresponds very well with the traditional engineering design process, thereby creating a shared frame of reference.

## CONCLUSION

The paper discusses the challenges to CWE presented by Functional Product Development. It has been suggested that functional product development requires new tools and methods which in turn create new challenges for collaborative working environments. One such new tool, an activity-based simulation environment for a hardware-based service, has been presented above and shown to be useful. These new tools and methods also create opportunities for new research within the field of distributed collaborative work, since functional product development implies a need for increased distribution of people in terms of time-zones, distance and competence. The work shows that existing initiatives from the hardware development domain are applicable for the FPD domain. It has also been made plausible that a concurrent simulation approach that includes hardware as well as business development aspects may be developed, building on traditional engineering tools and approaches (Isaksson, Keski-Säppälä & Eppinger, 2000; Smith & Murrow, 1999; Dias & Blockley, 1994) as well as approaches found, loosely speaking, in the business development domain (Pretorius & Steyn, 2005; Nilsson, 1999; Chowdary & Prakash, 2005; Paper & Chang, 2005).

The suggested approach poses significant challenges not only with respect to tools and methods for collaborative engineering, but also industrial collaborative work as a whole.

Distributed work in the context of functional products requires ability to distribute knowledge effectively amongst many different team members. The simulation model discussed in this article is an attempt to display engineering-design-related information differently, based on an actual engineering design process. The simulation of a hardware-based service process may be used to improve the predicted outcome of the process, which may then be offered as a function in a total offer.

Development and use of the suggested modular activity-based process simulation modeling approach enables relevant activity-based analysis throughout the process, which will ultimately improve product quality while optimizing the chosen variable, for example, cost or throughput time. The model can be used throughout the different stages of the development process, regardless of geographic location, for optimizing an actual engineering design process and integrating the engineering and business disciplines. This may enable design for best function by simulation-driven design of the functional product lifecycle.

Future work includes optimization of the tool. The model will be further developed in terms of its accuracy with respect to the activities within the design process and the value created thereof. One way to do this is to further develop the model to better account for the pareto optimal solution to the two-dimensional problem of finding the most efficient distribution of resources in terms of cost and throughput time.

## ACKNOWLEDGMENT

The project has been financed by the Swedish National Aviation Engineering Research Programme (NFFP) through the Polhem Laboratory, both financially supported by VINNOVA. The author would like to thank Thomas Gustafsson and Bengt-Olof Elfström at Volvo Aero and Tobias Larsson of Luleå University of Technology for valuable support and interesting discussions. Finally, thanks goes to the informants for their time and patience.

## REFERENCES

Alonso-Rasgado, T., Thompson, G., Elfström, B. (2004). The design of functional (total care) products, *Journal of Engineering Design*, *15*(6), 515-540.

Boart, P. (2005). *Life Cycle Simulation Support for Functional Products*, Licentiate Thesis, Luleå University of Technology, lISSN 1402-1757 / ISRN LTU-LIC--05/20--SE / NR 2005:20.

Burge, J. (1999). *Design Rationale*, Draft Technical Report, Worchester Polytechnic Institute.

Bylund, N., Isaksson, O., Kalhori, V., Larsson, T (2004). Enhanced Engineering Design Practice using Knowledge Enabled Engineering with Simulation Methods. *Proceedings of Design 2004*.

Chowdhary, N., Prakash, M. (2005). Service Quality: revisiting the Two Factors Theory, *Journal of Services Research*, *5*(1).

Cross, N. (2000). Engineering design methods – Strategies for Product Design, New York, John Wiley & Sons.

Danesh, A., Kock, N. (2005). An experimental study of process representation approaches and their impact on perceived modeling quality and redesign success, *Business Process Management Journal, 11*(6), 724-735.

Davidson, W.H. (1993). Beyond re-engineering: the three phases of business transformation, *IBM Systems Journal, 32*(1), 65-79.

Dias, W.P.S., Blockley, D.I. (1994). The integration of product and process models for design , *Design Studies 15*(4).

EC (2005) Collaboration@Work, *The 2005 report on new working environments and practices* (October), Commission of Information Society and Media.

Holtzblatt, K., Jones, S. (1993). Contextual Inquiry: A Participatory Technique for System Design, in *Participatory Design: Principles and Practice*, Hillsdale, New Jersey.

Isaksson, O., Keski-Säppäl, S., Eppinger, S.D. (2000). Evaluation of design process alternatives using signal flow graphs, *Journal of Engineering Design, 11*(3), 211–224.

Kanter Moss, R. (1999). Change Is Everyone's job: Managing the Extended Enterprise in a

Globally Connected World. *Organizational Dynamics, 28*(1),.7-23.

LaCourse, D.E. (1996). *Handbook of Solid Modelling*, McGraw-Hill.

Larsson, T., Larsson, A., Karlsson, L. (2001). A Modular Approach to Web Based Multibody Dynamic Simulation, *International CIRP Design Seminar, Design in the New Economy.*

Löfstrand M., Larsson, T., Karlsson, L. (2005). Demands on Engineering Design Culture for Implementing Functional Products, *Proceedings of the International Conference on Engineering Design*, Melbourne.

Nemiro, J.E. (2004*). Creativity in Virtual Teams, Key Components for Success*, Pfeiffer/John Wiley and Sons.

Nergård, H.., Ericson, Å., Bergström, M., Sandberg, S., Larsson, T., Törlind, P. (2006). Functional Product Development – Discussing Knowledge Enabling Technologies, *International Design Conference, Design 2006,* Dubrovnik, Croatia.

Nilsson, A.G. et al. (1999). *Perspectives on Business Modelling, Understanding and Changing Organisations*, Springer-Verlag.

O'Donnell, E. (2005). Enterprise risk management: A systems-thinking framework for the event identification phase. *International Journal of accounting information systems, 6*(3), 177-195.

Paper, D., Chang, R-D. (2005). The State of Business Process Reengineering: A Search for Success Factors, *Total Quality Management,* 16(1), 21–133.

Porter, M. E. (1998). *Competitive strategy. Techniques for analyzing and strategic flexibility: A performance dilemma in designing new product development configurations.* Simon & Schuster: New York.

Prasad, B. (1997). *Concurrent Engineering Fundamentals, Integrated Product Development*, Prentice Hall.

Pretorius, C.J., Steyn, H. (2005). Knowledge management in project environments, *African Journal of Business Management, 36*(3).

Sharp, A., MacDermott, P. (2001). *Workflow Modeling: Tools for Process Improvement and Application Development*, Artech House Publishers, Norwood, MA.

Shostack, L.G.(1987). Service Positioning through Structural Change, *Journal of Marketing, 51*(1), 34-43.

Smith, R.P., Morrow, J.A. (1999). Product development process modeling, *Design Studies, 20*(3), 237-261.

Smith, P.G., Reinertsen, D.G. (1997). *Developing Products in Half the Time*, John Wiley and Sons.

Tinnilä, M. (1995). Strategic perspective to business process redesign, *Business Process Re-engineering & Management Journal, 1*(1), 44-59.

Ulrich, K.T., Eppinger, S.D.(1995). *Product Design and Development*, McGraw-Hill.

Wheelwright, C., Clark, K. (1992). *Revolutionising Product Development – Quantum Leaps in Speed, Efficiency and Quality*, the Free Press, New York.

Yin, R.K. (1994). *Case Study Research, Design and Methods*, Sage Publications.

# Chapter XV
# Managing Operational Business Processes with Web–Based Information Technologies

**Ned Kock**
*Texas A&M International University, USA*

## ABSTRACT

*Traditionally management schools of thought that emphasize certain types of work structures usually appear earlier than information technologies (IT) geared at supporting those work structures. This situation has undoubtedly changed recently, arguably around the mid-1990s, with the explosion in the commercial use of the Internet and particularly the Web. This calls for the development of a generic framework that ties together relevant management ideas that help organizations strategically and operationally align themselves with new Web-based IT. Our goal with this chapter is to provide some basic elements that can be used by managers and researchers as a starting point to develop this generic framework. As such, we focus on a particular set of activities associated with team coordination and communication in production and service delivery business processes through the Internet and the Web.*

## INTRODUCTION

Traditionally, management thinking has preceded and quite possibly driven the adoption and use of information technologies (IT) in organizations. That is, management schools (of thought) that emphasize certain types of work structures usually appear earlier than IT geared at supporting those work structures. This situation has undoubtedly changed recently, arguably around the mid-1990s, with the explosion in the commercial use of the Internet and particularly the Web. The emergence of e-commerce, e-trade, e-business, and other *e-'s* has clearly led to creation of new organizational forms, management challenges, and related management ideas (see, e.g., Kock, 2008). For example, the Web has led to the development or expansion of:

- "Internet startups", whose market value vastly exceeds what traditional price/earnings standards for company market valuation stipulate, placing these companies in an advantageous competitive position right at their inception due to the initial amount of capital that is available to them.
- "Internet portals", whose market value depends much more heavily on the number of visitors (first time or repeat) they can draw than on their revenues, profitability or other traditional market value measures.
- "Virtual organizations", which operate with no or little of physical assets and distribution channels.
- "Boundaryless organizations", in which geographical barriers to teamwork and market reach are virtually eliminated.

The examples above only scratch the surface as far as the potential that this "disruptive technology" which is the Internet can have on organizational structure and, in consequence, management thinking. The adoption of management ideas that are aligned with the collaboration potential afforded by the Internet and the Web can place companies in tremendously advantageous positions in their industries, at least at a certain point in the evolution as organizational entities, as illustrated by Dell Computer, Federal Express, E-Trade and Amazon.com. The reasons for this are many, and range from the capacity to benefit from lower barriers to new entrants, to the ability to attract large infusions of capital at the beginning of their life cycle, to the development and continuous use of highly streamlined distribution and workflow management processes.

## NEW ORGANIZATIONAL MODELS SUPPORTED BY THE WEB AND KEY MANAGEMENT SCHOOLS OF THE 1900s

At the time of writing, the type of management thinking discussed above was not well defined and shaped in the form of a single management school. Nevertheless, is has been easy to find organizations trying to adapt ideas from old and existing management schools to the new environment of Web-based IT. Table 1 summarizes key management schools that emerged in the late 1900s, before the use of the Web became widespread.

Trying to adapt ideas from old and existing management schools (such as those in Table 1) to the new environment of Web-based IT has its advantages, but is difficult to implement in practice. There are two key reasons for this. The first is that some of the new Web-based IT have emerged to support new organizational forms that are often incompatible with one single management school. The second reason is that existing management schools usually propose ideas that are, at some level, contradictory, often because they were developed on the premise that other management schools proposed ideas that did not work in practice (e.g., reengineering vs. total quality management). Moreover, given the tendency of business writers to focus on one or a few business ideas and propose them as a panacea, it is difficult to find a good match between single existing management schools and emerging Web-based IT. What is needed is a generic framework that ties together relevant management ideas that help organizations strategically and operationally align themselves with new Web-based IT.

It is beyond the scope of this chapter to propose a new management school. Even "describing" in the detail a new management school would increase the length of this discussion beyond what is expected from a chapter. Given this, a first step towards a new management framework to help organizations benefit from modern Web-based

*Table 1. Key management schools of the 1900s*

| Management school | Main figure(s) | Period | Main thesis |
|---|---|---|---|
| Total quality management | Deming, Juran | Began in the 1950s, first in Japan, reaching the US in the 1980s | Organizational improvement should focus on processes, not problems, and related quality issues. Productivity improvement cannot be realized without quality improvement. Line employees and customers, not only managers, should be deeply involved in quality improvement initiatives. |
| Organizational learning | Revans, Argyris, Senge | Began in the 1960s | Workers as well as managers can continuously improve the organization in which they work by freely sharing and questioning their knowledge and personal beliefs in a trusting organizational environment. |
| Excellence | Peters, Kanter | Began in the 1980s | Excellent organizations change continuously in order to satisfy their customers. This change is both top-down and bottom-up, i.e., it is driven by managers as well as line workers. |
| Reengineering | Hammer, Davenport | Began in the 1990s | Organizations should radically redesign their processes from time to time in order to remain competitive. This redesign should be top-down, i.e., primarily led by top managers. |

IT is proposed and discussed in the next section. Our goal is to provide some basic elements that can be used by managers and researchers as a starting point for a broader management model. As such, we focus on a particular set of activities associated with team coordination and communication in production and service delivery business processes.

## A SIMPLE FRAMEWORK FOR SUPPORTING PROCESSES WITH WEB-BASED IT

A great deal of my work since the late 1980s has revolved around the use of IT to support different forms of teamwork. Since 1997, several colleagues and I have been working with a number of companies in the Philadelphia Metropolitan Area in the analysis and redesign of their business processes, leveraging the resources provided by the Web to support new intra-organizational processes,

through "intranets", and new inter-organizational processes, through "extranets". Some of the companies we have worked with toward this end were Prudential Insurance, Metro One Telecommunications, Sheraton Hotels, Day & Zimmermann, Lockheed Martin, Delaware Investments, Penn Mutual and Andersen Consulting.

After several projects, each involving different managers, consultants and key employees, some patterns started to emerge that seemed relatively independent of characteristics of the organization, processes, or people involved. While the organizations and processes targeted had their own peculiarities, we seemed to invariably arrive at a similar final result. (Interestingly, the same was generally true in controlled experiments; see, e.g., Kock et al., 2008). This final result was, in all projects, a new process (we analyzed and redesigned over 30 processes from more than 15 organizations from 1997 to 2000). Processes analyzed included marketing, sales, inventory control, production, distribution, and service delivery.

Production and service delivery processes were the most frequent types of processes redesigned. In these, some generic features were particularly similar across redesigned processes in different companies. These are illustrated in Figure 1 and can be summarized as follows:

**A Web-based workflow control module**, represented in Figure 1 by the oval described as "Process automation application (workflow control module)". This is a computer application module that automates the execution of a process, from beginning to end, reminding process team members of tasks under their responsibility and allowing them to update the execution status of those tasks. This module populates a **process execution database** that stores data about process execution, represented in the figure by the drum symbol described as "Process execution database".

**A Web-based customer query module**, represented in Figure 1 by the oval described as "Process automation application (customer query module)", whose main function is to give customer access to process execution status data. For customers requesting an external telephone line repair, for example, this module would provide information about repair status.

**A Web-based OLAP (Online Analytical Processing) application**, represented in Figure 1 by the oval described as "OLAP application", whose main function is to allow the process manager to generate (and customize the generation of) process metrics periodically. Process metrics provide a simplified view of the productivity and

*Figure 1. A generic model to implement processes enabled by Web-based IT*

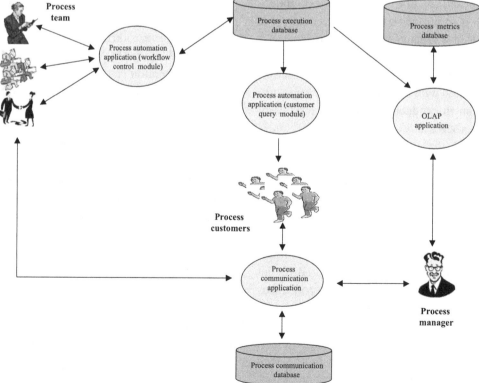

quality of a process and can be used for continuous improvement of the processes.

**A Web-based process communication application**, represented in Figure 1 by the oval described as "Process communication application", which populates and provides access to a **process communication database**. This application supports continuous communication between the process manager, process customers, and process team and may incorporate the following Web-based components:

- **A repository of summarized process metrics and process improvement initiatives** aimed at improving the outcomes of the metrics. Usually the process manager maintains this repository.
- **A discussion forum** that allows process customers to communicate with each other as well as with process team members and the process manager.
- **A knowledge base** with key data needed by process team members to execute their respective activities in the process, and process customers, so they can use outputs of the process more efficiently and effectively. In the case of a help desk process, for example, this knowledge base would contain equipment and software support information to be used by process customers for self-help.

## A PRACTICAL EXAMPLE: A WEB-BASED "HELP DESK"

One of the most common processes of IT organizations that provide technology support to parent companies is the "help desk" process. It is through the help desk process that internal users are enabled to do their work using IT. Help desk activities include new accounts (e.g., email, proxy, dial-up, selected applications) creation, office applications training, general hardware and software support, network cabling set up, and database

hosting, among others. The help desk process is a key process for both IT organization and parent company. The IT organization's budget is often defined by the quality and volume of help desk-related services provided to internal IT users.

A practical implementation of a help desk process using the Web-based IT model discussed in the previous section is shown in Figure 2. The relative position and shape of the main process elements is the same as in Figure 1 so that the reader can easily relate generic elements (shown in Figure 1) with their counterparts in the implementation example shown in Figure 2.

In this practical implementation, the user interface is a Web browser (e.g., Netscape Navigator, Internet Explorer etc.) and, as such, is common to all users. All applications are Web-enabled and run on Web servers (or clusters of Web servers). The communication medium between Web servers and browsers is the Internet (although it could have been an intranet or local area network supporting Web communication protocols). This configuration allows any of the process "actors" (i.e., process manager, process team members and process customers) to use the system anywhere-anytime. Specific implementation elements are discussed below.

**A Web-based workflow control module**, is implemented as a help desk job allocation and escalation application, developed using ColdFusion (a Web development platform commercialized by Allaire Corporation) by a third-party software developer (and modeled after the popular Remedy Help Desk system). This application populates an Oracle **help desk database** that stores data about help desk "jobs" (e.g., requests for support and follow-up activities).

**A Web-based customer query module**, is implemented as a help desk job query application, developed with Java Server Pages (or Servlets, which are standard pieces of Java code that run on the Web server), which allows IT users to monitor the status of their help desk jobs. This application runs on the same group of Web servers (which

*Figure 2. A Web-based "help desk" implementation of the generic Web-based IT model*

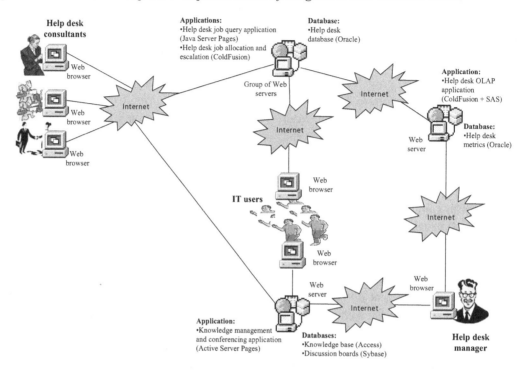

could be seen as one large Web server) as the help desk job allocation and escalation application and performs queries against the same help desk database populated by that application (although without modifying the database).

**A Web-based OLAP (Online Analytical Processing) application**, is implemented as a help desk OLAP application, developed using ColdFusion and SAS (an OLAP application development platform), that allows the help desk manager to generate (and customize the generation of) help desk quality and productivity metrics periodically. The application populates an Oracle help desk metrics database. Examples of metrics are number of help desk jobs of a certain category (e.g., network troubleshooting) solved within 2 hours of the request for help, number of complaints by IT users, number of help desk jobs handled by a particular individual or group of individuals, percentage of recurring problems etc.

**A Web-based process communication application**, is implemented as a knowledge

management and conferencing application, developed with Active Server Pages (standard pieces of VBScript code – itself similar to Microsoft's Visual Basic language code – that run on the Web server), which populates and provides access to two databases: **an Access knowledge base and a Sybase discussion board database**. The application also allows the help desk manager to post process metrics periodically, which are converted by the application into standard HTML and shown as a series of static Web pages. This application supports continuous communication between the help desk manager, IT users, and the help desk team. It incorporates the following Web-based components:

- **A discussion forum** that allows IT users to communicate with each other as well as with help desk consultants and the help desk manager in a more personal and less structured way than through help desk jobs. This discussion forum also works as a continuous two-way information exchange forum between local IT "gurus" (e.g., a salesperson who knows a lot about a sales IT application and who helps his colleagues in the Sales Department) and help desk consultants.

- **A knowledge base** with key knowledge needed by help desk consultants to execute their respective activities in the process. This knowledge base is also used by selected IT users (e.g., the local IT "gurus" mentioned above) for self-help.

## LINKS WITH DIFFERENT MANAGEMENT SCHOOLS AND RELATED IDEAS

It is important to stress that the process redesign initiatives that led to variations of the generic model discussed here were guided by a common methodology called MetaProi, which stands for Meta-process for Process Improvement (see Kock, 1999). In spite of this, the fact that the model shown on Figure 1 emerged from process redesign efforts involving different people in different companies is still remarkable. After all, senior management and consultants were involved, and they agreed that the new processes were either optimal or close to optimal. This convergence is also an indication of the existence of underlying management ideas that are likely to surface if awareness about current Web-based IT potential exists. Further inspection also suggests that even though these management ideas, which surfaced in process redesign discussions, are not tied to a single management school, they are obviously aligned with several schools (as shown on Table 2).

The "Process feature(s)" column on Table 2 describes features of the generic process model that are highly dependent on IT, particularly in the last two rows (repository, discussion forum, and knowledge base). Those features would not have been present if senior management was not willing to implement the management ideas described in the first column of Table 2, which in turn became more popular with the emergence of four contemporary management schools: total quality management, organizational learning,

*Table 2. Management ideas, related schools and process features*

| Management idea | Management schools | Process feature(s) |
|---|---|---|
| Direct management control on teams should be reduced to a minimum. Process-level control should be automated as much as possible. | Excellence, Reengineering. | Workflow control automation. |
| Customers should have instant access to process execution status. | Total quality management, reengineering. | Automated customer query support. |
| Process metrics should be periodically analyzed and used to incrementally improve processes. | Total quality management. | OLAP-based process metrics generation. |
| Customers should be allowed access to process performance data and related process improvement initiatives, and asked for their advice on how to improve processes. | Excellence, total quality management, organizational learning. | Process metrics and improvement initiatives repository, discussion forum. |
| Customers should be given full and decentralized access to process-related data so they can solve some process-related problems themselves. | Reengineering, organizational learning. | Process knowledge base. |

excellence, and reengineering. Still, one cannot convincingly argue that management thinking is driving the use of the technology. Not only do these four management schools differ significantly from each other, but they also have a different following (e.g., organizational learning proponents often suggest their management school as a "softer" and more "people-oriented" alternative to reengineering). It is more likely that modern Web-based IT force the adoption of management ideas that do not have a single and coherent source.

The idea that information technology should drive organizational design has been proposed by many business thinkers, including reengineering co-inventor Tom Davenport (1993) – in fact, this was one of the early areas of disagreement between him and other proponents of reengineering led by Hammer and Champy (1993). Yet, letting information technology define how processes are structured shifts a great deal of the responsibility on how to manage organizations to software developers and systems integrators, who arguably do not know the processes of the organizations they serve as well as their (internal or external) customers do. Moreover, software developers and system integrators need to sell their products and services to many organizations in order to maximize their profits. This is bound to decrease potential competitive advantages for their corporate customers. After all, if you have the same processes and enabling technologies as your competition, how can you possibly get ahead of them?

## CREATING VIRTUAL COMMUNITIES OF PROCESS TEAM MEMBERS, USERS AND MANAGERS

From a practical perspective, the generic process model discussed above can be seen as an "archetype process", which can be used as a "template" for the design of optimal business processes. After all, it is based on a number of process redesign

efforts that led to the same high-level result. Using it may save organizations precious time and resources that would otherwise be wasted "reinventing the wheel".

From a more philosophical perspective, the process model can be seen as a first step in the direction of a new management school. This new school's principles should guide the selection and implementation of Web-based IT to enable optimal processes, rather than the other way around. One of the key concepts underlying this new management school is that of "virtual communities" of process team members, users and managers, brought together in creative ways through the use of Web-based IT. Such virtual communities should, among other things, promote collaboration between customers and suppliers, by allowing them to communicate and share information and knowledge independently of traditional time and distance constraints.

## ACKNOWLEDGMENT

A previous version of this chapter has been published in the journal *Communications of the ACM*; the author thanks the journal's publisher for permission to use the article as a basis for this chapter. The author would like to thank John Nosek and Allen Lee for enlightening discussions on the Web's potential for business process management. Thanks are also due to Mark Nissen and Keith Snider for comments and suggestions on a presentation at the Naval Postgraduate School on one of the empirical projects that served as a basis for this chapter.

## REFERENCES AND FURTHER READING

Argyris, C. (1992). *On organizational learning.* Cambridge, MA: Blackwell.

Ashkenas, R., Ulrich, D., Jick, T., & Kerr, S. (1995). *The boundaryless organization*. San Francisco, CA: Jossey-Bass.

Christensen, C.M. (1998). *The innovator's dilemma: When new technologies cause great firms to fail*. Cambridge, MA: Harvard Business School Press.

Davenport, T.H. (1993). *Process innovation*. Boston, MA: Harvard Business Press.

Davidow, W.H., & Malone, M.S. (1992). *The virtual corporation*. New York, NY: HarperCollins.

Deming, W.E. (1986). *Out of the crisis*. Cambridge, MA: Center for Advanced Engineering Study, Massachusetts Institute of Technology.

Grudin, J. (1994). CSCW: History and focus. *IEEE Computer*, 27(5), 19-26.

Hammer, M., & Champy, J. (1993). *Reengineering the corporation*. New York, NY: Harper Business.

Kock, N. (1999). *Process improvement and organizational learning: The role of collaboration technologies*. Hershey, PA: Idea Group Publishing.

Kock, N. (Ed) (2008). *Encyclopedia of e-collaboration*. Hershey, PA: Information Science Reference.

Kock, N., Danesh, A., & Komiak, P. (2008). A discussion and test of a communication flow optimization approach for business process redesign. *Knowledge and Process Management*, 15(1), 72-85.

Peters, T.J., & Waterman, R.H., Jr. (1982). *In search of excellence*. New York, NY: Harper & Row.

Senge, P.M. (1990). *The fifth discipline*. New York, NY: Doubleday.

# Chapter XVI
# Vision, Trends, Gaps and a Broad Roadmap for Future Engineering

**Jan Goossenaerts**
*Eindhoven University of Technology, The Netherlands*

**Frank Possel-Dölken**
*RWTH Aachen University, Germany*

**Keith Popplewell**
*Coventry University, UK*

## ABSTRACT

*New challenges result from the virtualization and distribution of product development activities. This article analyzes problems of cooperative engineering as well as methods and tools for the virtual engineering of extended products. Based on these analyses, a broad road map is proposed that articulates public- and civil-sector roles in coping with future engineering challenges. With a strategic horizon, the public-sector role targets the creation of a knowledge-intensive global business ecosystem conducive to balanced civil-sector innovation and sustainable growth. The civil-sector roles evolve tactics that implement proven cooperative and virtual engineering practices with a focus on value creation.*

## INTRODUCTION

This road map has been drafted on the basis of gaps identified at two expert workshops organized by the IMS (Intelligent Manufacturing Systems) NoE Special Interest Group 6 on Collaborative Engineering of Virtual Products. A first workshop took place during the IMS Forum held in May 2004 in Como, Italy. A second took place during the Design of Information Infrastructure Systems for Manufacturing (DIISM) Conference in October 2004 in Toronto, Canada. The input of these workshops have been analyzed and positioned in a strategic research and technology development road map with specific attention to articulating requirements that are aligned to stakeholder needs and opportunities offered by technology.

E-collaboration solutions in product life cycles promise to increase value for stakeholders, to shorten time to market, to handle the increasing complexity of products, and to lower the costs of development and ownership. In cooperative engineering (CE) the focus is on the organizational aspect of product development. In virtual engineering (VE) the focus is on the technological infrastructure that enables and supports CE and the life cycles of extended products.

The three-cycle model of product development (Gausemeier, 2004) identifies the major issues of holistic product development as strategic product planning, virtual product development, and virtual production system development. Both the organizational and technological perspectives matter for all these cycles. Moreover, both perspectives extend into the social domain: Product stakeholders also affect the product life cycle via regulations, transportation, marketing, usage, repair and upgrade, take-back, and recycling and disposal, and there is a need for intimate information sharing among all product and production stakeholders (Kimura, 2005).

Increasingly strong social demands and constraints and environmental considerations direct manufacturing activities and product use to be more resource saving and environmentally benign. Moreover, industry must be globally competitive. Information technology promises to accommodate both requirements (Kimura, 2005).

With a focus on total benefit and cost of ownership, and socioenvironmental impacts, the socioindustrial global community must adopt a practice of collaborative product development, and it must achieve a high maturity level in obtaining and structuring data and knowledge from external and internal sources. A powerful e-collaboration environment bundling VE methods and solutions,

tools, and infrastructure must enable advanced practices.

## VISION, TRENDS, ENABLERS, AND PRACTICES FOR FUTURE ENGINEERING

### A Global Context and its Emerging Vision

Over the past decade, the international community has articulated desirable outcomes, including social and environmental ones. It has achieved consensus about global development goals, such as the Millennium Development Goals[1] (Sachs et al., 2005), and environmental targets, such as the Kyoto Protocol. Reporting frames such as that of the Global Reporting Initiative[2] help organizations to report on environmental and social outcomes in addition to profits or losses. In the new growth paradigm, the precompetitive and postcompetitive phases of the knowledge production process (Yoshikawa, 1994) can be addressed in a more mature manner. The paradigm recognizes the broad context within which products are developed and production capabilities develop. The paradigm also admits ICT's enabling role in achieving development goals such as sustainability and inclusivity. Kimura (2005) lists critical issues for the result-focused management of knowledge in the pre- and postcompetitive phases of product life cycles. Virtual and cooperative engineering require institutions, solutions, and practices regarding knowledge and idea flows that cannot escape the public-civil context.

The emerging vision is to achieve, society-wide, an excellent level of holistic harmonization and fit of technologies, organizational concepts, and company and market culture. The "improvement of the state of manufacturing industries as a whole" envisioned in the IMS[3] program (Yoshikawa, 1994) includes industries' ability to respond to global and local challenges and to contribute to realizing public policies while delivering value to the civil sector.

## Trends and Collaboration Enablers

The vision requires the integration of societal and organizational approaches, technical solutions, and company culture into an innovation and development environment that is result and customer focused, high performance, and leading in quality.

Trends in cooperative engineering that support the vision include product life cycle management (PLM); networked, team-oriented, interdepartmental and intercompany process collaboration; product development as an integrated, formalized enterprise business process; increasing systematic innovation and knowledge management; and the setup of virtual enterprises of small and medium-sized companies (SMEs).

In virtual engineering, the supporting trends include engineering object management and new approaches for distributed data and knowledge models; the development of aligned market-, industry-, and company-specific standards for data exchange between different applications; and development application integration (DAI) and enterprise application integration (EAI) based on portal or peer-to-peer technologies.

The social domain also sees new institutional practices that aim to respond to challenges of the technology-intensive network economy.

Wettig (2002) and Bilalis and Herbert (2003) describe the new approach to technical harmonization and standardization that was defined in an EU (European Union) Council Resolution of May 1985. It introduces a clear separation of responsibilities between the EU legislator and the European standards bodies CEN, CENELEC, and ETSI in the legal framework, allowing for the free movement of goods. Dul, Vries, Verschoof, Eveleens, and Feilzer (2004) illustrate how this approach delivers concerted directives and standards in the ergonomics area.

Experimental intellectual property schemes aim for a new balance between the public benefit from creation and the private reward for creators (the creative commons; Lessig, 2001).

An international framework to promote access to data is being promoted. An emerging complex cyber infrastructure is rapidly increasing our ability to produce, manage, and use data. As research becomes increasingly global, data intensive, and multifaceted, it is imperative to address national and international data access and sharing issues systematically in a policy arena that transcends national jurisdictions. Open access to publicly funded data provides greater returns from the public investment in research, generates wealth through the downstream commercialization of outputs, and provides decision makers with facts needed to address complex, often transnational problems (Arzberger et al., 2004).

## Collaboration Practices

To achieve the vision, a road map must leverage the current state of practice and technology. For product development today, software applications are the most important tools. They facilitate the entire development process and manage electronically nearly all documents generated as part of product development and project management. CAD, FEM, simulation, document management, multimedia, and office communication are among the 13 different types of software applications that Robert Bosch GmbH applied in 2002 (Eversheim, 2002).

Large companies, such as in the automotive industry, as well as SMEs in the tool and die industry and sheet-metal processing must set up internal standards and interfaces to cope with the heterogeneous system environment and data exchange problems in the product development process. All face the challenges of customer-oriented job-shop manufacturing with increasingly short delivery times. In the tool and die industry, the CAD-CAM-NC chain is the major optimization target for cutting down lead times. Individual commercial software systems were integrated into a company-specific CAD-CAM-NC environment. This technical trend is accompanied by PLM, an extended management approach with a holistic view on all life cycle phases of products, from creation to disposal. For job-shop producers this means, for instance, integrating sales business processes with product development processes. Mass-production companies strive for life-cycle-spanning, IT-supported business processes from marketing through development and production, to sales and service (Figure 1).

In the machine tool industry, most European players are SMEs with limited financial and personnel resources. Yet, machine tools are among the most complex mechatronic products. They face some of the highest requirements concerning mechanical design, the usage of the latest electronic equipment, and advanced software solutions for control, operator support, and maintenance. Machine tools are also subject to requirements that are of public interest, such as the protection of the health and safety of users, and the protection of the environment. In order to keep up with growing customer requirements and competition from overseas, this industry is investing heavily into research and deployment of the virtual machine tool (VMT).

First, the VMT vision and concept calls for a coupled design environment for machine tools and related components. This environment must be based on commercial CAE applications and must allow for bidirectional exchange of product models between the development phases: design, component design and calculation, FEM, analytic mechanical analysis with multibody simulation, and performance evaluation and optimization by matching calculation results with measured machine tool behavior (Figure 2). Second, the VMT vision also extends to the mechatronic development domains, such as the design of electronic circuits with E-CAD systems, controls architecture development, controls programming, and control system simulation. Furthermore, current research focuses on the coupling of machine tool simulation and process simulation.

The VMT concept also has a long-term perspective. It calls for integrated development environments that offer holistic support for mechatronic design. In the machine tool industry, environments with integrated data models are not available yet. Recent closer collaboration of CAE software vendors with automation providers and machine tool builders may lead to more integrated development environments building upon extended product data management systems.

*Figure 1. Product life cycle data management (Source: BMW, WZL)*

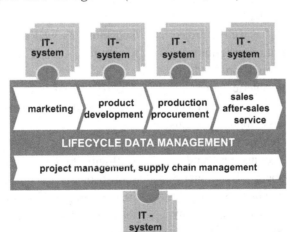

*Figure 2. Virtual machine tool design (Source: WZL)*

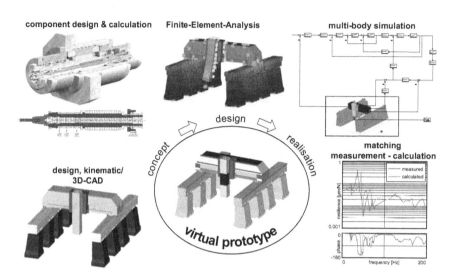

Because of their high complexity, mechatronic products like machine tools require domain-specific product models suited to the various development teams and stakeholders involved. In the longer term, various domain-specific product models need to be integrated as part of a DAI platform. Agent-oriented approaches provide the necessary means to set up information environments where the objects of a unified product model (UPM) can be flexibly linked and jointly administered while different stakeholders access only domain-specific views (Figure 3). Klement (2005) has developed a PDM platform that can consistently manage product data objects from different engineering domains as well as project management. Via an application programming interface (API), a CAE application loads its internal data objects into the generic data model of the agent platform and links to data objects of other applications. The CAE application thus becomes a tool providing a specific view onto the overall agent-managed product and project data structure, offering domain-specific functionality for manipulating selected data objects.

Pockets and chains of excellence exist today. Yet, with respect to the vision of society-wide excellence enabled by global e-solutions, gaps emerge as local excellence is contrasted with the more common obsolescence. The socioindustrial fabric faces sustainability challenges. Collaboration objectives cut across all multistakeholder product development and product-use activities. Collaborative design maturity must be enhanced. More than just being a technical challenge, this also is a sociotechnical challenge for a global IT-reliant work system.[4]

If the vision points in a direction, and as proven ICT-based solutions and experimental institutions demonstrate opportunities and feasibility, gaps and problems still exist in practices, knowledge and tools, as well as in the institutional infrastructure.

## Conflicts of Interests and Competence Gaps

The dynamism in the IT sector does not match well with the long investment horizons in some industries, such as process industries, or the limited learning means of others, such as SMEs. In these industries, collaboration along the product life cycle meets many nontechnical hurdles. A

*Figure 3. Multiagent approach for engineering object management gaps (Source: WZL)*

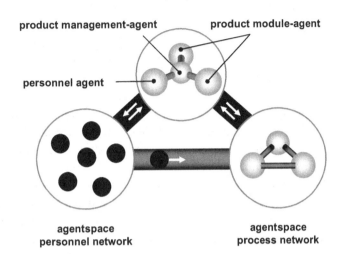

process-industry sector study into the adoption of product data standards (Dreverman, 2005) illustrates problems in the network of plant life cycle stakeholders.

A first problem is data interpretation differences among the stakeholders. In the case of process plants, these stakeholders are engineering, procurement, and construction (EPC) contractors; plant owners; and equipment vendors. The engineering data differs greatly from the operational data. Plant owners actually need a fraction of this engineering data. They impose compliance to their own standards, but have decreasing knowledge of which data they actually need. EPC contractors, on the other hand, often work strictly to contract specifications and do not proactively participate in formulating improved specifications. As a result, plant owners end up with much unnecessary and redundant data. Fear of revealing critical information to competitors is a second problem. EPC contractors and also equipment vendors are reluctant to cooperate due to fear of revealing critical information to competitors. A third problem is the short learning curve. A plant is only built once and the frequency of projects is low. A slight change of parameters results in a greatly different design, and even when an exactly identical plant is built,

the second plant differs significantly due to rapid progression of the technology used.

Traditionally, plant owners did engineering in-house and hence have developed in-house standards. Today, plant owners often impose the use of in-house standards and software solutions on the EPC contractors. The multitude of such standards causes a need for multiple mappings and higher costs. This problem is amplified as equipment vendors differ significantly regarding their data readiness. Bigger vendors may be able to deliver in the required format, but many small suppliers use old systems or sometimes only deliver paper drawings.

The human factor is another major cause of problems. In global multi-office engineering, it is very hard to really cooperate in design. This is because of differences in the style and taste of engineers. Aligning these different styles may cost more than the advantages of cooperation. For this reason, in the process industry, global engineering is mainly done at the unit and module level. Second, there is an envisioning gap between technical opportunities and available experience on the user side. The high technical competencies of VE solution providers often face little experience and strong reservations against VE technologies by far too many product developers. Third, there is the system complexity for holistic VE solutions, which possibly overstrains the capabilities of most users, provided that software intelligence does not significantly increase.

## Legacy and Application Gaps

Legacy systems are forming a big hurdle to broad innovation. The system environment is heterogeneous and today's VE applications lack interfaces for facilitating and supporting integrated information technology. This impedes the deployment and implementation of VE approaches. To take the innovation barrier, significant investments are required. Currently used CAE applications are large-scale engineering environments that need to be fundamentally adapted in order to support integrated product life cycles.

Computing power is still insufficient for integrated simulation environments. This concerns particularly the simulation of complex automation and control solutions with respect to real-time behavior. Also, setting up virtual models of machinery or entire production systems requires extensive efforts. The success and benefits of simulation experiments on the other hand can in many cases not be predicted for sure. In addition, the integration of these virtual worlds into standardized development workflows is lacking. The commercial market for integrated simulation environments is just beginning to emerge.

## Cross-Sectorial Gaps

The adverse legacy systems, competence gaps, and conflicts of interest all contribute to not achieving collaboration objectives.

Investments in collaboration technologies for the product life cycle exhibit strong network effects. These are complementary relationships in value creation among adopters of a common standard (Farrell & Klemperer, 2003) or joint technical infrastructure. For such technologies, lock-in situations are common, and the lack of expectation

sharing among stakeholders may be just one factor of adoption inertia (Au & Kauffman, 2005). The value proposition must be articulated. A possible approach is to use the technique of the counterfactual model and social saving that originated in the 19th century for estimating the cost-reducing or resource-saving effect of railroads (Fogel, 1979). Gallagher, O'Conner, Dettbarn, Gilding, and Gilday (2004) have quantified the cost estimate of inadequate interoperability by comparing the current state of interoperability with a hypothetical counterfactual scenario in which electronic data exchange and availability is fluid and seamless. The resulting 2002 cost figure of $15.8 billion for the U.S. capital facilities supply includes design, engineering, facilities management and business processes software systems, and redundant paper records management across all facility life cycle phases.

In general, there is a lack of systematic approaches and support tools for the capture, evolution, and reuse of knowledge applicable in the support of collaboration between departments or companies. Generic knowledge of the process of collaboration can be identified as applicable to almost all industrial sectors, as can sector-specific knowledge dependent on market and technological factors (Popplewell & Harding, 2004). Companies or virtual enterprises generate knowledge of their own collaboration issues, which, if captured and maintained, forms a growing body of enterprise experience that improves decision making and hence all measures of performance (i.e., financial, environmental, societal, etc.). Such knowledge at all levels is dynamic and expanding, and support tools must be able to use a wide range of techniques for knowledge capture, discovery, and retrieval. Areas with weak systematics and generics include the following.

- Integrated models for product life cycles: There exist no holistic reference models for different application domains that describe domain-specific product life cycles.

- The methodological and technical support for integrated product, project, and production information management: Business processes continue to be inefficient because companies still lack the holistic understanding of their networked product development processes, their customer-focused project management, and their production and operations management.

- Formalized product life cycle workflows: The implementation of VE methods must be embedded into a sophisticated organizational approach that specifies and standardizes company-specific workflows of how to proceed in the development of products and processes.

## Institutional Gaps in the Knowledge Economy

At present, software vendors and standards bodies are the principals of the systematic and generic. For leading software vendors, lock-in of the customer base is the strategic objective. Standards bodies are ill-equipped to counteract monopolistic strategies in rapidly transforming and emerging markets. The public-sector weakness in the face of market dynamism structurally concurs with obsolete practices for managing public knowledge assets.

Free riding and undersupply plague knowledge that becomes a pure and global public good. An actor that lacks the knowledge used to create value in a modern economy suffers from an idea gap (Romer, 1993). Whereas the partial and temporary monopoly power that is granted by patents, or by control of a large fraction of the market, lock-in, or network externalities, may act as motivators for intentional efforts to produce and transmit knowledge (Kurtzman, 2003; Romer), there is as yet no consensus on the basic institutional infrastructure for market exchanges when knowledge is the good exchanged.

The Global Public Goods Task Force (2005, p. 22) summarizes:

*Most governments are heavily involved in regulating the production and dissemination of knowledge, using two instruments—(i) intellectual property laws that protect the rights of patent and copyright holders, and (ii) support for the common knowledge platform via funding of research in specific areas and protection of common use rights. However, the balance between the two kinds of systems has been tilting increasingly towards private intellectual property during the past 20 years, reflecting the pursuit of national commercial interests in the absence of international standards. The bottom line is a major contraction of the common knowledge platform, which is prejudicial to public interests.*

For today's innovators, the relentless expansion of the current legal apparatus may be generating a highly fragmented and complex system of rights whose management incurs high transaction costs, with the effect of discouraging those types of creative activities that cannot afford such additional costs (Ramello, 2005). The "tragedy of the anti-commons" (Heller, 1998) is the name of the institutional failure that is looming with the trend to stronger patent systems and the patchwork approach to intellectual property in information products (Pendleton, 2005). The open-source movement (Lerner & Tirole, 2001) and the creative-commons licensing contracts (Lessig, 2001) are emerging practices at the other extreme. Neither of the extremes seems to establish the appropriate balance between the public benefit from creation and the private reward for the creator.

## A BROAD ROAD MAP FOR FUTURE ENGINEERING

The gap analysis shows a problem space that spans both the civil and public sector and surpasses the solution portfolio of any engineering or social science discipline on its own. Improving the state of manufacturing industries and engineering as a whole is beyond the means of the manufacturing, engineering, and software communities. The connectedness of the global fabric is widely recognized. To overcome our inability to make engineering, manufacturing, and e-collaboration solutions part of concerted practices that respond to both global and local challenges, we must also expose the industry's embedding in the global community as an engine of growth and as a beneficiary of right-sized institutions and new technologies.

## A Broad Road Map

On the challenges for society and organizations, Zall Kusek and Rist (2004, p. xi) state, "As demands for greater accountability and real results have increased, there is an attendant need for enhanced results-based monitoring and evaluation of policies, programmes, and projects."

Civil and public stakeholders must take aligned steps to cooperatively deliver extended markets and products that create sustainable prosperity. Virtual engineering e-collaboration technologies promise to make these steps affordable, but only if key participants purposely embark on a complex cooperative performance improvement program—institutional and organizational. Complementary scopes of public- and civil-sector roles must be supported by dedicated decision and reporting frames. Those of the Millennium Project and the Global Reporting Initiative must be further refined to serve as a yardstick for progress and a resource for planning.

The road map is broad because it calls upon multiple stakeholders; addresses problems with strategic, tactical, and operational horizons in the dimensions of space and time; and calls for collaboration objectives expressed with respect to a comprehensive range of outcomes, including the social and environmental.

In a global cooperative context, a road map must identify tasks for a large number of actors

and stakeholders who together can achieve the scaling of excellence from their current pockets to society. Society is subject to the developments in and the limits of its natural and physical environment: the baseline and vulnerability context. Within this context, the excellent society should achieve bold development goals, as expressed in the Millennium Development Goals and the Kyoto Protocol. This society also is a community of value-exchanging actors moving into increasingly advanced uses of content, ICT, and application software to achieve outcomes that contribute to a total system of environment, economy, society, and culture (Monnai et al., 2005).

Gaps are diverse, and conflicting trends exist. Concerted tasks to overcome gaps must be allocated to the natural stakeholders, that is, those responsible for the assets involved, and these stakeholders must enact a results-based monitoring and evaluation of their processes and projects. Where conflicting trends inhibit total welfare, decision frames must be established first before courses of action are decided (Zall Kusek & Rist, 2004). For the purpose of this broad road map, the stakeholders will be subdivided into two classes: those pursuing public benefit within a strategic to tactical horizon, and those pursuing private reward within a tactical to operational horizon.

## A Public Sector that Enables Collaborative Product Development

The public sector, including stakeholders such as academia and research institutes, standards bodies, and regulators, must facilitate collaborative product development. Often, the asset concerned is knowledge or institutional infrastructure. Knowledge has one of the oldest traditions of international cooperation. Stakeholders in the public sector must rearticulate their purposes and their role models, taking into consideration the balancing of public and civil interests. There needs to be a transparent international dialogue, and a process with a view to achieving a knowledge consensus, on the appropriate balance between private intellectual property and knowledge in the public domain (Global Public Goods, 2005). In a global economy, this consensus must be shared globally. Academia and research institutes must then ensure that their activities, in particular, research target finding, the publication of results, dissemination approaches, and education, are informed also by the knowledge consensus. They must ensure open access to data for greater returns from the public investment.

The global public sector must give adequate attention to the provision of knowledge as a global public good, and to the removal of hurdles that prevent its flow. With a strategic horizon, the international community must design and deploy an improved knowledge exchange infrastructure that is as pervasive as the international financial infrastructure and plays a special role as a conduit that lets productive ideas flow across the globe. Without this, change processes of most civil-sector stakeholders will continue to be poorly guided, slow, and laborious at best, and wrong or unfeasible in most cases. The Global Programs of the World Bank (World Bank Operations Evaluation Department, 2004) may offer one possible instrument to address this challenge. The proposals of the International Task Force on Global Public Goods describe a road map with far-reaching changes.

The requirements framework of the improved knowledge exchange infrastructures must be built upon systematic and generic contributions such as integrated models for product life cycles; methodological and technical support for integrated product, project, and production information management; and formalized product life paths.

Immediate action is possible for the principles regarding the establishment of access regimes for digital research data from public funding, to which 34 OECD member governments declared their commitment. Contracts regarding publicly funded research could include clauses that implement these principles for all contractors in line with their focus on public or private utility (thus

reducing the contractual incompleteness that currently reigns in most knowledge exchanges, and encourages free riding and rent-seeking aims). Simultaneously, supporting infrastructural services should be identified or be implemented where gaps exist. Examples in this area are the Global Biodiversity Information Facility (GBIF)[5] and the Interoperability Service Utility envisioned in the *Enterprise Interoperability Research Roadmap* published by the European Commission (Li, Cabral, Doumeingts, & Popplewell, 2006).

For the civil-sector stakeholders, the transformations of the knowledge exchange infrastructure and the articulation of private and public phases in the product knowledge life cycle should have several implications. Where current contracts are shallow and suffer from contractual incompleteness, knowledge economy contracts should be knowledge aware and have a broader scope. Supported by a more capable market and knowledge exchange institutions, social and environmental values will become part of dedicated clauses in future contracts that will determine responsibilities, rights, and liabilities in product life cycles. This will reduce risks of breakdown in contractual relations, stimulate local content in global supply chains, and lead to improved socioenvironmental impact of product life paths. Civil-sector stakeholders should avoid the trap of hyperbolic discounting[6] in their dealings with environmental and social values and with knowledge. Whenever knowledge on a product is captured by any stakeholder, this must be done early and comprehensively to allow for further sharing beyond the private boundary, and with transparent reflection of its hosting frame of reference in the knowledge evolution.

A second area for immediate action is the application of the area of virtual engineering software and data of the new approach to technical harmonization and standardization (Bilalis & Herbert, 2003). The lack of interoperability of software for product development has long been addressed by standards alone (STEP) without strategic support from directives. Yet, there is a sound argumentation for institutional intervention where market failures support rent seeking by software vendors and where interventions do not lock in the market. Consider that left-right conventions do not harm the mobility utility on a network of roads (Arthur, 1994). Moreover, user-owned data can be separated from application-added data through a proper architectural style (Goossenaerts, 2005).

## Collaboration-Based Competences in the Civil Sector

Knowledge infrastructure and right-focused institutions will imply significant social savings and value construction opportunities for the civil-sector actors. Today's engineering and production companies are embarking on substantial changes in the area of virtual engineering. Software and services turnover for the digital factory is predicted to show annual increases of approximately 35% in the next 5 years. However, there is no single threaded path into the future, and information and communications technologies show a rapid and disruptive evolution. Hence, there are manifold issues that need to evolve and finally merge in order to establish a culture and technological environment for efficient networked product life cycles. Changes in practices are required. Many of these changes involve network effects. Enhanced knowledge infrastructures, right-sized institutions, and alliance approaches (van de Ven, 2005) will accelerate value construction by market participants. Below we address scenarios for the gaps that were highlighted in the article.

The resolution of conflicts of interest is achieved by the improved fitness of the public-sector infrastructure, which clearly identifies public knowledge and models, and separates them from their proprietary complements. This will facilitate companies to establish processes and culture that will spur and enable dynamic cooperation with suppliers, customers, or even competitors if required. A virtual enterprise is a temporary, project-oriented cooperation of companies established in order to

handle projects that none of the partners could do alone (Zheng & Possel-Dölken, 2002).

As cross-sectorial gaps are overcome, knowledge sharing, intelligent collaboration, and knowledge discovery will be facilitated. Knowledge sharing between product stakeholders will increasingly rely on shared information models. Recent research in system interoperability must be applied to increase the level of automation in the sharing of information. Beyond current workflow management, intelligent collaboration must embody and apply as wide a range as possible of knowledge of collaboration, the relevant industrial sector, the value chain, and the partners to identify and resolve potential decision conflicts at the earliest possible point, before avoidable expense is incurred. The volume of knowledge potentially available to support collaborative engineering is too vast to be adequately embedded in support agents through conventional elicitation and encoding. The capabilities of knowledge-based support agents must be extended with knowledge discovery methods (e.g., data mining) that derive new insights from current and historical information stored in structured hybrid knowledge bases with crisp open or private boundaries.

Investments in new applications or in legacy conversion can then be rooted in a proven and rich joint technical infrastructure. Where simultaneous engineering can be considered as state of the art in most advanced engineering firms, the next step will be systemic, networked engineering approaches that link the expertise and knowledge of past engineering projects with new engineering tasks across interdepartmental and intercompany boundaries. Networked engineering requires multidimensional modeling frameworks specified by metamodels that describe the structure and rules for application-specific models. These modeling frameworks facilitate integration activities in business information management, EAI, as well as vertical integration on the level of manufacturing execution systems (MES). Also in product development, integrated (vendor-specific) software environments emerge. One of the major tasks for information technology for the next 10 years will be the development of solutions on how to integrate the increasing number of "integrated peninsulas" into a flexible framework for integrated PLM where different stakeholders and application domains engage in information networks.

The short-term task in the domain of work management is the development of reference activity models and their extension by methods and tools for the automated, context-sensitive generation of workflows. Intelligent workflow generation is based on semantic networks and domain ontology (Weck, Hoymann, & Lescher, 2004).

Regarding applications, simulation approaches need to be combined in order to optimize not just the development of single manufacturing steps, but to focus on entire process chains. In order to achieve and guarantee lead times, product quality, production costs, and customization amongst other things, we need to analyze the production processes beginning with the very raw material for the different component threads, as well as customization processes, to finally merge into a single product, such as a machine tool or automobile (virtual process chains). Step by step we move to augmented reality: Product simulation, factory process flow simulation, and the simulation of automated manufacturing and assembly systems all become similar to the information and computer systems used to plan and control real-world product use and production.

## CONCLUSION

Virtual engineering and e-collaboration technologies represent foundational cornerstones of the digital revolution in engineering, product development, and product use. Yet technological capabilities only slowly translate into improved sustainability and inclusivity of the socioeconomic fabric in which the products evolve and emerge. The excellence that is achieved in some pockets does not scale out due amongst other things to

market or institutional failures and the limited cooperative maturity they perpetuate. Beyond being a CAE technology road map, a road map for future engineering must pay attention also to the restoration of the dynamic balance between the public and civil sector. This broad road map articulates some pathways that build upon the current technological capabilities and also leverage trends in global governance, the knowledge economy, modeling, and methodology.

## ACKNOWLEDGMENT

The authors thank all SIG 6 members and all participants to the Idea Factory sessions in Como, May 2004, and Toronto, October 2004, for sharing views and knowledge. Special thanks are due to Eiji Arai, Paul van Exel, Fumihiko Kimura, Frank Lillehagen, John Mills, Janusz Szpytko, and Klaus-Dieter Thoben for their comments on drafts of this article. The authors also wish to acknowledge the Commission of the European Communities for their support of the IMS Network of Excellence within which the road map was developed.

## REFERENCES

Alter, S. (2003). 18 reasons why IT-reliant work-systems should replace the "IT-artifact" as the core subject matter of the IS field. *Communications of the Association for Information Systems, 12*, 366-395.

Arthur, W. B. (1994). Competing technologies, increasing returns, and lock-in by historical small events. In W. B. Arthur (Ed.), *Increasing returns and path dependence in the economy* (pp. 13-32). Ann Arbor, MI: The University of Michigan Press.

Arzberger, P., Schroeder, P., Beaulieu, A., Bowker, G., Casey, K., Laaksonen, L., et al. (2004). An international framework to promote access to data (policy forum). *Science, 303*, 1777-1778.

Au, J. A., & Kauffman, R. J. (2005). Rational expectations, optimal control and information technology adoption. *Information Systems and E-Business Management, 3*(1), 347-370.

Bilalis, Z., & Herbert, D. (2003). IT standardization from a European point of view. *Journal of IT Standards and Standardization Research, 1*(1), 46-49.

Brecher, C. (2002). Effiziente entwicklung von werkzeugmaschinen: Mit virtuellen prototypen direkt zum marktfähigen produkt. In W. Eversheim, K. Klocke, T. Pfeifer, & M. Weck (Eds.), *Wettbewerbsfaktor produktionstechnik: Aachener perspektiven* (pp. 157-190). Aachen, Germany: Shaker.

Cooper, R. G. (2002). *Top oder flop in der produktentwicklung. Erfolgsstrategien: Von der idee zum launch*. Weinheim, Germany: Wiley-VCH.

Dreverman, M. (2005). *Adoption of product model data standards in the process industry*. Unpublished master's thesis, Eindhoven University of Technology, USPI-NL & Department of Technology Management.

Dul, J., Vries, H. d., Verschoof, S., Eveleens, W., & Feilzer, A. (2004). Combining economic and social goals in the design of production systems by using ergonomics standards. *Computers & Industrial Engineering, 47*(2/3), 207-222.

Eversheim, W. (2002). Mit e-engineering zum i³-engineering (with e-engineering to i³-engineering). In W. Eversheim, K. Klocke, T. Pfeifer, & M. Weck (Eds.), *Wettbewerbsfaktor produktionstechnik: Aachener perspektiven* (pp. 127-155). Aachen, Germany: Shaker.

Eversheim, W., & Schuh, G. (2004). *Integrierte produkt- und prozessgestaltung*. Berlin, Germany: Springer.

Farrell, J., & Klemperer, P. (2003). Coordination and lock-in: Competition with switching costs and network effects. In R. Schmalensee & R. Willig (Eds.), *Handbook of industrial organization 3*. Amsterdam: North Holland.

Fogel, R. W. (1979). Notes on the social saving controversy. *The Journal of Economic History, 39*(1), 1-54.

Gallagher, M. P., O'Conner, A. C., Dettbarn, J. L., Jr., Gilding, A., & Gilday, L. T. (2004). *Cost analysis of inadequate interoperability in the U.S. capital facilities industry* (NIST GCR 04-867).

Gausemeier, J. (2004). Strategische produkt- und technologieplanung: Systematische entwicklung von produkt- und produktionssystemkonzeptionen. *Proceedings of the XI Internationales Produktionstechnisches Kolloquium PTK 2004* (pp. 99-109).

Global Public Goods, Secretariat of the International Task Force. (2005). *Meeting global challenges: International co-operation in the national interest. Towards an action plan for increasing the provision and impact of global public goods*. Retrieved from http://www.gpgtaskforce.org

Goossenaerts, J. B. M. (2004). Interoperability in the model accelerated society. In P. Cunningham & M. Cunningham (Eds.), *eAdoption and the knowledge economy: Issues, applications, case studies* (pp. 225-232). Amsterdam: IOS Press.

Goossenaerts, J. B.M. (2005). A domain model for the IST infrastructure. In D. Konstantas, J.-P. Bourrières, M. Léonard, & N. Boudjlida (Eds.), *Interoperability of enterprise software and applications* (pp. 373-384). Berlin, Germany: Springer.

Heller, M. (1998). The tragedy of the anticommons: Property in the transition from Marx to market. *Harvard Law Review, 111*, 621-688.

Kimura, F. (2005). Engineering information infrastructure for product life cycle management. In

E. Arai, J. Goossenaerts, F. Kimura, & K. Shirase (Eds.), *Knowledge and skill chains in engineering and manufacturing: Information infrastructure in the era of global communications* (pp. 13-22). Berlin, Germany: Springer.

Klement, R. (2005). *Agentenbasiertes produktdatenmanagement.* Unpublished doctoral dissertation, RWTH Aachen University, Aachen, Germany.

Kurtzman, J. (2003). The knowledge economy. In C. W. Holsapple (Ed.), *Handbook on knowledge management 1: Knowledge matters* (pp. 73-87). Berlin, Germany: Springer.

Lerner, J., & Tirole, J. (2001). The open source movement: Key research questions. *European Economic Review, 45,* 819-826.

Lessig, L. (2001). *The future of ideas: The fate of commons in a connected world.* New York: Random House.

Li, M., Cabral, R., Doumeingts, G., & Popplewell, K. (2006). *Enterprise interoperability research roadmap.* Retrieved from ftp://ftp.cordis.europa.eu/pub/ist/docs/directorate_d/ebusiness/ei-roadmap-final_en.pdf

Monnai, T., Arai, E., Oda, J., Tomiyama, T., & Hotta, A. (2004). *A proposal of design vision for artifact design and production in the 21st century: A perspective from the design engineering section of the National Committee for Artifact Design and Production.* Tokyo: Science Council of Japan.

Pendleton, M. D. (2005). Balancing competing interests in information products: A conceptual rethink. *Information & Communications Technology Law, 14*(3), 241-254.

Perelman, M. (2003). *The perverse economy.* New York: Palgrave MacMillan.

Popplewell, K., & Harding, J. A. (2004). Impact of simulation and moderation through the virtual enterprise life-cycle. In K. Mertins & M. Rabe (Eds.), *Experiences from the future: New methods and applications in simulation for production and logistics* (pp. 299-308). Berlin, Germany: IPK Berlin.

Ramello, G. B. (2005). Intellectual property and the markets of ideas. *Review of Network Economics, 4*(2), 161-180.

Romer, P. (1993). Idea gaps and object gaps in economic development. *Journal of Monetary Economics, 32*(3), 543-573.

Sachs, J. (2005). *The UN Millennium Project: Investing in development. A practical plan to achieve the Millennium Development Goals.* New York: The United Nations Development Program.

Van de Ven, A. H. (2005). Running in packs to develop knowledge-intensive technologies. *MIS Quarterly, 29*(2), 365-378.

Weck, M., Hoymann, H., & Lescher, M. (2004). Effizienz und flexiblität beim mobilen einsatz von AR im service. *WT Werkstattstechnik, 94*(5), 242-246.

Wettig, J. (2002). New developments in standardisation in the past 15 years: Product versus process related standards. *Safety Science, 40*(1-4), 51-56.

World Bank Operations Evaluation Department. (2004). *Addressing the challenges of globalization: An independent evaluation of the World Bank's approach to global programs* (1st ed.). Washington, DC: The International Bank for Reconstruction and Development & the World Bank.

Yoshikawa, H. (1994). Intelligent manufacturing systems: Technical co-operation that transcends cultural differences. In H. Yoshikawa & J. Goossenaerts (Eds.), *Information infrastructure systems for manufacturing* (IFIP transaction B-14, pp.19-40). Amsterdam: Elsevier North Holland.

Zall Kusek, J., & Rist, R. C. (2004). *Ten steps to a results-based monitoring and evaluation system: A handbook for development practitioners.* Washington, DC: The International Bank for Reconstruction and Development & the World Bank.

Zheng, L., & Possel-Dölken, F. (2002). *Strategic production networks.* Berlin, Germany: Springer.

## ENDNOTES

1    See http://www.developmentgoals.org/

2    The GRI was launched in 1997 as a joint initiative of the U.S. nongovernmental organization Coalition for Environmentally Responsible Economies (CERES) and the United Nations Environment Programme with the goal of enhancing the quality, rigour, and utility of sustainability reporting. The initiative has enjoyed the active support and engagement of representatives from business, nonprofit advocacy groups, accounting bodies, investor organizations, trade unions, and many more. Together, these different constituencies have worked to build a consensus around a set of reporting guidelines with the aim of achieving worldwide acceptance. The Global Reporting Initiative (2002) Sustainability Reporting Guidelines can be found at http://www.globalreporting.org.

3    www.ims.org

4    A *work system* is a system in which human participants and/or machines perform work using information, technology, and other resources to produce products and/or services for internal or external customers. IT-reliant work systems are work systems whose efficient and/or effective operation depends on the use of IT (Alter, 2003).

5    GBIF is an interoperable network of biodiversity databases and information technology tools that enables users to navigate and put to use the world's vast quantities of biodiversity information to produce national economic, environmental, and social benefits (http://www.gbif.org/).

6    Hyperbolic discounting is a term economists use to refer to the tendency of people to apply lower discount rates to events in the far future and high discount rates to events in the near future (Perelman, 2003).

*This work was previously published in International Journal of e-Collaboration, Vol. 3, Issue 4, edited by N. Kock, pp. 1-20, copyright 2007 by IGI Publishing (an imprint of IGI Global).*

# Section IV
# Advanced Conceptual and Theoretical Issues

# Chapter XVII
# The Ape that Used E-Mail:
## An Evolutionary Perspective on E-Communication Behavior

**Ned Kock**
*Texas A&M International University, USA*

**Vanessa Garza**
*Texas A&M International University, USA*

## ABSTRACT

*This chapter reviews theoretical research on e-communication behavior, identifying two main types of theories: technological and social. Based on this review, it provides the rationale for the development of a new theory that is neither technological nor social. The new theory is based on evolution theory, whose foundations were laid out by Darwin. Three theoretical principles are developed from evolution theory: media naturalness, innate schema similarity, and learned schema variety. The chapter concludes by illustrating how the theoretical principles can be used as a basis for the development of a simple predictive model in the context of an online broker.*

## INTRODUCTION

Given the title of this chapter, it is prudent to begin it with a clarification. This chapter is not about a chimpanzee or gorilla that used e-mail. It is about a much more modest (no chimpanzee or gorilla has ever been shown to have been able to speak intelligently, much less send and receive e-mail) yet important topic, namely the multimil-lion-year development of our biological apparatus for communication and how it affects electronic communication (e-communication) behavior.

### Defining E-Communication and E-Communication Behavior

The *e* in *e-communication* stands for *electronic*, so the term e-communication refers to, essentially, any form of computer-mediated communication plus more traditional forms of electronic communication, such as telephone communication (since the telephone is also an electronic device). The term e-communication includes computer-mediated communication over the Internet as well as over other computer network infrastructures, thus also including computer-mediated communication that takes place through group decision-support systems and local-area-network-based communication tools.

*E-communication behavior* refers to the behavior of users toward e-communication technologies. For example, it has been shown that individuals in groups engaged in knowledge-intensive tasks and interacting primarily over e-mail tend to take 5 to 15 times longer on average to prepare and make individual contributions (i.e., electronic postings) than if they were interacting face to face only (Kock, 1998, 1999, 2005). In this case, what could be called "decreased contribution speed," with contribution speed being measured in words per minute, is a component of e-communication behavior, or the behavior of the users toward e-mail. Behavior toward e-communication tools is described in two main ways: (a) by contrasting the behavior of people using e-communication tools with the behavior of people in the absence of e-communication tools (i.e., interacting face to face), and (b) by contrasting the behavior of people using e-communication tools that incorporate different elements (e.g., asynchronous vs. synchronous electronic conferencing).

E-communication has its roots in the 1960s, when the first e-mail systems emerged, largely running on mainframe computers. In those early days, only a tiny minority, largely made up of people who spent their working days in front of a computer screen, used computers for communication (Sproull & Kiesler, 1991). For the majority of people, face-to-face (FtF) conversation, telephone calls, and paper-based documents were the communication media of choice.

The interconnection of mainframes, followed by desktop computers, through networks and the Internet, has changed the above picture dramatically, making e-communication an alternative choice for many business and social interactions. Significant technological innovations made this choice even more attractive, such as the group sense fostered by features of computer conferencing systems, the synchronicity and facilitation features of group decision-support systems, and virtual-presence features of video-enhanced media spaces, which were made feasible by extensive applied research as well as the advent of cheaper technology and increasing bandwidth and connectivity.

Increased use of e-communication media has led to demands from business and government for a better understanding of e-communication behavior. These demands were met by intensive empirical and theoretical research in the 1980s and 1990s, which have led to the development of several theories that can be classified into two main groups—technological and social—theories that have been essentially in a tug-of-war for many years. Technological theories have been traditionally deterministic in the sense that they have tried to provide a basis for predicting e-communication behavior based on a finite number of variables. Social theories have in many cases been developed to overcome limitations of technological theories, claiming that technological theories are oversimplified. Nevertheless, social theories have been, more often than not, unable to provide a useful basis on which to predict e-communication behavior. While technological theories provide a simplified view of e-communication, usually focusing on communication media and collaborative tasks as predictive factors, social theories try to understand e-communication as a social and very complex phenomenon, and often end up being more explanatory and descriptive than predictive.

Rather than joining the tug-of-war between technological and social theories, perhaps a desirable alternative line of action would be to try to think outside the box and devise a theoretical model that is neither purely technological nor social. This is the choice made in this chapter, which uses evolution theory (i.e., a biological theory) to explain e-communication behavior. In doing so, it provides a logical basis on which the implicit assumption made by technological theories that individual behavior is uniform and predictable can be understood. However, instead of arguing that individual behavior is uniform, this chapter shows that there are biological influences that induce individuals to present similar behavior. Moreover, these biological influences are isolated from social influences, the latter also being seen as strong and equally important. This isolation provides a basis for a unified understanding of e-communication behavior as a combination of biological and social influences, as well as an understanding of constraints posed by communication media and collaborative tasks.

This chapter is organized as follows. In the "E-Communication Behavior Theories" section, a brief theoretical review of research on e-communication behavior is conducted. The review identifies two main types of theories, technological and social, and provides the rationale for the development of a new theory that is neither technological nor social. The next section, "The Evolution of our Biological Apparatus for Communication," discusses how communication evolved over millions of years in the human species; this discussion is focused on traits that are relevant for the understanding of behavior toward e-communication technologies. The section "Key Theoretical Principles" follows with principles developed from evolution theory that have a direct application to our understanding of e-communication behavior. The section "Using the Theoretical Principles to Predict the Behavior of Customers of an Online Broker" illustrates how the theoretical principles can be used as a basis for the development of a simple predictive model tying media naturalness to customer satisfaction and revenues at an online

broker. Finally, the conclusion summarizes the main points of the chapter and suggests future research directions.

## E-COMMUNICATION BEHAVIOR THEORIES

Technological theories of e-communication place particular emphasis on the fit between task and medium as a determinant of the communication process and outcomes. That is, the foci of these theories are the communication medium and the task being accomplished through it. Examples of technological theories are the media richness theory (Daft & Lengel, 1986; Daft, Lengel, & Trevino, 1987; Lengel & Daft, 1988), the gains and losses model (Alavi, 1994; Nunamaker, Dennis, Valacich, Vogel, & George, 1991), and the task-technology fit theory proposed by Zigurs and Buckland (1998).

Among technological theories, perhaps the best known is the media richness theory (Daft & Lengel, 1986; Daft et al., 1987; Lengel & Daft, 1988), which has been quite influential among e-communication tool developers and researchers (Jackson & Purcell, 1997; Kock, 1998; Kock, Lynn, Dow, & Akgün, 2006; Lee, 1994; Markus, 1994) even though it was developed before the advent of most of the e-communication tools in use today. The media richness theory argues that rational individuals predictably favor the use of specific communication media to accomplish certain tasks. The media richness theory classifies different communication media according to a richness scale that features FtF interaction at the top and printed documents at the bottom, with e-communication media somewhere in between (Lee, 1994; Markus, 1994). A key hypothesis of the media richness theory is that rich media are more appropriate to support equivocal communication (which is likely to occur in complex tasks) than lean media, and that aggregate data about rational individual media choices would consistently support this hypothesis.

Social theories of e-communication place emphasis on the role of the social environment and socially constructed information-processing schemas (i.e., mental information-processing structures) in defining behavior toward e-communication technology. Examples of these theories are the social influence model (Fulk, Schmitz, & Steinfield, 1990), critical mass theory (Markus, 1990), adaptive structuration theory (DeSanctis & Poole, 1994; DeSanctis, Poole, Dickson, & Jackson, 1993; Poole & DeSanctis, 1990), and the technology metastructuration model (Orlikowski, Yates, Okamura, & Fujimoto, 1995).

A historical analysis of theoretical developments in e-communication suggests that many social theories have been developed to fill a gap arguably left by previous technological theories. An influential study conducted at a large risk-management service provider by Markus (1994) illustrates this link. The study builds on the social influence model and shows that social influences can shape individual behavior toward e-communication media in ways that are inconsistent with the media richness theory's predictions (Daft et al., 1987). Markus convincingly questioned the rigidity of the richness scale proposed by the media richness theory by showing that social pressures can change some attributes of e-communication media seen as static by the theory. For example, the study showed that pressure from senior managers on their subordinates to reply promptly to e-mail sent to them increased feedback immediacy, a feature of the e-mail medium that the media richness theory claimed to be static; therefore, e-mail was shifted up from its relative position on the media richness scale.

By focusing on the communication medium and task, technological theories implicitly assume that behavior and outcomes are determined only by those factors and not by specific characteristics of the individuals interacting through the communication medium. That is, technological theories implicitly assume that, for each specific combination of communication medium and task, individuals will behave in very similar and predictable ways. This has probably been the main target of criticism from social theoreticians, who argue that social characteristics of individuals interacting through a communication medium to perform a task and characteristics of the environment surrounding those individuals are as important, if not more, to determine behavior and task outcomes as are medium and task characteristics.

There are pros and cons to the debate regarding technological vs. social theories. On the positive side, it has provided plenty of fuel for research; technological as well as social theorists have published many research papers, often with new and interesting points. On the negative side, it has led to a generalized perception that, since all theories that incorporate strong predictive elements are attacked and their flaws uncovered, e-communication behavior is to a large extent unpredictable (DeSanctis et al., 1993; Postmes, Spears, & Lea, 1998; Trevino, Webster, & Stein, 2000; Zigurs, Buckland, Connolly, & Wilson, 1999).

Joining the tug-of-war between technological and social theories is not necessarily a bad thing and is probably better than ignoring theory altogether. However, if we try to think outside the box (i.e., from a perspective that is neither technological nor social) about this tug-of-war and its underlying assumptions, we may be able to make significant progress toward a unified theory of e-communication. One key assumption made by the proponents of technological theories is that individual behavior is not only predictable but also uniform. Social theories argue otherwise, based on the assumption that a complex web of social factors and interactions influences individual behavior. Perhaps the solution to the problem is to try to isolate those influences that are uniform across individuals from those that are not. While social theories have already established that social influences are not uniform, varying depending on social background and culture (whose diversity today is not only celebrated, but also encouraged), technological theories have failed to identify the source of uniform influences implicit in their hypotheses. This source, this chapter argues, is our biological communication apparatus.

## THE EVOLUTION OF OUR BIOLOGICAL APPARATUS FOR COMMUNICATION

One of the fundamental premises of evolution theory, whose foundations were laid out by Darwin (1859/1966), is that all living organisms evolved from one common ancestor through a process that follows a few simple laws (Boaz & Almquist, 1997; Campbell, 1992; Dawkins, 1986, 1990; Dozier, 1992; Gould, 1977; Isaac, 1993; McCrone, 1991; Wills, 1993; Wilson, 1998).

- **The Inheritance Law:** Offspring inherit a large proportion of their parents' biological characteristics through their genes. The similarity between the combined genetic code of the parents and that of the offspring is very high.
- **The Mutation Law:** When members of a species generate offspring, natural genetic mutations occur that lead the offspring to develop biological characteristics that are different from those of the parents. These genetic mutations are usually incremental and arbitrary.
- **The Natural Selection Law:** Those offspring whose new biological characteristics give them an edge for survival and mating over the others are the most likely to pass the genes responsible for those biological characteristics to their own offspring.

According to evolution theory, the human species also evolved, according to the laws listed above, over millions of years, which suggests that it shares certain biological characteristics with all living beings, particularly those closer to it in evolutionary terms such as the great apes

(e.g., gorillas and chimpanzees). The evolutionary pace set by the evolution laws is usually very slow (Boaz & Almquist, 1997; Lorenz, 1983), leading to the development of physical, behavioral, and cognitive traits over long periods of time. These periods may span thousands or millions of years and are contingent on breeding speed and mortality rates. In the case of the human species, this process is not believed to have led to significant physical and cognitive modifications in the last 100,000 years (Campbell, 1992; Dawkins, 1986; Dozier, 1992; Wills, 1993; Wilson, 1998).

During the vast majority of the evolutionary processes that led to the human species, human beings and their ancestors communicated FtF. Research evidence suggests that facial expressions and simple sounds were extensively used for communication as early as 5 to 2 million years ago by Australopithecus afarensis and africanus, who were members of the australopithecine genus (Boaz & Almquist, 1997). This behavioral trait, also found in modern primates and many other mammals, has been refined over millions of years, leading to the appearance of the first rudimentary forms of speech and later complex speech (Isaac, 1993; Laitman, 1993). Only very late in the evolutionary process that led to the human species is there evidence of communication through pictorial representations, mostly in the form of cave paintings, which can be seen as early manifestations of written communication (Campbell, 1992).

The development of a sophisticated biological apparatus to communicate through facial expressions and sounds was an important element in our evolution. Such an apparatus includes a complex web of facial muscles, nerves, and specialized brain functions that, research shows, could not have been developed for any purpose other than communication (Lieberman, 1998). For example, while only a small subset of our facial muscles is used for chewing, a much larger number is used for expression of thoughts and feelings. Also, the development of a larynx located relatively low in the neck, a key morphological trait that differentiates human beings from their early ancestors, considerably increased the variety of sounds that we can generate yet, at the same time, significantly increased our chances of choking on ingested food and liquids (Laitman, 1993; Lieberman, 1998).

Based on the discussion above, it is reasonable to assume that sounds were not frequently used alone for communication (e.g., only sounds, without gestures and facial expressions). Also, asynchronous (i.e., time-disconnected) communication would have required some form of sound or symbol (e.g., a pictorial representation) storage artifact. Paintings (mostly in caves), which are probably the most rudimentary of such storage artifacts, appeared late in the human evolutionary cycle, after complex speech was developed. Sound storage artifacts appeared only much later, after civilization was well established. Therefore, one can conclude that synchronous FtF communication, with the use of discrete sounds (which later developed into complex speech) and visual cues, has been the predominant mode of communication used by human beings over millions of years of evolution, and that our biological communication apparatus has been optimized for it. Our brain, in particular, seems to have been structured to excel in FtF communication (Lieberman, 1998; McCrone, 1991; Wills, 1993) by allowing us, for example, to derive a wealth of accurate information and meaning from facial expressions and tone of voice even when they contradict what is being said (e.g., when a person is lying or speaking in a delirious way).

## KEY THEORETICAL PRINCIPLES

The discussion above provides the basis for the development of principles that can help us understand e-communication behavior in ways that are significantly different from those presented by technological and social theories. In the discussion of the principles provided below, information-processing schemas (Bartlett, 1932, 1958; Cossete & Audet, 1992; Lord & Foti, 1986), which are mental information-processing structures, are referred to only as schemas. The goal of this chapter is to highlight the potential of evolution theory as a lens for understanding e-communication behavior, not to develop a detailed theory. Thus, we develop and discuss applications of only three principles even though many other principles could be developed based on a more in-depth review of evolution theory as it relates to the evolution of our biological communication apparatus.

- **The media naturalness principle:** Innate communication schemas bias an individual's perception of media naturalness. Media that incorporate all the elements of actual unencumbered FtF interaction (e.g., physical presence, ability to see and hear others, synchronicity) will be perceived as more natural for communication than other media, and therefore as requiring less individual cognitive effort (due to cognitive adaptation) to be used for communication than other media. The extent to which a communication medium incorporates actual FtF interaction elements defines its degree of naturalness.

- **The innate schema similarity principle:** Innate communication schemas are very similar across different individuals, therefore biasing media naturalness perceptions of different individuals in very similar ways.

- **The learned schema diversity principle:** Since the human brain is very adaptable, learned communication schemas (i.e., those that are not inherited, but acquired through interaction with the environment surrounding an individual, including the social environment) also influence media naturalness perceptions. However, this influence is not as uniform across different individuals as that of innate communication schemas. Therefore, learned communication schemas bias media naturalness perceptions of different individuals in different ways.

The three principles above illustrate both the power and the likely limitations of evolutionary-theory-based e-communication theories, and have been developed with that purpose in mind. The media naturalness principle and the innate schema similarity principle are complementary, whereas the learned schema variety principle highlights the fact that biology alone cannot explain the full complexity of e-communication behavior.

The media naturalness principle is a first step in the direction of developing an entirely new theory (or theories) that could replace the media richness theory and other similar technological theories. For example, the link between decreased naturalness and increased cognitive effort can be used to explain why people prefer to conduct certain collaborative tasks using media that incorporate elements of FtF communication like the ability to use gestures and tone of voice to aid communication as well as provide and obtain immediate feedback during the communication interchange (Daft et al., 1987). This link can also be used to explain why better outcomes can be generated through media of lower naturalness through compensatory adaptation (Kock, 1998; Kock et al., 2006) by providing a basis on which to hypothesize that low naturalness poses cognitive obstacles that individuals engaged in collaborative tasks may be able to overcome—a hypothesis that is incompatible with the media richness theory yet has been strongly supported by empirical evidence (Kock, 1998, 1999, 2005).

The innate schema similarity principle highlights one of the most important reasons why evolution theory should be used to explain and predict e-communication behavior: namely, its potential to explain innate influences that are common to all individuals, independently of cultural and social background. As the Internet makes the world smaller by bringing together people with completely different cultural and social backgrounds into virtual communities based on shared personal interests and common business purposes, it is important to develop a predictive theoretical model that can help us understand and anticipate, at a certain level and with perhaps a limited degree of certainty, behavioral traits of all of the members of those virtual communities. The innate schema similarity principle stresses the potential of evolution theory as a basis for the development of such a predictive theoretical model.

Finally, the learned schema diversity principle underscores evolution theory's inability to explain everything. That is, while it is important to be able to isolate the influence of innate schemas from that of learned schemas on e-communication behavior, which helps us apply the Cartesian "divide and conquer" method of scientific inquiry, e-communication behavior will always be the result of a combination of the innate and learned schema influences. For example, individuals who developed schemas (i.e., learned schemas) related to the use of e-mail by using it to perform equivocal tasks during many years would tend to see e-mail as a more natural medium to perform tasks of high complexity than other individuals who have not gone through the same experiential schema-development process. The influence of learned schemas, in this example, would partially suppress the influence of innate schemas, even though the innate schemas would still exist and have the same configuration as in other individuals.

## Using the Theoretical Principles to Predict the Behavior of Customers of an Online Broker

As a way of illustrating the use of the three principles discussed above, let us consider the case of an online broker and its customer support process. This example is based on an action research study previously conducted by one of the authors involving one mutual fund management firm and two online brokers. The goal of this illustration is to provide an example of how the theoretical principles can be used as a basis for the development of a simple predictive model tying media naturalness to customer satisfaction and revenues. The predictive model refers to the generic customer support process performed by the online broker, and can be extended to most online brokerages.

The main goal of the customer support process is to help customers buy investment products, which usually include money market instruments, stocks, bonds, mutual funds, and derivatives. The customer support process is implemented by means of a set of short interactions (i.e., with a duration that goes from a few minutes to a few hours) between the customer and online broker through communication media.

For a customer to buy or sell an investment product through the online broker, he or she must engage in a set of interactions with the online broker using one or more media. Thus, it can be said that the customer and the online broker engage in a set of interactions using $N$ different media that we may call $M_1, M_2, M_3...M_N$, where $N$ is the number of different media used to complete the task. For example, for the task of buying shares of a mutual fund, a customer may first obtain basic information about mutual funds from the broker's Web site (which is primarily text based), then conduct a live text-based chat online with one of the broker's customer representatives to understand how mutual funds operate, then go back to the Web site to understand the steps involved in making the purchase, then call the broker and chat with a customer representative over the telephone to clarify some issues regarding the purchase transaction steps, and then, finally, perform the purchase online using the broker's Web site. In this example, three main media—the Web site, a live text-based chat system, and the telephone—were used in five communication

interactions. Based on the media naturalness principle, it could be argued that these three media can be sorted in the following order of decreasing degree of naturalness: telephone, live text-based chat, and Web site. The telephone medium is the most natural of the three because it incorporates synchronicity and the ability to convey verbal cues, both present in the FtF medium. The live text-based-chat medium is the second most natural medium because it incorporates synchronicity, but not the ability to convey verbal cues. The Web site (which is primarily text based) is the least natural of the three because it does not incorporate either synchronicity or the ability to convey verbal cues.

The three principles, that is, media naturalness, innate schema uniformity, and learned schema variety, can be used to derive hypotheses related to the use of different media for the provision of customer support services by the online broker. These hypotheses refer to each of the customer support interactions. The hypothesis below is a direct application of the media naturalness principle.

**H1:** There is a negative causal link between the degree of the naturalness of the medium used for communication between the customer representative and customer, and the cognitive effort perceived by the customer in connection with the customer support interaction.

Previous computer-mediated communication studies that investigated perceived cognitive effort and satisfaction (Graetz, Boyle, Kimble, Thompson, & Garloch, 1998; Nunamaker et al., 1991) provide the basis on which to hypothesize that increased perceived cognitive effort is likely to lead to increased customer dissatisfaction with the service provided by the online broker, and thus increased likelihood of using the services of a competing online broker. This is compounded by the low cost associated with opening an account at a competing online broker and the weak bond that ties providers and customers in the online brokerage industry (Spiro & Baig, 1999). This can be summarized in two hypotheses.

**H2:** There is a positive causal link between the cognitive effort perceived by the customer and his or her degree of dissatisfaction with the customer support provided by the online broker.

**H3:** There is a positive causal link between the degree of dissatisfaction experienced by the customer during a customer support interaction with the online broker and the likelihood that the customer will use the services of a competing online broker.

The innate schema uniformity principle suggests that hypotheses H1, H2, and H3 are likely to hold for the majority of customers since it is primarily based on the influence of innate schemas possessed by all the members of the human species. This could be expressed as a hypothesis (which would in fact be a metahypothesis as it refers to the other hypotheses) but will be omitted in this illustration for simplicity.

The learned schema variety principle, on the other hand, suggests that learned schemas are likely to also play a role in how customers perceive their communication interactions with the online broker by moderating the causal link established in hypothesis H1 between media naturalness and cognitive effort. That is, the less the customer knows about buying and selling investment products using the services provided by the online broker, the stronger the negative effect of media naturalness on cognitive effort. This leads us to hypothesis H4.

**H4:** The mismatch between the knowledge possessed by the customer and that required to perform the task (i.e., buy or sell an investment product) positively moderates the negative causal link between the degree of naturalness of the medium used for communication between the customer representative and customer, and the cognitive effort perceived by the customer in connection with the customer support interaction.

Given that the theoretical model above refers to each customer support interaction, it is implicitly assumed that each interaction will have an impact on the likelihood that the user will move to a competing online broker. Previous studies on the nature of customer-provider relationships in the financial service industry (Macdonald, 1995; Walkins, 1992) suggest that it is reasonable to also assume that the impact of each interaction will be both incremental and cumulative in most cases (exceptions would be, e.g., single interactions in which dissatisfaction would be extreme, leading the customer to leave the broker at once).

Since the four hypotheses presented above have each a clear negative form (i.e., a respective null hypothesis), they (as well as the causal model that summarizes them) can be tested and therefore disproved or shown to appropriately explain the results obtained from the study. This can be accomplished through positivist case and action research studies, and, less ideally, laboratory experiments or surveys of online brokers. Current trends in the use of communication media in the online brokerage industry provide support for the hypotheses above as they suggest a link between customer satisfaction and loyalty, and the use of communication media that incorporate elements of FtF interaction (e.g., synchronicity, the ability to see and hear the other party, etc.) to support customers (Dodson, 2000).

## CONCLUSION

This chapter provides a brief theoretical review of research on e-communication behavior, which identifies two main types of theories—technological and social—and the rationale for the development of a new theory that is neither technological nor social. This new theory is based on evolution theory, whose foundations were laid out by Darwin, particularly as it relates to how communication evolved over millions of years in the human species. Finally, key theoretical principles are developed from evolution theory that have a direct application to our understanding of e-communication behavior and can be used in the development of a new theory of e-communication behavior. An application of these principles is provided through the development of a simple predictive model tying media naturalness to customer satisfaction and revenues in an online broker.

Why is it important to try to understand e-communication behavior based on evolution theory? Two main reasons can be given to answer this question. First, evolution theory provides a scientific basis on which to ground key hypotheses of technological theories. For example, the media richness theory proposes a richness scale but does not explain why different media are perceived according to that scale. This chapter shows that the richness scale proposed by the media richness theory is partly supported by evolution theory. If one assumes that some technological theories need to be refined and not replaced by a new theory, which may be the case, evolution theory can be very useful in their refinement and scientific grounding.

Second, evolution theory can be used as a basis for the development of an e-communication behavior theory that, while perhaps incorporating some of the hypotheses of certain technological theories, will be free from their previously identified flaws. Again, using the media richness theory as an example, the media naturalness principle replaces, with advantages, the static richness scale hypothesis of the media richness theory. As noted before, several studies succeeded in showing fatal flaws in this hypothesis by providing evidence, for example, that the media richness scale is not static (Markus, 1994), and that richness is not inherent in a communication medium and can vary depending on who is involved in the communication act (Lee, 1994). In fact, the static richness scale hypothesis proposed by the media richness theory has proven to be its main weakness as it opens the door, for instance, to the argument that a medium richer than FtF (e.g., a "super-rich" virtual-reality-based medium) will be even better than FtF for tasks involving intense communication. What is argued here, in contrast, is that any non-FtF medium will be perceived as less natural than FtF. One of the reasons for this is because our biological apparatus for communication has been optimized by Darwinian evolution for FtF communication. This implies that the users of a super-rich virtual-reality-based medium will also perceive it as less natural, thus requiring more cognitive effort for communication (because, e.g., it may induce perceived information overload) than the FtF medium.

The widespread use of e-communication technologies today is only matched by the increasing uncertainty about the effects of these technologies on humans. Given this, the search for reliable theories that help us predict e-communication behavior is strongly warranted. This chapter is a first step in that search and a small one toward the final goal of e-communication researchers, which is to develop a grand theory that can be used to explain e-communication behavior in its full complexity. Evolution theory alone will never lead us to such a grand theory, but it will be instrumental in its development.

## ACKNOWLEDGMENT

We would like to thank Amotz Zahavi, Geoffrey Miller, and Donald Hantula for comments and suggestions regarding the connection between evolutionary biology and evolutionary psychology principles and some of the ideas proposed in this chapter. An earlier version of this chapter was published as an article in Volume 5 of the journal *Communications of the Association for Information Systems* (AIS); we thank the journal's publisher for permission to use that article as a basis for this chapter.

# REFERENCES

Alavi, M. (1994). Computer-mediated collaborative learning: An empirical evaluation. *MIS Quarterly, 18*(2), 159-174.

Bagozzi, R. P. (1980). *Causal models in marketing.* New York: John Wiley & Sons.

Bartlett, F. (1932). *Remembering: A study in experimental and social psychology.* Cambridge, MA: Cambridge University Press.

Bartlett, F. (1958). *Thinking: An experimental and social study.* New York: Basic Books.

Boaz, N. T., & Almquist, A. J. (1997). *Biological anthropology: A synthetic approach to human evolution.* Upper Saddle River, NJ: Prentice Hall.

Campbell, B. C. (1992). *Humankind emerging.* New York: HarperCollins.

Cossete, P., & Audet, M. (1992). Mapping of an idiosyncratic schema. *Journal of Management Studies, 29*(3), 325-348.

Daft, R. L., & Lengel, R. H. (1986). Organizational information requirements, media richness and structural design. *Management Science, 32*(5), 554-571.

Daft, R. L., Lengel, R. H., & Trevino, L. K. (1987). Message equivocality, media selection, and manager performance: Implications for information systems. *MIS Quarterly, 11*(3), 355-366.

Darwin, C. (1966). *On the origin of species.* Cambridge, MA: Harvard University Press. (Original work published 1859)

Davis, J. A. (1985). *The logic of causal order.* London: Sage.

Dawkins, R. (1986). *The blind watchmaker.* New York: W.W. Norton & Company.

Dawkins, R. (1990). *The selfish gene.* Oxford, UK: Oxford University Press.

DeSanctis, G., & Poole, M. S. (1994). Capturing the complexity in advanced technology use: Adaptive structuration theory. *Organization Science, 5*(2), 121-147.

DeSanctis, G., Poole, M. S., Dickson, G. W., & Jackson, B. M. (1993). Interpretive analysis of team use of group technologies. *Journal of Organizational Computing, 3*(1), 1-29.

Dodson, J. (2000, September 18). It's time to chat with your customers. *Internetweek.* Retrieved from http://www.internetwk.com/ebizapps/col091800.htm

Dozier, R. W., Jr. (1992). *Codes of evolution.* New York: Crown Publishers.

Fulk, J., Schmitz, J., & Steinfield, C. W. (1990). A social influence model of technology use. In J. Fulk & C. Steinfield (Eds.), *Organizations and communication technology* (pp. 117-140). Newbury Park, CA: Sage.

Gould, S. J. (1977). *Ever since Darwin: Reflections in natural history.* New York: W.W. Norton & Company.

Graetz, K. A., Boyle, E. S., Kimble, C. E., Thompson, P., & Garloch, J. L. (1998). Information sharing in face-to-face, teleconferencing, and electronic chat groups. *Small Group Research, 29*(6), 714-743.

Isaac, G. L. (1993). Aspects of human evolution. In R. L. Ciochon & J. G. Fleagle (Eds.), *The human evolution source book* (pp. 263-273). Englewood Cliffs, NJ: Prentice Hall.

Jackson, M. H., & Purcell, D. (1997). Politics and media richness in World Wide Web representations of the former Yugoslavia. *Geographical Review, 87*(2), 219-239.

Kock, N. (1998). Can communication medium limitations foster better group outcomes? An action research study. *Information & Management, 34*(5), 295-305.

Kock, N. (1999). *Process improvement and organizational learning: The role of collaboration technologies.* Hershey, PA: Idea Group Publishing.

Kock, N. (2005). *Business process improvement through e-collaboration: Knowledge sharing through the use of virtual groups.* Hershey, PA: Idea Group Publishing.

Kock, N., Lynn, G. S., Dow, K. E., & Akgün, A. E. (2006). Team adaptation to electronic communication media: Evidence of compensatory adaptation in new product development teams. *European Journal of Information Systems, 15*(3), 331-341.

Laitman, J. (1993). The anatomy of human speech. In R. L. Ciochon & J. G. Fleagle (Eds.), *The human evolution source book* (pp. 56-60). Englewood Cliffs, NJ: Prentice Hall.

Lee, A. S. (1994). Electronic mail as a medium for rich communication: An empirical investigation using hermeneutic interpretation. *MIS Quarterly, 18*(2), 143-157.

Lengel, R. H., & Daft, R. L. (1988). The selection of communication media as an executive skill. *Academy of Management Executive, 2*(3), 225-232.

Lieberman, P. (1998). *Eve spoke: Human language and human evolution.* New York: W.W. Norton & Company.

Lord, R. G., & Foti, R. J. (1986). Schema theories, information processing and organizational behaviour. In H. P. Sims & D. A. Gioia (Eds.), *The thinking organization* (pp. 20-48). San Francisco: Jossey-Bass.

Lorenz, K. (1983). *The waning of humaneness.* Boston: Little, Brown & Co.

Macdonald, J. (1995). Quality and the financial service sector. *Managing Service Quality, 5*(1), 43-46.

Markus, M. L. (1990). Toward a critical mass theory of interactive media. In J. Fulk & C. Steinfield (Eds.), *Organizations and communication technology* (pp. 194-218). Newbury Park, CA: Sage.

Markus, M. L. (1994). Electronic mail as the medium of managerial choice. *Organization Science, 5*(4), 502-527.

McCrone, J. (1991). *The ape that spoke: Language and the evolution of the human mind.* New York: William Morrow and Company.

Nunamaker, J. F., Dennis, A. R., Valacich, J. S., Vogel, D. R., & George, J. F. (1991). Electronic meeting systems to support group work. *Communications of ACM, 34*(7), 40-61.

Orlikowski, W. J., Yates, J., Okamura, K., & Fujimoto, M. (1995). Shaping electronic communication: The metastructuring of technology in the context of use. *Organization Science, 6*(4), 423-444.

Poole, M. S., & DeSanctis, G. (1990). Understanding the use of group decision support systems: The theory of adaptive structuration. In J. Fulk & C. Steinfield (Eds.), *Organizations and communication technology* (pp. 173-193). Newbury Park, CA: Sage.

Postmes, T., Spears, R., & Lea, M. (1998). Breaching or building social boundaries? Side-effects of computer-mediated communications. *Communication Research, 25*(6), 689-715.

Rice, R. E. (1992). Task analyzability, use of new media, and effectiveness: A multi-site exploration of media richness. *Organization Science, 3*(4), 475-500.

Spiro, L. N., & Baig, E. C. (1999, February 22). Who needs a broker? *Business Week, 3617*, 113.

Sproull, L., & Kiesler, S. (1991). Computers, networks and work. *Scientific American, 265*(3), 84-91.

Trevino, L. K., Webster, J., & Stein, E. W. (2000). Making connections: Complementary influences on communication media choices, attitudes, and use. *Organization Science, 11*(2), 163-182.

Walkins, J. (1992). Information systems: The UK retail financial services sector. *Marketing Intelligence & Planning, 10*(6), 13-18.

Webster, J., & Trevino, L. K. (1995). Rational and social theories as complementary explanations of communication media choices: Two policy-capturing studies. *Academy of Management Journal, 38*(6), 1544-1573.

Wills, C. (1993). *The runaway brain: The evolution of human uniqueness.* New York: Basic Books.

Wilson, E. O. (1998). *Consilience: The unity of knowledge.* New York: Alfred A. Knopf.

Zigurs, I., & Buckland, B. K. (1998). A theory of task/technology fit and group support systems effectiveness. *MIS Quarterly, 22*(3), 313-334.

Zigurs, I., Buckland, B. K., Connolly, J. R., & Wilson, E. V. (1999). A test of task-technology fit theory for group support systems. *Database for Advances in Information Systems, 30*(3), 34-50.

*This work was previously published in E-Collaboration in Modern Organizations: Initiating and Managing Distributed Projects, edited by N. Kock, pp. 1-13, copyright 2008 by Information Science Reference (an imprint of IGI Global).*

# Chapter XVIII
# Metaphors for E–Collaboration:
## Nonprofit Theatre Web Presence

**Julie E. Kendall**
*Rutgers University, USA*

## ABSTRACT

*What constitutes regional commerce? What creates and enhances a regional identity? In the United States, regions can be quite large and may even cover geographical territory from several surrounding counties or states. They are larger than any one individual company, shopping street, or district. Regional cooperation of commercial businesses is often manifested through special events, cooperative advertising with coordinated signage, extended opening hours, and special discounts that contribute to building a sense of community, and which eventually develop a sense of region. The political and environmental exigencies for the creation and expansion of regions have meant an increase in the popularity and importance of regions and a subsequent movement to enhance and differentiate their identities. We now see the rise of regional governments, water authorities, and educational institutions among many others. One little-explored idea has been the use of e-collaboration to forge, reinforce, and sustain a regional identity via the virtual world. Although geographical separation of many miles might dictate that bricks-and-mortar theatres cannot easily collaborate physically (i.e., they cannot share costumes, props, ushers, and so on), the possibility of e-collaboration opens potential opportunities for attracting wider audiences, reaching and ultimately casting fresh talent, and building reciprocal audiences who possess a passion for the arts and who have the means and desire to travel to attend performances throughout the geographical region. In this study, a methodology built on the conceptual foundation of metaphor research was used to comprehend and then interpret the Web presence of 15 nonprofit theatres that comprise the total regional theatre of southern New Jersey that exists on the Web. In order to add additional insight, our earlier research findings from working with off-Broadway and regional theatre festivals were extended to analyze the Web presence of the theatres in southern New Jersey. We contribute to the literature by systematic and deep investigation of the strategic importance of the Web for nonprofit theatre groups in the southern New Jersey region. In addition, our use of the metaphor methodology in order to create a telling portrait of what transpires on the Web in relation to nonprofit organizations is also an original contribution. Our work is meant to heighten the awareness of administrators to the rapidly accelerating need for the strategic use of e-collaboration. We propose that with the use of the Web, administrators can move toward creating a regional theatre Web presence for South Jersey, one which would make use of an evolutionary metaphor. To this end, we suggest the use of an organism metaphor. Through the creation of reciprocal hyperlinks, theatres can be supported in improving their practice of colocation on the Web, wherein they will be taking strides to cooperate as a regional theatre community.*

## INTRODUCTION

Web presence is the perception of influence and organizational identity that organizations attempt to create in their customers and Web site visitors. Used as a strategic positioning instrument, Web presence goes well beyond the basic graphics, text, and hyperlinks that are the building blocks of a Web site. The Web presence of the organization should have a positive effect on its operations, meaning that these operations should be made easier, faster, and more efficient and effective. An organization's competitiveness is expected to be sharpened through a strong Web presence so that it will gain additional market share, expand operations into new markets, and attract additional customers (Abuhamdieh, Kendall, & Kendall, 2000, 2002, 2007).

Developing an organizational Web presence is expected to enhance the organization's adaptation and growth by enhancing its relationship with its customers. This will make the organization more alert to its customers' needs and expectations. This translates into a good outlook for an organization's growth prospects.

Nonprofit organizations traditionally lag behind commercial enterprises in their approach to implementing integrated information technology, particularly in the area of developing a strategic IT plan. This occurs for a number of reasons, but they include the lack of expertise and knowledge concerning the importance of information technology to an organization (specifically in the performing arts community), the lack of a predictable source of funding for endeavors that are earmarked as exclusively for IT development, and reticence to include IT as a funding priority when grant requests are made. Additionally, many funding agencies specifically will not grant requests for standard items required to build IT infrastructure, such as computers, software, and expertise to develop information systems and IT policy. Because of these concerns, oftentimes information technology enhancements are not even broached (Te'eni & Kendall, 2004).

I chose to look at an exhaustive list of regional theatres that have a Web presence in southern New Jersey (widely known to residents as South Jersey). South Jersey is made up of eight counties and has a population of about 2.3 million people (U.S. Census Bureau, 2003). This fairly densely populated region can support a number of different theatre groups, but the theatres are spread over the region.

As surprising as it may seem, creative arts have a critical part to play in the economy of New Jersey and in the economy of South Jersey as well. A report published in 2000 that examined the economic impact of arts funding in New Jersey a decade ago found that $18 million in NJSCA funding resulted in $1 billion of annual economic activity in New Jersey. The findings showed that during that time there was over $546 million in direct spending by arts groups and over $474 million in ancillary spending by visitors. This generated $27 million in tax revenue, over 17 million audience members including 4.5 million schoolchildren, and over 11,000 jobs involving over 47,000 artists and over 700 arts groups (*The Arts Mean Business: A Study of Economic Activity, 2000. NJSCA/ArtPRIDE*, 2000).

Mindful of the potential economic and cultural impact of regional performing arts groups in New Jersey, I set about to systematically examine how theatres currently use their presence on the Web, and to recommend how they can improve their service by changing their Web metaphors and how they can cooperate and collaborate with other theatres in the region.

## METHODOLOGICAL APPROACH

In beginning my research, I set as one of my standards to be inclusive rather than exclusive in identifying theatres to study. I subsequently identified 15 nonprofit regional theatres that had developed and maintained a Web presence. I conducted original research seeking to identify nonprofit theatres located in southern New Jersey using several different search engines including Copernic Agent Professional and Google. Copernic uses more than 1,000 search engines, consults multiple search engines at once, combines their results, removes duplicates, and keeps the best information gathered from the search engines it queries. Membership listings in arts alliance organizations including the Artpride New Jersey, Discover Jersey Arts Online, the New Jersey Theatre Alliance, New Jersey Theatre League, and the South Jersey Cultural Alliance.

When I began to determine which metaphor was in play on each theatre Web site, I used two different approaches. One approach was to read and interpret the language used on the Web pages in order to determine the presence or absence of predominant metaphors that I had already identified in organizational users of other information systems and in systems development methodologies (J. E. Kendall & Kendall, 1994).

Another way to observe what metaphor was foremost in serving as an organizing concept on a theatre's Web site was to assess the visual and multimedia elements of the Web page to understand the content, design, and technical elements of the pages. I examined the theatre Web sites using eight dimensions provided as guidelines for Web designers (K. E. Kendall & Kendall, 2005). The eight dimensions include (a) overall appearance (layout and composition), (b) use of graphics, (c) use of color, and the use of sound or video, (d) use of new technology and products, (e) content, (f) navigability (internal and external links), (g) site management, and (h) communication with users. By assessing both the language employed and the technical elements adopted, I was able to determine what metaphor was representative of each theatre Web site.

Metaphors shape the way we think. By using words and visual aspects that people understand and believe in to make linkages with the new and unfamiliar, a metaphor enables the person who hears it to envision a new reality. Metaphors assert that one object actually is another (Weaver, 1967). Invoking a metaphor means opening the door for a listener to use all previous associations in approaching a new subject.

Researchers have argued the power of metaphors to shape our very reality (Duncan, 1968; Graber, 1976; Lakoff & Johnson, 1980). Ott (1989, pp. 29-30) notes, "Metaphors help organization members put meaning into things they experience and realize apparent contradictions and paradoxes they encounter. Metaphors help organizations tie their parts together into meaningful wholes." For example, saying, "Time is money," calls into play many interrelated ideas, including that time is a means of payment, that it perhaps can be spent like money, and that things like time off can be earned or banked. The user is informed of a variety of possible courses of action because of the entailment aspect of the original metaphor.

In the past 20 years or so, organizational researchers have recognized the importance of metaphors. Morgan (1986, pp. 12-13) in his pioneering work goes even further by concluding, "By using different metaphors to understand the complex and paradoxical character of organizational life, we are able to manage and design organizations that we may have not thought possible before."

Metaphor analysis was first used in the study of management information systems by J. E. Kendall and Kendall (1993), who built on the seminal work of Clancy (1989) concerning business metaphors. Clancy identified six metaphors commonly found in organizations: the journey, game, war, machine, organism, and society. Kendall and Kendall observed three other basic business metaphors: the jungle, zoo, and family, which pointed out weaknesses in the organization that Clancy did not identify in his work. The authors proceeded to map the attributes of the nine metaphors to the development of different types of information systems and then hypothesized the likelihood of success given the organizational climate and the presence of particular metaphors. Further information about metaphors in systems development can also be found in J. E. Kendall and Kendall (1994).

## CLASSIFYING THE WEB SITES OF SOUTH JERSEY THEATRES

The Web sites seemed to cluster around seven of the nine metaphors introduced earlier. Of the 15 Web presences evaluated, three were classified as portraying a jungle metaphor, three evidenced a family metaphor, three called forth a journey metaphor, one evoked a machine metaphor, two used the society metaphor, two used the game metaphor, and one represented an organism metaphor. None of the theatre Web presences were classified as exhibiting a strategic war metaphor or a chaotic zoo metaphor. Table 1 provides a summary of the metaphors and the southern New Jersey theatre Web sites that correspond to each metaphor.

### Enacting the Jungle Metaphor on South Jersey Theatre Web Sites

The jungle metaphor is one that typically requires a guide to help secure a path out of the jungle. All three of the sites identified could be characterized by the sentiment, "Once we get through this season, maybe we'll have time to construct a real Web site."

*Table 1. Organizing metaphors found on theatre Web sites and how they cluster*

| Web Presence Metaphor | Southern New Jersey Theatres |
|---|---|
| Jungle | Foundation Theatre of Burlington County College<br>East Lynne Theater Company<br>Department of Fine Arts of Rutgers-Camden |
| Family | Bridge Players Theater Company<br>Mainstage Center for the Arts<br>Sketch Club Players |
| Journey | Cumberland Players<br>The Road Company<br>Surflight Theatre |
| Machine | Haddonfield Plays and Players |
| Society | Burlington County Footlighters<br>Fine & Performing Arts Center at Cumberland County College |
| Game | Puttin' on the Ritz<br>Triple Threat Foundation for the Arts |
| Organism | Holly City Repertory Theatre |

The Foundation Theatre Company in residence at the Geraldine Clinton Little Theatre of the Burlington County College Web site contains the motto of the school, "We Can Get You There," displayed in the upper right-hand corner of the home page. Unfortunately, that slogan stands in ironic contrast to the search function provided, which does not help the visitor locate theatre productions. There is a hyperlink on the page to the calendar of events, which brings up a page of 12 radio buttons that the user can click on to designate that they are looking for a subject such as performing arts or student government events. The page features a phone number for the box office to get further information, but there is no way to book online or even to request information online. Neither is there any way for the organization to capture visitors' information when they visit the site.

Another theatre in the category of jungle metaphor is the East Lynne Theater Company in Cape May. The Web site is situated inside a shell of the sponsor NewJersey.com, which is an electronic consortium of New Jersey newspapers that display paid advertising. They offer free Web hosting and Web page set up for community groups. As a result, the pages appear in a generic frame, with links to the main site and a chance to build one's own site, so there is no specific design that conveys the mission or feeling of the theatre's Web presence. It is very difficult to locate this URL (uniform resource locator). The free frame provided by NJ.com is chaotic and confusing. Going to the "Links" page eventually brings up a series of 11 hyperlinks that refer to a grab bag of local tourism sites, and professional and amateur theatre Web sites. One link is broken, and another, when clicked on, brings up a page with the message "Being reconfigured." There is no clear organization; the page serves as more of a friendly list of theatres and other interesting Cape May tourist sites that someone has hastily put together. The hyperlinks do not appear to be diligently maintained or shaped in any particular

way. They are overgrown with possibly irrelevant links.

The third Web site in the jungle metaphor category is that of the Department of Fine Arts of Rutgers-Camden. The maze of links is disorderly and confusing. Although there is a link on the page to the Rutgers Camden Center for the Arts, there are no reciprocal links to the theatre division of the fine arts department. In fact, clicking on a link to Rutgers lands the visitor in a central Rutgers University site, not the Rutgers-Camden site. Many synergies are being missed.

It is interesting to note that two of the three Web sites evidencing the jungle metaphor are schools (one a university, the other a community college). It is possible that these Web sites will always evince a metaphor chaotic in nature, even when they are developed more completely, simply due to their missions as schools that serve a diverse constituency.

## Using the Family Metaphor on South Jersey Theatre Web Sites

Families tend to have more than one goal. Parents and children may love each other but may not see each other's point of view. The Web sites all communicate their family approach with the message of "We are a community; you are welcome to our house."

The Web site of the Bridge Players Theater Company is designed to use a graphic of theatre curtains as the frame. There is an original icon that is a drawing of the Tacony-Palmyra Bridge with the two masks of drama—comedy and tragedy—superimposed over the bridge. The Web site is enthusiastic but amateurish. It is clear that no voluntary help with the site is turned away; therefore, the results are somewhat uneven. Some of the Web pages are consistent in design, and others are not. Some things are almost touchingly naïve (such as the request for people not to use files that are posted openly) and are not password protected. The site includes a generic message board and a visitor guest book that permits linking to other people's URLs without a screening of the links for appropriateness to the overall Web presence. The security problems and the patched-together feel of the Web site certainly make it seem homespun. It is a friendly site and everyone is invited to participate.

The Mainstage Center for the Arts of Blackwood also clusters into the family metaphor. The Web site is lively and friendly, showing children's handprints on the main page, which includes links labeled "Theater," "Kids," "Harmony", "Music," "Dance," "Home," "Contact," "Mission History," and "Audition," as well as "Upcoming Events." The slogan reads, "Quality family entertainment at affordable prices!" There are nine different fonts used on the white background of the home page. There is also an icon showing an award from the *Courier-Post* newspaper as one of the "2000 Best of South Jersey" along with a sentence that reads, "Ranked One of the Best Arts and Entertainment Centers of South Jersey Five Years in a Row!" and a link to the *Courier-Post Online*; the site also links to the New Jersey State Council on the Arts and the Discover New Jersey Arts Web sites. In addition, this is the only Web site I examined that partners with Greatergood.com, which in turn partners with many e-commerce merchants, donating 15% of purchases from the participating e-commerce merchants to the Mainstage Center for the Arts. The mission stresses the positive benefits of engaging youth in theatre arts as a way to address increasing violence in society.

The third Web site that displays a family metaphor is the Sketch Club Players, Inc., of Woodbury (SCP). This Web site features a small logo of the company: the dramatic masks of tragedy and comedy intertwined, with the name of the company surrounding the masks in a circle. On the right-hand side are five clip-art images from popular clip-art packages, which give the Web site a familiar and homespun look. These are not hyperlinked, however. Everyone, regardless of their particular talent, is encouraged to participate. This particular family is very proud of their dwelling, stating, "We are proud to own our building, and we work hard to keep improving it." The site is hosted at Geocities.com, which is a commercial site that offers free Web hosting, or Web hosting for a nominal fee. Unfortunately, the design result is still somewhat amateurish. The link leading to the history of SCP ends with the comment "SCP hopes to keep supporting the performing arts in Gloucester County for many more years!" Their community involvement and their commitment to welcoming everyone is a very clear family message.

## Employing the Journey Metaphor on South Jersey Theatre Web Sites

The journey metaphor invokes a goal and a struggle to reach the goal. The sentiment expressed overall by a theatre using this metaphor is "We try new things; some succeed, some don't. We continually discover what our patrons want; we will eventually get there."

The Cumberland Players performing at the Little Theatre in Vineland, Cumberland County, are clearly on a voyage of discovery. The journey metaphor is also emphasized by one of the reviews chosen for the Web site from the Atlantic City Press, which reads in part, "Instead of performing the same old overdone musicals and Neil Simon plays, the Cumberland Players are challenging area theatergoers with quality work." Although the box office is not online, the form page has been made quite functional. This is the only site in the group studied to include a navigational bar at the bottom of the printable ticket order form. The theatre is making full use of the navigational qualities of the Web in that way, and that plays nicely into its use of the journey metaphor as well. The site is well maintained and frequently updated, and appears eager to take visitors to new places. In response to a current arts funding crisis, the Web site has enabled two e-mail links, one to the New Jersey legislators and one to the governor of New Jersey, which permit people to request that the governor not suspend funding for the arts. The Cumberland Players "Links" page features the Discover NJ Arts alliance page as the first link, and has a series of links that do indeed permit the user to discover different arts alliances groups. The links encourage exploration, and descriptions of each link, as well as the icon to click on, are presented. This page is informative and leads visitors to check each link because of its vivid descriptions of what each link contains (much as a travel brochure might).

The Road Company of Williamstown in Gloucester County is another theatre group whose Web site evokes the journey metaphor. Even its name is evocative of a journey. The Web site is a mixture of clip art and animation, and features several links and a good deal of thought about where the company has been and where it is going. Clicking on the link "Theater Information" brings up the statement:

*We're called The Road Company for a reason: we don't own a theater; we rent wherever we perform. For many years, that rented home was The Grand Theater in Williamstown. We performed over 30 shows in our years there. But with the current owners' decision to no longer use it for rentals; we once again have hit the road.*

When I wrote to the group on another matter regarding an inappropriate link that was listed on the Web site (the owner of the domain had changed to a dorm Web-cam pay site), they were incredibly responsive and remedied the problem immediately by removing the link.

The third theatre using the journey metaphor is that of the Surflight Theatre of Beach Haven. On the left-hand side is a gray navigational bar with links such as "Home," "What's Playing," "Tickets," "About Surflight," "Our Programs," "Support Surflight," "Volunteer," and "Jobs at Surflight." The "Mailing List" link is displayed but not enabled; "Seating Chart" is enabled as is

"Contact Us," however the "Site Map" is not a link. The home page shows two color photographs of two upcoming performances. Also included is a link to respond to the proposed arts funding budget cuts for New Jersey, and a number of icons for a variety of theatre alliances are shown. Clicking on the link "About Surflight" brings up a lovingly told chronicle of the historical journey of the theatre company thus far. Each attempt at something new is described; most, such as the summer children's breakfast or going not for profit, are described as great successes. There is a genuine feeling of discovery and exploration conveyed on this page.

## Enacting the Machine Metaphor on One South Jersey Theatre Web Site

If you have ever heard anyone praise a well-organized enterprise by remarking that "It runs like a well-oiled machine," you understand what makes a machine metaphor. For the theatre enacting this type of metaphor, we can characterize the sentiment as "We designed a series that should apply to all; three musicals, and three classic plays each year."

The Web presence of the Haddonfield Plays and Players is the only one of the 15 theatre Web sites examined to evince a machine metaphor. The left-hand column is a list of 11 links headed by the ubiquitous hit counter numbering in the 16,000s, which is the number of visitors reportedly coming to the site since January 12, 2002. The link called "Database" brings up a page that claims to be a historical database that includes all the shows and full casts from past productions. There is a simple search function where the visitor can enter either a name or the name of a show, and bring up a separate screen where the information requested is displayed. The database and all other functions seem to work properly, but the traditionally warm, welcoming feeling of the other theatres employing the family metaphor is absent; absent also is the explorative spirit shown in the theatres with Web presences that I have characterized as having a journey metaphor. The machine metaphor as enacted here holds predictability and order, with several subscription series designed to apply to all.

## The Society Metaphor and South Jersey Theatre Web Sites

Rules as a mainstay for the maintenance of the society is a strong feature of this metaphor. Theatres with this type of presence embody the sentiment "We do not allow exchanges or refunds. Payment for next year's series must be received no later than..." and so on.

On the Burlington County Footlighters Web site, clicking on "Order Tickets" brings up a page titled "Easy Internet Ticket Order Form," which leads the visitor to believe that this transaction can be completed online. However, upon further reading, it is clear that you need to print out the form and mail it back to the theatre. No e-mail or e-commerce transactions are permitted. Further, the theatre only takes checks; it does not have the ability to process credit cards. These rules are explicitly stated throughout. It mentions that the Web site's message board is moderated and thanks visitors for behaving in accordance with its rules. The link for auditions includes an agreement that the actors will follow the rules of the house regarding behavior before, during, and after the show. Included in the rules is the topic of paying dues. This preoccupation with the rules is highly consistent with the society metaphor, but this is the only Web site of the 15 that went to this extent to ensure compliance. Rules feature prominently on the Web site. The visitor gets the idea that the Footlighters have been in business a long time (since 1938), and one of the reasons for their longevity is that they spell out all of the rules, and they communicate them clearly. For instance, on the ticket order form, subscribers are instructed to print all information clearly, with an additional, wry comment that states, "We are not handwriting experts."

The second South Jersey theatre that embodies the society metaphor is the Fine & Performing Arts Center (FPAC) at Cumberland County College in Vineland. Rules are greatly in evidence on several of the pages. These include the "Rental Info" page, still within the frame of the county college, which gives a text version of the policies and procedures renters must follow in order to rent the Fine & Performing Arts Center. The frame gives the Web site an orderly look, and permits the visitor to orient easily to the information on the page and to navigate easily around the site. More rules are given on the "Stage Specs" page, which provides technical information necessary to set up a show within FPAC. This information is currently linked to the rental information and not hidden away from the casual browser who is looking at the site as an audience member or performer. The rules and technical data can be overwhelming to patrons who just want to find a good production for the weekend. The "Links" page features six links and two of them are to performing-arts or theatre-alliance-type sites, one is to another theatre group discussed in an upcoming section, and one is to a nearby symphony group. Those sites do no appear to have reciprocal links with the Fine & Performing Arts Center.

## The Game Metaphor and South Jersey Theatre Web Sites

In the game metaphor, the leader is often described as a coach, and the game is one of a competitive sport. The sentiment expressed by theatres possessing the game metaphor can be summed up as, "We strive to be better than the competition; we will continue to improve and win the hearts of theatregoers. We will win all of the awards." Two South Jersey theatres evoke this metaphor: Puttin' on the Ritz of Oaklyn, and Triple Threat of Cherry Hill.

Puttin' on the Ritz in Oaklyn is intending to win the big game, and all of the competitions leading up to it as well. Its slogan appears at the top of the home page—"Quality theatre, simply done"—and on each associated page there is a further definition of quality shown in maroon lettering at the top of the page. Tickets must be reserved via phone with a credit card or a subscription can be mailed on a form from the Web site with check or credit card payment. The box office is not online. Puttin' on the Ritz runs a children's theatre as well as the main theatre. The main theatre produces six shows a year, five of which are musicals from the past.

Triple Threat Foundation for the Arts of Cherry Hill has a competitive advantage in that they used online ticketing for about a year for most of their shows. The Web site resembles a corporate Web site and the links on the left-hand side are very revealing of the game orientation. They begin with the link, "News> TTFA takes 'Civil War' to competition for the NJ Theatre League Competition." This is the only theatre Web site to mention the competition though several of the regional theatres will compete in it. Another link brings up the news that three actors who performed at Triple Threat are now going to appear in the national touring company of *The Music Man*. The group is clearly proud of them, and considers them team members as well as winners. Triple Threat definitely has a goal to be professional in everything it does. In its children's performing-arts pages, the end of the page advertising classes states, "Triple Threat Students Succeed," which heads a boxed display of alumni names and those who have gone on to professional jobs. This is a very different arena to compete in, and except for the Puttin' on the Ritz Web presence, the other theatres do not aspire to this goal of professionalism, quality, or success in a bigger arena.

## The Organism Metaphor and One South Jersey Theatre

The organism metaphor is a balanced metaphor that allows the entity to grow. In the realm of community theatre, the sentiment of the organism

metaphor can be articulated as "We are a growing theatre; we are helping develop new plays and new talent."

The Holly City Repertory includes among its priorities on the "Mission" page producing and developing original works that have not been previously produced and works "produced outside of an educational institution." It also offers workshops and classes "to improve our company" and "to offer another creative outlet for local artists." Its mission statement concludes with the expression, "collaborating with any and all area artistic groups to create a nurturing, culturally rich atmosphere which will foster economic growth through tourism." The theatre's Web presence, including the graphics, layout, design, and content, is highly evocative of the organism metaphor. The Web site includes a link to the Riverfront Renaissance Center for the arts, which has an elaborate Web site featuring the cultural and community life of Millville, New Jersey, as well as many links to sites on the subject. It also has a link to the Glasstown Arts District, which has a reciprocal link to the Holly City Web site as well as to Cumberland County. Holly City Repertory's selection of plays to produce, events to sponsor, and calls for participation in the key activities of nurturing and growing through producing original works are all different ways to express the idea of cultivating the organism.

## E-COLLABORATION AND NONPROFIT THEATRES

Examining the 15 Web sites systematically through the use of metaphors has brought many observations to the fore, and many insights have been realized. The following section examines the possibilities for e-collaboration of the theatres based on the metaphor currently evoked by their Web presence. E-collaboration has been broadly defined as the following: "Collaboration using electronic technologies among different individuals to accomplish a common task" (Kock, 2005).

This section focuses on how the metaphor is hindering or enabling the theatre, and expressly recommends changes in the Web presence metaphor being used that I believe will produce positive outcomes for the theatre in question.

The evocation of the jungle metaphor by three of the theatres can be interpreted to mean that the development of a Web presence is not a high priority or even a priority at all. If the theatres desire success in the future, it is imperative that they give thought, careful attention, and monetary resources to developing a Web presence that fulfills their missions. This responsibility can no longer be neglected or mischaracterized as an afterthought or an add-on. Ideally, as the organizations are experiencing strategic planning, they will also give thought to what their Web sites should contain, who should design them, and maybe even more critically, who will maintain and update them. If they are educational institutions trying to create a Web presence, they will always need to retain a broad constituency and thereby will always need to maintain a Web presence that appeals through a variety of metaphors. The jungle metaphor does not appear to be conducive to e-collaboration.

At first glance, one might argue that the family metaphor might encourage e-collaboration. A detailed analysis of the Web sites, however, shows that these organizations are quite protective of their families. They encourage their audiences to remain loyal and would also prefer that their actors continue acting with them, rather than pursuing opportunities with other theatre groups. In the end, these theatre families act as typical families do. Individual family members seek the companionship of members of other families, but entire families rarely have a reason or opportunity for collaboration with another entity. If the theatres evincing this metaphor desire to become more goal oriented, they will need to systematically evaluate their IT plans and possibly change the family metaphor that they are portraying via their Web presence. For now, the theatres have

no overarching goals, but instead recognize that each member of the family has a life beyond the theatre group.

The journey metaphor highlights the fact that theatre productions are often a journey where obstacles are encountered and eventually overcome in order for the show to go on. When this metaphor appears on a theatre's Web site, the theatre shares its adventures with the patrons. The theatres must, as a matter of course, review whether the chaos of the journey remains appealing to their staff, patrons, and board members. The strong goal orientation of the journey metaphor makes it a good choice for Web presence for these South Jersey theatres. Their well-conceived Web sites are easily navigable and are excellent at depicting the spirit of exploration. Those on the journey do not necessarily seek to be rescued when storms develop; rather they would prefer to struggle through and eventually reach their intended destination on their own. These theatres show no interest in collaboration at the present time and may need to change their metaphor so that not everything they attempt involves a struggle.

There was only one theatre in my population of Web sites in the Southern New Jersey region with a Web site that evoked a well-oiled machine. The theatre has set a clear goal and exists in an orderly environment. The availability of a searchable database on the Web site in order to locate performers and productions is one dimension of the machine metaphor that is working well for it. However, a machine metaphor does not permit creativity and is essentially boring. Without creativity, the group employing a machine metaphor is in danger of becoming a de facto club rather than a community theatre. In general, the machine metaphor is not a positive one for regional theatres to pursue in their Web presence and certainly does not encourage cooperation.

There were two organizations evoking the society metaphor in the group of the Southern New Jersey theatres. Both of the organizations evoking the society metaphor are well established and highly rule based. Although societies try to cooperate, the societies involved can rarely agree on common goals and tend to be bound by the rules they set up. One may look to the United Nations in general or the Kyoto accords in particular as examples of the attempt to make societies cooperate with one another. In the final analysis, the society metaphor is not useful for facing changes that require the group to adopt a more collaborative position. I recommend that eventually those organizations evincing the society metaphor in their Web presences will need to rethink and redesign them to include a regionally cooperative metaphor.

There were two theatres with Web presences that evinced the game metaphor. The game metaphor as a Web presence can function in a number of successful ways for the theatre groups. In the cases of the two theatre groups here, the metaphor was supportive in fostering a competitive stance. The two groups are quite different. One is old, and the other is rather newly established. One has grown up with the Web, while the older one is just now recognizing the importance of a Web presence for maintaining a competitive position and is hiring professional help for the Web site's development and maintenance. Both organizations display Web sites that are visually and textually furthering their metaphor of the game. The team-building aspect of the game metaphor is a positive aspect of this Web presence. The game metaphor will allow these theatres to move to a regional cooperative rather than a competitive stance.

In an analogous situation, sports teams belong to leagues. The NFL (National Football League) negotiates contracts with television executives and shares the revenue among 32 different teams that comprise the league. This is merely one example of how a game metaphor can provide support for collaboration. Regional theatres can benefit from the same approach and consequently the game metaphor is flexible enough for them to embrace these strategic changes.

There was only one theatre that displayed the organism metaphor in the 15 southern New Jersey theatre Web sites that I studied. Developing a

Web presence with an organism metaphor affords a theatre company a great deal of flexibility. It permits growth, change, and experimentation that other metaphors do not. The organism is a very positive metaphor for regional theatre Web presence. It allows the expression of creativity balanced by the requisite discipline to adapt and grow. It accommodates many different types of participants and an abundance of new ideas, and it can serve as a liberating metaphor for an organization.

Working together, the regional theatres can all be part of the same garden. They can allow one of the sponsoring agencies discussed earlier in the study to cultivate the garden. Once a theatre group recognizes that by using an organism metaphor it need no longer be constrained by its own history, past participants, or play choices, its ability to attract and retain participants will be exhilarating.

Based on my assessment of the 15 southern New Jersey theatre Web sites, I believe that I can identify which regional theatres are more likely to collaborate with others in terms of a strategic Web affiliation. The theatres have already developed Web sites that demonstrate that they are willing and able to be part of an umbrella organization. These theatres have existing Web sites that, under scrutiny, invoke metaphors of the game or organism. Less likely to use e-collaboration are those theatres that adopt a society, journey, or family metaphor. Even less likely to cooperate regionally are the three theatres that are still hacking their way out of the metaphoric jungle on their Web sites.

## SUCCESSFUL WEB METAPHORS IN THE THEATRE INDUSTRY

Now that I have identified regional theatres that invoke the game and organism metaphors, the next step is to look for instances of successful leagues and gardens in the theatre industry.

In New York City, large professional theatres that are located within a defined neighborhood are referred to as Broadway theatres. The group that promotes Broadway shows is called The League of American Theatres and Producers, Inc. (http://www.LiveBroadway.com). The league began in 1930 as The League of New York Theatres, and its mission is to heighten awareness of and interest in Broadway theatre as well as to support the creation of more profitable theatrical productions. The league also negotiates collective bargaining agreements with all theatrical unions and guilds, maintains relevant research archives, and supports charitable efforts.

Although it is called a league, The League of American Theatres and Producers behaves more like a gardener. The emphasis is on cultivation, and the membership is so diverse that each of the members has its own way of nurturing shows. The league's membership consists of theatre owners and operators, Broadway and touring company producers, Telecharge and Ticketmaster, booking agents, hotels, and newspapers and magazines such as the *New York Times* and *The New Yorker*. Under the Live Broadway banner, the league brings to Broadway fans live plays as well as other theatrical events and services like the Tony (Antoinette Perry) Awards (together with The American Theatre Wing) and small annual shows such as *Broadway on Broadway* and *Broadway Under the Stars*.

Broadway's location possesses a distinct advantage in attracting theatregoers. All of the Broadway theatres are located in a relatively compact site, and the theatres benefit from the fact that theatregoers will notice a sign for a new play when leaving a show they have just seen. Marquees are powerful symbols, and the patron who notices the show a theatre is currently producing may decide to see that play or a future production.

We have long known that locating similar businesses together in clusters often helps the businesses perform better than those that are in dispersed locations. Recent research examines the geographical concentration of Internet industries (Kolka, 2002), hotelling (Huck, Muller, & Vriend, 2002), restaurant locations (Mariani, 2001), and the location of retail outlets (Netz & Taylor, 2002). For a complete look at location theory, readers should see the volume by Wesolowsky (2001). Many factors come into play when location decisions are made. Jacoby (2000) studied the location of e-commerce hot spots and pointed to the attitudes of store owners, customers, and their communities in making location decisions. Of interest in our study of regional theatre Web presence is that he also found that regions and the country could come into play in location decisions.

A more focused study asks the question about what exactly transpires within a cluster of similar businesses. Baptista (2000) looked at the clustering of technological firms in a region to find out whether innovations would diffuse faster because of their proximity to each other. While traditional location theory endorses the advantages to be found through locating similar businesses together in geographical clusters, the regional theatres of South Jersey cannot capitalize on building clusters of theatres into a theatre row (such as was recently accomplished in Manhattan on 42nd Street between 9th and 10th avenues, where a collection of five theatres are now available for rental). The theatres are geographically dispersed around eight separate counties. Indeed, many of the theatres were not built as theatres originally, so their individual locations within a community can vary widely from main street, a college campus, or an even an out-of-the-way residential neighborhood. Just heightening awareness of the existence of the theatre and then getting an audience to commit to attending performances in unknown locations is a challenge for all of the regional theatres.

E-commerce provides an answer for some of the location and publicity problems the theatres are experiencing. Just as with any business, theatres need to communicate with their audience the *who*, *what*, *when*, *where*, *why*, and *how* of their mission. In addition, theatres need to demonstrate their connection to the community and in particular their potential relevance in the lives of their audience members. This includes posting descriptions of their current offerings, creating offers that appeal to a variety of audience members such as weekend subscription packages and subscriptions to performances especially for children, and so on. The theatres need to communicate the locations of their theatres, the names and resumes of the current cast members, and information on how interested volunteers can support the companies through contributions of time or talent. In the past, newspaper advertisements were the most widely used vehicles for heightening awareness. In addition, theatres attempted to increase the number of series subscribers whiles also garnering repeat ticket sales from pleased audience members. Long-running shows that are seen by great numbers of theatregoers (shows such as *Phantom of the Opera* or *The Producers* come to mind) are able to rely on word of mouth for a continuous stream of eager theatre goers, but small, regional theatres often have very truncated production runs, often only over one Friday, Saturday, and Sunday. The expense of radio and television ads tend to put them out of the reach as communication tools of most regional nonprofit theatres.

A highly identifiable Web site with e-commerce features such as online ticketing and meaningful, organized links is an ideal place to promote current productions. Since patrons of theatres are educated and have sufficient disposable income to attend cultural events, they tend to have the means and desire to search for information on the Web. This turns out to be a rather one-sided relationship between the patrons who are online and the theatres putting on shows. While audience members may be online seeking local, live theatre productions, the regional theatres studied here do not possess the people, technical expertise, time, or budget to create a Web presence that will attract and retain people to the Web site.

From our study thus far, we have learned that the regional theatres that attempt a Web presence try to do so on their own separately from other theatres, without professional help or a template, starting with the basics. The volunteers who develop these initial Web sites create what it is in their power to do. Often, the question of a match between a theatre's Web site and its organizational mission is never even considered in this process.

It has been said that although modern transportation systems conquered the tyranny of distance, e-commerce can be credited with eliminating distance altogether. However, the process of helping audience members locate and then go to the Web site adds another dimension to distance. Even using the output from a familiar search engine such as Google, a theatregoer must still make informed choices about which of the listed links he or she will follow. The problem of electronically traveling to a different theatre Web site when one is already on one is that there is usually no information given about how to make this electronic journey. Location theorists tell us that there are distinct benefits that can accrue when similar businesses locate in proximity to each other. Making the e-commerce world of the theatre smaller and having sites "closer together" can have many beneficial effects. The way we characterize this internal and external navigational distance in e-commerce is through the term *e-distance*.

For the professional Broadway stage, we can see that theatres are connected in two important but different ways. One way is through their common ownership by a large, parent corporation. Eight Broadway theatres and 35 entertainment venues throughout the United States are owned by the Nederlander Producing Company of America. Its rival is the Shubert Organization, which is the parent of 17 Broadway theatres. Tickets for any of the productions at any of these theatres are sold by a common online ticket agency. The Shubert Organization owns Telecharge, and Ticketmaster is labeled as the world's largest ticket retailer by most sources. When an audience member arrives at these online ticket-agency Web sites, there is much to see and do. For instance, the sites provide a synopsis of the play and promote ready navigation among any of the current productions purveying tickets on the sites. For a small handling fee, audience members can purchase their tickets online at both sites. The entire theatre world comes alive on the Web on sites such as Playbill.com and Broadwayd.com, with daily postings of backstage gossip, show reviews, and photo opportunities at the fall of the first curtain.

Centralized online ticketing is not purely the province of Broadway shows. Some off-Broadway shows cooperate in a joint online box office called Ticket Central, where customers can buy tickets online for a dozen different plays. Clicking on a link called "In the Neighborhood" takes the Web site visitor to a neighborhood restaurant page, embellished with links to the Web sites of the restaurants listed. Even detailed parking instructions are presented. Part of the strategic alliance that was put together includes tie-ins for offering ticket holders discounts for parking and close-by restaurants if theatregoers display their evening's ticket stubs. The listing of the restaurants' links within the "In the Neighborhood" theme is very apt since the inculcation of community and a sense of helping each other is emphasized among all of the businesses present on this site.

Of the 15 regional theatres examined in South Jersey, only one of them features online ticket purchases for patrons. A few of the theatres do include links to local restaurants in their cities. The Holly City Repertory of Millville, New Jersey, is one of these.

The theatre alliance Web sites create links to multiple theatres in South Jersey, but the links are not often provided (by the theatres) in the reverse direction. When the links are displayed, they are presented in a hodgepodge, without apparent organization. If a patron is curious, he or she must click on the link to see where it leads.

Some of the added links are no longer functional and some have changed destinations: the theatres' Web sites are not maintained sufficiently to catch errors, missing links, or inaccuracies.

## CONCLUSION

In this period of uncertainty in funding prospects, the theatres in South Jersey need to join together. They can do this by e-collaboration that will permit them to link to one another on the Web or by setting up an umbrella organization that handles all ticketing and provides links to each of the regional theatres. In this way, theatres will be able to increase the level of interest among patrons. Rather than seeing themselves merely as members of a city or county arts community, the theatres can change their Web presence both rhetorically and visually to fashion a regional identity that can enable them to build knowledgeable audiences, obtain funding, and discover a broader range of acting talent.

Currently, the e-distance that separates the 15 regional nonprofit South Jersey theatres is greater than the true geographical distance among them. Several arts alliance groups, among them, Discover NJ Arts, New Jersey Theatre Alliance, New Jersey Theatre League, NJTheatre.com, and South Jersey Cultural Alliance, have created (as an overt manifestation of their expressed strategic mission to champion collaboration in the arts) Web presences that organize and display several of the New Jersey theatre links. However, the regional theatres do not collaborate with each other in promoting each others' productions. The New Jersey Theatre Alliance is currently doing trial runs of online ticket purchasing, but individual seats for requested performances are not available.

It is still a challenge for a theatregoer to locate a regional theatre production on the Web. Browsing a current schedule or bringing up detailed information about a play now showing means that the audience member must know all of the

URLs for the theatres they would like to attend, or they must keep going back to one of the several theatre arts alliance Web sites for more links. The theatres present in southern New Jersey do not yet link directly to each other, so that means that the audience member becomes burdened with browsing.

There are only one or two instances where regional theatre Web sites are providing reciprocal links with other theatre companies. To make matters worse, some artistic directors jealously guard the resumes of the actors who work with the company from season to season, explicitly discouraging actors from working at another area theatre. The paramount goal then becomes to inculcate loyalty to a particular theatre company rather than perfecting the actor's craft, pooling area talent, sharing limited funding resources, or improving the overall quality of the South Jersey theatre experience. Actors who participate in regional nonprofit acting roles often feel quite comfortable with playing in any of the many regional theatres, taking their talents with them as they audition for yet another role. However, individual theatres have not adopted the perspective that permits them to visualize themselves as a collaborative community.

With those considerations aside for a moment, I recommend that the theatres follow through on their impulses toward creating a regional identity so that they are truly drawing audiences, talent, ideas, and funding from the region. This can be manifested metaphorically in their Web presence by rewriting content to widen the language to include more of a sense of community, or by adding more language reflective of a competitive game or a growing organism.

Specifically, the Web sites can be changed to ensure e-collaboration via inclusion of reciprocal links, especially for nearby theatres that have seasons that are clearly different. For example, a theatre season without musicals that presents several original dramas or an experimental theatre linking with another that does outstanding community outreach are prime candidates for this type of cooperation. Theatre Web sites can also be linked to other arts alliance Web sites. Theatre companies may also consider e-collaboration for the purpose of creating an exclusively regional Web site for southern New Jersey theatres that uses a different metaphor (perhaps the game or organism metaphor) that is able to reconceptualize individual theatre offerings as a lively and growing regional resource.

## NOTE

This research was conducted as part of a fellow award made by the Walter Rand Institute of Public Affairs at Rutgers University, Camden. The author is grateful for the generous support and encouragement of the Rand Institute faculty and staff during the course of the fellowship. It was a fruitful and productive relationship.

## REFERENCES

Abuhamdieh, A. H., Kendall, J. E., & Kendall, K. E. (2000). Beyond e-commerce: Evaluating the strategic impact of Web presence for nonprofit organizations. In M. Swink (Ed.), *Proceedings of the Decision Sciences Institute* (pp. 567-569). Atlanta: Decision Sciences Institute.

Abuhamdieh, A. H., Kendall, J. E., & Kendall, K. E. (2002). An evaluation of the Web presence of a nonprofit organization: Using the balanced scorecard approach in ecommerce. In R. Traunmuller (Ed.), *Information systems: The e-business challenge* (pp. 209-222). Boston: Kluwer Publishing.

Abuhamdieh, A. H., Kendall, J. E., & Kendall, K. E. (2007). E-commerce opportunities in the nonprofit sector: The case of New York Theatre Group. *International Journal of Cases on Electronic Commerce, 3*(1), 29-48.

*The arts mean business: A study of economic activity, 2000. NJSCA/ArtPRIDE.* (2000). NJ: NJ Foundation/Rutgers University Graduate School of Education.

*The arts in New Jersey: A study of economic activity 1992-93.* (n.d.). NJ: NJSCA/South Jersey Cultural Alliance/Eagleton Institute, Rutgers University.

Baptista, R. (2000). Do innovations diffuse faster within geographical clusters? *International Journal of Industrial Organization, 18*(3), 515.

Clancy, J. J. (1989). *The invisible powers: The language of business.* Lexington, MA: Lexington Books.

Duncan, H. D. (1968). *Symbols in society.* New York: Oxford University.

Graber, D. A. (1976). *Verbal behavior and politics.* Chicago: University of Illinois Press.

*LiveBroadway.com.* (2005). Retrieved January 2005 from http://www.liveBroadway.com

Huck, S., Muller, W., & Vriend, N. J. (2002). The East End, the West End, and King's Cross: On clustering in the four-player hotelling game. *Economic Inquiry, 40*(2), 231-241.

Jacoby, C. (2000). E-commerce hot spots. *Corporate Location, 3,* 18.

Kendall, J. E., & Kendall, K. E. (1993). Metaphors and methodologies: Living beyond the systems machine. *MIS Quarterly, 17*(2), 149-171.

Kendall, J. E., & Kendall, K. E. (1994). Metaphors and their meaning for information systems development. *European Journal of Information Systems, 3*(1), 37-47.

Kendall, K. E. (2000). Ecommerce aesthetics: Ecommerce for ecommerce's sake. *Information Resources Management Journal, 13*(3).

Kendall, K. E., & Kendall, J. E. (2005). *Systems analysis and design* (6th ed.). Upper Saddle River, NJ: Prentice Hall.

Kock, N. (2005). What is e-collaboration? *International Journal of e-Collaboration, 1*(1), i-vii.

Kolka, J. (2002). Silicon mountains/silicon molehills: Geographic concentration and convergence of Internet industries in the US. *Information Economics and Policy, 14*(2), 211.

Lakoff, G., & Johnson, M. (1980). *Metaphors we live by.* Chicago: The University of Chicago Press.

Mariani, J. (2001). The implications of your location. *Restaurant Hospitality, 85*(8), 20.

Morgan, G. (1986). *Images of organization.* Beverly Hills, CA: Sage Publications.

Netz, J. S., & Taylor, B. A. (2002). Maximum or minimum differentiation? Location patterns of retail outlets. *The Review of Economics and Statistics, 84*(1), 162.

Ott, J. S. (1989). *Organizational culture perspective.* Chicago: The Dorsey Press.

Te'eni, D., & Kendall, J. E. (2004). Internet commerce and fundraising. In D. Young (Ed.), *Effective economic decision-making by nonprofit organizations* (pp. 167-189). New York: The Foundation Center.

U.S. Census Bureau. (2003). Retrieved from http://eire.census.gov/popest/data/counties/tables/CO-EST2001-08/CO-EST2001-08-34.php

Weaver, R. M. (1967). *A rhetoric and handbook.* New York: Holt, Rinehart, and Winston.

Wesolowsky, G. O. (2001). Lectures on location theory. *INFOR, 39*(1), 124.

*This work was previously published in E-Collaboration in Modern Organizations: Initiating and Managing Distributed Projects, edited by N. Kock, pp. 14-30, copyright 2008 by Information Science Reference (an imprint of IGI Global).*

# Chapter XIX
# User Satisfaction with E–Collaborative Systems

**Jeffrey Wong**
*University of Nevada, USA*

**Kevin Dow**
*Kent State University, USA*

**Ofir Turel**
*California State University, USA*

**Alexander Serenko**
*Lakehead University, Canada*

## ABSTRACT

*E-mail is a critical component of most e-collaborative environments. This chapter describes an application of the American Customer Satisfaction Index (ACSI) framework to model the antecedents and consequences of customer satisfaction with e-mail systems. The ACSI framework is an established methodology in the marketing literature and appeared to be useful to assess the antecedents and consequences of individual satisfaction in many more circumstances than external customer purchases. We surveyed e-mail users to gather data to utilize in an ACSI model modified for e-mail systems. Our findings indicate that the ACSI model can yield useful insights into factors that contribute to and result from user satisfaction.*

## INTRODUCTION AND BACKGROUND

Information and communication technologies are the foundation for collaborative efforts that allow geographically dispersed individuals to work as a team (Kock, 2005). E-mail is one such ICT. The widespread use of e-mail technologies demonstrates its importance as a communication medium. For example, in 2003, 31 billion e-mail messages were sent daily worldwide with an average of 56 e-mails per e-mail address and 174 e-mails per person (Industry Canada, 2004). Furthermore, over 600 million people worldwide were using e-mail systems by the end of 2004 (Radicati Group Inc., 2004). The phenomenal number of users was brought about partially by the declining costs of computing, fees for long-distance communication (Sproull & Kiesler, 1991), and advances in computer and telecommunications technologies. Continuing advances in technology and the globalization of business will likely increase the widespread use of e-mail.

The prolific use of e-mail has also introduced some problematic situations. For example, user overload has resulted from the widespread use of e-mail as a communications medium (Sherwood, 2002). At the same time, the increasing number of unsolicited commercial e-mail messages (typically regarded as junk mail or spam) has exacerbated the information overload problem. Unwanted communication has been credited as being one of the most critical components of e-mail overload (Hinde, 2002).

The number of unsolicited messages is growing significantly and may soon account for more than half of all e-mail traffic (Krim, 2003). One explanation for this growth is that senders find it more expensive to target their e-mail messages to potential customers rather than simply send the same message to large distribution lists (Gopal, Walter, & Tripathi, 2001). Additionally, there are insufficient and ineffective antispam regulations in place. At the moment, only 26 countries have mandated antispam laws, leaving the opportunity for legal spamming activities in more than 100 other countries.

From the perspective of e-mail service providers, the negative effects of spam may hinder customer retention and acquisition. The magnitude of e-mail communication represents a potentially lucrative business opportunity for e-mail service providers. For them, the volume of e-mails and subscribers can translate into advertising dollars and in some cases, user fees. Accordingly, it is believed that spam can have crucial effects on both users' use of e-mail and on e-mail service providers' profitability. Our study seeks to contribute

to the literature by studying the antecedents and consequences of user satisfaction with e-mail, and to explore the potential impact of spam on user satisfaction.

To survive in the competitive environment of technology services, it is essential to both attract and retain customers. User satisfaction is a critical factor in the determination of loyalty to a service provider (Reichheld, 2003). Customer turnover can be costly because of resources expended to replace customers lost, and the possibility of damage to an e-mail provider's reputation. Findings from empirical studies suggest that when customers perceive a firm is providing superior products or services, those firms enjoy higher financial returns than firms with less satisfied customers (Anderson & Fornell, 2000).

We employ the American Customer Satisfaction Index (ACSI) model developed in the 1990s (Fornell, Johnson, Anderson, Cha, & Bryant, 1996) in our study. The ACSI was created by leading researchers in customer satisfaction, Claes Fornell and Eugene Anderson, to measure overall customer satisfaction in a way that can be compared between companies or between industry segments. Customer satisfaction has increasingly become important as companies have become service oriented, and customers are faced with many alternative providers from which to choose services and products. The ACSI has become one of the most frequently utilized satisfaction measures in the marketing literature.

The value of customer satisfaction measured by the ACSI is derived from the premise that without satisfied customers, current and future revenue streams are jeopardized. The ACSI was designed to measure customer satisfaction in a standardized way that would provide insights into the consumer economy for companies, industry trade associations, and government agencies. The developers of the ACSI felt that their methods would help to meet the need for an overall measure of the consumption experience. The index measures the quality of goods and services as perceived by those who consume them, and is designed primarily to explain customer loyalty.

There are two principal concepts underlying the ACSI model. First, the constructs of the model represent different types of customer evaluations that can only be measured indirectly. This is why the ACSI uses a multiple-indicator approach that measures customer satisfaction as a latent variable. Second, the ACSI is built on a series of cause and effect relationships that allows the antecedents and consequences of overall user satisfaction to be examined. In the case of this chapter, we examine user satisfaction with e-mail systems. Figure 1 illustrates the modified ACSI model and relationships between variables used in our study. The goal of this model is to present a set of causal relationships among several quality-related constructs. These variables will be further discussed in the next section where we develop the relationships tested in this chapter.

The remainder of the chapter is structured as follows. The next section develops the relationships that are tested through the ACSI framework. The subsequent section outlines the research methodology and statistical results. The discussion, conclusion, and directions for future research are provided in the last section.

## ACSI ELEMENTS AND FRAMEWORK

This study uses the ACSI framework to generate a score for e-mail services so that a comparison with other services may be made. This score, coupled with the causal model, depicts the perceptions, beliefs, and behaviors of e-mail users. As depicted in Figure 1, overall customer satisfaction has two antecedents and two consequences as proposed by Fornell et al. (1996). We have modified the model for this study by omitting the variables related to the perceived value construct because the e-mail services are generally free for any given Internet service provider.

The primary research questions addressed in this chapter result in five testable hypotheses. A secondary research question is also addressed.

**RQ 1.** What are the relationships among the antecedents and consequences of customer satisfaction with electronic mail?

**RQ 2.** What is the level of customer satisfaction with electronic mail measured by the American Customer Satisfaction Index?

*Figure 1. The e-mail services customer satisfaction model (Adapted from the American Customer Satisfaction Model by Anderson and Fornell, 2000)*

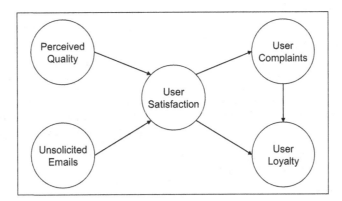

Satisfaction with e-mail is a users' reaction to their judgment of the state of fulfillment (Oliver, 1997). Users have a set of perceptions regarding their e-mail based on either previous experience or external influences. While using their e-mail system, these perceptions are compared with their actual experience, and a set of beliefs regarding the extent to which the e-mail service has met their expectations is developed. As a result, individual e-mail users adjust their perceptions accordingly.

The ACSI represents a customer-centered quality measurement system to evaluate the performance of individual companies, industries, economic sectors, and national economies. The index is calculated quarterly for many industries, including information technology. The ACSI is available for online news and information services, portals, search engines, online retailers, and telecommunications companies.

The contemporary literature presents a variety of models that measure the degree of customer satisfaction with products or services (Bansal, Irving, & Taylor, 2004). In our study, the ACSI was used because it demonstrates good psychometric capabilities and enables the generation of a standardized satisfaction score, which is comparable across industries and sectors.

The quality of an e-mail system positively influences the level of user satisfaction with it. It is derived from the degrees of personalization and reliability of the e-mail service. Further, the number of unsolicited e-mail messages, which is frequently cited as the major e-mail dissatisfaction reason, is posited to have a direct negative effect on satisfaction. Accordingly, the related hypotheses we test are as follows.

**H1:** Perceived quality will have a positive association with the level of customer satisfaction.

**H2:** The number of unsolicited spam messages received by a user is negatively associated with the level of customer satisfaction.

Prior research has found that satisfaction has a positive effect on both loyalty and retention (Bolton, 1998; Gerpott, Rams, & Schindler, 2001) and a negative effect on the number of customer complaints (Anderson & Fornell, 2000; Kim, Park, & Jeong, 2004). Marketing scholars have argued that in industries where some switching barriers exist, it is more valuable to examine loyalty than to measure retention. In high-switching-barrier industries (such as e-mail), customers that are dissatisfied might still remain with their service provider. In these industries, disloyal customers that remain with a company due to these high switching costs may ultimately have a negative effect on new customer acquisition as they share their opinions and beliefs with others (Reichheld, 2003).

In the case of e-mail systems, there are at least two potential switching barriers. First, for Web-based systems, one main barrier is the e-mail address (which is not portable to other service providers). In general, users find it inconvenient to regularly change their e-mail addresses because they have to locate all people and notify them about the change. Second, in the case of PC-based applications, the main barriers are the cost associated with the purchasing of new software, for example, Microsoft Outlook, and the setup efforts. It follows that the extent of user satisfaction is negatively associated with an individual's propensity to either formally or informally complain about services. At the same time, user satisfaction with e-mail positively influences the degree of loyalty to a specific e-mail system. User loyalty is a favorable attitude toward a specific e-mail system that leads to choosing the same system given a need for a new e-mail application. Accordingly, the related hypotheses we test are the following.

**H3:** The level of customer satisfaction is negatively associated with the frequency of user complaints.

**H4:** The level of customer satisfaction is positively associated with loyalty.

Following the ACSI framework, we test the relationship between the endogenous outcomes of overall satisfaction. There are no direct ways to test the efficacy of how an e-mail company deals with handling customer complaints. However, if a customer becomes satisfied with the way their complaints were handled, this treatment could engender loyalty. On the other hand, if the customer is dissatisfied with the manner in which complaints are addressed, the effect on loyalty would be expected to be negative. Therefore, we can only hypothesize that an association exists. Accordingly, the related hypothesis we test is the following.

**H5:** The frequency of user complaints is associated with loyalty.

## METHOD AND DATA ANALYSIS

### Survey Instrument and Construct Measures

A survey was used to sample participants from a population of e-mail users. All responses were kept anonymous and only limited demographic data were collected to determine the nature of the sample. This voluntary survey was administered to 200 undergraduate and graduate students. Two hundred surveys were administered and 186 surveys were returned. Eight instruments were either incomplete or partially complete and were excluded from data analysis. The final sample for analysis consisted of 178 usable responses.

The measures used in this study were adopted from previously validated instruments (Fornell et al., 1996) and also from existing literature to create measures for the five constructs used in this study to minimize the potential for measurement error. While it is acknowledged that all latent measures are imperfect, using existing and previously validated measures provides more of a consensus for appropriate representation of the constructs detailed in this chapter.

Perceived quality is simply an individual's judgment about the e-mail system and relates to the perception of quality based on how well the product fits personal requirements and whether expectations about reliability are met. Satisfaction is a measure of an individual's experience based on his or her evaluation of the e-mail system and can be thought of as the overall evaluation of the total consumption experience. Customer loyalty expresses an individual's intended behavior related to the e-mail system and it is operationalized with a single item used to reflect an individual's likelihood to remain loyal to the e-mail system. Customer complaints can be thought of the voicing of dissatisfaction and is measured with a single dichotomous item to reflect whether or not individual users have complained about their e-mail system. If subjects have complained, then they indicated to what extent have they have done so. Unsolicited e-mail is a categorical representation of the number of unsolicited e-mails received by the user on a daily basis.

Respondents to the survey indicated their age, sex, name, and type of the most frequently utilized e-mail system. In addition, actual e-mail usage details, such as the number of messages sent or received daily (excluding spam) and time spent working with an e-mail application were reported. The development of the research instrument followed an iterative process to ensure face validity of the survey. Specifically, a small group of information technology practitioners and academics was consulted and asked whether the items proposed in the instrument adequately measured the desired constructs. As a result of their feedback, several minor modifications were made.

## Descriptive Statistics

The participants surveyed in this study represented a diverse sample. Their ages ranged from 18 to 50 with 51% of the participants male and 49% female. On average, respondents utilized their respective e-mail system for 5 years; the amount of time ranged from 3 months to 14 years. Table 1 outlines descriptive statistics for each of the items used in the survey. Table 2 outlines the Pearson correlations among the variables included in this study.

It should be noted that the correlation between perceived quality and satisfaction is relatively high. We believe, however, that this does not threaten the validity of the model for several reasons. First, the loadings of these items on the constructs to which they belong are higher than their cross-loadings. Second, these two constructs represent an independent and a dependent variable that are expected to be correlated. Third, other studies that utilized or adapted the American Customer Satisfaction Index framework also report high correlations between quality and satisfaction. All of these studies argue that there is a reasonable statistical support to treat quality and satisfaction as being distinctly different from each other. For example, researchers have consistently uncovered a high correlation between quality and satisfaction (Babakus, Bienstock, & Scotter, 2004; O'Loughlin & Coenders, 2004). Overall, it should be noted that even though some of the correlations in our model are fairly high, they are still within the norm, and as such are not inconsistent with the discriminant validity of our constructs.

*Table 1. Descriptive statistics*

| CONSTRUCT | ITEM | N | MEAN | STD. DEVIATION | SKEWNESS | KURTOSIS |
|---|---|---|---|---|---|---|
| Quality | QUALITY 1 | 178 | 7.06 | 1.31 | -0.83 | 1.47 |
| | QUALITY 2 | 178 | 7.38 | 1.41 | -0.52 | 0.05 |
| | QUALITY 3 | 178 | 7.25 | 1.60 | -0.56 | 0.30 |
| Unsolicited E-Mails | | 177 | 2.29 | 1.61 | 1.06 | 0.28 |
| ACSI | ACSI 1 | 178 | 7.28 | 1.43 | -0.52 | 0.85 |
| | ACSI 2 | 177 | 6.59 | 1.39 | -0.43 | -0.13 |
| | ACSI 3 | 178 | 6.72 | 1.51 | -0.43 | -0.13 |
| Loyalty | | 176 | 6.94 | 1.96 | -0.60 | 0.13 |
| Complaints | | 175 | 0.22 | 0.46 | 2.24 | 6.91 |

*Table 2. Correlation matrix of variables in model*

| | Perceived Quality | Unsolicited E-mails | ACSI | Customer Complaints | Customer Loyalty |
|---|---|---|---|---|---|
| Perceived Quality | 1.000 | | | | |
| Unsolicited E-mails | -0.114 | 1.000 | | | |
| ACSI | 0.828 | -0.079 | 1.000 | | |
| Customer Complaints | -0.105 | 0.203 | -0.187 | 1.000 | |
| Customer Loyalty | 0.531 | 0.021 | 0.573 | -0.085 | 1.000 |

## The American Customer Satisfaction Index

To help understand the results of the survey, it is important to understand how the ACSI is calculated. The ACSI was calculated for e-mail systems (both in the aggregate and for each individual e-mail provider) based on the formula suggested by Anderson and Fornell (2000):

$$ACSI = \frac{\sum_{i=1}^{3} w_i \cdot \bar{x}_i - \sum_{i=1}^{3} w_i}{9 \cdot \sum_{i=1}^{3} w_i} \times 100, \qquad (1)$$

where $w_i$ represents the weight of the $i^{th}$ item obtained from the outer model generated by PLS, and represents the average of the $i^{th}$ item that loads on the ACSI construct.

## Analysis

Prior to any analysis of the model, it is important to confirm the reliability and validity of measures used in this study. As such, we examine item reliability, convergent validity, and discriminant validity.

**Item reliability.** Item reliability indicates whether the indicators for a particular latent variable measure that latent variable only. Guidelines provided by Hair, Anderson, Tatham, and Black (1995) were used in determining the item reliability for each latent variable. Following their suggestion, only items with loading greater than or equal to 0.50 were retained. As can be seen in Table 3, each of the factor loadings are above the minimum threshold of 0.50. As such, all individual items were retained for the final structural model.

**Convergent validity.** Construct validity indicates the degree to which an observable variable represents the variable of interest, which may only be indirectly observed. It is measured with Cronbach's alpha using a popular rule of thumb at 0.70 (Fornell & Larcker, 1981). All values obtained exceed this value and therefore convergent validity has been satisfied.

**Discriminant validity.** Discriminant validity represents the extent to which measures of a given construct differ from measures of other constructs in the same model. Essentially, a latent construct should share more variance with its indicators than it shares with other latent constructs. To assess this, Fornell and Larker (1981) suggest the use of the average variance extracted: simply the average variance shared between a construct and its measures. The average variance extracted is obtained by the sum of the loading squared, divided by the number of items in the construct. This measure should be greater than the variance

*Table 3. Loadings and cross-loadings for each item and construct*

|  | **Perceived Quality** | **ACSI** | **Unsolicited E-mail** | **Complaints** | **Loyalty** |
|---|---|---|---|---|---|
| PQ1 | 0.863 | 0.702 | -0.073 | -0.132 | 0.402 |
| PQ2 | 0.888 | 0.735 | -0.069 | -0.099 | 0.491 |
| PQ3 | 0.841 | 0.708 | -0.129 | -0.042 | 0.484 |
| ACSI1 | 0.818 | 0.864 | -0.094 | -0.160 | 0.543 |
| ACSI2 | 0.547 | 0.778 | -0.101 | -0.156 | 0.345 |
| ACSI3 | 0.698 | 0.893 | -0.037 | -0.163 | 0.541 |
| JUNK | -0.104 | -0.089 | 1.000 | 0.185 | 0.062 |
| UC | -0.105 | -0.187 | 0.185 | 1.000 | -0.085 |
| UL | 0.531 | 0.537 | 0.062 | -0.085 | 1.000 |

(squared correlation) shared between the latent construct and other latent constructs in the model. Each construct passed the test for discriminant validity, and the loadings and cross-loadings for each construct can be found in Table 3.

## RESULTS

### Structural Model

We employed partial least squares using the PLS Graph software package (Chin, 2001) to evaluate our model. Statistically significant levels of the estimated path coefficients were determined using the bootstrap procedure. The t-values we obtain are estimates of the bootstrap path coefficient divided by the standard error.

Figure 2 and Table 4 show the results of PLS analysis. The significant paths indicate that three of the five hypotheses are supported. Specifically, as hypothesized, the path coefficient from perceived quality to user satisfaction (0.829, p<0.01) provide support for H1, which stated that the quality of an e-mail application is positively associated with user satisfaction. The results do not support H2. This suggests that spam does not have a strong effect on user satisfaction. The path coefficient from user satisfaction to user complaints (-0.187, p<0.05) supports H3, which said user satisfaction is negatively associated with complaints. H4, stating user satisfaction is positively associated with the degree of loyalty, is supported by the results (0.578, p<0.01). Finally, the path coefficient from user complaints to user loyalty was not statistically significant and does not support H5. In summary,

*Figure 2. Results of statistical testing*

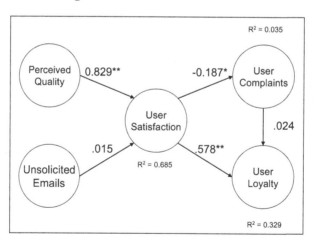

*Table 4. Table of statistical testing*

| Hypothesis | Estimate | T-value | P-value | Supported? |
|---|---|---|---|---|
| H1: PQ → ACSI | 0.829 | 30.682 | <0.01 | supported |
| H2: JUNK → ACSI | 0.015 | 0.334 | not significant | rejected |
| H3: ACSI → UC | -0.187 | 2.437 | <0.05 | supported |
| H4: ACSI → UL | 0.587 | 8.394 | <0.01 | supported |
| H5: UC → UL | 0.024 | 0.297 | not significant | rejected |

most of the hypothesized linkages in the ACSI model were supported by our findings.

## American Customer Satisfaction Index Results

An average ACSI score for all of the e-mail services was calculated to be 65.5, as seen in Table 5. This table is presented to get a sense of ACSI scores for other industries in North America for Quarter 4 of 2003. Table 5 further outlines the specific comparison of e-mail systems. As can be seen, the satisfaction score for e-mail service ranks just below that of the airline industry, and just above that of cable and satellite TV.

## DISCUSSION

Our findings largely support the relationships between the elements of the ACSI model, suggesting that the ACSI is a feasible measurement of customer satisfaction related to e-mail usage. The degree of perceived quality of an e-mail application appears to strongly influence an individual's level of satisfaction with this e-mail system. A more satisfied e-mail user complains less about his or her e-mail experience and dem-

*Table 5. Current ACSI Scores for select industries in North America*

| Sector | ACSI |
|---|---|
| Search Engines | 79 |
| Personal Computers | 77 |
| Portals | 76 |
| Computer Software | 74 |
| News & Information | 73 |
| Fixed Line Telephone Service | 70 |
| Network/Cable TV News | 69 |
| Wireless Telephone Service | 66 |
| E-Mail Systems | 65.5 |
| Cable & Satellite TV | 63 |

onstrates a high degree of loyalty to a particular e-mail system.

An interesting finding of our study is that unsolicited e-mail making it through the many spam filters of e-mail providers was not a significant determinant of customer satisfaction. This finding is surprising because the literature seems to indicate that spam is a real problem to e-mail users. We suspect that, in general, issues that are beyond the control of the technology do not seem to negatively impact the level of satisfaction with this e-collaborative technology. As such, users appear to be coping with these downside issues better than the experts would have predicted.

Alternatively, this finding may be partially explained by the motivational premises of attribution theory. This theory explains how people make causal explanations about events and describes the processes and behavioral outcomes of those rationalizations. According to attribution theory, people tend to give credit to themselves for events with positive outcomes and blame the external environment for events with a negative outcome.

When a spam e-mail message arrives, a person spends some time to determine the relevance of this message and to delete it. This is a negative outcome situation that e-mail users may blame on external factors, such as the quality of an e-mail system, a spammer, the lawmakers delaying antispam legislation, and so forth. Research in the area of human-computer interaction (HCI) suggests that people tend not to hold software responsible for mistakes, problems, or bugs because users expect computer applications to be generally unreliable (Lieberman, Rosenzweig, & Singh, 2001). Therefore, it is plausible that a recipient of spam attributes it to factors not associated with their e-mail application. For example, a spammer is considered directly responsible for the spam, not the e-mail service provider whose spam filters did not detect and remove the spam.

On the surface, the ACSI calculated for e-mail services appears to be relatively low compared with those of related products and services in other industries in North America. However, the proper way to use the ACSI score may be to compare scores from one period to the next instead of in a cross section among other goods and services. Alternatively, comparisons to similar services are more meaningful than industry or sector cross-sectional comparisons.

Finally, we found no evidence of a relationship between a user's tendency to complain about an e-mail system and his or her level of loyalty to the particular e-mail service. This may be due to high switching barriers that prevent people from moving from one e-mail system to another. Even though an e-mail service might be free of charge, the change of an e-mail address, time to install a new application, and software acquisition costs create high switching barriers for e-mail users. Therefore, even though people complain about their e-mail experience, they tend to stay with their current e-mail system. In addition, there are few substitutes for e-mail.

## CONCLUSION

Satisfaction with e-mail systems is an important topic because of the significant role that e-mail plays in communication and e-collaboration. Our study employs the ACSI customer satisfaction model to offer insights into the antecedents and consequences of user satisfaction with e-mail systems.

We find evidence that perceived quality is a determinant of user satisfaction. In turn, user satisfaction is positively related to user loyalty, and negatively associated with user complaints. Our findings generally support the ACSI model of customer satisfaction. Surprisingly, unsolicited e-mail was not a statistically significant determinant of user satisfaction, which was an unanticipated finding based upon the literature discussing the potential effect of spam on e-mail

users. Additionally, user complaints did not appear to have an effect on user loyalty, as some of the literature on customer loyalty might suggest. The findings of this chapter may be of value not only to e-mail users and e-mail providers, but also to researchers interested in other e-collaborative technologies.

Our study has its limitations. The sample consisted mostly of young Canadian students, which may not be generalizable to the entire e-mail user population. However, we feel that this population has strong familiarity with and dependence on e-mail, making it typical of regular e-mail users (Fallows, 2002). Ideally, it would have been preferable to survey a larger sample that draws from a cross section of individuals that includes people from business and governmental sectors and who are of heterogeneous geographical dispersion, using a wider variety of e-mail systems. Future research may employ a broader cross section of e-mail users to modify, validate, or expand on our findings.

## REFERENCES

Anderson, E. W., & Fornell, C. (2000). Foundations of the American Customer Satisfaction Index. *Total Quality Management & Business Excellence, 11*(7), 869-882.

Babakus, E., Bienstock, C. C., & Scotter, J. R. V. (2004). Linking perceived quality and customer satisfaction to store traffic and revenue growth. *Decision Sciences, 35*(4), 713-737.

Bansal, H. S., Irving, P. G., & Taylor, S. F. (2004). A three-component model of customer commitment to service providers. *Journal of the Academy of Marketing Science, 32*(3), 234-250.

Bolton, R. N. (1998). A dynamic model of the duration of the customer's relationship with a continuous service provider: The role of satisfaction. *Marketing Science, 17*(1), 45-65.

Chin, W. W. (2001). *PLS-Graph user's guide, version 3.0.* Soft Modeling Inc.

Fornell, C., Johnson, M. D., Anderson, E. W., Cha, J., & Bryant, B. E. (1996). The American Customer Satisfaction Index: Nature, purpose, and findings. *Journal of Marketing, 60*(7), 7-18.

Fornell, C., & Larcker, D. F. (1981). Evaluating structural equation models with unobservable variables and measurement error. *Journal of Marketing Research, 18*(1), 39-50.

Gerpott, T. J., Rams, W., & Schindler, A. (2001). Customer retention, loyalty, and satisfaction in the German mobile cellular telecommunications market. *Telecommunications Policy, 25*(4), 249-269.

Gopal, R. D., Walter, Z., & Tripathi, A. K. (2001). Admediation: New horizons in effective email advertising. *Communications of the ACM, 44*(12), 91-96.

Hair, J. F., Jr., Anderson, R. E., Tatham, R. L., & Black, W. C. (1995). *Multivariate data analysis with readings* (4th ed.). Englewood Cliffs, NJ: Prentice Hall.

Hinde, S. (2002). Spam, scams, chains, hoaxes and other junk mail. *Computers & Security, 21*(7), 592-606.

Industry Canada. (2004). *The digital economy in Canada: Unsolicited commercial electronic mail (SPAM).* Retrieved July 30, 2004, from http://e-com.ic.gc.ca/epic/internet/inecic-ceac. nsf/en/h_gv00170e.html#stats

Kim, M. K., Park, M. C., & Jeong, D. H. (2004). The effects of customer satisfaction and switch-ing barrier on customer loyalty in Korean mobile telecommunication services. *Telecommunication Policy, 28*(2), 145-159.

Kock, N. (2005). What is e-collaboration. *International Journal of e-Collaboration, 1*(1), i-vii.

Krim, J. (2003, March 13). Spam's cost to business escalates: Bulk e-mail threatens communication arteries. *The Washington Post*, p. A01.

Lieberman, H., Rosenzweig, E., & Singh, P. (2001). Aria: An agent for annotating and retrieving images. *IEEE Computer, 34*(7), 57-62.

Oliver, R. L. (1997). *Satisfaction: A behavioural perspective on consumer.* Boston: Irwin Mc-Graw-Hill.

O'Loughlin, C., & Coenders, G. (2004). Estimation of the European customer satisfaction index: Maximum likelihood versus partial least squares. Application to postal services. *Total Quality Management & Business Excellence, 15*(9-10), 1231-1255.

Radicati Group Inc. (2004). *Market numbers summary update.* Palo Alto, CA.

Reichheld, F. F. (2003). The one number you need to grow. *Harvard Business Review*, 46-54.

Sherwood, K. D. (2002). *Overcome email overload with Microsoft Outlook 2000 and Outlook 2002: Get through your electronic mail faster.* Palo Alto, CA: World Wide Webfoot Press.

Sproull, L., & Kiesler, S. B. (1991). *Connections: New ways of working in the networked organization.* Cambridge, MA: The MIT Press.

# Chapter XX
# Organizational Sense of Community and Listserv Use:
## Examining the Roles of Knowledge and Face-to-Face Interaction

**Anita Blanchard**
*University of North Carolina at Charlotte, USA*

## ABSTRACT

*This study examines how a Listserv affects its members' sense of community (SOC) with the sponsoring organization. It was expected that the Listserv would increase members' knowledge about and participation in the sponsoring organization department, which, in turn, would increase their SOC. The study examined Listserv members and nonmembers before and after implementation of the Listserv. As expected, Listserv membership increased knowledge and face-to-face activity, and knowledge and face-to-face activity increased sense of community. However, there was ironically no effect of Listserv membership on sense of community. These findings challenge previous theories about the development of sense of community while nonetheless demonstrating the positive effects of Listserv membership.*

## INTRODUCTION

Organizations can use one-way, information-dispersing Listservs to keep their members informed and connected. Listservs are group distribution e-mails in which members can conveniently send messages to one e-mail address, usually the Listserv name, instead of all of the individual members' e-mail addresses. Sometimes organizations assign members to Listservs, but often members choose to join a particular Listserv to stay informed about the organization or topics relevant to the organization.

Work organizations can use Listservs to keep employees updated on policies, announcing the entry or departure of key personnel, changes in benefits, and upcoming social events (e.g., the company picnic). Educational organizations can use Listservs to inform students about upcoming classes, research and internship opportunities, and extracurricular student activities (e.g., clubs). Social and professional organizations can use them to inform members of club-relevant announcements, involvement opportunities, and organize upcoming face-to-face (FtF) events. For example, alumni clubs can make announcements and promote viewing parties for athletic events; professional networking clubs can promote job opportunities and their monthly meetings.

These organizations may expect that this type of Listserv keeps Listserv members informed and active in the organization. However, how does the Listserv affect the Listserv members' greater attachment to the sponsoring organization? Researchers believe that electronic collaboration technologies such as e-mail and the Internet can increase members' attraction to and affiliation with their communication partners (Adams-Price & Chandler, 2000; Meier, 2000; Mesch & Levanon, 2004; Walther, 1996). Does this relationship extend to increasing affiliation with the larger organization?

This chapter will examine the relationship between an informational Listserv and organizational affiliation. Specifically, it will examine how a Listserv affects the amount of information members feel they have about the organization sponsoring the Listserv, the amount of face-to-face interaction members have with other members of the organization, and subsequently, a particular form of organizational affiliation: organizational sense of community (SOC). The next section examines the research on computer-mediated communication (CMC) and organizational sense of community.

## Organizational Sense of Community

Sense of community has a long history within the community psychology literature. Sarason

(1974) was one of the first researchers to identify that community members' feelings about each other and the community itself are important to the community's successful functioning. SOC leads to satisfaction with and commitment to the community, and is associated with involvement in community activities and problem-focused coping behavior (McMillan & Chavis, 1986).

McMillan and Chavis (1986) developed the SOC construct by defining it as an individual's feelings of membership, identity, belonging, and attachment with a group. Their descriptive framework of SOC has been widely accepted because of its theoretical base and its qualitative empirical support. This framework has four dimensions.

- **Feelings of membership:** Feelings of belonging to, and identifying with, the community.
- **Feelings of influence:** Feelings of having influence on, and being influenced by, the community.
- **Integration and fulfillment of needs:** Feelings of being supported by others in the community while also supporting them.
- **Shared emotional connection:** Feelings of relationships, shared history, and a "spirit" of community.

Recently, SOC has been gaining attention in a variety of groups and organizations including work organizations (Burroughs & Eby, 1998; Chavis & Pretty, 1999; Chipuer & Pretty, 1999; Clark, 2002; Obst & White, 2005), schools (Bess, Fisher, Sonn, & Bishop, 2002; Chipuer & Pretty; Royal & Rossi, 1999), and membership groups (Harris, 1999; Zaff & Devlin, 1998). SOC has even been reported in online groups (Blanchard & Markus, 2003; Foster, 2004; Koh & Kim, 2003; Roberts, Smith, & Pollock, 2002; Rodgers & Chen, 2005). In work organizations, SOC has been linked to positive outcomes including increased job satisfaction and organizational citizenship behavior (Burroughs & Eby, 1998), and less work-family conflict (Clark, 2002).

SOC may be particularly relevant for organizations and groups using Listservs to disperse information and encourage participation. Certainly, there is a need for these organizations, particularly the membership organizations in which participants are not formally tied to the organization, to strengthen their participants' affiliation.

What contributes to organizational sense of community? Burroughs and Eby (1998) tested a framework of the antecedents and outcomes of their organizational SOC measure, which was based on McMillan and Chavis' (1986) measure. They hypothesized that employees' need for affiliation and tenure, the size of the work group, the number of friends one has in the group, transactional contracts (e.g., use of organizational programs and services), and relational contracts (i.e., employees' organizational commitment and the organizations' commitment to the employees) would lead to SOC. However, only relational contracts made a significant positive contribution.

Other researchers used their own SOC measures and tested factors contributing to them. Clark (2002) found that supportive supervision and the intrinsic value of the work lead to her measure of SOC. Royal and Rossi (1999) found that organizational variables (perceived orderliness of students and support for innovation) and time-related variables (employee tenure and time spent interacting with others) led to SOC (as they defined it) in a school. Schuster (1998) examined the processes of exchanging support that led to SOC (as she defined it) in a writers' group in an assisted care home for the elderly. García, Giuliani, and Wiesenfeld (1999) concluded that the community's history was an important factor in creating SOC. Zaff and Devlin (1998) found that the amount of interaction between community members and components of the physical environment led to SOC.

The findings from these previous studies can be grouped into two broad categories. The first is history or knowledge about the community. In a very complicated model, McMillan and Chavis (1986) predicted that knowledge about the community and its history is integral to SOC. Garcia et al. (1999) examined this relationship and found that knowledge about the community contributes to SOC. Thus, knowledge and information about the organization should increase SOC.

Can computer-mediated communication, then, increase knowledge? As Listservs are a communication medium, it seems quite reasonable that Listserv participants will increase their information about the sponsoring group or organization. Sproull and Kiesler (1991) have even shown that employees increased their attachment to the organization through participating in group e-mails like Listservs. This increased attachment was even more pronounced for employees who had been marginalized within the organization by working second shift (Huff, Sproull, & Kiesler, 1989). By reading informational e-mails sent to groups, members may increase their knowledge and information of the organization (Huff, Sproull, & Kiesler, 1989). Recent research has shown that information distributed online had a stronger effect on communication and participation than either elevation or print media (Nah, Veenstra, & Shah, 2006).

Two questions arise. About whom exactly does knowledge increase? With whom does SOC potentially increase? We argue that it is the organizational entity itself that sponsors the Listserv and subsequently sends out relevant information about the entity and its members. The sponsoring organizational entity could be the entire organization, an organizational department (e.g., a student's academic major), or a membership or social club. Indeed, equal access to information such as that dispersed through an organizational Listserv increases members identification with a target entity (Connaughton & Daly, 2004). Therefore, the first two hypotheses for this study are the following.

**Hypothesis 1:** Listserv membership is positively related to knowledge about the sponsoring organization.

**Hypothesis 2:** Knowledge about the sponsoring organization is positively related to SOC.

The second broad category of antecedents of SOC is the interaction, usually FtF, with other members of the community (Burroughs & Eby, 1998; Royal & Rossi, 1999; Zaff & Devlin, 1998). Clearly, members have to interact with each other to develop an SOC. There are quite likely intervening mechanisms between interacting and the development of SOC, but few researchers have addressed this. Possibilities include the exchange of support (Clark, 2002; Schuster, 1998) and organizational commitment (Burroughs & Eby, 1998).

Can the Listserv also increase FtF interaction between organizational members? If the sponsoring organization has opportunities for members to interact FtF, then potentially, yes. An information-dispersing Listserv can publicize involvement opportunities for its members. Examples include advertising about the company picnic, schools providing information about extracurricular activities, or membership organizations providing information about networking meetings. Indeed, recent research has found that members of a neighborhood Listserv are likely to know more people in their FtF communities (Mesch & Levanon, 2004). Thus, the next two hypotheses are as follows.

**Hypothesis 3:** Listserv membership is positively related to FtF activity in the sponsoring organization.

**Hypothesis 4:** FtF activity is positively related to SOC.

Although the effect of Listserv membership on increasing information and FtF activity and its subsequent effect on SOC are important, ultimately, what drives this intervention is being able to connect Listserv membership to increasing SOC. Therefore, we expect there to be a mediating relationship of information and FtF activity between Listserv members and SOC (see Figure 1). The final hypothesis addresses this issue.

**Hypothesis 5:** The relationship between Listserv membership and sense of community will be mediated by knowledge about the organization and FtF activity in the organizational department.

The next section describes the organizational context in which the study occurred.

## Study Context

The Listserv used for this study was an informational Listserv implemented for the students of a large, urban southern California university.

*Figure 1. Proposed model of how a Listserv affects sense of community*

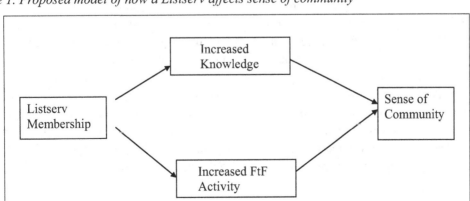

This Listserv was primarily developed to provide the primarily commuter student population with information about academic departments. Thus, in this study the sponsoring organization is the students' academic departments.

The communication on this Listserv tended to be one way; that is, professors and student leaders posted messages about administrative information, upcoming social events, and employment opportunities. The Listserv was used to advertise jobs, internships, research assistant positions, advisement information, club activities, and other information relevant for the students. Messages were posted at least once a week. Few discussions occurred on this Listserv. It can be described as an information-sharing organizational Listserv.

## METHOD

### Participants

Participants were advanced undergraduate students (i.e., juniors and seniors) of two academic departments within a large, urban university in southern California. The psychology (i.e., the test) department implemented a Listserv for its students while the sociology (i.e., the control) department did not. These two departments were chosen for comparison because of their similar size within the university and their similar social science orientation.

Data were collected at the beginning (before implementation of the Listserv) and the end of the academic school year (after implementation). During the first data collection, students were recruited during class periods with 327 psychology students and 239 sociology students participating. Although students could choose not to complete the surveys without penalty, nearly all of the students who were offered the survey participated. Thus, the difference in responses for the two departments reflects the difference in sizes between the two departments.

After the first round of data collection, participants in the psychology department were told about a new group e-mail system (i.e., the Listserv) that would provide useful information to them about upcoming events and news from the department. They were also instructed on how to join the Listserv.

During the second data collection, surveys were mailed to students' homes using addresses the students provided during the first round of data collection. Data were matched back to the first data collection resulting in a total of 266 usable surveys, a 47% response rate from the first data collection. The attrition between the first and second data collection is largely due to collecting data within the classroom in the first round and sending the surveys to participants' home addresses in the second. Even with a follow-up postcard, many participants did not return the second survey.

At this point, it was determined that not all of the psychology students who had the opportunity joined the Listserv. This meant that instead of two groups of participants (psychology test group and sociology control group), there were three groups of participants: psychology students who chose to join the Listserv (*N*=66), psychology students who did not choose to join the Listserv (*N*=112), and sociology students who did not get the opportunity to join the Listserv (*N*=88).

The demographic characteristics of the participants are similar across all three groups including age (mean=26.7, sd=8.0), years at the university (mean=3.58, sd=.54), days spent on campus (mean=3.56, sd=1.22), and minutes spent commuting (mean=31.31, sd=20.07). However, there were fewer women among the sociology participants (69%) as compared to the psychology students who were members of the Listserv (82%) and those who were not (89%).

## Measures

*Knowledge.* Knowledge was measured by listing four statements about how much the students knew about the department. These four statements were "I generally know about things going on in this department," "I know about research opportunities," "I know about changes in classes," and "I know about upcoming student events in the department." These topics were typical of the information posted on the Listserv. Participants responded on a scale of 1 (*strongly disagree*) to 6 (*strongly agree*). A reliability analysis on these variables in the first data collection period produced a coefficient alpha of 0.82. The variables were combined into a scale of knowledge.

*FtF activity.* Face-to-face activity was measured by asking students about their membership in departmental student organizations (e.g., the Psi Chi psychology honors club), their participation in research and internship activities (e.g., a professor's research group), and their attendance of meetings within the department (see Appendix A). Responses ranged from 0 (*not a member*) to 5 (*very active member*) for the student organizations, and 0 (*none*) to 5 (*5+*) for the number of meetings attended. A reliability analysis on this scale in the first data collection period produced a coefficient alpha of 0.70, which is low but acceptable. The variables were combined into a scale of active participation.

*Sense of community.* Sense of community was measured using a modified version of the Sense of Community Index (Chipuer & Pretty, 1999). This index has been used in many organizations including educational organizations. Statements were modified to reflect participants' potential affiliation with their academic departments. Sample items include "I think this is a good department for me to be a student," "I feel at home in this department," and "It is important for me to be a student in this department." Responses ranged from 1 (*strongly disagree*) to 6 (*strongly agree*). A reliability analysis was also performed on this scale in the first data collection period, producing a coefficient alpha of 0.64.

This is a low reliability score, but it is considered typical of the Sense of Community Index (Chipuer & Pretty, 1999). This measure is widely considered to have a strong theoretical basis (Chipuer & Pretty; Long & Perkins, 2003; Obst, Smith, & Zinkieqicz, 2002; Obst & White, 2004). Several SOC researchers have conducted confirmatory factor analysis of this scale, which has yielded somewhat contradictory results (e.g., Long & Perkins, 2003; Obst & White, 2004). These researchers have found that although they can improve upon the overall Sense of Community Index, with which this study's low reliability score concurs, their subsequent exploratory factor analyses propose quite different subfactors of sense of community. Chipuer and Pretty argue that until these measurement issues are resolved, researchers should continue to use the combined Sense of Community Index so that comparisons can be made across studies. Therefore, the variables were combined into an overall SOC score.

## RESULTS

Descriptive analyses of the data are presented in Tables 1 and 2.

Data were checked for analysis following the guidelines of Tabachnik and Fidell (2001). Because the FtF activity scale was highly skewed, it was transformed using an inverse function. This decreased problems with skewness and kurtosis so that it would not violate assumptions of normality and could be used in linear regression analyses. A consequence is that for this transformed scale, lower numbers represent more actual FtF activity. Table 2 shows the correlations between the research variables.

A potential problem of this study's research design is its quasi-experimental nature; participants could not be randomly assigned to academic departments and thus preexisting differences could account for any changes that occur after Listserv implementation. To test for preexisting differences, a one-way ANOVA (analysis of variance) was conducted comparing the study's measures before Listserv implementation for the sociology students, psychology Listserv members, and psychology nonmembers. None of the preimplementation measures reported in Table 1 were significantly different between the three groups. Additionally, because gender was different for the sociology department as compared to the psychology department, further analyses were conducted to determine if gender was related to the study variables: It was not.

To test the hypotheses, we conducted path analyses using the following logic. First, we collected measures of all the variables of interest in both time periods. We expected that measures from the first data collection (e.g., SOC 1) would

be reliable predictors of the same measures in the second round of data collection (e.g., SOC 2). If our hypotheses are supported, then the hypothesized variable would have a reliable relationship above and beyond the measures from the first data collection. We assessed whether the relationship was above and beyond by examining the beta weights from regression equations. Additionally, because we have three groups to compare (sociology, psychology without the list, and psychology with the list), we used contrasts to test the effects of using the Listserv. The two groups we contrasted were (a) the psychology Listserv members against the psychology nonmembers, and (b) the psychology Listserv members against the sociology students. Finally, the number of years at the university was used as a control variable. This is considered conceptually similar to the tenure data found to be related to SOC in previous research (Royal &

*Table 1. Descriptive analyses of study variables*

|  | Preimplementation | | | Postimplementation | | |
|---|---|---|---|---|---|---|
|  | **Psych With List** | **Psych No List** | **Sociology** | **Psych With List** | **Psych No List** | **Sociology** |
| Knowledge | 2.93 (.89) | 2.93 (1.00) | 2.94 (1.02) | 3.67 (.79) | 3.18 (1.17) | 3.17 (1.00) |
| Inv. Activity | 0.92 (.20) | 0.94 (.16) | 0.95 (.17) | 0.80 (.26) | 0.87 (.22) | 0.95 (.16) |
| SOC | 4.04 (.42) | 4.01 (.42) | 4.12 (.45) | 4.26 (.58) | 4.18 (.66) | 4.22 (.59) |

*Note: There were 66 psychology Listserv members, 112 psychology nonmembers, and 88 sociology students. Inverse (inv.) activity is the inverse of the activity scale to deal with problems of skewness and kurtosis.*

*Table 2. Correlations between study variables*

|  | 1 | 2 | 3 | 4 | 5 |
|---|---|---|---|---|---|
| 1. Pre-Knowledge | (.82) |  |  |  |  |
| 2. Pre-Inv. Active | -0.19** | (.70) |  |  |  |
| 3. Pre-SOC | 0.45*** | -0.16** | (.64) |  |  |
| 4. Post-Knowledge | 0.43*** | 0.00 | 0.33*** |  |  |
| 5. Post-Inv. Active | -0.19* | 0.61*** | -0.09 | -0.11 |  |
| 6. Post-SOC | 0.38** | -0.02 | 0.54*** | 0.59** | -0.15* |

*Note: Pre means preimplementation of the Listserv. Post means postimplementation of the Listserv. The numbers on the diagonal are the reliability coefficients from the first round of data collection. * p<.05, ** p<.001, *** p<.001*

Rossi, 1999), but was not an object of focus for this study.

The hypothesis testing strategy included (a) testing that the Listserv increased knowledge and FtF interaction as expected (Hypotheses 1 and 3), (b) testing that knowledge and FtF interaction increase SOC as expected (Hypotheses 2 and 4), and finally (c) that knowledge and FtF interaction mediate the relationship between Listserv membership and SOC.

To test Hypothesis 1, stating that the Listserv increased knowledge about the sponsoring organization, we examined whether Listserv membership increased knowledge above and beyond the original measure of knowledge. The results of this analysis show that Listserv membership is positively related to knowledge for the psychology Listserv members compared to the psychology non-Listserv members ($\beta$=.12, p<.05), and for the psychology members compared to sociology members ($\beta$=.12, p<.05; see Table 3). Therefore, Hypothesis 1 is supported. Participation in the Listserv reliably explained participants' knowledge about the department above and beyond their previous knowledge about the department.

To test Hypothesis 3, which said that the Listserv increased FtF activity in the sponsoring organization, we examined whether participation in the Listserv increased FtF activity above and beyond the original measure of FtF activity. The results in Table 4 show that although Listserv membership significantly explains FtF activity above and beyond previous FtF activity as compared to the sociology students ($\beta$=-.24, p<.001), it does not show these results when compared to the other psychology students ($\beta$=-.00, p=.99). Therefore, Hypothesis 3 is partially supported.

To test Hypotheses 2 and 4, which state that knowledge and FtF activity increase SOC, we conducted one hierarchical regression model. Table 5 shows the results of testing the effects of knowledge and FtF activity on SOC. Knowledge, FtF activity, and SOC from before Listserv implementation are entered in Step 2 as baseline measures. In Step 3, knowledge and FtF activity after implementation are entered to determine if they explain SOC beyond baseline. From the results, we can conclude that SOC at the beginning of the study strongly predicts SOC at the end of the study ($\beta$=.40, p<.001). However, both knowledge ($\beta$=.35, p<.001) and FtF activity ($\beta$=-.12, p=.06) at the end of the study are also related to SOC, although knowledge has a much stronger relationship than FtF activity. A total of 45% of

*Table 3. Testing Hypothesis 1: Listserv increases knowledge*

| Variable | B | SE B | β |
|---|---|---|---|
| Step 1 | | | |
| Academic Year | .11 | .12 | .06 |
| Step 2 | | | |
| Academic Year | .00 | .11 | .00 |
| Pre-Knowledge | .46 | .08 | .42** |
| Step 3 | | | |
| Academic Year | .00 | .11 | .02 |
| Pre-Knowledge | .45 | .06 | .42** |
| Psych List to No List | .15 | .08 | .12* |
| Psych List to Sociology | .17 | .09 | .12* |

*Note: $R^2$ = .00 for Step 1. $\Delta R^2$ = .17 for Step 2 (p<.001). $\Delta R^2$ = .04 for Step 3 (p<.001). * p<.05, ** p<.001*

*Table 4. Testing Hypothesis 3: Listserv increases FtF activity*

| Variable | B | SE B | β |
|---|---|---|---|
| Step 1 | | | |
| Academic Year | -.00 | .03 | -.13* |
| Step 2 | | | |
| Academic Year | .00 | .02 | .01 |
| Pre-Inv. Activity | .77 | .07 | .61** |
| Step 3 | | | |
| Academic Year | .00 | .02 | -.03 |
| Pre–Inv. Activity | .74 | .07 | .58** |
| Psych List to No List | -.00 | .02 | -.00 |
| Psych List to Sociology | -.00 | .02 | -.24** |

*Note: $R^2 = .02$ for Step 1. $\Delta R^2 = .35$ for Step 2 (p<.001). $\Delta R^2 = .06$ for Step 3 (p<.001). ** p<.001*

*Table 5. Testing Hypotheses 2 and 4: Knowledge and FtF activity increase SOC*

| Variable | B | SE B | β |
|---|---|---|---|
| Step 1 | | | |
| Academic Year | -.00 | .07 | -.03 |
| Step 2 | | | |
| Academic Year | -.01 | .06 | -.07 |
| Pre-Knowledge | .11 | .04 | .19** |
| Pre-Activity | .15 | .19 | .05 |
| Pre-SOC | .56 | .07 | .47*** |
| Step 3 | | | |
| Academic Year | -.01 | .06 | -.08 |
| Pre-Knowledge | .00 | .04 | .07 |
| Pre-Activity | .29 | .22 | .08 |
| Pre-SOC | .48 | .07 | .40*** |
| Post-Knowledge | .20 | .03 | .35*** |
| Post-Activity | -.30 | .17 | -.12ᵗ |

*Note: $R^2 = .00$ for Step 1. $\Delta R^2 = .33$ for Step 2 (p<.001). $\Delta R^2 = .12$ for Step 3 (p<.001). ᵗ p=.06, * p<.05, ** p<.10, *** p<.001*

the variance of SOC is explained by this model as indicated by the adjusted values for $R^2$. Thus, Hypotheses 2 and 4 are supported.

To test Hypothesis 5, regarding knowledge and FtF interaction mediating the relationship between Listserv membership and SOC, we used Baron and Kenny's (1986) mediation testing strategy.

This strategy includes testing that (a) Listserv membership is related to knowledge and FtF interaction, (b) Listserv membership is related to SOC, and (c) when knowledge and FtF interaction are entered in a hierarchical regression after Listserv membership, these two variables decrease the relationship of Listserv membership to SOC.

Because Hypotheses 1 and 3 complete the first step of this strategy, the next step is to test that Listserv membership increased SOC above and beyond the original measure of SOC. The results of this analysis show that Listserv membership did not increase SOC (see Table 6). Therefore, Hypothesis 5 is not supported.

Because there is no direct relationship between Listserv membership and SOC, we cannot test Hypothesis 5 stating that this relationship is mediated by knowledge and FtF activity (Baron & Kenny, 1986). There can be no indirect (i.e., mediated) relationship if there is no direct one.

## Exploratory Analysis

The results of these analyses are perplexing. Listserv membership increases knowledge about the sponsoring organization and FtF activity within it. Knowledge and FtF activity increase SOC. The model appears to hold; however, because there is no direct link between Listserv membership and SOC, the indirect effects of Listserv membership on SOC approach zero. Therefore, the parts of knowledge and FtF activity that are related to SOC are independent of those related to Listserv membership.

Why is there no effect of the Listserv on SOC? Reflecting upon the findings, we conclude that Listserv membership increases participants' amount of knowledge. Members of the Listserv have access to more information simply by being members of the Listserv. This is verified in the data by increased knowledge for the Listserv group compared to both its internal and external control groups. Thus, the Listserv increased how much people knew about what was going on in the department.

The data also support the conclusion that information is related to SOC. That is, as people know more about the department (i.e., they have more objective knowledge), they have a greater SOC. However, because Listserv membership (with more objective knowledge) did not have a direct effect on SOC, we questioned the direction of this relationship. Instead, we considered whether SOC could lead to a perception of more knowledge. That is, people with a strong SOC believe they know more about what is going on in the department apart from any objective increases in knowledge.

Therefore, we questioned whether the direction of the relationship between SOC and information in the original model is correct. We regressed the relationship of Listserv membership and SOC on

*Table 6. Testing Hypothesis 5: Listserv increases SOC*

| Variable | | B | SE B | β |
|---|---|---|---|---|
| Step 1 | | | | |
| | Academic Year | .00 | .07 | -.02 |
| Step 2 | | | | |
| | Academic Year | -.01 | .06 | -.06 |
| | Pre-SOC | .67 | .06 | .55*** |
| Step 3 | | | | |
| | Academic Year | -.01 | .14 | .00 |
| | Pre-SOC | .67 | .07 | .55*** |
| Psych List to No List | | .00 | .04 | .02 |
| Psych List to Sociology | | .00 | .05 | .04 |

*Note: $R^2$ = .00 for Step 1. $\Delta R^2$ = .30 for Step 2 (p<.001). $\Delta R^2$ = .00 for Step 3 (p=.70). * p<.05, ** p<.001*

knowledge. Table 7 presents the results of this exploratory analysis.

These analyses show that, indeed, Listserv participation and SOC are both independently related to the participants' knowledge about the department. SOC is strongly related ($\beta$=.44, p<.001) while Listserv membership is more moderately related; knowledge is higher for the Listserv members compared to psychology nonmembers of the Listserv ($\beta$=.10, p=.06) and the sociology students ($\beta$=.12, p<.05).

We also questioned the direction of the relationship between SOC and FtF activity. We regressed SOC along with Listserv membership on FtF activity. Table 8 presents the results of this analysis. While FtF activities in the first time period have the strongest relationship to FtF activities at the end of the study ($\beta$=.60, p<.001), SOC ($\beta$=-.17, p<.001) and Listserv membership for the psychology students as compared to the sociology students ($\beta$=-.23, p<.01) are also strongly related to FtF activity at the end of the study.

The two exploratory analyses challenge our research model. In particular, the data are better explained by using information and FtF activity as criteria instead of predictor variables. We propose, then, that the direction of the relationship between information with FtF activity and SOC was incorrect. Knowledge and FtF activity are not mediators of the relationship between Listserv membership and SOC. Instead, knowledge and FtF activity are outcomes of Listserv participation and SOC. Model 2 revises the original model to reflect the results.

## DISCUSSION

The purpose of this research was to examine the effects of Listserv implementation on the sponsoring organization's members. It was expected that the Listserv would increase participants' knowledge about as well as their FtF activity in the Listserv's sponsoring organization, in this case, an academic department. It was then expected that knowledge

*Table 7. Exploratory analysis regressing sense of community and Listserv membership on knowledge*

| Variable | B | SE B | $\beta$ |
|---|---|---|---|
| Step 1 | | | |
| Pre-Knowledge | .38 | .07 | .35*** |
| Pre-SOC | .36 | 14 | .17** |
| Step 2 | | | |
| Pre-Knowledge | .30 | .06 | .27*** |
| Pre-SOC | .00 | .14 | -.04 |
| Post-SOC | .78 | .11 | .45*** |
| Step 3 | | | |
| Pre-Knowledge | .30 | .06 | .27*** |
| Pre-SOC | -.00 | .14 | -.03 |
| Post-SOC | .75 | .11 | .44*** |
| Psych List to No List | .13 | .07 | .10$^\tau$ |
| Psych List to Sociology | .17 | .08 | .12* |

*Note: $R^2$ = .20 for Step 1 (p<.001). $\Delta R^2$ = .14 for Step 2 (p<.001). $\Delta R^2$ = .03 for Step 3 (p<.001). $^\tau$ p=.06, * p<.05, ** p<.01, *** p<.001*

*Table 8. Exploratory analysis regressing sense of community and Listserv on FtF activities*

| Variable | B | SE B | β |
|---|---|---|---|
| Step 1 | | | |
| Pre-Activities | .77 | .07 | .61*** |
| Pre-SOC | .00 | .03 | .00 |
| Step 2 | | | |
| Pre-Activities | .78 | .07 | .62*** |
| Pre-SOC | .00 | .03 | .11 ᵗ |
| Post-SOC | -.01 | .01 | -.19*** |
| Step 3 | | | |
| Pre-Activities | .76 | .06 | .60*** |
| Pre-SOC | .00 | .02 | .08 |
| Post-SOC | -.01 | .02 | -.17** |
| Psych List to No List | .00 | .02 | .01 |
| Psych List to Sociology | -.01 | .02 | -.23*** |

*Note: $R^2$ = .37 for Step 1 (p<.001). $\Delta R^2$ = .02 for Step 2 (p<.01). $\Delta R^2$ = .05 for Step 3 (p<.001). ᵗ <.10, * p<.05, ** p<.01, *** p<.001*

*Figure 2. Revised proposed model*

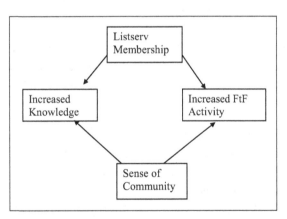

and FtF activity would increase the members' SOC, thus mediating the relationship between the Listserv and the members' SOC.

The results show that although the Listserv is related to participants' knowledge and FtF activity, and that subsequently knowledge and FtF activity are related to participants' SOC, there was no relationship between the Listserv and sense of community. Instead and ironically, the Listserv and SOC together independently affect knowledge and FtF activity. A new model is proposed that reverses the relationship between SOC and FtF activity and knowledge.

This model challenges much of the current research about the antecedents of SOC. Previously, research has argued that knowledge and FtF activity increase SOC (Burroughs & Eby, 1998; García et al., 1999; Royal & Rossi, 1999; Zaff & Devlin, 1998). However, much of this research has been conducted qualitatively or through cross-sectional survey research. Thus, it is possible that SOC researchers have confused the direction of this correlational relationship.

Although the Listserv did not increase SOC as anticipated, it did affect knowledge about and potentially FtF activity in the sponsoring organization, which are in and of themselves worthy outcomes. Thus, the results of this study concur with other research demonstrating the effects of participation in electronic media on increased information and FtF interaction. Therefore, increased knowledge and FtF activity may be important goals for organizations who want to keep their members informed and active. We argue that the Listserv potentially affected FtF activity because the psychology Listserv members had higher FtF activity than the sociology students but not more than the psychology nonmembers. It is possible that the psychology department simply became more active without relation to the Listserv. However, it is also possible that the Listserv's ability to advertise about upcoming events and activities increased participation among members as well as nonmembers as they discussed during regular student interactions.

These findings are especially encouraging because the Listserv, as an electronic collaboration technology, itself was quite simple. It was not interactive in that members did not hold discussions on it. Instead, the Listserv consisted of one-way communications about opportunities and events. A more interactive Listserv might elicit more of an affective response from its members (e.g., Koh & Kim, 2003; Rodgers & Chen, 2005; Weis et al., 2003). However, interactive Listservs are harder to develop and maintain due to the time requirements on their members. Additionally, the focus of the effects in a more interactive Listserv may be directed toward the Listserv and not the sponsoring organization (Liao, Troth, & Griffith, 2002).

That the Listserv increases FtF activity is particularly intriguing. An information-dispersing Listserv is a very passive medium for its members. That it was able to increase FtF interactivity for the department in which the Listserv was implemented is encouraging. It also points out where organizations may be able to increase the organizational attachment of their members. For instance, if the FtF interactions foster the development of relationships and exchange of support, which were not measured in this study, then the interactions could help develop SOC as predicted by the model. Thus, FtF interactions and SOC could be part of a reinforcing cycle in which the Listserv could draw in new members for FtF interactions. Although not examined in this study, increased information and FtF activity may affect other desirable organizational outcomes such as organizational commitment or involvement. Future research should consider what other desirable outcomes for dispersed organizational members may be affected by Listservs.

Finally, this research can be used as a lesson for organizations who wish to increase their members' affiliation through an information-dispersing Listserv only. It may not be the best use of their time, resources, and money to use a Listserv solely for increasing their members' affiliation. Even though it can increase their members' knowledge, it will not directly affect their affiliation with the organization. Additional or different media may be required.

*Limitations and strengths.* Participants in this study were not randomly assigned to be members of the Listserv. Even though there were no significant differences between the groups at the start of the study, participants were self-selected into Listserv membership. Clearly, the members of the Listserv are different from the nonmembers because they had the opportunity and chose to join the Listserv. An alternative explanation of the findings is that Listserv joiners are more likely to be more curious about and involved in the organization. Thus, there could be some personality trait that explains their changes in knowledge and FtF activity.

However, the members who joined this Listserv may, in fact, be similar to members of other Listservs in which members must choose to join. Most Listservs require that the members join them instead of being assigned to them. Additional research should address this issue by examining both randomly assigned and self-selected Listserv members.

Additionally, the student population may limit some of the study's generalizability. For example, students and traditional employees are likely to differ in their feelings of affiliation with their work groups, departments, and overarching organizations. For employees, work groups and organizations may be the primary focus of their affiliation outside the home, whereas these commuter students may have less developed affiliation because they do not spend as much time on campus as employees do at an organization. This research may be most generalizable to nontraditional employees such as telecommuters who rely more on collaboration technologies to stay informed or to membership groups such as voluntary social or professional organizations who do not interact with each other on a daily basis. As with all research, findings must be replicated in different populations to strengthen their conclusions.

A strength of this research, however, is that it controls for levels of the variables of interest before and after implementation of the Listserv. We are in a better position to assess the relationship between SOC, and information and FtF activity after the Listserv implementation because we have a better understanding of what occurred before the Listserv.

## CONCLUSION

This research examined how implementing a Listserv affects sense of community for the sponsoring organization's members: It did not. Instead, it demonstrated that a Listserv can increase knowledge about and face-to-face activity within an organization; interactivity and knowledge do not directly increase feelings of community.

What then are the broader implications for this study? Managers, school administrators, and membership group coordinators can and should use their Listservs to share information and promote FtF interactions. This is a simple use of an easy collaboration technology that can take advantage of the active involvement of few to reward the passive involvement of many.

However, we should not expect that an information-distributing Listserv alone will promote feelings of affiliation for the sponsoring organization. Instead, at this time, research suggests that affiliation will increase during exchanges of information and particularly support (Clark, 2002; Schuster, 1998). The question remains as to whether these exchanges need to occur primarily face to face or if exchanging information and support through collaborative technologies will create feelings of affiliation (like those suggested by virtual communities) to the sponsoring organization. Managers and researchers who wish to increase affiliation for their members will need to pursue these questions further.

Electronic collaboration technologies vary drastically in how much members interact within them and how much effort is required for them to be successful. Information-dispersing Listservs have a place in the arsenal of communication technologies as a very simple tool to keep members informed about and, potentially, active in their organizations.

## REFERENCES

Adams-Price, C. E., & Chandler, S. (2000). The star fleet ladies auxiliary: Evolution of an online women's mailing list. *CyberPsychology and Behavior, 3*(5), 811-816.

Baron, R. M., & Kenny, D. A. (1986). The moderator-mediator variable distinction in social psychological research: Conceptual, strategic and statistical considerations. *Journal of Personality and Social Psychology, 51*, 1173-1182.

Bess, K. D., Fisher, A. T., Sonn, C. C., & Bishop, B. J. (2002). Psychological sense of community: Theory, research, and application. In A. T. Fisher, C. C. Sonn, & B. J. Bishop (Eds.), *Psychological sense of community: Research, applications and implications.* New York: Kluwer Academic/Plenun Publishers.

Blanchard, A., & Markus, M. L. (2003). The experienced "sense" of a virtual community: Characteristics and processes. *The Data Base for Advances in Information Systems.*

Burroughs, S. M., & Eby, L. T. (1998). Psychological sense of community at work: A measurement system and explanatory framework. *Journal of Community Psychology, 26*, 509-532.

Chavis, D. M., & Pretty, G. H. (1999). Sense of community: Advances in measurement and application. *Journal of Community Psychology, 27*(6), 635-642.

Chipuer, H. M., & Pretty, G. H. (1999). A review of the Sense of Community Index: Current uses, factor structure, reliability and further development. *Journal of Community Psychology, 27*, 643-658.

Clark, S. C. (2002). Employees' sense of community, sense of control, and work/family conflict in Native American organizations. *Journal of Vocational Behavior, 61*, 92-108.

Connaughton, S. L., & Daly, J. A. (2004). Identification with leader: A comparison of perceptions of identification among geographically dispersed and co-located teams. *Corporate Communications, 9*(2), 89-103.

Foster, P. M. (2004). Psychological sense of community in groups on the Internet. *Behaviour Change, 21*(2), 141-146.

García, I., Giuliani, F., & Wiesenfeld, E. (1999). Community and sense of community: The case of an urban barrio in Caracas. *Journal of Community Psychology, 27*, 727-740.

Harris, J. (1999). The idea of community in the study of writing. In L. Ede (Ed.), *On writing research: The Braddock essays 1975-1998* (pp. 260-271). Boston: Bedford.

Huff, C. W., Sproull, L., & Kiesler, S. (1989). Electronic communication and organizational commitment: Tracing the relationship in a city government. *Journal of applied social psychology, 19*, 1371-1391.

Koh, J., & Kim, Y.-G. (2003). Sense of virtual community: A conceptual framework and empirical validation. *International Journal of Electronic Commerce, 8*(2), 75.

Liao Troth, M. A., & Griffith, T. L. (2002). Software, shareware and freeware: Multiplex commitment to an electronic social exchange system. *Journal of Organizational Behavior, 23*(5), 635-653.

Long, D. A., & Perkins, D. D. (2003). Confirmatory factory analysis of the Sense of Community Index and development of a brief SCI. *Journal of Community Psychology, 31*(3), 279-296.

McMillan, D. W., & Chavis, D. M. (1986). Sense of community: A definition and theory. *Journal of Community Psychology, 14*, 6-23.

Meier, A. (2000). Offering social support via the Internet: A case study of an online support group for social workers. *Journal of Technology in Human Services, 17*(2-3), 237-266.

Mesch, G. S., & Levanon, Y. (2004). Community networking and locally-based social ties in two suburban localities. *City & Community, 2*(4), 335-351.

Nah, S., Veenstra, A. S., & Shah, D. V. (2006). The Internet and anti-war activism: A case study of information, expression, and action. *Journal of Computer Mediated Communication, 12*(1).

Obst, P., & White, K. M. (2005). An exploration of the interplay between psychological sense of community, social identification and salience. *Journal of Community & Applied Social Psychology, 15*, 127-135.

Obst, P. L., Smith, S., & Zinkieqicz, L. (2002). An exploration of sense of community: Part 3. Dimensions and predictors of psychological sense of community in geographical communities. *Journal of Community Psychology, 30*(1), 119-133.

Obst, P. L., & White, K. M. (2004). Revisiting the Sense of Community Index: A confirmatory factor analysis. *Journal of Community Psychology, 32*(6), 691-705.

Roberts, L. D., Smith, L. M., & Pollock, C. M. (2002). MOOing till the cows come home: The sense of community in virtual environments. In C. C. Sonn (Ed.), *Psychological sense of community: Research, applications, implications*. New York: Kluwer Academic/Plenum.

Rodgers, S., & Chen, Q. (2005). Internet community group participation: Psychosocial benefits for women with breast cancer. *Journal of Computer Mediated Communication, 10*(4).

Royal, M. A., & Rossi, R. J. (1999). Predictors of within-school differences in teachers' sense of community. *Journal of Educational Research, 92*, 259-267.

Sarason, S. B. (1974). *The psychological sense of community: Prospects for a Community Psychology*. San Francisco: Jossey-Bass.

Schuster, E. (1998). A community bound by words: Reflections on a nursing home writing group. *Journal of Aging Studies, 12*(2), 137-148.

Sproull, L., & Kiesler, S. (1991). *Connections: New ways of working in the networked organization*. Cambridge, MA: MIT Press.

Tabachnik, B. G., & Fidell, L. S. (2001). *Using multivariate statistics* (4th ed.). Needham Heights, MA: Allyn & Bacon.

Walther, J. B. (1996). Computer mediated communication: Impersonal, interpersonal and hyperpersonal interaction. *Communication Research, 22*, 33-43.

Weis, R., Stamm, K., Smith, C., Nilan, M., Clark, F., Weis, J., et al. (2003). Communities of care and caring: The case of MSWatch.com®. *Journal of Health Psychology, 8*(1), 135-148.

Zaff, J., & Devlin, S. (1998). Sense of community in housing for the elderly. *Journal of Community Psychology, 26*, 381-398.

## APPENDIX A

Are you a member of the following groups in the psychology/sociology* department? If so, please indicate your level of activity in these groups:

## PSI CHI/PSSA*

Other (Please Indicate): _____

How many semesters have you been supervised in an internship by a psychology/sociology* professor?

How many semesters have you participated in a research activity or project with a professor outside of class?

How many meetings or activities sponsored by the psychology faculty or staff have you attended?

How many meetings or activities sponsored by the psychology students have you attended?

*Note: This part of the survey was tailored to each department and either contained psychology or sociology as well as the specific departmental clubs Psi Chi or PSSA.*

*This work was previously published in E-Collaboration in Modern Organizations: Initiating and Managing Distributed Projects, edited by N. Kock, pp. 42-59, copyright 2008 by Information Science Reference (an imprint of IGI Global).*

# Chapter XXI
# Agile IT Outsourcing

**Boris Roussev**
*University of the Virgin Islands, USA*

## ABSTRACT

*Agile methods are lightweight, iterative software development frameworks used predominantly on small and mid-sized software development projects. This chapter introduces a project structure and management practices creating agile conditions for large software projects outsourced either offshore or onshore. Agility is achieved by slicing a large project into a number of small projects working in agile settings. Development is divided into research and development activities that are located on-site, and production activities located off-site. The proposed approach makes agile methods applicable to the stressed conditions of outsourcing without compromising the quality or pace of the software development effort. Creating an agile environment in an outsourcing project relies on maintaining a balance between the functions and sizes of on-site and off-site teams, on redefining the developers' roles, and on reorganizing the information flow between the different development activities to compensate for the lack of customers on-site, team colocation, and tacit project knowledge.*

## INTRODUCTION

We live in a digital world where any activity not requiring a physical presence can be outsourced to any place that is connected to the Internet. Even the term *physical presence* comes with a qualification. Information and communication technologies enable cooperation in a distributed mode. Technologies, such as groupware and videoconferencing, are increasingly becoming feasible for organizations to use in distributed projects.

Advances in ICT have been essential for loosening the spatial constraints on software development. The largely digital nature of software development allows changing its geography of provision. The combination of low labor costs, technological sophistication, satisfactory (but not outstanding) project management skills, and successful software establishment makes south Asia a particularly attractive location for software production outsourcing (Dossani & Kenney, 2003). However, the decision to outsource software production is not a simple matter of upside (Natovich, 2003). Product and project managers have been looking for ways to mitigate risks in outsourcing projects to maximize reward (Craumer, 2002). Even though the total contract value of IT outsourcing transactions continues to increase (Hale, Souza, Lo, Adachi, & Babaie, 2005; Technology Partners International [TPI], 2005), many large organizations are bringing key IT projects back in house because outsourcing contracts have failed to meet expectations (Huber, 2005).

Agile methods (Agile Alliance, 2001; Beck, 1999; Schuh, 2005; Sridhar, Mahapatra, & Mangalaraj, 2005) are popular software development processes designed for use on small to mid-sized software projects. They are based on the notion that object-oriented software development is not a rigidly defined process, but an empirical one that may or may not be repeated with the same success under changed circumstances.

Agile methods are based on four critical values: simplicity, communication, feedback, and courage, informing a set of key practices (Pollice, 2004), which will be considered in more detail later. Boehm and Turner (2004, p. 27) define agile methods as "very light-weight processes that employ short iterative cycles; actively involve users to establish, prioritize, and verify requirements; and rely on tacit knowledge within a team as opposed to documentation." However, many of the agile practices seem to be incompatible with the context of outsourcing, especially when outsourcing offshore; for example, agile practices work better when there are customers on-site, team colocation, short life cycles, and the value of embracing change. Above all, agile methods are applicable mainly to small and mid-sized projects because of many of the characteristics of agile development. For example, smaller, colocated teams require

fewer lines of communication and less coordination efforts, can use less formal development processes, can reach an agreement faster, and can adapt to change more rapidly (Schuh, 2005; Stephens & Rosenberg, 2003).

In the past, there have been several attempts to reproduce the conditions for agility in large projects. To the best of our knowledge, no such attempt has been made for outsourcing projects. Pollice (2001a, 2001b), Evans (2004), and Boehm and Turner (2004) propose to scale up agile methods by balancing agility and discipline. Pollice and Evans, for instance, look for common ground between agile and RUP (Jacobson, Booch, & Rumbaugh, 1999), while Boehm and Turner try to get the best of both agile and plan-driven (waterfall) worlds. In contrast, Kruchten (2004) proposes to scale down large projects to meet the agile "sweet spot" based on experience reported in Brownsword and Clements (1996) and Toth, Kruchten, and Paine (1993). The sweet spot, or in other words the ideal agile context, is characterized by a small team of developers sharing common values, team colocation, customers on-site, and a short life cycle.

In this work, we show how to reengineer large outsourcing projects to benefit from the sweet spot of agile methods while avoiding its "bitter spot." The proposed approach makes agile methods applicable to the stressed condition of both offshore and onshore outsourcing environments without compromising the quality of the software development effort. Creating a context congenial to agile methods hinges on balancing the functions and sizes of on-site and off-site teams, on redefining the developers' roles, and on reorganizing the information flow between the different development activities.

The rest of the chapter is structured as follows. Next it examines some critical issues in outsourcing software development activities. Then it presents the structure of the agile outsourcing project. The chapter then elaborates on the inception and architectural activities in agile outsourcing, which are crucial to slicing large projects into multiple, relatively independent agile projects. Next it discusses some of the challenges likely to be experienced by outsourcing suppliers when applying the proposed approach, and finally it concludes.

## OUTSOURCING SOFTWARE DEVELOPMENT ACTIVITIES

### What can be Outsourced?

When the software development process is considered in its totality, it appears to resist relocation because software production requires face-to-face interactivity with clients (and among codevelopers), for example, during user requirements elicitation and testing. The development workflow has to be parsed into activities requiring different levels of interactivity, and the less client-communication-intensive activities can be potentially outsourced.

The software complexity chain is frequently described as a series of processes, each of which is less complex than the earlier one (Akella & Dossani, 2001). The initial processes are less labor intensive but more complex than the later ones. The complexity of a process is roughly inverse proportional to its labor intensity. The pyramid

model in Figure 1 gradates the processes in terms of labor, complexity, risk, and communication intensity.

Theoretically, outsourcing is possible for all the levels of the complexity pyramid, but there are important differences of how outsourcing for each level is likely to be implemented. The processes at or closer to the pyramid's apex, such as domain knowledge acquisition, architecture design, and technology determination, are objectively more difficult to outsource (King, 2005). Moving up the complexity pyramid entails establishing an intimate client-supplier rapport and acquiring knowledge about the client's core and critical activities.

IT client activities can be divided into core and noncore on the one hand and critical and noncritical on the other hand. Core activities are services that differentiate a firm from its competitors and they are key to its continued growth. Noncore activities are the firm's noncompetitive services, such as payroll and human resources. Within both core and noncore activities, there are activities crucial to their functioning, termed critical activities. The higher the pyramid level is, the more communication intensive the activities become, and the bigger the demand grows for domain, architectural, and design knowledge. Adopting agile methods can help outsourcing suppliers move up the value chain because agile methods address the issues enumerated above.

*Figure 1. Activities and pyramid of labor*

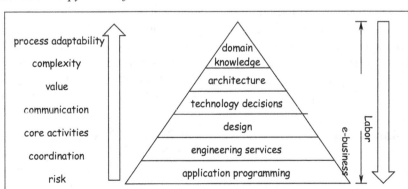

## Interactivity

Interactivity always comes across as a stumbling block for outsourcing (King, 2005). Interactivity has two dimensions: interaction among codevelopers and interaction with clients. Requirements elicitation and acceptance testing are the activities requiring the most active involvement on the part of the client, which makes them impossible to outsource.

The greater the need of codevelopers to interact across a set of different activities of the software process, the higher the risk threshold of outsourcing a subset of the activities is. Outsourcing the entire set of activities might be considered as a way of retaining interactivity at the new location. However, if some activities cannot be outsourced because that would disrupt the interaction with the client, then outsourcing the others might need careful consideration.

## Rethinking of Earlier Cost-Benefit Decisions

The lower cost of highly skilled personnel calls for the rethinking of established cost-benefit decisions. For example, the much lower cost of software engineers in India compared to the United States (Dossani & Kenney, 2003; Outsourcing Institute, 2004) makes it feasible to increase the density of software inspections (Gilb & Graham, 1993) or to dispel managers' doubts about the feasibility of pair programming (CeBASE, 2004). Other activities that are candidates for reconsideration are regression and integration testing, iteration planning, and metrics for tracking project progress. In all of the above-mentioned practices, lower labor costs can change the break-even point, and thus create new sources of revenue.

## Risks in IT Outsourcing

A recent study based on the managerial assessment of overall risk in in-house IT development projects identifies six critical risk factors: (a) the lack of customer involvement, (b) requirements volatility, (c) ill-fitting software methods, (d) the lack of formal project management practices, (e) dissimilarity to previous projects, and (f) project complexity (Laplante & Neill, 2004; Tiwana & Keil, 2006). In addition, there are some unique risks at play for clients of outsourcing projects related to controlling vendor involvement (Choudhury & Sabherwal, 2003). These unique risks can be divided into intractable risks and unforeseen risks (Taylor, 2006). Intractable risks are those risks that resist mitigation actions despite managers' best efforts to address them. Unforeseen risks appear unlikely to affect project outcomes, even if a project involves active risk assessment, but they have significant impact in later development stages.

The most common intractable risk is overoptimistic schedules and budgets, or in other words, schedule and budget management. The most likely unforeseen risk is inflated client expectations, or trust. Understanding and managing overoptimistic schedules and budgets, and client trust are critical for both clients and vendors.

The best strategy to avoid underestimation of budgets and schedules is to do costly presale requirements analysis. However, even if carried out, the results of such analysis can be compromised by the presale team's desire to secure the project by placing a winning bid, which is characteristic of both small and large companies (Jiang, Klein, & Discenza, 2002). A more effective risk mitigation approach is to factor out the presale requirements specification activity into a stand-alone, chargeable consulting activity (Taylor, 2006).

In general, iterative and incremental software methods employ project scoping to assess the functionality that must be delivered, the resources that must be allocated to deliver this functionality, and the time to implement the software system (Kruchten, 2000). Typically, both in-house and outsourced software projects are overscoped. According to the Standish Group (2003), 53% of all projects cost 189% of their estimates. The project scope is the underpinning for project planning. The project plan creates the breakdown work structure, defines iterations, sets targets as major and minor milestones, allocates resources, and creates incentives.

Agile methods, in particular, do not rely on a detailed project plan. Their assumption is that as the project unfolds, some features will evolve while other features will be dropped altogether because they do not bring the expected value, the external environment has changed, or the customers' understanding of these features has evolved. In other words, agile methods do not overpromise unrealistic schedules and budgets.

Client trust and satisfying client expectations are extremely important to vendors as they depend on client referrals and references. One of the main factors for the success of agile methods is the improved communication line between clients and developers. Agile methods rely on a shared vocabulary and improved communication. This results in improved traceability between client needs and resultant software artifacts. In agile methods, the goal of the development team is to become part of the customer's discourse, or context. From a communications standpoint, agile software development can be viewed as a discursive communication model in which the vendor responds to client requests with increments—pieces of executable functionality produced in one iteration (Roussev & Rousseva, 2006). The customer tests each increment, after which the communication cycle repeats. In the testing subprocess, or the ensuing discourse between client and vendor, the customer may become aware of a compelling necessity to redefine needs. The process of constant reassessing of client needs decreases the extent of the client's disconfirmation of expectations, thus leading to improved customer satisfaction.

## Problems Experienced by Outsourcing Suppliers

Levina and Ross' (2003) research on outsourcing vendors' value proposition indicates that cost, quality, and project management skills are the three most important attributes of value to clients. Success in IT development outsourcing projects is predicated on factors related to vendors' core competencies (Prahalad & Hamel, 1990), complementarities of the core competencies (Milgrom & Roberts, 1990), and the following capabilities of the development team: technical knowledge, domain expertise, and management skills, including client management (Akella & Dossani, 2001; Levina & Ross, 2003). Offshore developers face problems in acquiring advanced domain knowledge as they are geographically separated from their clients' business environments and more often than not have a different background and culture (Dossani & Kenney, 2003; Outsourcing Institute, 2004). The lack of advanced domain knowledge can lead to misunderstanding of client expectations and misinterpretation of client needs (Kruchten, 2000). The latter may be further compounded by the suppliers' business interaction, client coordination and communication style, and the shortage of project management expertise, including planning, scheduling, and progress monitoring (Akella & Dossani). The end result is inadequate quality.

Quality in outsourcing contexts should be considered on a much larger scale than merely in terms of defects, usability, maintainability, reliability, and performance (Akella & Dossani, 2001). Outsourcing clients define quality of work as the possession of advanced domain knowledge, adherence to schedules, high coordination between client and supplier, adaptability, and mature software processes, for example, SEI/CMM (Paulk, Curtis, Chrissis, & Weber, 1993) and ISO 9001 (International Organization for Standardization) certifications, coupled with transparency (i.e., observability) and outcome measurability (Kirsch, Sambamurthy, Ko, & Purvis, 2002). As a consequence, clients attribute project failure mostly to poor coordination, communication, and scheduling. In addition, clients expect suppliers to be very responsive and to push beyond the stated goals by engaging actively in identifying new problems and opportunities, and offering innovative solutions. Clients anticipate outsourcing suppliers to become part of their teams and to advise them on which components and activities to outsource and which ones to keep in house. The major impediment to satisfying these client expectations is the low value-added levels of activities (see Figure 1) on which most offshore software firms operate. Typically, offshore vendors undertake projects in the areas of applications development, testing, and maintenance, while the high-end work, such as developing the IT strategy, building the software architecture, designing the system, integrating the project with enterprise packages, and designing custom components, are all discharged by firms in developed countries (Akella & Dossani, 2001; R. Akella & R. Dossani, personal communication, 2004).

Another issue with outsourcing suppliers is employee turnover. The rapid growth of outsourcing suppliers at popular offshore locations has created a dynamic labor market with a big demand for lead developers for new projects. As a consequence, turnover levels can be extremely high, which could have an adverse impact on product quality as later hires may not have adequate qualifications or time to make the transition to the new development environment (technology, software process, and domain expertise; Mezak, 2005).

In an environment where communication lines with clients and end users suffer by time difference, cultural issues, language barriers, business practices, and lack of advanced domain knowledge, project management skills and coordination with clients become even more critical to project success. However, management at offshore locations is often characterized by culture-bound, hierarchical administrative styles instead of the more efficient and beneficial leadership through role modeling (Akella & Dossani, 2001).

To sum up, the major causes for outsourcing failure can be attributed to the lack of advanced domain knowledge, poor communication and coordination with clients, immature management and scheduling practices, insufficient experience in higher-value-added activities (e.g., architecture design), and last but not least, inadequate quality. There is also the danger of losing touch with the local and national environments.

The problems experienced by outsourcing suppliers can be objective or subjective. For instance, it is objectively difficult to communicate effectively with a remote client. The lack of expertise in project scheduling is, on the other hand, subjective because it is not universally true. More often than not, a lot more could be done to alleviate subjective problems rather than objective ones.

Based on the above analysis, we can divide the problems experienced by outsourcing suppliers into three categories: (a) communication problems, involving the relationship and coordination with remote clients, (b) problems due to less technical know-how, such as a lack of domain expertise, experience in building software architectures, design experience, and quality thereof, and (c) management problems, involving project controlling and scheduling. In order to deliver successful software products, outsourcing supplier firms need to address the communication, technical know-how, and management issues listed above.

## THE AGILE OUTSOURCING PROJECT

In this section, we present an agile method of software development geared toward the context of outsourcing.

## Core Agile Practices

Agile methods are iterative and incremental. In an iterative process, the activities that were performed earlier in the process are revisited later. Revisiting activities provides developers in areas such as requirements engineering and software architecture with the opportunity to correct mistakes they have made. The iterative model implies more interactions among the various management and technical groups. It is a means of carrying out exploratory studies early on in a project when the team develops the requirements and discovers a suitable architecture.

Some important agile practices are the following (Beck, 1999).

- **Embracing change:** Respond to change quickly to create more value for the customer.
- **Fast cycles:** Deliver small releases frequently, implement the highest priority functions first, speed up requirements elicitation, and integrate daily.
- **Simple design:** Strive for a lean design and restructure (refactor) the design to improve communication and flexibility or to remove duplication, while at the same time preserve the design's behavior.
- **Pair programming:** To quote from Beck (1999), "if code reviews are good, we'll review code all the time." With pair programming, two programmers collaborate side by side at one machine. This quality-control practice also helps disseminate tacit **knowledge among the team members.**
- **Test-driven development:** This is a quality-control technique where a developer first writes a test, and then writes the code to pass that test.
- **Tacit knowledge:** There is a preference for project knowledge in team members' heads rather than in documents.

- **Customers on-site:** Continuous access to a customer helps to resolve ambiguities, set priorities, establish scope and boundary conditions, and provide test scenarios.
- **Colocation:** Developers and on-site customers work together in a common room to enhance tacit project knowledge and deepen members' expertise.
- **Retrospection:** This is a postiteration review of the work done and work planned. This reflective activity facilitates learning and helps improve the estimates for the rest of the project.

The enumerated practices (or disciplines) can be divided into three broad categories: (a) communication, for example, in pair programming and sharing tacit knowledge, (b) management, for example, in planning, scrums (short, daily planning sessions in which the whole team takes part), short cycles, and frequent delivery, and (c) technical, for example, in test-driven design, simple design, and refactoring. These categories correspond to the three groups of problems commonly experienced by outsourcing suppliers, as discussed previously.

The fast cycle of agile methods gives business stakeholders multiple and timely feedback opportunities, which makes agile methods explorative (aiding in architecture discovery and requirements verification) and adaptive to change. There is a broad consensus that agile methods perform well on small and mid-sized projects in dynamic environments (Pollice, 2001a, 2001b), for example, in e-commerce. What is seen as problematic with agile methods is that they lack formal project management practices, such as formal and sufficiently detailed plans, schedules, budgets, and milestones. Tiwana and Keil's (2004) study strongly suggests that formal project management practices have the power to reduce project risk substantially.

The feasibility-impact grid in Figure 2 shows how we map the core agile practices to the outsourcing suppliers' concerns discussed earlier.

*Figure 2. Impact of agile practices on outsourcing suppliers' concerns*

| Practices\Concerns | Domain expertise | Architecture | Design | Scheduling | Communication | Coordination | Quality |
|---|---|---|---|---|---|---|---|
| **Customer onsite** | √ | | | | √ | | |
| Fast cycle | | √ | √ | | √ | | √ |
| **Embracing change** | | √ | | √ | | | √ |
| Test-driven development | | √ | | | | | √ |
| Refactoring | | | √ | √ | | | |
| Simple design | | | √ | | | | √ |
| Retrospection | | √ | | | √ | √ | √ |
| Risk mitigation | | | | √ | | | |
| Tacit knowledge | | | √ | | √ | √ | |
| **Co-location** | | | √ | | √ | √ | |
| Planning game | | | | √ | | √ | |
| Scrums | | | | √ | | √ | |
| Pair-programming | | | √ | | | | √ |
| Immediate customer feedback | √ | √ | | | √ | | √ |

Agile practices incompatible with outsourcing are highlighted. A checkmark in a cell indicates that the agile discipline listed in this cell's row heading can alleviate the concern listed in this cell's column heading.

One concern, not listed in Figure 2, is employee turnover. Agility could break the impact of high turnover as several core practices, for example, preference for tacit knowledge, pair programming, and retrospection, make it possible for new team members to be brought quickly up to speed.

## Structuring the Agile Outsourcing Project

The main question we address below is how to reproduce the conditions ideal for agility in an outsourcing project.

Even a quick look at the core agile practices above would reveal that some of them are incompatible while others are not entirely consistent with the context of outsourcing, for example, having customers on-site, colocation, short life cycles, and embracing change. Above all, agile methods can be applied only to small projects.

Kruchten (2004) proposes to scale down large projects to meet the agile sweet spot. The author describes the organization of a large project as an evolving structure, starting out as one, colocated team, which over time is transformed to a team of teams (with a tree-like structure). Kruchten also suggests organizing the iterative process into four typical RUP phases as shown in Figure 3 (Kruchten, 2000). Each phase shifts the focus of the development effort onto a different activity. A phase consists of one or more iterations, where iterations can be thought of as mini waterfalls.

The structure of the agile outsourcing project is based in Kruchten's approach. However, in an agile outsourcing project, the primary goal is not to slice a big project into multiple agile subprojects (which might be required anyway), but to outsource the project to one or more agile teams, which are colocated at a remote site and share common culture and educational background.

The structure of the development process is illustrated in Figure 4. The phases of the life cycle are separated between research and development (R&D) activities and production activities, as suggested in Royce (2002). R&D is carried out

*Figure 3. Typical RUP phases of the iterative process*

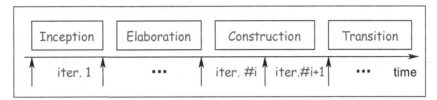

*Figure 4. Team structure of agile outsourcing*

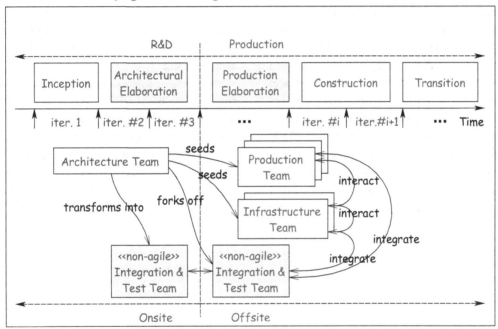

on-site, that is, close to the client, while production takes place off-site. Elaboration is split between R&D and production. The two new phases are called architectural elaboration and production elaboration.

A team comprised of requirements engineers and architects starts the development process. The team is a mix of developers from the client's organization and from the outsourcing supplier. Initially, this team focuses on the business case, vision document, and system requirements. The team works closely with the client in a typical agile setting. The team's objective, however, is not to deliver executable code (a must in agile methods), but to set up an architectural prototype, including prioritized system-level use cases.

When the team has enough clarity on key architectural choices, it can set about building and testing an architectural prototype. Toward the end of the architectural elaboration phase, when the architecture stabilizes, additional teams are created off-site. Each new team is seeded preferably with two members of the architecture team. For large projects, the early architectural prototype is used to slice the project into smaller, considerably independent agile projects. Each agile project owns part of the system architecture.

The seed developers transfer domain expertise from the client to the supplier's site. Some of them are employees and managers from the client's organization. The seed developers take on several roles. They lead the teams, serve as local architects, act as customer surrogates, communicate with the initial architecture team, and, if necessary, communicate directly with the client. This organization creates near-perfect conditions for agility in each off-site team.

Each agile off-site team works on a subsystem and develops its detailed subsystem use-case model, hence the second elaboration phase, named production elaboration in Figure 4.

For small projects, one off-site production team will suffice to develop the complete code. For large projects, however, several production teams might be necessary to do the job. In addition, one or more infrastructure teams must be set up to develop common elements such as middleware, services, and any reusable assets. The customers for the infrastructure teams are all other teams. Thus, no matter how many teams are spawned off-site, they all work in agile conditions even though predominantly with customer surrogates.

It is important to use a common software tool to reduce the risk of miscommunication, track and communicate project requirements, identify replicated modules, map test cases to requirements, and successfully integrate the outputs from the agile teams into builds.

The context diagrams in Figure 5 model the environments in which the different off-site teams operate. Note the dual nature of seed developers. On the one hand, a seed developer impersonates a customer, and on the other hand, he or she is part of the team.

The interactions of off-site teams with the real customer are supposed to be infrequent and mediated by the seed developers and the architecture team.

For large projects, somebody needs to put together the builds delivered by the production and infrastructure teams, and test the assembled system. This job is assigned to the integration and test team, or integration team for short. The testing engages the client so that the client's feedback can situate the project and steer the future effort.

*Figure 5. Context diagrams for off-site teams*

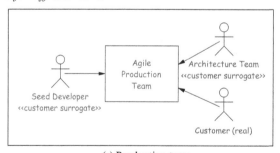

(a) Production team

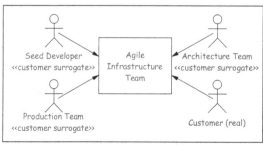

(b) Infrastructure team

The problem with the integration team is that it gets input from the off-site teams but receives feedback from the client. Normally, the input and the feedback are coming from the same place, that is, the customer. To account for this anomaly, we split the integration team into two teams: one located on-site and the other off-site (see Figure 4). Both integration teams derive directly from the initial architecture team. This guarantees that the developers in charge of integration and testing thoroughly understand the client's needs.

A problem with the proposed organization is that of fault propagation. For example, a defect committed by one of the production or infrastructure teams can propagate through the integration process before the client detects it. Owing to the late stage of its detection, isolating and removing such a defect is expensive.

We have provisioned for two floodgates preventing fault propagation: (a) the seed developers in each off-site team and (b) the test engineers in the integration team. Since they all come from the primary architecture team, it is very likely that they would be able to detect many defects, which are normally revealed with help from customers.

The only two teams operating in a nonagile environment, but still in an iterative and incremental mode, are the on-site and off-site integration teams.

The iterations (heartbeats) of both the agile and integration teams can be best illustrated with the dual-beat structure shown in Figure 6. Striking a balance between the lengths of the agile and integration iterations is the underlying objective of the management team.

The management team, comprised of all local team managers, is led by the managers of the integration teams. We do not show the management team as a separate box in Figure 4 because management is thinly distributed across all teams.

Since all off-site teams reside in the same country, and most probably in the same city, there are no cultural differences to overcome, and communications among production, infrastructure, and integration teams are not as ineffective as they are with geographically distributed teams. The management team is in a favorable position because good communication is a prerequisite for effective coordination.

*Figure 6. Nested iterations*

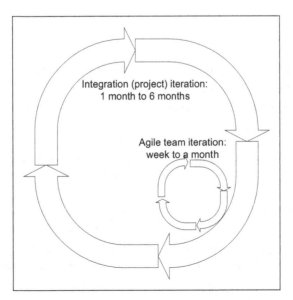

## ACTIVITIES AND WORKFLOWS

In this section, we discuss the activities in an agile outsourcing project.

### Inception Phase

During inception, the emphasis is on the user requirements. A user requirement is a specification of what the system must do. As user requirements are elicited, they are organized into use cases (Jacobson, 1987). Use-case descriptions can smoothly scale to large and small systems alike. They promote refinement and traceability from system-level usage goals down to low-level (subsystem, component, and instance) usage goals. Use cases are sufficiently flexible to be used in highly iterative and incremental development environments (Jacobson et al., 1999), as the one proposed in this work.

If a system consists of several subsystems, use-case analysis can be applied recursively to the subsystems as well. This defines clearly the requirements and responsibilities of each subsystem. Subsystem-level use cases are derived from the system-level use cases and the system architecture (the architectural decomposition of the system into subsystems).

### Architectural Elaboration

The on-site team carries out the architectural elaboration. The goals of the architecture team are to partition the system into multiple semantic domains centered on different subject matters, to define the architectural decomposition of the system into subsystems, and to map system-level use cases to subsystem use cases.

### Domain Modeling

A domain is a subject area with a shared vocabulary (Mellor, Kendall, Uhl, & Weise, 2004), for example, as in a user interface (UI) or payment transaction management. Each domain contains many classes organized around a single subject matter. Most domains require specialized expertise, for example, experience and knowledge in UI design or in payment transaction management. It makes sense to allocate the modeling of a domain to a developer with domain knowledge in that particular subject area.

Since a domain model captures precisely the conceptual entities of a single subject matter, it can be said that domain models are logical models. Logical models are in sharp contrast to subsystem models, which are pieces of the physical system. Typically, a physical subsystem is constructed from instances of several logical models. For example, a collaboration realizing a system-level use case would involve instances from a UI domain, a business logic domain, a transaction management domain, a persistent storage domain, and a security domain. Domain modeling leverages scarce domain knowledge normally limited to very few team members and shields the rest of the team from the domain implementation detail. For example, to make an object persistent, a developer needs only to mark its class or one of its attributes as persistent, and a persistent software entity is automatically generated at compile time using the knowledge locked in the persistent storage domain model. The result is a simplified development process, where only a few developers need detailed knowledge about domain technicalities.

Domains, unlike objects, are not elemental, but just like objects they are cohesive. The classes and components in a domain are tightly coupled and interdependent, and yet the domain is autonomous; that is, its classes and components are decoupled from entities lying outside the domain boundary. Once constructed, domain models have greater longevity than an application because they evolve independently of other domain models out of which the application is built; in other words, they become corporate assets and the biggest units of reuse.

In UML (unified modeling language), developers represent the containment hierarchy of a system through an aggregation of subsystems. A subsystem is defined as a subordinate system within a larger system. The subsystems define the large-scale physical architecture of the system.

## Model Organization

For small systems, the subsystem structure can be organized by use cases. The system model is divided into subsystems of related use cases. This model organization is straightforward and allows tracing requirements easily to model elements. The downside of the use-case-based model organization is that it does not scale up well and encumbers reuse. Developers are forced to reinvent similar classes in collaborations realizing different use cases.

For large systems, we propose to derive the subsystem structure from the requirements model and the domain model.

A UML package is a container for modeling elements (Jacobson et al., 1999). It is an organizational unit defining a name space for the modeling elements it contains. The top-level packages of the domain-based system model are (a) a system use-cases package, (b) domains package, (c) infrastructure package, (d) subsystems package, and (e) builds package. The system use-cases package contains system-level use cases and their actors. The domain package has one subpackage for each domain. The infrastructure domain is a special type of domain. Infrastructure domains contain services and extension points for system communication and infrastructure, and they are dependent on the selected implementation technology, for example, RMI/J2EE or CORBA. The infrastructure package contains one subpackage for each infrastructure domain. Each infrastructure subpackage is assigned to an infrastructure team. Several production teams may use the classes and components realizing the services of an infrastructure subpackage. The subsystem package contains one package for each subsystem, that is, the classes and components of a subsystem. A large subsystem package can be recursively divided into subpackages until the size of the leaf packages becomes manageable. A subsystem package normally refers to the classes of several domain packages. Finally, the builds package, containing the system test model, is divided into subpackages, one per prototype, to allow for easy management of incremental builds.

The domain-based model organization scales up well to large projects for three main reasons. First, subsystem package decomposition can be applied recursively, resulting in subsystems realizing subsystem use cases. Second, classes from different domains may be reused in different settings and deployments of the designed system, and third, domain models are assets that can be reused across projects.

There are two problems with the domain-based model organization. Developers tend to blur the distinction between domain models and subsystem models, and there is an overhead associated with maintaining two separate types of models: domain models (logical) and subsystem models (physical).

## Production Elaboration

All strategic decisions for the overall organization structure of the system have been made in the architectural elaboration phase. Production elaboration drills down inside the subsystems to specify the semantic objects whose collaborations deliver the system's structure and behavior. In production elaboration, the subsystem use cases are detailed and mapped to collaborations of components and objects using communication diagrams (Jacobson et al., 1999).

Next we show how packages are assigned to teams; for example, the architecture team is in charge of developing the system use cases and therefore owns the system use-cases package.

## CHALLENGES TO AGILE OUTSOURCING PROJECTS

Managers of agile outsourcing projects ought to be aware of the following challenges to project success.

The architecture team is the key to project success. It is of paramount importance that this team be a good mix of requirements analysts and architects. Members of the architecture team elicit requirements, build the primary system architecture, and subsequently take the roles of surrogate customers, local managers, and integration and test engineers, and communicate with customers throughout the entire life cycle.

Interteam dependencies reduce teams' abilities (especially affected is the infrastructure team) to test code and deliver builds. Production teams should provide the infrastructure team(s) with stubs early on so that the work of the infrastructure team(s) proceeds smoothly.

With multiple teams, there is always the danger of replicating functionality across teams. The proximity and common culture of the off-site teams work against the chances of duplicating functionality. The participation of the members of the architecture team, and later of the integration teams, in design reviews and software inspections helps detect replication early.

## CONCLUSION

In the late 1990s and early 2000s, agile methods took the imagination of software developers by storm. This fact clearly indicates that heavyweight methods have not been embraced wholeheartedly by developers and managers alike and are found either impractical or costly (or both) in many environments. In this chapter, we introduced a novel project structure creating agile conditions for large outsourcing software projects. We showed how to slice a large software project into multiple agile projects. We proposed to separate the development activities into R&D activities, carried out on-site and close to the client, and production activities, carried out off-site and possibly offshore. The on-site architecture team starts work on the project. In cooperation with the client, the architecture team develops the high-level use-case model of the system and completes an architectural prototype with the strategic decisions for the overall system structure. The agile off-site teams are seeded with members of the architecture team and start functioning toward the end of the architectural elaboration. The seed developers transfer domain expertise to the supplier's site and act as customer surrogates to help reproduce agile conditions off-site. Outsourcing entire sets of related production activities retains interactivity at the off-site location and reduces the project risk significantly.

*Table 1.*

| Packages | Team |
|---|---|
| System use-cases package | Architecture team |
| Domains package | Architecture team or reuse |
| Infrastructure domain packages | Infrastructure teams |
| Subsystem packages | Production teams |
| Builds package | Integration and test teams |

# REFERENCES

Agile Alliance. (2001). *Agile Alliance manifesto.* Retrieved from http://www.aanpo.org

Akella, R., & Dossani, R. (2001). *IT outsourcing and the software value chain: The Indian supplier during the downturn.* Proceedings of the IT Conference, Bangalore, India.

Beck, K. (1999). *Extreme programming explained: Embrace change.* Boston: Addison-Wesley.

Boehm, B., & Turner, T. (2004). *Balancing agility with discipline.* Boston: Addison-Wesley.

Brownsword, L., & Clements, P. (1996). *A case study in successful product line development* (Tech. Rep. No. CMU/SEI-96-TR-035). Software Engineering Institute.

CeBASE. (2004). *eWorkshop on software inspections and pair programming.* Retrieved from http://www.cebase.org

Choudhury, V., & Sabherwal, R. (2003). Portfolios of control in outsourced software development projects. *Information Systems Research, 14*(3), 291-314.

Craumer, M. (2002). How to think strategically about outsourcing. *Harvard Management Update, 7*(5).

Dossani, R., & Kenney, M. (2003). *Went for cost, stayed for quality? Moving the back office to India.* Stanford University, Asia-Pacific Research Center. Retrieved from http://APARC.stanford.edu

Evans, G. (2005). Agile RUP: Taming the Rational™ unified process. In L. Liu & B. Roussev (Eds.), *Management of object-oriented software development.* Hershey, PA: Idea Group.

Gilb, T., & Graham, G. (1993). *Software inspection.* Boston: Addison-Wesley.

Hale, K., Souza, R., Lo, T., Adachi, Y., & Babaie, E. (2005). *Forecast: IT services, worldwide,* *2005-2009.* Gartner. Retrieved June 2005 from http://www.gartner.com

Huber, N. (2005, May 3). Outsourcing "backlash" highlights need for IT leaders to sharpen management skills. *Computer Weekly,* pp. 24-27.

Jacobson, I. (1987). Object-oriented development in an industrial environment. *ACM SIGPLAN Notices, 22*(12), 183-191.

Jacobson, I., Booch, G., & Rumbaugh, J. (1999). *The unified software development process.* Boston: Addison-Wesley.

Jiang, J., Klein, G., & Discenza, R. (2002). Pre-project partnering impact on information systems projects, project team, and project manager. *European Journal of Information Systems, 11*(2), 86-97.

King, W. R. (2005). Outsourcing becomes more complex. *Information Systems Management, 22*(2), 89-90.

Kirsch, L. J., Sambamurthy, V., Ko, D., & Purvis, R. L. (2002). Controlling information systems development projects: The view from the client. *Management Science, 48*(4), 484-498.

Kruchten, P. (2000). *The rational unified process: An introduction.* Boston: Addison-Wesley.

Kruchten, P. (2004). Scaling down large projects to meet the agile "sweet spot." *The Rational Edge.* Retrieved from http://www.therationaledge.com

Laplante, P. A., & Neill, C. J. (2005). "The demise of the waterfall model is imminent" and other urban myths. *ACM Queue,* pp. 10-15.

Levina, N., & Ross, J. W. (2003). From the vendor's perspective: Exploring the value proposition in information technology outsourcing. *MIS Quarterly, 27*(3), 361-364.

Mellor, S. J., Kendall, S., Uhl, A., & Weise, D. (2004). *MDA distilled.* Boston: Addison-Wesley.

Mezak, S. (2005). *The seven deadly dangers of outsourced software development.* Retrieved April 2005 from http://www.accelerance.com

Natovich, J. (2003). Vendor related risks in IT development: A chronology of outsourced project failure. *Technology Analysis & Strategic Managements, 15*(4), 409-419.

Outsourcing Institute. (2005). Retrieved April 2005 from http://www.outsourcing.com

Paulk, M. C., Curtis, B., Chrissis, M. B., & Weber, C. V. (1993). Capability maturity model, version 1.1. *IEEE Software, 10*(4), 18-27.

Pollice, G. (2001a). RUP and XP: Part I. Finding common ground. *The Rational Edge.* Retrieved from http://www.therationaledge.com

Pollice, G. (2001b). RUP and XP: Part II. Valuing differences. *The Rational Edge.* Retrieved from http://www.therationaledge.com

Pollice, G. (2004). RUP and extreme programming: Complementing processes. In L. Liu & B. Roussev (Eds.), *Management of object-oriented software development.* Hershey, PA: Idea Group Publishing.

Roussev, B., & Akella, R. (n.d.). Agile outsourcing projects: Structure and management. *International Journal of e-Collaboration, 2*(4), 37-52.

Roussev, B., & Rousseva, Y. (2006). *Unreliable interlocutors in information systems development.* Proceedings of San Diego International Systems Conference, San Diego, CA.

Royce, W. (2002). The case for results-based software management. *The Rational Edge.* Retrieved from http://www.therationaledge.com

Russel, B., & Chattargee, S. (2003). Relationship quality: The undervalued dimension of software quality. *Communications of the ACM, 46*(8), 85-89.

Schuh, P. (2005). *Integrating agile development in the real world.* Hingham, MA: Charles River Media, Inc.

Sridhar, N., Mahapatra, R., & Mangalaraj, G. (2005). Challenges of migrating to agile methodologies. *Communications of the ACM, 48*(5).

Standish Group. (2003). *CHAOS research report.* Retrieved from http://www.standishgroup.com

Stephens, M., & Rosenberg, D. (2003). *Extreme programming refactored: The case against XP.* San Francisco: Apress.

Taylor, H. (2006). Critical risks in outsourced projects: The intractable and the unforeseen. *Communications of the ACM, 49*(11).

Technology Partners International (TPI). (2005). *Technology Partners International Inc. quarterly index.* Retrieved from http://www.tpi.net

Tiwana, A., & Keil, M. (2004). The one-minute risk assessment tool. *Communications of the ACM, 47*(11), 73-78.

Tiwana, A., & Keil, M. (2006). Functionality risk in software development. *IEEE Transactions on Engineering Management, 53*(3), 412-425.

Toth, K., Kruchten, P., & Paine, T. (1993). *Modernizing air traffic control through modern software methods.* Proceedings of the 38th Annual Air Traffic Control Association Conference, Nashville, TN.

*This work was previously published in E-Collaboration in Modern Organizations: Initiating and Managing Distributed Projects, edited by N. Kock, pp. 60-76, copyright 2008 by Information Science Reference (an imprint of IGI Global).*

# Chapter XXII
# Applying Pattern Theory in the Effective Management of Virtual Projects

**Ilze Zigurs**
*University of Nebraska at Omaha, USA*

**Deepak Khazanchi**
*University of Nebraska at Omaha, USA*

## ABSTRACT

*The management of virtual projects is fundamentally different from that of traditional projects. Furthermore, the research in this area comes from different reference disciplines and perspectives, and a unified view or theory of best practices does not yet exist. We use the theoretical frame of patterns to propose a unified view. We focus on three concepts as the underlying theoretical elements for identifying patterns of effectiveness in virtual project management: (a) coordination, (b) communication, and (c) control. As a first step in the identification of specific patterns, we conducted a series of virtual focus groups with participants from industry who had real experience with virtual projects. The brainstorming data from the focus groups were analyzed to develop an initial set of patterns. Based on this first step, we also present a structured process for the discovery and continuing validation of patterns of effectiveness in virtual projects, and discuss the issues involved in applying the process.*

## INTRODUCTION

Project management (PM) is a challenging activity in the best of circumstances, and it has become even more so in the virtual world. The increasingly popular use of virtual teams for dispersed projects has resulted in new challenges for both research and practice. We use the term *virtual projects* to refer to any project in which team members are at least partly geographically dispersed and rely on information and communication technologies to accomplish their work. The project team may be dispersed on other dimensions as well, for example, culturally or organizationally, but geographic dispersion is a minimal condition. The challenge in virtual projects is to go beyond a simple transfer of knowledge from traditional environments by developing a theoretically sound set of practices that are relevant for the virtual domain.

We use the theoretical frame of patterns to address this challenge in a novel way. Pattern theory was introduced in architecture (Alexander, 1965; Alexander, Ishikawa, Silverstein, Jacobson, Fiksdahl-King, & Angel, 1977) and was later applied to software design (Gamma, Helm, Johnson, & Vlissides, 1994) as a way of developing accepted solutions for specific problems in a defined context. We propose that patterns of effective management for virtual projects can be identified, applied, and validated. We focus on three concepts as the underlying theoretical elements for identifying such patterns, namely, communication, coordination, and control. Different types of projects can be expected to have different patterns for successful project management. The key research question for the study is the following: What patterns of communication, coordination, and control can be identified for the successful management of virtual projects? The answer to this question is important because it advances theory in a significant research domain while also providing practical advice to managers on a question of real importance.

Based on the theoretical foundation just described, we conducted an empirical study in order to identify patterns. Brainstorming comments and questionnaire data from a series of virtual focus groups provided the data for textual analysis. Themes in the text were identified and related to the theoretical model. This analysis was used to extract patterns of effective virtual project management. The next section provides the theoretical development of patterns and the definition

and background of key concepts. The method is then described, followed by the data analysis and results. The discussion section highlights the key findings and elaborates on additional issues related to validation and a process for the continuing discovery of patterns. The chapter concludes with a summary of the contributions as well as implications for research and practice.

## THEORETICAL FOUNDATION

The management of virtual projects is a complex phenomenon, and the relevant theory and concepts that govern that phenomenon come from different domains. We begin with a definition of key concepts in order to set the boundaries for the specific study that is described here. First, projects are defined and characterized in terms of a parsimonious typology. Second, virtuality is defined, and the role and nature of technology are developed. Third, key factors for managing virtual projects are presented. Fourth, the concept of patterns is defined. Each of these separate pieces is built on existing literature and presented in the context of our overarching theoretical frame.

### Typology of Projects

Projects are the lifeblood of organizational activity. A project can be defined as a "temporary endeavor undertaken to create a unique product or service" (Project Management Institute [PMI] Standards Committee, 1996, p. 4). Projects vary on many dimensions, including purpose, size, time span, urgency, scope, and complexity, and these dimensions are often overlapping. For example, are scope and complexity two independent characteristics of projects, or do they interact, or does one lead to or contribute to the other? These are not mere semantic arguments since a coherent characterization of projects is the first step to understanding and managing them.

A number of different typologies of projects exist based on dimensions such as cultural differences (Carmel & Agarwal, 2001), uncertainty vs. scope (Shenhar, 1998), type of coordination structure (Gassmann & Von Zedtwitz, 2003), and organizational characteristics (Evaristo & Munkvold, 2002). Three consistent themes can be observed in much of this literature, and we use these three themes as dimensions that characterize projects for the current study. First is complexity, which we define as the issues that have to be managed for successful completion of a project. Specifically, complexity is affected by team attributes such as size, culture, language, gender composition, personal characteristics, complementarity of resources, and the nature of project knowledge (Gassmann & Von Zedtwitz; Grant, 1996; Powell, Piccoli, & Ives, 2004; Royce, 1998). The second dimension is project scope, which we define as the boundaries of a project, including its duration and level of innovation (Gassmann & Von Zedtwitz). The third dimension is project risk, which encompasses unanticipated events that may affect successful completion. Risk may be programmatic, technical, quality related, logistical, or deployment related (Christensen & Thayer, 2001; IEEE, 2004).

If each dimension is characterized as low, medium, and high, the resulting typology of projects would have 27 different types. Our interest is in a more parsimonious examination so that we can ascertain key differences among the types that are at either end of the continuum vs. somewhere in the middle. Thus, we define three types of projects based on extreme and mixed values of each of the three dimensions. Table 1 shows the project typology for this research.

## Virtuality and Technology

The term *virtual* is generally defined in degrees or extent of virtuality rather than as a binary condition (Fiol & O'Connor, 2005). The greater the dispersion on various dimensions, the greater the virtuality of the entity, whether it is a team, a project, or an organization. Dimensions of dispersion include such factors as geography, time, function, organizational affiliation, culture, continuity of the relationship, or technology used for communication (Dubé & Paré, 2004; Espinosa, Cummings, Wilson, & Pearce, 2003; Katzy, Evaristo, & Zigurs, 2000; Watson-Manheim, Chudoba, & Crowston, 2002). Consistent with these generally accepted views, we define virtuality as the extent to which project members are dispersed on geographical and other dimensions and rely on information and communication technologies to carry out project goals.

Virtuality is not possible without information and communication technologies, and the nature and capabilities of those technologies vary widely. Media richness theory defines technology

*Table 1. Project typology*

| Project Type/ Dimension | Com-plexity | Scope | Risk | Example |
|---|---|---|---|---|
| **Lean** | Low | Narrow | Low | In-house software development project with multiple segments, within one organization though across multiple locations, having clarity of goals and resource allocation, and relatively established teams |
| **Hybrid** | Mixed levels of complexity, scope, and risk | | | Significant enhancement of customer relationship management application using systematic development approach, but with global heterogeneity in outside partnerships |
| **Extreme** | High | Wide | High | Multinational implementation of global supply chain application involving multiple units, varied cultural orientations, conflicting goals, different personalities, and varied resource infrastructures |

in terms of fixed characteristics (Daft & Lengel, 1986). Channel expansion theory suggests that perceptions and the use of a channel can evolve over time based on such characteristics as team members' knowledge of one another and the task context (Carlson & Zmud, 1999). Adaptive structuration theory views technology as being malleable through group interaction (DeSanctis & Poole, 1994).

It seems that both fixed and emergent characteristics should be accommodated in any definition of technology. In addition, the main functions of communication, process structure, and task support need to be provided (McGrath & Hollingshead, 1994; Nunamaker, Dennis, Valacich, Vogel, & George, 1991; Zigurs & Buckland, 1998). Hence, we define technology for virtual projects as consisting of an integrated and flexible set of tools for communicating among project members, structuring the process, and supporting task analysis and performance.

## Factors for the Management of Virtual Projects

Although there are many ways to classify key issues for the management of virtual projects, we propose that three major issues capture the essence of the majority of those different views, namely, communication, coordination, and control. We use these three concepts because they are intuitive and they have been consistently used in previous research and in practice (e.g., Goodbody, 2005). At the same time, we recognize the difficulty inherent in using these constructs since they are closely tied to each other. For example, it is well understood that control is a mechanism for mitigating coordination and communication challenges in virtual project teams. We are aware, as were previous researchers, that communication in all its forms is essential to achieving effective control and coordination. This apparent interaction suggests a level of confounding. However, this does not in any way take away from the fundamental

differences between these concepts and their relevance separately and together to the management of either virtual or traditional projects.

In the following paragraphs, we briefly discuss each of these concepts in turn, along with a justification for their importance and a summary of what is known from prior research. Given that our focus is on the identification of patterns, we keep the review at a summary level, sufficient to develop a broad understanding of the concepts that are relevant to this study.

We define communication as the process by which people convey meaning to one another via some medium through which they exchange messages and information in order to carry out project activities. Communication is fundamental to virtual projects, and a large body of research has accumulated from the study of virtual teams in a variety of contexts. Virtual team members can find it difficult to deal with different interaction styles and preferences (Sarker & Sahay, 2001), and they sometimes make rapid and negative attributions based on infrequent communication and perceptions of unresponsiveness (Cramton, 2001). Periodic face-to-face (FTF) meetings help to overcome communication problems by serving as reinforcement points for the confidence and trust that are required to work remotely (Maznevski & Chudoba, 2000; Shani, Sena, & Stebbins, 2000). Cultural differences can exacerbate communication problems due to differences in such things as preferences for interaction and debate (Massey, Hung, Montoya-Weiss, & Ramesh, 2001), expectations of compatibility (Rutkowski, Vogel, Bemelmans, & Van Genuchten, 2002), and frames of reference (Van Ryssen & Godar, 2000). Appropriate communication is also needed to develop and sustain trust (Jarvenpaa & Leidner, 1999; Pinsonneault & Caya, 2005) and to set and reinforce norms that support attention and commitment from team members (Cramton, 2001; Watson-Manheim & Belanger, 2002). Overall, the existing research reinforces the importance of communication and the explicit attention that must be paid to communication issues throughout the life of the virtual team (Martins, Gilson, & Maynard, 2004; Schubert, Leimstoll, & Romano, 2003). This is even more important in the context of research that has found the amount of communication declines as teams move higher on the virtualness continuum (Martins et al.).

Coordination is the second major issue for the management of virtual projects. We define coordination as the mechanisms through which people and technological resources are combined to carry out specified activities in order to accomplish stated goals (Crowston, 1991; Grant, 1996). Coordination is a wide-ranging concept that requires action related to the task, team member roles, member relations, time, norms or values, language and culture, and even media (Zigurs, Evaristo, & Katzy, 2001). Zalesny, Salas, and Prince (1995) suggest that there are four components of coordination: identifying goals (i.e., the objectives of joint activities), mapping goals to activities (what specific activities are needed), mapping activities to actors (who does what), and managing interdependencies (sequencing and synchronizing activities). Contextual and organizational factors such as training, trust, and team cohesion can affect coordination (Chinowsky & Rojas, 2003). Dependencies within teams need to be managed (Malone & Crowston, 1994), and appropriate structures must be put into place (Gassmann & Von Zedtwitz, 2003). Cultural differences can also negatively impact virtual team coordination (Maznevski & Chudoba, 2000). Finally, reward systems can affect coordination (Burke, Aytes, & Chidambaram, 2001). Achieving and sustaining coordination occurs over time rather than as a single event (Turvey, 1990); as such, it requires the expertise and experience of team members (Zalesny et al.). In sum, coordination presents significant challenges to virtual teams, not the least of which is that it occurs through communication and thus includes interaction effects.

The third and final issue is control. We define control as the process of monitoring and measuring

project activities so as to anticipate and manage variances from project plans and organizational goals (Hendersen & Lee, 1992; Kirsch, 1996; Project Management Institute, 2004). In this definition, monitoring may require the development of a variety of mechanisms for assessing behavioral actions and project outcomes so as to take corrective actions as needed. For example, in the virtual project context, the challenge of control could relate to establishing standards for assessing team member performance, communication of progress, establishment of norms for team member interaction, structuring of teams, or use of collaborative technology. It should also be noted that our definition of control does not preclude the use of a portfolio of control modes as suggested by Kirsch. Finally, the challenges associated with controlling projects are closely tied with coordination and communication issues. For example, temporal distance exacerbates coordination and control problems directly or indirectly through its negative effects on communication (Carmel & Agarwal, 2001). Thus, some organizations move toward reducing collaboration complexity by giving up control and transferring ownership to foreign entities, or by taking the full project ownership to the domestic entity (Carmel & Agarwal). Other challenges that impact control in virtual projects include reinforcing project objectives (Chinowsky & Rojas, 2003), monitoring and measuring issues, the collaborative infrastructure (Evaristo & Munkvold, 2002), the client's knowledge of the systems development process (Kirsch et al., 2002), and group leadership (Homsky, 2003).

This necessarily brief review highlights the many factors that can have an impact in virtual project environments, showing the complexity involved in seeking generalizations. Our approach in dealing with this complexity was to start with the typology and identify the three key dimensions for management. We recognize that our choice of communication, coordination, and control as the key dimensions of our typology could be argued or made differently. However, the prevalence of these three dimensions in the literature of project management, including PMI (2004), supports their importance.

We argue that the managerial practices of communication, coordination, and control combine with virtuality effects to imply different types of technology needs. We also expect differences across the three project types. Table 2 shows the implications for technology needs for each project type in terms of managerial concerns and

virtuality effects. The next step is to use pattern theory to look for significant practices that could make a difference.

## Pattern Theory

Pattern theory is a key starting point for our research and a natural perspective for understanding, at a somewhat abstract level, effective practices for virtual project management. Patterns help to make sense of complex behavior by looking for

*Table 2. Project types and implications for technology needs*

| Project Type | Dominant Mana-gerial Concern | Virtuality Effects | Technology Needs |
|---|---|---|---|
| Extreme<br><br>(High complexity, broad scope, high risk, e.g., mission-critical virtual project) | Commun-ication | Relatively difficult to build shared context while virtual project team is dispersed and physical contact is rare<br><br>Differences in culture, team experience, language, gender, personalities, resources, infrastructure, and historical knowledge exacerbate the difficulties of communication. | High communication:<br><br>Rich context communication tools, lateral communication channels, e.g., videoconferencing, Web-based information-management portal |
| Hybrid<br><br>(Varying levels of complexity, scope, and risk, e.g., Y2K [Year 2000] bug) | Coordi-nation | Units/partners that do not share mutual project knowledge might underperform due to miscommunicated needs.<br><br>Differences in culture, team experience, language, gender, personalities, resources, infrastructure, and historical knowledge are moderated by the existence of rapport among some project members. | High process structure:<br><br>Virtual collaboration systems and knowledge management tools, lateral and vertical communication channels |
| Lean<br><br>(Low complexity, narrow scope, low risk, e.g., maintenance virtual project) | Control | Virtual project team already has an established shared context; however, absence of physical interactions might hinder successful project completion<br><br>Heterogeneity on various dimensions (culture, team experience, language, gender, personalities, resources, infrastructure, and knowledge management) is not a critical factor because it is managed by prior experience within and across team members and through sharing of historical repository of project experiences | High information processing:<br><br>Project management/workflow tools, CASE tools, software configuration management tools, vertical communication channels |

the regularities in such behavior. Pattern theory arose in architecture and the work of Alexander (1965) and Alexander et al. (1977), who developed patterns for common architectural design problems, for example, the "bathing room" or "bed cluster." To quote Alexander (1965),

When we build something good, when we build a system that works well, we must ask what is it about this that makes it good? Why is it good? What are its essential qualities that will allow us to build something completely different but which is good in the same way.

Patterns are analogous to recurring themes, familiar processes, rules of thumb, or standard procedures. Patterns provide holistic "abstractions of experiences" that are profound in some way and can be implemented to solve problems in a specific context. To some extent, patterns are a means of communicating insights about a problem domain to others. Patterns do not have to be distinct from each other; in fact, if they are linked in some way, then that allows us to develop a pattern language.

Formally, a pattern is defined as a three-part rule that expresses a relationship among a specific context, a problem, and a solution (Alexander et al., 1977). Alexander's work was carried over into software engineering and popularized in object-oriented design by the "Gang of Four" (Gamma et al., 1994). There are many ways to document specific patterns, but common practice is to include the key elements of the context, problem, and solution. An example of a pattern from object-oriented development is shown below (adapted from Gamma et al.) in the same format that we later use to describe our derived virtual project patterns.

## Singleton

- **Context:** There are certain actions that need to be coordinated by a single object across the entire application, for example, the print spooler and file manager.

- **Problem:** How do you provide a single instance of a class that is easily accessible?
- **Solution:** Ensure that only one instance of a class is created, and provide a global point of access to it. (Note that at this point, the actual code for implementing the Singleton pattern could also be provided.)

Some work has been done on patterns in the context of collaborative work. Schuemmer (2003) proposed a structure for sociotechnical patterns that could be used to support collaboration. Fernandez, Holmer, Rubart, and Schuemmer (2002) specified patterns for designing groupware tools with the goal of developing a common vocabulary. Völter (2002) presented patterns specifically for project management, naming them "anti-patterns" because they represented the antithesis of common knowledge for basic project management techniques. To our knowledge, no one has applied pattern theory in a systematic way to the management of virtual projects.

Essentially, we are arguing that the major components of the framework—project type, technology, and virtuality—all affect the managerial dimensions of communication, coordination, and control, which in turn affect project outcomes. Considerable existing research addresses these major components, but it is not our intent to reargue that research here. Instead, we view pattern theory as providing a new way to bring these components together. Thus, and as stated earlier, our research question asks what patterns of communication, coordination, and control can be identified for the successful management of virtual projects.

## RESEARCH METHOD

We devised a study that represents a first step in examining our research question. We used a grounded theory approach because such an approach is particularly useful to explore complex and dynamic phenomena in organizational settings (Glaser & Strauss, 1971). Participants in the study were businesspeople who had experience with being members of a virtual team. They interacted asynchronously in a series of virtual focus groups, brainstorming ideas on the factors that contributed to the success or failure of virtual projects. A presession questionnaire and the brainstorming ideas from the focus groups served as the data from which we inductively derived our patterns.[1]

Twenty-nine individuals from five different firms committed to participate in the virtual focus groups, with 14 people completing all phases of the study. Each focus group was an asynchronous brainstorming session conducted via Web-based groupware, with a separate session conducted for each company. All five firms were global companies: Two were software and service providers, one was a technology manufacturer, one a services company, and one a research and engineering firm. Each participant was asked to respond about a project in which he or she had participated within the last 12 months, thus each participant was responding about a different project. The project descriptions ranged from Web site development to systems integration, to the development of customer support applications.

The virtual focus groups were conducted using WebIQ™ (http://www.webiq.net), a Web-based meeting support application that includes capabilities for building an agenda, conducting electronic brainstorming, and administering questionnaires. Each participant was given an individual log-in and password. After logging in, participants filled out a questionnaire that asked about a specific virtual project in which they had participated within the last year. Responses to brainstorming questions were instructed to be about that same project. Participants then had a 72-hour window in which to brainstorm ideas about the following two questions.

1. What specific management and team member practices contributed to the effectiveness of your project?
2. What specific management and team member practices contributed to the ineffectiveness of your project?

The instructions asked participants to think broadly to include individual behaviors, processes, technologies, and tools as they applied to both of the questions.

The questionnaire data provided the basis for classifying each project with respect to the typology. The following characteristics of the project were derived.

- Project complexity (average of eight questions related to complexity)
- Project scope (average of three questions related to scope)
- Project risk (average of six questions related to risk)

Project type was calculated as the mean of project complexity, scope, and risk. There was a natural break point between the top four projects (highest complexity, scope, and risk) and the bottom three projects (lowest complexity, scope, and risk). The four projects with the highest scores were identified as extreme projects; those with the lowest scores were identified as lean projects, and the remaining ones were identified as hybrid projects. The overall mean for extreme projects ranged from 3.94 to 4.08, while the overall mean for lean projects ranged from 2.00 to 2.68 (on a five-point scale). Hybrid project means ranged from 3.21 to 3.75, thus each break point between the three different project types was half a point between lean and hybrid and nearly a quarter of a point between hybrid and extreme. A total of 14 unique projects were reported: a different project by each participant who completed all the phases of the study. Two examples from each type of project show the diversity: (a) Lean projects may include the development of a Web site, or installing and testing a new version of an application, (b) hybrid projects include customer support and the enhancement of an application, and (c) extreme projects include large dual-shore development projects, or adding a new product line.

Project success and virtuality were also calculated from questionnaire items. Based on prior research, overall virtuality was assessed by asking participants to rate the number of organizations or firms represented by project team members and their temporal dispersion. Similarly, project success was measured by assessing the extent to which participants perceived that the project was completed on schedule and within budget, met goals and specifications, and was on the whole successful. These variables were used to evaluate the impact of virtuality and success across the proposed virtual project typology.

We developed a coding scheme to analyze the brainstorming text (see Table 3). Each complete idea from the two brainstorming questions was coded for references to communication, coordination, or control. Each idea could have more than one reference to a theme, as well as a reference to multiple themes. Each complete idea was also coded for any reference to a technology, and a plus or minus sign was used to show whether the technology was being referred to as having a positive or negative impact. The authors worked together initially to identify the codes, resolving disagreements through discussion. Remaining data were coded independently and then reviewed,

and discrepancies were resolved through discussion, with few disagreements.

## ANALYSIS AND RESULTS

This section provides descriptive information from the questionnaire data, followed by the key patterns that relate to coordination, control, and communication as derived from the virtual focus group data.

### Use of Technology

In the presession survey, participants were asked to rate the extent to which they used specific technologies to work with team members on the project. Our data confirm that e-mail is still the most-often-used technology for communication among virtual team members regardless of whether the project type is lean, hybrid, or extreme (see Table 4). The next most-used technology was various forms of the telephone, including conference calling and voice mail. The frequency rankings of e-mail and telephone use were true across all project types. Next in importance were face-to-face meetings, including an especially interesting result. The data show that team members make the most use of face-to-face communication in extreme and hybrid projects and very minimal use in lean projects. This is probably because lean projects are clear and have little complexity and scope, and could potentially be dealt with collaboratively via e-mail alone.

*Table 3. Coding scheme with examples*

| Text of Brainstorming Idea | Theme | Subcategory (if applicable) | Technology (if applicable) | +/- |
|---|---|---|---|---|
| Utilized the phone for discussion and error diagnosis/resolution | Communication | Meaning | Telephone | + |
| Good error logging capabilities of tools | Coordination | | Distributed PM tools | + |
| Daily checkpoint meetings amongst the developers and the architecture folks were crucial and added a lot value | Control | | | |

*Table 4. Use of technologies during virtual projects*

| Technology | Mean for Lean Projects | Mean for Hybrid Projects | Mean for Extreme Projects | Overall Mean | Overall Std. Dev. |
|---|---|---|---|---|---|
| E-mail | 4.65 | 5.00 | 5.00 | 4.93 | 0.27 |
| Telephone | 3.00 | 4.71 | 4.50 | 4.29 | 0.91 |
| Conference calling | 2.67 | 4.57 | 4.50 | 4.14 | 0.95 |
| Voice mail | 2.33 | 4.00 | 4.00 | 3.64 | 0.84 |
| Face-to-face meetings | 1.33 | 3.14 | 3.25 | 2.79 | 1.12 |
| Tools for group work, distributed PM tools, EMS, IM, shared whiteboard, and others | Ratings ranged from 1.00 to 2.00 | | | | |

Interestingly, there is also a clear break in the frequency with which participants used the more traditional e-mail and voice tools vs. the tools for group work that have been developed more recently. Such tools as simultaneous document editing and shared whiteboard were rarely used. It is also worth noting that distributed project management and electronic meeting systems were used very little across all project types. The means of usage are highest in hybrid projects for both of these tools, but even so, the means are still low. These two tools in particular support structure for group processes, but they require a greater learning curve and continuing reinforcement.

## Patterns for Effective Management of Virtual Projects

We argued that three theoretical elements should help to define patterns of project management, namely, communication, coordination, and control. Furthermore, technology was expected to constrain and enable how each element would be handled and the balance or pattern among elements. Thus, a potential design pattern for virtual project management would include descriptions of processes, best practices, factors, tools, and/or techniques that impinge upon coordination, communication, and control.

In this section, we detail some of the patterns that were identified for lean, hybrid, and extreme projects. Each pattern is based on the brainstorming data from the virtual focus groups. That is, for each type of project (lean, hybrid, extreme), we examined all the comments that were coded for each dimension of management practice (communication, coordination, control) and developed a pattern based on that set of comments. Multiple patterns could be generated from one set of comments.

Each pattern is described in terms of (a) the pattern's name, a descriptive word or phrase that captures its essence, (b) the context, a description of the situation to which the pattern applies, (c) the problem, a question that captures the essence of the problem that the pattern addresses, and (d) the solution, a prescription for dealing with the problem. The patterns presented here are a subset of all the patterns discovered during this study, showing examples of the key concerns in each type of project. The goal here is to provide the most critical patterns for a virtual context: those that could potentially be used as a check or safeguard against ineffective project management practices. Appropriate attention and management of communication, control, and coordination via the application of these patterns may offer help in improving or assuring the effectiveness of virtual project management practices. Table 5 shows the names of all patterns identified in our study; a subset is illustrated in the subsequent sections.[2]

*Table 5. Patterns by project type*

| Lean | Hybrid | Extreme |
|---|---|---|
| • ChangeControlCoordination | • ConflictResolution | • CoordinateHumanResource |
| • CommTime | • HumanExpertise | • ManageCommitment |
| • FlexWorkTime | • MeetingDesign | • ManageKnowledge |
| • Gatekeeping | • ProjectLeadership | • ManageTeamTraining |
| • ManagerialProjectControl | • RelationshipCoordination | • ManageVirtuality |
| • SharedResources | • RoleCoordination | • SharedUnderstanding |
| • TaskCoordination | • SharedResources | • Standardize |
| • TeamProjectControl | | |
| • VersionControl | | |
| Common across all project types: CommunicationCheck, FaceTimeCheck, and ScopeCreepCheck | | |

## Common Patterns

Communication is not only critical for all types of projects, but it impacts effective coordination and control as well. The importance of communication is reflected in the two example patterns presented below, both of which are common to all three types of projects. The patterns relate to communication among team members either generally via various media and/or by using face-to-face meetings. Participants working in lean projects were particularly concerned about communication. Since lean projects are neither complex nor large in scope, the study's participants handled them mostly via a virtual mode and predominantly used e-mail and regularly scheduled telephone conferencing for communicating with stakeholders. However, it was evident from participant comments that these patterns were also applicable to hybrid and extreme projects.

### CommunicationCheck

- **Context:** Team members do not have a shared understanding of project issues and solutions.

- **Problem:** How do you ensure effective communication among team members?
- **Solution:** Schedule periodic conferences using technologies that emphasize communication, for example, telephone and telephone conferencing, e-mail, and video-conferencing.

### FaceTimeCheck

- **Context:** Team members neither agree nor have a shared understanding of project issues, solutions, work processes, and documentation requirements.
- **Problem:** How do you ensure effective communication and build trust among team members?
- **Solution:** Schedule periodic face-to-face conferences by flying some team members, possibly by rotation, to different locations. Though costly, even occasional participation in FTF meetings over the lifetime of a project is very effective. FTF meetings can engender increased trust and engagement among team members and also help clarify various facets of the project and resolve issues and conflicts.

## Patterns in Lean Projects

Patterns identified in lean projects related to resource sharing, work schedule flexibility, and task, managerial, and team control issues. Issues included the sharing of information across virtual stakeholders, management of rework, change control and coordination, and management of scope creep. Participants in our study were particularly concerned about the negative impact of rework requests that cropped up without warning, primarily due to the absence of good communication and established coordination among stakeholders, project managers, and virtual team members. We provide examples of two patterns for lean projects that relate to control and coordination issues that are often encountered in projects of this type: ManagerialProjectControl and TaskCoordination.

### ManagerialProjectControl

- **Context:** The progress of the project is impeded due to inadequate information sharing between the project team members and the manager responsible for interacting with the client.
- **Problem:** How do you monitor project changes based on interactions with your client?
- **Solution:** Schedule periodic (weekly or daily, as needed) project review meetings for all or some team members with the project manager or manager interacting with your client(s). These meetings are used both to update the manager regarding the project status and to cull new information obtained from the project client(s) that may have a direct impact on project tasks.

### TaskCoordination

- **Context:** There is a complete disconnect between team members as new members are added.

- **Problem:** How do you ensure task coordination as new members are added to a team?
- **Solution:** Coordinate task assignment to new team members by clearly communicating revised roles and responsibilities along with timelines and tasks to all the team members. Ensure that everyone understands the assignment of new members in the team and convey this to all stakeholders and team members.

## Patterns in Hybrid Projects

Patterns in hybrid projects are related to such issues as meeting design, shared resources and infrastructure capabilities, team member role and relationship coordination, human expertise, conflict resolution, and project leadership. The following two patterns provide examples of critical issues in hybrid projects. The MeetingDesign pattern addresses the creation of an effective meeting environment for a variety of stakeholders in different situations. The RoleCoordination pattern addresses the issue of ensuring clarity in role responsibilities, another area where virtual projects are likely to suffer given the distributed nature of at least some project team members.

### Meeting Design

- **Context:** During meetings conducted via conference calls, your team gets bogged down in details that do not necessarily apply to many team members. This becomes increasingly complicated with a large number of project stakeholders.
- **Problem:** How do you develop a meeting environment that stimulates effective communication among all team members?
- **Solution:** Schedule periodic conferences using a variety of technologies that emphasize communication (e.g., telephone and telephone conferencing, e-mail, and videoconferencing). Design meetings

based on the following guidelines: (a) Use the participation of all stakeholders when the goal is to inform and develop a shared understanding of broad project goals and issues, (b) use selective participation of relevant stakeholders to deal with specific issues and challenges, and (c) keep meeting agendas short. Remember that people have short attention spans, particularly when you cannot see them. Anything more than an hour is probably better suited to a focused small meeting; consider having more meetings rather than long ones. Also consider which format would work best at meetings for the issues at hand.

## RoleCoordination

- **Context:** Your team members are unclear about their roles and responsibilities in the project. This is causing misunderstandings about project goals and resulting in a delayed project.
- **Problem:** How do you provide team members with a clear understanding of their individual roles and responsibilities in the project?
- **Solution:** Cleary define team members' roles and responsibilities and work processes at the outset. If new members are added, clearly communicate revised roles and responsibilities to all team members. Ensure that they all understand their assignments and provide them with the tools to deliver. Communicate roles, responsibilities, and work processes to all stakeholders and team members. If feasible, consider rotating members through different roles. Use technologies with a high process structure (such as virtual collaboration systems and knowledge management tools) to share information on the team's work processes and the roles and responsibilities of team members. Include team members in designing work processes and

delineating roles and responsibilities. This will increase team ownership.

## Patterns in Extreme Projects

Extreme projects are likely to need all of the patterns that were identified for hybrid projects. In addition, we identified patterns for extreme projects that related to the coordination between remote and local sites, management of virtuality, management commitment, standardization of processes and documentation, knowledge management, building a shared understanding of project requirements and processes, and appropriate and consistent training of all team members. We present two patterns for extreme projects that were particularly interesting and need specific attention from managers.

First, the ManageVirtuality pattern is particularly significant for extreme projects, which by definition involve a combination of high complexity, scope, risk, and varying levels of virtuality. Overcoming geographic and time-zone differences is not just critical for global teams, but can also matter within a single country. For example, one of the participants from the United States said that project notifications from the Pacific time zone would reach the central time zone later in the day, leaving less time for addressing issues and/or requiring team members to work outside of normal hours.

## ManageVirtuality

- **Context:** Your team is having difficulty with time-zone differences at both the national and global levels. This problem occurs especially during crunch time or crisis situations when communication is not prompt. As a result, the problem resolution process is delayed.
- **Problem:** How do you overcome time-zone and geographic differences and effectively engage all team members?

- **Solution:** Overcome or eliminate distance barriers due to time-zone and geography by providing activities that require intensive interaction and coordination (e.g., project initiation) through temporarily collocating team members. Require periodic site visits and travel by team members to different sites. Designate team member liaisons as focal points of coordination who spend some time in the home office location to become acculturated and informed about technical issues; liaisons can then transfer knowledge to local sites for day-to-day coordination. Assign team members in one geographic region (e.g., North and South America) to tasks requiring telephone or video-based interactions because they share time zones and thus can more easily schedule conferences.

The second example for extreme projects, the ManageKnowledge pattern, focuses attention on the importance of knowledge management and information sharing among stakeholders and the organization as a whole. One participant pointed to the effectiveness of a knowledge portal in the project as follows: "[W]e have a homegrown tool—knowledge portal which has features for collaboration, e-learning and knowledge management which was found really useful. It was a challenge to implement it but once the team started using it everyone saw the power and usefulness of the same."

## ManageKnowledge

- **Context:** Team members are unable to share intelligence and best practices, or to simultaneously edit master documents. In some instances, team members are not following established processes.
- **Problem:** How do you mobilize and share knowledge across the team and your organization?

- **Solution:** Start with input from project team members across the organization and build a repository of best practices, templates, learning tools, workflow standards, and examples of processes within standard methodologies. Make sure all members of the team have access to and can contribute to the knowledge portal.

## DISCUSSION

One issue that was reinforced throughout the projects in this study is the importance of communication. Regardless of the type of project, communication was mentioned time and time again as a fundamental necessity. Both prior research and our study reinforce the idea that communication is important in and of itself as well as through its relationship to coordination and control. All of these teams relied heavily on e-mail and voice media, which emphasize communication. Thus, the communication dimension of technology had the greatest priority, more so than process structure or information processing.

Our study also reinforced the importance of periodic face-to-face communication for virtual teams, a finding that is consistent with prior research (Maznevski & Chudoba, 2000). Participants emphasized the advantages of regular face-to-face meetings for some or all team members to help resolve issues and monitor progress. Periodic collocation of team members can help to establish ground rules and common understanding, which in turn facilitates communication and coordination when team members return to their distant home locations. This practice allows team members to build a social network, as well as stimulate the development of team identity, cohesion, and commitment that help to sustain members during dispersed periods (Davidson & Tay, 2003). Another interesting result related to technology was the relatively low use of distributed project management tools. Indeed, there was generally low use for all of the technologies that we would categorize as providing support for process structure or information processing. Clearly, there is much room for improvement in providing better tools and training for virtual teams in these areas.

In order to develop appropriate training, apply the right tools and use patterns effectively; one thing that managers must first be able to do is to assess the nature of the project and its context. This study provides an initial set of such assessment tools. We have described specific measures to identify the nature of a virtual project in terms of complexity, scope, risk, and virtuality. In addition, a technology inventory can be taken to identify the extent and type of technology support available. Managers can be provided with a simple project dashboard type of tool that elicits information on each of the aspects of the project and displays calculations on the measures (Khazanchi & Zigurs, 2007). The assessment can help to build a common vocabulary for the project team that will help to identify the key issues around which patterns will be identified.

The discovery and validation of patterns should be an ongoing process that is part of a continual learning approach for project managers and members. We recommend a five-step process: (a) Recognize and abstract an attribute or feature of virtual project management that affects the key issues of communication, coordination, or control, (b) define the recurring problem or system of conflicting forces that the feature solves, (c) define the context in which the feature is appropriate, (d) name and describe the pattern, and (e) continue to validate and refine the pattern. This five-step approach is described in more detail elsewhere (Khazanchi & Zigurs, 2007), but we have provided an example of one round of that process in this study. The brainstorming tools that were used in this project are a good example of tools that can support the important first step of this process.

## CONCLUSION

This study makes several contributions. First, we developed a project typology based on theoretically founded characteristics of projects. Second, we applied pattern theory to the practice of virtual project management in terms of coordination, control, and communication. Third, we collected data that identified a starting set of patterns for the effective management of lean, hybrid, and extreme virtual projects. Fourth, we developed a structured approach that is usable by other researchers.

The contributions to theory come from the development of concepts, the typology, and the pattern approach. We have elaborated the concepts of virtuality, communication, control, and coordination as they relate to virtual project management and developed a new typology and descriptions of extreme, lean, and hybrid projects. In addition, if at its core, pattern theory is the basis for developing a solution to a problem in a certain context; our study has identified an initial set of patterns in virtual project management across various types of projects. Indeed, there is still much to learn from the original concept of patterns. For example, in his speeches and other writings, Alexander (1996) has argued that patterns should also have a "moral component" and "create coherence, morphological coherence in the things which are made with it," and "be generative, [that is], allow people to create coherence, morally sound objects, and encourage and enable this process." We have not dealt with these aspects directly in our study, but they have the potential to contribute to a higher level of understanding. Also, patterns might be viewed as providing a bridge between virtual and traditional contexts. Earlier, we argued that virtuality is a continuum. Viewed that way, patterns can expand one's capability to operate effectively along the entire continuum, that is, to connect to what we already know from traditional practices and bridge the gap to virtual environments.

The contributions to research methodology arise from the measures and coding scheme. We have developed and implemented measures for the various concepts that drive the typology of virtual projects. We have also developed a coding scheme to analyze brainstorming text from virtual focus group sessions. In fact, we believe that our study is a relatively unique example of conducting research using asynchronous virtual focus groups with globally dispersed participants. This required the development of a complete set of protocols for managing, organizing, and conducting the data collection elements of the research.

Contributions to practice are in the patterns themselves. The patterns identified in the study can be utilized as critical checks and/or design principles for use in managing virtual projects. Managers of virtual projects can follow either a deductive or inductive process. A deductive approach would start with identifying the type of project (using the measures developed), then searching the patterns for that project type and applying the prescribed solution for each relevant problem. An inductive approach would start with a search of the pattern library, looking for any patterns that apply. If the problems fall primarily into one project type, then a manager can reasonably infer that this is the type of the project.

As with any study of this kind, several limitations apply. Firms and participants were selected from a convenience sample based on contacts developed by the authors. We recognize the limitations inherent in such a sample, but given that the study is only a first step and that the firms represented a good cross section of global industries, we believe that the data provide a good starting point. The patterns were derived from a limited data set. Even though we had participants from five different companies and a sufficient diversity of project types for our categorization, the generalizability of our conclusions is limited. In addition, even though the coding scheme was based on theory, there may be other relevant dimensions besides the ones we identified and used

in the development of patterns. The next steps for research follow naturally from the limitations of the study. Additional settings need to be examined and the concepts tested with additional data.

Some of our patterns are clearly related to each other in some way; this came about from the natural process of applying the grounded theory approach to our data. Inducing from the data that was provided during discussion in our virtual focus groups, we found that some patterns turn out to have similarities and apparent relationships. In fact, this is as it should be within the realm of pattern theory since it allows us to develop a pattern language as more patterns are discovered and a coherent structure of patterns in virtual project management evolves. Our study resulted in the identification of patterns for managing virtual projects; we do not lay claim to the uniqueness of all of these patterns. In fact, we are quite sure that many elements of these patterns already exist in some form in traditional PM or in other fields of endeavor. Further exploration of these patterns may result in the coalescing of some and/or expansion or redefinition of others.

We started with the goal of going beyond a cookbook approach to the management of virtual projects. The theoretical frame of patterns helps us make a large step toward that goal. One of the most intriguing aspects of the pattern approach is the idea that specific patterns themselves should fit together into a coherent pattern language that provides a higher level of understanding. A specific pattern is not a prescription, although a pattern could be used to create a prescription in a specific context. Patterns are generic and more akin to the idea of universal laws than to prescriptions. Consistent with Alexander's ideas, patterns should help to create new processes and help organizations to continue to change and adapt. Patterns as a set represent an abstraction of something important: They provide a language for communication and action, and they embody a value set. It is these aspects of patterns that can provide that higher level of understanding.

The results from this study provide immediate and practical guidance for managers of virtual projects, as well as providing a strong foundation for the necessary next steps in research. Those steps entail studying how people use patterns in a systematic way, how people adapt them, and how pattern use reveals what really matters across a variety of contexts. The pattern perspective provides an essential cross-level view—a view of specific practices for success as embodied in individual patterns, as well as the systemic view that comes from their combination in a pattern language.

## ACKNOWLEDGMENT

The research was partially supported by a grant from the Project Management Institute.

## REFERENCES

Alexander, C. (1965). *Notes on the synthesis of form.* Cambridge, MA: Harvard University Press.

Alexander, C. (1996, October). The origins of pattern theory, the future of the theory, and the generation of a living world. *ACM Conference on Object-Oriented Programs, Systems, Languages and Applications (OOPSLA).* Retrieved from http://www.patternlanguage.com/archive/ieee/ieeetext.htm

Alexander, C., Ishikawa, S., Silverstein, M., Jacobson, M., Fiksdahl-King, I., & Angel, S. (1977). *A pattern language: Towns, buildings, construction.* Oxford University Press.

Burke, K., Aytes, K., & Chidambaram, L. (2001). Media effects on the development of cohesion and process satisfaction in computer-supported workgroups: An analysis of results from two longitudinal studies. *Information Technology & People, 14*(2), 122-141.

Carlson, J. R., & Zmud, R. W. (1999). Channel expansion theory and the experiential nature of media richness perceptions. *Academy of Management Journal, 42*(2), 153-170.

Carmel, E., & Agarwal, R. (2001). Tactical approaches for alleviating distance in global software development. *IEEE Software*, 22-29.

Chinowsky, P. S., & Rojas, E. M. (2003). Virtual teams: Guide to successful implementation. *Journal of Management in Engineering, 19*(3), 98-106.

Christensen, M. J., & Thayer, R. H. (2001). *The project manager's guide to software engineering's best practices.* Los Alamitos, CA: IEEE Computer Society.

Cramton, C. D. (2001). The mutual knowledge problem and its consequences for dispersed collaboration. *Organization Science, 12*(3), 346-371.

Crowston, K. (1991). A coordination theory approach to organizational process design. *Organization Science, 8*(2), 157-175.

Daft, R. L., & Lengel, R. H. (1986). Organizational information requirements, media richness and structural design. *Management Science, 32*(5), 554-571.

Davidson, E. J., & Tay, A. S. M. (2003). Studying teamwork in global IT support. *Proceedings of the 36th Hawaii International Conference on Systems Sciences.*

DeSanctis, G., & Poole, M. S. (1994). Capturing the complexity in advanced technology use: Adaptive structuration theory. *Organization Science, 5*(2), 121-147.

Dubé, L., & Paré, G. (2004). The multi-faceted nature of virtual teams. In D. J. Pauleen (Ed.), *Virtual teams: Projects, protocols, and processes* (pp. 1-39). Hershey, PA: Idea Group Publishing.

Espinosa, J. A., Cummings, J. N., Wilson, J. M., & Pearce, B. M. (2003). Team boundary issues across multiple global firms. *Journal of Management Information Systems, 19*(4), 157-190.

Evaristo, R., & Munkvold, B. E. (2002). Collaborative infrastructure formation in virtual projects. *Journal of Global Information Technology Management, 5*(2), 29-47.

Fernandez, A., Holmer, T., Rubart, J., & Schuemmer, T. (2002). Three groupware patterns from the activity awareness family. *EuroPLoP 2002: Seventh European Conference on Pattern Languages of Programs.*

Fiol, C. M., & O'Connor, E. J. (2005). Identification in face-to-face, hybrid, and pure virtual teams: Untangling the contradictions. *Organization Science, 16*(1), 19-32.

Gamma, E., Helm, R., Johnson, R., & Vlissides, J. (1994). *Design patterns: Elements of reusable object-oriented software.* Boston: Addison-Wesley.

Gassmann, O., & Von Zedtwitz, M. (2003). Trends and determinants of managing virtual R and D teams. *R & D Management, 33*(3), 243-262.

Glaser, B. G., & Strauss, A. L. (1971). *The discovery of grounded theory: Strategies for qualitative research.* Chicago: Aldine Publishing Company. (Original work published 1967)

Goodbody, J. (2005). Critical success factors for global virtual teams. *Strategic Communication Management, 9*(2), 18-21.

Grant, R. M. (1996). Toward a knowledge-based theory of the firm. *Strategic Management Journal, 17*, 109-122.

Henderson, J. C., & Lee, S. (1992). Managing IS design teams: A control theories perspective. *Management Science, 38*(6), 757-777.

Homsky, O. (2003). More patterns for group leadership. *EuroPLoP 2003: Seventh European Conference on Pattern Languages of Programs.*

IEEE. (2004). *IEEE Standard 1540-2004. IEEE standard for software life cycle processes: Risk management.* IEEE Press.

Jarvenpaa, S., & Leidner, D. (1999). Communication and trust in global virtual teams. *Organization Science, 10*(6), 791-815.

Katzy, B., Evaristo, R., & Zigurs, I. (2000). Knowledge management in virtual projects: A research agenda. *Proceedings of the 36th Hawaii International Conference on Systems Sciences.*

Khazanchi, D., & Zigurs, I. (2005). *Patterns of effective management of virtual projects: An exploratory study.* Newtown Square, PA: Project Management Institute.

Khazanchi, D., & Zigurs, I. (2007). An assessment framework for discovering and using patterns in virtual project management. *Proceedings of the 36th Hawaii International Conference on Systems Sciences.*

Kirsch, L. J. (1996). The management of complex tasks in organizations: Controlling the systems development process. *Organization Science, 7*(1), 1-21.

Malone, T., & Crowston, K. (1994). The interdisciplinary study of coordination. *ACM Computing Surveys, 26*(1), 87-119.

Martins, L. L., Gilson, L. L., & Maynard, M. T. (2004). Virtual teams: What do we know and where do we go from here? *Journal of Management, 30*(6), 805-835.

Massey, A. P., Hung, Y. C., Montoya-Weiss, M., & Ramesh, V. (2001). When culture and style aren't about clothes: Perceptions of task-technology "fit" in global virtual teams. *Proceedings of the 2001 International ACM SIGGROUP Conference on Supporting Group Work*, 207-213.

Maznevski, M. L., & Chudoba, K. M. (2000). Bridging space over time: Global virtual team dynamics and effectiveness. *Organization Science, 11*(5), 473-492.

McGrath, J. E., & Hollingshead, A. B. (1994). *Groups interacting with technology: Ideas, evidence, issues, and an agenda.* Thousand Oaks, CA: Sage Publications.

Nunamaker, J. F., Dennis, A. R., Valacich, J. S., Vogel, D. R., & George, J. F. (1991). Electronic meeting systems to support group work. *Communications of the ACM, 34*(7), 40-61.

Pinsonneault, A., & Caya, O. (2005). Virtual teams: What we know, what we don't know. *International Journal of e-Collaboration, 1*(3), 1-16.

Powell, A., Piccoli, G., & Ives, B. (2004). Virtual teams: A review of current literature and directions for future research. *The Data Base for Advances in Information Systems, 35*(1), 6-36.

Project Management Institute (PMI). (2004). *A guide to the project management body of knowledge* (3rd ed.). Newtown Square, PA.

Project Management Institute (PMI) Standards Committee. (1996). *A guide to the project management body of knowledge.* Newtown Square, PA: Project Management Institute.

Royce, W. (1998). *Software project management: A unified framework.* Reading, MA: Addison-Wesley, Inc.

Rutkowski, A.-F., Vogel, D., Bemelmans, T. M. A., & Van Genuchten, M. (2002). Group support systems and virtual collaboration: The HKNet Project. *Group Decision and Negotiation, 11*(2), 101-125.

Sarker, S., & Sahay, S. (2001). Information systems development by US-Norwegian virtual teams: Implications of time and space. *Proceedings of the 36th Hawaii International Conference on Systems Sciences.*

Schubert, P., Leimstoll, U., & Romano, N. C. (2003). Internet groupware systems for project management: Experiences from a longitudinal study. *Proceedings of the 16th Bled eCommerce Conference: eTransformation*, 611-631.

Schuemmer, T. (2003). Evolving a groupware pattern language. *ECSCW2003: Fifth International Workshop on Collaborative Editing.*

Shani, A. B., Sena, J. A., & Stebbins, M. W. (2000). Knowledge work teams and groupware technology: Learning from Seagate's experience. *Journal of Knowledge Management, 4*(2), 111-124.

Shenhar, A. J. (1998). From theory to practice: Toward a typology of project management styles. *IEEE Transactions on Engineering Management, 45*(1), 33-48.

Turvey, M. T. (1990). Coordination. *American Psychologist, 45*(8), 938-953.

Van Ryssen, S., & Godar, S. H. (2000). Going international without going international. *Journal of International Management, 6*, 49-60.

Völter, M. (2002). Hope, belief and wizardry: Three different perspectives on project management. *EuroPLoP 2002: Seventh European Conference on Pattern Languages of Programs.*

Watson-Manheim, M. B., & Belanger, F. (2002). Exploring communication-based work processes in virtual work environments. In *Proceedings of the 36th Hawaii International Conference on Systems Sciences.*

Watson-Manheim, M. B., Chudoba, K. M., & Crowston, K. (2002). Discontinuities and continuities: A new way to understand virtual work. *Information Technology & People, 15*(3), 191-209.

Zalesny, M. D., Salas, E., & Prince, C. (1995). Conceptual and measurement issues in coordination: Implications for team behavior and performance. *Research in Personnel and Human Resources Management, 13*, 81-115.

Zigurs, I., & Buckland, B. (1998). A theory of task/technology fit and group support systems effectiveness. *MIS Quarterly, 22*(3), 313-334.

Zigurs, I., Evaristo, R., & Katzy, B. (2001). *Collaborative technologies for virtual project management.* Washington, DC: Academy of Management.

## ENDNOTES

[1]  See Khazanchi and Zigurs (2005) for a complete copy of the questionnaire.

[2]  For complete details on the full set of patterns, see Khazanchi and Zigurs (2005).

*This work was previously published in E-Collaboration in Modern Organizations: Initiating and Managing Distributed Projects, edited by N. Kock, pp. 93-112, copyright 2008 by Information Science Reference (an imprint of IGI Global).*

# Compilation of References

Abrams, D., & Hogg, M. A. (1987). Language Attitudes, Frames of Reference, and Social Identity: A Scottish Dimension. *Journal of Language and Social Psychology, 6*(3-4), 201-213.

Abuhamdieh, A. H., Kendall, J. E., & Kendall, K. E. (2000). Beyond e-commerce: Evaluating the strategic impact of Web presence for nonprofit organizations. In M. Swink (Ed.), *Proceedings of the Decision Sciences Institute* (pp. 567-569). Atlanta: Decision Sciences Institute.

Abuhamdieh, A. H., Kendall, J. E., & Kendall, K. E. (2002). An evaluation of the Web presence of a nonprofit organization: Using the balanced scorecard approach in ecommerce. In R. Traunmuller (Ed.), *Information systems: The e-business challenge* (pp. 209-222). Boston: Kluwer Publishing.

Abuhamdieh, A. H., Kendall, J. E., & Kendall, K. E. (2007). E-commerce opportunities in the nonprofit sector: The case of New York Theatre Group. *International Journal of Cases on Electronic Commerce, 3*(1), 29-48.

Adams, G. L., & Lamont, B. T. (2003). Knowledge management systems and developing sustainable competitive advantage. *Journal of Knowledge Management, 7*(2), 142-154.

Adams-Price, C. E., & Chandler, S. (2000). The star fleet ladies auxiliary: Evolution of an online women's mailing list. *CyberPsychology and Behavior, 3*(5), 811-816.

Agile Alliance. (2001). *Agile Alliance manifesto.* Retrieved from http://www.aanpo.org

Ahuja, M. K., & Thatcher, J. B. (2005). Moving Beyond Intentions and Toward the Theory of Trying: Effects of Work Environment and Gender on Postadoption Information Technology Use. *MIS Quarterly, 29*(3), 427-459.

Ahuja, M. K., Galleta, D. F., & Carley, K. M. (2003). Individual centrality and performance in virtual R&D groups: An empirical study. *Management Science, 49*, 21-38.

Ajzen, I., & Fishbein, M. (1980). *Understanding attitudes and predicting social behavior.* Englewood Cliffs: NJ: Prentice-Hall.

Akella, R., & Dossani, R. (2001). *IT outsourcing and the software value chain: The Indian supplier during the downturn.* Proceedings of the IT Conference, Bangalore, India.

Alavi, M. (1994). Computer-mediated collaborative learning: An empirical evaluation. *MIS Quarterly, 18*(2), 159-174.

Alavi, M., & Leidner, D. E. (2001). Knowledge management and knowledge management systems: Conceptual foundations and research issues. *MIS Quarterly, 25*(1), 107-136.

Alem, L., & Kravis, S. (2004). Design and evaluation of an online learning community: a case study at CSIRO. *SIGGROUP Bulletin, 25*(1), 20-24.

Alexander, C. (1965). *Notes on the synthesis of form.* Cambridge, MA: Harvard University Press.

Alexander, C. (1996, October). The origins of pattern theory, the future of the theory, and the generation of a living world. *ACM Conference on Object-Oriented Programs, Systems, Languages and Applications (OOPSLA).* Retrieved from http://www.patternlanguage.com/archive/ieee/ieeetext.htm

Alexander, C., Ishikawa, S., Silverstein, M., Jacobson, M., Fiksdahl-King, I., & Angel, S. (1977). *A pattern language: Towns, buildings, construction.* Oxford University Press.

Allport, F.H. (1924). *Social psychology.* Boston: Houghton Mifflin.

Alonso-Rasgado, T., Thompson, G., Elfström, B. (2004). The design of functional (total care) products, *Journal of Engineering Design, 15*(6), 515-540.

Alter, S. (2003). 18 reasons why IT-reliant work-systems should replace the "IT-artifact" as the core subject matter of the IS field. *Communications of the Association for Information Systems, 12*, 366-395.

Anckar, B. (2002). Adoption drivers and intents in the mobile electronic marketplace: Survey findings. *Journal of Systems and Information Technology, 6*(2), 1-17.

Anckar, B., & D'Incau, D. (2002). Value creation in mobile commerce: Findings from a Consumer Survey. *The Journal of Information Technology Theory and Application (JITTA), 4*(1), 43-64.

Anderson, E. W., & Fornell, C. (2000). Foundations of the American Customer Satisfaction Index. *Total Quality Management & Business Excellence, 11*(7), 869-882.

Anderson, K. J., & Leaper, C. (1998). Meta-analyses of Gender Effects on Conversational Interruption: Who, What, When, Where, and How. *Sex Roles, 39*(3/4), 225-252.

Anderson, L.R., & Ager, J.W. (1978). Analysis of variance in small group research. *Personality and Social Psychology Bulletin, 4*, 341-345.

Andersson, R., & Olsson, A.-K. (1999). Fields of Education and Training. Manual. from http://europa. eu.int/comm/eurostat/ramon/nomenclatures/index. cfm?TargetUrl=LST_NOM

Andreu, R., & Ciborra, C. (1996). Organizational learning and core capabilities development: The role of IT. *Journal of Strategic Information Systems, 5*(2), 111-127.

Andrews, D., Nonnecke, B., & Preece, J. (2003). Electronic Survey Methodology: A Case Study in Reaching Hard-to-Involve Internet Users. *International Journal of Human-Computer Interaction, 16*(2), 185.

Antonakis, J., & Atwater, L. (2002). Leader distance: A review and a proposed theory. *Leadership Quarterly, 13*(6), 673-704.

Antonakis, J., & House, R. J. (2002). The full-range leadership theory: The way forward. In B. J. Avolio & F. J. Yammarino (Eds.). *Transformational and charismatic leadership: The road ahead* (Vol. 2, p. 3-33). Oxford, UK: Elsevier.

APQC. (2000). *Building and Sustaining Communities of Practice-Final Report*. Houston, TX: American Productivity and Quality Center.

Ardichvili, A., Page, V., & Wentling, T. (2003). Motivation and barriers to participation in virtual knowledge-sharing communities of practice. *Journal of Knowledge Management, 7*(1), 64-77.

Argyris, C. (1992). *On organizational learning.* Cambridge, MA: Blackwell.

Argyris, C., & Schon, D. A. (1978). *Organizational learning: A theory of action perspective.* Reading, MA: Addison-Wesley Publishing Company.

Argyris, C., (1999). *On Organizational Learning* (2nd Ed.). Mallden, MA: Blackwell.

Arrback, A., & Bjelkemyr, M. (2003). *System to Manage Guidelines for Design for Manufacture.* Technical report. Jönköping, Sweden: Department of Mechanical Engineering, School of Engineering, Jönköping University,

Arthur, W. B. (1994). Competing technologies, increasing returns, and lock-in by historical small events. In W. B. Arthur (Ed.), *Increasing returns and path dependence in the economy* (pp. 13-32). Ann Arbor, MI: The University of Michigan Press.

Arzberger, P., Schroeder, P., Beaulieu, A., Bowker, G., Casey, K., Laaksonen, L., et al. (2004). An international framework to promote access to data (policy forum). *Science, 303*, 1777-1778.

Ashkenas, R., Ulrich, D., Jick, T., & Kerr, S. (1995). *The boundaryless organization.* San Francisco, CA: Jossey-Bass.

Atwater, L. E., (1988). The relative importance of situational and individual variables in predicting leader behavior: The surprising impact of subordinate trust. *Group and Organization Studies, 12*(3), 290-310.

Atwater, L.E., & Yammarino, F.J. (1993). Personal attributes as predictors of superiors and subordinates perceptions of military academy leadership. *Human Relations, 46*(5), 645-668.

Au, J. A., & Kauffman, R. J. (2005). Rational expectations, optimal control and information technology adoption. *Information Systems and E-Business Management, 3*(1), 347-370.

Aubrey, B., & Kelsey, B. (2003). Further understanding of trust and performance in virtual teams. *Small Group Research, 34*(5), 575-619.

Avolio, B. (1999). *Full Leadership Development: Building the Vital Forces in Organizations.* Thousand Oaks, CA: Sage Publications, Inc.

Avolio, B. J., & Kahai, S. S. (2003). Adding the "e" to e-leadership: How it may impact your leadership. *Organizational Dynamics, 31*(4), 325-338.

Avolio, B., Kahai, S., & Dodge, G. E. (2001). E-Leadership: Implications for theory, research, and practice. *Leadership Quarterly, 11*(4), 615-668.

Axtell, C.M., Fleck, S.J., & Turner, N. (2004). Virtual teams: Collaborating across distance. In C.L. Cooper & I.T. Robertson (Eds.), *International review of industrial and organizational psychology* (Vol. 19) (pp. 205-248). Chichester: Wiley.

Babakus, E., Bienstock, C. C., & Scotter, J. R. V. (2004). Linking perceived quality and customer satisfaction to store traffic and revenue growth. *Decision Sciences, 35*(4), 713-737.

Bafoutsou, G., & Mentzas, G. (2002). Review and functional classification of collaborative systems. *International Journal of Information Management, 22*(4), 281–305.

Bagozzi, R. P. (1980). *Causal models in marketing.* New York: John Wiley & Sons.

Baker, W. E., & Faulkner, R. R. (2004). Social networks and loss of capital. *Social Networks, 26*, 91-111.

Balasubramanian, S., Peterson, R. A., & Jarvenpaa, S. L. (2002). Exploring the Implications of M-Commerce for Markets and Marketing. *Journal of the academy of Marketing Science, 30*(4), 348-36

Balthazard, P., Waldman, D. A., Howell, J., & Atwater, L. E. (August, 2002). *Modeling performance in teams: The effects of media type, shared leadership, interaction style, and cohesion.* Paper presented at the meeting of the Academy of Management, Denver, Colorado.

Bansal, H. S., Irving, P. G., & Taylor, S. F. (2004). A three-component model of customer commitment to service providers. *Journal of the Academy of Marketing Science, 32*(3), 234-250.

Baptista, R. (2000). Do innovations diffuse faster within geographical clusters? *International Journal of Industrial Organization, 18*(3), 515.

Barnes, S. & Huff, S. (2003). Rising Sun: iMode and the Wireless Internet. *Communications of the ACM, 46*(11), pp. 79-84.

Barnes, S., & Scornavacca, E. (2004). Mobile marketing: the role of permission and acceptance. *International Journal of Mobile Communications, 2*(2) 128-139.

Barney, J. (1991). Firm resources and sustained competitive advantage. *Journal of Management, 17*(1), 99-120.

Baron, R. M., & Kenny, D. A. (1986). The moderator-mediator variable distinction in social psychological research: Conceptual, strategic and statistical considerations. *Journal of Personality and Social Psychology, 51*, 1173-1182.

Bartlett, F. (1932). *Remembering: A study in experimental and social psychology.* Cambridge, MA: Cambridge University Press.

Bartlett, F. (1958). *Thinking: An experimental and social study.* New York: Basic Books.

Bass, B. M. (1990). *Bass & Stogdill's Handbook of Leadership: Theory, Research, and Managerial Applications.* New York, NY: Free Press.

Bass, B. M., & Avolio, B. A. (1990). *The multifactor leadership questionnaire.* Palo Alto, CA: Consulting Psychologists Press.

Bass, B. M., & Avolio, B. J. (1993). Transformational leadership: A response to critiques. In *Leadership Theory and Research: Perspectives and Directions* (pp. 49-80). New York: Academic Press.

Bauer, H.H., Barnes, S.J., Reichardt, T., & Neumann M.M. (2005). Driving consumer acceptance of mobile marketing: A theoretical framework and empirical study. *Journal of Electronic Commerce Research, 6*(3) 181-192.

Beasley, A. L. (2005). The Style Split. *Journal of Accountancy, 200*(3), 91-92.

Beck, K. (1999). *Extreme programming explained: Embrace change.* Boston: Addison-Wesley.

Bell, B.S., & Kozlowski, S.W.J. (2002). A typology of virtual teams: implications for effective leadership. *Group and Organization Management, 27*(1), 14-49.

Bell, P., & Linn, M. C. (2000). Scientific arguments as learning artifacts: Designing for learning from the Web with KIE. *International Journal of Science Education, 22*(8), 797-817.

Bentler, P.M. (1989). *EQS structural equations program manual.* Los Angeles: BMDP Statistical Software.

Bento, R., & Schuster, C. (2003). Participation: the online challenge. In A. K. Aggarwal (Ed.), *Web-based education: learning from experience table of contents* (pp. 156-164). Hershey, PA, USA IGI Publishing.

Beranek, P., (2000). The impacts of relational and trust development training on virtual teams: An exploratory investigation. Paper presented at the 33ʳᵈ *Hawaii International Conference on System Sciences.* Honolulu, HI.

Berg, B. L., (1989). *Qualitative Research Methods for the Social Sciences.* Needham Heights, MA: Allyn and Bacon.

Bess, K. D., Fisher, A. T., Sonn, C. C., & Bishop, B. J. (2002). Psychological sense of community: Theory, research, and application. In A. T. Fisher, C. C. Sonn, & B. J. Bishop (Eds.), *Psychological sense of community: Research, applications and implications.* New York: Kluwer Academic/Plenun Publishers.

Bilalis, Z., & Herbert, D. (2003). IT standardization from a European point of view. *Journal of IT Standards and Standardization Research, 1*(1), 46-49.

Bixby, A., Downs, B., and Self, M. (2006). A scheduling and capable-to-promise application for Swift & Company. *Interfaces, 36*(1), 69 – 86.

Bjurklo, M., & Kardemark, G. (1998). Social tests in a model for controlling the enhancement of competence. *Journal of Human Resource Costing and Accounting, 3*(2), 51-64.

Blake, R. R., & Mouton, J. S. (1994). *The managerial grid* (4th ed.). New York: Gulf Publishing.

Blanchard, A., & Markus, M. L. (2003). The experienced "sense" of a virtual community: Characteristics and processes. *The Data Base for Advances in Information Systems.*

Blattberg, R. C., & Deighton, J. (1991). Interactive marketing: Exploiting the age of Addressability. *Sloan Management Review, Fall*, 5-14.

Blomqvist, E., Levashova, T., Öhgren, A., Sandkuhl, K., & Smirnov, A. (2005). *Formation of Enterprise Networks for Collaborative Engineering*. Paper presented at the Post-conference proceedings of 3. Intl. Workshop on Collaborative Engineering, Sopron, Hungary.

Boart, P. (2005). *Life Cycle Simulation Support for Functional Products*, Licentiate Thesis, Luleå University of Technology, lISSN 1402-1757 / ISRN LTU-LIC--05/20--SE / NR 2005:20.

Boaz, N. T., & Almquist, A. J. (1997). *Biological anthropology: A synthetic approach to human evolution.* Upper Saddle River, NJ: Prentice Hall.

Boehm, B., & Turner, T. (2004). *Balancing agility with discipline*. Boston: Addison-Wesley.

Bolton, R. N. (1998). A dynamic model of the duration of the customer's relationship with a continuous service provider: The role of satisfaction. *Marketing Science, 17*(1), 45-65.

Boneva, B., Kraut, R., & Frohlich, D. (2001). Using e-Mail for Personal Relationships: The Difference Gender Makes. *American Behavioral Scientist, 45*(3), 530-549.

Boon, M. v. d. (2003). Women in International Management: An International Perspective on Women's Ways of Leadership. *Women in Management Review, 18*(3/4), 132-146.

Borgatti, S. P. (1997). Structural holes: Unpacking Burt's redundancy measures. *Connections, 20*, 35-38.

Borgatti, S. P., Everett, M. G., & Freeman, L. (2002). *Ucinet 6 for Windows*. Harvard: Analytic Technologies.

Bostrom, R. P., Anson, R., & Clawson, V. K. (1993). Group facilitation and group support systems. In L. M. Jessup & J. S. Valacich (Eds.), *Group Support Systems: New Perspectives* (pp. 146-168.). New York, NY: McMillan Publishing Company.

Bourhis, A., Dubé, L., & Jacob, R. (2005). The Success of Virtual Communities of Practice: The Leadership Factor. *Electronic Journal of Knowledge Management Volume, 3*(1), 23-34.

Brecher, C. (2002). Effiziente entwicklung von werkzeugmaschinen: Mit virtuellen prototypen direkt zum marktfähigen produkt. In W. Eversheim, K. Klocke, T. Pfeifer, & M. Weck (Eds.), *Wettbewerbsfaktor produktionstechnik: Aachener perspektiven* (pp. 157-190). Aachen, Germany: Shaker.

Bresnahan, J. (1998). Supply chain anatomy: The incredible journey. *CIO Enterprise Magazine*, August 15. [Retrieved from http://www.cio.com site on March 12, 2006.]

Brizendine, L. (2006). *The Female Brain*. USA: Morgan Road Books.

Brodbeck, F.C., Frese, M., Akerblom, S. et al. (2000). Cultural variation of leadership prototypes across 22 European countries. *Journal of Occupational and Organizational Psychology, 73*(1), 1-29.

Brownsword, L., & Clements, P. (1996). *A case study in successful product line development* (Tech. Rep. No. CMU/SEI-96-TR-035). Software Engineering Institute.

Bryman, A., (1993). Charismatic leadership in business organizations: Some neglected issues. *Leadership Quarterly, 4*, 289-304.

Buenger, V., Daft, R.L., Conlon, E.J., & Austin, J. (1996). Competing values in organizations: Contextual influences and structural consequences. *Organization Science, 7*(5), 557-576.

Bui, T., Bodart, F., & Ma, P. C. (1998). ARBAS: A formal language to support argumentation in network-base organizations. *Journal of Management Information Systems, 14*(3), 223-237.

Burge, J. (1999). *Design Rationale*, Draft Technical Report, Worchester Polytechnic Institute.

Burgoon, J. K., Buller, D. B., & Woodall, W. G. (1996). *Nonverbal communication: The unspoken dialogue* (2nd ed.). New York: McGraw-Hill.

Burke, G. J., and Vakharia, A.J. (2002). Supply chain management. In H. Bidgoli (Ed.), *Internet Encyclopedia*, New York: John Wiley.

Burke, K., Aytes, K., & Chidambaram, L. (2001). Media effects on the development of cohesion and process satisfaction in computer-supported workgroups: An analysis of results from two longitudinal studies. *Information Technology & People, 14*(2), 122-141.

Burroughs, S. M., & Eby, L. T. (1998). Psychological sense of community at work: A measurement system and explanatory framework. *Journal of Community Psychology, 26*, 509-532.

Burt, R. (1992). *Structural holes: The social structure of competition*. London: Harvard University Press.

Burt, R. (1997). The contingent value of social capital. *Administrative Science Quarterly, 42*, 339-65.

Burt, R., Hogarth, R. M., & Michaud, C. (2000). The social capital of French and American managers. *Organization Science, 11*, 123-47.

Burt, R., Janotta, J. E., & Mahoney, J. (1998). Personality correlates of structural holes. *Social Networks, 20*, 63-87.

Bylund, N., Isaksson, O., Kalhori, V., Larsson, T (2004). Enhanced Engineering Design Practice using Knowledge Enabled Engineering with Simulation Methods. *Proceedings of Design 2004*.

Campbell, B. C. (1992). *Humankind emerging*. New York: HarperCollins.

Carlson, J. R., & Zmud, R. W. (1999). Channel expansion theory and the experiential nature of media richness perceptions. *Academy of Management Journal, 42*(2), 153-170.

Carmel, E., & Agarwal, R. (2001). Tactical approaches for alleviating distance in global software development. *IEEE Software*, 22-29.

Carroll, A., Barnes, S.J., & Scornavacca, E. (2005). Consumers perceptions and attitudes towards SMS mobile marketing in New Zealand. *In Proceedings of the Fourth International Conference on Mobile Business (ICMB), Sydney, Au*stralia, July 11-13, pp. 434-440.

Carroll, J. M., & Rosson, M. B. (1996). Developing the Blacksburg electronic village. *Communications of the ACM, 39*(12), 69-74.

Carter, L., Haythorn, W., Shriver, B., & Lanzetta, J. (1951). The behavior of leaders and other group members. *Journal of Abnormal and Social Psychology, 46*, 589-595.

Cascio, W. F., & Shurygailo, S. (2003). E-leadership and virtual teams. *Organizational Dynamics, 31*(4), 362-376.

Cascio, W. F., & Shurygailo, S. (2003). E-leadership and virtual teams. *Organizational Dynamics, 31*, 362-76.

Castelfranchi, C. (1995). Guarantees for autonomy in cognitive agent architecture. In Wooldrige, M. and Jennings, N. R. (Eds.), *Intelligent Agents: Theories, Architectures, and Languages*, 890, 56-70. Heidelberg, Germany: Springer-Verlag.

Castells, M. (1996). *The Rise of the Network Society, The Information Age: Economy, Society and Culture, Vol. I*. Cambridge, MA; Oxford, UK: Blackwell.

CeBASE. (2004). *eWorkshop on software inspections and pair programming*. Retrieved from http://www.cebase.org

Chan, C. C. A., Monroe, G., Ng, J., & Tan, R. (2006). Conflict Management Styles of Male and Female Junior Accountants. *International Journal of Management, 23*(2), 289-295.

Chavis, D. M., & Pretty, G. H. (1999). Sense of community: Advances in measurement and application. *Journal of Community Psychology, 27*(6), 635-642.

Chen, L. (2005). *Optimal information acquisition, inventory control, and forecast sharing in operations management*. Dissertation thesis. Stanford, CA: Stanford University.

Cheng, F., Ryan, J.K., and Simchi-Levy, D. (2000). Quantifying the 'bullwhip effect' in a supply chain: the impact of forecasting, lead times, and information. *Management Science, 46*(3), 436 – 444.

Chi, L., & Holsapple, C. W. (2005). Understanding computer-mediated interorganizational collaboration: A model and framework. *Journal of Knowledge Management, 9*(1), 53-75.

Chidambaram, L., (1996). Relational development in computer-supported groups. *MIS Quarterly, 20*(2), 143-163.

Chin, W. W. (2001). *PLS-Graph user's guide, version 3.0.* Soft Modeling Inc.

Chinowsky, P. S., & Rojas, E. M. (2003). Virtual teams: Guide to successful implementation. *Journal of Management in Engineering, 19*(3), 98-106.

Chipuer, H. M., & Pretty, G. H. (1999). A review of the Sense of Community Index: Current uses, factor structure, reliability and further development. *Journal of Community Psychology, 27*, 643-658.

Choudhury, V., & Sabherwal, R. (2003). Portfolios of control in outsourced software development projects. *Information Systems Research, 14*(3), 291-314.

Chowdhary, N., Prakash, M. (2005). Service Quality: revisiting the Two Factors Theory, *Journal of Services Research, 5*(1).

Christensen, C.M. (1998). *The innovator's dilemma: When new technologies cause great firms to fail.* Cambridge, MA: Harvard Business School Press.

Christensen, M. J., & Thayer, R. H. (2001). *The project manager's guide to software engineering's best practices.* Los Alamitos, CA: IEEE Computer Society.

Clancy, J. J. (1989). *The invisible powers: The language of business.* Lexington, MA: Lexington Books.

Clark III, I. (2001). Emerging value propositions for m-commerce. *Journal of Business Strategies, 18*(2), 133-148.

Clark, S. C. (2002). Employees' sense of community, sense of control, and work/family conflict in Native American organizations. *Journal of Vocational Behavior, 61*, 92-108.

Claus, L., (2004). Too much of a good thing? Negative effects of high trust and individual autonomy in self-managing teams. *Academy of Management Journal, 47*(3), 385-400.

Clawson, V. K., & Bostrom, R. P. (1996). Research-driven facilitation training for computer-supported environments. *Group Decision and Negotiation, 5*(1), 7-29.

Clear, T. & Daniels, M., (2001). "*A Cyber-Icebreaker for an Effective Virtual Group?,*" 6th Annual Conference On Innovation and Technology In Computer Science Education (ITiCSE), June 25-27, Canterbury.

Cluts, M. M. (2003). *The evolution of artifacts in cooperative work: constructing meaning through activity.* Paper presented at the International ACM SIGGROUP Conference on Supporting Group Work 2003.

Coates, J. (1986). *Women, Men and Languages: Studies in Language and Linguistics.* London, UK: Longman.

Cohen, J. (1988). *Statistical power analysis for the behavioral sciences* (2nd edition). Hillsdale, NJ: Erlbaum.

Cohen, J., & Cohen, P. (1983). *Applied multiple regression/correlation analysis for the behavioral sciences* (2nd ed.). Hillsdale, NJ: Erlbaum.

Cohen, W. M., & Levinthal, D. A. (1990). Absorptive capacity: A new perspective on learning and innovation. *Administrative Science Quarterly, 35*(1), 128-152.

Conger, J.A., & Kanungo, R.N. (1988). The empowerment process: integrating theory and practice. *Academy of Management Review, 13*(3), 471-82.

Connaughton, S. L., & Daly, J. A. (2004). Identification with leader: A comparison of perceptions of identification among geographically dispersed and co-located teams. *Corporate Communications, 9*(2), 89-103.

Constant, D., Sproull, L., & Keisler, S. (1997). The Kindness of Strangers: On the Usefulness of Electronic Weak Ties for Technical Advice. In S. Kiesler (Ed.), *Culture of the Internet* (pp. 303-322). Mahwah, NJ: Lawrence Erlbaum Associates.

Cooper, R. G. (2002). *Top oder flop in der produktentwicklung. Erfolgsstrategien: Von der idee zum launch.* Weinheim, Germany: Wiley-VCH.

Coppola, N., Hiltz, S., & Rotter, N., (2004). Building trust in virtual teams. *IEEE Transactions on Professional Communication, 47*(2), 65-105.

Cosley, D., Frankowski, D., Kiesler, S., Terveen, L., & Riedl, J. (2005, April 2–7, 2005, ). *How oversight improves member-maintained communities.* Paper presented at the SIGCHI 2005 Conference on Human factors in Computing Systems, Portland, Oregon, USA.

Cossete, P., & Audet, M. (1992). Mapping of an idiosyncratic schema. *Journal of Management Studies, 29*(3), 325-348.

Costa, P. T. J., Terracciano, A., & McCrae, R. R. (2001). Gender Differences in Personality Traits across Cultures: Robust and Surprising Findings. *Journal of Personality and Social Psychology, 81*(2), 322-331.

Cramton, C. D. (2001). The mutual knowledge problem and its consequences for dispersed collaboration. *Organization Science, 12*(3), 346-371.

Craumer, M. (2002). How to think strategically about outsourcing. *Harvard Management Update, 7*(5).

Cross, Gary J. (2000). How e-business is transforming supply chain management. *Journal of Business Strategy*, 21(2), 36-39.

Cross, N. (2000). Engineering design methods – Strategies for Product Design, New York, John Wiley & Sons.

Cross, R., & Prusak, L. (2002). The people who make organizations go - or stop. *Harvard Business Review*, *June*, 5-12.

Cross, R., Parker, A., Prusak, L., & Borgatti, S. P. (2001). Knowing what we know, supporting knowledge creation and sharing in social networks. *Organizational Dynamics*, *30*, 100-20.

Crowston, K. (1991). A coordination theory approach to organizational process design. *Organization Science*, *8*(2), 157-175.

Cummings, J. N., & Cross, R. (2003). Structural properties of work groups and their consequences for performance. *Social Networks*, *25*, 197-210.

Cutmore, T. R. H., Hine, T. J., Maberly, K. J., Langford, N. M., & Hawgood, G. (2000). Cognitive and Gender Factors Influencing Navigation in a Virtual Environment. *International Journal of Human-Computer Studies, 53*, 223-249.

Daft, R. L., & Lengel, R. H. (1986). Organizational information requirements, media richness and structural design. *Management Science, 32*(5), 554-571.

Daft, R. L., Lengel, R. H., & Trevino, L. K. (1987). Message equivocality, media selection, and manager performance: Implications for information systems. *MIS Quarterly, 11*(3), 355-366.

Daghfous, N., Petrof, J. V., & Pons, F. (1999). Values and adoption of innovations: A cross cultural study. *Journal of Consumer Marketing, 16*(14), 314-331.

Danesh, A., Kock, N. (2005). An experimental study of process representation approaches and their impact on perceived modeling quality and redesign success, *Business Process Management Journal, 11*(6), 724-735.

Darwin, C. (1966). *On the origin of species*. Cambridge, MA: Harvard University Press. (Original work published 1859)

Davenport, T.H. (1993). *Process innovation*. Boston, MA: Harvard Business Press.

Davenport, T.H., and Harris, J.G., (2005). Automated decision making comes of age. *MIT Sloan Management Review*, 46(4), 83-89.

David, P., & McDaniel, R., (2004). A field study on the effect of interpersonal trust on virtual collaborative relationship performance. *MIS Quarterly, 28*(2), 183-227.

Davidow, W.H., & Malone, M.S. (1992). *The virtual corporation*. New York: Harper Collins.

Davidson, E. J., & Tay, A. S. M. (2003). Studying teamwork in global IT support. *Proceedings of the 36th Hawaii International Conference on Systems Sciences*.

Davidson, W.H. (1993). Beyond re-engineering: the three phases of business transformation, *IBM Systems Journal, 32*(1), 65-79.

Davies, F. (1989). Perceived Usefulness, Perceived Easy of use and user acceptance of Information Technology. *MIS Quarterly, 13*(3), 319-340.

Davis, D. D., Mihalescz, M., Bryant, J. L., Tedrow, L., Liu, Y., & Say, R. (2003, April). *Leadership in global virtual teams*. Paper presented at the meeting of the Society for Industrial and Organizational Psychology, Orlando, Florida.

Davis, F. D., Bagozzi, R. P., & Warshaw, P. R. (1989). User Acceptance of Computer technology: A comparison of two theoretical Models. *Management Science, 35*(8), 982-1003.

Davis, F.D., and Venkatesh, V. (1996). A critical assessment of potential measurement biases in the technology acceptance model: three experiments. *International Journal of Human-Computer Studies, 45*(1), 19-45.

Davis, F.D., Bagozzi, R.P., & Warshaw, P.R. (1992). Extrinsic and intrinsic motivation to use computers in the workplace. *Journal of Applied Social Psychology, 22*(14), 1111-1132.

Davis, J. A. (1985). *The logic of causal order*. London: Sage.

Dawkins, R. (1986). *The blind watchmaker*. New York: W.W. Norton & Company.

Dawkins, R. (1990). *The selfish gene*. Oxford, UK: Oxford University Press.

de Vreede, G. J., Boonstra, J., & Niederman, F. (2002). What is effective GSS facilitation? A qualitative inquiry into participants' perceptions. *System Sciences, 2002. HICSS. Proceedings of the 35th Annual Hawaii International Conference on*, 616-627.

Deaux, K. (1984). From Individual Differences to Social Categories. Analysis of a Decade's Research on Gender. *American Psychologist, 39*(2), 105-116.

Deming, W.E. (1986). *Out of the crisis.* Cambridge, MA: Center for Advanced Engineering Study, Massachusetts Institute of Technology.

Den Hartog, D. N., & Koopman, P. L. (2001). Leadership in organizations. In N. Anderson, D. S. Ones, H. K. Sinangil, & C. Viswesvaran (Eds.). *Handbook of Industrial, Work and Organizational Psychology* (Vol. 2, p. 166-187). London, England: Sage.

Denison, D.R., Hooijberg, R., & Quinn, R.E. (1995). Paradox and performance: Toward a theory of behavioral complexity in managerial leadership. *Organization Science,* 6(5), 524-540.

Dennis, A. R., & Valacich, J. S. (1999). Rethinking media richness: Towards a theory of media synchronicity. In R. H. Sprague (Ed.), *Proceedings of the 32nd Hawaii International Conference on System Sciences* (pp. 1-10). Los Alamitos, CA: IEEE Computer Society Press.

Dennis, A. R., Wixom, B. H., & Vandenberg, R. J. (2001). Understanding fit and appropriation effects in group support systems via meta-analysis. *MIS Quarterly,* 25(2), 167-193.

DeSanctis, G., & Poole, M. S. (1994). Capturing the complexity in advanced technology use: Adaptive structuration theory. *Organization Science,* 5(2), 121-147.

DeSanctis, G., Poole, M. S., Dickson, G. W., & Jackson, B. M. (1993). Interpretive analysis of team use of group technologies. *Journal of Organizational Computing,* 3(1), 1-29.

Deschamps, J. (1982). Social Identity and relations of Power Between Groups. In H. Tajfel (Ed.), *Social Identity and Intergroup Relations* (pp. 85-98.). UK: Cambridge University Press.

Dias, W.P.S., Blockley, D.I. (1994). The integration of product and process models for design, *Design Studies* 15(4).

Dickinger, A., & Haghirian, P. (2004). An investigation and conceptual model of SMS marketing. *In Proceedings of the 37th Hawaii International Conference on System Sciences (HICSS-37),* Hawaii, USA, January 5-8, CD-ROM.

Dickson, G., Limayem, M., J., L.-P., & DeSanctis, G. (1996). Facilitating computer supported meetings: A cumulative analysis in a multiple criteria task environment. *Group Decision and Negotiation,* 5(1), 51-72.

Dierickx, I., & Cool, K. (1989). Asset stock accumulation and sustainability of competitive advantage. *Management Science,* 35(12), 1504-1511.

Dodson, J. (2000, September 18). It's time to chat with your customers. *Internetweek.* Retrieved from http://www.internetwk.com/ebizapps/col091800.htm

Dore, R., (1983). Goodwill and the spirit of market capitalism. *British Journal of Sociology, 34*(4), 459-482.

Dossani, R., & Kenney, M. (2003). *Went for cost, stayed for quality? Moving the back office to India.* Stanford University, Asia-Pacific Research Center. Retrieved from http://APARC.stanford.edu

Dozier, R. W., Jr. (1992). *Codes of evolution.* New York: Crown Publishers.

Drazin, R., & Van de Ven, A. H. (1985). Alternative forms of fit in contingency theory. *Administrative Science Quarterly, 30*(4), 514-539.

Dreverman, M. (2005). *Adoption of product model data standards in the process industry.* Unpublished master's thesis, Eindhoven University of Technology, USPI-NL & Department of Technology Management.

Duarte, D.L., & Snyder, N.T. (1999). *Mastering virtual teams.* San Francisco: Jossey-Bass.

Dubé, L., & Paré, G. (2004). The multi-faceted nature of virtual teams. In D. J. Pauleen (Ed.), *Virtual teams: Projects, protocols, and processes* (pp. 1-39). Hershey, PA: Idea Group Publishing.

Dubé, L., Bourhis, A., & Jacob, R. (2005). The impact of structuring characteristics on the launching of virtual communities of practice. *Journal of Organizational Change Management, 18*(2), 145-166.

Dubrovsky, V. J., Kiesler, S., & Sethna, B. N. (1991). The equalization phenomenon: Status effects in computer-mediated and face-to-face decision making groups. *Human-Computer Interaction,* 6, 119-46.

Dul, J., Vries, H. d., Verschoof, S., Eveleens, W., & Feilzer, A. (2004). Combining economic and social goals in the design of production systems by using ergonomics standards. *Computers & Industrial Engineering, 47*(2/3), 207-222.

Duncan, H. D. (1968). *Symbols in society.* New York: Oxford University.

Eagly, A., & Johnson, B. (1990). Gender and the emergence of leaders: A meta-analysis. *Psychological Bulletin,* 108(2), 233-256.

Easley, R. F., Devaraj, S., & Crant, J. M. (2003). Relating collaborative technology use to teamwork quality and performance: An empirical analysis. *Journal of Management Information Systems, 19*(4), 247-268.

Ebner, W., & Krcmar, H., (2005). Design, implementation, and evaluation of trust-supporting components in virtual communities for patients. *Journal of Management Information Systems, 21*(4), 101-135.

EC (2005) Collaboration@Work, *The 2005 report on new working environments and practices* (October), Commission of Information Society and Media.

EC (2005). *i2010 – A European Information Society for Growth and Employment.* Brussels, Belgium: Commission of European Communities.

EC (2005b). *i2010 – A European Information Society for Growth and Employment: Extended Impact Assessment.* Brussels, Belgium: Commission of European Communities.

Edelsky, C. (1993). Who's Got the Floor? In D. Tannen (Ed.), *Gender and Conversational Interaction* (pp. 189-227). New York, NY: Oxford University Press.

Eden, C., & Ackermann, F. (2001). Group decision and negotiation in strategy making. *Group Decision and Negotiation, 10*(2), 119–140.

Eisenhardt, K. M., & Brown, S. L. (1998). Time pacing: Competing in markets that won't stand still. *Harvard Business Review, 76*(2), 59-69.

Eisenhardt, K. M., & Galunic, D. C. (2000). Coevolving: At last, a way to make synergies work. *Harvard Business Review, 78*(1), 91–101.

Eisenhardt, K. M., & Martin, J. A. (2000). Dynamic capabilities: What are they? *Strategic Management Journal, 21*(10), 1105–1121.

Elgh, F. (2004). A Generic Framework for Automated Cost Evaluation of Product Variants and Fabrication Plants. *Proceedings of Design Engineering Technical Conferences and Computers and Information in Engineering Conference,* (vol. 3). New York, NY: American Society of Mechanical Engineers.

Elgh, F. (2007). *Computer-Supported Design for Producibility – Principles and Models for System realisation and Utilisation.* Ph.D. thesis. Gothenburg, Sweden: Department of Product and Production Development, Chalmers University of Technology.

Elgh, F. (2007). Modelling and Management of Manufacturing Requirements in Systems for Automated Variant Design. In Loureiro, G., & Curran, R. (Eds.), *Complex Systems Concurrent Engineering* (pp. 321-328). London: Springer.

Elgh, F., & Cederfeldt, M. (2007). Concurrent Cost Estimation as a Tool for Enhanced Producibility – System Development and Applicability for Producibility Studies. *Journal of Production Economics*, 109(1-2), 12-26.

Espinosa, J. A., Cummings, J. N., Wilson, J. M., & Pearce, B. M. (2003). Team boundary issues across multiple global firms. *Journal of Management Information Systems, 19*(4), 157-190.

Evans, G. (2005). Agile RUP: Taming the Rational™ unified process. In L. Liu & B. Roussev (Eds.), *Management of object-oriented software development.* Hershey, PA: Idea Group.

Evans, P., & Wurster, T. S. (2000). *Blown to bits: How the new economics of information transforms strategy.* Boston, MA: Harvard Business School Press.

Evaristo, R., & Munkvold, B. E. (2002). Collaborative infrastructure formation in virtual projects. *Journal of Global Information Technology Management, 5*(2), 29-47.

Eversheim, W. (2002). Mit e-engineering zum i³-engineering (with e-engineering to i³-engineering). In W. Eversheim, K. Klocke, T. Pfeifer, & M. Weck (Eds.), *Wettbewerbsfaktor produktionstechnik: Aachener perspektiven* (pp. 127-155). Aachen, Germany: Shaker.

Eversheim, W., & Schuh, G. (2004). *Integrierte produkt- und prozessgestaltung.* Berlin, Germany: Springer.

Farrell, J., & Klemperer, P. (2003). Coordination and lock-in: Competition with switching costs and network effects. In R. Schmalensee & R. Willig (Eds.), *Handbook of industrial organization 3.* Amsterdam: North Holland.

Feng, S.C., & Song E.Y. (2000). Information Modeling of Conceptual Process Planning Integrated with Conceptual Design. *Proceedings of Design Engineering Technical Conferences and Computers and Information in Engineering Conference.* New York, NY: American Society of Mechanical Engineers.

Fernandez, A., Holmer, T., Rubart, J., & Schuemmer, T. (2002). Three groupware patterns from the activity awareness family. *EuroPLoP 2002: Seventh European Conference on Pattern Languages of Programs.*

Fine, C. (1998). *Clockspeed: Winning industrial control in the age of temporary advantage.* Reading, MA: Perseus Books.

Finholt, T., & Sproull, L. (1990). Electronic groups at work. *Organization Science, 1*, 41-64.

Fiol, C. M., & O'Connor, E. J. (2005). Identification in face-to-face, hybrid, and pure virtual teams: Untangling the contradictions. *Organization Science, 16*(1), 19-32.

Fishbein, M., & Ajzen, I. (1975). *Belief, Attitude, Intention, and Behavior: An Introduction to Theory and Research.* Reading, MA: Addison-Wesley.

Fisher, M. (1997). What is the right supply chain for you? *Harvard Business Review,* March-April, 105-117.

Fjermestad, J., & Hiltz, S.R. (2000). Group support systems: A descriptive evaluation of case and field studies. *Journal of Management Information Systems, 17*(3), 115-160.

Fogel, R. W. (1979). Notes on the social saving controversy. *The Journal of Economic History, 39*(1), 1-54.

Fontaine, M. (2001). Keeping communities of practice afloat: understanding and fostering roles in communities. *Knowledge Management Review, 4*(4), 16-21.

Forester, M. (1999). Deja vu discussion delivers message emphasizing value. *Chain Store Age, 75*(April), 12.

Fornell, C., & Larcker, D. F. (1981). Evaluating structural equation models with unobservable variables and measurement error. *Journal of Marketing Research, 18*(1), 39-50.

Fornell, C., Johnson, M. D., Anderson, E. W., Cha, J., & Bryant, B. E. (1996). The American Customer Satisfaction Index: Nature, purpose, and findings. *Journal of Marketing, 60*(7), 7-18.

Forrester, J. W. (1958). Industrial dynamics. *Harvard Business Review*, July-August, 37-66.

Foster, P. M. (2004). Psychological sense of community in groups on the Internet. *Behaviour Change, 21*(2), 141-146.

Freeman, L. C., Borgatti, S. P., & White, D. R. (1991). Centrality in valued graphs: A measure of betweenness based on network flow. *Social Networks, 13*, 141-54.

Frohlich, M.T. (2002). e-Integration in the Supply Chain: Barriers and Performance, *Decision Sciences*, 33(4), 537-556.

Fuchs-Kittowski, F. (2007). *Integrierte IT-Unterstutzung der Wissensarbeit.* Cologne: EUL Verlag.

Fulk, J., Schmitz, J., & Steinfield, C. W. (1990). A social influence model of technology use. In J. Fulk & C. Steinfield (Eds.), *Organizations and communication technology* (pp. 117-140). Newbury Park, CA: Sage.

Furst, S. A., Reeves, M., Rosen, B., & Blackburn, R. S. (2004). *Managing the life cycle of virtual teams. Academy of Management Executive, 18*(2), 6-20.

Gaither, N. and Frazier, G. (2002). *Operations Management,* 6th Edition, Cincinnati: Southwest.

Galbraith, J. (1973). *Designing complex organizations.* Reading, MA: Addison-Wesley.

Gallagher, M. P., O'Conner, A. C., Dettbarn, J. L., Jr., Gilding, A., & Gilday, L. T. (2004). *Cost analysis of inadequate interoperability in the U.S. capital facilities industry* (NIST GCR 04-867).

Gamma, E., Helm, R., Johnson, R., & Vlissides, J. (1994). *Design patterns: Elements of reusable object-oriented software.* Boston: Addison-Wesley.

García, I., Giuliani, F., & Wiesenfeld, E. (1999). Community and sense of community: The case of an urban barrio in Caracas. *Journal of Community Psychology, 27*, 727-740.

Gassmann, O., & Von Zedtwitz, M. (2003). Trends and determinants of managing virtual R and D teams. *R & D Management, 33*(3), 243-262.

Gausemeier, J. (2004). Strategische produkt- und technologieplanung: Systematische entwicklung von produkt- und produktionssystemkonzeptionen. *Proceedings of the XI Internationales Produktionstechnisches Kolloquium PTK 2004* (pp. 99-109).

Gefen, D. (2003). Tutorial Assessing Unidimensionality through LISREL: An Explanation and Example. *Communications of the Association for Information Systems, 12*(2), 1-26.

Gefen, D., & Ridings, C. (2005). If You Spoke as She Does, Sir, Instead of the Way You Do: A Sociolinguistics Perspective of Gender Differences in Virtual Communities. *The DATA BASE for Advances in Information Systems, 36*(2), 78-92.

Gefen, D., & Straub, D. W. (1997). Gender Differences in Perception and Adoption of E-mail: An Extension to the Technology Acceptance Model. *MIS Quarterly, 21*(4), 389-400.

Genesereth, M. R. and Ketchpel, S.P. (1994). Software agents. *Communications of the ACM*, 37(7), 48-53.

George, G., & Sleeth, R.G. (2000) Leadership in computer-mediated communication: Implications and research directions. *Journal of Business and Psychology, 15*, 287-310.

Gerpott, T. J., Rams, W., & Schindler, A. (2001). Customer retention, loyalty, and satisfaction in the German mobile cellular telecommunications market. *Telecommunications Policy, 25*(4), 249-269.

Gerstner, C.R., & Day, D.V. (1997). Meta-analytic review of leader-member exchange theory: Correlates and construct issues. *Journal of Applied Psychology, 82*(6), 827-844.

Gibson, C.B., & Cohen, S.G.(Eds.) (2003). *Virtual teams that work. Creating conditions for virtual team effectiveness.* San Francisco: Jossey-Bass.

Gilb, T., & Graham, G. (1993). *Software inspection.* Boston: Addison-Wesley.

Ginsberg, A., & Venkatraman, N. (1985). Contingency perspectives of organizational strategy: A critical review of the empirical research. *Academy of Management Review, 10*(3), 421-434.

Girgensohn, A., & Lee, A. (2002). *Making Web Sites be places for social interaction.* Paper presented at the ACM 2002 Conference on Computer Supported Cooperative Work.

Glaser, B. G., & Strauss, A. L. (1971). *The discovery of grounded theory: Strategies for qualitative research.* Chicago: Aldine Publishing Company. (Original work published 1967)

Global Public Goods, Secretariat of the International Task Force. (2005). *Meeting global challenges: International co-operation in the national interest. Towards an action plan for increasing the provision and impact of global public goods.* Retrieved from http://www.gpgtaskforce.org

Globally Connected World. *Organizational Dynamics, 28*(1),.7-23.

Goh, A. L. S. (2005). Harnessing knowledge for innovation: An integrated management framework. *Journal of Knowledge Management, 9*(4), 6-18.

Goldenberg, S., (1992). Thinking Methodologically. New York, NY: HarperCollins Publishers Inc.

Golembiewski, R. T., & McConkie, M., (1975). The centrality of interpersonal trust in group processes. C.L. Cooper (Ed.). *Theories of Group Processes.* New York: John Wiley & Sons, 131-185.

Gongla, P., & Rizzuto, C. R. (2001). Evolving communities of practice: IBM Global Services experience. *IBM Systems Journal, 40*(4), 842-862.

Goodbody, J. (2005). Critical success factors for global virtual teams. *Strategic Communication Management, 9*(2), 18-21.

Goossenaerts, J. B. M. (2004). Interoperability in the model accelerated society. In P. Cunningham & M. Cunningham (Eds.), *eAdoption and the knowledge economy: Issues, applications, case studies* (pp. 225-232). Amsterdam: IOS Press.

Goossenaerts, J. B.M. (2005). A domain model for the IST infrastructure. In D. Konstantas, J.-P. Bourrières, M. Léonard, & N. Boudjlida (Eds.), *Interoperability of enterprise software and applications* (pp. 373-384). Berlin, Germany: Springer.

Gopal, R. D., Walter, Z., & Tripathi, A. K. (2001). Admediation: New horizons in effective email advertising. *Communications of the ACM, 44*(12), 91-96.

Gould, S. J. (1977). *Ever since Darwin: Reflections in natural history.* New York: W.W. Norton & Company.

Graber, D. A. (1976). *Verbal behavior and politics.* Chicago: University of Illinois Press.

Grabher, G. (2002). The project ecology of advertising: Talents, tasks, and teams. *Regional Studies, 36,* 245-62.

Grabher, G. (2004). Learning in projects, remembering in networks? Communality, sociality, and connectivity in project ecologies. *European Urban and Regional Studies, 11,* 103-23.

Graetz, K. A., Boyle, E. S., Kimble, C. E., Thompson, P., & Garloch, J. L. (1998). Information sharing in face-to-face, teleconferencing, and electronic chat groups. *Small Group Research, 29*(6), 714-743.

Granovetter, M. (1992). Problems of explanation in economic sociology. In N. Nohria & R. G. Eccles (Eds), *Networks and organisations: Structure, form, and action* (pp. 25-56). Cambridge, MA: Harvard Business School.

Grant, R. M. (1991). The resource-based theory of competitive advantage: Implications for strategy formulation. *California Management Review, 33*(3), 114-135.

Grant, R. M. (1996). Toward a knowledge-based theory of the firm. *Strategic Management Journal, 17,* 109-122.

Gray, B. (2004). Informal Learning in an Online Community of Practice. *Journal of Distance Education, 19*(1), 20-35.

Gray, J. (1992). *Men are From Mars, Women Are From Venus*. New York, NY: HarperCollins.

Griffin, K., (1967). The contribution of studies of source credibility to a theory of interpersonal trust in the communication process. *Psychological Bulletin, 68*(2), 104-120.

Griffith, T., Fuller, M., & Northcraft, G. (1998). Facilitator influence in Group Support Systems. *Information Systems Research, 9*(1), 20-36.

Groover, M.P. (2001). *Automation, Production Systems, and Computer-Integrated Manufacturing*. Upper Saddle River, NJ: Prentice-Hall.

Gruber, T. R. (1993). A translation approach to portable ontology specifications. *Knowledge Acquisition, 5*(2), 199-220.

Grudin, J. (1994). Computer-Supported Cooperative Work: History and Focus. *IEEE Computer, May*.

Grudin, J. (1994). CSCW: History and focus. *IEEE Computer, 27*(5), 19-26.

Guiller, J., & Durndell, A. (2007). Students' Linguistic Behaviour in Online Discussion Groups: Does Gender Matter? *Computers in Human Behavior, 23*(5), 2240-2255.

Guimaraes, T., Cook, D., & Natarajan, N. (2002). Exploring the importance of business clockspeed as a moderator for determinants of supplier network performance. *Decision Sciences, 33*(4), 629-644.

Gutman, J. (1982). A Means-End Chain Model Based on Consumer Categorization Processes. *Journal of Marketing, 46*(Spring), 60-72.

Guzdial, M., Kolodner, J. L., Hmelo, C., Narayanan, H. Carlson, D. Rappin, N., Hubscher, R., Turns, J., & Newsletter, W. (1996). Computer support for learning through complex problem-solving. *Communications of the ACM, 39*(4), 43-45.

Guzzo, R. A., & Dickson, M. W. (1996). Teams in organizations: Recent research on performance and effectiveness. *Annual Review of Psychology, 47*, 307-38.

Haeckel, S.H. (1999). *Adaptive Enterprise: Creating and Leading Sense-and-Response Organizations*. Boston, MA: Harvard Business School Press.

Haghirian, P., & Madlberger, M. (2005). Consumer attitude toward advertising via mobile devices - an empirical investigation among Austrian users. In *Proceedings of the 13th European Conference on Information Systems*, Regensburg, Germany, May 26-28: http://is2.lse.ac.uk/asp/aspecis/20050038.pdf (Accessed February 21, 2006).

Hair, J. F., Jr., Anderson, R. E., Tatham, R. L., & Black, W. C. (1995). *Multivariate data analysis with readings* (4th ed.). Englewood Cliffs, NJ: Prentice Hall.

Hale, K., Souza, R., Lo, T., Adachi, Y., & Babaie, E. (2005). *Forecast: IT services, worldwide, 2005-2009*. Gartner. Retrieved June 2005 from http://www.gartner.com

Hammer, M. R., Bennett, M. J., & Wiseman, R. (2003). Measuring intercultural sensitivity: The intercultural development inventory. *International Journal of Intercultural Relations, 27*(4), 421-443.

Hammer, M., & Champy, J. (1993). *Reengineering the corporation*. New York, NY: Harper Business.

Han, J., & Han, D. (2001). A framework for analysing customer value of internet business. *Journal of Information Technology Theory and Application (JITTA), 3*(5), 25-38.

Han, S., Harkke, V., Landor, P., & Mio, R. R. d. (2002). A foresight framework for understanding the future of mobile commerce. *Journal of Systems & Information Technology, 6*(2), 19-39.

Hancock, J.T., & Dunham, P.J. (2001). Impression formation in computer-mediated communication revisited: An analysis of the breadth and intensity of impressions. *Communication Research, 28*, 325-347.

Handy, C., (1995). Trust and the virtual organization. *Harvard Business Review, 73*(3), 40-50.

Hannah, A., & Murachver, T. (1999). Gender and Conversational Style as Predictors of Conversational Behavior. *Journal of Language and Social Psychology, 18*(2), 153-174.

Hannam, R.G. (1997). *Computer Integrated Manufacturing – From Concepts to Realization*. Harlow, Great Britain: Addison Wesley Longman Ltd.

Hansen, M. T. (1999). The search-transfer problem: The role of weak ties in sharing knowledge across organizations subunits. *Administrative Science Quarterly, 44*, 82-111.

Hargadon, A., & Sutton, R. I. (1997). Technology brokering and innovation in a product development firm. *Administrative Science Quarterly, 42*(4), 716-749.

Harrington, S.J., & Ruppel, C.P. (1999). Telecommuting: A test of trust, competing values, and relative advantage.

*IEEE Transactions on Professional Communication,* 42(4), 223-239.

Harris, J. (1999). The idea of community in the study of writing. In L. Ede (Ed.), *On writing research: The Braddock essays 1975-1998* (pp. 260-271). Boston: Bedford.

Hart, P., & Saunders, C., (1997). Power and trust: Critical factors in the adoption and use of electronic data interchange. *Organization Science, 8*(1), 23-42.

Hart, R. K., & McLeod, P. L. (2002). Rethinking team building in geographically dispersed

Heckman, R., & Misiolek, N. I. (2005, January). *Leaders and followers in student online project teams.* Paper presented at 38th Hawaii International Conference on System Sciences, Waikoloa, HI.

Heller, M. (1998). The tragedy of the anticommons: Property in the transition from Marx to market. *Harvard Law Review, 111,* 621-688.

Hemphill, J.K. (1959). Job descriptions of executives. *Harvard Business Review, 37*(5), 55-67.

Henderson, J. C., & Lee, S. (1992). Managing IS design teams: A control theories perspective. *Management Science, 38*(6), 757-777.

Henderson, J. C., & Lee, S., (1992). Managing I/S design teams: A control theories perspective. *Management Science, 38*(6), 757-777.

Henoch, B., & Sandkuhl, K. (2002). Competence modelling as a basis for formation of SME-networks - the SME-chains approach. In *Proceedings of the WWDU 2002 Conference.*

Herring, S. C. (1993, January 20). Gender and Democracy in Computer Mediated Communication. *Electronic Journal of Communication 3(2)* Retrieved July 29, 2006, from http://www.cios.org/www/ejc/v3n293.htm

Herring, S. C. (1996). Posting in a Different Voice: Gender and Ethics in Computer-Mediated Communication. In C. Ess (Ed.), *Philosophical Perspectives on Computer-Mediated Communication* (pp. 115-145). Albany: State University of New York Press.

Herring, S. C. (1996). Two Variants of an Electronic Message Schema. In S. C. Herring (Ed.), *Computer-Mediated Communication Linguistic, Social and Cross-cultural Perspectives* (pp. 81-106). Philadelphia, PA: John Benjamins Publishing Company.

Hertel, G., Geister, S., & Konradt, U. (2005). Managing virtual teams: A review of current empirical research. *Human Resource Management Review,* 15(1), 69-95.

Hertel, G., Konradt, U., & Orlikowski, B. (2004). Managing distance by interdependence: Goal setting, task interdependence and team-based rewards in virtual teams. *European Journal of Work and Organizational Psychology,* 13(1), 1-28.

Hildreth, P., Kimble, C., & Wright, P. (2000). Communities of practice in the distributed international environment. *Journal of Knowledge Management, 4*(1), 27-38.

Hilmer, K., & Dennis, A. (2001). Stimulating thinking: Cultivating better decisions with groupware through categorization. *Journal of Management Information Systems, 17*(3), 93-114.

Hinde, S. (2002). Spam, scams, chains, hoaxes and other junk mail. *Computers & Security, 21*(7), 592-606.

Hinds, P. J., & Kiesler, S. (Eds.) (2002). *Distributed work: New research on working across distance using technology.* Cambridge: MIT Press.

Hinds, P., & Weisband, S. (2003). Knowledge sharing and shared understanding in virtual teams. In C.B. Gibson & S.G. Cohen (Eds.), *Virtual teams that work: Creating conditions for virtual teams effectiveness* (pp. 21-36). San Francisco: Jossey-Bass.

Hoch. J.E. (2007). *Verteilte Fuehrung in virtuellen Teams.* Dissertationsschrift an der Universität Kiel [*Distributed leadership in virtual teams,* PhD thesis]. URL: http://e-diss.uni-kiel.de/index.html

Hofer, C. W., & Schendel, D. (1978). *Strategy formulation: Analytical concepts.* St. Paul, MN: West Publishing Company.

Hofner Saphiere, D.M. (1996). Productive behaviors of global business teams. *International Journal of Intercultural Relations,* 20(2), 227-259.

Hofstede, G. (1980). *Culture's Consequences: International Differences in Work Related Values.* London, UK: Sage.

Hofstede, G., Neuijen, B., Ohayv, D. D., & Sanders, G. (1990). Measuring Organizational Cultures: A Qualitative and Quantitative Study Across Twenty Cases. *Administrative Science Quarterly, 35,* 286-316.

Hogg, M. A., & Tindale, R. S. (2005). Social identity, influence, and communication in small groups. In J. Harwood & H. Giles (Eds.), *Intergroup communica-*

tion: *Multiple perspectives* (pp. 141-164). New York: Peter Lang.

Hollander, E. P., (1964). *Leaders, groups, and influence.* New York: Oxford University Press.

Hollingshead, A. B., & Contractor, N. S. (1994, November). *The dynamics of leader consensus in continuing face-to-face and computer-mediated work groups.* Paper presented at the annual meeting of the Speech Communication Association, Chicago.

Hollingshead, A.B., & Contractor, N.S. (2002). New media and organizing at the group level. In S. Livingstone & L. Lievrouw (Eds.), *Handbook of new media* (pp. 221-235). London: Sage.

Holmes, J. (1992). Women's Talk in Public Contexts. *Discourse and Society, 3*(2), 131-150.

Holtzblatt, K., Jones, S. (1993). Contextual Inquiry: A Participatory Technique for System Design, in *Participatory Design: Principles and Practice*, Hillsdale, New Jersey.

Homsky, O. (2003). More patterns for group leadership. *EuroPLoP 2003: Seventh European Conference on Pattern Languages of Programs.*

Hong, S. J., & Tam, K. Y. (2006). Understanding the Adoption of Multipurpose Information Appliances: The Case of Mobile Data Services. *Information Systems Research, 17*(2), 162-179.

Hooijberg, R. (1996). A multidirectional approach toward leadership: An extension of the concept of behavioral complexity. *Human Relations*, 49(7), 917-946.

Hooijberg, R., & Choi, J. (2000). Which leadership roles matter to whom?: An examination of rater effects on perceptions of effectiveness. *Leadership Quarterly*, 11(3), 341-364.

Hooijberg, R., & Choi, J. (2001). The impact of organisational characteristics on leadership effectiveness models: an examination of leadership in a private and public sector organisation. *Administration and Society,* 33(4), 403-431.

Hooijberg, R., Hunt, J.G., & Dodge, G.E. (1997). Leadership complexity and development of the leaderplex model. *Journal of Management*, 23(3), 375-408.

House, R.J., & Aditya, R.T. (1997). The social scientific study of leadership: Quo Vadis? *Journal of Management, 23,* 409-473.

Huang, J. C., & Newell, S. (2003). Knowledge integration processes and dynamics within the context of cross-

functional projects. *International Journal of Project Management, 21*(3), 167–176.

Huber, N. (2005, May 3). Outsourcing "backlash" highlights need for IT leaders to sharpen management skills. *Computer Weekly*, pp. 24-27.

Hubka, V., Andreasen, M.M., & Eder, W.E. (1998). *Practical Studies in Systematic Design.* London, Great Britain: Butterworth.

Huck, S., Muller, W., & Vriend, N. J. (2002). The East End, the West End, and King's Cross: On clustering in the four-player hotelling game. *Economic Inquiry, 40*(2), 231-241.

Huff, C. W., Sproull, L., & Kiesler, S. (1989). Electronic communication and organizational commitment: Tracing the relationship in a city government. *Journal of applied social psychology, 19*, 1371-1391.

Huff, L. C., Cooper, J., & Jones, W., (2002). The development and consequences of trust in student project groups. *Journal of Marketing Education, 24*(1), 24-34.

Hunter, D., Bailey, A., & Taylor, B. (1995). *The Art of Facilitation.* Cambridge, MA: Perseus Book Group.

Huysman, M., Creemers, M., & Derksen, F. (1998). Learning from the environment: Exploring the relation between organizational learning, knowledge management and information/communication technology. In E. D. Hoadley & I. Benbasat (Eds.), *Proceedings of the 4th Americas Conference on Information Systems* (pp. 598-600). Atlanta, GA: Association for Information Systems.

Iacono, C. S., & Weisband, S., (1997). Developing trust in virtual teams. Paper presented at the *30th Annual Hawaii International Conference on System Sciences.* Honolulu, HI.

IEEE. (2004). *IEEE Standard 1540-2004. IEEE standard for software life cycle processes: Risk management.* IEEE Press.

Ilgen, D.R., & Hollenbeck, J.R. (1991). The structure of work: Job design and roles. In M.D. Dunnette & L.M. Hough (Eds.), *Handbook of industrial and organizational psychology* (pp. 165-207). Palo Alto, CA: Consulting Psychologists Press, Inc.

Industry Canada. (2004). *The digital economy in Canada: Unsolicited commercial electronic mail (SPAM).* Retrieved July 30, 2004, from http://e-com.ic.gc.ca/epic/internet/inecic-ceac.nsf/en/h_gv00170e.html#stats

International Labour Organization. (2004, September 18). International Standard Classification of Occupations, 1988 (ISCO-88). Retrieved September 19, 2005, from http://www.ilo.org/public/english/bureau/stat/isco/isco88/index.htm

Isaac, G. L. (1993). Aspects of human evolution. In R. L. Ciochon & J. G. Fleagle (Eds.), *The human evolution source book* (pp. 263-273). Englewood Cliffs, NJ: Prentice Hall.

Isaksson, O., Keski-Säppäl, S., Eppinger, S.D. (2000). Evaluation of design process alternatives using signal flow graphs, *Journal of Engineering Design, 11*(3), 211–224.

Jackson, M. H., & Purcell, D. (1997). Politics and media richness in World Wide Web representations of the former Yugoslavia. *Geographical Review, 87*(2), 219-239.

Jacobson, I. (1987). Object-oriented development in an industrial environment. *ACM SIGPLAN Notices, 22*(12), 183-191.

Jacobson, I., Booch, G., & Rumbaugh, J. (1999). *The unified software development process*. Boston: Addison-Wesley.

Jacoby, C. (2000). E-commerce hot spots. *Corporate Location, 3*, 18.

Jacucci, G., Pawlak, A., & Sandkuhl, K. (2005). Preface. In Jacucci, G., Pawlak, A., & Sandkuhl, K. (Eds.), *Proceedings of Challenges in Collaborative Engineering Workshop*. Jönköping, Sweden: Department of Computer & Electrical Engineering, School of Engineering, Jönköping University.

Jaeger, D., & Pekruhl, U. (1998). Participative company management in Europe: The new role of middle management. *New Technology, Work and Employment,* 13(2), 94-103.

Jarvenpaa, S. L., & Leidner, D. E. (1999). Communication and trust in global virtual teams. *Organizational Science, 10*(6), 791-815.

Jarvenpaa, S., Knoll, K., & Leidner, D., (1998). Is anybody out there? Antecedents of trust in global virtual teams. *Journal of Management Information Systems, 14*(4), 29-64.

Jarvenpaa, S., Shadow, T., & Staples, S., (2004). Toward contextualized theories of trust: The role of trust in global virtual teams. *Information Systems Research, 15*(3), 250-267.

Jarvenpaa, S.L., & Leidner, D.E. (1999). Communication and trust in global virtual teams. *Organization Science,* 10(6), 791-815.

Jarvenpaa, S. L., & Tanriverdi, H. (2002). Leading virtual knowledge networks. *Organizational Dynamics, 31,* 403-412.

Jiang, J., Klein, G., & Discenza, R. (2002). Pre-project partnering impact on information systems projects, project team, and project manager. *European Journal of Information Systems, 11*(2), 86-97.

Johnson, B. (1993). Community and Contest: Midwestern Men and Women Creating Their Worlds in Conversational Storytelling. In D. Tannen (Ed.), *Gender and Conversational Interaction* (pp. 62-80). New York, NY: Oxford University Press.

Johnson, C. M. (2001). A survey of current research on online communities of practice. *Internet and Higher Education, 4*(1), 45-60.

Jonassen, D., & Remidez, H., (2002). Mapping alternative discourse structures onto computer conferences. Gerry Stahl, (Ed.). *Computer Support for Collaborative Learning: Foundations for a CSCL Community.* Hillsdale, NJ: Erlbaum, 237-244.

Jones, S., & Marsh, S. (1997). Human-Computer-Human Interaction: Trust in CSCW. *SIGCHI Bulletin, 29*(3).

Judge, T. A., & Piccolo, R. F. (2004). Transformational and transactional leadership: A meta-analytic test of their relative validity. *Journal of Applied Psychology, 89,* 755-768.

Junglas, I. A. (2002). *U-Commerce an experimental investigation of ubiquity and uniqueness.* Unpublished Dissertation, University of Georgia, Athens.

Kahai, S, Sosik, J, & Avolio, B. (2004). Effects of Participative and Directive Leadership in Electronic Groups. *Groups & Organization Management, 29*(1), 67-105.

Kahai, S, Sosik, J., & Avolio, B. (1997). Effects of leadership style and problem structure on work group process and outcomes in an electronic meeting system environment. *Personnel Psychology, 50,* 121-146.

Kahai, S. S., & Avolio, B. J. (2006). Leadership style, anonymity, and the discussion of an ethical issue in an electronic context. *International Journal of e-Collaboration, 2,* 1-26.

Kahai, S. S., Sosick, J. J., & Avolio, B. J. (2003). Effects of leadership style, anonymity, and rewards on creativity-relevent processes and outcomes in an electronic meeting system context. *Leadership Quarterly, 14,* 499-524.

Kahai, S. S., Sosik, J. J., & Avolio, B. J. (2003). Effects of leadership style, anonymity, and rewards on creativity-relevant processes and outcomes in an electronic meeting system context. *Leadership Quarterly, 14*(4-5), 499-524.

Kahai, S. S., Sosik, J. J., & Avolio, B. J. (2004). Effects of participative and directive leadership in electronic groups. *Group & Organization Management, 29*(1), 67-105.

Kahai, S., & Avolio, B. (2006). Leadership Style, Anonymity, and the Discussion of an Ethical Issue in an Electronic Context. *International Journal of e-Collaboration, 2*(2), 1-26.

Kanter Moss, R. (1999). Change Is Everyone's job: Managing the Extended Enterprise in a

Kapoor, N., Konstan, J. A., & Terveen, L. G. (2005). *How peer photos influence member participation in online communities.* Paper presented at the 2005 Conference on Human Factors in Computing Systems.

Katz, D., & Kahn, R.L. (1978). *The social psychology of organisations.* New York: John Wiley.

Katzy, B., Evaristo, R., & Zigurs, I. (2000). Knowledge management in virtual projects: A research agenda. *Proceedings of the 36th Hawaii International Conference on Systems Sciences.*

Kayworth, T. R., & Leidner, D. E. (2002). Leadership effectiveness in global virtual teams. *Journal of Management Information Systems, 18*, 7-40.

Kayworth, T., & Leidner, D. E. (2000). The Global Virtual Manager: A Prescription for Success. *European Management Journal, 18*(2), 183-194.

Kayworth, T.R., & Leidner, D.E. (2001). Leadership effectiveness in global virtual teams. *Journal of Management Information Systems, 18*(3), 7-40.

Kelly, S. U., Sung, C., & Farnham, S. (2002). *Designing for Improved Social Responsibility, User Participation and Content in On-line Communities.* Paper presented at the SIGCHI conference on Human factors in computing systems.

Kelman, H. C., (1958). Compliance, identification and internalization: Three processes of attitude change. *Journal of Conflict Resolution, 2*(1), 51-60.

Kendall, J. E., & Kendall, K. E. (1993). Metaphors and methodologies: Living beyond the systems machine. *MIS Quarterly, 17*(2), 149-171.

Kendall, J. E., & Kendall, K. E. (1994). Metaphors and their meaning for information systems development. *European Journal of Information Systems, 3*(1), 37-47.

Kendall, K. E. (2000). Ecommerce aesthetics: Ecommerce for ecommerce's sake. *Information Resources Management Journal, 13*(3).

Kendall, K. E., & Kendall, J. E. (2005). *Systems analysis and design* (6th ed.). Upper Saddle River, NJ: Prentice Hall.

Kenny, D. A., Manetti, L., Pierro, A., Livi, S., & Kashy, D. A. (2002). The statistical analysis of data from small groups. *Journal of Personality and Social Psychology, 83*, 126-137.

Kerr, S., & Jermier, J.M. (1978). Substitutes for leadership: Their meaning and measurement. *Organizational Behavior & Human Performance*, 22(3), 375-403.

Khazanchi, D., & Zigurs, I. (2005). *Patterns of effective management of virtual projects: An exploratory study.* Newtown Square, PA: Project Management Institute.

Khazanchi, D., & Zigurs, I. (2006). Patterns for effective management of virtual projects: Theory and evidence. *International Journal of e-Collaboration, 2*(3), 25-49.

Khazanchi, D., & Zigurs, I. (2007). An assessment framework for discovering and using patterns in virtual project management. *Proceedings of the 36th Hawaii International Conference on Systems Sciences.*

Kickul, J., & Neuman, G. (2000). Emergent leadership behaviors: The function of personality and cognitive ability in determining teamwork performance and KSAS. *Journal of Business and Psychology, 15,* 27-51.

Kiesler, S. (1986, January-February). The hidden messages in computer networks. *Harvard Business Review,* pp. 46-54, 58-60.

Kilbourne, W., & Weeks, S. (1997). A Socio-economic Perspective on Gender Bias in Technology. *Journal of Socio-Economics, 26*(1), 243-260.

Kilduff, M., & Krackhardt, D. (1994). Bringing the individual back in: A structural analysis of the internal market for reputation in organizations. *Academy of Management Journal, 37*, 87-108.

Kilduff, M., & Tsai, W. (2003). *Social networks and organizations.* London: Sage.

Kim, M. K., Park, M. C., & Jeong, D. H. (2004). The effects of customer satisfaction and switching barrier on customer loyalty in Korean mobile telecommunication services. *Telecommunication Policy, 28*(2), 145-159.

Kimball, L., & Eunice, A. (1999). The virtual team: Strategies to optimize performance. *Health Forum Journal, 42*(3), 58-62.

Kimball, L., & Ladd, A. (2004). Facilitator toolkit for building and sustaining virtual communities of practice. In P. M. Hildreth & C. Kimble (Eds.), *Knowledge Networks: Innovation through Communities of Practice* (pp. 202-215). Hershey, PA: Idea Group Pub.

Kimura, F. (2005). Engineering information infrastructure for product life cycle management. In E. Arai, J. Goossenaerts, F. Kimura, & K. Shirase (Eds.), *Knowledge and skill chains in engineering and manufacturing: Information infrastructure in the era of global communications* (pp. 13-22). Berlin, Germany: Springer.

King, W. R. (2005). Outsourcing becomes more complex. *Information Systems Management, 22*(2), 89-90.

Kinney, S. T., & Panko, R. R. (1996). Project teams: Profiles and member perceptions - Implications for group support system research and products. *Proceedings of the 29th Annual Hawaii International Conference on System Sciences,* 128-137.

Kirche, E., Zalewski, J., Tharp, T. (2005). Real-time sales and operations planning with CORBA: Linking demand management and production Planning. In C.S. Chen, J. Filipe, I. Seruca, J. Cordeiro (Eds.), *Proceedings of the 7th International Conference on Enterprise Information Systems* (pp. 122-129). Washington, DC: IEEE Computer Society Press (in conjunction with ICEIS).

Kirkman, B. L., Rosen, B., Gibson, C. B., Tesluk, P. E., & McPherson, S. O. (2002). Five challenges to virtual team success: Lessons from Sabre, Inc. *Academy of Management Executive, 16*(3), 67-79.

Kirkman, D.P. (1998). Requirement Decomposition and Traceability. *Requirements Engineering,* 3(2), pp. 107-111.

Kirsch, L. J. (1996). The management of complex tasks in organizations: Controlling the systems development process. *Organization Science, 7*(1), 1-21.

Kirsch, L. J., (1997). Portfolios of control modes and IS project management. *Information Systems Research, 8*(3), 215-239.

Kirsch, L. J., Sambamurthy, V., Ko, D., & Purvis, R. L. (2002). Controlling information systems development projects: The view from the client. *Management Science, 48*(4), 484-498.

Klement, R. (2005). *Agentenbasiertes produktdatenmanagement.* Unpublished doctoral dissertation, RWTH Aachen University, Aachen, Germany.

Kluger, A.N., & DeNisi, A. (1996). The effects of feedback interventions on performance: A historical review, a meta-analysis, and a preliminary feedback intervention theory. *Psychological Bulletin, 119*(2), 254-284.

Knoke, D., & Kuklinski, J. H. (1991). Network analysis: Basic concepts. In G. Thompson, J. Frances, R. Levacic, & J. Mitchell (Eds), *Markets, hierarchies and networks* (pp. 173-82). London: Sage.

Kock, N. (1998). Can communication medium limitations foster better group outcomes? An action research study. *Information & Management, 34*(5), 295-305.

Kock, N. (1999). *Process improvement and organizational learning: The role of collaboration technologies.* Hershey, PA: Idea Group Publishing.

Kock, N. (2003). Action research: Lessons learned from a multi-iteration study of computer-mediated communication in groups. *IEEE Transactions on Professional Communication,* 46(2), 105-128.

Kock, N. (2004). The psychobiological model: Towards a new theory of computer-mediated communication based on Darwinian evolution. *Organization Science, 15,* 327-48.

Kock, N. (2005). *Business process improvement through e-collaboration: Knowledge sharing through the use of virtual groups.* Hershey, PA: Idea Group Publishing.

Kock, N. (2005). What is e-collaboration? *International Journal of e-Collaboration, 1*(1), i-vii.

Kock, N. (Ed) (2006). *Information systems action research: An applied view of emerging concepts and methods.* New York, NY: Springer.

Kock, N. (Ed) (2008). *Encyclopedia of e-collaboration.* Hershey, PA: Information Science Reference.

Kock, N., & Hantula, D. A. (2005). Do We Have e-Collaboration Genes? *International Journal of e-Collaboration, 1*(2), i-ix.

Kock, N., & Nosek, J. (2005). Expanding the Boundaries of E-Collaboration. *IEEE Transactions on Professional Communication,* 48(1), 1-9.

Kock, N., Danesh, A., & Komiak, P. (2008). A discussion and test of a communication flow optimization approach for business process redesign. *Knowledge and Process Management,* 15(1), 72-85.

Kock, N., Davison, R., Wazlawick, R., & Ocker, R. (2001). E-collaboration: A look at past research and future challenges. *Journal of Systems and Information Technology, 5*(1), 1-9.

Kock, N., Lynn, G. S., Dow, K. E., & Akgün, A. E. (2006). Team adaptation to electronic communication media: Evidence of compensatory adaptation in new product development teams. *European Journal of Information Systems, 15*(3), 331-341.

Kogut, B., & Zander, U. (1996). What do firms do? Coordination, identity, and learning. *Organization Science, 7*(5), 502-518.

Koh, J., & Kim, Y.-G. (2003). Sense of virtual community: A conceptual framework and empirical validation. *International Journal of Electronic Commerce, 8*(2), 75.

Kolka, J. (2002). Silicon mountains/silicon molehills: Geographic concentration and convergence of Internet industries in the US. *Information Economics and Policy, 14*(2), 211.

Konradt, U., Hertel, G., & Schmook, R. (2003). Quality of management by objectives, task-related stressors and non-task-related stressors as predictors of stress and job satisfaction among teleworkers. *European Journal of Work and Organizational Psychology, 12*(1), 61-79.

Konradt, U., Schmook, R., & Maelecke, M. (2000). Impacts of telework on individuals, organizations and families - A critical review. In: Cooper, C.L. & Robertson, I.T. (Eds.), *International review of industrial and organizational psychology* (Vol. 15, pp. 63-99). Chichester: Wiley.

Korsgaard, M. A., Schweiger, D. M., & Sapienza, H. J., (1995). Building commitment, attachment, and trust in strategic decision-making teams: The role of procedural justice. *Academy of Management Journal, 38*(1), 60-84.

Krackhardt, D. (1987). QAP partialling as a test of spuriousness. *Social Networks, 9*, 171-86.

Krackhardt, D., & Hanson, J. (1993). Informal networks: The company behind the chart. *Harvard Business Review, 71*, 104-11.

Krackhardt, D., & Stern, R. N., (1988). Informal networks and organizational crises: An experimental simulation. *Social Psychology Quarterly, 51*(2), 123-140.

Krim, J. (2003, March 13). Spam's cost to business escalates: Bulk e-mail threatens communication arteries. *The Washington Post*, p. A01.

Kruchten, P. (2000). *The rational unified process: An introduction*. Boston: Addison-Wesley.

Kruchten, P. (2004). Scaling down large projects to meet the agile "sweet spot." *The Rational Edge*. Retrieved from http://www.therationaledge.com

Kumar, K., & van Dissel, H. G. (1996). Sustainable collaboration: Managing conflict and cooperation in interorganizational systems. *MIS Quarterly, 20*(3), 279-300.

Kurtzman, J. (2003). The knowledge economy. In C. W. Holsapple (Ed.), *Handbook on knowledge management 1: Knowledge matters* (pp. 73-87). Berlin, Germany: Springer.

LaCourse, D.E. (1996). *Handbook of Solid Modelling*, McGraw-Hill.

Laffey, J., Musser, D., Remidez, H., & Gottdenker, J., (2003). Networked systems for schools that learn. *Communications of the ACM, 46*(9), 192-200.

Laitman, J. (1993). The anatomy of human speech. In R. L. Ciochon & J. G. Fleagle (Eds.), *The human evolution source book* (pp. 56-60). Englewood Cliffs, NJ: Prentice Hall.

Lakoff, G., & Johnson, M. (1980). *Metaphors we live by*. Chicago: The University of Chicago Press.

Lakoff, R. T. (1975). *Language and Woman's Place*. New York: Harper & Row.

Laplante, P. A., & Neill, C. J. (2005). "The demise of the waterfall model is imminent" and other urban myths. *ACM Queue*, pp. 10-15.

Larson, C. E., & LaFasto, F. M. J., (1989). *Teamwork: What must go right/what can go wrong*. Newbury Park, NJ: Sage.

Larsson, T., Larsson, A., Karlsson, L. (2001). A Modular Approach to Web Based Multibody Dynamic Simulation, *International CIRP Design Seminar, Design in the New Economy*.

Laso-Ballesteros, I., & Salmelin, B. (2005). AMI-endowed collaboration@work. In G. Riva, F. Vatalaro, F. Davide, & M. Alcaniz (Eds.), *Ambient Intelligence: The evolution of technology, communication and cognition towards the future of human-computer interaction (pp. 237-265)*. Amsterdam, The Netherlands: IOS Press.

Lave, J., & Wenger, E. (1991). *Situated Learning: legitimate peripheral participation*. Cambridge, UK: Cambridge University Press.

Lawler, E. J. (2005). Role of status in group processes. In M. C. Thomas-Hunt (Ed.), *Status and groups* (pp. 315-325). New York: Elsevier.

Lawler, E., (1992). *The ultimate advantage: Creating the high-involvement organization.* San Francisco: Jossey-Bass.

Leao, A. L. M. d. S., & Mello, S. C. B. d. (2002). *Conhecendo o valor do cliente virtual: Uma analize utilizando a teoria de cadeias de meios-fim.* Paper presented at the XXVI ENAMPAD, Salvador, Bahia, Brazil.

Lee, A. S. (1994). Electronic mail as a medium for rich communication: An empirical investigation using hermeneutic interpretation. *MIS Quarterly, 18*(2), 143-157.

Lee, E.-J. (2003). Effects of "Gender" of the Computer on Informational Social Influence: The Moderating Role of Task Type. *International Journal of Human-Computer Studies, 58,* 347–362.

Lee, H., Padmanabhan, V., and Whang, S. (1997). Information distortion in a supply chain: the bullwhip effect. *Management Science, 43,* 546 – 548.

Lee, H., Padmanabhan, V., and Whang, S. (1997). The bullwhip effect. *Sloan Management Review,* 38(3), 93-103.

Lee, H., Padmanabhan, V., and Whang, S. (2004). Information Distortion in a Supply Chain: The Bullwhip Effect/Comments on "Information Distortion in a Supply Chain: The Bullwhip Effect". *Management Science,* 50(12), 1875 – 1894.

Leidner, D. E., & Kayworth, T. (2006). Review: A Review of Culture in Information Systems Research: Toward a Theory of Information Technology Culture Conflict. *MIS Quarterly, 30*(2), 357-399.

Leidner, D., Alavi, M., & Kayworth, T. (2006). The role of culture in knowledge management: A case study of two global firms. *International Journal of e-Collaboration, 2*(1), 17-40.

Lengel, R. H., & Daft, R. L. (1988). The selection of communication media as an executive skill. *Academy of Management Executive, 2*(3), 225-232.

Lerner, J., & Tirole, J. (2001). The open source movement: Key research questions. *European Economic Review, 45,* 819-826.

Lesser, E. L., & Storck, J. (2001). Communities of practice and organizational performance. *IBM Systems Journal, 40*(4), 831-841.

Lessig, L. (2001). *The future of ideas: The fate of commons in a connected world.* New York: Random House.

Levina, N., & Ross, J. W. (2003). From the vendor's perspective: Exploring the value proposition in information technology outsourcing. *MIS Quarterly, 27*(3), 361-364.

Li, M., Cabral, R., Doumeingts, G., & Popplewell, K. (2006). *Enterprise interoperability research roadmap.* Retrieved from ftp://ftp.cordis.europa.eu/pub/ist/docs/directorate_d/ebusiness/ei-roadmap-final_en.pdf

Liao Troth, M. A., & Griffith, T. L. (2002). Software, shareware and freeware: Multiplex commitment to an electronic social exchange system. *Journal of Organizational Behavior, 23*(5), 635-653.

Lieberman, H., Rosenzweig, E., & Singh, P. (2001). Aria: An agent for annotating and retrieving images. *IEEE Computer, 34*(7), 57-62.

Lieberman, P. (1998). *Eve spoke: Human language and human evolution.* New York: W.W. Norton & Company.

Lin, F., & Sandkuhl, K. (2007). Polygon-Based Similarity Aggregation for Ontology Matching. In *ISPA Workshops* (pp. 255-264): Springer.

*LiveBroadway.com.* (2005). Retrieved January 2005 from http://www.liveBroadway.com

Löfstrand M., Larsson, T., Karlsson, L. (2005). Demands on Engineering Design Culture for Implementing Functional Products, *Proceedings of the International Conference on Engineering Design,* Melbourne.

Long, D. A., & Perkins, D. D. (2003). Confirmatory factory analysis of the Sense of Community Index and development of a brief SCI. *Journal of Community Psychology, 31*(3), 279-296.

Lord, R. G., & Foti, R. J. (1986). Schema theories, information processing and organizational behaviour. In H. P. Sims & D. A. Gioia (Eds.), *The thinking organization* (pp. 20-48). San Francisco: Jossey-Bass.

Lorenz, K. (1983). *The waning of humaneness.* Boston: Little, Brown & Co.

Lowe, K. B., & Kroeck, K. (1996). Effectiveness correlates of transformational and transactional leadership: A meta-analytic review of the MLQ literature. *Leadership Quarterly, 7*(3), 385-426.

Ludford, P. J., Cosley, D., Frankowski, D., & Terveen, L. (2004). *Think different: increasing online community participation using uniqueness and group dissimilarity.* Paper presented at the 2004 conference on Human factors in computing systems.

Lundqvist, M. (2005). *Context as a Key Concept in Information Demand Analysis.* Paper presented at the Proceedings of the Doctoral Consortium associated with the 5th Intl. and Interdisciplinary Conference on Modeling and Using Context (CONTEXT-05), Paris, France.

Lundqvist, M., & Sandkuhl, K. (2004). Modeling Information Demand for Collaborative Engineering. In Sandkuhl, K., & Kazmierski, T. (Eds.), *Proceedings of Challenges in Collaborative Engineering Workshop* (pp. 111-120). Jönköping, Sweden: Department of Computer & Electrical Engineering, School of Engineering, Jönköping University.

Lyytinen, K., & Yoo, Y. (2002). Issues and Challenges in Ubiquitous Computing. *Communications of the ACM, 45*(12), 63-65.

Macdonald, J. (1995). Quality and the financial service sector. *Managing Service Quality, 5*(1), 43-46.

Maier, A., Aguado, J., Bernaras, A., Laresgoiti, I., Pedinaci, C., Pena, N., & Smithers, T. (2003). *Integration with Ontologies.* Paper presented at Professionelles Wissensmanagement - Erfahrungen und Visionen. Luzern, Germany. Retrieved November 3, 2003, from www.ontoprise.de/documents/integration_with_ontologies.pdf.

Majchrzak, A., Malhotra, A., & John, R. (2005). Perceived individual collaboration know-how development through information technology–enabled contextualization: Evidence from distributed teams. *Information Systems Research, 16*(1), 9–27.

Majchrzak, A., Malhotra, A., Stamps, J., & Lipnack, J. (2004). Can absence make a team grow stronger? *Harvard Business Review, 82*(5), 131-137.

Malhotra, Y. (2000). Knowledge management and new organization forms: A framework for business model innovation. *Information Resources Management Journal, 13*(1), 5-14.

Malone, T. W., & Crowston, K. (1994). The interdisciplinary study of coordination. *ACM Computing Surveys, 26*(1), 87-119.

Malone, T. W., Grant, K. R., Lai, K.-Y., Rao, R., & Rosenblitt, D., (1987). Semi-structured messages are surprisingly useful for computer-supported coordination. *ACM Transactions on Information Systems, 5*(2), 115-131.

Malone, T., & Crowston, K. (1994). The interdisciplinary study of coordination. *ACM Computing Surveys, 26*(1), 87-119.

Manz, C. C., & Sims, H. P. (1987). Leading workers to lead themselves: The external leadership of self-managing work teams. *Administrative Science Quarterly, 32*, 106-128.

Manz, C.C., & Sims, H.P. (1993). *Business without bosses: How self-managing teams are building high performance companies.* New York: Wiley.

Mariani, J. (2001). The implications of your location. *Restaurant Hospitality, 85*(8), 20.

Markus, M. L. (1990). Toward a critical mass theory of interactive media. In J. Fulk & C. Steinfield (Eds.), *Organizations and communication technology* (pp. 194-218). Newbury Park, CA: Sage.

Markus, M. L. (1994). Electronic mail as the medium of managerial choice. *Organization Science, 5*(4), 502-527.

Marshall, C., & Novick, D. (1995). Conversational effectiveness and multi-media communications. *Information Technology & People, 8*(1), 54-79.

Martins, L. L., Gilson, L. L., & Maynard, M. T. (2004). Virtual teams: What do we know and where do we go from here? *Journal of Management, 30*(6), 805-835.

Massey, A. P., Hung, Y. C., Montoya-Weiss, M., & Ramesh, V. (2001). When culture and style aren't about clothes: Perceptions of task-technology "fit" in global virtual teams. *Proceedings of the 2001 International ACM SIGGROUP Conference on Supporting Group Work*, 207-213.

Mathieson, K. (1991). Predicting user intentions: comparing the Technology Acceptance Model with the Theory of Planned Behavior. *Information Systems Research, 2(3),* 173-191.

Mayer, R. C., Davis, J. H., & Schoorman, F. D., (1995). An integration model of organizational trust. *Academy of Management Review, 20*(3), 709-734.

Maznevski, M. L., & Chudoba, K. M. (2000). Bridging space over time: Global virtual team dynamics and effectiveness. *Organization Science, 11*(5), 473-492.

Maznevski, M.L., & Chudoba, K.M. (2000). Bridging space over time: global virtual team dynamics and effectiveness. *Organization Science, 11*(5), 473-492.

McAllister, D. J., (1995). Affect and cognition-based trust as foundation for interpersonal cooperation in organizations. *Academy of Management Journal, 38*(1), 24-59.

McCrone, J. (1991). *The ape that spoke: Language and the evolution of the human mind.* New York: William Morrow and Company.

McElroy, J. C. (1982). A typology of attribution leadership research. *Academy of Management Review, 7*, 413-17.

McElroy, J. C., & Shrader, C. B. (1986). Attribution theories of leadership and network analysis. *Journal of Management, 12*, 351-62.

McGrath, J. E. (1984). *Groups: Interaction and performance.* Englewood Cliffs, NJ: Prentice-Hall.

McGrath, J. E., & Hollingshead, A. B. (1994). *Groups interacting with technology: Ideas, evidence, issues, and an agenda.* Thousand Oaks, CA: Sage Publications.

McLaren, T., Head, M., & Yuan, Y. (2002). Supply chain collaboration alternatives: Understanding the expected costs and benefits. *Internet Research, 12*(4), 348-364.

McLeod, P. L., Baron, R. S., Marti, M. W., & Yoon, K. (1997). The eyes have it: Minority influence in face-to-face and computer-mediated group discussion. *Journal of Applied Psychology, 82*, 706-718.

McMillan, D. W., & Chavis, D. M. (1986). Sense of community: A definition and theory. *Journal of Community Psychology, 14*, 6-23.

Meier, A. (2000). Offering social support via the Internet: A case study of an online support group for social workers. *Journal of Technology in Human Services, 17*(2-3), 237-266.

Meixell, M.J. (2006). Collaborative Manufacturing for Mass Customization. [Retrieved on February 15 from the George Manson University at http://www.som.gmu.edu/faculty/profiles/mmeixell/collaborative%20Planning%20&%20Mass%20Customization.pdf ]

Meixell, M.J. and Gargeya, V.B. (2005). Global supply chain design: A literature review and critique. Transportation Research, 41(6), 531-550 [Retrieved on February 15, 2006 from the Science Direct web site resource at http://top25.sciencedirect.com/index.php?subject_area_id=4 .]

Mellor, S. J., Kendall, S., Uhl, A., & Weise, D. (2004). *MDA distilled.* Boston: Addison-Wesley.

Melville, N., Kraemer, K., & Gurbaxani, V. (2004). Information technology and organizational performance: An integrative model of IT business value. *MIS Quarterly, 28*(2), 283-322.

Mesch, G. S., & Levanon, Y. (2004). Community networking and locally-based social ties in two suburban localities. *City & Community, 2*(4), 335-351.

Meyerson, D., Weick, K. E., & Kramer, R. M., (1996). Swift trust and temporary groups, in R. M. Kramer and T. R. Tyler (Eds.). *Trust in Organizations: Frontiers of Theory and Research.* Thousand Oaks, CA: Sage Publications.

Mezak, S. (2005). *The seven deadly dangers of outsourced software development.* Retrieved April 2005 from http://www.accelerance.com

Michael, J., & Yukl, G. (1993) Managerial level and subunit function as determinants of networking behavior in organisations. *Group & Organisation Management,* 18(3), 328-351.

Microsoft (2003). *Internet &networking dictionary.* Redmond: Microsoft Press.

Millen, D. R., & Patterson, J. F. (2002). *Stimulating social engagement in a community network.* Paper presented at the ACM 2002 Conference on Computer Supported Cooperative Work.

Mintzberg, H. (1973). *The nature of managerial work.* New York: Harper and Row.

Mitchell, J. C. (1969). The concept and use of social networks. In J. C. Mitchell (Ed.), *Social networks in urban situations. Analyses of personal relationships in central African towns* (pp. 1-50). Manchester: Manchester University Press.

Mizruchi, M. S. (1994). Social network analysis: Recent achievements and current controversies. *Acta Sociologica, 37*, 329- 43.

Monnai, T., Arai, E., Oda, J., Tomiyama, T., & Hotta, A. (2004). *A proposal of design vision for artifact design and production in the 21$^{st}$ century: A perspective from the design engineering section of the National Committee for Artifact Design and Production.* Tokyo: Science Council of Japan.

Montoya-Weiss, M., Massey, A. P., & Song, M. (2001). Getting it together: Temporal coordination and conflict management in global virtual teams. *Academy of Management Journal, 44*, 1251-63.

Morgan, G. (1986). *Images of organization.* Beverly Hills, CA: Sage Publications.

Morris, C.G., & Hackman, J.R. (1969). Behavioral correlates of perceived leadership. *Journal of Personality and Social Psychology, 13,* 350-361.

Morrison, E.W., & Phelps, C. (1999). Taking charge: Extra-role efforts to initiate workplace change. *Academy of Management Journal, 42*(4), 403-419.

Mulac, A., Erlandson, K. T., Farrar, W. J., & Hallett, J. S. (1998). Uh-huh. What's That all About? Differing Interpretations of Conversational Backchannels and Questions as Source of Miscommunication Across Gender Boundaries. *Communication Research, 25*(6), 641-668.

Muller, F. (1999). *Mobile commerce report* [Internet]. Durlacher. Retrieved June 11, 2003, from the World Wide Web: http://www.durlacher.com/bbus/resreports.asp

Muller, M. J., & Carey, K. (2002). *Design as a minority discipline in a software company: Toward requirements for a community of practice.* Paper presented at the SIGCHI conference on Human factors in computing systems.

Murphy, P.R., & Jackson, S.E. (1999). Managing work role performance: Challenges for twenty-first-century organizations and their employees. In D.R. Ilgen & E.D. Pulakos (Eds.), *The changing nature of performance: Implications for staffing, motivation, and development* (pp. 325-365). San Francisco: Jossey-Bass.

Nah, S., Veenstra, A. S., & Shah, D. V. (2006). The Internet and anti-war activism: A case study of information, expression, and action. *Journal of Computer Mediated Communication, 12*(1).

Nahapiet, J., & Ghoshal, S. (1998). Social capital, intellectual capital, and the organizational advantage. *Academy of Management Review, 23*(2), 242-266.

Natovich, J. (2003). Vendor related risks in IT development: A chronology of outsourced project failure. *Technology Analysis & Strategic Managements, 15*(4), 409-419.

Nelson, K. M., & Cooprider, J. G., (1996). The contribution of shared knowledge to IS group performance. *MIS Quarterly, 20*(4), 409-432.

Nemiro, J.E. (2004*). Creativity in Virtual Teams, Key Components for Success*, Pfeiffer/John Wiley and Sons.

Nergård, H.., Ericson, Å., Bergström, M., Sandberg, S., Larsson, T., Törlind, P. (2006). Functional Product Development – Discussing Knowledge Enabling Technologies, *International Design Conference, Design 2006,* Dubrovnik, Croatia.

Netz, J. S., & Taylor, B. A. (2002). Maximum or minimum differentiation? Location patterns of retail outlets. *The Review of Economics and Statistics, 84*(1), 162.

Niederman, F., Beise, C. M., & Beranek, P. M. (1993). Facilitation issues in distributed group support systems. *Proceedings of the 1993 conference on Computer personnel research,* 299-312.

Niederman, F., Beise, C. M., & Beranek, P. M. (1996). Issues and concerns about computer-supported meetings: The facilitator's perspective. *MIS Quarterly, 20*(1), 1-22.

Nilsson, A.G. et al. (1999). *Perspectives on Business Modelling, Understanding and Changing Organisations,* Springer-Verlag.

Nilsson, P., & Andersson, F. (2004). Process-driven Product Development – Managing Manufacturing Requirements, In Horváth, I., & Xirouchakis, P. (Eds.), *Proceedings Fifth International Symposium on Tools and Methods of Competitive Engineering* (pp. 395-404). Rotterdam: Millpress.

Nonaka, I. (1991). The knowledge-creating company. *Harvard Business Review, 69*(6), 96-104.

Nonaka, I., & Takeuchi, H. (1995). *The knowledge-creating company: How Japanese companies create the dynamics of innovation.* New York: Oxford University Press.

Nonaka, I., Toyama, R., & Nagata, A. (2000). A firm as a knowledge-creating entity: A new perspective on the theory of the firm. *Industrial and Corporate Change, 9*(1), 1-20.

Nonnecke, B., & Preece, J. (1999). *Shedding light on lurkers in online communities.* Paper presented at the Ethnographic Studies in Real and Virtual Environments: Inhabited Information Spaces and Connected Communities, Edinburgh, Edinburgh, Scotland.

Noy, N.F., & McGuinness, D.L. (2001*). Ontology Development 101: A Guide to Creating Your First Ontology*, Stanford Knowledge Systems Laboratory Technical Report KSL-01-05 and Stanford Medical Informatics Technical Report SMI-2001-0880. Stanford University: Stanford Knowledge Systems Laboratory.

Nunamaker, J. F., Dennis, A. R., Valacich, J. S., Vogel, D. R., & George, J. F. (1991). Electronic meeting systems to support group work. *Communications of the ACM, 34*(7), 40-61.

Nunamaker, J. F., Dennis, A. R., Valacich, J. S., Vogel, D. R., & George, J. F. (1991). Electronic meeting systems to support group work. *Communications of ACM, 34*(7), 40-61.

O'Donnell, E. (2005). Enterprise risk management: A systems-thinking framework for the event identification phase. *International Journal of accounting information systems, 6*(3), 177-195.

O'Loughlin, C., & Coenders, G. (2004). Estimation of the European customer satisfaction index: Maximum likelihood versus partial least squares. Application to postal services. *Total Quality Management & Business Excellence, 15*(9-10), 1231-1255.

O'Neill, D. K., & Gomez, L. M., 1994. The collaboratory notebook: A distributed knowledge building environment for project learning. *Proceedings of ED MEDIA 94.* Vancouver B.C., Canada.

Obst, P. L., & White, K. M. (2004). Revisiting the Sense of Community Index: A confirmatory factor analysis. *Journal of Community Psychology, 32*(6), 691-705.

Obst, P. L., Smith, S., & Zinkieqicz, L. (2002). An exploration of sense of community: Part 3. Dimensions and predictors of psychological sense of community in geographical communities. *Journal of Community Psychology, 30*(1), 119-133.

Obst, P., & White, K. M. (2005). An exploration of the interplay between psychological sense of community, social identification and salience. *Journal of Community & Applied Social Psychology, 15,* 127-135.

Oeser, O.A., & Harary, F. (1964). A mathematical model for structural role theory, II. *Human Relations,* 17(1), 3-17.

Oliver, R. L. (1997). *Satisfaction: A behavioural perspective on consumer.* Boston: Irwin McGraw-Hill.

Orlikowski, W. J., Yates, J., Okamura, K., & Fujimoto, M. (1995). Shaping electronic communication: The metastructuring of technology in the context of use. *Organization Science, 6*(4), 423-444.

Ott, J. S. (1989). *Organizational culture perspective.* Chicago: The Dorsey Press.

Outsourcing Institute. (2005). Retrieved April 2005 from http://www.outsourcing.com

Pahl, G., & Beitz, W. (1996). *Engineering Design: A Systematic Approach.* London: Springer.

Pahl, G., & Beitz, W., (1996). *Engineering Design – A Systematic Approach.* London, Great Britain: Springer-Verlag Ltd.

Pan, S. L., & Leidner, D. E. (2003). Bridging communities of practice with information technology in pursuit of global knowledge sharing. *Journal of Strategic Information Systems, 12*(1), 71-88.

Panayotopoulou, L., Bourantas, D., & Papalexandris, N. (2003). Strategic human resource management and its effects on firm performance: an implementation of the competing values framework. *International Journal of Human Resource Management, 14*(4), 680-699.

Paper, D., Chang, R-D. (2005). The State of Business Process Reengineering: A Search for Success Factors, *Total Quality Management,* 16(1), 21–133.

Parks, M. R., & Floyd, K. (1995, January 10, 2003). Making Friends in Cyberspace. *Journal of Computer Mediated Communication 1(4)* Retrieved October 3, 2007, from http://www.ascusc.org/jcmc/vol1/issue4/parks.html

Paul, D. L. (2006). Collaborative activities in virtual settings: A knowledge management perspective of telemedicine. *Journal of Management Information Systems, 22*(4), 143-176.

Paulhus, D.L. (1991). Measurement and control of response bias. In J.P. Robinson, P.R. Shaver, & L.S. Wrightsman (Eds.), *Measures of personality and socialpsychological attitudes* (pp. 17-59). New York: Academic Press.

Paulk, M. C., Curtis, B., Chrissis, M. B., & Weber, C. V. (1993). Capability maturity model, version 1.1. *IEEE Software,* 10(4), 18-27.

Pawlak, A., Sandkuhl, K., Cholewa, W., & Indrusiak, L. (Eds.). (2007). *Coordination of Collaborative Engineering. 5. Intl. Workshop on Collaborative Engineering.* Krakow, Poland.

Pawlowski, S. D., Robey, D., & Raven, A. (2000). *Supporting shared information systems: boundary objects, communities, and brokering.* Paper presented at the 21st International Conference on Information Systems.

Pearce, C.L., & Conger, J.A. (2003). *Shared leadership: Reframing the hows and whys of leadership.* Thousand Oaks, CA: Sage.

Pendleton, M. D. (2005). Balancing competing interests in information products: A conceptual rethink. *Information & Communications Technology Law, 14*(3), 241-254.

Perelman, M. (2003). *The perverse economy.* New York: Palgrave MacMillan.

Peters, T.J., & Waterman, R.H., Jr. (1982). *In search of excellence.* New York, NY: Harper & Row.

Pfeffer, J., & Salancik, G. R. (1978). *The external control of organizations.* New York: Harper and Row.

Piccoli, G., & Ives, B., (2003). Trust and the unintended effects of behavior control in virtual teams. *MIS Quarterly, 27*(3), 157-180.

Pinsonneault, A., & Caya, O. (2005). Virtual teams: What we know, what we don't know. *International Journal of e-Collaboration, 1*(3), 1-16.

Podsakoff, P.M., & Organ, D.W. (1986). Self reports in organizational research: problems and prospects. *Journal of Management,* 12(4), 531-544.

Pollice, G. (2001). RUP and XP: Part I. Finding common ground. *The Rational Edge.* Retrieved from http://www.therationaledge.com

Pollice, G. (2001). RUP and XP: Part II. Valuing differences. *The Rational Edge.* Retrieved from http://www.therationaledge.com

Pollice, G. (2004). RUP and extreme programming: Complementing processes. In L. Liu & B. Roussev (Eds.), *Management of object-oriented software development.* Hershey, PA: Idea Group Publishing.

Poole, M. S., & DeSanctis, G. (1990). Understanding the use of group decision support systems: The theory of adaptive structuration. In J. Fulk & C. Steinfield (Eds.), *Organizations and communication technology* (pp. 173-193). Newbury Park, CA: Sage.

Popplewell, K., & Harding, J. A. (2004). Impact of simulation and moderation through the virtual enterprise life-cycle. In K. Mertins & M. Rabe (Eds.), *Experiences from the future: New methods and applications in simulation for production and logistics* (pp. 299-308). Berlin, Germany: IPK Berlin.

Porter, M. E. (1998). *Competitive strategy. Techniques for analyzing and strategic flexibility: A performance dilemma in designing new product development configurations.* Simon & Schuster: New York.

Postmes, T., & Spears, R. (2002). Behavior online: Does anonymous computer-mediated communication reduce gender inequality? *Personality and Social Psychology Bulletin, 28,* 1073-1083.

Postmes, T., Spears, R., & Lea, M. (1998). Breaching or building social boundaries? Side-effects of computer-mediated communications. *Communication Research, 25*(6), 689-715.

Powell, A., Piccoli, G., & Ives, B. (2004). Virtual teams: A review of current literature and directions for future research. *The Data Base for Advances in Information Systems, 35*(1), 6-36.

Prasad, B. (1997). *Concurrent Engineering Fundamentals, Integrated Product Development,* Prentice Hall.

Prescott, J. E. (1986). Environments as moderators of the relationship between strategy and performance. *Academy of Management Journal, 29*(2), 329-346.

Pretorius, C.J., Steyn, H. (2005). Knowledge management in project environments, *African Journal of Business Management, 36*(3).

Project Management Institute (PMI) Standards Committee. (1996). *A guide to the project management body of knowledge.* Newtown Square, PA: Project Management Institute.

Project Management Institute (PMI). (2004). *A guide to the project management body of knowledge* (3rd ed.). Newtown Square, PA.

Quinn, R.E. (1988). *Beyond rational management: Mastering the paradoxes and competing demands of high performance.* San Francisco: Jossey-Bass.

Quinn, R.E., Faerman, S.R., Thompson, M.P., & McGrath, M.R. (1996). *Becoming a master manager: A competency framework.* New York: John Wiley.

Radicati Group Inc. (2004). *Market numbers summary update.* Palo Alto, CA.

Ramello, G. B. (2005). Intellectual property and the markets of ideas. *Review of Network Economics, 4*(2), 161-180.

Ramesh, R., & Whinston, A., (1994). Claims, arguments, and decisions: Formalisms for Representation, Gaming, and Coordination. *Information Systems Research, 5*(3), 294-325.

Rangarajan, N., & Rohrbaugh, J. (2003). Multiple roles of online facilitation: An example in any-time, any-place meetings. *Group Facilitation: A Research and Applications Journal, 5,* 26-36.

Reagans, R., & Zuckerman, E. W. (2001). Networks, diversity, and productivity: The social capital of corporate R&D teams. *Organization Science, 12,* 502-17.

Reichheld, F. F. (2003). The one number you need to grow. *Harvard Business Review,* 46-54.

Reina, D., & Reina, M., (1999). *Trust and betrayal in the workplace.* San Francisco, CA: Berrett-Koehler.

Remidez, H., (2003). System structure design and social consequence: The impact of message templates on affectivity in virtual teams. Unpublished doctoral dissertation. University of Missouri, Columbia.

Ren, Y., Kraut, R., & Kiesler, S. (2007). Applying Common Identity and Bond Theory to Design of Online Communities. *Organization Studies, 28*(3), 77-408.

Rettie, R., & Brum, (2001). M. M-commerce: the role of SMS text messages. In *Proceedings of the Fourth Biennial International Conference on Telecommunications and Information Markets (COTIM 2001)*, Karlsruhe, Germany; http://www.ebusinessforum.gr/content/downloads/047_brum_mcommerce.pdf

Reynolds, T., & Gutman, J. (1988). Laddering Theory, Theory, Method, Analysis, and Interpretation. *Journal of Advertising Research, 28*(1), 11-31.

Rice, R. E. (1984). Mediated group communication. In R. E. Rice & Associates (Eds.), *The new media: Communication, research, and technology* (pp. 129-156). Beverly Hills, CA: Sage.

Rice, R. E. (1992). Task analyzability, use of new media, and effectiveness: A multi-site exploration of media richness. *Organization Science, 3*(4), 475-500.

Roberts, L. D., Smith, L. M., & Pollock, C. M. (2002). MOOing till the cows come home: The sense of community in virtual environments. In C. C. Sonn (Ed.), *Psychological sense of community: Research, applications, implications.* New York: Kluwer Academic/Plenum.

Roberts, P. W., & Amit, R. (2003). The dynamics of innovative activity and competitive advantage: The case of Australian retail banking, 1981 to 1995. *Organization Science, 14*(2), 107-122.

Robey, D., Ross, J. W., & Boudreau, M.-C. (2002). Learning to implement enterprise systems: An exploratory study of the dialectics of change. *Journal of Management Information Systems, 19*(1), 17-46.

Rodgers, R., & Hunter, J.E. (1991). Impact of management by objectives on organizational productivity. *Journal of Applied Psychology, 76*(2), 322-336.

Rodgers, S., & Chen, Q. (2005). Internet community group participation: Psychosocial benefits for women with breast cancer. *Journal of Computer Mediated Communication, 10*(4).

Rogers, E. M. (2003). *Diffusion of Innovations* (5th ed.). New York: Free Press. A division of Simon & Schuster, Inc. 1230 Avenue of the Americas.

Rokeach, M. (1973). *The nature of human values.* New York, NY: The Free Press a division of McMillan Publishing Co.Inc.http://www.wirelessreview.com/ar/wireless_numbers_sky/

Romano, N. C. J., Nunamaker, J. F. J., Briggs, R. O., & Mittleman, D. D. (1999). Distributed GSS facilitation and participation: field actionresearch. [Conference paper]. *System Sciences, 1999. HICSS-32. Proceedings of the 32nd Annual Hawaii International Conference on*, 1-12.

Romer, P. (1993). Idea gaps and object gaps in economic development. *Journal of Monetary Economics, 32*(3), 543-573.

Ropers, S. (2001). New business models for the mobile revolution. *EAI*(February), 53-57.

Rose, G., & Straub, D. W. (1998). Predicting General IT Use: Applying TAM to the Arabic World. *Journal of Global Information Management, 6*(3), 39-46.

Rosenthal, R., & Rosnow, R.L. (1991). *Essentials of Behavioral Research: Methods and Data Analysis.* Boston, MA: McGraw Hill.

Roussev, B., & Akella, R. (n.d.). Agile outsourcing projects: Structure and management. *International Journal of e-Collaboration, 2*(4), 37-52.

Roussev, B., & Rousseva, Y. (2006). *Unreliable interlocutors in information systems development.* Proceedings of San Diego International Systems Conference, San Diego, CA.

Royal, M. A., & Rossi, R. J. (1999). Predictors of within-school differences in teachers' sense of community. *Journal of Educational Research, 92*, 259-267.

Royce, W. (1998). *Software project management: A unified framework.* Reading, MA: Addison-Wesley, Inc.

Royce, W. (2002). The case for results-based software management. *The Rational Edge.* Retrieved from http://www.therationaledge.com

Russel, B., & Chattargee, S. (2003). Relationship quality: The undervalued dimension of software quality. *Communications of the ACM, 46*(8), 85-89.

Rutkowski, A.-F., Vogel, D., Bemelmans, T. M. A., & Van Genuchten, M. (2002). Group support systems and virtual collaboration: The HKNet Project. *Group Decision and Negotiation, 11*(2), 101-125.

Sachs, J. (2005). *The UN Millennium Project: Investing in development. A practical plan to achieve the Millennium Development Goals.* New York: The United Nations Development Program.

Sahin, F. and Powell Robinson, E.P. (2002). Flow coordination and information sharing in supply chains: review, implications, and directions for future research. *Decision Sciences, 33*(4), 505-536.

Salam, S., Cox, J.F., & Sims, H.P. (1997). In the eye of the beholder: How leadership relates to 360-degree performance ratings. *Group & Organizational Management, 22*(2), 185-209.

Sandkuhl, K., Smirnov, A., & Shilov, N. Configuration of automotive collaborative engineering and flexible supply networks. In P. Cunningham & M. Cunningham (Eds.), *Expanding the Knowledge Economy – Issues, Applications, Case Studies.* Amsterdam: IOS Press.

Santos, J., Doz, Y., & Williamson, P. (2004). Is your innovation process global? *MIT Sloan Management Review, 45*(4), 31-37.

Sarason, S. B. (1974). *The psychological sense of community: Prospects for a Community Psychology.* San Francisco: Jossey-Bass.

Sarker, S. & Wells, J. D. (2003). Understanding Mobile handheld Device use and Adoption. Communications of the ACM, 46(12), p.35-40.

Sarker, S., & Sahay, S. (2001). Information systems development by US-Norwegian virtual teams: Implications of time and space. *Proceedings of the 36ᵗʰ Hawaii International Conference on Systems Sciences.*

Sarker, S., & Sahay, S. (2003). Understanding virtual team development: an interpretive study. *Journal of the Association for Information Systems, 4,* 1-38.

Sarker, S., & Sahay, S., (2004). Implications of space and time for distributed work: an interpretive study of US-Norwegian systems development teams. *European Journal of Information Systems, 13*(1), 3-20.

Sarker, S., Valacich, J., & Sarker, S., (2003). Virtual team trust: Instrument development and validation in an IS educational environment. *Information Resource Management Journal, 16*(2), 35-55.

Satchwell, R., & Dugger, W. (1996). A united vision: Technology for all Americans. *Journal of Technology Education, 7*(2), 5-12.

Sawhney, M., Wolcott, R. C., & Arroniz, I. (2006). The 12 different ways for companies to innovate. *MIT Sloan Management Review, 47*(3), 75-81.

Sayer, A. (2000). *Realism and social science.* London: Sage.

Scardamalia, M., & Bereiter, C., (1994). Computer support for knowledge-building communities. *The Journal of Learning Sciences, 3*(3), 265-283.

Schlenoff, C., Ivester, R., Libes, D., Denno, P., & Szykman, S. (1999). An Analysis of Existing Ontological Systems for Applications in Manufacturing. *Proceedings of Design Engineering Technical Conferences and Computers and Information in Engineering Conference.* New York, NY: American Society of Mechanical Engineers.

Schneider, G.P., and Perry, J.T. (2000). *Electronic Commerce.* Cambridge, MA: Course Technology.

Schrott, G., & Glückler, J. (2004). What makes mobile computer supported cooperative work mobile? Towards a better understanding of cooperative mobile interactions. *International Journal of Human-Computer Studies, 60,* 737-52.

Schubert, P., Leimstoll, U., & Romano, N. C. (2003). Internet groupware systems for project management: Experiences from a longitudinal study. *Proceedings of the 16ᵗʰ Bled eCommerce Conference: eTransformation,* 611-631.

Schuemmer, T. (2003). Evolving a groupware pattern language. *ECSCW2003: Fifth International Workshop on Collaborative Editing.*

Schuh, P. (2005). *Integrating agile development in the real world.* Hingham, MA: Charles River Media, Inc.

Schuman, S. (2005). *The IAF Handbook of Group Facilitation: Best Practices from the Leading Organization in Facilitation.* San Francisco, CA: Jossey-Bass.

Schuster, E. (1998). A community bound by words: Reflections on a nursing home writing group. *Journal of Aging Studies, 12*(2), 137-148.

Schwarz, R. (2002). *The Skilled Facilitator.* San Francisco, CA: Jossey-Bass.

Schwarz, R., Davidson, A., Carlson, P., & McKinney, S. (2005). *The Skilled Facilitator Fieldbook: Tips, Tools, and Tested Methods for Consultants, Facilitators, Managers, Trainers, and Coaches.* San Francisco, CA: Jossey-Bass.

Scott, J. E. (2000). Facilitating interorganizational learning with information technology. *Journal of Management Information Systems, 17*(2), 81-113.

Selen, W., and Soliman, F. (2002). Operations in today's demand chain management framework. *Journal of Operations Management*, 20(6), 667-673.

Senge, P. M. (1990). *The fifth discipline: The art and practice of the learning organization*. New York, NY: Doubleday/Currency.

Senge, P., (1990). *The fifth discipline: The art and practice of the learning organization*. New York: Doubleday.

Shamir, B. (1999). Leadership in boundaryless organizations: Disposable or indispensable? *European Journal of Work and Organizational Psychology*, 8(1), 49-71.

Shani, A. B., Sena, J. A., & Stebbins, M. W. (2000). Knowledge work teams and groupware technology: Learning from Seagate's experience. *Journal of Knowledge Management, 4*(2), 111-124.

Shapiro, C., & Varian, H. R. (1999). *Information rules: A strategic guide to the network economy*. Boston, MA: Harvard Business School Press.

Sharp, A., MacDermott, P. (2001). *Workflow Modeling: Tools for Process Improvement and Application Development*, Artech House Publishers, Norwood, MA.

Shaw, M.E. (1981). *Group dynamics: The psychology of small group behavior*. New York: McGraw-Hill Book Company.

Sheard, J. (2004). *Electronic learning communities: strategies for establishment and management* Paper presented at the 9th annual SIGCSE conference on Innovation and technology in computer science education.

Shenhar, A. J. (1998). From theory to practice: Toward a typology of project management styles. *IEEE Transactions on Engineering Management, 45*(1), 33-48.

Sherwood, K. D. (2002). *Overcome email overload with Microsoft Outlook 2000 and Outlook 2002: Get through your electronic mail faster*. Palo Alto, CA: World Wide Webfoot Press.

Sheth, J. N., Newman, B. I. & Gross, B. L. (1991). *Consumption values and market choice: Theory and applications* (1991 ed.): South-Western Publishing Co.

Sheth, J. N., Newman, B. I., & Gross, B. L. (1991). Why we buy what we buy: A theory of consumption values. *Journal of Business Research, 22*, 150-170.

Shipper, F. (1991). Mastery and frequency of managerial behaviors relative to sub-unit effectiveness. *Human Relations*, 44(4), 371-388.

Short, J., Williams, E., & Christie, B. (1976). *The social psychology of telecommunications*. London, England: John Wiley and Sons.

Shostack, L.G.(1987). Service Positioning through Structural Change, *Journal of Marketing, 51*(1), 34-43.

Silver, M., (1988). User perceptions of decision support system restrictiveness: An experiment. *Journal of Management Information Systems, 5*(1), 51-65.

Simch-Levy, D., Kaminsky, P., Simchi-Levy, E. (2003). *Designing and managing the supply chain – concepts, strategies and case studies, Second Edition*. New York: McGraw-Hill.

Sivasubramaniam, N., Murray, W. D., Avolio, B. J., & Jung, D. L. (2002). A longitudinal model of the effects of team leadership and group potency on group performance. *Group and Organization Management, 27*, 66-96.

Smith, H. A., & McKeen, J. D. (2003). The Evolution of the KM Function. *Journal*. Retrieved from http://business.queensu.ca/knowledge/workingpapers/working/working_03-07.pdf

Smith, P.G., Reinertsen, D.G. (1997). *Developing Products in Half the Time*, John Wiley and Sons.

Smith, R.P., Morrow, J.A. (1999). Product development process modeling, *Design Studies, 20*(3), 237-261.

Sohlenius, G. (1992). Concurrent Engineering. *CIRP annals*, 41(2), pp. 645-655. Retrieved Mars 11, 2005, from http://www.cirp.net/publications.

Sorenson, O., Rivkin, J. W., & Fleming, L. (2005) *Informational complexity and the flow of knowledge across social boundaries*. Paper in Evolutionary Economic Geography. Utrecht: University of Utrecht.

Sorrentino, R.M., & Boutillier, R.G. (1975). The effects of quantity and quality of verbal interaction on ratings of leadership ability. *Journal of Experimental Social Psychology, 11*, 403-411.

Sosik, J. J., Avolio, B. J., & Kahai, S. S. (1997). Effects of leadership style and anonymity on group potency and effectiveness in a group decision support system environment. *Journal of Applied Psychology, 82*(1), 89-103.

Sosik, J. J., Avolio, B. J., Kahai, S. S., & Jung, D. I. (1998). Computer-supported work group potency and effectiveness: The role of transformational leadership, anonymity, and task interdependence. *Computers in Human Behavior, 14*(3), 491-511.

Sparrowe, R. T., Liden, R. C., Wayne, S. J., & Kraimer, M. L. (2001). Social networks and the performance of individuals and groups. *Academy of Management Journal, 44*, 316-25.

Spender, J. C. (1996). Making knowledge the basis of a dynamic theory of the firm. *Strategic Management Journal, 17*, 45-62.

Spiro, L. N., & Baig, E. C. (1999, February 22). Who needs a broker? *Business Week, 3617*, 113.

Sproull, L., & Kiesler, S. (1986). Reduceing social context cues: Electronic mail in organizational communication. *Management Science, 32*, 1492-512.

Sproull, L., & Kiesler, S. (1991). Computers, networks and work. *Scientific American, 265*(3), 84-91.

Sproull, L., & Kiesler, S. (1991). *Connections: New ways of working in the networked organization.* Cambridge, MA: MIT Press.

Sproull, L., & Kiesler, S. B. (1991). *Connections: New ways of working in the networked organization.* Cambridge, MA: The MIT Press.

Sridhar, N., Mahapatra, R., & Mangalaraj, G. (2005). Challenges of migrating to agile methodologies. *Communications of the ACM, 48*(5).

Standing, C., Benson, S., & Karjaluoto, H. (2005). Consumer perspectives on mobile advertising and marketing. In *Proceedings of the Australia and New Zealand Marketing Academy Conference*, Perth, Australia, December 5-7, pp. 135-141 [CD-ROM].

Standish Group. (2003). *CHAOS research report.* Retrieved from http://www.standishgroup.com

Staples, D. S., & Jarvenpaa, S. L. (2000). *Using Electronic Media for Information Sharing Activities: A Replication and Extension.* Paper presented at the 21st International Conference on Information Systems.

Staples, D.S., Wong, I. K., & Cameron, A. F. (2004). Best Practices for Virtual Team Effectiveness. In D. Pauleen (Ed.). *Virtual teams: Projects, protocols and processes* (pp. 160-185). Hershey, PA: Idea Group Publishing

Stasser, G., Vaughan, S. I., & Stewart, D. D. (2000). Pooling unshared information: The benefits of knowing how access to information is distributed among group members. *Organizational Behavior and Human Decision Processes, 82,* 102-116.

Staw, B. M. (1975). Attribution of the causes of performance: A new alternative interpretation of cross-sectional research on organizations. *Organizational Behavior and Human Performance, 13,* 414-32.

Stephens, M., & Rosenberg, D. (2003). *Extreme programming refactored: The case against XP.* San Francisco: Apress.

Stewart, C. M., Shields, S. F., & Sen, N. (2001). Diversity in On-Line Discussions: A study of Cultural and Gender Differences in Listervs. In C. Ess & F. Sudweeks (Eds.), *Culture, Technology, Communication: Towards an Intercultural Global Village* (pp. 161-186). Albany, NJ: State University of New York Press.

Stogdill, R.M. (1950). Leadership, membership, and organization. *Psychological Bulletin, 47,* 1-14.

Stogdill, R.M. (1974). *Handbook of leadership.* New York: The Free Press.

Straub, D. W. (1994). The Effect of Culture on IT Diffusion: E-mail and FAX in Japan and the U.S. *Information Systems Research, 5*(1), 23-47.

Straus, S.G. (1997). Technology, group process, and group outcomes: Testing the connections in computer-mediated and face-to-face groups. *Human Computer Interaction, 12*(3), 227-266.

Stuckey, B., & Smith, J. D. (2004). Sustaining communities of practice. *Proceeding of WBC2004 - The IADIS International Conference on Web-based Communities,* 24–26.

Suh, N.P. (1990). *The Principles of Design.* New York, NY: Oxford University Press.

Sultan, F. & R. B. Henrichs (2000). "Consumer preferences for Internet services over time: Initial explorations." Journal of Consumer Marketing 17(no. 5): 386-402.

Sultan, F. & Rohm, A. (2005). The Coming of the Era of "Brand in the hand" Marketing. MIT Sloan Management Review, 47(1), p.83-90.

Suthers, D., 1998. Representations for scaffolding collaborative inquiry on ill-structured problems. Paper presented at the *1998 AERA Annual Meeting.* San Diego, CA.

Swan, J. A., Scarbrough, H., & Robertson, M. (2002). The Construction of 'Communities of Practice' in the Management of Innovation. *Management Learning, 33*(4), 477-496.

Sweeney, J. C., & Soutar, G. N. (2001). Consumer Perceived Value: The development pf a multiple item scale. *Journal of Retailing, 77*(2001), 203-220.

Sweeney, J. C., Soutar, G. N., & Johnson, L. W. (1999). The Role of Perceived risk in the quality-value relationship: A study in a retail environment. *Journal of Retailing, 77*(1), 75-105.

Szykman, S., Racz, J., & Sriram, R. (1999). The Representation of Function in Computer-Based Design. *Proceedings of Design Engineering Technical Conferences and Computers and Information in Engineering Conference.* New York, NY: American Society of Mechanical Engineers.

Tabachnik, B. G., & Fidell, L. S. (2001). *Using multivariate statistics* (4th ed.). Needham Heights, MA: Allyn & Bacon.

Taggar, S. Hackett, R., & Saha, S. (1999). Leadership emergent in autonomous work teams: Antecedents and outcomes. *Personnel Psychology, 52*, 899-926.

Takahashi, M., Fujimoto, M., & Yamasaki, N. (2003, November 9–12, 2003). *The active lurker: influence of an in-house online community on its outside environment.* Paper presented at the 2003 international ACM SIGGROUP conference on Supporting group work, Sanibel Island, Florida, USA.

Tannen, D. (1991). Teachers' Classroom Strategies Should Recognize that Men and Women Use Language Differently. *The Chronicle of Higher Education, June 19*, B1-B3.

Tannen, D. (1994). *You Just Don't Understand Women and Men in Conversation.* New York, NY: Ballantine Books.

Tannen, D. (1995). The Power of Talk: Who Gets Heard and Why. *Harvard Business Review, 73*(5), 138-148.

Tarasov, V., & Lundqvist, M. (2006). Modeling collaborative design competence with ontologies. *International Journal of e-Collaboration: Special Issue on the State of the Art and Future Challenges on Collaborative Design, 3*(4), 46-62.

Tarassov, V., Sandkuhl, K., & Henoch, B. (2006). *Using ontologies for representation of individual and enterprise competence models.* Paper presented at the Proceedings of the Fourth IEEE International Conference on Computer Sciences Research, Innovation and Vision for the Future, RIVF 2006, Ho-Chi-Minh City, Vietnam.

Tarmizi, H., & de Vreede, G. J. (2005). A Facilitation Task Taxonomy for Communities of Practice. *Proceedings of the Eleventh Americas Conference on Information Systems*, 1-11.

Tarmizi, H., de Vreede, G. J., & Zigurs, I. (2006). Identifying Challenges for Facilitation in Communities of Practice. *System Sciences, 2006. HICSS'06. Proceedings of the 39th Annual Hawaii International Conference on, 1*, 1-10.

Tarmizi, H., de Vreede, G.-J., & Zigurs, I. (2007). A Facilitators' Perspective on Successful Virtual Communities of Practice. *Proceedings of the 13th Americas Conference on Information Systems.*

Taylor, H. (2006). Critical risks in outsourced projects: The intractable and the unforeseen. *Communications of the ACM, 49*(11).

Taylor, S., & Todd, P.A. (1995). Assessing IT usage: the role of prior experience. *MIS Quarterly, 19*(2),561-570.

Te'eni, D., & Kendall, J. E. (2004). Internet commerce and fundraising. In D. Young (Ed.), *Effective economic decision-making by nonprofit organizations* (pp. 167-189). New York: The Foundation Center.

Te'eni, D., (2001). Review: A cognitive-affective model of organizational communication for designing IT. *MIS Quarterly, 25*(2), 251-312.

Technology Partners International (TPI). (2005). *Technology Partners International Inc. quarterly index.* Retrieved from http://www.tpi.net

Teece, D. J. (2007). Explicating dynamic capabilities: The nature and microfoundations of (sustainable) enterprise performance. *Strategic Management Journal, 28*(13), 1319–1350.

Teece, D. J., Pisano, G., & Shuen, A. (1997). Dynamic capabilities and strategic management. *Strategic Management Journal, 18*(7), 509–533.

Teltzrow, M., & Kobsa, A. (2004). Impacts of User Privacy Preferences on Personalized Systems: a Comparative Study. In J. Karat, J. Vanderdonekt, C.-M. Karat & J. O. Blom (Eds.), *Designing personalized user experiences in eCommerce* (pp. 315 - 332). Norwell, MA: Kluwer Academic Publishers.

*The arts in New Jersey: A study of economic activity 1992-93.* (n.d.). NJ: NJSCA/South Jersey Cultural Alliance/Eagleton Institute, Rutgers University.

*The arts mean business: A study of economic activity, 2000. NJSCA/ArtPRIDE.* (2000). NJ: NJ Foundation/Rutgers University Graduate School of Education.

Tinnilä, M. (1995). Strategic perspective to business process redesign, *Business Process Re-engineering & Management Journal, 1*(1), 44-59.

Tiwana, A., & Keil, M. (2004). The one-minute risk assessment tool. *Communications of the ACM, 47*(11), 73-78.

Tiwana, A., & Keil, M. (2006). Functionality risk in software development. *IEEE Transactions on Engineering Management, 53*(3), 412-425.

Toth, K., Kruchten, P., & Paine, T. (1993). *Modernizing air traffic control through modern software methods.* Proceedings of the 38ᵗʰ Annual Air Traffic Control Association Conference, Nashville, TN.

Townsend, A. M., DeMarie, S. M., & Hendrickson, A. R. (1998). Virtual teams: Technology and the workplace of the future. *Academy of Management Executive, 12,* 17-28.

Townsend, J., & Donovan, P. (1999). *The Facilitator's Pocketbook.* Hants, UK: Management Pocketbooks.

Trevino, L. K., Webster, J., & Stein, E. W. (2000). Making connections: Complementary influences on communication media choices, attitudes, and use. *Organization Science, 11*(2), 163-182.

Tsang, M.M., Ho, S., & Liang, (2004). T. Consumer attitudes toward mobile advertising: an empirical study. *International Journal of Electronic Commerce, 8*(3), 65-78.

Tsui, A.S. (1984). A role set analysis of managerial reputation. *Organizational Behavior and Human Performance,* 34(11), 64-96.

Turban, E. & Aronson, J., (2001), *Decision Support Systems and Intelligent Systems.* Upper Saddle River, NJ: Prentice-Hall Inc.

Turban, E., McLean, E., & Wetherbe, J. (2002). *Information Technology for Management: Transforming Business in the Digital Economy* (Third ed.). Milton, Queensland: John Wiley & Sons.

Turvey, M. T. (1990). Coordination. *American Psychologist, 45*(8), 938-953.

Tushman, M. L. (1979). Work characteristics and subunit communication structure: A contingency analysis. *Administrative Science Quarterly, 24,* 82-98.

U.S. Census Bureau. (2003). Retrieved from http://eire.census.gov/popest/data/counties/tables/CO-EST2001-08/CO-EST2001-08-34.php

Ullman, D. G. (1997). *The Mechanical Design Process.* Singapore: McGraw-Hill Book Co.

Ulrich, K.T., Eppinger, S.D.(1995). *Product Design and Development,* McGraw-Hill.

UNESCO Institute for Statistics. (2003, November 25). International Standard Classification of Education (ISCED 1997). Retrieved September 20, 2005, from http://www.uis.unesco.org/ev.php?ID=3813_201&ID2=DO_TOPIC

Vakharia, A.J. (2002). E-business and supply chain management. *Decision Sciences,* 33(4), 495-504.

Valkeavaara, T. (1998). Human resource development roles and competencies in five European countries. *International Journal of Training and Development,* 2(3), 171-189.

Van de Ven, A. H. (2005). Running in packs to develop knowledge-intensive technologies. *MIS Quarterly, 29*(2), 365-378.

Van der Heijden, H. (2004). User acceptance of hedonic information systems. *MIS Quarterly, 28*(4), 695-703.

Van der Velde, M.E.G., Jansen, G.W.E., & Vinkenburg, C.J. (1999). Managerial activities among top and middle managers: self versus others perceptions. *Journal of Applied Management Studies,* 8(2), 161-174.

Van House, N. A., Butler, M. H., & Schiff, L. R. (1998). *Cooperative knowledge work and practices of trust: Sharing environmental planning data sets.* Paper presented at the ACM Conference on Computer Supported Cooperative Work.

Van Ryssen, S., & Godar, S. H. (2000). Going international without going international. *Journal of International Management, 6,* 49-60.

Vassileva, J., & Sun, L. (2007). An Improved Design and a Case Study of a Social Visualization Encouraging Participation in Online Communities. In J. M. Haake, S. F. Ochoa & A. Cechich (Eds.), *Groupware: Design, Implementation, and Use* (Vol. 4715, pp. 72-86).

Venkatesh, V., & Agarwal, R. (2006). A Usability-Centric Perspective on Purchase Behavior in E-Channels. *Management Science, 52*(3), 367-382.

Venkatesh, V., & Brown, S. A. (2001). A longitudinal investigation of personal computers in homes: adoption determinants and emerging challenges. *MIS Quarterly, 25*(1), 71-102.

Venkatesh, V., & Morris, M. G. (2000). Why Don't Men Ever Stop to Ask for Directions? Gender, Social Influence, and their Role in Technology Acceptance and Usage Behavior. *MIS Quarterly, 24*(1), 115-139.

Venkatesh, V., Morris, M.G., Davis, G.B., & Davis, F.D. (2003). User acceptance of information technology: toward a unified view. *MIS Quarterly, 27*( 3), 425-479.

Völter, M. (2002). Hope, belief and wizardry: Three different perspectives on project management. *EuroPLoP 2002: Seventh European Conference on Pattern Languages of Programs.*

Wakertin, M. E., Sayeed, L., & Hightower, R. (1997). Virtual teams versus face-to-face teams: An exploratory study of a web-based conference system. *Decision Sciences, 28*(4), 975-996.

Walkins, J. (1992). Information systems: The UK retail financial services sector. *Marketing Intelligence & Planning, 10*(6), 13-18.

Walther, J. B. (1992). Interpersonal effects in computer-mediated interaction: A relational perspective. *Communication Research, 19,* 52-90.

Walther, J. B. (1996). Computer mediated communication: Impersonal, interpersonal and hyperpersonal interaction. *Communication Research, 22,* 33-43.

Walther, J. B. (1996). Computer-mediated communication: Impersonal, interpersonal, and hyperpersonal interaction. *Communication Research, 23,* 3-43.

Walther, J. B., & Bunz, U. (2005). The rules of virtual groups: Trust, liking, and performance in computer-mediated communication. *Journal of Communication, 55,* 828-846.

Walther, J. B., & Tidwell, L. C. (1995). Nonverbal cues in computer-mediated communication, and the effect of chronemics on relational communication. *Journal of Organizational Computing, 5,* 355-378.

Walther, J. B., Loh, T., & Granka, L. (2005). Let me count the ways: The interchange of verbal and nonverbal cues in computer-mediated and face-to-face affinity. *Journal of Language and Social Psychology, 24,* 36-65.

Warkentin, M., & Beranek, P. M. (1999). Training to improve virtual team communication. *Information Systems Journal, 9,* 271-89.

Watson-Manheim, M. B., & Belanger, F. (2002). Exploring communication-based work processes in virtual work environments. In *Proceedings of the 36th Hawaii International Conference on Systems Sciences.*

Watson-Manheim, M. B., Chudoba, K. M., & Crowston, K. (2002). Discontinuities and continuities: A new way to understand virtual work. *Information Technology & People, 15*(3), 191-209.

Weatherall, A. (1998). Re-visioning Gender and Language Research. *Women and Language, 21*(1), 1-9.

Weaver, R. M. (1967). *A rhetoric and handbook.* New York: Holt, Rinehart, and Winston.

Webster, J., & Trevino, L. K. (1995). Rational and social theories as complementary explanations of communication media choices: Two policy-capturing studies. *Academy of Management Journal, 38*(6), 1544-1573.

Webster, J., & Wong, W. K. P. (2003, April). *Comparing traditional and virtual group forms: Identity, communication and trust in naturally occurring project teams.* Paper presented at the meeting of the Society for Industrial/Organizational Psychology, Orlando, Florida.

Weck, M., Hoymann, H., & Lescher, M. (2004). Effizienz und flexiblität beim mobilen einsatz von AR im service. *WT Werkstattstechnik, 94*(5), 242-246.

Wegge, J. (2006). Communication via videoconference: Emotional and cognitive consequences of seeing one's own picture, affective personality dispositions and disturbing events. *Human Computer Interaction, 21*(3), 273-318.

Weill, P., & Olson, M. H. (1989). An assessment of the contingency theory of management information systems. *Journal of Management Information Systems, 6*(1), 59-85.

Weis, R., Stamm, K., Smith, C., Nilan, M., Clark, F., Weis, J., et al. (2003). Communities of care and caring: The case of MSWatch.com®. *Journal of Health Psychology, 8*(1), 135-148.

Weisband, S. P. (1992). Group discussion and first advocacy effects in computer-mediated and face-to-face decision making groups. *Organizational Behavior and Human Decision Processes, 53,* 352-380.

Weisband, S. P., Scheider, S. K., & Connolly, T. (1995). Computer-mediated communication and social information: Status salience and status differences. *Academy of Management Journal, 38,* 1124-1151.

Weisband, S., Schenider, S., & Connolly, T. (1995). Computer-mediated communication and social information: Status salience and status differences. *Academy of Management Journal, 38,* 1124-51.

Wenger, E. C. (2001). Supporting Communities of Practice: A Survey of community-oriented Technologies, Available from http://www.ewenger.com/tech

Wenger, E. C., McDermott, R., & Snyder, W. M. (2002). *Cultivating Communities of Practice: A Guide to*

*Managing Knowledge.* Boston, MA: Harvard Business School Press.

Wernerfelt, B. (1984). A resource-based view of the firm. *Strategic Management Journal, 5*(2), 171-180.

Wesolowsky, G. O. (2001). Lectures on location theory. *INFOR, 39*(1), 124.

West, C., & Zimmerman, D. (1983). Small Insults: A Study of Interruptions in Cross-sex Conversations between Unacquainted Persons. In B. Thorne, H. Kramarae & N. Henley (Eds.), *Language, Gender and Society* (pp. 103-118). Rowley, MA: Newbury House.

Wettig, J. (2002). New developments in standardisation in the past 15 years: Product versus process related standards. *Safety Science, 40*(1-4), 51-56.

Wheeler, B. C. (2002). NEBIC: A dynamic capabilities theory for assessing net-enablement. *Information Systems Research, 13*(2), 125-146.

Wheelwright, C., Clark, K. (1992). *Revolutionising Product Development – Quantum Leaps in Speed, Efficiency and Quality*, the Free Press, New York.

Wiesenfeld, B.M., Raghuram, S., & Garud, R. (1999). Managers in a virtual context: The experience of self-treat and its effects on virtual work organizations. In C.L. Cooper & D.M. Rousseau (Eds.), *The virtual organization* (pp. 31-44). Chichester: Wiley.

Wiggins, B., & Horn, Z. N. J. (2005, April). *Explaining effects of task complexity in computer-mediated communication: A meta-analysis.* Paper presented at the meeting of the Society for Industrial and Organizational Psychology, Los Angeles, CA.

Williamson, O.E., (1975). *Markets and hierarchies.* New York: The Free Press.

Wills, C. (1993). *The runaway brain: The evolution of human uniqueness.* New York: Basic Books.

Wilson, E. O. (1998). *Consilience: The unity of knowledge.* New York: Alfred A. Knopf.

Winograd, T., (1987-1988). A language/action perspective on the design of cooperative work. *Human-Computer Interaction, 3*(1), 3-30.

Wixom, B., & Todd, P.A. (2005). A theoretical integration of user satisfaction and technology acceptance. *Information Systems Research, 16*(1), 85-102.

Woodruff, R. B. (1997). Customer Value: The Next Source of Competitive Advantage. *Journal of the Academy of Marketing Science, 25*(2), 139-153.

Wooldridge., M. and Jennings, N.R. (1995). "Intelligent agents: theory and practice." [Retrieved on February 15, 2006 from GRACO web site at http://www.graco.unb.br/alvares/DOUTORADO/disciplinas/feature/agente_definicao.pdf.]

World Bank Operations Evaluation Department. (2004). *Addressing the challenges of globalization: An independent evaluation of the World Bank's approach to global programs* (1st ed.). Washington, DC: The International Bank for Reconstruction and Development & the World Bank.

Wu, J.-H., & Wang, S.-C. (2004). What drives mobile commerce? An empirical evaluation of the revised technology acceptance model. *Information & Management, 42*(5), 719-729.

Yang, O., & Shao, Y. (1996). Shared leadership in self-managed teams: a competing values approach. *Total Quality Management, 7*(5), 521-534.

Yates, S. J. (2001). Gender, Language and CMC for Education. *Learning and Instruction, 11*(1), 21-34.

Yin, R.K. (1994). *Case Study Research, Design and Methods*, Sage Publications.

Yoo, W. S., Suh, K. S., & Lee, M. B. (2002). Exploring the Factors Enhancing Member Participation in Virtual Communities. *Journal of Global Information Management, 10*(3), 55-71.

Yoo, Y., & Alavi, M. (2004). Emergent leadership in virtual teams: what do emergent leaders do? *Information and Organization, 14*(1), 27-58.

Yoo, Y., & Alavi, M. (2004). Emergent leadership in virtual teams: What do emergent leaders do? *Information and Organization, 14*, 27-58.

Yoshikawa, H. (1994). Intelligent manufacturing systems: Technical co-operation that transcends cultural differences. In H. Yoshikawa & J. Goossenaerts (Eds.), *Information infrastructure systems for manufacturing* (IFIP transaction B-14, pp.19-40). Amsterdam: Elsevier North Holland.

Yukl, G. (1989). Managerial leadership: A review of theory and research. *Journal of Management, 15*(2), 251-289.

Yukl, G. A., (2006). *Leadership in organizations* (6th ed.). Upper Saddle River, NJ: Pearson Prentice Hall.

Yun, G. W., & Trumbo, C. W. (2000). Comparative response to a survey executed by post, e-mail & web form. *Journal of Computer Mediated Communication, 6*(1).

Zaccaro, S. J., & Bader, P. (2002). E-leadership and the challenges of leading E-teams: Minimizing the bad and maximizing the good. *Organizational Dynamics, 31*(4), 377-387.

Zaff, J., & Devlin, S. (1998). Sense of community in housing for the elderly. *Journal of Community Psychology, 26*, 381-398.

Zahra, S. A., & George, G. (2002). The net-enabled business innovation cycle and the evolution of dynamic capabilities. *Information Systems Research, 13*(2), 147-150.

Zalesny, M. D., Salas, E., & Prince, C. (1995). Conceptual and measurement issues in coordination: Implications for team behavior and performance. *Research in Personnel and Human Resources Management, 13*, 81-115.

Zall Kusek, J., & Rist, R. C. (2004). *Ten steps to a results-based monitoring and evaluation system: A handbook for development practitioners.* Washington, DC: The International Bank for Reconstruction and Development & the World Bank.

Zeithaml, V. A. (1988). Consumer Perception of Price, Quality, and Value: A Means-End Model and Sythesis of Evidence. *Journal of Marketing, 52*(July), 2-22.

Zhang, X., Prybutok, V. R., & Strutton, D. (2007). Modeling Influences on Impulse Purchasing Behaviors during Online Marketing Transactions. *Journal of Marketing Theory & Practice, 15*(1), 79-89.

Zheng, L., & Possel-Dölken, F. (2002). *Strategic production networks.* Berlin, Germany: Springer.

Zhu, K., & Kraemer, K. L. (2002). E-commerce metrics for net-enhanced organizations: Assessing the value of e-commerce to firm performance in the manufacturing sector. *Information Systems Research, 13*(3), 275-295.

Zigurs, I. (2003). Leadership in virtual teams: Oxymoron or opportunity? *Organizational Dynamics, 31*, 339-51.

Zigurs, I., & Buckland, B. (1998). A theory of task/technology fit and group support systems effectiveness. *MIS Quarterly, 22*(3), 313-334.

Zigurs, I., & Buckland, B. K. (1998). A theory of task/technology fit and group support systems effectiveness. *MIS Quarterly, 22*(3), 313-334.

Zigurs, I., & Buckland, B. K. (1998). A theory of task/technology fit and group support systems effectiveness. *MIS Quarterly, 22*(3), 313-334.

Zigurs, I., & Kozar, K. (1994). An exploratory study of roles in computer-supported groups. *MIS Quarterly, 18*(3), 277-297.

Zigurs, I., (2002). Leadership in virtual teams: Oxymoron or opportunity. *Organizational Dynamics, 31*(4), 339-351.

Zigurs, I., Buckland, B. K., Connolly, J. R., & Wilson, E. V. (1999). A test of task-technology fit theory for group support systems. *Database for Advances in Information Systems, 30*(3), 34-50.

Zigurs, I., Evaristo, R., & Katzy, B. (2001). *Collaborative technologies for virtual project management.* Washington, DC: Academy of Management.

Zimmerman, D., & West, C. (1975). Sex-roles, interruptions and silences in conversation. In B. Thorne, H. Kramarae & N. Henley (Eds.), *Language and Sex: Difference and Dominance* (pp. 89-101). Rowley, MA: Newbury House.

# About the Contributors

**Ned Kock** is professor and founding chair of the Division of International Business and Technology Studies at Texas A&M International University. He holds degrees in electronics engineering (BEE.), computer science (MS), and management information systems (PhD). Ned has authored several books, and published in a number of journals including *Communications of the ACM, Decision Support Systems, European Journal of Information Systems, IEEE Transactions, Information & Management, Information Systems Journal, Information Technology & People, Journal of Organizational Computing and Electronic Commerce, MIS Quarterly*, and *Organization Science*. He is the Editor-in-Chief of the *International Journal of e-Collaboration*, associate editor of the *Journal of Systems and Information Technology*, and associate editor for Information Systems of the journal *IEEE Transactions on Professional Communication*.

* * *

**Pedro Antunes** is associate professor at the University of Lisboa. His research interests address the design, development and assessment of collaborative technologies, focusing in particular on complex socio-technical interactions such as electronic meetings and group decision and negotiation. He has published more than 70 papers on these topics and participated in more than 40 conference program committees. He is Steering Committee Member of CRIWG - International Workshop on Groupware. Since 2000, he has also been project evaluator and reviewer for the European Commission in several thematic areas.

**Gert-Jan de Vreede** is Kayser distinguished professor at the Department of Information Systems & Quantitative Analysis at the University of Nebraska at Omaha, where he is director of the Institute for Collaboration Science. His research focuses on collaboration engineering, the theoretical foundations of (e)-collaboration, and the transfer of collaborative technology and work practices. His articles have appeared in journals such as *Journal of Management Information Systems, Communications of the ACM, Communications of the AIS, Small Group Research, DataBase, Group Decision and Negotiation, Journal of Creativity and Innovation Management, International Journal of Technology and Management, Journal of Informatics Education and Research, Simulation & Gaming*, and *Simulation*.

**Fredrik Elgh** is assistant professor in Product Development at the department of Mechanical Engineering at the School of Engineering, Jönköping Unversity. He holds a MSc in mechanical engineering from Jönköping University, Sweden and PhD in product and process development from Chalmers

University of Technology. His research interests include design methodology, computer supported engineering design, cost engineering, and design for producibility. Prior to the academic career he worked in the furniture industry as a production engineer.

**Lior Fink** is a faculty member in the Department of Industrial Engineering and Management, Ben-Gurion University of the Negev. He holds a bachelor's degree in psychology and economics, a master's degree in social-industrial psychology – both from Bar-Ilan University – and a PhD in information systems from Tel Aviv University. Prior to his doctoral studies, Lior gained substantial industry experience working as an organizational development consultant. In his last position, he headed the organizational development unit in one of Israel's largest IT organizations. After receiving the Fulbright Post-Doctoral Scholar Award in 2006, he spent one year at the UCLA Anderson School of Management. Lior's articles have been published or accepted for publication in a number of journals including the *Data Base for Advances in Information Systems, International Journal of e-Collaboration, Journal of the Association for Information Systems*, and *Journal of Information Technology*. His current research interests focus on the strategic value of IT infrastructure, enterprise-wide systems, and collaborative technologies and on strategic aspects of IT markets.

**David Gefen** (gefend@drexel.edu) is associate professor of MIS at Drexel University, Philadelphia USA, where he teaches Strategic Management of IT, Database Analysis and Design, and VB.NET. He received his PhD in CIS from Georgia State University and a Master of Sciences in MIS from Tel-Aviv University. His research focuses on trust and culture as they apply to the psychological and rational processes involved in ERP, CMC, and e-commerce implementation management, and to outsourcing. David's wide interests in IT adoption stem from his 12 years of experience in developing and managing large information systems. His research findings have been published in *MISQ, ISR, IEEE TEM, JMIS, JSIS, The DATA BASE for Advances in Information Systems, Omega: the International Journal of Management Science, JAIS, CAIS,* and elsewhere. David is an author of a textbook on VB.NET programming. David is on the editorial boards of *MISQ, DATABASE* and *IJeC*.

**Nitza Geri** is head of Undergraduate Management Studies at the Department of Management and Economics at The Open University of Israel and a member of the Chais Research Center for the Integration of Technology in Education. She holds a BA in accounting and economics, an MSc in management sciences and a PhD in technology and information systems management from Tel-Aviv University. She is a CPA (Israel) and prior to her academic career she had over 12 years of business experience. Her research interests and publications focus on various aspects of the value of information, and information systems adoption and implementation, which include: strategic information systems, e-business, value creation and the Theory of Constraints, managerial aspects of e-learning systems adoption and use. Personal site: http://www.openu.ac.il/Personal_sites/nitza-geri.html

**Julia E. Hoch** works as research and teaching assistant at the Department of Work-, Organizational- and Social Psychology at the University of Technology, Dresden, Germany. She studied psychology at the University of Kiel and University of Wuerzburg, Germany, and holds a doctor in psychology from the University of Kiel, Germany. She worked as research and teaching assistant at the University of Kiel and the University of Technology, Munich, Germany. Her research interests include leadership in virtual teams, shared leadership and work motivation in teams.

**Heikki Karjaluoto** (heikki.karjaluoto@ *econ.jyu.fi*) is research professor of Marketing at the University of Jyväskylä, Finland. He received his DSc in marketing from University of Jyväskylä, Finland in 2002. His research interests concern electronic business in general and mobile business in particular. He has published extensively on electronic business in marketing and information system journals, and has collaborated with several researchers in Finland and abroad and with Finnish high-tech companies in research projects.

**Elias T. Kirche** is associate professor of Computer Information Systems and Decision Sciences at the Lutgert College of Business, Florida Gulf Coast University. He received a PhD in operations management from University of Houston (2002). Dr. Kirche is a member of the Decision Science Institute and the Production and Operations Management Society. His professional work experience includes project management and quality control systems. He is recipient of Aspen Technology scholarship to develop Advanced Planning and Scheduling (APS) case studies. Dr. Kirche research interests are: activity-based costing, supply chain optimization models, empirical research and theory testing.

**Udo Konradt** is a full professor and chair of the Department of Work and Organizational Psychology at the University of Kiel, Germany. He holds a doctor in psychology from the University of Bochum, Germany. He has authored several books on electronic human resource management, and published in scholarly journals including *International Journal of Human-Computer Interaction, Behavior and Information Technology, European Journal of Work and Organizational Psychology, Journal of Applied Social Psychology*, and *Small Group Research*. His research interests include collaboration in distributed (virtual) teams, electronic human resource management, and dispersed leadership.

**Magnus Löfstrand** (PhD) is a researcher at the Division of Computer Aided Design at Luleå University of Technology in Sweden. He holds an MSc in mechanical engineering from Luleå University of Technology. His research interests include product development and in particular functional product development in a business-to-business, extended enterprise setting. The focus is on supporting product development processes with tools and methods in order to enable faster development of new and innovative solutions to industrial needs and opportunities. Application areas are mainly in the aerospace and automotive industry.

**Patricia Mcmanus** (p.mcmanus@ecu.edu.au) is a PhD student in the School of Management Information Systems. Her PhD is investigating the decisions related to the adoption of m-services. She is currently lecturing in business information systems and marketing at the University of Western Sydney.

**Narasimha Paravastu** is an assistant professor of MIS at the Metropolitan State University, Minneapolis, MN. He received his PhD from Drexel University, Philadelphia PA.

**Walter Rodriguez** is director of research and professor of Information Systems at the Lutgert College of Business, Florida Gulf Coast University. He received his PhD in engineering project management from University of Florida in 1982. Dr. Rodriguez was holder of the Alico Chair in Operations and chair of the Information Systems and Decision Sciences Department at FGCU. He founded and chaired the Engineering Computer Graphics Program at Georgia Tech (1985-1993) and was awarded the Harvard Foundation Medal (1994) and a postdoctoral fellowship (Information Technology) at the Massachusetts

Institute of Technology (1996), while holder of the Louis Berger Endowed Chair at Tufts University. During the last 25 years, he has obtained continuous National Science Foundation, NASA and private industry sponsored grants in the systems development, collaborative decision-support, distributed learning technologies, and multi-project management areas. Dr. Rodriguez has published over 120 refereed articles in prestigious business and engineering journals and proceedings.

**Craig Standing** (c.standing@ecu.edu.au) is professor of Strategic Information Management in the School of Management at Edith Cowan University, Australia. His current research interests are in the areas of electronic markets, IS evaluation and mobile commerce. He has published in the *European Journal of Information Systems, IEEE Transaction on Engineering Management, Information & Management* and *European Journal of Operational Research*.

**Susan Standing** (s.standing@ecu.edu.au) is a research assistant in the Web Centre, School of Management, Edith Cowan University, Western Australia. She holds a degree in accounting and information management and has worked on a number of funded research projects. Her research interests include accounting information systems and electronic marketplaces.

**Staffan Sunnersjö** is professor of Machine Design in the department of Mechanical Engineering at the School of Engineering, Jönköping Unversity. He holds a MSc and a PhD in mechanical engineering from Aston University, Birmigham UK, 1976. He has published three books and more than 40 papers in scientific journals, conference proceedings and other technical publications. Earlier works are oriented towards structural dynamics and stress analysis, while later works deal with design methodology and computer support. Prior to the academic career he worked in the power generation industry and the shipbuilding industry and subsequently became manager for the Engineering Design division at the Swedish Institute for Production Engineering Research.

**Vladimir Tarasov** is assistant professor at the Centre for Evolving IT in Networked Organisations (CENIT), Jönköping University. He received PhD in computer science from Petrozavodsk State University, Russia, in 1996. He took a PhD course in St. Petersburg Institute for Informatics and Automation of the Russian Academy of Sciences, Russia, in 1991-1993. He received MSc in mathematics from Petrozavodsk State University in 1990. He works in a number of research projects in the fields of information logistics, ontological engineering, and collaborative engineering. He also manages the master's programme in information engineering and teaches in the areas of: software engineering, development of distributed applications, and information logistic. He has published 28 scientific papers.

**Janusz Zalewski** is professor of Computer Science and Engineering at Florida Gulf Coast University. He holds a PhD in computer science from Warsaw University of Technology (1979). Previously, he held academic positions at Embry-Riddle Aeronautical University and University of Central Florida. Dr. Zalewski worked on projects for Superconducting Super Collider, Lawrence Livermore National Laboratory, NASA, FAA and Nuclear Regulatory Commission, as well as for a number of private companies, including Lockheed Martin, Harris, Boeing and others. His research interests are: software engineering, real-time systems, computer networks and distributed systems.

**Halbana Tarmizi** is a PhD candidate in the College of Information Science and Technology at the University of Nebraska at Omaha. He holds a Master's degree in Telecommunications from Michigan State University and a Dipl.-Ing. in electrical engineering from Aachen University of Technology (Germany). His research interests include collaboration technology, online communities, and virtual teams. He is currently working on participation issues in communities of practice. He has published and presented his work in the *International Journal of e-Collaboration, e-Service Journal* as well as conferences such as the AMCIS, HICSS and MWAIS.

**Ilze Zigurs** is professor and Department Chair of Information Systems and Quantitative Analysis in the College of Information Science and Technology at the University of Nebraska at Omaha. She holds the Mutual of Omaha distinguished chair of Information Science and Technology, and also served as the founding director of the doctoral program in Information Technology. In 2007, she was named a fellow of the Association for Information Systems. Dr. Zigurs' research examines design, implementation, and use of collaboration technologies, particularly in virtual teams and projects. She has co-published with Deepak Khazanchi a book on patterns of effectiveness in virtual projects. Professor Zigurs was formerly a senior editor for the *MIS Quarterly* and Department Editor for the *IEEE Transactions on Engineering Management*.

# Index

## W